1978

Merry Christmas
to a lovely _____
Martha (MacIntosh) Bowers
from her lucky husband
Bob

THE CLANS, SEPTS, AND REGIMENTS
OF THE SCOTTISH HIGHLANDS

PLATE I.

THE CLANS, SEPTS, AND REGIMENTS

OF THE

SCOTTISH HIGHLANDS

BY

FRANK ADAM, F.R.G.S., F.S.A.(Scot.)

REVISED BY

SIR THOMAS INNES OF LEARNEY

LORD LYON KING OF ARMS
K.C.V.O., ADVOCATE

SEVENTH EDITION

W. & A. K. JOHNSTON & G. W. BACON LTD.
EDINBURGH AND LONDON

First published 1908
Second Edition 1924
Third Edition 1934
Fourth Edition 1952
Fifth Edition 1955
Sixth Edition · · · · 1960
Seventh Edition · · · · 1965

PRINTED IN GREAT BRITAIN BY W. & A. K. JOHNSTON & G. W. BACON LTD.
EDINA WORKS, EASTER ROAD, EDINBURGH, SCOTLAND

PREFACE

WHEN Mr. Frank Adam launched *Clans, Septs, and Regiments of the Scottish Highlands*, he provided Scots folk all over the world with exactly the sort, and size, of book which they wanted ; and notwithstanding the difficulties and limitations under which he produced it, the work filled, in a preliminary way, what was an obvious public demand, although experience showed that it lacked treatment of many points which were to become steadily of more and more practical importance if clanship and the Highland spirit were to be successfully preserved. With the development of scientific historical research, and the publication of such works as those of Drs. John Cameron, I. F. Grant, Agnes Mure Mackenzie, and many other specialised searchers, it became evident that the book, as Adam last issued it, was no longer abreast of current knowledge or modern requirements. That is often the case with such books ; and then one of two things happens : either the work fades into being less and less consulted, with ultimate oblivion, or else it takes, under adequate revision, a permanent place in literature as a living and standard work. In the latter manner, John Erskine's *Principles of the Law of Scotland* (under the editorship of Sheriff Nicolson, and again of Sir John Rankine, K.C.), and *Boutell's Heraldry* (under first Aveling, and later Wheeler-Holohan), have passed into " standard works." I had been asked to correct a number of actual errors, armorial and other, in the Third Edition ; and when a Fourth became necessary, the inadequacy of the existing text to fulfil modern requirements, or to deal with or incorporate the new facts and branches of the subject essential to its purpose, became evident. The publishers therefore resolved that *Clans, Septs, and Regiments* should be brought up to date and take its place in Scottish literature as a permanent " Encyclopædia of Clanship."

To revise the work of a deceased author must always be a matter of anxious care ; but here much of the revision has consisted in introducing fresh authoritative matter ; and as it is my literary practice to cite the authorities relied on, so, since many of these authorities are subsequent to 1908, or in books which had not come under Adam's notice, no explanation seems needed for the consequent additions and adjustments of the text. These, I take it, would have commended themselves to Adam, who was himself always seeking fresh information ; and when one considers that he wrote from Malaya, and at a distance from research facilities, he achieved a relatively notable work. In some respects he naturally formed his narrative and his views upon the then—and locally—available material. Where, however, he had expressed personal views on which I differ, I have commented on, or referred to, his own expressions.

One dominant difference will, however, be found in the scheme and motif of the present edition. Adam thought that " the clan *system* is dead, but that a clan-*spirit* survives." In law and social organisation, the " clan system " is *still* quite " alive " ! No legislation " destroyed it," though (by planning and welfare interference) like even the ordinary familial authority within the home, much has been done to *limit* the *patria potestas* to such an extent that (as in the decline of Rome) home-life marriage and the clan-spirit give place to moral weakness, and a lack of the security and happiness which a strong family organisation gives. Too often it is the " clan-*spirit*" which is, I will not say " dead," but in a very anæmic condition. In most quarters, however, the clan-spirit remains as strong and vigorous as ever ; and amongst the things borne home to me is the insistent demand amongst Clansfolk, Clan Societies, and the younger generation of those no longer resident in their native homes where custom lives on, for definite information about the essentials of clan-life and organisation, and the symbolic-ceremonial and customs, upon which the handing down of tradition, and thus the perpetuation of the strength and vigour of a race, depend.

Here is therefore one chord of difference between the present edition and its predecessors, and one well touched upon in two stanzas of a well-known poem of my old friend, the late Rev. T. Ratcliffe Barnett :

> The old days and the old ways,
> And the world as it used to be,
> How the heart longs for the old days—

and though with a vague sense that somehow " the clan-spirit " still had a message for those of Highland blood, yet, as an " exiled Scot " far from the land of pine and heather, it was rather as of an intangible and vanished past that Adam wrote. In this edition the reader will find a different—and a sterner—treatment of almost every angle of clanship. Hark to the Rev. Barnett's next lines, which ring out like a trumpet call :

> For the old days and the old ways
> Are the life of the days to come—

and the present edition does not spare in effort to let clansfolk learn why—and how—they can all share in keeping alive our ancient social system, which is still rooted in Scottish Law, and is the basis of Scottish character.

In an age of possible scientific destruction, which might, for modern civilisation, perhaps be not unlike that which befell the civilisations of Greece and Rome, let us bear in mind that *the one continuant entity*,

which survives when powerful states have melted away, is *The Tribe,
The Family, The Clan.* Artificial riches and glory, metropolitan ex-
travagance, wealth and conceit, lead to, and end, nowhere. They and
theirs fade out again and again. Ultimately the world belongs to the
man with " three acres and a cow " (sixty or so acres in the Highlands !)
—the crofter—(and many a chieftain's *duthus* was little more), that is,
to the *Family* grouped faithfully around a *duthus*, loved with honest
pride and preserving traditions and genealogy ; gathered around and
connected with " the hearth of the race "—their Chieftain's home ; to
feudo-tribal monarchy and clanship, *The Family*, as a proud and land-
loving hereditary group, based upon honouring the Fifth Commandment.

In Scotland we are fortunate that, in a great measure, our " auld
lawes "—on which tenure and clan organisation were based—have in
their essentials survived until now from their age-old evolution in the
early days of our Picto-Scottish patriarchal organisation ; and it is
these which have preserved in Caledonia so much of its ancient
structure, character and outlook. To the continuance of these—our
laws of heritage, tenure, marriage and succession—do we owe it that
there is still a Scotland, and that we are not like the seven lost kingdoms
of the English Heptarchy. But in the greater movement, and publicisa-
tion of mass civilisations, of present times, the demand has been
insistent for more precise and collected information on these vital
matters, especially in relation to the patriarchal tribe-groups, so that
Scots folk, and the children of the Clans, wherever they settle, may
preserve the vitality of those age-old hereditary Highland institutions,
that were so securely enshrined in the Laws of Scotland, which
Southern politicians—when (from certain provisions in the Treaty of
Union) they found that they could not abolish them as readily as they
would have wished—have instead, in not a few cases, sought to destroy,
trying by groundless propaganda to wheedle the Scots into abandoning
the very laws whereby their ancient and native civilisation and their
high national character have actually been preserved.

Of our ancient Highland customs and organisation, much will (in
an order rather more methodically marshalled and inter-related than
elsewhere) be found set forth here. This, with the new material
gathered from Highland records, and incorporated in the Fourth and
present editions of *Clans, Septs, and Regiments of the Scottish Highlands,*
will accordingly be of wide *practical* assistance to Highland institutions
at home and all over the Empire, and, indeed, " the world o'er "
wherever " the heart is Highland."

THOMAS INNES OF LEARNEY.

EDINBURGH.
September 1964

CONTENTS

PART I

HISTORY OF THE CLAN SYSTEM

ix

PART V

CLAN INSIGNIA AND HERALDRY

PART VI

CLAN LISTS AND STATISTICS

LIST OF PLATES

Armorial Shield: The King of Scots. *Lyon Register*, I., 14.

I

Ancient Alba and the Rise of the Highland Clan System—400 B.C. to A.D. 1286

WHO were the Celts, the Picts, and the Gaels? Whence came they? and, Who were the progenitors of the Highlanders of Scotland? are questions which have never been fully and finally answered, though archæology is now gradually uncovering scientific data bearing on such questions.

Britain in prehistoric days appears to have been but sparsely populated. Indeed, the greater portion of what is now known as the Highlands of Scotland was covered by dense forests. The Celts, Albans, or Gaels, who superimposed themselves on the aboriginal inhabitants of Britain, formed part of a conquering race, which, advancing from the confines of Asia, spread themselves over the greater part of Europe.[1] Sufficient evidence exists to prove the influence of such a race throughout Europe, despite the absence of details of their history and their conquests. Both ancient and modern geography attests the influence of the Celtic immigration, while to the present day many names in European geography show distinct evidence of their Celtic origin.

It is known that in early days a State, named Albania, existed on the north-east of the kingdom of Armenia. Though this was not Celtic, a Celtic province of Galatia existed in Asia Minor. In modern Albania, on the shores of the Adriatic, the clan system is still in full swing and the national garb is a species of kilt. Mrs. Will Gordon, in *A Woman in the Balkans* (Nelson, 1918), says : " The different tribes [of Albania] wage war one against another, just as the old clan feuds existed in Scotland years ago. In some of the hill fastnesses also they wear a kind of tartan kilt very similar to the Scot, and the bagpipe is the national instrument of the Highlander here." In the " Gallia Transalpina " of the Romans are the Rhone or " red river " (*ruadh-abhainn*) and the Garonne or " rough river " (*garbh-abhainn*). In

---

[1] Thus Mr. F. Adam. The question, however, is whether in many cases tribal districts in Scotland are not still peopled by original inhabitants who settled in the " sparsely populated " country. That, at any rate, is the tradition of many of our old Highland families, and, like Sir George Mackenzie, I see no reason to doubt that in many cases such tradition is well founded. It, of course, partly depends on what one regards as such—I take it not a stray raider, but those who made a settled home.

Northern Spain, while the name of the province of Galicia is derived from its people, the Gallegos, this forms a markedly tribal district, the adjacent Basque provinces being regarded by many as Celtic, and the heraldic administration of the " Chronicler Kings of Arms " of Royal Spain is most closely analogous to that of the Lyon Court in Scotland.[1]   In France the nobiliary and social practice of Celtic Brittany are closely related to the customs of Scotland and Ireland. In the British Isles we find the Gael perpetuated in the names Galway in Ireland and Galloway in Scotland, while the ancient name of the kingdom of Scotland was Alba.   The name still survives in the titles Duke of Albany and Marquis of Breadalbane.

The question when the stream of Celtic emigration from the mainland of Europe to the British Isles commenced, has been often debated.

It is now thought the Celts became the governing race during the " Second Iron Age," 400–300 to 100 B.C., and that they imported *La Tène* culture, so-called from the discoveries at a great Celtic settlement near Neuchatel.[2]

Controversy has long raged on the origin of the Picts, but it is widely held the early settlers, " Picts," of north and east Scotland entered from the north-east.   They are now thought a Bronze Age people (T. Wainwright, *Problem of the Picts*, p. 159), from whom derived the matrilinear succession which later became the basis of Scottish Common Law.   A third stream emigrated to Ireland from Spain.

That the Picts, including the tribe of the " Catti," came in from across the North Sea, seems preserved in tribal legends referred to in a source not usually consulted by prehistorians, namely Nisbet's *System of Heraldry*, which records this as the tradition alike of the Catti, the Sutherlands, and the Murrays, original inhabitants of the province of Moray,[3] and that they were divided into kindreds and clans.   Curle's map[4] shows that the race which produced the pre-Christian characteristically " Pictish " sculptured stones were settled on the Elgin and Sutherland coasts of the Moray Firth (especially at what I might call the Duffus and Dunrobin centres—and these, be it noted, are respectively the *duthus* of the two clans mentioned by Nisbet), and in Mar and Strathspey, intermixed with early Christian

---

[1] *Juridical Review*, September 1940.

[2] The latest views on these questions will be found in I. F. Grant, *Lordship of the Isles*, chap. IV., and C. L. Curle, " Chronology of Early Christian Monuments in Scotland," *Pro. of Soc. of Antiquaries, Scotland*, LXXIV., p. 60.

[3] *System of Heraldry*, I., pp. 253, 259.   I am not impressed with Professor Watson's suggestion that the place-names of north-eastern Scotland were a series of mere adjectivally-qualified nostalgic reiterations of the word " Ireland."

[4] *Pro. Soc. of Antiquaries, Scotland*, LXXIV., p. 61, diag., p. 112.

versions, and other slightly later groups of their particular monuments occur in Angus and round St. Andrews.[1]

This Pictish nation, which was strongly clannish, even in pre-historic times, which adopted a Christianity intertwined with clan totemism, and which resolutely favoured the panelled cross, is that which became the basis of the Scottish nation, though from 843 to 1034 (Kenneth MacAlpine to Malcolm II.), it was ruled by kings who were Dalriad Scots in the male line.

The Celts whom Cæsar found in England were probably descendants

[1] Curle remarks, as their especial characteristics : (a) in adopting Christianity they developed the tall slabs engraved with their own version of the cross and not the free standing crosses of Dalriada ; (b) beyond the holy symbol of the cross they were " singularly uninterested in Christian themes " ; (c) the cross is accompanied by decorative carvings of animals and incidents, whereof " the source and meaning . . . are obscure " ; but, adds Curle, (d) there are " traces of totemism in the clan names of the Picts and their preoccupation with animal art might have its source in this. . . ." " Legends and folk-tales very probably account for many other motives " (pp. 114–115). Looking to traditions such as that preserved by Nisbet, and the foregoing observations, one may conclude that the Picts were intensely clannish, and that their religion and monuments were closely related to their tribal organisation, Christianity being adopted in general, but, as regards the particular, woven into the individual art and legend of each tribe. This, then, is the prehistoric *fundamentum* of the race which was the base of *Alba*—Caledonian Scotland.

Certain of the objects—rods, circles, etc.—found on many of the stones and surrounding the cross, or on the reverse, have been shown to be subject to orderly arrangement, though its import is unsettled. I think they are obviously insignia of rank, and that Dr. Douglas Simpson's query—How this can be reconciled with an otherwise " anonymous " monument ?—lies in the concept of tribo-clan succession, and the theory that each successive chief is *MacGartnaigh*, or what-ever it may be, and " undertakes the name." The Scottish clans were, as we shall see, extremely *duthus*-conscious, and, in the case of the " tribe of the land," a chief bearing the re-embodied " name " is not so much anonymous as con-tinuous " representer," and such stones may well commemorate the sepulture or fame of the successive chiefs (thereby relating Christianity and ancestor-worship), and the " combinations " of symbols may be found to denote degree of rank, or extent of chiefship, or over-chiefship. A monument with repetition might commemorate two or three distinct chiefs, or the junction of two lines ; and—looking to the Pictish, and our common law of succession—the mirror and comb symbols may relate to a " chieftainess " or to a monument erected by such or at a time when the succession had passed through a female, or indeed by the heiress and her husband (cf. Cameron, *Celtic Law*, p. 237).

Indeed the Hilton of Cadboll stone clearly shows an heretrix-chief and her shadow-husband behind. The " crescent device " probably denotes a chieftainly diadem and the " V-rod " addition an indication of actual regnancy. Such considerations, from a " tribal " angle, may suggest a basis for further research along the lines explained by Dr. Simpson in *Stones of Scotland* (Batsford), pp. 17–18. The Moniefieth stone (*Proc. Soc. Antiq. Scot.*, LXXIV., p. 111) seems to me analogous to a " preheraldic " composition in the style of the staircase tower at Huntly Castle, for why should two of the " evangelists " be arrayed so differently from the others ? Assuming the uppermost carving is the Crucifixion, my impression is that the second tier are priests, the third secular chiefs, and that the person beneath is more probably a local harper than David—at any rate a very similar design to the sixteenth-century Irish chief's harper illustrated in R. Bruce Armstrong, *The Irish and Highland Harps*, p. 6 (MacSweyn's Feast).

of Celts who had migrated there from what is now France. Indeed, to the present day, there is much affinity between the Bretons of Brittany (the ancient Armorica) in France and their Welsh kinsmen (and the same might be said of the Cornish, whose language is now almost extinct). Between the French Celts, on the one hand, and their Scottish, Highland, Irish, and Manx kinsmen, on the other—particularly indeed the Scots—there has always remained a very close tie, of which the armorial fleurs-de-lys of the respective Royal arms were regarded as a symbolic link ; whilst, as is well known, the Scots long enjoyed the right of being treated as naturalised subjects in France, whilst the tribal development of Scotland and the *ancien régime* was, as John Riddell, the great peerage lawyer, emphasises, very closely similar.

To this and the succeeding period appear to belong a number of the old folk-tales, of fights between the agile swordsmen and " giants " living in caves and armed with clubs, and the " rescue " by the former of princesses. These are tales which preserve vague memories of struggles in the still unsettled region, between invading warriors armed with bronze and iron weapons, imposing themselves on a burlier but more primitive race, whose daughters or widows were as likely as not the " princesses " who became the wives of the better-armed captains.

It is, accordingly, worth notice that even in these virtually prehistoric days an element of continuity of " succession " is apparent in folk-lore, which we find perpetuated in the subsequent heraldry of the Middle Ages, for, in a remarkable number of cases, the armorial supporters of a baron's coat of arms are a couple of " wild men with clubs," who seem thus symbolised as the " supporters " in the sense of followers of the subsequent *capitani tribuum*, with whom Craig, the great feudal jurist of Scotland, identifies the Baronage of Scotland,[1] and which he, like our modern scientists, relates to the development of the clan system.

The Romans invaded Britain in A.D. 43. From shortly after that until A.D. 410 all England and Wales, as well as the south of Scotland as far as the Wall of Antoninus (from Forth to Clyde), formed a province of the Roman Empire.

The part of Britain with which our narrative has the most concern (namely, that portion situated to the north of the Wall of Antoninus) was styled by the Romans " Caledonia." The native Caledonians preserved their wild independence, for which they were not less in-

---

[1] The remarkable prevalence of these armorial " savages " as supporters is remarked by most of our heraldic writers, (cf. Seton, *Law and Practice of Heraldry*, p. 263, and Stevenson, *Heraldry in Scotland*, p. 244,) and even prior to the tournaments, at which they were represented in life ; others even remark that such " wild men " are the supporters appropriate to be granted to any baron, when no other creature is relevant. Evidently they represent in earliest form the " native men " mentioned in so many Highland charters, and heraldry thus carries us back to, and explains, the transition of the facts underlying our folk-lore into medieval history and armorial symbolism.

debted to their poverty than to their valour. Their incursions were frequently repelled and chastised, but their country was never subdued. Later the people of this region became known to the Romans as Picts.

In A.D. 208 the Emperor Severus invaded Caledonia, penetrating as far as Burghead on the Moray Firth, but even the might of the Roman Empire failed to invade the part of Scotland now known as the mid, north, and west Highlands. Severus died at York in A.D. 211, and thenceforth the Romans gave Caledonia a wide berth.

A chief seat of the Caledonians at this period seems to have been Dunkeld, and Schiehallion their " fairy mountain." Inverness, however, was the military centre of the Pictish monarchs, and rose in importance during the fourth century A.D. The two leading clans in Alba or Caledonia had by this time come to be the *Orcs* (the Boar Clan) and the *Cats* (the Cat Clan). No doubt these had become Royal dynasties, and their names would be related to, or represented by, their totem animals. The descendants of the Caledonians, whose ancestors inhabited the seaboard, have a considerable strain of Scandinavian blood, attributable to the various Norse invasions and settlements on the coasts of Scotland, from the middle of the eighth century until the final expulsion of the Norsemen in 1266. The Caledonian Picts called their land " Alba," and themselves Albans or Albiones, and they were also termed " Cruithne," a term which was applied by old writers not only to the Caledonian Celts but also to the Celts of Ireland. By the Welsh, the Caledonian Picts and their kinsmen in Ireland were designated *Gwyddyl*, the former being usually distinguished by the appellation of *Gwyddyl Fichti*, or Gaelic Picts.

Ptolemy, the geographer, states that, in the second century, the Caledonians consisted of thirteen tribes.[1] These appear to have been subsequently merged in the two great divisions of Dicaledones and Verturiones.

Subsequent to the death, in A.D. 211, of the Emperor Severus, Roman Britain enjoyed comparative peace for nearly a century. In the early part of the fourth century, however, we find Roman Britain being raided from the north by the Caledonians or Picti ; its western coasts harried by the Scotti from Ireland ; while, on the east, the coast was exposed to the attacks of the Angles and Saxons. These invaders appear to have made no discrimination between Romans and Britons. Two and a half centuries of subjection appears to have had the Britons depending almost entirely for defence on the military might of Rome. Towards the middle of the fourth century another race, named the Attacotti, or Attacotts, make their appearance as raiding the northern portion of the Roman British frontier. Historians are divided as to who these Attacotti can have been.

To repel the invasions of Saxons, Scots, Attacotts, and Caledonians, fresh Roman reinforcements were despatched to Britain under the general, Theodosius, who achieved complete success in A.D. 369.

[1] Appendix No. I.

Peace was, however, not of long duration ; for, in A.D. 400 and in A.D. 406, Roman reinforcements were being hurried to Britain to repel and chastise the Caledonian patriots. In A.D. 407, however, when troubles were thickening round Italy, the Roman forces were withdrawn from Britain, never to return. In A.D. 410 the Emperor Honorius abandoned Britain, and the inhabitants of south Britain were left to their own devices, to preserve the independence granted to them. On several occasions they implored the assistance of their whilom lords against enemies who were attacking them by sea and by land. These appeals were met with a deaf ear, for the Romans were then themselves at grips with the barbarians, who ultimately overturned the Roman Empire of the West. Despairing, therefore, of any other means of saving themselves, the Romanised south British, in A.D. 449, by promising the Saxons subsidies and territory, enlisted that race for a time as their allies. The combined efforts of Briton and Saxon were successful in defeating the Picts. Ultimately the Saxons turned on their British hosts, and after a series of bloody engagements subjugated the greater part of them. The remnants of the defeated British kept independence in remote and inaccessible and mountainous parts of the country, such as Cornwall, Wales, Cumberland, and Westmorland (which became the British Cumbrian kingdom of Reged), Strathclyde (Scottish Cumbria), and Galloway, leaving the lowland and fertile districts of south Britain to the Saxons. The epoch which saw the overthrow of the British by the Saxons was also remarkable for the conversion to Christianity of the Picts by St. Ninian or Ringan, who was himself a Strathclyde Briton, and from this mission and a train of holy men, such as St. Colm, St. Drostan, and St. Modan, eastern Scotland and the Southern Picts were converted to Christianity long before St. Columba ever set foot on Iona.[1]

The sixth century was a momentous one in the annals of Pictavia or Caledonia, for during this period the Irish or Dalriadic Scots successfully invaded western Pictavia and, under King Fergus, established the kingdom of Dalriada there in A.D. 503. It is no less remarkable for the conversion of the Northern Picts to Christianity by St. Columba, who landed on the shores of the small island of Hy, or Iona, from Ireland, in A.D. 563.

The Dalriadic Scots are believed to have come from Antrim, from Dal-Riada, so named from its chief, Carbre-Riada. The Dalriadic colonists were under the leadership of Fergus, *mor mac* Erc, a descendant of Carbre-Riada.

With Fergus came his two brothers, Loarn and Angus. The southern boundary of the Dalriadic territory in Scotland was the Firth of Clyde, while on the east the boundary between the Dalriads and the Picts was a chain of mountains, then known as Drumalban. After the Dalriadic Scots had firmly settled in Scotland, their possessions appear

---

[1] F. Knight, *Early Christianising of Scotland*, p. 304 and *op. cit.* W. D. Simpson, *The Historical St. Columba*, pp. 35–39.

to have been divided among four tribes. These were (1) the *Cinel Lorn*, descended from Loarn, one of the three brothers already mentioned; (2 and 3) the *Cinel Gabran* and the *Cinel Comgall* descended, respectively, from two sons of Domangart, son of Fergus; while (4) the *Cinel Angus* derived their descent from the third brother, Angus.

The Cinel Lorn occupied that part of Argyllshire now known as Lorne; the Cinel Gabran had the districts of Argyll proper and Kintyre; the Cinel Comgall had the territory of Comgall, now known as Cowal; and the Cinel Angus had for their share the islands of Islay and Jura. Beyond these, districts in the north, between Lorne and Ardnamurchan, including Morvern, Ardgour, probably part of Lochaber, as well as the island of Mull, appear to have formed debatable ground, whose population was Pictish, while the Scots had colonies among them. The capital of the Dalriadic Scots was Dunadd, in the neighbourhood of Crinan, while Dunolly, at modern Oban, was the chief fortress of the Cinel Lorn.

The fourth nation found in Scotland towards the middle of the seventh century was that of the Angles. By A.D. 650 the Angles, under Oswald of Bernicia, had extended their sway as far north as the Forth. Ida founded the Angle kingdom of Bernicia, which extended from the Forth on the north to the Tees on the south, with Bamborough for its capital. Bernicia was bounded on the west by the kingdom of the Strathclyde Britons (Scottish Cumbria, *i.e.* Clydesdale, Ayrshire, Dumfriesshire, Peeblesshire, Selkirkshire, and upper Roxburghshire). This Strathclyde kingdom, of which Alcluith or Dunbarton was the capital, was bounded on the north by *Clach nam Breatannach* (Glenfalloch), and on the south included Cumberland, which had been part of the British kingdom of Reged (or English Cumbria).

Before the establishment of Christianity amongst the Picts the religion of the nation was Druidism. The origin of the name is wrapped in obscurity, but the Druidical religion seems to have included fire-worship, and involved a great deal of tribal religion akin to totemism or ancestor-worship. To this day in Scotland there are many evidences of such attributes of Druidism. For example, Beltane Day (the 1st of May) is the day of the " white " or magic; there is also the festival of *Samhain*, or Hallowe'en, which is *Samfuin* —summer end. The weeks following these, 6th May and 6th November, are still the dates of the " Head Courts " of the Lord Lyon King of Arms—representative of the Celtic Druid historians, later the High Sennachie of the Scottish kings.

During the period of the supremacy of the Druidical religion, Scotland was populated by a large number of distinct tribes, each under its own chief, and these chiefs under the district provincial *righ*, *i.e.* district kings, though, of course, the independence of each tribe was very great. " Thus every district became a petty independent state . . . a sort of hereditary monarchy." [1] It would appear that

---

[1] D. Stewart of Garth, *Sketches, &c., of the Highlanders of Scotland*, 1825, p. 24.

B*

each of the tribes had its own " Druids," respectively priest, sennachie, and dempster or judge of the tribe, but the Druids [1] regarded themselves as an Order and Hierarchy, and just as the chiefs formed a nominal group under their *Ard-righ*, so the Druids appear to have been organised in what one might call a hierarchy or college, evidently under the precedency of the chief Druid of the Pictish High King. In time of war, it was the custom of the tribes to arrange themselves under the banner of one supreme war-leader, entitled *ceann-cath*. This war-leader, chosen for his military efficiency, was, as Robertson points out in *Early Scottish Kings*,[2] distinct from the hereditary chiefs and high chief, whose status was that of Representative of the Community, and not necessarily the executive war-leader or commander-in-chief.

The Druidical order consisted of three classes : the *Bardi*, or Poets, the *Vates*, or Priests, and the highest branch of the order, the *Deo-Phaistein*, who acted as lawgivers and instructors of the principles of religion. An Archdruid presided over the complete order ; and it can well be understood how this hierarchy was able to wield a power which surpassed any authority of king or chief. The Druids enjoined the cultivation of memory and forbade the committing of history to writing. Versification was practised in order that the mind might retain a greater hold of the subject. Even the laws of the country were preserved in rhyme, and in this manner had to be orally mastered ; and, similarly, the genealogies of the kings, chiefs, and chieftains, were orally handed down by the high sennachies and tribal sennachies, who thus wielded a tremendous power in matters of succession to office or to property.

It can easily be imagined, therefore, that when Christianity supplanted " Druidism " in Celtic Scotland, a bitter struggle must have taken place between the Christian priesthood and those of the older Druidic religion. Traces of this are preserved in the life of St. Columba, and indeed are found in the Scottish coronation service, where the division of ceremonial duties between the Bishop and the Lyon, indicates an engrafting on the older pagan ritual of chiefly " inauguration " the Christian concept of Ordination of the Sovereign. It has been suggested that when Christianity came in, the missionaries would in their zeal have done all in their power to destroy the ancient religion and its practices. This, however, is far from being the case, for, unlike a modern missionary with a military force not so far behind him, the primitive saints were obliged to convert or perish, and in the process of conversion to be exceedingly diplomatic and extraordinarily

---

[1] So much nonsense has been written about " Druids " that some care has to be used in employing this term. There is no doubt, however, that such a priestly-juristic order existed, though the details of its tenets, organisation, and ceremonies are still very limited—largely, no doubt, owing to the oral transmission of their lore.

[2] See " Analysis," *Notes and Queries*, 15th August 1942, p. 96.

adaptable.   In these circumstances, innumerable survivals of the earlier tribal cults have subsisted throughout Christian Scotland, and were cleverly engrafted by the early saints, with the practice and ritual of the Christian and Catholic religion ; indeed, it was not until after the Reformation, when there arose a sudden resurgence of the earlier rites and primitive beliefs—popularly denoted " witchcraft "— that effective steps were taken by the Reformed Church, and the Government authorities of the seventeenth century, to suppress the remains of the Druidical religion.

Whilst the Druid priests all but disappeared with the advent of the Christian religion, saving a brief resurgence as the local " devils " of the post-Reformation witch-cultus, the bardic and sennachiedal branch survived in two forms : (a) the Royal heralds ; (b) the tribal bards. It would be difficult to say that the second of these is even yet extinguished. They subsisted in many of the greater clans down to the middle of the eighteenth century. The office of *Ri-seannachie*, with supreme jurisdiction in matters of genealogy, and the duty of preserving the Royal pedigree (and, in the Inaugurator's scarlet robe of office, declaiming it at coronations), passed down into the " Principal Herald " of our medieval history, for heraldry " as pertaining to " the sennachie's office, was added to his duties so that the chief of the sennachiedal branch of the " Druids " evolved into the Lord Lyon King of Arms, whose " brethren heralds," pursuivants, and macers, comprising the college of seventeen individuals, preserved the form of the primitive bardic incorporation, and in the seventeenth century Garter Sir William Dugdale pointedly observes that the heraldic " visitations " were similar to those of the bards (*i.e.* the *cuairt* of the Celtic Druid sennachies), whilst the British heralds and kings of arms were in use to be inaugurated like the Druids by the gift of a gold or silver cup.[1]

The sixth century was an important one in the history of the Highlands, marking both the establishment of the throne of Dalriada and the Columban monastery of Iona, and also the conversion of the Pictish *Ard-righ*, King Brude MacMaelchon ; whilst in Dalriada, King Aidan MacGabran was inaugurated as a Christian king by Columba. On Aidan's defeat by the Anglian king, Ethelfrid, in A.D. 603, the latter's two sons, Oswald and Oswiu, assumed sway over large tracts of southern and central Scotland. But " a comparatively brief experience of Anglian rule and aggressive tactics (as usual) stirred Pictland to its depths. . . . Then arose a strong and heroic national leader in Brude III. (Brude MacBile) who proved the Bruce of his time," [2] who defeated the Angles at Nectansmere. He later became the champion of, and much extended the ambit of, the Columban Church, whose practice became that of all Pictland.

King Nechtan MacDerile, having, in A.D. 710, been converted to the ideas of Rome and Canterbury by Abbot Coelfrid, the Columbans were expelled.[1]

King Angus of Pictland, styled *MacFergus* ("King Hungus" of legend), carried the religious development of Scotland, and consequently its inter-related constitutional and tribal development, a great step farther when he introduced the cult of St. Andrew in 757. In 756 he had, with Edbert, King of Northumbria made a successful campaign against the kingdom of Strathclyde but on returning eastward, Symeon of Durham records that, between "Ovania" and "Newburgh" a disaster overwhelmed Edbert's army. Scottish tradition fills in the picture : The Northumbrian army commanded by "Atholstan" seems to have swung north into East Lothian threatening the Pictish kingdom. A vision of St. Andrew's Cross in the sky, with the Pictish bishops promise of victory, encouraged the Picts to attack. Having annihilated Edbert's army at Athelstaneford, Angus returned to Fife, where at the headland of Kilrymount he was duly met by St. Regulus, who had just landed with the—alleged—sacred relics, and thereupon was founded what in due time became the Archepiscopal See and Burgh of St. Andrews. King Angus I died in 759.

In A.D. 836, Alpin, virtually the last of the Dalriadic Scottish kings, fell near Laicht Castle, on the ridge which separates Kyle from Galloway. The accession of the son of Alpin, Kenneth MacAlpin, to the kingdom of the Scots, marks the beginning of a new epoch in the history of the Highlands. Historians disagree as to the manner of the fusion of the Picts with the Dalriadic Scots. Kenneth had ruled his father's kingdom of Dalriada for a few years prior to A.D. 843, when the death of Eoghann, King of the Picts, opened to him the succession, apparently through his mother being a Pictish princess. His right to the throne was apparently not readily admitted. No doubt Kenneth's sovereignty of Dalriada was regarded as an obstacle to his becoming *Ard-righ Albainn*—just as there is a tendency to prevent the merging of two ancient noble families or houses. The Pictish nobles seem to have resisted his claim. At any rate, there seems to have followed a conference at Scone—which had become the sacred centre of Pictavia —where, at a banquet, or conclave, Kenneth apparently met the "Seven Earls" of Alba. Whatever they were going to do, Kenneth —by what is vaguely termed "the treachery of Scone"—had all seven murdered, and thereupon seems to have been inaugurated *Ard-righ* without further question. At any rate, Kenneth MacAlpin became king of the united Picts and Scots in A.D. 843, and was crowned at Scone not long after in the Pictish monastery on the ancient Stone of Destiny, which to the present day is the Coronation Stone for all the British monarchs. This Stone (see Appendix No. II.) was taken in 1296 by the English king, Edward I., to Westminster, where it has

---

[1] Iona was sacked by the Vikings in A.D. 825. Whilst many of the wonderful treasures of Iona were then lost, relics of St. Columba were later transferred to Dunkeld, which then became the chief seat of the Celtic Church in Pictland.

since remained. In 1328, though its return was not demanded in the Treaty of Northampton, it was purposed to restore the Stone to Scotland; the citizens of London, however, would not permit of its removal. The early capital of King Kenneth was Dunstaffnage (in Argyll); however, shortly after his accession to the kingship of the united Picts and Scots the capital of the kingdom was transferred to Scone, where the historic " Moot Hill " became thenceforth the legal centre of *all* Scotland, as it already was of Pictland.

The close of the ninth century saw all Caledonia united under one monarch, and its inhabitants known as *Gaedhil*, or Gaels. Contemporaneously, however, with the period of fusion between Picts and Scots, and the foundation of a monarchy, which became that of united Scotland, the coasts of Scotland and the Western Isles were being harried and dominated by the Norsemen. The Norse inroads commenced in the north about A.D. 750, and in the Western Isles about A.D. 794. These at first were mere piratical forays. However, a century later, an important revolution in Norway led to the foundation of Norwegian kingdoms of the Western Isles and Orkney and in the north of Scotland. The year A.D. 872 saw Harold Harfagar established as the first king of all Norway. Many of Harold's opponents then fled from Norway and formed piratical settlements among the Scottish Isles, whence they issued to harry the coasts of Norway. In order to stop these forays, the Norwegian king fitted out an expedition, subdued the piratical Norsemen, and added the Isles to the Crown of Norway. About A.D. 894 a second Norse territory was formed in Scotland, consisting of Caithness, Sutherland, and part of Ross, Inverness, and Argyll. The Western Isles of Scotland, with the Isle of Man, were termed by the Norsemen the *Sudreys*, to distinguish them from Orkney and Shetland, which the Norwegians designated the *Nordereys*. The name *Sudrey* is still perpetuated in the designation of the English bishopric of *Sodor* and Man.

It was not until 1266 that the Norwegians were finally expelled from Scotland, except the Orkney and Shetland Islands. The Danes never obtained a footing in the Highlands of Scotland. The part of Scotland ravaged by them was the south-east coast.

Constantine II., the son of Aedh, and grandson of King Kenneth MacAlpin, occupied the throne of Alba between A.D. 900 and A.D. 942.

In A.D. 908 the direct line of the sovereigns of the Britons of Strathclyde became extinct, and Donald, the brother of Constantine, King of Alba, was, under the machinery appropriate when the throne became *de jure* and *de facto* vacant, elevated to fill the vacant throne. This paved the way to the eventual uniting of the kingdoms of Alba and Strathclyde under one monarch.

Malcolm MacKenneth (1005–1034) was perhaps the greatest of the lawgivers amongst our Celtic sovereigns, and indeed amongst the earliest of our Scottish legal codes is that intituled " The Laws of King Malcolm MacKenneth." How far the diction preserves or includes the acts of King Malcolm is a matter of dispute, but the early chroniclers all remark upon his juristic achievements, amongst one of which was the crystallising of the law of succession, which became, and still remains, the law and order of common law succession in the law of Scotland. The tribal system of succession in relation to the *gilfine, derbhfine, iarfine,* and *indfine,* was so complicated that Irish historians doubt if it can ever have really worked in practice, as it was laid down in theory. It was of such a complicated nature that wrangles about what it meant, and how it was applied, led to bloody family dissensions at almost every succession. Malcolm MacKenneth therefore evolved a simpler and more direct evolution of the *derbhfine* system, which preserved the principle and continuity of the Celtic structure, whilst eliminating the difficulties and grounds for dispute which had existed in the system introduced from Ireland. For some time naturally the collateral heirs, due under the confusing system of alternate succession between the chiefs of two, or three, *derbhfines,* raised trouble when the succession devolved upon the direct heir through a son or daughter, but before long the simplicity and wisdom of King Malcolm's law was recognised, the more so, perhaps, because from its analogy to the divine law of succession laid down in Numbers xxvii., it naturally received the full endorsement of the Christian Church.

Under Malcolm II., whose reign lasted thirty years, the kingdom made material progress. The Danes, who had made a raid on the coast of Moray, were so severely defeated that they abandoned all further attempts to effect a settlement in Scotland. In 1018 Malcolm, along with his tributary, Eugenius the Bald, King of Strathclyde, invaded Northumbria, and inflicted a crushing defeat on Eadulf Cudel, the Earl of that province, at Carham on the Tweed. The result was the cession to the Scottish king of the rich district of Lodoneia, or Lothian. This included not only the territory comprised by the three Lothians, but Berwickshire and lower Teviotdale, as high as Melrose on the Tweed. It was about this time, too, that the Caledonian kingdom began to be named *Scotia* by chroniclers. By the Gaelic inhabitants, however, their land was, as it still is, designated *Alba.*

Eugenius, King of the Strathclyde Britons, died in the year the Battle of Carham was fought. With him expired the direct MacAlpin line of the kings of Strathclyde. Duncan, grandson and eventual successor to King Malcolm of Scotland, was selected, evidently by nomination of the *Ard-righ,* in order to effect the union of the kingdom, to fill the vacant British throne.

On the death in 1034 of Malcolm II. without male issue, he was succeeded, under the new law, by his grandson, Duncan I., son of his daughter the Princess Bethoc, or Beatrice, and her husband Crinan, Hereditary Abbot of Dunkeld and Dull, who, as stated above, was already King of the Britons of Strathclyde. Duncan was a young man and had the reputation of being a good king, and his reign lasted until 1040, when, after a defeat at the hands of the Norsemen, he was slain near Elgin by Macbeth, Mormaer of Moray.

Macbeth thereupon ascended the Scottish throne in right of his wife *Gruoch nighean Bode*, who under the older alternating order of succession would have, apparently, had a claim to the throne, and tradition probably does not err in attributing to her influence Macbeth's action in disposing of the young Duncan who was apparently not a very effective military leader. Macbeth appears to have made an excellent sovereign, but, from the circumstances of his succession, naturally found himself in opposition to the Church, and consequently was given a bad reputation. He was eventually, in 1057, defeated and slain at Lumphanan, in Mar, by Malcolm, son of Duncan I. The victorious prince was crowned at Scone as Malcolm III. Malcolm is, however, better known to history as Malcolm *Ceann-mór* (or big-head), so named owing to the peculiar shape of his head.

The reign of Malcom Ceann-mór was remarkable for a variety of circumstances, which tended towards the drifting of the monarch from his Gaelic to his Lowland subjects, but which contributed indirectly to the development of the Highland clan system.

Malcolm contributed to the organisation and development of Scotland as a united and organised kingdom, and, moreover, to the high degree of tribal development in Scotland, which we recognise in the clan system. About 1066 Malcolm selected for his settled capital, Dunfermline, the picturesque little city in the old Pictish province of Fife, and so much did the Royal house become attached to the cathedral city founded there in this reign that Dunfermline Abbey became the place of sepulture of many Scottish monarchs in place of Scone, which, however, with its historic moot hill, still remained the official centre and constitutional seat of the Scottish sovereigns and the spot where their coronations took place. About the very time at which Malcolm settled at Dunfermline occurred the Norman Conquest of England, as a result of which a number of noble Saxon families fled to Scotland, where they were well received by the king, who assigned them grants of land. What actually happened was, as Professor Rait explains,[1] that the kings " did not interfere with the ownership of land as it existed before these grants ; the result of his intervention was ultimately to confirm it. What the king gave his friends consisted rather of rights over land than of land itself." The *dominium utile*, as it is called, remained with the Celtic chieftains and their dependents, and by the new tenure they got a legal security for ownership ; new lords only got their castle, the demesne, and right of a following, whilst they also got the *dominium directum*, namely, presiding in the new Baron Court as a local Parliament. Among the refugees were Edgar the Atheling, the rightful heir to the English Saxon throne, who was accompanied by his mother and his sister Margaret. While later the Norman barons merely consolidated existing Celtic land usages, Margaret, on the

[1] *The Making of Scotland*, p. 27.

other hand, made social innovations. The Princess Margaret was espoused by King Malcolm in 1070, and as she obtained a great influence over her husband, the queen was instrumental in introducing many Saxon innovations at the Scottish Court. Among these was the supersession of Gaelic as the court language by Saxon. Queen Margaret used all her influence to replace the rites of the Celtic Church by those of Rome. She had frequent discussions on the subject with the Scottish clergy whose language was Gaelic. On those occasions, we are told, King Malcolm, who spoke both the Gaelic and Saxon languages, acted as interpreter.

These events we have narrated led to the introduction into Scotland of many new names. Indeed, the introduction of surnames into Scotland is attributed to this reign. The *Chronicles of Scotland* relate that " He [Malcolm] was a religious and valiant king ; he rewarded his nobles with great lands and offices, and commanded that the lands and offices should be called after their names." It is not to be supposed that he did this specifically, but he did bring about a state of progress wherein the chiefs of tribes came to be named from, or gave names to, their *duthus*, and began to use such names.

Malcolm Ceann-mór, after a prosperous reign, was killed at the siege of Alnwick, in Northumberland, in 1093. The king's family were then all under age, and his brother Donald (known as " Donald Bane ") succeeded to the Scottish throne as Donald III. During the short reign of this sovereign he acquired a considerable measure of popularity among his Gaelic subjects by the expulsion from Scotland of many of the Saxon immigrants, who had been settled in the kingdom by his brother and predecessor. Donald Bane thus reigned along with Eadmund, eldest-surviving son of Malcolm and Margaret. This is usually represented as a usurpation, or assertion by Donald of a supposed earlier system of collateral succession. It is overlooked that under one of the old Scoto-Celtic laws which long survived, and to which attention is drawn by Skene [1] and Fordun, if the heir, either male or female, was under fourteen, the nearest agnate (heir-male), became chief or king for life, but when the heir attained majority he also reigned jointly with his—if we may so describe it—" trustee for life," and a situation arose in which there was a " joint reign." In primitive days it was no doubt difficult for the heir, on coming of age, completely to dispossess a man who had during the minority taken all the effective threads of power into his own hands, and a joint reign was perhaps in those days the expedient least likely to lead to civil war or domestic tragedy. However, in 1097, this joint form of monarchy was brought to an end through intervention of Edgar Atheling (brother-in-law of Malcolm Ceann-mór), who succeeded in dethroning both Donald Bane and Eadmund and placed Eadgar, next brother of Eadmund, on the throne. His reign was an unfortunate one, for during it the Norwegian king, Magnus, surnamed Barefoot, succeeded in obtaining possession of the Western Isles and Kintyre.

[1] *Highlanders*, p. 105.

Eadgar died in 1107 and was succeeded by his next brother, who became king under the style of Alexander I. King Alexander probably ruled over a still smaller territory than his brother and predecessor, as what remained of the Scottish territory was divided between himself and his younger brother David. Alexander ruled over the territory north of the Forth and Clyde as well as the debatable land, including Edinburgh, with the title of king. His brother David, on the other hand, became ruler of the rest of Lothian and Cumbria with the title of Prince of Cumbria. Through his wife, Matilda, daughter of Waltheof, Earl of Northumberland, David became Earl of Northampton and Lord of Huntingdon, in England. These English honours were retained by the Scottish Royal Family until the War of Independence.

On the death of Alexander I. in 1124, he was succeeded by David, Prince of Cumbria, his brother, and the Scottish territories became once more united. During Alexander's reign a serious rebellion broke out in the ancient province of Moray. This was subdued by the king in 1116, when a large tract of territory was confiscated.

A further influx of foreigners into Scotland took place in the reign of King David, this time of Normans as well as of Saxons. Grants made by the king to his new subjects, Saxons and Normans, were in what are now known as the Lowlands of Scotland, and were feudal ones, namely a written grant by knight-service, in which the older Celtic system of landholding was gradually placed on record and incorporated in the great new and businesslike system of feudal tenure, under which, in Scotland, as in early medieval France, the family, as an organised unit, was given permanent recognition in law, and in connection with the fief, *mesnie*, or in Gaelic, *duthus*. The Normans were by far the greatest business-men of the Middle Ages ; they were quick to perceive the immense social value and practical advantage of the organised family which we recognise pre-eminently in the clan system, and the machinery which they had adopted in France, although somewhat unpopular in England where it had to be imposed after the Conquest, and the national defeat of Hastings, nevertheless instantly appealed to the Scottish king and his Celtic nobles as a highly popular institution for effective co-ordination and perpetuation of the Celtic family system. At a later period some of these non-Celtic families (of whom the Frasers and the Gordons may be cited as notable examples) obtained a footing in the Highlands, where they soon became *Hiberniori quam ipsi Hiberni*, more Highland than the Highlanders. Indeed, the latter of the above-named families (the Gordons) attained such power in the Highlands that their chiefs came to be known as " the Cocks of the North."

Moray, however, was not long at rest ; for, in 1130, during the absence of King David in England, Angus, Earl of Moray, along with Malcolm, his brother, sons of Heth, Earl of Moray, raised another rebellion. The revolt, however, was not only completely quelled by the king, but the Celtic Earldom of Moray was forfeited. It was not revived until after the Battle of Bannockburn, when the Earldom of Moray was conferred by King Robert the Bruce on his nephew, Sir Thomas Randolph.

In 1139, Stephen, King of England, ceded to David's son the whole Earldom of Northumberland, with the exception of the castles of Newcastle and Bamborough, and to David, Cumberland.

David's reign lasted till 1153. He was remarkable for the liberal donations made by him to the Church. Indeed, of such a munificent description were these benefactions, that they drew from King James VI. the regretful complaint that David was " ane sair sanct for the crown."

David's eldest son, Henry, having predeceased him, his successor was his grandson, Malcolm IV., who was only twelve years of age at the time of his accession. Young as the king was he soon showed an aptitude for government, though he had a short reign of twelve years only, as he died in 1165. He had to deal with several insurrections, one of the most serious being that of the " Maister Men," namely, several of the great earls who objected to the king's continental expedition to the siege of Toulouse, and it is likely an attempt was made to dethrone him, which would apparently have been successful had good generalship not prevented the development of an anticipated rebellion in Moray, as well as others in Ross and Galloway. During this reign the latter—which had hitherto been ruled by its own princes —was brought into immediate subjection to the Scottish Crown. In Moray, which had proved the most recalcitrant of the Scottish provinces, apparently on account of the tradition of the Macbeth claim, King Malcolm instituted a mass-readjustment of population, many of the troublesome Morays being given lands in Ross-shire and in the south of Scotland, whilst the swampy tracts in the Laigh of Moray were feued by knight-service to men competent to drain the marshes and become loyal vassals of the king. The most striking feature of the reign is that all these improvements were effected by amicable arrangement, for in 1160 King Malcolm effected a treaty with Somerled, Lord of the Isles, who had been supporting the MacHeth party in Moray, and which presumably related to these arrangements. Nevertheless, they quarrelled four years later in 1164, when, their opposing armies having met at Renfrew, Somerled was either killed in battle or, as some say, murdered in his tent. Whilst Malcolm thus succeeded by firmness and diplomacy in materially consolidating his realm, he was nevertheless obliged in 1157 to cede the Scottish possessions in Northumberland and Cumberland to Henry II. of England.

The proceedings in Moray connected with the MacHeth rebellion also bear on the history of the Clan Murray (whose centre was the Castle of Duffus) and the Clan Mackay, which claims descent from *MacHeth*. If so, their seat as *Ri Moreb* was presumably the Castle Hill of Elgin, whilst possibly their territory comprehended the " dominium " of Kilmalemnock, with the " thaneages therein " as one charter expresses it. If so, there was evidently rivalry between the race of

MacHeth and the race of Freskin for the " representation "—indicated by the title "de Moravia." The Crown and Somerled seem to have agreed that the MacHeth line be transferred to the remotest corner of Scotland—Strathnaver, the Crown thus securing the main fortress of Moray, whereupon the House of Freskin took the style " de Moravia," as the principal house of the race left in Moray. Freskin, in this view, had an interest to concur in the expulsion of the line which claimed the " kingship " of Moray and the Castle Hill of Elgin.

Malcolm IV. was succeeded by his brother William I., surnamed the Lion, who occupied the throne until 1214, and is famous in history as the king who first adopted the lion rampant as his heraldic device. During an expedition in 1174 into England with the view of recovering the possessions ceded by his predecessor to Henry II., King William was taken prisoner by the English. He was released at the end of the year ; not, however, until as a condition of his release, the Scottish king had agreed to do homage for his kingdom to the monarch of England, and to give, as pledges for this, the castles of Roxburgh, Berwick, Jedburgh, Edinburgh, and Stirling. During the reign this disgraceful treaty was, however, abrogated by Richard Cœur-de-Lion in 1189 in consideration for the payment by Scotland of 10,000 merks, equal to over £20,000 in silver weight. Of course the purchasing power was immensely greater. Whilst all claims on the Scottish monarchs for homage for Scotland were expressly abrogated, it was stipulated that homage by the Scottish to the English sovereigns should continue for the fiefs and titles held by the former in England.

In 1187 at an important battle—Mamgarvie—Donald MacWilliam, the great-grandson of Malcolm Canmore by Ingibiorg, his first wife, and thus Canmore's lineal heir, was slain, and the position of the line of William the Lion thus firmly established upon the throne. William's successor, Alexander II., did a good deal to consolidate the kingdom, and in 1230 finally crushed the claims of the House of MacWilliam to the throne of Scotland, Gillescop MacWilliam being slain, and his little daughter cruelly put to death at the cross of the burgh of Forfar to extinguish the line.

In 1234, during the reign of King Alexander II., son of William the Lion (1214–1249), occurred the death of Alan, last Prince of Galloway. This Prince left no male issue. King Alexander, therefore, despite the opposition of the inhabitants of the principality (who naturally held that, in any event, the heir of line should, by the custom of the country, have succeeded), overcame all resistance and annexed the principality of Galloway to the kingdom of Scotland, dividing it into three feudal districts.

During the Royal campaign in Galloway material aid was rendered to the king by Farquhar Macintagart, second Earl of Ross. In recognition of the Earl's services he received a grant of land in Galloway, of which his successors retained possession for the best part of two centuries. This grant to one of the chiefs of the northern Highlands may be one of the reasons for finding in that province surnames, which in several cases are identical with those borne by families in the Highlands of Scotland. Alexander II. was sympathetic to the ideals of the Highland chiefs and paid several visits to the western coasts, on the last of which he died on the Isle of Kerrera near Oban.

Alexander III., son of Alexander II., who occupied the throne between the years 1249 and 1286, had the distinction of commanding the Scottish army at the decisive Battle of Largs in 1263, when the Norwegians, under Haco, their king, were completely defeated and finally driven from Scotland. It was not, however, until the reign of King James VI., on that monarch's marriage to Anne, Princess of Denmark, that the Orkney and the Shetland Isles were, by treaty, added to the kingdom of Scotland.

King Alexander was killed in 1286 at Kinghorn, in Fife, owing to the fall of his horse over a cliff. His sole heir was his grand-daughter, Margaret, Princess of Norway. After a " reign " of four years the young heiress to the Scottish Crown died, however, on the voyage to Scotland, and the whole of Scotland was, as a consequence of this untimely death, suddenly plunged into confusion and woe. This period of trouble did not come to an end till, at the beginning of the following century, the kingdom emerged triumphantly from her troubles after the Battle of Bannockburn. The close of the thirteenth century, however, while inaugurating a disastrous period for Scotland, was also noteworthy in that it also heralded the commencement of the Highland clan system, and the War of Independence really had the effect of establishing Scotland as the model tribal kingdom which has become so famous in world history. Indeed, but for the accession of the heroic Bruce, and his accurate conception of the proper model for a free feudal realm in which liberty could really flourish under the wholesome clan-family organisation, Scotland would, under a continuance of the line of Alexander III., probably have sunk into an Anglian province crushed under centralised governance.[1]

The end of the Celtic-Atholl dynasty has been said to mark also the decline of the old Celtic Church, but notices of the Culdees are found at least down to 1332—the year of Dupplin—but its formal influence had virtually ceased before the end of Alexander's reign. Had this not been so, it would almost certainly have also recovered its position under the Bruce. Its influence, however, continued, as we shall see, to modify Roman practice, and to receive Papal sympathy down to the Reformation ; the enemies of the Culdees appear rather to have been fanatic minor proselytes and their sin-conscious patrons, than the princes of the Holy See and the Scottish Episcopate.

Queen Margaret was a narrow-minded and ill-tempered virago,[2] completely under the dominance of her confessor, Turgot, who had inspired her with an intense dislike of the Celtic Church. She exerted such influence upon her husband, so impressed her religious views

[1] Professor Rait, *The Making of Scotland*, p. 62.   [2] *Per* J. R. N. Macphail, K.C.

upon her sons, that a campaign for " conversion " of the Celtic Church to the more recently evolved Roman doctrines was embarked upon. The Celtic Church defended itself vigorously, so its ultimate absorption was achieved not by persecution but by a gradual process of filling Culdee benefices, as they fell vacant, by priests qualified according to the later Roman tenets. The most active of the successors of Malcolm Ceann-mór in this course was King David I., who, partly from ecclesiastical influence and partly from a belief that the founding of abbeys would assist in developing the resources, and facilitating the government of the country, made immense grants to the now fashionable monastic orders which were spreading through Christendom, but which were moved by motives quite different (the saving of their own monkish souls) from the tribo-religious functions of the Celtic Abbacies—or indeed the episcopates of the Church of Rome. The latter existed to propagate religion internationally in a beautiful form, whilst the Celtic Church-monachist existed to preserve and impart that same religion, consonantly with the local art and tradition of each Celto-tribal realm. The lesser clans which did not, like the Righ and Mormaers, have abbeys, also continued each to venerate the local co-arb (heir) of the primitive saint by whom the tribe had been led from paganism into the fold of Christianity.

The Celtic Church was thus essentially a clan-church,[1] though it was later merged in the Roman system. Coincidentally with the development of this we find the English archbishops endeavouring to assert their supremacy over the Scottish clergy. These English pretensions were strenuously and successfully resisted by the Scottish sovereigns ; for, in 1188, Pope Clement III., in a Bull addressed to King William the Lion, recognised the independence of the Scottish Church, and declared " the Church of Scotland to be the daughter of Rome by special grace, and immediately subject to her." However, the Culdee star continued to pale before the rising sun of continental monasticism, and a century and a half later the name of Culdee disappears from the annals of Scotland.

The Celtic Church, like every other institution in Scotland, was tribal and hereditary. It was monachistic rather than episcopal, more analogous to the hereditary priesthood of early civilisations (cf. the Levites of the Old Testament), and the tendency was evidently for each provincial kingship or tribe to have its own saints and hereditary, but uncelibate, monastic organisation. " The soul of Celtic monachism was Christianity, but its body was the tribe or family," as Dr. G. G. Coulton says,[2] continuing :

Celtic monasticism, then, was founded on the tribal or family principle as was the society around it. The monastery with its endowments were

---

[1] The " Culdees " (Céle Dé, servants of God) do not seem to have been co-extensive with the whole Celtic Church, but one of the branches of its monastic element.

[2] G. G. Coulton, Scottish Abbeys and Social Life, 1933, pp. 16–17,

the possessions of a particular family, and as a natural consequence they became something still more unusual in monastic history—they became hereditary. Columba named his own cousin as his successor [1] and 120 years passed before there was any free election of an abbot of Iona. Out of the first eleven abbots, nine were certainly of Columba's family. The common Celtic title for the successors of saints like Patrick or Columba [2] in their abbacies was *co-arb*, which literally means " heir," and throws the emphasis upon inheritance rather than upon choice or appointment. [3]

Six centuries later, when a few representatives of this Celtic Church survived under the name of Culdees, we find that the Abbot of Abernethy is also lord of the lordship of Abernethy, and that he not only grants tithes out of his property there, but asserts that property to be the inheritance of himself and his heirs.

This seems really an instance of the identity of chief and high priest, a doctrine refurbished at the Reformation in the Crown as Head of the Church ; but in the Celtic form this, I think, applied only to certain families, those of the hereditary abbots, who thus formed an hereditary tribal priesthood. The organisation of the Celtic Church thus differed fundamentally from that of the " regular " monastic orders of the Roman Church, and also in important aspects from the —later—regulations adopted by the Church of Rome.

In accordance with tribal principles the old Celtic priesthood was traditionally a married one—in that respect like the Greek Orthodox Church, but with a different significance—and this subsisted even in the Scoto-Roman Church where, of course, the custom of the priests perpetuating the old Celtic practice of a married clergy, was frowned on by the officials of the Roman Church—and later seized on as a handle for opprobrious propaganda by Calvinist reformers—who were as opposed to the Celtic as to the Roman Church.

The Celtic abbeys were thus the seats of lines of hereditary abbots whom the Roman chroniclers chose inaccurately to describe as " lay abbots," and it was this tribal priesthood of these abbacies which evolved, and for centuries developed, the beautiful series of carved

---

[1] Here we have an instance of what I might call " ecclesiastical tanistry." It illustrates exactly what was the corresponding practice in the tribe itself ; tanistic testate succession was the rule—" election," and later intestacy, was an expedient to cover an unusual emergency.

[2] I feel great doubt about the identity of perambulating saints, as described in G. A. F. Knights's *Archæological Light on the Early Christianising of Scotland.* Travelling conditions, and the span of life, would surely have made it impossible for them to impress their personality on so many districts, and looking to the long period involved and the tribal character of religion, I feel many are different, and strictly local " saints "—who may, of course, have been named after, and derived Christianity from, " the original saint " of the name.

[3] This would be absolutely true of the period subsequent to Malcolm McKenneth, but as elsewhere indicated I think in the earlier tribal period the concept of heir was primarily tanist—nominee—the member whom the chief had selected for his re-embodiment, and who thus got his *universitas*, or heirship. I, of course, agree with Dr. Coulton that the emphasis was on Inheritance.

monuments which are found all over the Highlands including Pictland.
Each of the great tribal districts had some peculiar variety of the
Cross or other ornaments indicating the high degree of local individuality
which has ever continued throughout the old local divisions of Scotland
in matters alike lay and ecclesiastical.

The beautiful Celtic Church was anathema to the imported
monastics (then obsessed with asceticism) and St. Bernard denounced
the hereditary monasteries of Scotland and Ireland as " an abominable
custom " but gives the interesting information that " men suffered
no bishop to be appointed but from men of their own tribe and family,
and this execrable succession was of no recent date, for some fifteen
generations had now gone by in this wickedness. . . . Before Celsus
(Primate of Ireland) there had been eight generations (or primates) of
married [1] men not in orders [2] yet imbued with letters." [3]

That these hereditary prelates, and their monks, were " imbued
with letters " (which the Bernardine ascetics were not !) and exponents
of fascinatingly beautiful art (which the early Bernardines foreswore),
the magnificent Celtic missals and other " ancient books " of Celtic
monasticism amply testify. Moreover, they were nobles—and proud of
it. Indeed, it was a dispute with St. Finbar regarding the copying of one
of these volumes that led to the princely St. Columba settling at Iona.

It is only necessary to examine what the Viking raids have left of
their beautiful workmanship and carving to realise that this tribal
priesthood had raised religion to a far far higher standard than contemporary continental clergy, and that the religious arts and culture
which were being handed down by these clan abbots from father to
son were an entrancing contrast to the " save-my-own-soul " rules of
early continental monasticism before it blossomed into the " custom
of Cluny," the great Burgundian abbey which, under the especial appro-
bation of the Papacy, developed the tradition of " splendour in the
worship of God," and which—like its daughter-house of Paisley in
Scotland—was more in accord with the traditions of the Celtic Church.

Coulton points out that the medieval monks themselves achieved
but little in art and scrivening, but both as regards building, and the
scriptorium, excepts " the really vigorous days of the Celtic Church." [4]
Such being the effects of hereditary ecclesiasticism—as with other
hereditary effort [5]—it is interesting to find he observes, even in the
mid-fifteenth century, that " St. Columba's monastery of Iona had,
naturally kept something of the colour of its original Christianity . . .
(and) . . . a remarkable survival from those days of tribal monasticism," [6] but extraordinarily inconsequent to describe it as " the
bad old tribal tradition," this being the tradition of the only Church

---

[1] Married priests are still licensed by the Pope (*Sunday Mail*, 4th November
1951, p. 10). So Celtic practice was not *fundamentally* incompatible.
[2] Presumably Celtic orders. [3] *Scottish Abbeys and Social Life*, 1933, p. 44.
[4] *Ibid.*, pp. 159, 189. [5] F. F. Brentano, *Old Regime in France*, pp. 61–71
[6] *Abbeys and Social Life*, p. 225.

and period, in which he admits there was vigorous monastic activity in art and learning !

At Iona, St. Margaret had endeavoured to introduce the non-Celtic monastical practices, and, after the Norse desecrations, Reginald Mac Somerled, by 1203, installed Benedictine monks, regarding whom there was a dispute with the *co-arb* of St. Columba, and the Celtic Church apparently retained an office of " Prior of Iona " and still influenced the whole character of the settlement. Consequently, the position was that until the fifteenth century Iona was continuing the grand traditions of its Celtic past, and its abbots were of princely and noble rank, until the death of Abbot MacFingon. Then an ignoble appointee, Abbot Dominic, resolved to break with Celtic tradition and decided that in future no one of noble rank should be admitted, when, of course, the whole standard of culture and religious splendour would have declined.[1]

The low-born monks introduced by the unworthy Dominic based their plot for destroying the ancient Celtic character of the monastery of Icolmkill on the ground that the then deceased Abbot Fingon, had, by a formal contract, openly made the usual and proper provision for the Lady Moire—in Celtic rule, his wife, and under Scoto-Roman terminology " honourably as concubine "—to whom, in Celtic law, he was proving (as Dr. Warrack expresses it of the Parson of Stobo),[2] an " exemplary husband."

The terminology employed in the deed to comply with the ruling Canon Law principles of St. Andrews, was none too flattering, but it was a compromise, and the fact is that the Popes did endeavour to find, and apply, a compromise with Celtic tradition, and granted successive appointments to the issue of these unions between " a priest and an unmarried woman " (for which there are many Scottish petitions) ;   and   this   " ancient   Celtic   priestly   marriage "—not " monastic abuse," as Coulton calls it—was duly " supported by the head of the Church,[3] the low-born monks snubbed, and Lachlan, *duine-uasail* of Clan Maclean, a meet successor of the noble Columban monks, duly admitted ; whilst towards the end of the century, another Mackinnon Abbot was amongst those who beautified the Cathedral. The Church of Scotland seems fortunately to be steadily finding its

---

[1] The Celtic system was based on the family pyramid, in which the best of taste in craftsmanship or other attainments was fostered in hereditary families. It was by the gradual and continued spreading of these liberal attainments, from a purely preserved stock of each, that the high level of tribe-attainment was achieved. Similarly, hereditary craftsmen were noble-like, or " masters " of their own work ; and the co-ordinating of these—very noble—efforts lay with the chieftainly and abbatical *derbhfines* of *daoine-uasal*. Cutting out this capacity for applying, or functions, of a nation's " nobility " has invariably led to cultural decline, if not reversion of the entire national stock to cultureless savagery—as in the case of the Inca civilisation in Peru, when their *noblesse* was all but extinguished by the Spaniards.

[2] J. Warrack, *Domestic Life in Scotland*, pp. 40, 61.

[3] *Ibid.* p. 226.

way back to the early principles and beautiful ideas and architecture of the Celtic Church.[1]

There is still much evidence of the principles of the Celtic Church in Scottish religious sentiment, and these were, of course, present even in the time of Roman Catholic hierarchy, for the Scottish prelates were ever vigorously patriotic, and whilst adopting many of the Catholic ways the older Celtic traditions persisted beneath. The " Scottish Sabbath " is directly derived from that observed in the Celtic Church, and just as that Church was abbatical, the early bishops were in Scotland subsidiary to the tribal abbots.[2]   Since abbacies were an indigenous form of religious institution in Scotland, it is significant that, whilst bishops were abolished, Abbot and Prior, as ecclesiastical titles, were not, and continued to be used and applied long after the Reformation.

The ministers who officiate in our many abbey churches (such as Iona, Paisley, Dunkeld, Dunfermline, Glenluce), and priories—such as that of the Culdees at Monymusk—are actually entitled to the old Scottish terms of Abbot and Prior.   Moreover, since it is now recognised that the Cross may, in a Scottish kirk, be depicted in a panel behind, though apparently not on, the Communion table, there is again scope for displaying the symbol of the Christian religion in the Church of Scotland.   The Cross in a panel above and behind the Communion table—as erected in the Thistle Chapel, St. Giles' Cathedral, and unveiled by King George VI., 29th July 1943—is exactly in accordance with the arrangement still seen in St. Columba's cave at Loch Coalisport, an arrangement which, it has been surmised, was fashioned by the saint himself.[3]   Reinstatement of the holy symbol in this manner so identified with St. Columba himself developed in the beautiful coloured and jewelled Celtic and square-ended Pictish crosses seen on the old sculptured stones, and glowing with gold and enamel, would make Scottish churches again worthy of comparison with those of other branches of the Christian faith, and re-emphasise what our Celtic and Pictish art has to offer to the service of God and the identification of reverent beauty with the National Church.

[1] In 1925, however, the Church of Scotland made a profound mistake in abolishing, or consenting to abolition of, the territorial character of kirks and the heritable character of the family pew, which, until then, had been related to the ownership and occupancy of land.   That is, the Church of Scotland had throughout (even after the Reformation) been related to the family and the land —that is to tribality.   The chief's, or laird's, pew, complete with arms and banner (cf. G. Scott Moncrieff, *Stones of Scotland*, p. 69), still survives, wisely, by "custom" —no doubt a faint sense of its basic significance surviving, for it is really the symbol of " the family " as an institution, and, as will be seen, an aspect which traced the National Church back to the earliest and most characteristic features of Scotland's ecclesiastical and secular civilisation.

[2] *Scotland the Ancient Kingdom*, p. 169.

[3] I. F. Grant, *Lordship of the Isles*, p. 79.

II

The Highlands and Clanship under the House of Bruce

DURING the long reign of Alexander III., named "the Peaceable," Scotland had enjoyed a "Golden Age" of steady progress, in which arts and organisation had developed, but in consistency with the traditions of Ancient Alba ; and people long looked back on the happy days of his reign. It is stated to mark the "evolution of the Highland clan system," which really means that during this progressive period the old customs had been peacefully shaped under the guidance of a sovereign and nobility sympathetic to the nation's ancient past, into the mould which was to give them permanence even through the stress which was to follow. Tribo-feudalism—the "organisation of the family"—had secured perpetuation of what Professor G. G. Coulton terms "Tribality and Inheritance" as the basis of the Scottish social and legal system ; and accordingly we find its flower— Clanship—becoming apparent in the realm of the young king who had been so characteristically inaugurated with the full ceremonial of an *Ard-righ Albainn,* and his complete genealogy declaimed according to Celtic custom by the red-robed High Sennachie, who, sometime during this reign, was also invested with the supreme control of Scottish heraldry, as appertaining to his office of Supreme Judge of Genealogies—a matter of such importance in the Celtic kingdom.

Though King Alexander, by his first wife, had two sons and a daughter, both princes had died childless by 1283, whilst his daughter Margaret, Queen of Norway, had also died, leaving by her husband, King Eric, an only child, Margaret, celebrated as "Maid of Norway," sole grandchild of King Alexander. Since he had no other near relatives, and those nearest were men with too many foreign interests, the situation for Scotland was a grave one ; and though the King subsequently married Joleta de Dreux, daughter of an ancient noble house in France, he immediately summoned the Estaits of Scotland, where, in order to obviate the possibility of trouble (the trouble which eventually proved so disastrous), the Maid of Norway, who in any event was the heir-at-law under the law of Malcolm MacKenneth, was also solemnly received as heir-designate, *i.e.* "Tanist," to the throne of Scotland.

All too soon afterwards, on 19th March 1286, as Thomas the

Rymer prophesied, Alexander III. perished in riding to rejoin his bride by dark, his horse falling over " the King's Crag " at King-horn ; and the succession devolved, alike by law and tanistry, upon the little nine-year-old Maid of Norway, thereupon, for four years, Margaret, Queen of Scots.

A Regency was at once appointed, consisting of three nobles for Ancient Alba (be-north the Forth) and three for southern Scotland ; and negotiations were entered into for Margaret's marriage with Edward, Prince of Wales, whereby (with full guarantees for the retention of Scotland's federal independence) the Union of 1603 would have been effected towards the close of the thirteenth century.

Meantime, the Maid being a " pupil " (*i.e.* under twelve or fourteen), Robert Bruce (grandfather of the patriot, and one of the collateral heirs) claimed (*a*) that he had been verbally (and apparently in open Council) nominated next heir to the throne if King Alexander died without issue ; and (*b*) conveniently omitting any reference to the little Norwegian princess, that if the Crown became *de facto* and *de jure* vacant, it lay with the " Seven Earls of Scotland " (who represented the " seven sons of Cruithne the Pict ") to choose the king, and he accordingly threatened the Regents. It may be assumed that he further designed to assert his right, from the girl-princess's tender age, that he would be entitled, if she arrived, to rule as Donald Bane had done, under the Celtic principle of the " joint-reign," described by Fordun.[1] Robert Bruce, however, held large estates in England ; Edward had got a Papal dispensation for his son's marriage to the Maid, and obviously " had no use for " a resuscitation of the " joint-reign " idea, nor maybe for a plea that the Maid, as a Norwegian subject, was ineligible as heir, so that, the Crown being " vacant," Bruce might claim as next nominee.[2] Bruce and the Seven Earls subsided with remarkable suddenness, presumably on a hint from Edwardian and Papal sources that there was, so far as they were concerned, no question of vacancy or joint-reign in the Celtic sense, though obviously the Prince of Wales would have become King of Scots *jure uxoris* (as Darnley did two and a half centuries later). The arrangements and independence of Scotland were solemnly provided for in the Treaty of Birgham, 18th July 1290. Unfortunately the Maid (on whose behalf Anthony, Bishop of Durham, as her Lieutenant, had taken over the kingdom) died at Kirkwall, on her way to Scotland in September 1290.

The contingency so long foreseen had now occurred, and the ancient realm of Scotland became the subject of contention between

[1] W. F. Skene, *Highlanders of Scotland*, 1902 edition, p. 105.

[2] The pleadings in question are fragmentary, but might yet be more fully read by modern X-ray photography. In the light of what is now known the above seems in short the tenor of Bruce's pleas and " threats " to the Regents of Scotland.

a dozen greedy litigants, whilst Edward of England had been baulked in his plan for securing the Union of the Crowns in a legitimate and amicable manner under guarantees which would have proved more satisfactory than those of the seventeenth century and of 1707.

An incautious letter from the northern Regent, the Bishop of St. Andrews, gave Edward the opportunity to announce that he had been invited to adjudicate between the claimants.[1]

Edward duly came to Norham, accompanied by his northern barons, and politely, from the depth of his pity and affection for poor Scotland (!) offered to do justice to all. Edward was indeed perhaps the greatest jurist of his age, and accompanied by Chief Justice Brabazon, and the supposedly quite independent apostolic notary, Johannes Erturi de Cadomo, inveigled the Scots magnates to permit him to adjudicate, whilst he had no difficulty in getting the mass of greedy claimants to do something more—to acknowledge him as Lord Paramount, and so give him a better title to decide. With nine of the eleven ready to make this submission, Bruce and Baliol felt they would only prejudice their claims if they stood out. The " English Justinian " accordingly proceeded to business—not as an " arbiter," but as president of a court, the peculiar character of which has until quite recently been entirely overlooked. The " paramountcy " business was a semi-private stroke of business with the claimants. What was prepared for deciding the great issue was something far more interesting.[2]

He convened a Court modelled, it is now perceived, upon the Centumviral Court, the " Court of the thirty-five Tribes " of ancient Rome, and accordingly of such an unusual nature as to disarm popular criticism. Indeed it was a most skilful and popular move, for it

---

[1] On hearing a rumour of the Maid's death, Bruce had approached Scone with an alleged army, intending to make good a reversionary claim under his nomination by the deceased king. Bishop Fraser, however, was a supporter of Baliol's claim as heir-at-law, and to forward this begged that Edward would approach the Border to " comfort the people, obviate bloodshed and help to place on the throne the man who had the proper title." Dispute has raged as to whether the Bishop betrayed his country.

[2] The great " multiplepoinding "—if I may so term it—for the Crown of Scotland has never been properly described, or reported, though it is by far the most momentous of all British " trials." A quite readable account of it will be found in J. Hill Burton's *History of Scotland*, II., pp. 202–259, which should be compared with Dr. Neilson in the *Scottish Historical Review*, XVI., p. 1, and some comments in W. C. Dickinson, *Court Book of the Barony of Carnwath*, p. xxx. Burton by no means understood the drift of many parts of the proceedings, and points which to him seemed " anomalous " (always a dangerous sort of expression, and one which too often merely covers " what we don't understand ") are capable of most interesting explanation from other sources. Moreover, many of the damaged pleadings, supposed last century to be incapable of further elucidation, could probably now be more amply deciphered by scientific photography. A full re-examination of the whole would throw much important light on ancient Scottish laws and principles of succession and procedure.

acknowledged the fact that Scotland was a thoroughly tribal kingdom. Nothing was more likely to appeal to such a clannish realm. Of course it gave the great English jurist ample opportunity to juggle with " procedure " (ultimately for deep-laid ends) ; but it is not possible to say that his Court-centumviral did not, on the whole, behave (according to its lights, and the procedure adopted) with strict— indeed too strict—judicial formality.[1]

The structure of this court-tribal was 105 persons, 104 " tryours " under King Edward's presidency. Twenty-four were chosen from his English barons, and eighty were Scottish, forty chosen by Bruce and forty by Baliol, recognised as the principal contestants. What remains a matter for further searching examination, is just why these numbers were selected, and what bearing they may have had on the tribal structure of Scotland. Allowing for the vacant throne, or substituting the so-called " Lord Paramount " or his Chief Justice *ad hoc*, the Scottish tryours would have numbered eighty-one— nine times nine, which is curiously just the equivalent of nine *derbhfines*.[2]

In this connection, one recollects Sir Æneas Macpherson's curious advice to Cluny, that in clan disputes he should, as chief, avoid personal intervention, but appoint three persons "from each house " (perhaps from his clan being " the tribe of the three brothers ") and act in accordance with their report.[3]

This appears to be simply the creation of an *ad hoc derbhfine* ; and one notes Professor Hogan's observation that questions of succession in Celtic Ireland seem to have been settled by the Royal *derbhfine* itself.[4] It seems possible that Edward somehow evolved a judicature embodying, in effect, not only some concept of the "Seven Earls and the Communitas," which Bruce had brought forward at an earlier period, but also two other groups to represent Lothian and Galloway. Conceivably there was some native tradition of such a conclave and that it represented the true nature of what the Seven Earls in their

[1] That is to say, it demonstrated the same inimical attitude towards tribal custom, which is noticed in Stair's *Institutions*, of the seventeenth century, and in the Court of Session in the nineteenth and the present century. Only in the *Courts of Chivalry* have sympathy and respect been shown (throughout the ages) for these ancient principles so closely bound up with the *jus familare*. Land having fallen *in commercie*, Law Courts have fallen into thinking of little beyond the money values, or, when they do (*e.g.* a recent decision of an eminent Lord Chancellor) drop into platitudes of assessing human values in " days of happiness," forgetting that many of the most important contributions to the community have been made by people racked by pain and long done with " happiness." Tribal law more sensibly assessed human values in *cows*, aptly recognising that capacity to function is ultimately dependent on Meat and Milk.

[2] J. Cameron, *Celtic Law*, p. 112.

[3] *The Loyall Dissuasive* (Scot. Hist. Soc. edition), p. 86.

[4] " Irish Law of Kingship," p. 249, in *Proceedings of the Royal Irish Academy*, XL.

protest had alluded to as the " Seven Earls and the Communitas "
(evidently the "seven" each with the barons of his province [1]) ;
whilst clearly Lothian and Galloway had to be considered when
Scotland be-south the Forth was involved.[2] If this should have been
so, the reason why there should have been twenty-four English
assessors would form a further subject for speculation ; unless indeed
they were simply to make up the 105 of the classical *curia centumvirale*,
and from their skill and practice in jurisprudence would assist the
" Lord Paramount "—in more ways than one! By this stage the
" paramountcy " question had been disposed of, through all the
competitors and their supporting magnates having acquiesced—as
above mentioned, the *Communitas* of Scotland had lodged objections,
which, however, had been ruled "not to the point" (*non efficax*) ;
and, sad to say, the meticulous John de Cadomo managed to slip
recording the details of this in his monumental roll. Unfortunately
for his reputation, enough subsists in Rishanger's *Chronica* to
prove there was that which the roll should have included,[3] but which
the " English Justinian " evidently did not wish on record !

---

[1] Cf. Aikman, *History of Scotland* ; Fraser Tytler, *History of Scotland*, I., 372 ;
Proc. Soc. Ant. Scot., vol. 77, p. 171, n. 3. Documents therein cited show us
that the barons and chiefs were the *Communitas*, and we must recollect that every
baron was in law and nature *chef de famille*.

[2] Not only in Peerage cases, such as that of the *Earldom of Mar*, but in most
of our more serious histories, allusion is made to this body of the " Seven Earls,"
who undoubtedly (as such) intervened in this great *Cause-Royal*. Historians,
however, have maintained the greatest reserve in treating of a subject which has
appeared so " shadowy," and on which so little has come down in " legal record."
In the light of so much fresh knowledge on tribal institutions and their relationship to early British history, it would no longer be right to evade the issues, and
assistance to be gained in assessing the course of events and development of
jurisprudence, which may depend on more serious examination of such matters.
I can simply draw attention to these rather marked features, and their possible
bearing, as lines for further research, and co-ordination of facts "curious " in
themselves, but constructively suggestive when related one to another, in the
light of modern knowledge.

[3] Much discussion has centred on who this *Communitas* was. Historians are
now satisfied it could not, and did not, mean the " Estait of the Burghs," nor
popular representative of what is called " the people." It is, I think, equally clear
just what it really was, for the *magnatus et tecius communitatis* of certain early
charters are the *comitum, baronum et proborum hominorum* of others. In these
days—and the more so in tribe-clannish realms—constitutional theory took no
cognisance of individuals, but only of communities and their representers. The
earls and barons were the magnates, each in principle chiefs and representatives
of all within their jurisdictions, and each with their own court for those within
their *potestas*, just as in earlier times the chiefs of clans were the real *Proceres
Regni* (*Loyall Dissuasive*, pp. 22, 37, 98). There were, however, many Thanes
(*Tigh-airn*), freeholders, and chieftains, " holding " directly of the Crown by
titles less than *in liberam baroniam*, yet who were equally the " representatives
of communities," to whom they stood in the position of *chef de famille* ; and it
was evidently these smaller *tenants in capite* (including chiefs of " honourable
clans" recognised as incorporeal fiefs, no doubt) who protested for the independence
of Scotland.

The great tribunal now entered on " the merits " of the claims given in by the claimants, of whom it very soon became clear that three (or four) [1] alone involved serious matters for consideration— though all were buttressed by numerous " red-herrings," the worse

---

[1] Eric, King of Norway, entered a claim, in the capacity of father of the deceased Maid of Norway, which Hill Burton dismisses with the quip that it " must surely have disturbed the gravity even of the decorous court of the Lord Superior." He forgets that, under the " modern " Scots law unhappily and inequitably laid down by a mere majority decision in " the case of John Gilbert," an obscure 16th-century suitor (since the Maid had succession and, through her so-called Lieutenant, Anthony Beck, possession of the kingdom) her father as nearest agnate, and not her maternal heirs of the Scottish blood-royal, would in a matter of ordinary heritage (most unrighteously), inherit. It is, accordingly, of the most vital importance to find that it was decided *in foro*, in a cause determined according to what had obtained in the court of Alexander III., and the 13th-century law of Scotland (*Scots Peerage*, Atholl, p. 33), regarding " earldoms, baronies, and other impartible tenures," that King Eric failed in his claim. Indeed, as Craig, the celebrated feudalist observes (*Jus Feudale*, II. 17, 9) regarding Gilbert's case, " in more important matters many of the judges changed their minds." Of these an example is the Court of Session's decision in 1633, regarding peerages (*Oliphant* v. *Oliphant*, Morrison's *Dictionary of Decisions*, cf. *D. of Dec.*, 10027), descending to heirs-general, that the honour must follow the line flowing from the grantee ; and in arms likewise, herein lies the real point of Lord Justice-Clerk Aitchison's opinion, 27th March 1941, that he would not follow the (modern) feudal law to such length as would " involve that the arms would transmit to a stranger " (1941 S.C. 686). This heraldic term—actually " stranger-in-blood "—of course in no way relates to the blood-descendants of a daughter, or heir female, and arises only in relation to a title-by-progress and a collateral ascendant. It is, moreover, intimately related to Sir G. Mackenzie's observation that a title in a " disponee " of arms under a name and arms clause is regarded as " in the nature of an original title " (*Works*, II., p. 616 and *Notes and Queries*, 20th April 1940, p. 273) " equivalent to an original right " if it proceed on a " resignation " ; and gives vital point to the distinction in form of making up such title by rematriculation to the child of an heiress, who succeeds as of right " for she was heiress herself " (noticed by Lord Jamieson in 1941 S.C. 706), and a regrant on resignation arising out of a procuratory or other writ in favour of an heir of tailzie ; and points to the necessity for great care in drafting the destinatory clause of such a confirmation or regrant, lest a divertion from the old blood, such as arose in the resettlement of the Lordship of Sinclair, should inadvertently be perpetrated. As regards heirs-general inheriting arms by succession, the repeated emphasis (Mackenzie, *Works*, II., p. 615), that arms descend " as it were a crown " ; and both Seton (*Law and Practice*, p. 331) and Stevenson (*Heraldry in Scotland*, p. 336) on the analogy of the descent of arms to the descent of a Crown, and in Scotland to the Crown, as it was adjudicated in this great court-tribal of 1292. In this then—as so frequently—the Law of Arms preserves the Law and Practice of the ancient tribo-feudal succession unwarped by the ideas of commerce and profit prevalent in " ordinary courts of law." In regard to this, one may remark that, unlike the Roman law, our chivalric Laws of Arms decline to recognise the *Familiæ Emptor*, and a " sale " of arms or Representation would be regarded as disgraceful. Settlements and tailzies of arms and chiefships accordingly bear to be " for grave and weighty considerations "—which at any rate sounds better, though these may also involve substantial assets. The point, however, is that the motive (into which the Crown in peerage transfers would—and Lyon in arms-transfers still must—look) is the " weill and standing of the houss " (cf. F. F. Brentano, *Old Regime in France*, p. 42).

the claim the more of those. Of these claimants, a tabulation will be the simplest explanation :

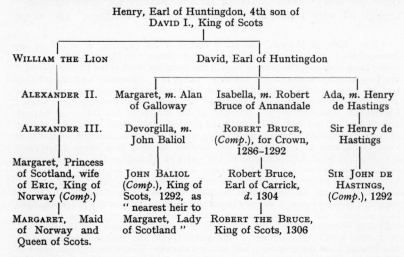

Henry, Earl of Huntingdon, 4th son of
DAVID I., King of Scots

WILLIAM THE LION — David, Earl of Huntingdon

ALEXANDER II. — ALEXANDER III. — Margaret, Princess of Scotland, wife of ERIC, King of Norway (*Comp.*) — MARGARET, Maid of Norway and Queen of Scots.

Margaret, *m.* Alan of Galloway — Devorgilla, *m.* John Baliol — JOHN BALIOL (*Comp.*), King of Scots, 1292, as " nearest heir to Margaret, Lady of Scotland "

Isabella, *m.* Robert Bruce of Annandale — ROBERT BRUCE, (*Comp.*), for Crown, 1286–1292 — Robert Bruce, Earl of Carrick, *d.* 1304 — ROBERT THE BRUCE, King of Scots, 1306

Ada, *m.* Henry de Hastings — Sir Henry de Hastings — SIR JOHN DE HASTINGS, (*Comp.*), 1292

Bruce maintained (1) that Alexander II. had nominated him heir, in the event of his dying without issue and that Parliament had confirmed that ; (2) that Alexander III. had verbally designated him heir if he died without issue, at the time the Maid of Norway was nominated and confirmed heir to her grandfather ; and (3) *separatim*, that at common law, amongst the issue of heirs-portioners, he, as son of Isabella, was one degree nearer than either Baliol or Hastings, and so behooved to succeed.

Baliol maintained that (1) as representative of the eldest sister Margaret, he was heir-at-law of the Maid, and entitled to succeed her in the kingdom she had herself inherited ; (2) supposing Bruce proved the nomination by Alexander II., that King did not " die childless," but was admittedly succeeded by Alexander and Margaret, so the nomination was superseded ; (3) that the nomination by Alexander III. was not substantiated, and likewise void. Hastings, of course, claimed that the kingdom should be divided amongst the representatives of the three daughters.

King Eric's plea, as above mentioned, was as heir-at-law *qua* nearest agnate to the Maid, his daughter, in the heritage to which she had duly succeeded and died in possession.

The eighty Scottish tryours reported that the succession to the kingdom of Scotland fell to be determined by the rules applicable to " earldoms, baronies and other impartible tenures " (naturally thaneages and chiefships and feudal superiorities), and on a second remit, that earldoms were not partible, but that baronies were partible. That is, the lands of a barony were divided amongst heirs-portioners, but the castle or *caput baroniae*, being indivisible went to the eldest daughter at common law (*Court Book of the Barony of Carnwath*) ; it was also determined that the remoter representative of the eldest daughter excluded the nearer descendant of a younger daughter—a ruling which, when it came to be applied, had the effect of postponing Bruce to Baliol. It was, however, strictly in accordance with the " Law of Malcolm MacKenneth," and what had been settled by William the Lion *in curia Regis*, in the case of the Countess of Atholl succession,[1] and was accordingly, so far as it went, perfectly good Scoto-Celtic law. The serious aspect, however, was that the Court, adapted for being influenced by the English twenty-four (who at certain points were alone consulted), succeeded in ruling out both the nominations in favour of Bruce—which do not seem to have been even admitted to probation ; and thus several vital principles of the old Celtic law (several aspects of which came to be considered later in our peerage practice) were excluded from consideration, and it would be of the greatest interest to ascertain more about the Bruce's pleadings on these points, and their relation to the protests of the *Communitas*, and on behalf of the Seven Earls.

These issues it would seem, technically speaking, would have involved the question of whether a " second heir " as well as the " Tanist " could be appointed ; and whether, if the Tanist, duly succeeding, died without himself nominating (or as in the case of the Maid age seven, being unable to nominate), the " nomination-over " by Alexander III. revived in effect (supposing it to be proved to have been made), as if the Maid had never succeeded ; or whether the Crown became an intestate heritage on her demise.

This latter seems to have been the sentiment of the great tribunal (though it so brushed the points aside that it does not seem to have pronounced on this matter on which it had prevented proof being led). The manner in which this part of the matter was disposed of probably explains why the succession to the Crown was, during the fourteenth century, on several occasions made the subject of specific and statutory tailzies, comprehending not merely a single *Tanist* or *Designatus*, but calling a tailzied line of heirs. The House of Bruce, in fact, did not forget what had occurred in 1292 ; but strange to say, in spite of their solemnity, these tailzies of the Crown made in the fourteenth century were, as Professor Hannay pointed out in 1938,[2] completely disregarded when the contingency ultimately arose in the case of Mary Queen of Scots ; and likewise, upon the death of Elizabeth, a dying nod was held to have superseded the formal settlements of Henry VIII.—so much importance, it would appear, had been attached to the untrammelled power of sovereignty, *i.e.* of an *Ard-righ*. Similarly (save under the Strict Entail Act of 1685) any heir-in-tail

---

[1] *Scots Peerage*, I., p. 423. The earldom did not pass to the heir-male collateral of Earl Patrick.

[2] *Maclean of Ardgour Evidence*, s.v. Professor Hannay.

could, by Scots law, take the appropriate steps to alter an existant
tailzie ; though, not being allodial, the intervention of his superior
(*i.e.* higher chief, or the Crown—in arms, the Lord Lyon) was necessary
to complete the resettlement.

In this respect it is to be observed that, in reply to the demands
for " Homage " Alexander III. had replied, " To homage for my
kingdom of Scotland no one has any right but God alone, nor do I
hold it of any but of God," [1] just as " Duncan, by the Grace of God,
Earl of Fife," had in 1177 set forth his allodial title to his province.[2]
The principle was affirmed by Statute 1, Charles II., cap. II. and has
more than once—as in the marriage settlements of Mary Queen of
Scots [3]—saved Scotland from annexation.

The subject of nomination (tanistry) having been thus ruled
out as inapplicable to the actual circumstances, and the meticulous
De Cadomo having—so unfortunately !—overlooked recording that
decidedly interesting part of the proceedings (he blamed, for certain
omissions, a lawsuit with the Archbishop of Canterbury, which,
he said, was taking up his time)—the more interesting as it was the
one which went to the roots of the Bruce's claim—the Court proceeded
to deliver judgement (and on the " record " a just one, according
to the laws of Malcolm MacKenneth, and the decisions cited from the
Courts of William the Lion). This was pronounced in the Castle of
Berwick in November, 1292, by the mouth of Chief Justice Brabazon,
finding John Baliol nearest lawful heir to Margaret, Lady of Scotland,
in the Crown and Kingdom.[4]

Thus the great court-tribal at any rate administered law and
justice in as exemplary a manner as could, I suppose, be expected,
and the only constitutional blot on the proceedings [5] was that the
greedy foreign claimants had acquiesed in the theory of Edward's
" Paramountcy." King Edward would, no doubt, have argued that
his power to convene the Court and act in the matter depended on
that as a preliminary ; the Scots have always maintained, as we have
seen the Seven Earls and the baronage maintained, that his position
was that of *arbiter*, not *Paramount*. Technically he should have been
appointed *ad hoc* Dempster or *Judex*, and by the Regents ; but that
would not have suited his deeper plans, which next materialised.

The right of Baliol having been judicially established, it followed,
from Edward's theory of Paramountcy, that he had to be invested
and do homage, and to pay the fees due to the various English officials
at a vassal's homage. Naturally there were no precedents on this,

[1] Register of Dunfermline, p. 217.   [2] *Scots Peerage,* IV., p. 6.
[3] Pitscottie, *History of Scotland*, II., p. 126.
[4] R. Neilson, *Scottish Historical Review*, XVI., pp. 1, 7.
[5] The exclusion of Nomination was regrettable, but, from a legal point of
view, not other than the sort of mistakes which judicatures are only too liable
to make in tackling questions they do not understand—or don't want to ! The
suspicious thing is that the exclusion thereof was not most explicitly dealt with
in the notarial record.

and no fee ascertainable as applicable for the kingdom of Scotland, so the sorry farce of inventing such had to be covered up in much verbiage. More than that, the Treaty of Birgham, only eighteen months old, stood as a most awkward monument of Scottish independence, and proved a source of no small worry to the " Lord Paramount." In doing homage, poor Baliol did his best—alleging that not yet being invested as King, he could not use the Royal Seal of Scotland, so he sealed the Act of Homage only with his personal " Baliol " seal. He deserves honour for this resourceful plan to save the independence of the Royal House and Kingdom.

Edward might have been ready to let matters proceed gently— as indeed he was ; but the English Parliament thought otherwise, and a base moneylender's prosecution was devised, obviously, as the next step in reducing Scotland's freedom. In *Moigne v. Roger*, this usurer appealed from the Scottish Court to the Lord-Superior's Parliament of England. Parliament not only sustained the competency of the appeal ; but notwithstanding even the disapprobation of King Edward, who foresaw an impossible situation was being created, the English Parliament insisted that King John Baliol must appear personally at the Bar of the English Parliament. A few more appeals, and the " King of Scots " would have found himself little other than permanent Attorney-General for Scotland in the English High Court ! Even Edward conceded the propriety of Baliol being allowed to consult the people of his kingdom about this. This scheme of the Westminster politicians, however, led to a declaration of war, in which Baliol was defeated, and obliged to resign the Crown in July 1296 ; and Edward then made his triumphal progress through Scotland, collecting forced Declarations of Homage, and on his return journey stole the Coronation Stone from Scone.

Next year, goaded by the brutal treatment of the English governors, Sir William Wallace slew William de Hasilrigg, so-called " Earl of Clydesdale " and raised the Royal Standard (*vexillum regium*, as he carefully calls it) on behalf of King John Baliol, " in name of the illustrious John, by God's Grace, King of Scotland," for the Scots maintained he had been illegally coerced in the pretended resignation of his Crown.

Wallace, appointed Guardian of Scotland on behalf of his King (then Edward's captive), fought gloriously, first in battle, and later, it appears, in the Papal Court, whence a Bill in 1298 directed Edward to desist his aggression, and emphasised that his claims to Paramountcy were, even on his own actings, unsound. In 1305 Wallace fell— betrayed for £100 by " the Fause Menteith " and his own valet ; but the proceedings of the English Parliament in the following September, annexing Scotland to England, and cancelling the ancient *Laws of the Bretts and Scots* as " unsuited to civilisation " (the well-known English, and political, view of everything familial or tribal), consolidated the national will to resistance, and young Robert the Bruce, now heir to his grandfather's rights as nominee (tanist) of Alexander III., failing that monarch's own issue, saw that the moment had come to raise once more the Scottish Royal Banner.

It is now proper to say something regarding the character of the Scottish War of Independence ; and that can hardly be better expressed than in the words of Professor W. B. Hunter Marshall (University of Manitoba), who scouts the false idea that this was " the common people of Scotland struggling against an alien nation . . . without adequate support and leadership from their natural leaders the barons, who were in reality an alien aristocracy introduced by David I. and his descendants."

After emphasising that " it was amongst the barons and freeholders that we find the dogged resistance to aggression," Professor Marshall continues : " Firstly, it is untrue to say that the greatei barons were an alien aristocracy. In many cases they were the male descendants of the old Celtic nobility, accustomed, no doubt, to life at an itinerant Court, but with their roots in a Celtic background." In 1296 the Earls of Lennox, Strathearn, Atholl, Fife, Mar, Ross, and Caithness, at least, were Celtic by race, while in addition those of Carrick, Menteith, Angus and Buchan were descendants of Celtic heiresses. . . . Of even the Norman members of the baronage, he adds that they had been established for five or six generations and lived away from the Court in a Gaelic atmosphere. The ability which the Celt has for incorporating alien military aristocracies is well known. Of the alleged " English estates," he points out, " what a comparatively small quantity of land was actually held by Scotsmen in England. . . . The history of most of the great nobles of the period shows that the general bias was towards actively opposing Edward."

Of the political tactics of the Bruces, he explains how these had always " the intention of coming forward once Edward had destroyed the prestige of the Comyns. . . . The best proof of this and of Carrick's personal policy is the secret alliance concluded by him with the greatest of moderates, Bishop Lamberton of St. Andrews, within a month of the surrender (to Edward) of Comyn."

As regards the, supposed, disastrous effects of the war, he points out that " at no time was there an effective English occupation of Scotland for more than a few months, and that the elaborate administrative systems set up in 1296 and again in 1305 had never a lengthy existence except in Lothian and along the Border." [1] Such circumstances explain why, in spite of material damage, the old Celtofeudal and Scottish character of the country progressed unaltered, indeed strengthened by the hatred engendered by the brief experience of English domination.

The Red Comyn, Baliol's nephew, having apparently sought to resist the Bruce's renewal of his claim by designation (tanistry), and attempted to betray him, was slain at Dumfries, and on 27th

[1] *Scottish Notes and Queries*, 3rd series, IX., pp. 108–111.

March 1306, in the Chapel-Royal at Scone, the patriot King was inaugurated with the ancient ceremonial, and (the *Lia Fail* and ancient crown having been removed by Edward) was crowned with a circlet, whose gold is traditionally embodied in the present crown of Scotland,[1] placed on his head by the noble Isabella de Fife, Countess of Buchan, who, in the absence of her renegade brother, performed the hereditary function of the chief of the race of MacDuff.

The Scottish Coronation embodied the formal " Inauguration " of a Celtic *Ard-righ*, and embraced three distinct features : (1) The inaugural rites of the Pictish monarchy, including investiture by the sub-king (later Earl) of Fife : (2) the inaugural rites of the kings of Dalriada, including the declamation of the Royal lineage back to Fergus Mor MacEarc, by the High-Sennachie (who evolved into the Lord Lyon King of Arms, whose judicial robe of crimson velvet is that of the Celtic Royal Sennachie) ; (3) the Christian-Episcopal rites of ordination as a Christian king, to which anointing was added by Papal consent from the reign of David II.

Space precludes us rehearsing the stirring annals of Scotland's War of Independence, many of which took place in the Highlands,[2] as when the MacDougall chief reft from Bruce's shoulder the historic brooch :

> Thence in triumph wert thou torn,
> By the victor hand of Lorn !
> When the gem was won and lost,
> Widely was the war-cry tossed.

When at last, on that memorable 23rd June 1314, beneath the hoary walls of Stirling,

> The Bruce's royal standard blazed

and the gallant army of the patriot king was marshalled for the final defence of Scotland's right,

> With these, the valiant of the Isles
> Beneath their chieftains ranked their files
> In many a plaided band.

The Drummond chief had strewn the field with those iron-spiked " caltraps " which were to bring down the mail-clad knights of England, and which are still commemorated in the Earl of Perth's coat of arms and motto " Gang warily."

Twenty-one clans had followed their chiefs to the field : Cameron, Campbell, Drummond, Fraser, Grant, Macdonald, Macfarlane, MacGregor, Mackay, Mackenzie, Mackintosh, Maclean, Macpherson,

---

[1] The crown of Scotland is preserved in state in Edinburgh Castle along with the other " honours of Scotland." Far from having " never been used " since the Union, the " honours " were (as of old) duly borne in state before George IV. in 1822, so our Scottish Regalia still hold a constitutional and useable function in Great Britain, and are not (as English writers love to pretend) a mere obsolete relic.

[2] E. Barron, *The Scottish War of Independence*, is the best account of this memorable struggle.

Morrison, Munro, Robertson, Ross, Sinclair, Stewart, Sutherland, and, of course, the clans in Randolph's great Earldom of Moray. The Cummings, MacDougalls, and MacNabs were on the Edwardian side, and suffered accordingly. At the climax of the struggle, tradition says it fell to Clan Donald to turn the day, on Bruce's call :

> One effort more, and Scotland's free !
> Lord of the Isles, my trust in thee
> Is fast as Ailsa Rock :
> Rush on with Highland sword and targe,
> I, with my Carrick spearmen charge,
> Now, forward to the shock !

Of Clan Cholla's share in the victory, Clan Ranald's motto, " My hope is constant in thee," preserves the memory.

After the seventeen stormy years (1297–1314) the glorious victory of Bannockburn established once more the rightful heir of the Celtic monarchy in open untrammelled possession of the kingdom which he had inherited by tanistry, and reconquered from the English. We are here concerned with what King Robert did to preserve and perpetuate the ancient civilisation of Scotland.

Having, by sad experience, learnt that hereditary settlements " made of record by being done in open court " were liable to be defeated, he was careful to settle the succession to the Crown by recorded statutes, first in 1315, and subsequently in 1318, when the principle of succession laid down was that enunciated by Malcolm MacKenneth, and subsequently affirmed by the Centumviral-court of 1292. It settled the Crown most explicitly on heirs-general, carefully defined. In that same year, by the ancient bardic ceremonial of the gift of a golden cup, along with the honour of knighthood, the Bruce invested a new Lord Lyon King of Arms, and in the person of his nephew, the celebrated Thomas Randolph, he revived the historic Earldom of Moray. Randolph's sister was married to a Murray, and it is possible his mother was some descendant of the old line.

In May of 1328, the Treaty of Northampton fully recognised the independence of Scotland, set forth in the Barons' Declaration of Arbroath,[1] 1320, so that on his death in 1329 King Robert saw his work accomplished. His son and successor, David II., was but five years old at his accession, and for three years Randolph ruled as Regent. In 1332, shortly after his death, Edward, son of John Baliol, with Edward III.'s assistance, invaded Scotland, and though he won the Battle of Dupplin, and had a sham coronation as England's vassal on 24th September 1332, was, three months later, ignominiously

---

[1] The clause in the Declaration that any king who submitted Scotland to England would be driven out, is said to have been introduced by Bruce's own desire and only represents the principle that any chief who, without consent of the Heads of Houses of his clan or family purposes to put them under a stranger, *ipso facto* vacates his chiefship/kingship. (Sir George Mackenzie, *Works* II., p. 446). It just emphasised this piece of *Jus Familiae* to the Pope, Emperor, etc.

chased out of Scotland. The new Regent (Douglas) was, however, defeated at Halidon Hill in 1333 ; and in the following year the young King David was sent for safety and education to the Court of France where he was trained in all the principles of chivalry, and saw France in the closing days of its great and popular tribe-feudalism, before the long misery of the Hundred Years War descended on that fair country. Meantime, under the leadership of Sir Andrew Moray of Bothwell, and the Bruce's grandson, Robert the High Steward, successively Regents, and through the resistance of such gallant people as " Black Agnes," Countess of Dunbar, the insurgent adherents of Baliol were resisted and expelled, Edward Baliol finally leaving the country in 1339. By 1341 the Citadel of Edinburgh was recovered ; and King David, now seventeen, returned to assume the Government.

It is now important to say something about the reign of David II., which has been extraordinarily misrepresented. It is described as " one of the dead periods of Scottish history, which it is preferred to ignore " ; " an inglorious reign, of which the less said the better "—and so on. When one finds a period treated in that manner, the scientific enquirer is prompted only to examine it more carefully, and to seek the " reason why "—the more so since the reign of David II. is comparatively well documented, and a period of colour and progress in which both romance and sociology leap to the eye. Why then this silence ? The fact is that the reign of David II. witnessed a strong revival of the ancient national traditions of Scotland, a veritable Celtic revival, in which the march of progress, broken since 1292, again surged forward, and in which we perceive, amidst the galaxy of medieval colour and pageantry, the resurgence of many ancient traditions, offices, and organisations. The pattern of Scotland as a consolidated tribal kingdom was becoming clear. A sufficiency of records is now available to enable historians to demonstrate its entrancing texture ; but in spite—indeed because—of that very fact coupled with another contemporary reason, this gallant and fruitful reign has been traduced by authors who uniformly like to present Scotland as a dismal land of kill-joys, and shut their eyes to its days of colour and inherent national expression. The other reason was that the unfortunate effect of his second marriage created a matrimonial scandal at which the Church took offence, and led to the clergy turning upon him, whilst the rougher baronage, expostulating at his diplomatic course in Government, grumbled politically. Nevertheless, apart from the— quite accidental—circumstance of his capture and ransom, his reign was most successful, and that ransom was assuredly far cheaper than a long series of wars would have been !

In November 1331, the young king (aged 8) was crowned at Scone, with all the ceremonial, tribal and heraldic, pertaining to the ancient monarchy which his father had so gloriously restored ; and he was further, by Papal authority, the first Scottish monarch to be anointed, a part of the ceremony performed by the Bishop of St. Andrews.

This heralded a policy of the revival of tribalism, and the further encouragement of all that was best and brightest in the chivalric tribe-feudalism he learnt at the Court of France—our ancient ally— a land still running in the ancient mould in which the king was " father of all the fathers," and every fief a " family unit," in which the *chef de famille* " reigned " with a " family council," and in which this happy and organised family life had not been warped by the brutal " free companies " of the Hundred Years War. Nor had the post-Richelieu *noblesse dorée* (largely composed of be-titled monopolists and financiers posing as an aristocracy and actually completely different from the ancient *noblesse champètere* which retained its popularity right down to the Revolution), drawn the machinery of Government away from the feudal baronage, which has ever had to rule its domains in accordance with popular wishes, and which feudal units alone represented in a practical form " Government of the people by the people and for the people."

Accordingly these five brilliant years, 1341–46, wherein our later historians say that " nothing of importance " occurred, evince from the Treasurer's Accounts and the Registers of the Great Seal, that peaceful progress—and of the right kind, including the encouragement and development of clanship—was making rapid strides, and the good old days of Alexander III. were being renewed. As sovereign of a tribal kingdom, David II. realised, and his interest in heraldry and chivalry taught him, the signal importance of the clan spirit. Three generations earlier, in the days of good King Alexander, one had seen *Ken-kynol* (Celtic chiefship) treated as honourable heritage conveyable by charter in feudal form, and it was in David II.'s reign (the very time when Dr. Cameron, Dr. Mackay Mackenzie, and, indeed, Mr. Adam, concur that clanship was taking definite form) that we find a whole series of Crown charters of chiefship of clans. As Cameron and Mackenzie, the two modern scientific experts, explain,[1] the old Celtic institutions had not been abolished. On the contrary they had been merged into feudal form—preserved in the enduring machinery of the great state-socialism or family-organisation, known as feudalism ; and in the reign of David II. we duly find them not only being perpetuated by this convenient and effective machinery, but even in the nearest Latin equivalents to the old titles. In 1343, Donald Edgar had a charter of the office of *Capitaneus de Clanmacgowin*.[2] In the following year, 1344, there is another charter,

---

[1] Evidence of John Cameron, Ph.D., and W. Mackay Mackenzie, LL.D., in *Maclean of Ardgour* v. *Maclean* proof, 1938.

[2] Great Seal, I., App. II., No. 882. The terms *Captain, Captal, Caporal* were at that time, and later, used throughout Europe as description of the chief or head of a tribe or family, and were so used in Scottish deeds (A. Macbain, Editor, Skene's *Highlanders of Scotland*, 1902 edition, pp. 406, 413). It was not until seventeenth-century writers that an attempt was made to suggest that " captain " meant something other than chief. It was mere unsound pleading

" anent the Clan of Clanconnan and who should be captain thereof," [1] terminology which makes it clear that the king, as *Ard-righ*, was, like the High Kings of Ireland, intervening to settle a dispute, and— not indeed judicially, but by his paternal prerogative—settling whc should hold the chiefship. In the same year another charter tr Michael McGorth provides *quod sit capitanus de parentela de Kenelman*,[2] which the English Index entitles " Carta anent the clan of Kenelman," thus identifying *parentela* with *clan* ; and " parentela " of course may apply to descent either by male or female—it is a most neutral term ; whilst John M'Kennedy had a charter of the captaincy of the " Clan of Muntercasduff," [3] which means, when the Gaelic is translated, " the clan of the blackfooted people." [4]

Not only these, but other old Celtic offices such as *Maer* and *Toishachdorach*, were being made the subject of charters ; and it is plain that the chivalric young king was in full sympathy with his Celtic kingdom.

In 1346, in response to a request from his ally, France, an expedition became, regrettably, called for against the English ; and for this the king assembled one of the greatest armies ever summoned in Scotland, which included the warriors of the Isles. The noble host assembled at Perth, Scotland's ancient capital ; but the unfortunate murder, by the Earl of Ross, of Reginald of the Isles, caused some of the Highlanders to withdraw. The army duly crossed the border ; but at Neville's Cross, near Durham, a hurried engagement brought disaster to the Scottish army, and King David, after a gallant defence, became the prisoner of Edward III., at whose Court he spent eleven years of captivity. Edward III., however, was the very mirror of chivalry ; and at his splendid Court, King John of France was also in nominal duress, though no prison could have been more pleasant or profitable for men of honour than that wonderful galaxy of all that legend, records, and art could do to create the atmosphere of King Arthur's Britain as troubadours had loved to picture it. Apart from the magnitude of the ransom demanded, David was magnanimously treated ; and eleven years later, in 1357, he returned (after several temporary visits) to Scotland as sovereign and free a monarch as when he fell into Edward's hands, and right enthusiastically he was

—argument ; and the term we find applied in the seventeenth century to war- leaders appointed *ad hoc* was " Commander of the Clan," and not " Captain " (*Historical Papers*, New Spalding Club, pp. 357, 358, 362, 368 ; *Tartans of the Clans and Families of Scotland*, pp. 38 n. 10, 50 n. 7 ; Craig, *Jus Feudale*, I. 8, 2 original and Lord Clyde's edition).

[1] Great Seal, I., App. II., No. 912.   [2] *Ibid.* No. 913.   [3] *Ibid.* No. 914

[4] Can it have been some of such a darkly accoutred tribe, whom O'Curry records in a description of three Picts at an Irish Court : " Three great brown (haired) men. . . . They wore three short, black cowls, reaching to their elbows, and long hoods to their cowls. They had three enormous black swords, and three black shields over them ; and three black (handled) broad green spears over them " (D. A. Mackenzie, *Scotland the Ancient Kingdom*, p. 105).

C*

received by his Scottish lieges, for the Regency of the High Steward had not been quite so impartial and firm, as perhaps it should.

The heavy ransom was a weighty burden, but David had observed the benefits of trade, and—really one might say a skilled " economist " —he had persuaded Edward that if the ransom was to be forthcoming, trade must flow to pay it.

For the next ten years Scotland enjoyed prosperity on an unexampled scale. Trains of Scottish merchants passed to and from England and the Continent unhindered ; chivalric little companies of Scottish knights travelled abroad, spreading the fair fame and courage of Scotland in all the courts of Europe—precursors of those who were to found trade and social ties 200 years later. King, lords, chieftains, and merchants passed to and from London and Windsor, with a regularity and goodwill reminiscent of eighteenth- or nineteenth-century cosmopolitanism, whilst yet King David was fostering all that was best in art, beauty, clanship, and pride of race and country. Kill-joys and war-mongers were, of course, thoroughly disgruntled (just as they were over the equally peaceable and cultured Court of James III.) ; but the older chroniclers say of David II. only : " He was a man of distinguished virtue, just and humane, and (as regards his capture and ransom) appears to have been unfortunate rather than incapable." [1]   It was left for nineteenth-century historians, who should have known better, to hurl obloquy upon this clever and cultured king, largely because of the discovery of various " documents " in England, from which it transpires that Edward's magnanimity may well have been directed to securing from the childless king a conveyance of the throne of Scotland to one of his sons instead of to the High Steward. David made no mystery of this ; indeed, with masterful grasp of constitutional government, he openly brought home these " insulting " suggestions, submitted them to his Parliament, and then when this then healthily functioning body indignantly rejected them, declared that " Never would they consent that an Englishman should reign over them," the King, " affecting to be satisfied, passed on to other matters." [2]   The Steward took it seriously, and for a short time there was friction ; David cleared this up and made the Steward's son, the future Robert III., Earl of Carrick—a quiet but chivalric indication that David's heart was sound. Strangely enough, even modern historians like Rait have not perceived that David simply " played with " Edward III., dragging on continuous " negotiations " about the settlement desiderated by the Plantaganet, and, without ever breaking off the matter, laid the burden (as he was constitutionally entitled to do) upon the Scottish Parliament, and by this clever policy gave England nothing, but gained for Scotland many years of good trade, culture, and prosperity, " constant amicable correspondence between the merchants of both countries, and a

[1] Aikman's *History of Scotland*, II., p. 39.
[2] Tytler's *History of Scotland*, II., p. 116.

commercial intercourse of unexampled activity." Meantime his Parliament was passing numerous progressive laws for the better administration of the growing Scotland—the Scotland wherein clanship and tribalism were finding their feet firmly, as the pillars on which Scottish grandeur should be erected ; and these laws were emanating not from a " surly baronage " but from the early Lords of the Articles, and thus being evolved under the eye of King David himself. With his Highland subjects, David was naturally on happy terms. Disturbances had now and then to be settled, but this a tribally-minded king could easily effect ; and towards the end of his life, in 1369, he returned from one of his northern progresses having conducted negotiations of a most progressive character with the Lord of the Isles and other Highland chiefs, which he completed " with great ability and success." Chivalry and clanship evidently agreed well even in the fourteenth century ; and such an honourable and kingly sovereign was sure to appeal to the chiefs. In 1362, Queen Joanna, the little English princess, who had so loyally supported her husband's difficult but sagacious policy, died, and for his second wife, King David chose Margaret, Lady and heiress of Logie, a fair daughter of the fateful race of Drummond, and a fascinating widow. For a time all went, apparently, well enough ; but she not only estranged King David from his nephew and heir, the Steward, but presently gave cause for which the King obtained a divorce, though little has ever been found about the mystery. Queen Margaret vanished abroad ; and the Steward and King David were reconciled.[1]

Two years later, at the early age of forty-seven, King David II. died in his great new tower at Edinburgh, and left to Robert II., first of the Royal House of Stewart, a kingdom well and truly founded upon the basis of feudalism [2] and clanship which were to be the pillars of staunch loyalty that stood unshaken for the Stewart line, until the Cardinal of York—again by tanistry—indicated George III. as his heir in the jewels and honours of the hereditary regal line, flowing from the parental kingship of Alba and Dalriada. Such, then, is a survey of the critical period wherein Scottish clanship took shape and became the outstanding feature of Scotland's social organisation.

T. I. OF L.

[1] Can it be that she planned to impose an " heir " upon the country, and that the Steward unmasked the plot ? King David was eventually convinced and, having (no doubt on one of the grounds then competent) obtained annulment of the marriage, was reconciled with his nephew.

[2] Of Scotland's popular early pattern non-class tribo-feudalism, the learned Lord Crawford says : " A peculiar element mingled from the first in the feudality of Scotland, and has left an indelible impress on the manners and habits of thought in the country . . . the blood of the highest noble in the land was flowing in that of the working peasant, at no great interval. This was a subject of pride on both sides." (*Lives of the Lindsays*, 117, 119 ; and cf. *Pro. Soc. Ant. Scot.*, 79, p. 122.)

III

The Highland Clan System under the Royal Stewarts and down to the Battle of Culloden

WITH the accession of Robert II. in 1371, a new chapter in Scotland's history opened, and the glorious dynasty of Bruce was succeeded by the romantic House of Stewart. Since the family name altered, I say " a new dynasty," though the blood of Marjory Bruce and her great father, King Robert, of course passed down into the Stewart line, which now came to wear the crown in which was incorporated the slender fillet which Isabella of Fife had placed on King Robert's brow that day when he was handed the sword which regained for Scotland its freedom and the " auld laws " of tanistry and feudo-clanship. These would have speedily perished under Plantaganet sway.

The days of the second Robert were wild and romantic, for he was an elderly man by the time he succeeded, and both his nobles and his princes were more than he could well manage. But in these chivalrous days the Scotland of the clan system was fast taking its permanent shape, and so much of family annals are now forthcoming, that, as regards clan history, one must pass from the general to the particular history of individual clans.

The Bruces had replaced Celtic Scotland, its traditions and its spirit, upon the records of our national history ; and though recorded no doubt for the most part in Latin and the braid Scots of vernacular records, let us recollect that this feudal Scotland of charters and registers was a Scotland which had now safely based itself on the spirit of the tribe, on all that was permanent and perpetuable in the Celtic system ; and that (save for a few backslidings such as those of James I.—who has been too much belauded for being too little a Scotsman) the Stewarts were themselves personally identified with the all-permeating spirit of clanship, and, following the immemorial custom of the *Ard-righ*, spent their autumns in the tartan upon the hills of Atholl, Stirling, and Braemar.[1]

In 1396 Robert III. is stated to have issued another (and no doubt, one of the last) " gift of chieftainry," of the " haill Clan Chattan," probably in 1409, upon Chief Ferquhard's abdication, and in 1406

---

[1] Fordun gives a dramatic account of " the Hunting in Atholl," and the charters of my own chief include writs granted *apud Lonquhard-an-ree in Marre*— the Royal hunting-hut.

certainly he, by Royal charter, confirmed the resettlement of the *Ceann-cinnidh* of the race of Carrick [1] treating it, as I have elsewhere explained, as an incorporeal honourable hereditament.

The Laws of Arms were crystallising; dignities of *nobilitas minor*— (honours below peerage, save land baronies, which were *in commercio*) were being held to have been entirely remitted to the Royal King of Arms, who, as High-Sennachie, and Judge-Ordinary in Genealogies (as Lord Lyon Burnett describes him in a Lyon Office MS.), was held the proper delegate of the Crown " as appertaining to his sphere of duty " to act in all such matters both by grants, confirmations, and the " making up of titles "—for the Law of Arms treated them as most honourable forms of heritable property.[2]

In a tribal kingdom, naturally a special Department of State was essential to deal in an expert manner with such things, which two and a half centuries later Lord Lyon Erskine could vouch from his official " Registers," these being carefully in the plural.

It is right to emphasise that throughout these two centuries, 1300 to 1500, Scotland was not a distracted nation shattered by internecine feuds. On the contrary, it was a civilised and progressive realm, rapidly developing under the beneficent colourful and happy regime of feudo-clanship, and heredito-tribal spirit of the family. As Hume Brown has so aptly expressed it—though popular writers continue to ignore what he has written :

Scotland had no tale to tell like that of the Wars of the Roses in England, and she had no such bloody and protracted feud as that between the Burgundians and the Armagnacs in France. If she had incidents like the murder of James I. and the exploits of the Wolf of Badenoch, it would be easy to find a parallel to these in any other country, but . . . the nation did not spend its life in misery and . . . there was a steady expansion of the people along every line of progress.[3]

Lord Crawford likewise remarks of Scotland at this period : " the scene presented a favourable contrast with that of England." [4]

Such were the happy conditions which obtained in a feudo-clannish kingdom, and social historians quite overlook that, whilst this social organisation led to numerous minor and picturesque " clashes," in

---

[1] Great Seal, I., No. 509.

[2] *Juridical Review*, Sept. 1940, p. 198.

[3] Hume Brown, *History of Scotland*, I., p. 150. As regards James I. he takes the same view as here indicated, which Sir Robert Graham's prophecy has at long last proved right, that this King would eventually be reckoned " a cruel tyrant," whose policy towards the old Celtic earldoms was, in Lord Crawford's view, " harsh and iniquitous " (*Earldom of Mar in Sunshine, &c.*, pp. 251–254). Even so, murder of the King/Chief was indefensible ; but, being " ferocious." he should have been placed under a Regency (see *infra*). Unfortunately, the good Regent and Highland chiefs had no idea of the policy which James had imbibed during the long years of his imprisonment in England, the very doctrines which consistently proved so fatal to peace and happiness in Ireland.

[4] *Earldom of Mar in Sunshine, &c.*, p. 252.

which little material damage was done, and few or no lives lost, feudalism was a system which from its very structure prevented the possibility of organised aggression (another reason why mischievous-minded statesmen hated a system which cramped their evil ambitions, alike at home and abroad). The feudal army, with its " forty day " service, was incapable of being used for a campaign of conquest ; hence for evil designs of that nature power-politicians resorted not to the feudo-clan levies, but to subterfuges like " scutage," " mercenaries," and the marauding " free companies " (*i.e.* free of wholesome feudal, namely " family," laws and obligations), who, upon the Continent, so harassed the baronage and their happy self-governing fiefs.

In Scotland, whilst the clans and baronage eagerly adopted all the glorious romance, courtesy, and gaiety of chivalry, they set themselves firmly against the institution of a standing army, or taxation to support such a " guard," emphasising that it would weaken the defensive strength of the clans and fiefs, and that, as regards the tax burdens, the Crown was " King of Scots," not " King of Scotland "— thus emphatically repudiating the doctrine of English lawyers that the land was the inherent property of the State.[1] As we have seen, the theory in Scotland was that it was " allodial," and held by *prima occupatione,* " under God " and the virtually inalienable home of each tribal race.

The devotion of Scotland and the Highlands to the ideals of chivalry, " the refining effects of (which) upon the manners and customs of the Middle Ages cannot be overestimated," [2] was soon shown in an incident wherein the Highlands vied with the most gallant and romantic incidents of Froissart's *Chronicles of Europe.*

The clan system, which we have seen growing during the reigns of Alexander II. and the Bruce sovereigns, came more spectacularly into the sphere of Parliament in 1390, when *Alastair Mor mac-an-Righ,* Earl of Buchan, and " Wolf of Badenoch," in consequence of a dispute with the Bishop of Moray regarding, amongst other things, the Wolf's handfasting with Mariota *nighean* Athyn, with the help of " wild, wikkid hielandmen " burnt Elgin Cathedral in June 1390, and about the same time, to make good his claim to lands in Strathnairn, resisted by the Sheriff of Angus, swept down through the Grampians, defeated and slew the Sheriff, his adherents including one *Slurach* with the whole *Clanqwhevil,* now regarded as being Shaw, and the Clan Chattan,[3] in consequence of which the Wolf and the clan were put to the horn. It is now observed that the Wolf's force had both a tribal and a feudal aspect, features which I have shown are largely interdependent.

At any rate these incidents are the first evidences of the clan system in its new relation to Lowland law. The Wolf, having done

---

[1] J. H. Burton, *History of Scotland,* IV., p. 6.
[2] H. Norris, *Costume and Fashion,* II., p. 71.
[3] Skene, *Celtic Scotland,* III., p. 300.

penance, died, and in 1394 was buried in state within the ancient Celtic cathedral of Dunkeld. Clanqwhevil, we are, within some two years, to meet again in still more romantic circumstances.

During 1396 occurred the celebrated combat on the North Inch of Perth, where, in order to settle a question of dispute, the exact nature of which has not been preserved, before King Robert III. and his Court, thirty representatives of the Clan Chattan encountered an equal number of the " Clan Kay " (the precise identity of the contestants is, however, uncertain). In this contest the Clan Chattan were the victors, not, however, before they had lost nineteen of their number. Of the Clan Kay, twenty-nine bit the dust. The remaining man escaped by swimming across the Tay. In the Clan Chattan it was handed down that this contest was between the Davidsons, as " eldest cadet " of Clan Chattan, and the Macphersons, as " heir-male," obviously for the honour of " principal cadet " under the heir-of-line chief, The Mackintosh, and the aftermath of their quarrel at the Battle of Inver-nahavon. That the Macphersons won the positions of a place at the right of Mackintosh and *Ceann Cath* within Clan Chattan (the normal right of the " principal cadet " being thus allocated to a house which was not the " first cadet ") can only suggest the unpredictable result of a trial by combat (App. XXIX.).

The interesting feature of this clan fight upon the North Inch is that it originated in a suggestion of Lord Lindsay, and is accepted by Drs. Neilson and Skene (see p. 609) as a contest in a Scottish Court of Chivalry, and to have been based upon the analogy with the celebrated chivalric engagement of the " Thirty against Thirty," recorded in the *Chronicles* of Sir John Froissart. Its social significance lies in the official acknowledgement of clanship and clan disputes, as matters of honour falling within the scope of the laws of chivalry, and determinable by combat *in curia militaris* ; that is to say, according to the principles of heraldic chivalry, with which the future history of clanship has been so closely bound up, for in those days quarrels about a right to arms, badge, or banner were likewise determinable by combat in the Court of Chivalry, and it was not until the following century that the forms of the civil law were substituted in what became the Lyon Court for the more primitive arbitrament of battle as the procedure for the determination of such family disputes.[1]

The year 1411 marks another epoch in the history of the Gael, when Donald, Lord of the Isles, who had become heir to the Earldom of Ross, descended into the Lowlands with the intention of sacking Aberdeen and dispersing the forces of the Duke of Albany, Regent of the kingdom. The Regent had usurped the earldom, which he had bestowed on his son, John Stewart, Earl of Buchan. Some ten thousand Highlanders assembled beneath the banner of the Lord of the Isles at Harlaw, about eighteen miles from Aberdeen. One of three old

[1] Cf. H. W. C. Davis, *Medieval England*, s.v. " Court of Chivalry," p. 234 ; also cf. *Sources and Literature of the Law of Scotland*, pp. 382–383.

ballads about this famous conflict, preserves a curiously realistic refrain suggesting the drone of the bagpipes which were thus already the war-pipes of a Highland army :

> Yes, *we* cam frae the Hielans man,
> An *we* cam a the wye,
> An we *saw* MacDonnell and his men
> As *they* cam in frae Skye ;
> Wi' a drei, drei, drei-de-dronnelie,
> Drei-de-dronnelie, driee.

The Highland army was met at " the Red Harlaw " by the Regent's force under Alexander Stewart, Earl of Mar. On the 24th of July a bloody but indecisive battle was fought, when about five hundred of Mar's force were killed, including many Lowland barons, besides Sir Robert Davidson, Provost of Aberdeen, with many burgesses.[1] In 1424, however, the earldom of Ross was restored to the MacDonalds by King James I., on his release from his long captivity in England.

King James I., having been captured shortly before the death of his father Robert III., had spent the first eighteen years of his reign a captive in England, where, however, he had the opportunity of acquiring many useful and artistic attainments in the Court of the Plantagenets. He also learnt perhaps more than would have been good for the clan system, about the English system of parliamentary and representative government, as a centralised system by means of which the English baronage were in process of being subjected to centralised authority, and whereby it was in due course also intended to subjugate the Irish chiefs and laws to London domination. King James accordingly returned to Scotland with the intention of executing far-reaching reforms of an " authoritarian " character, and complete with a popular slogan that he was going to " make the Key keep the Castle, and the Bracken Bush keep the Cow." In the parliamentary sphere he designed to reorganise the feudo-tribal Great-Council of Scotland into a House of Lords and House of Commons, upon the pattern which had developed in fourteenth-century England, and for this purpose, to supplement the feudo-Celtic earldoms, each related to its *duthus*, by a purely personal peerage.[2]

[1] The old ballad's remark :

> There wes not sen King Kenneth's days
> Sic strange intestine crewel stryf
> In Scotland sene, as ilk man says,
> Quhair mony lichtlie lost thair lyfe ;

strongly suggests, what careful reading of many dramatic medieval encounters indicates, that in feudo-clan strife the damage and loss of life was relatively small ; and did not really interfere with cultural progress.

[2] It has been pointed out at great length in many of the articles and a number of the appendices in the recent voluminous *Complete Peerage*, that the intention of the thirteenth- and fourteenth-century Plantagenet kings was probably not to create a hereditary peerage, but merely to summon as *ad hoc* Lords-of-Parliament,

In Scotland, where the " Order of Earls " represented the old Celtic *mormaer* and provincial *righ*, the new peers came to be regarded as an extension of this comital order who all sat arrayed in velvet robes, upon the *palatium* and regal bench of the Scottish parliament, under the *Ard-righ* as holding the imperial Crown of the so-to-speak federal states of the realm of Scotland ; but so closely was the Scottish tribal system built up in the theory of the *duthus*, that right down to the union of 1707 the Scottish peers and parliament were able to regard their dignities as in a manner related at least to the moot hill of each lordship, just as the office of *Ard-righ* was inseparable from the great moot hill of Scone.

King James's parliamentary reforms were accordingly but partially adopted, and the Great-Council of Scotland continued largely to retain its tribal character. Unfortunately King James's other policy, which commenced with not undeserved punishment upon some of the great magnates who had abused their position during his imprisonment, developed into a general campaign to suppress the great earls, and to build up a centralised authoritarian bureaucracy. In pursuit of this policy for the anglicisation of Scotland, and extirpation of the great tribal divisions, the forfeiture of the House of Albany was followed by the ruthless confiscation of the earldoms of Strathearn, Lennox and Mar, and the Celtic spirit of the trusty Scottish nobility having been aroused to the apprehension that what was intended was nothing less than the suppression of the ancient Celtic organisation of the country, and of the sturdy local independence which had stood Scotland in such good stead through its former trials, culminated in popular resentment, and in Sir Robert Graham's, none the less indefensible, parricidal murder of King James at Perth in 1437.

An important acquisition to the Scottish kingdom was effected in 1467, during the reign of King James III. A large sum of money was due from Scotland to Denmark, being the arrears of " the annual of Norway " as it was called, the annuity of one hundred marks, due to Norway for the cession of the Hebrides, or Western Isles, settled by

---

those of the magnates who best suited the king and his advisers at a given moment. It has further been suggested by the editors of this work that the legal evolution of the Barony-in-fee, or ancient hereditary personal peerage of England, was largely due to the English heralds and the Court of Chivalry. If that view be well founded, as I readily believe, Britain certainly owes to the College of Arms and Court of Chivalry a tremendous debt of gratitude, though what the *curia militaris* determined was simply what one would expect any court of *noblesse* to regard as the reasonable and lawful interpretation of a Writ of Summons. If these had been interpreted, as the *Complete Peerage* suggests was the true intent of the Plantagenet sovereigns, the House of Lords would not have been a national *consilium* or impartial chamber of any description whatever, but the most egregious house of " yes-men " ever conceived by any tyrant or dictator. The sovereign or his advisers would on each occasion have contented themselves with summoning merely the puppets whom they intended should give formal acquiescence to the policy and legislation initiated by the ruling caucus at the tyrant's elbow.

the treaty of 1266, entered into after the defeat of Haco, King of Norway, at the Battle of Largs. James I. had obtained some settlement respecting this annuity. It had, however, again been permitted to fall into arrears, and the amount of the debt had become uncertain.

Under the influence of Charles VII. of France, an arrangement for settlement of the matter was made between Scotland and Denmark. James III. wedded Margaret, Princess of Denmark, to whom her father promised a dowry of 60,000 crowns and also renounced all claim to the arrears of the annuity payable on account of the cession of the Hebrides. When the time came for paying the dowry, only 2,000 crowns were forthcoming in cash. As a pledge for payment of the remainder the Orkney Islands were assigned to the Scottish Crown in lieu of 50,000 crowns, and shortly afterwards the Shetland Islands for the balance of 8,000 crowns. These pledges were never redeemed, and both Orkney and Shetland were formally annexed to Scotland by treaty, when King James VI. of Scotland married Anne, Princess of Denmark. The artistic and cultured James III. took, apparently, a keen interest in the Highlands, and a force of Highlanders is stated to have formed part of the Royal army at Sauchieburn.

If the "variand purpur tartar, browdin with thrissillis and a unicorne" which formed the drapery and curtains of James III.'s bed in 1488, was the "Royal Tartan,"—and though "tartar" does not necessarily mean what we now call tartan, it sounds a little like a description of the Royal sett—this particular Royal apartment must have been an early example of a style of which there are a number of (not over ancient) examples in Scottish castles, and which, with golden thistles and silvered unicorns, must have been decidedly gorgeous.

The hold of the Scottish monarchs over the Western Isles was further consolidated towards the close of the century by the downfall of the last Lord of the Isles, and the end of the regal power exercised by these island princes. In 1493 John, Lord of the Isles, was forfeited, and the lordship of the Isles was annexed to the Crown of King James IV. The title of Lord of the Isles became one of those borne by the Duke of Rothesay, eldest son of the sovereign. John, the forfeited Lord of the Isles, died at Dundee in 1498, and was buried in the abbey of Paisley. His forfeiture added greatly to the power and influence of the Clans Mackenzie and Maclean, more especially to the former.

The successors of King James IV. kept steadfastly in view ways and means for bringing the clans directly under the Royal influence. Many were the devices adopted for arriving at this desired consummation. The favourite device, however, was that of encouraging one clan to attack another, and thereby to weaken the power of each. Another was cancelling on subtle pretexts the feudal charters by which the Western chiefs held their ancestral possessions and offering them mere tenancies at will instead. The object of this was that they could be evicted easily and their lands handed over to financial companies. This could not be done where they had got feudal charters.

James IV., however, took a kingly interest in his Highland vassals, many of whom fought with him at Flodden, and he even learnt the Gaelic. His son—" The Knight of Snowdoun, James FitzJames "— James V., maintained, on the whole, happy relations with the Highlanders, made a number of progresses in the North and West Highlands, and wore the Highland dress. From these chivalrous Stewart sovereigns, clanship and its customs received understanding and encouragement at Court, as again occurred in the troubled days of the seventeenth century, when it was mainly on their Highlanders that the Stewart kings had to rely. Towards the close of James V.'s reign was looming, and burst in that of the fair Mary Queen of Scots, the storm of the " Reformation," whose tenets were in so many ways inimical to Gaelic culture and the harmony of family life. In the Highlands, as elsewhere, the new creed was not only to uproot many of the old gay customs, but also to stunt for an appreciable time the growth and revival of most Scottish arts and accomplishments.

The Church of Rome, probably unaware of the slender material resources of Scotland, had, by extracting " pious donations " from kings and nobles, acquired a tremendous proportion of the wealth and lands of the kingdom, and this concentration in the hands of a celibate clergy, compared with the old tribal monasteries of Scotland, led to criticism not lessened from the heavy contributions exacted by the Popes, to which was presently added heavy national taxation. The double burden quickly ruined the abbeys ; the doctrines of the Reformers led to criticism of the Church's authority ; and the chiefs began demanding the return of the lands their ancestors had been induced to hand over to the Church. Under Cardinal Beaton a statesmanlike readjustment would probably have been achieved, and the old traditions carried on ; but in 1559 John Knox proved only too able a propagandist of the doctrines of Calvin, who has been well· described as " a sick man with a sick man's bitter hatred for all that was beautiful and gay and that tended to make life more cheerful." [1] Within a short time untold mischief had been done to the glorious antiquities and ancient culture of Scotland.

The year 1559 was memorable for acts of vandalism, which resulted in almost all the Scottish ecclesiastical records and also the beautiful illuminated manuscripts and libraries of the cathedrals and abbeys being destroyed. Since the Church Courts and chartularies also covered a great sphere of daily life, the loss of those records is a great one to social and clan history. The destruction, commenced by King Edward, was completed by vandals aroused by Knox's sermons. Not content with wrecking the ancient churches and cathedrals of Scotland, and burning their archives and the beautiful manuscripts and paintings which enshrined the successive stages of our native art, and the craftsmanship of jewelled reliquaries and carvings of the old Celtic saints, the Reformers' rebel army, on 28th June 1559, burned the palace, abbey,

[1] H. van Loon, *Arts of Mankind*, p. 32.

and church of Scone. These being the repository of the records of the kingdom (as Scone was the scene of the coronation of the Scottish monarchs), many priceless archives of our country were lost. Thanks, however, to the energy shown by the burgesses of Glasgow (who rose against the Reformers' vandal gangs, and protected their ancient cathedral), the original duplicate of the treaty of 1328 with King Edward III. of England was saved, as it was deposited in the archives of Glasgow Cathedral. Rob. Johnston, a zealous Protestant writer, but a lover of his country, writing in 1655 (*Hist. Rerum Britan.*) of the irreparable injuries Knox had occasioned to Scotland, characterises him as a man " famous for the burning of churches, and for the renewing, in his native country, the barbarous devastation of the Vandals."

The Highlanders, and north-eastern Scotland, never sympathised with these sin-obsessed kill-joys, and consequently in the succeeding generation were found ranked with the Cavaliers and those who fought to preserve the tradition, beauty, and colourful customs of their ancestors.

The first time a list of Highland clans appears to have been embodied in an Act of Parliament is in that of 1587, in which is given a Roll of " The Names of the Landislordis and Baillis of Landis in the Hielandis and Ilis." In 1594 another Roll was compiled. As pointed out in *Macrae* v. *Macrae* (Lyon Court, 1909) these are in no sense " Rolls of Clans " or anything of that sort ; they are Rolls of certain clans which had been proving troublesome ! There never at any time was a " Roll of Clans " as such. As regards the feudal nature of clanship, it is noticeable that in these " Rolls " chiefs are bound up with Landlords and Bailies, the latter, as previously indicated, often holding the office of War Leader or *Ceann Cath.*

In 1597 several Acts of Parliament were passed relating to the Highlands and Islands. One of these provided for the erection of three Royal burghs in the West Highlands—in Kintyre, Lochaber. and Lewis respectively. These burghs are now the modern ones, Campbeltown, Fort William, and Stornoway. Another Act in that year was entitled, " That the inhabitants of the Ilis and Hielandis shaw their haldings (*i.e.* charters)." According to the terms of this Act, all persons possessing or pretending to possess a right to lands in the Highlands and Islands were ordered to exhibit their titles to the Lords of Exchequer on the 15th of May 1598, and, at the same time, to give suitable security for their future good conduct towards their king, their neighbours, and such as desired to trade with them. The penalty of non-compliance or inability to comply with these commands was forfeiture of property, whether real or pretended. Over a great part of the Highlands feudal charters had almost necessarily been obtained, at all events by the greater vassals, but as regards the smaller estates, many were still held by tenures which had not been committed to writing, and had only been, after the old manner, made of record by being " done in open court," *i.e.* by " real investiture " in the Clan or Provincial Council.[1] In other cases the Crown superior, such as the Lord of the Isles or other magnate who held only charter title, had been forfeited, and in consequence of this, or of the destruction of parchments in local wars, numbers of the chiefs and chieftains were, as the Government shrewdly expected, unable to implement the provisions of a statute which, however reasonable it might seem to the lairds in the neighbourhood of Edinburgh, had a sinister and ulterior motive when applied to the Highlands. The matter became, therefore, a most serious one to almost everyone concerned. True, in some cases clanspeople were in occupation of lands of which the nominal feudal possession had been given to strangers, though the tenants of these lands followed *not* their feudal superior, but the chief of their clan. Still, however, in the majority of cases, the matter of compliance with the first command contained in the Act (the production of title-deeds) was an utter impossibility. The lands had been in the possession of the chieftains and their *uasail* from time immemorial, and the charter by which the most of them was held was not by parchment-tenure but that of the sword, *i.e.* " Scottish Service " and under verbal grants of which the " record " was the oral tradition of the witnesses, *e.g.* " at the Black Stones of Iona " or grouped around the crest of Dundonald ; whilst four generations of tenure as by right, gave a perpetual and indefeasable right of " perfect " property subject only to payment of that " share of the produce " due to the chief. Then, again, there were some lands which had been held from the Lords of the Isles, now forfeited. As to the matter of the chiefs finding suitable securities for their behaviour, such was also an almost impossible matter. A Campbell was not likely to stand security for a MacDonald, nor a Mackay for a Gunn ! The real object of the Act was evidently to provide the Crown with a legal pretext for appropriating territory still held under the old allodial tenures, *i.e.* " under God."

There are no records extant to inform us of the nature of the proceedings before the Lords of the Exchequer. From what we know,

---

[1] See Appendix VIII. illustrating that MacDonald conferred Land Rights which were confirmed by oath at the Black Stones of Iona. As explained in Dr. Cameron's evidence in the *Ardgour* case (Appendix XXX.), the Celtic system was very like feudalism ; but, as we see, it was made of record by witness and not by writing, which was dangerous. As Rait says : " The new great men of the kingdom held of him [the King] by written charters, and the old Celtic nobility were glad to follow their example and to secure their rights " (*Making of Scotland*, p. 27). The *Ard-righ*, as in Ireland, had also the ultimate jurisdiction to settle disputes about succession to the *duthus* and to chiefship, and such came to be determined when necessary by the *Ri-Sennachie*, the Lord Lyon, whose judgements, as of Druidic origin, or following trial by combat in his court, it was *geiss* to gainsay (F. Knight, *Early Christianising of Scotland*, p. 52). The Heraldic visitation was noticed, even in Wales, *per* Garter Dugdale, to have taken the place of the *cuairt* conducted " as the Bards did heretofore " (A. Wagner, *Heralds and Heraldry*, p. 3, and *Sources and Literature of the Law of Scotland*, Stair Society, p. 382. See also p. 607 *infra*, App. XXIX).

however, many of the Highland chiefs, when asked to exhibit proof of their titles, produced their own sword along with a body of their clansmen, and proudly pointed to these as their titles of possession.

In many cases, no doubt, the Act was enforced by conferring a new Crown charter on payment of a substantial composition ; in other words, the unfortunate Highlanders were made to buy back their own lands, or agree to pay the Crown a handsome feu-duty.

It has, however, been suggested by Skene and others, that one of the consequences of this Act was the hurried composition of histories of the clans and fictitious charters, nearly all tracing their descent, not from Pict or Scot, but from Irish, Danish, Norse, or Norman adventurers. One is, however, utterly at a loss to see how anyone improved their position in regard to this statute by compiling a faked pedigree, adducing their origin from a foreigner. Such a compilation would have served no purpose as an answer to the requirements of the Act, and some other reason must be sought for the histories of that character. That some of the chiefs may have concocted fictitious charters is possible. The more general practice appears to have been to adduce evidence, accurate or inaccurate, that the ancient writs had been destroyed in fires or wars ; and a number of Crown confirmations of land in the west proceed upon such narrative. In a number of cases the original holding had in fact, until then, continued to be allodial. In other cases it held by grant from the Lord of the Isles, either by charter, or by ceremony at the " Black Stones." In cases of such feu-holdings under the Lord of the Isles, the Edinburgh bureaucrats evolved the theory that, unless confirmed by the Crown, they became voided by the forfeiture of the Lord of the Isles, so another ground was found for expropriating Highlanders, or making them repurchase their own lands. Parliament indeed endeavoured to prevent charters being granted to them at all !

On the completion of the Report by the Royal Commissioners under the Act of 1597, Lewis, Trouterness in Skye, Harris, Dunvegan, and Glenelg were declared at the king's disposal. Being largely allodial, and therefore pre-eminently not the property of the King of Scots, the Crown arguing from the very absence of Crown charters prepared to steal what had never belonged to it ! The Government then threw off the mask, and in 1598 these territories were conveyed to a company belonging to the East Coast, known as the " Fife Adventurers." These speculators arranged to begin by colonising the Island of Lewis. Their contract with the Crown bound them " to plant policy and civilisation in the hitherto most barbarous Isle of Lewis, with Rona-Lewis and Trotternish, and to develop the extraordinarily rich resources of the same for the public good and the king's profit." In this contract, however, and the dealing with it, no account was taken of the ideas of the inhabitants. Before long, the Government in Edinburgh found that they had reckoned without their host. After three attempts to take possession and a succession of struggles which lasted for twelve years, the Adventurers were, in 1610, obliged to resign their claims. As a sequel to the struggle between Highlander and Lowlander, Lewis passed from the MacLeods to the MacKenzies, afterwards Earls of Seaforth.

Prior to the union of the Crowns of Scotland and England under James VI., the efforts of the Crown and Parliament to weaken the Highland clan system had invariably ended in failure. Circumstances altered after 1603. The king's English advisers were ever alert to make use of any opportunity for weakening the northern sister kingdom, and subordinating its interests to those of the more powerful " predominant partner." The Highlanders held the balance of power in Scotland ; and as the clans, for the most part, were Episcopalians or Catholics, they were regarded with bitter and fanatical feelings by the ruling faction in the Low Country, who had become largely Presbyterian. Although Lowland Scots and the English were equally jealous of each other, still, as their common object was to weaken the Highland clans, an unnatural alliance was formed, having that object in view. The first-fruits of the campaign were an Act of Parliament, in 1608, abolishing all the heritable jurisdiction of the chiefs of clans ; placing their castles at the disposal of the Crown ; ordering the breaking up and destruction of the " galleys, berlings, and lymphads " (vessels) of the Island clans. The Government's first stage to " progress " was accordingly to destroy the existing beautiful and effective system of island communications ! Next they prohibited the use of guns, bows, and two-handed swords by the clanspeople. The chiefs were compelled to send their children as hostages to Edinburgh, under penalty of death. These measures were followed, in 1609, by the Statutes of Icolmkill,[1] nine in number, viz. : (1) Obedience to the Reformed Kirk ; the keeping of the Sabbath ; abolition of handfasting.[2] (2) Establishment of inns throughout the Highlands. (3) Limitation of the number of the household and the followers of the chiefs. (4) All persons found *sorning* (*i.e.*, living at free quarters upon the poorer inhabitants) to be tried as thieves and oppressors. (5) The fifth statute was one manifestly directed to destroying the considerable trade which, in those days, existed between France and the Highlands of Scotland, and diverting it to the Lowlands, for the benefit of the Lowland Scots and the English. Power was given to any person whatever to seize, without payment, wine or *aqua vitæ* imported for sale by a native merchant. If an Islander should buy any of the prohibited articles from a mainland trader, he would be fined £40 for the first offence, £100 for the second, and for the third offence loss of

---

[1] It is shocking to think that the name of this sacred Hebridean isle was tacked to their code for suppression of Highland law and customs.

[2] This is the system of subsidiary left-hand marriages for a year and a day, of which there were three degrees of "honourable connection" below that of the " first wife " (J. Cameron, *Celtic Law*). Their issue had been " legitimate " under Celtic law, and appear later to have been the *naturali* children, as distinct from *bastardi*, springing from unformalised connections.

his whole possessions and movable goods. Individuals, however, were to be allowed to brew as much *aqua vitæ* as their own families might require. The wine required for consumption by chiefs and gentlemen was to be purchased in the Lowlands. (6) Every gentleman or yeoman possessed of sixty cattle should send his eldest son, or, if he had no male children, his eldest daughter,[1] to school in the Lowlands, and maintain his child there till it had learned to speak, read, and write English. (7) Forbade the use of any description of firearms, even for the destruction of game. (8) The maintenance of bards " and other idlers " was forbidden. The gentry were forbidden to encourage them ; while the unfortunate bards (who were the sennachies or chroniclers of clan history) were threatened first with the stocks, and then banishment. (9) Provisions for enforcing the preceding Acts.

At first sight it might appear that the above statutes were framed with the benevolent idea of civilising the Highlands and imparting instruction to their inhabitants. The true purpose, however, was to destroy the tribo-Celtic civilisation, and to pave the way for the exploitation of the Highlands by companies like the Fife Adventurers. The Highlands were far from being either uncivilised, or without instruction or codes of law. On the contrary, like all tribal and feudal organisation in which there was " government of the people, by the people, for the people," in the only true sense of the term, and in which there was a close association of the chief and chieftains and their families with the people of the district, there was naturally a very high level of civilisation.

There were schools of language, music, and architecture. True, English was not taught, but, on the other hand, Latin (which was at this period the language of diplomacy) was familiar to most Highland gentlemen. The Highlands were famed for their manufactures, smiths, and jewellers. These rural craftsmen were, of course, usually hereditary, son or son-in-law succeeding father, and each generation accumulating further skill and pride in their vocation. As Brentano says of the similar old tribal civilisation of provincial France and Brittany, by preserving the family tradition in the practice of each calling, the industrial arts drew great advantage. Children profited by all the experience and practice their forefathers had acquired ; the son became as proud of his calling as of his name. Progress and changes came harmoniously by degrees, under the influence of the taste and genius of each new generation.[2] The clans exported manufactures, timber, stone, and fish to the continent of Europe, and received in exchange various articles of commerce. Wine was plentiful in the

---

[1] Compare the Law of Anjou and Maine which likewise, in absence of sons, treated the eldest daughter in all respects as a male for purpose of succession (Brentano, *Old Regime in France*, p. 43). In Statute 6 the Government recognised that an eldest heir-portioner would become chieftainess if there was no tailzie.

[2] I. F. Grant, *Social and Economic Development of Scotland*, p. 252 and *Lordship of the Isles*, pp. 414–418. Cf. F. F. Brentano, *Old Regime in France*, p. 70.

Highlands until the seventeenth century. In the *Costume of the Clans* we are told that the fine wrought-iron gateway on the steps of the river terrace to the Castle of Donibristle was sent from Holland in exchange for stone from the Highlands.

While those of the Statutes of Icolmkill, which were aimed at damaging the commerce of the Highlands, appear only too well to have succeeded in their object, the provisions regarding the disarmament of the Highlanders were more honoured in the breach than in the observance. Had it been otherwise, the risings of 1715 and 1745 might never have taken place.

In 1603 occurred the famous conflict between the Clan Gregor and Clan Colquhoun, which led to the excessively drastic measures taken against "the Children of the Mist." An inter-clan meeting projected for settling some disputes was, it is claimed, treacherously selected by Colquhoun of Luss for collecting a force of eight hundred men, with which he planned to wipe out the Macgregors. The Laird of MacGregor, however, got warning, and came prepared to fight or negotiate as the case might be. When the blow struck, the Clan Gregor, though a smaller force, cut the Colquhouns to pieces, and enraged at Colquhoun's treachery, committed terrific carnage in the ensuing rout, commemorated in the *Lady of the Lake* :

> Proudly our pibroch has thrilled in Glenfruin,
> And Banochar's groans to our slogan replied ;
> Glen-Luss and Ross-Dhu, they are smoking in ruin,
> And the best of Loch Lomond lie dead on her side.

The shocking massacre (by the Bastard of Glenstrae) at Bannachra, and the procession of sixty Colquhoun widows with their husbands' " bloody shirts," so shocked King James, that this (like any other unusual atrocity in feudo-clan life) led to really crushing penalties. Argyll was given letters of fire and sword against the Clan Gregor, whose name was proscribed ; and MacGregor, having surrendered to MacCailean, under promise that he " would take him out of Scottish ground," this Argyll did by sending him out of the kingdom to Berwick whence he was brought back and promptly hanged.

During the middle years of the seventeenth century occurred the Great Civil War between Charles I., the representative of constitutional and tribal monarchy, and the insurgent parliamentarians, eventually led by Oliver Cromwell. The dispute embodied both a religious and a secular aspect, and it was the junction of those which led to its extent. In England and part of Lowland Scotland, the narrow doctrines of Calvinism, and the dislike of ceremonial which that narrow-mindedness inspires, had taken root. In the Highlands, though the Old Church had not been Romish (in the later sense), yet the hierarchy of abbots and chapters, the stately ritual, and the gay processions and spectacular beauties of prelatical religion naturally appealed to the clansmen with their love of colour and tradition. On this ground they were (saving the Campbells and a few others) solidly on the side of Episcopacy and the stateliness of the old forms of religion. On the secular side, the struggle (shorn of high-sounding propaganda) was simply that King Charles, for defence of the realm against foreign dangers, saw that a fleet had to be built ; and the " new rich " of England, the merchant princes and those who had invested Tudor gains in various forms of wealth, were determined that they should not be taxed directly for the navy, but that the costs should be defrayed by indirect taxation on the poorer people. They further resented the olden courts by which people, who (as was none too seldom in those days) defeated the ends of justice in ordinary courts, could be made amenable if need be before courts composed of persons of their own standing, or completely incapable of being intimidated. The war thus became a struggle between Ritualism and Crown upholding the right to tax according to means, and narrow Puritanism, allied to the " new rich," determined that the Crown should not make them pay for the national defence.

The clans stood solidly for the old order of the constitution, and under the leadership of the gallant Marquess of Montrose fought nobly for King Charles against the Roundhead kill-joys.

After the murder of King Charles in 1649, and that of Montrose and several other clan chieftains in 1650, the Scottish nation, staunch at heart for the principles of tribalism and monarchy, immediately rallied to their lawful sovereign, Charles II., who had been proclaimed in Scotland as heir to his murdered father, " the Martyr King." Once more at Scone, on 1st January 1651—although the brutal Roundheads were already pressing across the Lothians—a King of Scots was crowned at Scone with all the ceremonial of the ancient monarchy, as preserved in the official report upon the Scottish coronation, prepared in 1628 for the Privy Council by Sir Jerome Lindsay of Annantland, Lord Lyon King of Arms, whose successor, Sir James Balfour of Denmiln, the Lord Lyon Antiquary, functioned, though the ceremony was given peculiar twists to suit the dominant Lowland Presbyterians, and Argyll, in place of a Thane of Fife, set the crown on Charles's head, whilst the Reverend Dr. Douglas prayed sanctimoniously anent " the sins of the king, and the sins of the king's house "—and of everybody else, according to the gloomy tenets of his creed—and finally hailed him as " the only covenanted king in the world." All too soon after the Cromwellian dictator set his heel upon the neck of Scotland, and after subverting even the national Courts of Justice, passed a pretended " Union " with England, under which the clan system and its feudal forms (so hateful to the English mentality) would soon have been extinguished.   Fortunately after " Old Noll's " unlamented death, his great General—Monck—who had been Commander-in-Chief of the army of occupation in Scotland, and who spent some time at Inverness, saw that in hereditary monarchy alone lay the future of a nation's liberty, and—may we surmise ?—inspired by the Scottish sense of loyalty to these principles, brought about the Restoration, and thereby gave back Scotland her liberty, laws, and native tribal institutions.

Charles II. always retained a warm affection for the land in which he had first borne his ancient crown, and his relations with the Highland chiefs were cordial. In those days the trouble was with the Lowland fanatics who bewailed the resumption of gaiety and cere-monial which followed the Restoration. At Holyroodhouse, part of which had been burnt by Cromwell, King Charles directed his great architect, Sir William Bruce, to restore the southern portion of the old palace with an elevation to conform to the characteristically Scottish tower of James IV., whose apartments are so closely associated with the life of Mary Queen of Scots. Over the old gateway of the palace, beside the tressured lion of the Royal arms, was the proud inscription, " *Nobis hæc invicta miserunt* 106 *proavi* " (" One hundred and six ancestors have handed us down these emblems unconquered "). This being the *leitmotif* of the whole palace, it was the natural and brilliant concept that a great collection of state portraits should be formed (so far as possible elaborated from originals in various other places), and should be the decoration of the principal apartment of the palace, the immense picture gallery. It was a truly clannish idea ; it made the whole concept of the palace a living embodiment of that inheritance and tribality and of high-spirited family continuity, which is the touchstone of the Scottish, and particularly the Highland, character.[1]

The year 1688 is a notable one, as it witnessed the last clan contest in the history of the Highlands. MacDonell of Keppoch, disdaining to hold by a sheepskin (*i.e.*, a parchment deed) the lands of Glenroy from Mackintosh of that Ilk, who had obtained a Crown charter of the disputed territory, encountered the forces of the Clan Mackintosh, commanded by their chief, at Mulroy (*Meall Ruadh*), in Lochaber. The Mackintoshes were completely defeated, their chief was made prisoner by the MacDonells, and he was compelled to renounce his claim to the lands in question. However, in requital for Keppoch's temerity, his lands were laid waste by a strong body of regular troops.

During the reign of King James VII., the clans stood faithfully by their high-chief, the *Ard-righ*, and kept coldly aloof from the blood-thirsty fanatics who, calling themselves " Godly men," steeped their disordered minds in the cruellest passages of the Old Testament, and maintained the right to assassinate their theological enemies—as

---

[1] Critics of these portraits, who suggest they are almost all imaginary, have overlooked that Sir G. Mackenzie, who was sufficiently near the time to know, states that at the coronation of Charles I. (" the Martyr ") a series of the Royal portraits was put on view—" their pictures were exposed, and noblest actions recited "—evidently a feature of the ceremonies (*Works*, II., p. 362). This shows that a pre-Restoration, and no doubt crude, series of Royal portraits existed in 1633. Moreover, the Royal genealogy was, he says, declaimed in the usual manner, though this is not specifically mentioned in the usual accounts of the 1633 coronation.

indeed they did Archbishop Sharp—whenever they felt a " call," apparently their euphemism for a homicidal impulse ! When it became essential to keep these unbalanced Covenanter-enthusiasts in check, it was on " the Highland Host," eight thousand of the clans, that King James and his general, the gallant Claverhouse, depended to save the country, and during their occupation of the unruly Lowlands, it has been stated that not one Whig actually lost his life—an example of the mild but firm order which a hereditary clan-army was able to maintain.

The king's generous and progressive endeavours to remove sectarian controversy by introducing general freedom of religion roused the Covenanters to fresh fury, and Marlborough's treachery to his Sovereign, when Dutch William's invasion took place, led to the unfortunate King James resorting to flight, when his loyal Scottish generals, Dumbarton and Claverhouse, urged the resistance which the nation expected. Unfortunately the Crown was left vacant (by the fatal gesture of throwing the Great Seal into the Thames—whence the Dutchman recovered it), and the Prince of Orange thus usurped the Crown. In Scotland the return of Lord Balcarres, chieftain of the " Lightsome Lindesays," and Claverhouse, now Viscount of Dundee, hero of the " gallant Grahams," was too late to prevent a pack-voted convention betraying Scotland to the foreigner and the Puritan fanatics. There was nothing left for Claverhouse, King James's Commander-in-Chief, but, as he nobly expressed it, " to go whither the spirit of Montrose should direct him," and to exclaim as in Scott's stirring lines :

> There's lands beyond Pentland, and hills beyond Forth,
> If there's Lords in the South, there are Chiefs in the North,
> And wild dunnie-wassels three thousand times three
> Will cry, Heigh ! for the bonnets o' Bonnie Dundee.

The clans rallied loyally to the banner of the *Ard-righ's* general, and the gallant army advanced into Atholl to battle with the traitors in the service of the Dutch invader.

> Strike and drive the trembling rebels
> Backwards o'er the stormy Forth ;
> Let them tell their pale Convention
> How they fared within the North.
>
> Let them tell that Highland honour
> Is not to be bought nor sold,
> That we scorn their Prince's anger
> As we loathe his foreign gold.

At Killiecrankie the traitor army under Mackay of Scourie was completely routed, but in the hour of victory, Viscount Dundee fell, and with him the star of the Stewarts, for King James had no other general at hand capable of securing the fruits of Dundee's last victory.

Is there any here will venture
To bewail our dead Dundee ?
Let the widows of the traitors
Weep until their eyes are dim !
Wail ye may full well for Scotland—
Let none dare to weep for him !
See, above his glorious body
Lies the royal banner's fold !
See, his valiant blood is mingled
With its crimson and its gold !

Open wide the vaults of Atholl
Where the bones of heroes rest ;
Open wide the hallowed portals
To receive another guest !

Sir Evan Cameron of Lochiel kept the clans together during the winter ; and in spring Major-General Thomas Buchan, brother to the Laird of Auchmacoy, arrived with a commission from King James, appointing him Commander-in-Chief, and around him gathered the remnants of the loyal clans—Macdonalds, Macleans, Camerons Macphersons, and the Grants of Glenmoriston and Inneses of Coxton. Unfortunately this gallant force was surprised and defeated, 1st May 1690, at " the Bonny Haughs o' Cromdale," in Strathspey.

At the time of the Revolution of 1688-1689, which resulted in the fall of the ancient Stuart dynasty, the Scottish Highland clans were with, but few exceptions, distinguished for their attachment to the Stuarts. The reason for this was essentially the clansmen's instinct of continuity, and the knowledge that the House of Stuart had learnt its lesson, and stood for " the old days and the old ways " of Scotland's native civilisation, whilst the supporters of " Dutch William " were essentially those inimical to our indigenous system of tribalism or clanship.[1]

[1] Adam, in an astounding passage containing more than one *non sequitur*, says : " On the death of King James V. without male issue, the sovereign ceased to be the *Ard-righ*, or overlord, of the Highland clans ; for by the law of tanistry, as already shown, the succession was strictly limited to the male line. On King James V.'s death, therefore, the chiefship of the Clan Stewart passed to the Earl of Lennox, whose eldest son, Darnley, was the father of King James VI. In this manner, therefore, the chiefship of the Royal clan reverted to the Crown." If Adam had been right, which he is not, how could the office of *Ard-righ* ever have passed into the House of Stewart ? James V. actually knew more than Adam when he said : " It came wi' a lass and it will gang wi' a lass." Moreover, by his marriage with Mary Queen of Scots, Darnley became *jure uxoris* King of Scots, and was so proclaimed that very evening, this being in accordance with the ancient law of Scotland, and the very principle in virtue of which Macbeth claimed the Crown in right of Gruoch his wife. All the modern evidence is that this " male " idea had no part in Celtic law. It was not even set forth as a stateable hypothesis in the clan disputes of the seventeenth century and is not adduced in the *Loyall Dissuasive* where, as Dr. Cameron observes, if it had been stateable the elaborate arguments in that book would have been unnecessary. No! the " heir-male " theory was invented by the wicked Lord Lovat after he had failed to abduct the heiress, and it was a theory seized upon avidly by Anglo-Hanoverian propagandists to secure quick extinction of the Scottish and Highland chiefly houses.

It was not " feudalism " which was unpopular with the Highlanders ; the clan system *was* feudal.   Indeed, the Lordship of the
Isles itself was organized on " feudal " lines.   It was the commercial
mis-application of feudalism against which the clans fought, as they
did against the English idea of direct Crown holdings, which weakened
chief and clan.

As in the days of Charles I., King James had promised to reorganise
the charters of superiority, under which Campbells and other grasping,
or disaffected, chiefs had secured feudal chieftaincy. over clans and
branches which should, according to strict feudal law, have been either
holding direct of the Crown, or have had their estates properly grouped
under the feudal dominions of their hereditary clan-chiefs.   Such
promises for rescinding of charters obtained through financial and
other forms of pressure and " commercialisation " of the old feudalism,
by the Houses of Argyll and Cogeach, had been promised by Montrose,
but prevented by his execution.   Both Charles II. and James VII.
had renewed these promises, which indeed were necessary to restore
the prerogative of the Crown, and curb the ill-gotten predominance
of the Whig clans.

Soon after Killiecrankie, William of Orange, well aware of the
importance attached by the clans to these promises, entered into a
treaty—executed at Achallader in Glenorchy—that he would implement the promises of the Stuart kings and free them from overlordship into which they had, by ostensible " commercial " transactions
and settlements of debts, been placed under feudal dominance of the
Whigs ; the Crown and Royalist chiefs having thereby been deprived
of their trusty vassals.

On their part, the clans agreed to disband their forces and swear
allegiance to King William, provided that King James would approve
of their doing this.   When the clans retired to their respective districts
on the faith of this treaty, pending the reply from King James, William,
who though in honour bound to keep his forces where they were till
King James's mandate to the clans had been received by them, gave,
on the contrary, orders to the army to advance and take up such
positions as would give him the command of the various clan districts.
However, the Duke of Leinster, who commanded the forces in Scotland,
intimated to Queen Mary (who was ruling the country during the
absence of her husband in Flanders) the violation of the treaty.   The
Queen thereupon countermanded King William's order, pending the
return of the messengers who had been sent to her father to obtain his
approval of the treaty entered into by the Highland clans with her
husband.   King James, well aware what his faithful clans would be
made to suffer if they refused to submit to the new Government, gave
his permission to them to take the oath of allegiance to William and
Mary.

How King William, aided by the Master of Stair, did all in his
power to prevent the chiefs taking the oath of allegiance to his Govern-

ment within a specified time, and thus to provide himself with a pretext for exterminating them and their clansfolk ; how he failed to do this in all but one case (that of MacIan, Chief of the MacDonalds, or MacIans of Glencoe) ; how the perfidious massacre of Glencoe was the result ; and how Dutch William's name has been handed down to the execration of posterity, are matters well known in history. The massacre of Glencoe took place during the night of the 12th of February 1692, after the Government troops had been hospitably entertained by MacIan and his clansfolk. When Stair learned that MacIan had been prevented taking the oath of allegiance to the new Government until after the period for doing so had expired, he penned a letter in which the following passage occurs : " Argyll tells me that Glencoe hath not taken the oath, at which I rejoice. It is a great work of charity to be exact in rooting out that damnable set." What Dutch William and his creature, Sir John Dalrymple, Master of Stair, Under-Secretary for Scotland, were prepared to do to the clans had they not taken the oath of allegiance is evident. " The letter is still extant," says Lord Macaulay, " in which he [Stair] directed the commander of the forces in Scotland how to act if the Jacobite chiefs should not come in before the end of December." " Your troops," writes Stair, " will destroy entirely the country of Lochaber, Lochiel's lands, Keppoch's, Glengarry's, and Glencoe's. Your power shall be large enough. I hope the soldiers will not trouble the Government with prisoners ! "

The massacre of Glencoe in 1692, followed by the failure of the Darien Scheme of 1695 (when King William did all in his power to cripple both Highland and Lowland Scottish commerce), and the disgraceful circumstances under which the Union between Scotland and England was effected in 1707, all contributed to make Celtic Scotland ripe for the rising, which took place when on the 6th of September 1715, John, Earl of Mar (most ancient of Celtic earldoms), who had been unwisely insulted by George I., raised the Royal Standard on the historic " Braes of Mar," and proclaimed " the Chevalier," son and heir of James VII., as " James VIII." As the old song has it :

The Standard on the Braes o' Mar is up and streaming rarely,
The gathering pipe on Lochnagar is sounding lang and sairly,
The Hieland men frae hill and glen, wi' belted plaids and glitt'ring blades,
Wi' bonnets blue and hairts sae true, are comin' late and early.

Had the Highland army at that juncture been commanded by a Dundee instead of by the Earl of Mar, whose interests lay in Scottish architecture and town-planning, history might have been different. At Sheriffmuir, November 1715, the Royalist army virtually defeated the Hanoverians, and the Chevalier had landed in Scotland ; but initiative was lacking ; the gains were not followed up, and ere long " James VIII." re-embarked (at Montrose), the rising subsided, and a few prominent Jacobites were executed.

Ten years later a blow was struck at clanship by the statute of 1725, euphemistically designated the " Disarming Act," and other legislation was directed to suppress the popular Highland " Huntings " in which the whole population joined. This unfortunate piece of legislation was indeed, in a sense, the precursor of the modern " Deer Forest " idea, which superseded the ancient Highland form of the sport. General Wade was commissioned to enforce these measures, and proved a reasonably popular man in an unpleasant duty ; but his underlings, such as Edmund Burt, the hated tax-gatherer at Inverness, treated the Highlanders with the brutal contempt characteristic of the Anglo-Saxon to everything un-English.[1] Their administration was described as a " haughty, keen, and unsupportable government " which the people of Inverness found " impossible for us to bear." Burt and his hectoring colleagues " shew up the English law " and " damned the law of Scotland" openly in the city. The General was also authorised to construct military roads throughout the Highlands, and to erect a chain of forts along the Great Glen of Scotland, through which the Caledonian Canal now runs, as well as to maintain a sloop of war on Loch Ness. These measures were adopted principally in order to overawe the Episcopalian and Roman Catholic inhabitants of that part of the Highlands, who were the warmest adherents of the House of Stuart. It may here be pointed out parenthetically, as an example of the irony of fate, that one of General Wade's forts in the Great Glen (Fort Augustus) is now a Catholic monastery. The roads, however, proved a most useful improvement, though ironically enough, their first military service was to the army of Prince Charles in 1745 !

In the year 1725, a number of independent companies was recruited among the clans which were believed to be favourably disposed to the House of Hanover. These companies formed a kind of military police, for the purpose of preserving law and order in the districts garrisoned by them. The companies were designated *Am Freiceadan Dubh*, or the Black Watch, owing to the appearance of their dark tartan, which contrasted strikingly with the scarlet uniforms of the *Saighdearan Dearg*, or Red Soldiers.

In 1738 that far-seeing statesman, Lord President Forbes of Culloden, submitted to the Government a plan which he had devised for utilising the warlike nature of the Highland clans, and at the same time thereby attaching them to the existing government.[2]

Two years later the Black Watch was formed into a regiment of the line, as the 43rd Regiment. A couple of months before the Rising of 1745, a second Highland regiment was raised, under the designation of Loudoun's Highlanders. During the events of " the '45," the Black Watch was stationed in the south of England, but Loudoun's Highlanders remained in the north.

On 25th July 1745 Prince Charles Edward Stuart, bearing a Com-

[1] J. B. Salmond, *Wade in Scotland*, p. 104.
[2] For details of the scheme see page 440.

mission of Regency from his father, the Chevalier de St. George, as " James VIII.," landed at Arisaig,[1] and took up residence at Borodale, where he was received by Angus Macdonald, the tacksman, and Macdonald of Glenaladale with a bodyguard of a hundred *daoine-uasail* of Clan Ranald. The " news frae Moidart " soon sped through the Highlands ; and Lochiel, after some hesitation about commencing the rising without French troops trained to resist the tactics of the Hanoverian soldiery, having declared he would " share the fate of my Prince," the clans were summoned, and ere long Gordon of Glenbucket arrived with assurances from the Jacobites of the north-east.

On 19th August the Royal Standard was raised, in the name of King James VIII. and the Stuart cause, at Glenfinnan, on the shores Loch Shiel and unfurled by Lord Tullibardine.

> When in deep Glenfinnan's valley
> Thousands on their bended knees
> Saw once more that stately ensign
> Waving in the Northern breeze,
> When the noble Tullibardine
> Stood beneath its weltering fold,
> With the Ruddy Lion ramping
> In its field of tressured gold.
> When the mighty heart of Scotland
> All too big to slumber more
> Burst in wrath and exultation
> Like a huge volcano's roar.

The Marquis then read the Chevalier's Commission :

JAMES VIII., by the Grace of God, King of Scotland, England, &c., &c., having always borne the most constant affection to Our ancient Kingdom of Scotland from whence We derive Our royal origin and where Our progenitors have swayed the sceptre with glory through a longer succession of kings than any monarchy upon earth can at this day boast of ; . . . We see a Nation always famous for valour . . . reduced to the condition of a province . . . in consequence of this pretended union, grievous and unprecedented taxes have been laid on and levied with severity . . . and these have not failed to produce . . . poverty and decay of trade . . . Our faithful Highlanders, a people always trained up and inured to arms, have been deprived of them . . . and a military government has been effectually introduced as in a conquered country . . . a remedy can

---

[1] The Prince had set sail in the French ship *La Du Teillay* on 21st June, accompanied by " the Seven Men of Moidart " : (1) William, Marquis of Tullibardine, (2) Sir John Macdonald, (3) Angus Macdonald, brother to Kinlochmoidart, (4) Sir Thomas Sheridan, an Irishman, (6) Francis Strickland, an Englishman, (5) Thomas O'Sullivan, and (7) the Rev. George Kelly. They landed at Eriska, off South Uist, on 23rd July, the first Scot to greet the Prince —who was still incognito—being MacNeil of Barra's piper (a friend of Duncan Cameron, a follower of Old Lochiel's who might well have been reckoned amongst the " Men of Moidart "). Next day the ship sailed on to Loch-nan-uamh in Arisaig and the Prince landed. On 11th August he went to Kinlochmoidart.

never be obtained but by Our restoration to the Throne of Our ancestors, into whose royal heart such destructive maxims could never find admittance . . . We are fully resolved to act always by the advice of Our parliaments, and to value none of Our titles so much as that of common *Father of Our People*, which We shall ever show Ourselves to be by Our constant endeavours to promote the quiet and happiness of all Our subjects.

Glenfinnan now resounded with the martial strains of the pibroch, and by evening the Prince found himself at the head of a brave and resolute army, which next morning commenced its march upon the Scottish capital. On the 4th September the Prince, superbly attired in tartan, his trews laced with gold, rode into the "Fair City" of Perth, where the Chevalier was again proclaimed, and having established his headquarters in the house of Viscount Stormont, the Prince Regent there received the Duke of Perth, Lord Airlie, Strowan-Robertson, and Oliphant of Gask, whose granddaughter, Caroline Oliphant, Lady Nairne, was later on to make Scotland ring with her wonderful Jacobite lyrics.[1] On the 11th September, the Prince's army marched from Perth *en route* for the capital; the Highlanders crossed the Forth in the face of Colonel Gardner's Dragoons, and after a visit to Lord Kilmarnock at Callander House, the Prince and his army advanced towards Edinburgh, whose Lord Provost, on 16th September, received the commands of Charles, as Prince Regent, to "receive Us as in duty bound" into "the capital of His Majesty's ancient Kingdom of Scotland," and a deputation of the Council having waited on the Prince (but settled nothing), the return of their coach to its stable in the Canongate enabled Locheil, Keppoch, and Ardshiel to capture the historic Netherbow Port and by daybreak Edinburgh was in the hands of the Highlanders, whilst Prince Charles, preceded by a hundred pipers and attended by the Duke of Perth and Lord Elcho (*i.e.* the chiefs of Drummond and Wemyss), amidst general acclamations made his way to Holyroodhouse and took up residence in the palace of his Royal ancestors. The Prince on this occasion wore a tartan coat, red velvet breeches and knee boots, a blue velvet bonnet laced with gold, bearing the "white cockade," and upon his breast the star of St. Andrew. That same day, at the Mercat Cross of Edinburgh, Roderick Chalmers of Portlethen, Ross Herald, proclaimed the Chevalier as "James VIII." Within a month of the raising of the Standard, Prince Charles had restored the Stuarts' rule in the Scottish capital. Three days later, the Highland army, under the personal command of the Prince, marched eastward to meet the now advancing forces of the Elector, under General Sir John Cope, and at Prestonpans,

---

[1] It is pleasant to record that the dignity of Lord Nairne, forfeited in consequence of the devoted Jacobitism of John, 3rd Lord Nairne, was restored to Caroline's husband, William, as 5th Lord, in 1824, at the instance of George IV., on account of his appreciation of her Jacobite songs, which breathe such devotion to the spirit of monarchy and chiefship.

on 21st September, annihilated the Hanoverian army, whose general, the notorious Cope, was amongst the first to fly. Prince Charles was now in peaceable possession of the whole of Scotland (save Edinburgh Castle and a few other forts), and had he followed the advice of those who urged him to denounce the hated Union, and summon a Scottish Parliament, the Stuart dynasty would have been again restored to its ancient throne ; but his mind was set upon " the Court of St. James," and preparations made instead for an invasion of England. Meantime the Prince maintained a brilliant court at Holyroodhouse— levées each morning, followed by meetings of the Council, and after dining in public, in the ancient regal manner, followed brilliant balls, attended by all the rank and fashion of the Scottish capital, which once again basked in the radiance of a resident court, and as Lord President Forbes remarked :

All Jacobites became mad, all doubtful people became Jacobites, and all bankrupts heroes, who talked of nothing but hereditary right and victory. What was more grievous (to Hanoverians) . . . and . . . much more mischievous . . . all the fine ladies, if you except one or two, became passionately fond of the Young Adventurer, and used all their arts and industry for him.

The Lord President, moreover, prepared another memorial for the information of Government, showing the approximate military strength of the clans. This totalled some 23,000 claymores, though in the memorial the Lord President omitted to take note of some of the smaller clans. Wade had estimated that the military strength of the clans well affected to the Hanoverian dynasty, was about 8,000 men. These consisted chiefly of Campbells, Sutherlands, Frasers, Grants, Rosses, Roses, Munros, and Forbeses. From the foregoing it can easily be seen in what direction the feelings of the clans lay. The Lord President used all his powerful influence to prevent the Highland chiefs calling out their clans on behalf of Prince Charles. In many cases his efforts were crowned with success, and both chief and clansmen remained neutral during the great struggle. In several instances, however, though the chief remained at home, his clans-people joined the Jacobite army, and were commanded by one of the clan chieftains. In one case, however, that of the Captain of Clan Chattan (Mackintosh), who was serving with the Hanoverian forces, the clan was called out by his wife, the Lady Mackintosh (Anne Farquharson of Invercauld), who raised two battalions, and placed them under the command of MacGillivray of Dunmaglas. It is well known how bravely these men acquitted themselves during the campaign, and especially at Culloden. If the truth were known, it is highly probable that, had the restraining influence of some of the Highland chiefs not been exercised, nine-tenths of the clansfolk would have been found on the side of Prince Charles during the Rising of

" the '45." The clanspeople regarded that Prince as the lawful representative of their supreme chief, or *Ard-righ* ; a chief whom, according
to the Highland idea, Parliament had no authority to depose. The
de facto King, George, on the other hand, was looked upon, not
only by the Highlanders, but also by a large section of the Lowland
population of Scotland, as a usurper, and a " wee, wee, German
lairdie ! "

The humanity and consideration of Prince Charles Edward
towards his vanquished enemies was as praiseworthy as the conduct of his opponents was infamous in its atrocity towards their
captives.

On the evening of 31st October, after six glorious weeks at Holyroodhouse, Prince Charles and his army moved southward, and on
the 8th November crossed the border " wi' a hundred pipers an a',
an a'." The expedition progressed as wonderfully as his Scottish
campaign ; Carlisle was captured, and the Jacobite army, in high
spirits, swept down into the Midlands ; but its leaders began to grow
anxious when the promised aid from the English Jacobites failed to
materialise. Moreover, disputes had arisen amongst the leaders,
particularly between Murray of Broughton, the Prince's secretary,
and Lord George Murray (younger brother of Lord Tullibardine), his
best general.

Consternation, however, struck the Whigs in London, when the
Jacobites, skilfully avoiding Cumberland's army, got between it and
London, and within 127 miles of the metropolis. The Elector had
ordered his yacht and embarked his valuables ; War Minister, the
Duke of Newcastle, retired to prepare for " eventualities " ; and a
further advance of perhaps a day's march would probably have left
the Prince in possession of the kingdom. But on the 5th December,
at a Council of War, Lord George advised retreat, and such was the
influence of his character that many of the chiefs acquiesced. The
Prince did his best to alter the fatal decision ; his gallant army was
staggered when, without reason, their uninterrupted advance was
reversed. For the star of the Stuarts, and for those who shrank in
the moment of victory, the decision spelt disaster. Had the Prince
remained in Edinburgh, he could have held Scotland for the Stuarts.
Had he boldly proceeded from Derby to London, he would have
recovered for his father all three crowns. Once the retreat commenced,
it became speedily evident that he could retain nothing even of what
he had won be-north the Border, and the retrocession which commenced on the 6th of December concluded on the Muir of Drummossie
on the fatal 16th of April.

> Fatal day whereon the latest
> Die was cast for me and mine,
> Cruel day that quelled the fortunes
> Of the hapless Stuart line.

Bring my horse and blow the trumpet,
Call the riders of FitzJames.[1]
Let Lord Lewis head the column,[2]
Valiant Chiefs of mighty names !

Hark ! the bagpipes fitful wailing :
Not the pibroch loud and shrill,
That, with hope of bloody banquet,
Lured the ravens from the hill,
But a dirge both low and solemn
Fit for ears of dying men
Marshalled for their latest battle,
Never more to fight again.

The star of the House of Stuart was extinguished for ever at the Battle of Culloden on 16th of April 1746. The sun set that day on scenes of savagery and blood, and the sunrise of the following day ushered in an epoch of butchery and terror, presided over by the cruel Duke of Cumberland ; an epoch which in savagery, has only been surpassed in modern history by the bloody orgies of the French Revolution of 1790–1793.[3]

[1] The Duc de FitzJames was a natural son of King James VII.

[2] Lord Lewis Gordon, a younger son of George, Duke of Gordon. He raised the celebrated regiment of cavalry from the north-east of Scotland. His sister, Lady Jean Gordon, married to a son of the Earl of Aberdeen, whilst residing at Fyvie, had with her son gone out to see the Duke of Cumberland's army march northwards. The Duke, in passing, having stopped to ask who she, a very handsome lady, was, she proudly replied, " I am the sister of Lord Lewis Gordon."

[3] It is remarkable that Adam should draw this parallel, because it is a closer one than might at first appear. In each case the intention was to substitute the soul-less administrative state for the natural feudo-clan family-state. The French Revolution, as is now well known, was the result of an undutiful plot by the dastardly Duc d'Orleans (" Citizen Egalité "), combined with plans of Frederick of Prussia to bring down the power of France, both of which were fostered by the crazy political fanatics who had dabbled in " Reason " as expounded by atheistical philosophers. The character of these subversists was essentially anti-familial individualism, opposed to the hallowed family-concept ; and the coups d'états were carried through by hired " thugs " against the wishes of the French people, who had expressed a desire for retention of the seigneurial Courts, which, as must be repeated, were popular and truly " democratic " self-governing councils (cf. F. Brentano, Old Regime in France, p. 133 ; W. C. Dickinson, Baron Court Book of Carnwarth, XCIII., CVIII.–XVII.).

La Bruyère's notorious false description of the French peasantry : " We see certain wild animals, male and female, spread over the country . . . clinging to the soil which they dig and turn up . . . and are in fact men. They retire by night into their dens, where they live on black bread . . . they spare others the trouble of sowing, plough . . ." but this—urban—writer (whose name not inaptly denotes " fog ") adds, " in town one is brought up in utter indifference to things rural," and, adds Brentano, " doubtless he wished to give us a personal example " (Brentano, Ibid. p. 259). For the truth one turns to Retif de la Bretonne : " In the evening at supper (the father) looked like a patriarch . . . twenty-two at table including the ploughman . . . and the vine dressers " ; Marmontel : " (grandmother) used to show me the provisions she had made for

The Highlands were practically laid waste by the Government troops, and the inhabitants, men, women, and children butchered, while those of the Highland chiefs who had not succeeded in making good their escape were executed under circumstances of extreme barbarity. So savage the nature and so vindictive towards Highlanders was the policy of the Government that in 1753 (seven years after Culloden) it brought to the block Dr. Archibald Cameron (a brother of Lochiel), who had, after the events of 1746, escaped to the Continent. In 1753 the doctor, believing that Government revenge had been satiated, ventured to return to his native country. His return to Scotland, however, was but the signal for his doom.

After a series of romantic and dangerous adventures in the Highlands, during which he went as far west as the Long Island, Prince Charles succeeded in reaching Arisaig on 19th of September 1746, and in making his escape to France on board a French vessel, along with a band of his unfortunate fellow-exiles. During one critical period of the Prince's wanderings in the Hebrides, his safety was assured and his escape from his enemies ultimately compassed in consequence of the devotion of the heroic Flora MacDonald, daughter of MacDonald of Milton, in South Uist, and step-daughter of Mac-Donald of Armadale, in Skye. In June 1746, when the Prince was hiding in Benbecula, it became evident the Redcoats were in such force that his capture was at last inevitable. Lady Clanranald and Flora, however, managed to arrange that the Prince should be taken across to Skye in a six-oared boat, disguised as Flora's maid, and this she successfully accomplished, in spite of close military scrutiny, and on 28th–29th June, being nearly overwhelmed by a storm during the

the winter, her bacon, hams, sausages, pots of honey . . . the sheepfolds clothed the women and children, my aunts spun the wool . . . the young people nearby would come in and help . . . making an enchanting picture "; Bouveret (peasant wedding) : " in addition to the fine clothes of the bride, and a head-dress of embroidery . . . there would be strains of pipes . . . and afterwards a sumptuous banquet and rustic dances." " The seigneur . . . would take part in these rustic weddings " (Brentano, *Ibid.* p. 269) ; Dr. Rigby (tourist) : " all the people look happy." And of the results of " Liberté, Egalité, Fraternité " (so called) : " The France of patronal and feudal traditions, that picturesque, energetic France . . . teeming with life and colour—the old ' family ' France—was dead. We were in the presence of an administrative France " ; and " When the Revolution had ended . . . the number of officials had increased tenfold " (Brentano, *Ibid.* p. 366).

Of that sorry France—of the shoddy " Empires " and the sordid " republics " —we know the sorry story ; scandal succeeding scandal, until it finally sank in the disgrace of 1940—the inevitable retribution of nations which turn away from the Fifth Commandment and the principles of the family, that is, the clan. In Scotland the " administrative " machine never reached the French stage—at least not in the eighteenth and nineteenth centuries—and our Scottish feudalism remained the popular tribo-feudalism of the twelfth to thirteenth century (cf. Brentano, *Ibid.* p. 139, with E. Crawford, *Lives of the Lindsays*, I., p. 119, *Scot. Ant. Soc.*, 79, p. 122). Adam's simile is thus a sound one; but in Scotland, fortunately, " the clan " survived Culloden, and our tribo-feudalism has lasted another two hundred years and made Scotland famous.

THE HIGHLAND CLAN SYSTEM UNDER THE ROYAL STEWARTS 71

night—a journey commemorated in the well-known " Skye Boat Song " :

> Speed bonny boat like bird on the wing !
> Onward ! the sailors cry ;
> Carry the lad that is born to be King
> Over the sea to Skye.

Successfully turning the point of Waternish, they landed safely at Mugstot, the seat of Sir Alexander Macdonald of Sleate, who, though a Jacobite at heart, was away in attendance on the Duke of Cumberland ; but his wife, Lady Margaret, being an enthusiastic Jacobite, was able to transfer the Prince to further safety in the house of Kingsburgh. Flora afterwards became the wife of MacDonald of Kingsburgh, whence she and her husband and family eventually emigrated to America, from which, however, she returned to spend the last years of her life in her native land.

It speaks volumes for the fidelity and incorruptibility of the Highlanders that, although the Government had offered a reward of £30,000 for the capture of Prince Charles Edward, dead or alive, and though this was known throughout the Highlands, still not a man could be found to soil his hands or besmirch the name of the Highlanders by doing anything towards gaining the fortune above alluded to.

Besides the sums paid as compensation for the reduction to merely nominal powers of hereditary jurisdictions, an amount of £152,000 was divided among those who had not taken part in the Rising of 1745. Of this sum, the House of Argyll appears to have had the lion's share.

For long after Culloden, the history of the Highlands is but a record of outrage and butchery, perpetrated by a licentious soldiery, encouraged by their savage commander, William, Duke of Cumberland, who had a grant of £25,000 per annum voted him by the British Parliament, as a reward for his policy of converting the Highlands of Scotland into a desert, and exterminating their unfortunate inhabitants!

On 12th August 1746 came the Disarming Act, 1746, 19 Geo. II., c. 39, entitled : " An Act for the more effectual disarming the Highlands in Scotland ; and for more effectually securing the Peace of the said Highlands ; and for restraining the Use of the Highland dress."

In addition to provisions for disarming the Highlands, and for prohibiting the wearing of the Highland dress or the use of tartan, the Act, *inter alia*, enacted severe penalties against the persons of any teachers who omitted to pray for the King by name, and for all the Royal family. It was also enacted that " in case he [the teacher] shall resort to or attend Divine Worship in any *Episcopal* Meeting House not allowed by the Law, every person so offending . . . shall, for the first Offence, suffer imprisonment for the Space of Six Months ; and for the Second, or any subsequent Offence . . . shall be adjudged to be transported, and accordingly shall be transported to some of his Majesty's Plantations in America for Life."

The Disarming Act was followed in 1747 by the Heritable Jurisdictions Act, which abolished all the greater heritable jurisdictions
such as Lordships and Bailliaries of Regality, Constabularies, and
Stewartries, whilst it reduced the jurisdictions of free barony to such
nominal powers as the imposition of penalties not exceeding 3/4
sterling, or two hours in the stocks. Otherwise, however, the old
jurisdiction of barony, which in 1600 Sir Thomas Craig had explained
was synonymous with, and a perpetuation of, the jurisdiction of the
capitani tribuum, continued, so that in Scotland the Baron Court, or
formalised local family-legislature and judicature of each baronial
duthus, is still a surviving living entity, and a link with the old days
of a self-governing Scotland. The insistence, however, with which
this statute was pressed and forced through Parliament against the
wishes of the people of Scotland, shows how thoroughly the Hanoverian
Government understood the inseparable relationship of clanship and
feudalism, and that the clan system could only be effectively attacked
through damaging the feudal framework by which it had been preserved. Notwithstanding the Act, however, the Baron Courts continued to function for another twenty or thirty years, and the " Statutes
and Ordinances " which were formerly made (and in principle would
still be) in these little legislative bodies, still survive in the " Estate
Regulations," mutually signed by landlord and tenant, and which
still in several cases maintained the old stately phraseology that they
are drawn up " for the governing of the estate." Modern people are
seldom told that the true nature of these heritable jurisdictions was a
miniature council or parliament in which the affairs of the little state
were ruled by the baron, with the council and inhabitants of his
cuntrie. Each Baron Court was a microcosm of the Royal parliament
of the realm of Scotland. These little popular local councils made
their Statutes and Ordinances " by and with the advice and consent of the haill tenants and commons of the said barony " for the
administration of local business, appointed the " four *birleymen* " or
arbiters who settled ordinary disputes and then sitting as a judicature,
acquitted or convicted delinquents. The function of the laird or his
baron-bailie was solely to carry out the judgement of this people's
court, either by fine or other appropriate penalty.

Miss Grant estimates, however, that only a fraction of the Court's
time was taken up with these " police court " proceedings. The bulk
of the business was the settlements of civil disputes between the
tenants, and operating the " communal working of the joint farms,
preservation of woods, and enforcement of acts of parliament." [1] Or,
as the 8th Duke of Argyll explained it :

Great estates were then generally erected into baronies, that is to say,
districts with a regular system of rural government in which the tenantry

---

[1] *Social and Economic Development of Scotland* p. 185, and W. C. Dickinson,
Baron Court Book of Carnwath, pp. lix–lxix.

of various classes took part under a president who represented the proprietor and was called the Bailie.[1]

In the light of what has been thus recently set forth of the real nature of " feudalism," I think that in her admirable survey of Scottish economics Miss Grant would now have paused before writing : " so lacking were the Scots throughout the whole period in any development of the power of actually and practically governing themselves." [2]

That is precisely what they *did* achieve, and by the only machinery capable of achieving it. They, like the Swiss, had grasped what the victims of " efficient centralised government " are now realising, that

Individuals and small groups . . . at least . . . can be moral and rational to a degree unattainable by large groups, for as numbers increase personal relations between members of the group, and members of other groups become more difficult . . . and finally . . . impossible.[3]

That is precisely why clanship and feudalism were effective and popular, and why bureaucrats and politicians hate such a form of organisation, with its gay kaleidoscope of freedom so different from the hideous uniformity of the modern regimented state.

Accordingly the Scottish people had no desire to see their local councils, the centres of popular local self-government, either abolished, or even restricted,[4] any more than the people of olden France desired the similar so-called " seigneurial jurisdictions " to be abolished in France.[5] In the face of the local popularity of these clan councils and baronial courts, it is at first sight extraordinary to read the vehement (though discreetly indefinite) denunciations of them by industrial capitalist politicians. The explanation is that in these little tribo-feudal parliaments, in which alone there was true government " of the people by the people," it was impossible to exploit the land and people on it, as the new type of industrialists were planning to do when they had expropriated the ruined chieftains. The closing-down of the Baron Court was the necessary antecedent to the " clear-ance " of the clansmen and the " planned " exploitation of the sheep-run, not to add the substitution of the selfish stalker's " Deer Forest " for the popular " Huntings " of the old Highland regime described by Taylor, the " Water Poet." Argyll is quite plain about it :

An improved system of agriculture could not even be begun without emancipation of the individual from the clogging effects of ignorant and effete communities." [6]

---

[1] J. Fyffe, *Scottish Diaries and Memoirs*, p. 565.
[2] *Social and Economic Development of Scotland*, p. 204.
[3] Aldous Huxley, *Grey Eminence*, p. 247.
[4] *Chartulary of Couper*, p. 299 ; *Social and Economic Devel. of Scotland*, p. 186.
[5] *Old Regime in France*, p. 133.
[6] J. Fyffe, *Scottish Diaries and Memoirs*, p. 565.
D*

The nature of the " improvements " we shall see later on ; be it here noted that these self-governing family-councils of the people themselves were brushed aside and stigmatised as " ignorant and effete " !

A few years were to show that in the clan system there were far more feudal rights than feudal wrongs ; and when the little feudal judicatures, by which these rights were rendered effective, had been extinguished in all but name, the clansman was helpless against the southern bondholders, who had in the meantime shackled too many of even those of the Highland chiefs who had escaped the actual forfeitures which followed the last Jacobite rising.

NOTE.—Whilst it indeed appears that the conduct of the Clan-army (p. 60) during the " Killing Time " was exemplary, Sir G. Mackenzie's " Vindication " (*Works*, II., 341) though disclosing Puritan " atrocities " not ordinarily mentioned, is not convincing. Both sides were equally cruel and intolerant ; but it was the Privy Councillors, and ecclesiastics associated with them, who at each stage were responsible for the brutalities, and not the military commanders. Indeed, Dalyell of the Binns resigned his command after the murder of the Covenanters taken and spared by him at Rullion Green.

Adam took the view that the Reformation and Presbyterian Kirk had a deleterious effect on the clans. As indicated, they did affect Celtic art and music. In other respects, both from its relatively strong local courts, and its Old Testament regard for patriarchal aspects, ceremonial (*e.g.* of baptism), parental responsibility, and heraldic decoration, the Church of Scotland (as compared with Episcopacy, which was weaker in territoriality and familialism) tended to foster the spirit of clanship.

IV

The Highlands after Culloden

IT is no doubt difficult for Scotsmen to write impassively of the methods which were employed by the Whig Government for placating (?) the Highlands after the Battle of Culloden, but a distinguished English writer (Lord Mahon, *History of England*) has said :

Quarter was seldom given to the stragglers and fugitives, except to a few considerately reserved for public execution. No care or compassion was shown to their wounded ; nay more, on the following day most of these were put to death in cold blood, with a cruelty such as never perhaps before or since has disgraced a British army. Some were dragged from the thickets or cabins where they had sought refuge, drawn out in line and shot, while others were dispatched by the soldiers with the stocks of their muskets. One farm building into which some twenty disabled Highlanders had crawled, was deliberately set on fire the next day, and burnt with them to the ground. The native prisoners were scarcely better treated, and even sufficient water was not vouchsafed to their thirst. . . . Every kind of havoc and outrage was not only permitted, but I fear we must add encouraged. Military licence usurped the place of law, and a fierce and exasperated soldiery were at once judge, jury, executioner. . . . The rebels' country was laid waste, the houses plundered, the cabins burnt, the cattle driven away. The men had fled to the mountains, but such as could be found were frequently shot ; nor was mercy granted even to their helpless families. In many cases the women and children. expelled from their homes and seeking shelter in the clefts of the rocks, miserably perished of cold and hunger ; others were reduced to follow the track of their marauders, humbly imploring for the blood and offal of their own cattle which had been slaughtered for the soldiers' food. Such is the avowal which historical justice demands. But let me turn from further details of these painful and irritating scenes, or of the ribald frolics and revelry with which they were intermingled, races of naked women on horseback for the amusement of the camp at Fort Augustus.

These summary murders of the rank and file of the Highlanders went side by side with the judicial murders of the upper ranks. It was not for a year, nor yet two or three, that this era of terror continued. Robert Louis Stevenson vividly illustrated this in the circumstances of the Appin murder in 1752, which resulted in the condemnation by a packed jury of James Stewart of the Glens, and his subsequent execution.

After 1746 large areas of the Highlands were forfeited to the Crown. These were placed under the management of the Court of Exchequer which was responsible to the Commissioners of the Treasury. Most of the authority of the Court of Exchequer was delegated to factors, and the Commissioners of the Treasury laid down a rule that as factor no Highlander should be eligible.

The unfortunate clansmen, who happened to be occupants of the forfeited estates, thus had an early experience of the dead hand of bureaucratic administration of land by " state " officials responsible only to impersonal departments. The friendly feudo-tribal clan relationship to chief, chieftain, and *duine-uasail*, was no longer present on these estates ; where not only was their little local council, the Baron Court, not held, but in cases of administrative oppression there was for them no remedy at the hands of the Crown and judicature, for it is too frequently forgotten that amongst the greatest advantages of systems of sub-infeudation and landlord and tenant, is that, in the event of dispute, the Crown holds a balance between the Superior and Vassal, or Laird and Tenant. Under the soulless rule of state adminis-trators, the clansman became—as must always be the case with a state-ridden peasantry—a slave in all but name ; and it was fortunate for the Scottish people that, in the later eighteenth century, steps were forced through Parliament for restoring a number of these old clan estates to the representatives of the ancient chiefs, though the Baron Courts (local parliaments), having had their powers reduced (*they were not abolished*), were seldom convened, which was a pity, as emblems of self-government should be kept functioning.

Some were fortunate enough still to be under their old chiefs, by whom they were treated as of yore. The tacksmen, or *daoine-uasail*, forming the gentry of the clan, chafed, however, under the altered conditions of affairs. The Government's discouragement of Baron Courts deprived them of an effective share in the management of the estates and property such as they had exercised under the happier feudal sway. Many of them, with their retainers, left the country and formed settlements in America, where they could wear their loved national garb, and be free from the persecutions of an alien Govern-ment. Between 1757 and 1763 the ordinary clansmen, to a certain extent, found congenial employment in serving in the Highland regi-ments, which were formed on the outbreak of war between France and Great Britain. The fortunes of these Highlanders are told in Chapter XIV. On the conclusion of peace in 1763, most of these High-land regiments were disbanded, and the men composing them had to look for other occupations. North Carolina appears to have claimed most of the Highland emigrants who left Scotland immediately after " the '45." After the conclusion of the war with France emigration to North Carolina again set in. This new wave of emigration commenced about 1769. Between that date and 1776 new circumstances had arisen, which contributed still more strongly to foster the spirit of emigration.

Emigration was in itself nothing new, and indeed a healthy feature in a prolific and expanding people with a fine empire to colonise. In the Middle Ages the Scots had migrated in large numbers to Europe, and made their way gallantly. After the opening of our American empire, it was both natural and expedient that Highlanders should take a share in peopling it ; and, as we shall see, they were—to the great advantage of Canada—both able and willing to do so. It has been estimated that in 1747 the population of the Highlands was about 230,000, whilst in 1795, it was, in spite of emigration, about 325,000, and by 1821, 447,000. Since the productive capacity had not, nor could then be doubled, there was bound to be poverty, and occasionally famine ; whilst the subdivision of crofts led to far greater congestion than had existed in the former runrig " fairm-touns." The proper course was assuredly to have inculcated that the numerous younger children should—like the younger sons of the lairds —make their way abroad ; and there was an empire waiting to receive them and requiring—as it still requires—just such settlers. Unfortunately the western folk did not in this show the practical resourcefulness of those on the east coast ; and when the essential migration took place, it was effected in masses which uprooted the parent stocks as well, and, largely on that account, caused the bitterest ill-feeling. This arose partly from the greater portion of the chiefs seeking to retain their growing clan around them, and failing to realise the situation that must develop.

Pennant, who made two tours in the Highlands of Scotland (in 1769 and 1772), tells one long tale of the condition of woe and wretchedness which he witnessed. In 1770 a famine broke out ; and the following year a (hardly altogether) " strange passion for emigration " seized many of the survivors. Clever people in the shipping business saw that something could be made of this, and that by telling wonderful tales of an American Eldorado, they could make a great deal of money by shipping Highlanders abroad, as their ancestors had shipped sheep and cattle. Whilst a few of the chiefs were induced by various means (i.e. financial pressure skilfully enforced) to join the " ramp," the greater number were struck with consternation at the manner in which the shipping adventurers were, by specious tales of wealth, wheedling their people on to the filthy transports in which too many died before they ever reached the shores of the New World. The deplorable aspects were the conditions surrounding the transport, and that the exodus was fostered by the emigration agents stirring up discontent, which led, not to the emigration of the surplus young people, but to the uprooting of the local stocks from which they sprang. This mischief was facilitated by a depreciation of the currency (or call it " inflation "), which again operated during the Napoleonic Wars.

The old produce-rents had been converted into " money " rents ; [1] the money had depreciated, and no longer represented the laird's " third " of the produce of the land (which he required, to fulfil his chiefly functions effectively). Faced with a demand for readjustment, the tacksmen became a ready prey to those promising a fortune in America. Moreover, the Government had in the generation following Culloden, encouraged the chiefs to live in the south and have their children educated there. They were quite unable to support the expenses of life in England, or to mingle with wealthy English aristocracy.[2]

The result was too often that debt was incurred, so that presently both chief and clansmen found themselves in a state of poverty. The astute business-politicians were at hand ready to inculcate an immediate remedy for both, which, as usual, was dubbed " progressive plans for developing the Highlands." Tempting rents for large tracts of Highland territory for sheep-runs were offered to the now bond-ridden chiefs by Lowland farmers financed by astute financiers. This usually resulted in the inhabitants of the straths and glens being more or less forcibly removed to barren tracts and coastlands, in order to make room for a few Lowland shepherds. The dispossessed Highland population to some extent found a precarious livelihood in fishing, crofting, weaving, and in the all-too-short lived kelp-burning, whilst many others were driven into the slum towns, where the aforesaid

---

[1] It is necessary to explain that " rent " is not so much " money per acre." The true nature of agricultural rent is a share of the produce between the owner and occupier of the land, and from the earliest times—and as the Dunvegan Records show, also in the Highlands—the produce was divisible in thirds : one for resowing, and, of the two others, one to the laird and one to the tenant, who thus shared the increase equally. The increase of cattle was similarly divisible. Out of their respective " halves " each party had obligations to fulfil, which consisted largely in the paying of wages in kind ; but, as money payments became commoner (and taxes, etc., had to be paid in money), it became the practice to commute part of the rent, and, lately, all of it, into cash sums subject to readjustment when a fresh lease was arranged. This system, convenient in itself if money values and produce prices had remained constant (which they do not), has in fact led to all the disputes about " fair rents " and so forth. In old days there were no such disputes in the modern sense, as, good or bad, the crop was divided (and the minister likewise " drew his teind " in kind). If the crop was good, the rent was good, and *vice versa*. Likewise, if prices were high, both parties got the benefit in disposing of what they wished to sell of their " share," and, if prices were bad, the rent was automatically " reduced " as the laird's share was of less value. Whilst " grain rents " (and some stock rents) have continued even to the present time, and the " fiars prices," which mark the commutation value of such rents where a " conversion " is desired, are still judicially " struck " each year in the Sheriff Courts, the Agricultural Holdings and Crofting Acts neglected this fundamental aspect of the " land question," and the Land Court was directed to fix " fair rents " and " equitable rents " (which was simply begging the question), instead of being directed to ascertain the estimable produce of the holding if cultivated according to the rules of good husbandry.

[2] *Book of Dunvegan*, Spalding Club.

financiers were preparing to exploit their labour, and thus by ruining chief, tacksman, and clansman alike, to make fortunes.

Whilst the latter developments related rather to the second wave (following the 1782 famine), the concatenation of over-population, famine, financial (inflation) disorganisation, shipping-propaganda, and the outlook of the chiefs educated in England, led to disastrous consequences.

In 1773 the celebrated Dr. Johnson, and his friend Boswell, made their famous " Tour of the Hebrides," and their account presents a perhaps more lucid presentation than others of the state of affairs.

Amongst the chiefs they visited were Sir Alexander Macdonald of Sleate, afterwards 1st Lord Macdonald, and his neighbour, Norman MacLeod of MacLeod. Johnson remarked most strongly the difference between these two Highland chiefs, both of whom were young men. MacDonald had received an English upbringing, and was quite out of touch with his clansfolk. MacLeod, on the contrary, had been educated in Scotland, and as the sequel will show, had the interests of his followers deeply at heart. Boswell remarks :

Sir Alexander MacDonald having been an Eton scholar and being a gentleman of talents, Dr. Johnson had been very well pleased with him in London. But my fellow traveller and I were now full of the old Highland spirit, and were dissatisfied at hearing of racked rents and emigration, and finding a chief not surrounded by his clan. Dr. Johnson said : " Sir, the Highland chiefs should not be allowed to go farther south than Aberdeen. A strong-minded man like Sir James MacDonald may be improved by an English education, but in general they will be tamed into insignificance." . . . My endeavours to rouse the English-bred chieftain, in whose house we were, to the feudal and patriarchal feelings proving ineffectual, Dr. Johnson this morning tried to bring him to our way of thinking. . . . We attempted in vain to communicate to him a portion of our enthusiasm.

Of MacLeod, Boswell says :

Dr. Johnson was much pleased with the Laird of MacLeod, who is, indeed, a most promising youth, and with a noble spirit struggles with difficulties and endeavours to preserve his people. He has been left with an encumbrance of forty thousand pounds debt, and annuities to the amount of thirteen hundred pounds a year. Dr. Johnson said of him, " If he gets the better of all this, he'll be a hero ; and I hope he will. I have not met a young man who had more desire to learn, or who has learnt more. I have seen nobody that I wish more to do a kindness to than MacLeod."

Pennant, who had visited Skye the previous year, says of MacLeod :

A gentleman of the most ancient and honourable descent, but whose personal character does him infinitely higher honour than this fortuitous distinction. To all the milkiness of human nature, usually concomitant on youthful years, is added the sense and firmness of more advanced life.

He feels for the distresses of his people, and insensible of his own, instead of the trash of gold, is laying up the treasure of warm affection and heart-felt gratitude.

MacLeod had succeeded to the chiefship during the previous year, on the death of his grandfather. In 1785 MacLeod (then a General) wrote his memoirs, from which the following is extracted :

In the year 1771 a strange passion for emigrating to America seized many of the middling and poorer sort of Highlanders. The change of manners in their chieftains since 1745 produced effects which were evidently the proximate cause of this unnatural dereliction of their own, and appetite for a foreign country. The laws which deprived the Highlanders of their arms and garb would certainly have destroyed the feudal military powers of the chieftains ; but the fond attachment of the people to their patriarchs would have yielded to no laws. They were themselves the destroyers of that pleasing influence. Sucked into the vortex of the nation, and allured to the capitals, they degenerated from patriarchs and chieftains to land-lords ; and they became as anxious for increase of rent as the new-made lairds—the *novi-homines*—the mercantile purchasers of the Lowlands. Many tenants whose fathers for generations had enjoyed their little spots, were removed for higher bidders. Those who agreed at any price for their ancient *lares*, were forced to pay an increase without being taught any new method to increase their produce. In the Hebrides especially this change was not gradual but sudden, and baleful were its effects. The people, freed by the laws from the power of the chieftains, and loosened by the chieftains themselves from the bonds of affection, turned their eyes and their hearts to new scenes. America seemed to open its arms to receive every discontented Briton. To those possessed of very small sums of money, it offered large possessions of uncultivated but excellent land, in a preferable climate—to the poor it held out large wages for labour ; to all it promised property and independence. Many artful emissaries, who had an interest in the transportation or settlement of emigrants, industriously displayed these temptations ; and the desire of leaving their own country for the new land of promise became furious and epidemic. Like all the other popular furies, it infected not only those who had reason to complain of their situation or injuries, but those who were most favoured and most comfortably settled. In the beginning of 1772 my grandfather, who had always been a most beneficent and beloved chieftain, but whose necessities had lately induced him to raise his rents, became much alarmed by this new spirit which had reached this clan. Aged and infirm, he was unable to apply the remedy in person ; he devolved the task on me ; and gave me for an assistant our nearest male relation, Colonel MacLeod of Talisker. The duty imposed on us was difficult ; the estate was loaded with debt, encumbered with a numerous issue from himself and my father, and charged with some jointures. His tenants had lost in that severe winter above a third of their cattle, which constituted their substance ; their spirits were soured by their losses and the late augmentations of rent ; and their ideas of America were inflamed by the strongest representations and the example of their neighbouring clans. My friend and I were empowered to grant such reductions in the rents as might seem necessary and reasonable ; but we found it terrible to decide between the justice to creditors, the necessities of an ancient family which we ourselves represented, and the claims and distresses of an impoverished tenantry. To God I owe, and I trust will ever pay, the most fervent thanks that this terrible task enabled us to lay the foundation of circumstances (though then unlooked for) that I hope will prove the means not only of the rescue, but the aggrandisement of our family. I was young, and had the warmth of the liberal passions natural to that age. I called the people of the different districts of our estate together; I laid before them the situation of our family—its debts, its burthens, its distresses; I acknowledged the hardships under which they laboured; I described and reminded them of the manner in which they and their ancestors lived with mine; I combated their passion for America by a real account of the dangers and hardships they might encounter there; I besought them to love their young chieftain, and to renew with him their ancient manners; I promised to live among them; I threw myself upon them; I recalled to remembrance an ancestor who had also found his estate in ruins, and whose memory was held in the highest veneration; I desired every district to point out some of their oldest and most respected men to settle with me every claim; and I promised to do everything for their relief which in reason I could. My worthy relation ably seconded me, and our labour was not in vain. We gave considerable abatements in the rents; few emigrated; and the clan conceived the most cordial attachment to me, which they most effectively manifested.

Let us now look at the other side of the picture! The foregoing shows what a chief brought up among his clanspeople was able to do in retaining their affections. His neighbour, Johnson's " English-bred chieftain," was, on the other hand, getting on badly with his tacksmen and people—there being little show of sympathy between them and a chief with colourless English ideas.

Do not, however, the striking contrasts between MacLeod and MacDonald of nearly a century and a half ago point to a moral in our own times? Why must the children of so many of our old Highland families be sent for their education to the south of England? Are there no first-class public schools in Scotland [1] that the children

---

[1] Adam mistakes the whole issue: a " public school " of the English type does not differ in its results from being situated in Scotland, when it holds that teaching of Scottish history " fosters the narrow spirit of insularity which it is the duty of every schoolmaster to combat." But the true objections to the system are that it often fosters a different set of loyalties which cuts across the clan sentiment and estranges the boy from the traditions of his country, home, and family, and the acquaintance with the world gained by the Scottish rural day schools. Our urban schools now too often reflect, not the stately, olden, Scottish character, but the uncouth degeneracy of the " Scotch comic " and the soured democrat. The home-bred Highland laddie can as often as not still take his place with dignity in any sphere or company at home or abroad. The feudo-clannish system give every child culture, manners, and pride; the stigma which really attaches to the industrio-urban education (whether " democratic " or " authoritarian ") is that it at any rate seems to make a virtue of vulgarity and inculcate an un-Scottish hatred of courtlieness, i.e. good family manners and the Clan spirit.

of Highland chiefs must be sent for their education to England ? We cannot help feeling that the mere fact of a young chief spending his youth among English surroundings does much to impair his usefulness in later life, when he is called to take his place as the head of the clan. The author has had many years practical experience of the benefit, nay, the necessity, of being able to converse with dependents in their own language. Putting, therefore, sentimental considerations entirely to one side, and looking at the matter from a cold and business point of view ; are not the personal interests of a Highland chief more likely to be more forwarded when he has been brought up on Scottish soil, and is able to converse with his dependents in the Gaelic, which is the language of their daily use, and which was the tongue spoken by his own forefathers ?

From 1759 to 1776 there was a constant flow of emigrants from the Highlands to North America. Between 1763 and 1775 alone it is estimated that upwards of 20,000 Highlanders left Scotland for the New World. Among the emigrants were Flora MacDonald, the heroine of 1746, with her husband, Allan MacDonald of Kingsburgh, who arrived in North Carolina in 1774. At the close of the American War of Independence, during which Kingsburgh fought on the British side, Flora and her husband returned to Scotland. She died in 1790, and was buried in the churchyard of Kilmuir, Skye. Highland emigrants in their new American homes freely wore the Highland dress, and were not forbidden the music of the *piob-mhòr*, which was at that period prohibited in the Highlands by Government as a " weapon of war."

On the outbreak of the American War in 1775, not only were the Highlanders in America loyal to the mother-country, but they raised a regiment in her support (the 84th Royal Highland Emigrant Regiment). At the conclusion of the war, the Highlanders, resisting all offers made to them by the new nation, crossed the border and settled in Canada. Of these early emigrants, the Earl of Selkirk says :

> The people of Breadalbane and other parts of Perthshire, as also those of Badenoch and Strathspey and part of Ross-shire, have generally resorted to New York, and have formed settlements on the Delaware, the Mohawk, and Connecticut rivers. A settlement has been formed in Georgia by people chiefly from Inverness. Those of Argyllshire and its islands, of the Island of Skye, of the great part of the Long Island, of Sutherland, and part of Ross-shire, have a like connection with North Carolina, where they have formed the settlements of Cross Creek. Some people from Lochaber, Glengarry, etc., who joined the settlements in New York at the eve of the American War, took refuge in Canada. The people of Moydart again, and some other districts in Inverness-shire, with a few of the Western Isles, are those who have formed the Scottish settlements of Pictou, in Nova Scotia, and of the Island of St. John.

In 1782–1783 a famine in the Highlands occurred on the failure of the potato crop. As a result of this another wave of emigration to

Canada set in. So alarmed were the Highland chiefs at the prospect of their territories becoming depopulated, that they did all in their power to stay the departure of the emigrants, in some cases to the extent of invoking the influence of the Government. In 1786 a meeting of noblemen and gentlemen was held in London, at which the Earl of Breadalbane stated that five hundred persons had resolved to emigrate from the estate of Glengarry. A resolution was thereupon adopted by the meeting, agreeing to co-operate with the Government, in order to frustrate the design. This attitude gives the lie to " slush " writers who suggest that the chiefs " deserted their people " and hounded them off the land. On the contrary, most of them sought to keep them there. It was the apostles of " progress " who were determined to have the Highlanders cleared out. The tide of emigration continued to flow apace. Between 1801 and 1804 there was another exodus, which included the emigration of the Glengarry Fencibles (described in Chapter XIV.), who settled in Ontario, Canada, in a district to which they gave the name of their own loved home, Glengarry.

The closing years of the eighteenth and the opening ones of the nineteenth century witnessed the final extinction of the Royal House of Stuart, which had exercised such a powerful effect on the destinies of the Highlands. The Chevalier, James Stuart (*de jure* James VIII.), died in exile in 1766, and Prince Charles Edward succeeded to the phantom crown. " Bonnie Prince Charlie's " later years were those of a soured and disappointed man. Unfortunately he had given way to the solace of the wine-cup in place of maintaining the stately resignation which had marked his father's years of exile. His last years were *not* sordid (see H. Tayler, *Prince Charlie's Daughter*) ; but his petulant character would, as a king, have brought difficulties. It was a clouded halo that now surrounded the " Adventurer " of 1745 :

> Let the shadows gather round me
> While I sit in silence here
> Broken-hearted as an orphan
> Watching by his father's bier. . . .
>
> Suppliant-like for alms depending
> On a false and foreign court,
> Jostled by the flouting nobles,
> Half their pity, half their sport.
>
> Fitting for the throneless exile
> Is the atmosphere of pall
> And the gusty winds that shiver
> 'Neath the tapestry on the wall.
>
> Bitter tears and sobs of anguish,
> Unavailing though they be.
> Oh, the brave—the brave and noble,
> That have died in vain for me !

Let, however, censorious critics of the evening of the life of Prince Charles pause for a moment, and compare the Prince's chivalrous and humane character as evinced during the period when his star was in the ascendant, with that of his successful rival, the stolid George II., who cared not for " bainting or boetry," and ask themselves which man was likely to have made the best monarch ? Though exiled and broken by the failure of his once-bright hopes, Prince Charles showed in many instances the gracious traits he inherited from Scotland's Royal line ; and though across the sea, in Scotland

> The olden times have passed away
> And weary are the new,
> And the fair white rose has faded
> In the garden where it grew,

the clansmen clung to their love of *Tearlach Og*, the Young Chevalier, and in the glens and clachans continued to sing

> You trusted in your hielan' men,
> They trusted you, dear Chairlie . . .
> Better lo'ed ye canna be,
> Will ye no come back again ?

With the death of Prince Charles without legitimate issue in 1788, the hopes of the Jacobites practically ended. His brother, Henry, Duke of York, was a Cardinal in the Roman Church, so at a meeting of the non-juring Episcopalian bishops of Scotland at Aberdeen on 24th April 1788, it was resolved to pray for King George III. in the services of the Church. Henry, Cardinal Duke of York, died at Rome in 1807, aged eighty-two. The evening of his life was a chequered one. The French Revolution despoiled him of his property both in France and in Italy. When the French took possession of the Papal territories, they drove Cardinal York from his residence at Frescati, and, after confiscating or destroying his property, left the Head of the House of Stuart absolutely destitute. The old man then retired to Venice. It does the charactei of George III. credit, that, upon learning of the destitute circumstances of his unfortunate rival, he settled an annuity of £4,000 per annum on the Cardinal, who, in due course, settled on him the Coronation Ring and the Sovereign's Chivalric Orders which had been worn by King Charles I.

By George IV. a stately monument was erected in St. Peter's, Rome, to the memory of James Stuart, the Chevalier, and his sons, Charles Edward and Henry, whose ashes repose beside those of their father. The heir-of-line of the Royal House of Stuart is now by descent from Henrietta, daughter of King Charles I., the ex-Queen, Prince Ruprecht *de jure* King of Bavaria.

The " regal " representation in the technical and legal sense devolved upon King George III. in virtue of the last Stuart, Henry,

Cardinal of York's settlement upon him of the remaining Crown jewels,[1] the Coronation Ring, and Badges of St. Andrew and of the Garter, which had descended to him from King Charles I. George III. thus succeeded the last of the Stuarts as constitutional and legitimist monarch and *Ard-righ Albainn*, and became sovereign not only under the parliamentary Act of Settlement but also by the Law of Tanistry ; and, as such, the kings of the Royal House of Windsor are to-day, by tanistry, and as representatives of the Stuart line, also the legitimist representatives of our ancient lines of monarchs. During the later nineteenth and early part of the present century, a few misguided people were in the habit of sending white roses to the Queen of Bavaria and her son, Ruprecht, the present *de jure* King of Bavaria. These ignorant and disloyal people completely overlooked that, by the Law of Tanistry and the implications of the Cardinal York's settlement of his Crown jewels (which was much more explicit than Queen Elizabeth's dying acknowledgment of James VI. as her heir in the English Crown), the Sovereigns of the House of Windsor are, by our British and historical principles of nomination and tanistry, unquestionably legitimate and tribal sovereigns as well as holding the throne by parliamentary title.

But to return from the realms of Jacobitism and romance to the painful subject of the exodus of the Highlanders from their native country. While, during the period between 1746 and the beginning of the nineteenth century, it was the clanspeople who were the principal sufferers, the first half of the nineteenth century saw the disappearance (especially in the West Highlands) of clansfolk and chiefs alike. While, previous to the commencement of the nineteenth century, it had been the aim of the landlords to stay the flood of emigration, now their efforts were exerted in the opposite direction.

The hideous propagandists of vulgar wealth were loudly proclaiming the identification of progress with pelf, and planning the soulless new world of big industrialism. Towards the close of the eighteenth century one of these disciples of " progress," touring through Caithness to seek fresh fields for investment, on observing a couple of hundred happy young harvesters in the cornfields of the Laird of Mey (afterwards 12th Earl of Caithness), remarked that this was quite uneconomic, and that some twenty or thirty people with efficient implements could have harvested the whole crop. To-day, no doubt, four men and a tractor-combine could have harvested a great deal more than the whole home farm of Barrogill, but could these two hundred kinsmen and followers of Sinclair of Mey have been better or more happily employed on an autumn day, than gathering the cornfields of Mey ?— and was the world to be a better place if four should be left and the

---

[1] This transmission to King George of these Regalia jewels was something completely different from legacies of documents, etc. The Cardinal made it clear that he regarded himself as " Henry IX.," so that so far as he was concerned, the transmission was from sovereign to sovereign, and thus a proper act of Tanistry.

other 196 (whom proper implements could have helped to leisure) were herded to the reeking cities ?

In the early nineteenth century, too many Highland lairds were stampeded by the raucous howls of these purveyors of " progress and planning," and amongst those who fell most deeply into the much-trumpeted snare was the Marquis of Stafford, who married the young Countess of Sutherland, and subsequently, after being eulogised by the disciples of " progress " as one of the most enlightened magnates in the country, was created Duke of Sutherland. To the Highlanders, the schemes so lauded by economists and scientists were anathema. In order to convert his wife's ancient clan territory into a " planner's paradise," he—for the good of the people—and in accordance with the best scientific advice, perpetrated the forcible expatriation of the Sutherland clansfolk who were settled in new " model " villages at various points along the coast, whilst the policy became notorious as " the Sutherland evictions." Nemesis was, as usual, upon the track of those who followed the advice of the materialistic politico-scientists —backed in this clearance policy by Government " Emigration Agents " whose business it was to get as many Highlanders out of the Highlands as possible. As I have already emphasised it was not the lairds and chiefs who favoured this. They did everything they could to prevent it (see pp. 80, 83). Life in the Highland clachans may have been " poor " and simple ; but, except when overcrowded, for which the shores of the New World were the waiting field of settlement, the feudo-clan system was a sound economic family organisation ; and the people had a right to live the life they loved, and from which, under the old feudo-clan law, they could not have been evicted. The new economic system, based on sheep and sport, proved, like too many financial schemes, a disastrous failure ; and the trim new villages in which clansmen had been crowded became hollow haunts of rankling desolation.

Kelp, or rather the ruin of the kelp industry on the coasts of the Highlands, was the cause of the effacement of many of the old land-marks, the exile of clansfolk and their chiefs, and the passing of large districts in the Highlands into the hands of strangers. The manu-facture of kelp from sea-weed was first introduced into the West Highlands in 1735. It was not, however, till about 1750 that the manufacture of the article assumed proportions of any magnitude. The clansfolk, who had been transferred from the glens and straths to the sea coast, had been encouraged to take up kelp manufacture which then presented a rising market. About 1800, prices reached high-water mark, at £22 per ton ; and, though a fall subsequently occurred, still, between 1798 and 1822, the average price was about £10, 10s. per ton. Owing to a succession of adverse circumstances, however, the price had by 1831 declined to £2. Misfortunes, it is truly said, never come singly ! In 1837, 1846, and 1850 severe famines accentuated the prevailing distress. A fresh exodus of Highlanders set in, and many of the old ancestral estates passed from the hands of the ruined chiefs into the possession of alien proprietors. By 1850 many of the West Highland chiefs were that in name only, owing to their having had to part with the clan territories. The new proprietors who took their places had neither time nor sentiment for those who remained of the unfortunate clanspeople ! If all the newcomers had behaved so humanely to their tenants as the late Sir James Matheson, the new owner of the Lewis, Highland grievances might have been remarkable by their rarity. Unfortunately, too many of them were Englishmen imbued with a conception of private sport very different from the old " Highland huntings," or even what they themselves were accustomed to in English fox- or stag-hunting. It is hardly surprising that these men made themselves and sport very unpopular in Scotland.

Another aspect of emigration was broached by Dr. Keltie—in language which shows he did not himself grasp the full implication of his observation—namely, that the " Scotch Poor Law Act," by imposing a local poor rate, created a financial position which virtually forced an immediate emigration policy, and gave scope to the Association of Highland proprietors, who at the time of the potato famine of 1837, endeavoured to organise a system in which emigrants could be assured of assistance, instead of being left at the mercy of the shipping speculators. Dr. Keltie says :

Formerly the poor widows and orphans and destitute persons were relieved by the parish minister from the poor's box, by voluntary subscriptions, which enabled the extremely needy to receive four or five shillings the quarter ; and this small pittance was felt on all hands to be a liberal bounty. The landlord added his five or ten pound gift at the beginning of the year, and a laudatory announcement appeared in the newspaper.[1] But the Act for the relief of the poor of Scotland now provides that a rate shall be levied on the tenant or occupier, and some of those who formerly paid £10 per annum, and were deemed worthy of much commendation, have now to pay £400 per annum without note or comment.[2]

Now, it is true enough, that the Act would often have had the

---

[1] Few Highland Celtic proprietors would have been able to give anything approaching such a subscription (in 1837, £10 was a large sum in the Highlands). English plutocrat purchasers would. The lavish distribution of " bounty " (attempts to purchase local popularity) were, of course, quite absent from the old clan system, where, in any event, there was extremely little money in circulation and " subscriptions " or " charity " were regarded as an insult. Indeed, one of the modern abuses is the manner in which " profiteer sportsmen " not only patronisingly throw money about, but scornfully state that if Scots local lairds (who, of course, have not made fortunes out of industrial slum-slavery) can't do so, like English gentlemen, they ought to clear out. The clan system was based on family organisation and mutual assistance in emergencies (a seasonal abstract of rent or distribution of meal was not " charity "), not " charitable bounty," and, as we have explained, " the hearth of the race " is not a subject to be parted with, since it is the focus of the whole clan or branch.

[2] Tiegelle's " Hints on the Hebrides."

effect of imposing a sudden rise of such a sum on the rates, and thereby wiping out the whole free income ; for £400 in those days was as much as maintained many a West Highland chieftain's household. The result was to put the " staff " out of employment (adding to the burden), and that the producing portion of the inhabitants had to carry an insupportable burden of " the destitute." This had at no time been " part " of the clan, or of any other, family system ; and the obvious solution was that those who could not support themselves should carve out a lairdship for themselves in the Dominions ; just as the cadets of preceding generations had taken service all over Europe. The regrettable fact was that the " Improvers " had altered the estate systems in such a manner as to produce more money, whilst supporting fewer persons on the land.

The " Emigration " epoch may be summarised as follows : Between 1745 and 1821, the population of the Highlands, in spite of emigration, increased from 330,000 to 447,000 ; and with a great new empire to be peopled it was, in any case, expedient and proper that a vigorous and prolific people like the Highlanders should—as they did—contribute to peopling the Dominions. The movement commenced normally ; but was soon encouraged by shipping-speculators, who endeavoured to stir up grievances (arising out of the readjustment of rents to the inflated money values [1]) in order to secure larger " human cargoes." The famine of 1771 led to a sudden (not so) " strange passion " amongst the increasing population, to seek the richer lands of the New World. The chiefs (with the exception of those reared in England) were alarmed and shocked at the exodus, and did their best to retain their clansmen, even at great sacrifice to themselves. They had necessarily to readjust the rents to new money values, since otherwise they could not fulfil their duties either as chiefs or landlords ; but, apart from the scandal of the emigration speculators (who landed the unfortunate emigrants in a state of destitution, and deserted them), the movement was a healthy imperial one, as is evidenced from the continued rise of the Highland population at home. So much so, indeed, that the further famine of 1782–1783 led to an increased migration, but still left a rising population behind. By this time, however, " Improvers " and business speculators were—with full Government approval—casting their net over Scotland in general, and the Highlands in particular, as a sphere in which money could be made by clearing land for sheep-walks at rents enhanced by the Napoleonic Wars, whilst the lairds were relieved not only of the increased income, but even of the estate as an asset, by being (also under the slogan of " improvement ") propagandised into borrowing vast sums at impossible interest, to make extravagant roads, buildings, etc., of a character which soon became out of date ; whilst the Entail Acts were abolished, so that the financiers could get a grip of the land as security, and thenceforth held both chiefs and clansmen

[1] *Book of Dunvegan*, II., p. 63.

to ransom. At this stage, under the whoops of "improvement," came the "clearances" under which the old clan-organised life was uprooted (a reflex of the reactionary " Rights of Man " [1] *motif* of the French Revolution), the promise of kelp- and fishing-fortunes in place of family tradition held out—a bubble which burst with the slump in kelp, and the potato disease famines of 1837 and 1850. This time, the old townships—the breeding-stock of the clans—had been shattered ; and a decline, of which the end has not been reached, fell on the Highlands.

Dr. Keltie continues :

Notwithstanding the immense number of people who have emigrated from the Highlands during the last hundred years, the population of the six chief Highland counties, including the Islands, was in 1861 upwards of 100,000 more than it was in 1755. In the latter year the number of inhabitants in Argyll, Inverness, Caithness, Perth, Ross, and Sutherland was 332,332 ; in 1790–1798 it was 392,263, which, by 1821, had increased to 447,307 ; in 1861 it had reached 449,875. Thus, although latterly, happily, the rate of increase has been small compared with what it was during last century, any fear of the depopulation of the Highlands is totally unfounded.

The next few decades were to show how groundless was this foolish complacency, and how little reason there was to be " glad " that the Highlands were ceasing to provide the men and women to guard and labour the Dominions. The emigration agents and the speculative financiers had done their worst ; but the Highlands still maintained their people, though disturbed in balance and tradition. Now came public administration ; and within a few decades the Highlands had, by the combined efforts of politicians and their schemes, been reduced to a decaying wilderness, in which the rural population had been virtually halved, the greater number of the chieftains ruined. What had been the home of a vigorous race became the silent playground of industrial profiteers.

One new attack on the clan system took the form of the " Crofters Act," which, in so far as it gave fixity of tenure met with Highland approval, but there were insidious innovations. Rents were drastically " reduced " without investigation of, or relation to, production ; and the temper of the Crofting Commission, etc., was such as to put a premium on lazy-farming ; whilst tenants were led into sinking capital in foolish improvements or works proper to the laird, which led to endless grievances and disappointments. The crucial provision was that transferring the management and settlement of all disputes— even between one tenant and another—to the Bureaucracy.[2] This,

---

[1] That was " man " as a selfish individual, as distinct from the member of an organised family. The terms *Liberté, Egalité*, were not accompanied by *Fraternité* until the nineteenth century. The whole " family " idea was anathema to the 1789 revolutionary.

[2] W. Douglas Simpson, *Book of Dunvegan*, II., p. 122.

of course, was a sinister blow at the clan sentiment, in which the chief is the natural, and proper, administrator of the *duthus*, and amenable to local influence—which the Bureaucracy is not.

The Act, like its successors, proved a complete failure ; " crofts " disappeared at a greater rate than the Commission created them ; the reason being that all the traditions and ideals which alone led to people loving, and living on, the land were being destroyed.

Whilst political machinery was thus initiating its campaign against the clan system, other influences were fortunately tending to preserve and develop clanship. During the latter half of the nineteenth century emigration, instead of, as before, being principally confined to North America, flowed also to Australia, South Africa, and New Zealand. Highland sentiment in the latter country is particularly strong.

If the economic chronicle of the Highlands in the nineteenth century was a chequered one, culturally it marked the resurgence of the Celtic spirit after the oppression which followed Culloden. It was the age of the " Romantic Revival " ; and we certainly owe it to Sir Walter Scott, and the Waverley novels and " The Lady of the Lake," that attention was drawn at the critical juncture to Highland culture. His genius it was which brought George IV. to Edinburgh in 1822 ; and he did more than anyone else to restore Scottish and Highland traditions and ceremonial to the Court. The *Historical Account of the Royal Visit*, 1822, is a most important record of the resuscitation of many things which (though subsisting locally in Scottish custom) had, so far as the Court was concerned, been locked away—like the regalia. One may add that, on that occasion, " The Honours of Scotland " were again actually used by His Majesty—being, as of old, carried in state before him through the streets of Edinburgh. As a contemporary bard expressed himself :

> The Crown that circled Bruce's helm
> Once more the Douglas' hand shall raise ;
> The sword that rescued Bruce's realm
> Be guarded by the De la Hayes.

> The children of the heath and yew
> Come harness'd down from glen and strath,
> Plant o'er their crests the White and Blue,
> And swell the *Righ gu Brath*.

But Scotland owes no less a debt to King George himself, who so thoroughly entered into the spirit of his ancient kingdom, whose toast at the great banquet in Scotland's Parliament Hall on 24th August 1822 was : " All the Chieftains and All the Clans of Scotland, and God bless the Land o' Cakes." MacGregor's Highland toast of the *Ard-righ* was : " The Chief of Chiefs—The King."

Well did a contemporary bard express the sentiment of the welcome:

> Our chieftains they crowd round the greatest of all,
> The first in the field, and the first in the hall ;
> To so mighty a Master 'tis given to few,
> So fair and so willing a homage to do.
>
> When he musters his kinsmen, the best shall not fail
> His standard to bow, and his bonnet to veil.
> From a long line of chiefs his dominion began,
> His vassals a host, and a People his clan !

Fifteen years later, the accession of his niece, the Queen-Empress Victoria, in 1837, placed the Highlands under the rule of a sympathetic sovereign who had the welfare of her Highland subjects deeply at heart, and who, for the first time for about one and a half centuries, made her Court and Royal home, often for a considerable part of the year, in the Highlands, reviving in many ways the life of the old Scottish Court. It later became the fashion for " smart people " to sneer at " Balmoral " and all it stood for ; but of Queen Victoria we may say, " The hairt's aye the pairt that maks us richt or wrang," and that she succeeded in gathering together many, still existing, threads of the Highland past, which had been so shattered in the eighteenth century. The astonishing thing is how few mistakes she made in the things that eventually matter. It was Victoria who resumed the practice of marrying the members of the Royal family into the old aristocracy (as had been the practice of the olden Scots kings), who extended the Royal *derbhfine*-rank to issue of her daughter, and who, as a matter of principle [1] restored old Scottish peerage-titles, realising as H.M. did, their broad-based tribal significance, and encouraged the perpetuation of the old Celto-feudal titles and clan traditions. Her reign saw the revival, not only of the great Highland gatherings, but of many lesser ones, and, had Parliament dealt with Highland economics in the sympathetic manner in which the Queen had with Highland traditions, many a glen would have been a livelier place to-day.

Time has worked strange changes in places and matters relating to the Highlanders and the Highlands. In Canada, America, South Africa, Australia, and New Zealand there must be a body of Highlanders who, united, far outnumber those left in the old country. All those Dominions have their Highland societies, had their kilted Highland regiments, hold their Highland gatherings. It is, however, in our premier colony, Canada, that the flame not only of Highland sentiment, but of Highland nationality has been especially kept alive. It should never be forgotten that, in times when use of the Highland garb and tartan were subject to severe penalties in Scotland, and the bagpipe prohibited, the Highland garb was worn by the settlers in

[1] *Queen Victoria's Letters,* 1874.

Canada, and the strains of the *piob-mhòr* heard among the depths of the American forests.

True! the clan system has put forth branches which, however vindictively " Death Duties " and administrators hack at the gnarled trunks of the clan civilisation of Scotland, flourish in the sister dominions beyond the seas and on which, it may truly be said, the sun never sets!

Alexander Macleod of Muiravonside,
1735.

DAVID, MASTER OF NORTHESK,
LORD ROSEHILL, 1719.

ALEXR. BAYNE OF RIRACHIES,
1745.

Archery Medals showing Eighteenth-Century Tartan Clothing.
Procs. of Society of Antiquaries of Scotland, XXVIII.

PART II

Structure of the Clan System

V

The Clan System Described

AMONGST the social organisations of the world, perhaps none has so captured public imagination as the Scottish clan system. The reason is not difficult to find, for it has carried down, into the modern world, the great principles of Tribality and Inheritance, from which people have elsewhere so often strayed, but to which the human race ever returns for inspiration.

"Celtic Scotland," says Miss Grant, "like the ancient society of the Gael in Ireland, was not a democracy. In Ireland there was strong aristocratic feeling;"[1] whilst another recent author even more emphatically expresses himself: "There was nothing democratic[2] in the constituents of the clan system. It presents to our view a series of social grades from the chief down to the bondsmen which makes it in effect the most aristocratic of communities."[3] This "most aristocratic of communities," however, was based in name and theory upon the family, for clan, that is, "children," is the Gaelic equivalent of "family," and our Scottish chiefs and barons were quick to perceive that, in a family, there can be no class-divisions, and accordingly developed the most magnificent aristocracy in the world, wherein "noct only the nobilitie but the hail people," as Bishop Leslie explains, "tak an inordinate pride" in noble birth, and in which "pride of ancestry, directed as it was amongst this people, produced very beneficial effects on their character"[4] and "proud as a Scot" became a saying all over Europe.

The clan was a feature of Gaelic organisation that the Scots had

[1] *Lordship of the Isles*, p. 409.

[2] As regards the use made of this word, and its import, a recent writer has observed, "The word Democracy is seldom defined. Indeed, it is hard to discover from any of the innumerable current writings what the word is meant to signify at the present time. It is one of those words which often change their meaning, and sometimes lose whatever meaning they ever had." (*Nineteenth Century*, October 1943, p. 146). The writers quoted are presumably using it in the "1789" sense when it was unquestionably a "word of evil sense" connoting a reactionary attack on every aspect of family organisation and the gracious forms of cultured tribal life.

[3] W. C. Mackenzie, *Highlands and Islands of Scotland*, p. 89.

[4] Stewart of Garth, *Sketches of the Highlanders*, 1825, p. 50.

brought with them from Ireland, although it may already have existed in Scotland among the Picts.[1]   In Scotland, however, the clan system was more markedly localised than in Ireland, and " all through the history of the Highlands the territorial connection was a strong one " ; [2] a sentiment which is corroborated by later expert investigation [3] and which indeed explains the survival not only of the clan system, but of Scotland as a tribal nation.

Whilst tribal poems such as those of " Deirdre," " Cuchullin," and the " Feiné " naturally deal largely with action and exploits, even these show the depth of local land attachment, e.g. in the " Song of Deirdre " :

> Glendarua ! O Glendarua !
> My love to him that is its heir !

shows a concept of the *duthus* or inheritance-land, with an individua " heir," and that such rights extended to forest and hunting grounds is commemorated in the " Cradle Song of the Lord of the Isles " :

> All her rowans, all her hazel,
> All her birdland, all her stagland,
> Child of Islay, shall be thine.

The fact, however, that—as we shall see—the clan itself was, like the land it occupied, " heritage," and this " clan " bound to the chief by the bond of kinship, gave the whole structure an intense and beautiful aspect which has throughout the ages made the relationship of chieftain and his people to " their " land—the clan-land—something utterly different from the commercial ideas of " private property " as an " investment."   Of course, its produce-yield was of essential economic importance, since the clan had necessarily to subsist ; but whilst the modern economist thinks of nothing but what he can get out of land to fill his purse and his belly, we find in the feudo-tribal clan-and-land nexus that the group gets something more— much more—than the sordid " economist " imagines, namely, the inspiration and incentive of an ancestral attachment in which every hill, glen, and stone of the *duthus* gives abiding pleasure to generation after generation,[4] far transcending the vulgar " amusements " and futilities with which " democracy " and " authoritarianism " alike,

---

[1] *Social and Economic Development of Scotland*, p. 151.
[2] *Ibid.* p. 495.   [3] See Appendix XXX.
[4] Many agricultural difficulties in the Dominions and America—" dust-bowl farming " and desert expansion—arise from the non-existence of the clan spirit and land organisation, based on " The Family " and " Tradition."   Clansfolk farming overseas, if they are to keep the clan spirit and its good agriculture must take the long-term " family " view based on devotion to their own holding, determination to cling to it and develop it.   The chimney-piece of stone or cement, if the owner be of *duine-uasail* grade, should be engraven with the duly matriculated coat-of-arms, and the family should be brought up to realise that the holding is to be treasured, worked for, and kept in the branch.

PLATE II.

MACDONALD CHIEFTAIN.

From Sculpture at Killian, Kintyre
showing quilted Celtic War-dress
and Armorial Shield.

(*Courtesy of Ian Finlay, Esq.*)

PLATE III.

PORTRAIT OF A HIGHLAND CHIEF, *c.* 1660.

From the painting by J. Michael Wright, showing *Breacan-feile* and style of Doublet fashionable at the Restoration, also early form of Feather-Bonnet.

endeavour to fill the aching void in the minds of their soul-weary " masses."

From the *Book of Deer* we learn that there were already clans and an organised land system in the pre-" feudal " Scotland of the eleventh century ; and further from the " shares " (of agricultural produce) we can see from " Deer *Notitiæ* "[1] that the tribal " shares " due to ascending hierarchies of *Toishach*, *Mormaer*, and *Ard-righ*, namely the *Cain* and *Cuiddiche* (*i.e.* produce-" rent " and " entertainment "), were already in operation, and that whatever their early outlook, they had already become closely related to the soil, for even a pastoral tribe must occupy some land, and when others come around demarcate its own district, so that land to cultivate and a chief to rule are the two primary essentials of developing civilised organisations. Whilst successive waves of immigrants evidently formed the settlers of Scotland, it seems long to have been sparsely peopled, and one sees no reason to doubt that many of these " tribes of the land "[2] were more or less the first effective possessors of their districts—for many old Scottish families claim that none were known to have held their property before and that neither history nor tradition knows of any earlier holders of their *duthus* ; or—*e.g.* the Forbeses—that their progenitor O'Conochar killed a bear and took possession of the district it had rendered uninhabitable ; and the Fletchers of Achallader, and other families, who claim that their ancestors were the first who " raised smoke and boiled water on that land." Such " titles to land " are by possession (which Grotius, the celebrated Dutch jurist, held is the only legitimate right to land, and which is still the title whereby a sovereign " acquires " a desert island, etc.). It is an " allodial " title, *i.e.* " by the Grace of God." The Earl of Fife held by this so late as the twelfth century, and the story of the building up of Scotland, as an organised feudal kingdom, is the conversion of these " allods " into " fiefs " held " of the King." The " resignation " of the allod was made by " staff and baton " and the new feudal tenure (with its guarantee of protection and fixity of tenure) was made by charter.[3]

Whilst the feudal pyramid, with the king as High-Chief at the top, fitted in excellently as a measure for giving permanence to the clan and tribal system (see p. 100), what we have to consider, in seeking the beginnings of the clan system, is the nature of the pre-feudal basis of land settlements ; and experts have taken different views on whether the " allod " (as we may call it) was the property of the eponymus and chiefs, or of " the tribe." The view of modern experts is that it was the property of the chiefs.[4]

[1] Conveniently available in J. Cameron's *Celtic Law*, p. 205.

[2] Earl of Crawford, *Earldom of Mar in Sunshine and Shade*, p. 165 ; but the successor was non-Salic.

[3] *Juridical Review*, September 1940, p. 196 ; H. Hallam, *Europe in the Middle Ages*, 1838 edition, I., p. 167.

[4] I. F. Grant, *Social and Economic Development of Scotland*, p. 485 ; Innes of Learney, *Tartans of the Clans and Families of Scotland*, p. 17, n. 4.

E

The matter, however, is not so simple, when one considers that each of these groups had its own *jus familiare*, and it would probably be safer to conclude that the relationship of people to land varied considerably in each tribe. The Lords of the Isles and other West Highland magnates certainly held their great domains in their own name, and their right to it was such that they, of their own motion, made grants of it. This and other factors certainly indicates that the land was, in the contemporary view, the chief's " property." [1]

So, however, was the " clan " itself—for we find it a heritable subject, of which even a female could be " heretrix " and that it, or its chiefship, was capable of grant by charter.[2] In Roman law, the *familia* was, however, a subject which could even be bought and sold— cf. the *familiæ emptor*. Under feudal and chivalric law, which so stresses the honour and dignity of " The Family," it is transmissable only by solemn settlement, and for what Lyon Court resettlements term " grave and weighty considerations," to which the Lord Lyon " interpones " the regal assent on behalf of the *Ard-Righ*.

On the Continent an allod was often equally divisible amongst the noble descendants of the " founder " (the chief getting the house and hearth). This was obviously an unsatisfactory system, which was modified by *jus familiare*, but in a number of the most ancient estates —at any rate in Alba, where there seems earlier written evidence to work on than as regards Dalriada—there are certain features which do suggest a form of what might be called a modified " tribal " land-holding. It is noticeable that just as the Mormaer/Earl/*Righ*, never " owns " the whole territory of the earldom, but only holds great estates in the district over which he reigns, similarly, both in the thaneages and in the estates which we can trace back to the allodial era (such as Forbes and Skene), there is a marked distinction between the " dominical lands " (as they seem called in later charters) and the " tenandria " or remaining portions of the territory ; but which I agree with Miss Grant [3] is something quite different from the demesne, cottarage, commonty, and waste of the English " manorial system."

In the case of the " Lordship of Forbes," the *duthus*—including the ancient " castle hill," at the very northern point of the whole, and Drumminnor, the medieval stone castle—forms only about one-quarter of the estate, which seemed conventionally divided in four sections.[4] Now this " old *duthus*," the " inheritance-land " (anciently

---

[1] *Social and Economic Development of Scotland*, p. 487.
[2] Kenkynol, R.M.S. I., No. 509, &c.
[3] *Social and Economic Development of Scotland*, pp. 61, 247.
[4] Tayler, *House of Forbes*, pp. 274–275. I surmise these were more than merely four " sale lots " for the sale of 1770, and that they may well have represented the " four quarters " for which birleymen were appointed in baronies and mairs, in earldoms and sheriffdoms (cf. *Baron Court Book of Carnwath*, p. cxv.).

orba or *erbsa*) and the dominical lands and " Thaneston " of the thaneages, are obviously the mensal land which descended with the chiefship, and the possession whereof was regarded as the necessary concomitant of " real " chiefship.[1] Later we find that the dignity and title was " annexit to " and descended to the inheritor [2] of the Moot Hill (for the Moot Hill of Scone *per se* was regarded as the " territory " identified with the High-Chiefship/*Ard-righ*), or " principal dwelling-place/chief chymmes " ; and within this the hall and chief hearth (over which the arms hung or were carven).[3] Later still we find that the " subject " could be the arms (and where it existed the seal),[4] " heritable property " though incorporeal, and the machinery whereby Representer/Chiefship was operated.[5]

Having thus indicated the character and evolution of the *duthus*, we must examine the remainder of the " cuntrie "—part of which was the wood and pasture, and uncultivated, but not necessarily uncultivable, ground ; and the parts " set " *in tenandria*, or in other forms of tenure to occupiers. The consensus of opinion appears to be that a custom existed, under which at any rate the more prominent holdings in it were " sett " by the chief to his younger sons at easy rents (which we must recollect meant share of produce), and that in subsequent generations when fresh cadet-sons had to be provided for, the remotest of these favoured tenants was required to remove, so that a younger son of the reigning generation might be provided for.[6]

[1] Skene, *Celtic Scotland*, III., p. 145 ; cf. Adam in third edition of this work, p. 545, " Chiefs in name only owing to their having parted with the clan territory "; and Mackay Mackenzie in *Maclean of Ardgour Evidence*, p. 227, " Do you know of any examples of a person being regarded as head or chief of the clan or family who did not own the territory ? " *A.* " No. I think the two things incompatible. What is the good of a chief who did not own land and did not have a following." With this one compares the view in both Northern and West Coast family manuscripts that a house became " extinct " when it lost its whole lands. Of course we shall see this modified to retention of certain vital key subjects. Under " commerce " and proscription, lands were only too prone to get lost, but something heritable had to descend—ultimately the arms, standard, and banner.

[2] I use this word advisedly, as I think did Lord Aitchison, even where the " inheriting " was under a trust settlement, which Maine & Pollock liken to a tribal chiefship settlement (*Ancient Law* per Pollock at p. 238).

[3] J. Riddell, *Peerage Law*, pp. 109–110 ; Crawford, *Earldom of Mar in Sunshine and Shade*, pp. 120–124 ; Brentano, *Old Regime in France*, p. 44 ; J. Starcke, *Primitive Family*, pp. 47, 164 ; Innes of Learney, *Law of Succession in Ensigns Armorial*, p. 48 ; " The Scottish Parliament," *Juridical Review*, 1933, XLV., pp. 10, 12.

[4] *Stuarts of Castle Stuart*, p. 248.

[5] *Tartans of the Clans and Families of Scotland*, p. 27 ; Mackenzie's *Works*, II., p. 618.

[6] The cadet line which had enjoyed the holding for one or two generations, would, however, have collected some assets and be expected to be able to acquire a holding of his own " in the market " ; or, if he failed in that, to merge in the general body of the clan.

Skene illustrates this from the practice of his own family wherein Tillybirloch and other adjoining lands, some eight miles from Skene, were kept for these provisions;[1] and it is evident that the "system" was closely related to the groups of *derbhfine* and *gilfine* described on p. 170, and that certain effects followed from a theory that three complete generations of tenure gave the fourth generation an indefeasible property in a holding so continuously occupied ; which became *duthus* to that line in the fourth generation.[2] Clearly, when one fell to pass "out of" the *derbhfine* (or "true family") into the *iarfine* or *duthaig-n' daoine* (as the extent of the organisation might provide), one had to be evicted from the holdings allocatable to *derbhfine*-members. If, however, the later generations of the main line were weak in numbers, one can see there might not be enough cadets to "take up" such holdings, with the result that a former line might manage to "hold" into the fourth generation ; whereupon that holding became "property" in him, and a line of branch-chieftains arose on that holding.

When the feudal system replaced the *allod*, the possibility of acquiring fortuitous property-rights ceased, and sub-feus had to be based on deliberate feu-charters, whilst cadets no longer had to be evicted to prevent them acquiring *duthus*-right. In both respects the feudal tenure was conducive to fixity of tenure, and consequently an improvement, which as Miss Grant says (and we may thus emphasise), "contributed to the stability of the clan system"[3] and to the effective "organisation of the family." The tack and the feu thus succeeded these earlier *derbhfine*, or maybe "kindly" occupancies, and if the tack precluded acquiring property, the feu at once ensured it, and in either case there was certainty of "where one stood," and unpleasantness over continual displacement of the remotest cadet was obviated.

The distinction between the *duthus* and the remainder of the

---

[1] *Memorials of the Family of Skene of Skene*, pp. 24, 37, 49 ; where W. F. Skene denominates them "tanistry lands," a most inaccurate and unsuitable description, since neither the lands which were acquired and held feudally, nor these settlements, had anything to do with "tanistry," *i.e.* nomination. I fancy he took the term from "Eudox's" and "Iren's" discourse in a book written by Edmund Spencer (*c.* 1584). The phrase which evidently struck Skene was "no property passed," and certainly these cadets had "no property," but it was to a quite different thing Eudox was referring, *i.e.* the principle that the "country" was the inalienable property of the race. Exactly the same idea permeated Scandinavian *Udal* tenure—still existent in Orkney. That, however, is quite a different thing from the allocation of the land within the race and under the chief. Similarly, his rash suggestion of an analogy to the Kentish "gavel" has drawn forth the scorn of modern authorities (*e.g.* Dr. Mackay Mackenzie), and just as the transient occupancy has nothing whatever to do with, or similarity to, "tanistry," so the dislocation of holdings has neither similarity with nor analogy to the English "gavel."

[2] The "four generations" are also found in the Hungarian tribe system (Ruvigny, *Nobilities of Europe*, 1910, p. 107).

[3] *Social and Economic Development of Scotland*, p. 515.

" native country " does, however, point to a variety of the allod
peculiar to Scotland—and indeed Hungary—in which, instead of being
equally divisible or entirely undivisible, there was a system of gradual
stepping down (just as we have seen in social ranks) ; and in a sense,
a sort of " tribal property " in the country distinct from the indivisible
property of successive chiefs in the *duthus*. In Scotland, however,
the importance of chiefship/chieftaincy was such as to give the chief
tremendous power in determining the manner and extent of occupancy
of the " undominical lands " (if I may invent an *ad hoc* phrase), which
in effect made the whole " his " property (just as it became under
feudal law), and which explains what Trevelyan and Miss Grant point
out, that the chief treated the land as a subject of which he could make
heritable grants, and such grants were made—as at the Black Stones
of Iona—in quite pre-feudal form, by testimony of witnesses, and with
perpetuity of tenure.[1]

The chief's patriarchal duty to the clan, however, paralleled by
the feudal provision that every man find himself a lord, ensured that
the chief must, some way or other, look after the clansmen in his
" cuntrie " ; though in other cases we find he *per se* could enter into
obligations to remove both himself and them *en masse*.[2] We thus find
a very high development of patriarchal power, and most ample interpretation of the doctrine of " Representership," and all that flowed
from this elementary concept of *eponymus* and *parentela*.

As Miss Grant expresses it :

> The clan was a hybrid institution, a mixture of tribal tradition cluster-
> ing about the *ipso facto* landholder of the soil—whether he held possession
> by feudal charter, lease or feu, or by mere sword-right—and the chiefs
> largely because of the inefficiency of the Lowland authorities continued
> to fulfil the functions of the tribal leader.[3]

I should say, not from inefficiency, but because every care had been
taken to see that the centralised Government should *not* be able to
destroy the healthy local self-government on " family " principles.
She emphasises elsewhere that :

> It was by means of feudal institutions that the rising clans made good
> their position and especially by means of feu-farm.[4]

> In practice feudalism and the clan system were very much alike (and),[5]
> all through the Highlands the territorial connection was a very strong one.[6]

It will accordingly be desirable for really understanding these
observations, to realise exactly what this " feudalism " really was,

---

[1] *Social and Economic Development of Scotland*, pp. 485–487 ; *Lordship of
the Isles*, pp. 407, 409.
[2] *Social and Economic Development of Scotland*, p. 517.
[3] *Lordship of the Isles*, p. 327.
[4] *Social and Economic Development of Scotland*, p. 516.
[5] *Ibid.* p. 514.   [6] *Ibid.* p. 495.

when the full significance of the enthusiastic adoption of the feudal system in Scotland, and throughout the Highlands, will at once become yet more strikingly evident.

Since popular writers still propagate the mischievous doctrine (designed by English politicians for the destruction of the Scottish social system) that there existed a conflict between feudalism and clanship, it is right to state, here and now, that not only was this completely negatived by the celebrated experts called as witnesses in the *Ardgour* proof, 1938 (Appendix XXX), but that it has been abandoned by every responsible or well-informed modern historian. I have already quoted Professor Rait, and, proceeding to a prejudiced Englishman, Professor Trevelyan says : " It is a pathetic fallacy to suppose that the tribal land was the people's or that they lived in rustic felicity until the chiefs, in a sudden access of wickedness, took it from them after ' the '45 ' " [1] ; whilst of Miss Cunningham's ill-constructed thesis (*The Loyal Clans*) he observes : " I do not think she has proved that the root of Highland Jacobitism was objection to feudal jurisdiction." [2]

Professor Dickinson, in the *Court Book of the Barony of Carnwath*, says of the early Celtic insurrections : " The revolts were not against feudalism as such . . . they were against the attempts of successive kings to introduce feudal tenure *de Rege Scotie* in place of a feudal tenure of (*i.e.* under) the Earl " (p. xvii, n. 4) and of the Moray revolts as being directed " against the new centralising power—homage and tenure to the King of Scotland instead of to the Celtic Earl " (*ibid.* p. lvi, n. 1).

Whilst a more popular historian, Agnes Mure Mackenzie, aptly endorses the foregoing, and gives the lie to the myth of feudal oppression. Of the social system in the Highlands she says :

---

[1] Ramillies, *England Under Queen Anne*, p. 216 : a brilliantly written and condensed, but, as regards Scotland, non-understanding, and on many points unbalanced, book—I mean in that he has placed weight on, for example, H. G. Graham, whose *Social Life in Scotland in the* 18th *Century* is a travesty of actual conditions.

[2] *Ibid.* p. 423. Assuredly not, since these jurisdictions were simply local self-government (see W. C. Dickinson, *Court Book of the Barony of Carnwath*, pp. lx., lxxx., cviii., cxiii.). Trevelyan (unwitting, or ignoring, that they were " government of the people, by the people, and for the people," in its purest and most effective form) with English obstinacy says (p. 267) that they were " oppressive to the people subject to them, and were a hateful anachronism in the eyes of English lawyers and statesmen," and at p. 188 that the people (whom he admits were most independent) were yet, he supposes, living " in a position of servitude at once feudal and economic." It would be far more accurate to say that the chief or laird was living in a constitutionally restricted atmosphere wherein he had to manage his estate according to the rulings of his tenantry ; and that, as I have shown above (p. 72), is precisely why Baron Courts were quietly " put in cold storage." They have never been " abolished," and are still one of the few remaining institutions embodying popular self-government.

It was feudal in the strict historical sense . . . which combines the feudal nexus of land tenure, a general neo-military basis with another not found conjoined with them out of Scotland, and which historians in consequence are apt to overlook.[1]

Looking to Brentano's exposition of the French twelfth- to thirteenth-century tribo-feudalism (see pp. 120, 143) we could hardly say so much now, but rather that historical feudalism has been concealed from the public by the chimera of a political picture (like La Bruyère's, see p. 69) invented by pre-bureaucrats for the destruction of " the family " and clan. Of the myth of " feudal oppression " already criticised by Professor G. G. Coulton,[2] Miss Mure Mackenzie aptly observes :

A man whose life and property depended on the willing service of his followers and whose only police were these same followers, had to behave himself reasonably well so far as they, at any rate, were concerned. He might murder his wife, carry off his neighbours, burn another chief's castle or rise against the king ; but to do these things, or to prevent someone else from doing them to himself, he had to depend on the clansmen who were his tenants, who were Highlanders with a sense of their dignity and as much right to the tartan as himself.[3]

The only documented modern work which perpetuates the exploded doctrine is W. C. Mackenzie's *Highlands and Isles of Scotland*, p. 87, in a paragraph which exhibits its own confutation. After stating that clanship differs " in essence from the feudal system," he proceeds :

What, then, was the clan system ? It differed from the tribal system for the *tuath* or tribe came to have the connotation of " country " and thus had a territorial basis independent of consanguinity.[4]

The essential feature of the clan system is denoted by its name *Clann*, children. It was the offspring of tribalism ; kinship lay at its root. The members of the clan from its chief downwards were supposed to be united by the common bond of blood relationship. Strictly speaking, that

---

[1] A. Mure Mackenzie, *History of Scotland in Modern Times*, p. 41.

[2] *Scottish Abbeys and Social Life*, p. 128.

[3] *History of Scotland*, p. 42. Moreover, if the *chef de famille* or clan chief— and they are synonymous—proved too unwilling to accept the advice of his " family/clan council " (see I. F. Grant, *Social and Economic Development of Scotland*), they, by judicial interdiction, or by placing in honourable " keping and fermance " in some friend's castle (*Familie of Innes*, p. 97 ; *Sketches of the Highlanders*) prevented a " misguidit " chief from destroying his clan or family by reckless conduct.

[4] So, of course, had the clan, for we speak of the " clan countries," *An duthaig MacLeod* (" Macleod's country "), and so on ; the very statutes refer to " pretence of blude or place of their duelling " ; whilst what popular writers set forth as a parliamentary " Roll of Highland Clans " is in our statute book intituled " Roll of Landlordis and Bailies in the Highlands."

relationship was a fiction. . . . The name was the binding link between the members of the clan.[1]

The feudal system, of which homage and vassalage were the essential features, was in some respects fundamentally opposed to the clan system, yet in practice the principles of land tenure were much the same under both systems. Now "homage," the courtly oath of fidelity and devotion by one noble to another, and the paternal kin, are likewise the very essence of clanship.

No one who reads Brentano's and Miss Mure Mackenzie's expositions of "historical feudalism" will fail to perceive that W. C. Mackenzie has built his distinction on complete misapprehension of what "feudalism" is, and, therefore, like Miss Cunningham, failed to understand why the two "systems" were much the same, and one an "integral part" of the other. The blunt historical truth is that they were the same, and as Dr. John Cameron and Dr. Mackay Mackenzie expounded in the *Ardgour* evidence, the one slipped into the other. As I explained it in *Tartans of the Clans and Families of Scotland*, p. 15, the feudal system proved the most excellent machinery for preserving and giving legal effect to clan customs—or as Brentano even more accurately says, was "the organisation and extension of the family"—and the homage was due to the Crown as "father of all the fathers."

What has caused many to assume that clanship must in some way differ from feudalism, is the subsistence of the clan, even apart from the landed fief. But exactly the same thing occurs in the case of an "armorial family." The historical truth (as again set forth in the *Ardgour* evidence, see Appendix XXX) is that the clan and family themselves were legally conceived as, and treated as, incorporeal feudalised fiefs. This is amply established by the Crown charters of the *Kenkynol*, and other chiefships in the thirteenth to fourteenth centuries, and by Lord Lyon Erskine's finding that a woman could be heretrix of a clan. Lyon in 1672 regarded the clan as an incorporeal heritable subject, whilst, in 1717, Grant of Grant regarded "the Clan Grant" as a subject which he could pass on to his son as "a present" (see p. 125). The "family" or "clan" is, however, always based on a fief, because to be an "honourable community" which has been "received into the *noblesse*" of the realm, it must, in the person of its "representer," have been granted or conferred, a "family seal of arms," and a coat of arms is a feudalised property,[2] the family is an "incorporation,"[3] and all the scientific modern evidence concurs that "clan and family mean exactly the same thing" (Appendix XXX, Dr. Lachlan Maclean

---

[1] This is nonsense. Until the mid-eighteenth century the ordinary clansman had no "name" in that sense—it was the characteristic of the so-called "Lowland" names !

[2] *Maclean of Ardgour* v. *Maclean*, 1941, following *Macdonell* v. *Macdonald*, 1826. Shaw & Dunlop, 371.

[3] Sir H. Maine, *Ancient Law*, pp. 205, 211 ; cf. *Old Regime*, p. 5.

Watt). This explains also why a clan chief, as chief of a " baronial family " may be " baron " without holding land *in liberam baroniam*,[1] by *e.g.* succeeding to a baronial coat of arms, or amongst several such *in familia*, to that which carries with it the " representation " of the clan/family as a noble incorporation. This somewhat detailed explanation will make it evident why there has been so much confusion about " what a clan is," and just how a clan does fit easily into the nobiliary and feudal law of Scotland, as indeed explained by Sir George Mackenzie:

Our kings derive not their power from the people . . . (but from) the right of paternal power which is stated in them ; . . . for every man is born subject to his own parents,[2] who, if they were not subject to a superior power, might judge and punish them . . . and do all other things that a king could do, as we see the patriarchs did in their own families.[3]

These descriptions are, of course, equally applicable to the patriarchal organisations of the family and the clan,[4] upon the *duthus* or fief in Scotland, namely the " chieftane of the cuntrie," expressly described in the Act, 1587, c. 59, s. 11, and the provisions in the Act of 1593 [5] regarding

chiftanis and chieffes of all clannis and the principallis of the brancheis of the saidis clannis . . . and depending upoun the directionis of the saidis Capitanis chieffes and chiftanis be pretence of blude or place of thare duelling . . . (to enter pledges for good behaviour).

The Scottish chieftain, like the analogous *chevetaignes-segneurs* of old Gaul was " revered by his family, honoured by his tenants, and awful to his domestics. . . . He kept his own seat by the fire, or at table, with his hat on his head." [6]

In maintaining this co-ordinated family establishment, *i.e.* " clan," in which all were regarded as the kinsmen, near or remote, of the chief (but skilfully divided into branches and sub-branches), the clan-cuntrie was, as Burt and all the other early observers notice, of the greatest importance ; and

the rents are chiefly paid in kind . . . and what they call the customs, as sheep, lambs, poultry. . . . By what has been said you may know how necessary the rent called custom is to the family of a Highland chief.[7]

---

[1] Cf. *Court Book of the Barony of Carnwath*, p. lix.

[2] Amongst brothers not " equal." The heir has precedence over the rest. The American " family " system is anti-familial, *i.e.* anti-familial, since " the family ", from its nature (and the 5th Commandment) accords honour and obedience to its chief, and branch-chieftain, who are accordingly *in loco parentis*. The family as an institution depends on this.

[3] *Works*, II., p. 446.   [4] *Ibid.* p. 447.   [5] A.P.S., IV., p. 40.

[6] J. G. Fyffe, *Scottish Diaries*, p. 63, s.v. Elizabeth Mure. The term " awful " simply means " awe-inspiring." For French equivalent cf. Brentano, *Old Regime in France*. As regards the custom of the chief alone wearing his hat, the hat was the sign of patriarchal jurisdiction, hence the cap of velvet within the crown and coronets, and also the baronial *chapeau* of Heraldry. See Chapter XV. *infra*, and *Proc. of the Soc. of Ant. Scot.*, vol. 79, pp. 111, 148 (Robes of the Feudal Baronage). The *hat* is a marked symbol of chiefship.

[7] E. Burt, Letters, No. 21.

E*

Whilst each clan, and its clan-cuntrie (which might as often as not include many detached estates, as well as the original allod and *duthus*) was thus, as Garth explains, and Burt contemptuously noticed, a little principality, and as I have elsewhere explained (see p. 139), modelled in descending degrees on the court of the *Ard-righ*, none the less each clan, and indeed each branch-family, had, and developed, its own customs and traditions ; so that whilst the general stateliness, and ceremonial was in each case that appropriate to a little " court," pride was maintained, and monotonous uniformity obviated, by each developing its own family tradition, and glorifying the history and incidents of its own successive *tighearn*.

Of the greater, and historic, tribal divisions—those which formed the " kingdoms " of the Mormair-Earls, the *Righ* of early history— the following is the generally accepted survey ; and it is noticeable that each of these seemed divided into a major and a slightly subsidiary section ; a feature also found in the older thaneages and supposedly representing the sphere and *duthus* of the earliest cadet of the Celto-regal line of *Righ* ; though possibly in many cases representing the territory of a still lesser " king " of independent origin, for the Mormaer-ships, like Scotland itself, must have been built up (on " adoptive " principles) from still more localised allodial patriarchates.

According to Pictish traditions Ancient Alba or Pictavia was divided into seven provinces, which number corresponded with the seven sons of Cruithne, the traditionary founder of the Pictish nation. These seven provinces, again, were divided among tribes, or *tuaths*.

The internal organisation of Pictavia was, according to Skene (*Celtic Scotland*) as follows : " The unit was the *Tuath* or tribe ; several Tuaths formed a *Mortuath* or great tribe ; two or more Mortu-aths a *Coicidh* or province ; and at the head of each was a *Ri* or king ; while each province contributed a portion of its territory at their point of junction to form a central district, in which the capital of the whole country was placed, and the *Ri* or king, who was elected to be its *Ard-ri* or sovereign, had his seat of government." In this account the provinces are termed " regna " or kingdoms. Under each province was the " sub-regio " or *Mortuath* with its Regulus or *Ri mortuath*, and composed, no doubt, of a certain number of *tuaths* or tribes, with their chiefs or *Ri tuaith* ; and where the four southern provinces met was the central district in which the capital, Scone, the seat of the *Ard-righ Albainn* was placed. At the period to which the description of the provinces given us by Andrew, Bishop of Caithness, belongs (1165), this organisation had been so far modified that the title of *Ri* or king is no longer borne by the heads of the tuath or tribe and the mortuath or sub-region, but at the head of the tuath is the *Toisach*, and of the mortuath the Mormaer. The title *Mormaer* means great mair or officer, but in its earlier form the title was apparently *Mor-aer*, great chief, and the *m* interjected.

The seven Pictish provinces of Caledonia were : (1) *Fib*, (2) *Cé*,

(3) *Athfotla,* (4) *Fortriu,* (5) *Cat,* (6) *Fidach,* (7) *Circhend*—each of them was divided into two districts, and they may be roughly apportioned as follows :

(1) *Fife* and *Fothreve* (the peninsula between Forth and Tay), or the modern counties of Fife, Clackmannan, and Kinross.

(2) *Moravia* ; sub-districts, Moray and Ross. This province consisted of the counties of Ross and Cromarty, and parts of Elgin, Nairn, Inverness, Banff, and Argyll.

(3) *Atholl* or *Athfodla* ; sub-districts, Atholl (in Perthshire) and Breadalbane and the district of Gowrie.

(4) *Strathearn* ; sub-districts, Strathearn (east Perthshire) and Menteith (parts of south Perthshire, Stirlingshire and Dunbartonshire).

(5) *Caithness* ; sub-districts, Caithness (*Gallaibh*) and Strathnaver (Sutherlandshire).

(6) *Mar* ; sub-districts, Mar and Buchan (in Aberdeen and Banff shires).

(7) *Angus* ; sub-districts, Angus (Forfarshire) and Mearns (Kincardineshire).

It is noticeable that each of these great tribal provinces is comprised of two divisions, whilst of these each is again sub-divided : *Mar* into *Mar* and *Garioch* ; *Buchan* into *Buchan* and *Formartine.* These probably in each case reflect the *duthus* of the " eldest cadet " who had been given a great appanage.

During the tenth century *Cat* (Caithness and Strathnaver) was conquered by the Norsemen, and disappeared from the kingdom of Alba. In its place we find the province of *Arregaithel.*[1] This included the territories of the Dalriadic Scots, and embraced the west coast districts from the north of the Firth of Clyde to Loch Broom.

From this division of the people into clans and tribes under separate chiefs arose many of those institutions, feelings, and usages which characterised the Highlanders. The nature of the country almost necessarily prescribed the form of their institutions. Proud alike of their ancestry—traditionally derived from the founder-chief—and of their little district, the *duthus* or " native cuntrie," and being determined to preserve their independence, the Highlanders long defended themselves in those strongholds which are ever the sanctuaries of national liberty, the " everlasting hills." The division of their country into so many straths, glens, and islands, separated from one another by mountains or arms of the sea, gave rise as a matter of necessity to still greater individuality amongst each of these little local societies or clans. Every district became, *de facto,* an independent state. In this way the population of the Highlands, though possessing a community of customs and the same characteristics, was divided into separate communities, each under a separate jurisdiction. A patriarchal

[1] Argyll and Lorne. Actually this remained Dalriada but *Mar* and *Buchan* raised themselves to separate status, and so retained the number (7) of the historic Pictish Mormairs—the " seven earls ".

system of government, a sort of hereditary monarchy founded on custom and regulated by laws and ancient family tradition, was thus established over each community or clan in the person of the chiefs. This system continued in full vigour till about the year 1748.

As a consequence of the separation which was preserved by the different clans, matrimonial alliances were rarely made with strangers, and hence the members of the clan were generally related to one another by ties of consanguinity or affinity. While this double connection tended to preserve harmony and goodwill among the members of the same clan, it also tended, on the other hand, to excite a spirit of animosity between rival clans, when an affront or an injury was offered by one clan to another, or by individuals of different clans. In spite, however, of this inter-clan rivalry and animosity, history has shown that whenever the liberties of Scotland were menaced, the clans united under the sovereign's banner in defence of their country's interest. The battles of Bannockburn and those fought by the Highland clans under the banner of Prince Charles during the Rising of " the '45," are notable examples of this.

Although the chief enjoyed immense power over his clan in the different characters of administrator, leader, and judge, all of which might or might not be exercised by him or her in person, but any one of which might be delegated to an *ad hoc* war leader or *judex* (dempster), the authority of the chief was nevertheless far from absolute, owing to the principle of the family council or clan council, under which the chief, although parent and represener of the community comprehending his clan, nevertheless acted constitutionally in concert with the *conseil de famille* composed of the heads of houses, and by whose advice and assent he was guided on matters of family policy, and who in some cases, where necessary, even took steps to place a foolish or improvident chief under supervision. In a small clan or family, such council might be quite an informal one, but in the greater clans, and in the case of the Lord of the Isles, it amounted to a full and formal parliament, like those even yet found in many of the great families of Europe. In the feudal organisation of the tribal territories, this council became formalised as the Court of the Barony, by which legislation for the administration of the estate and people thereof was "statuted and ordained by and with advice and consent" of the whole tenants and vassals thereof, in fact a miniature but very formal parliament ; and this as a judicature also administered justice with the chief or baron as presiding judge, and upon whom, through his officer of court, and four or six halberders armed with Lochaber axes, the judgement of the court or legislation of the little baronial " clan-parliament," fell to be administered. Each such clan or family could have its own particular laws, peculiar to itself, equivalent to what the Romans termed the *jus familiare*. The custom of the clan or of its concomitant the barony, extended even to their having their own scale of weights and measures. We must at all times remember that the clan was an organisation represented by its chief in respect of his being the representer of the real or traditional founder of the community, and that the organisation was bound up in the *duthus* or clan country and its heart the family home, and the head of the fief, in order that each such community should continue to possess its central point, its pivot, the family hearth, above which are emblazoned the armorial bearings of the chief.

As the system of clanship, like that of chivalry, was calculated to cherish a warlike spirit, the young chiefs and heads of families tended to be regarded or despised according to their military or peaceable disposition. Martin stated, and subsequent writers have repeated, that every heir or young chieftain of a tribe was obliged to give a public specimen of his valour before he was owned and declared governor or leader of his people, who obeyed and followed him upon all occasions.

No one, however, cites any concrete instance—far less series of such ; and the " rite " is nowhere recorded as part of a chief's inauguration. It is probably a garbled version of symbolic " victory " over the forces of evil, expected of a chief or sovereign.[1]

The political constitution of a clan was as follows :

1. The Chief, or *Ceann-Cinnidh*, who according to the principle of tanistry was either heir-at-law (by right of succession under the law of Malcolm MacKenneth), heir of tailzie under a specific destination, or heir by tanistry under the act or deed of nomination by the preceding chief ; and prior to the intestate succession and heritage law of Malcolm MacKenneth, the principle of tanistry included, to cover the contingency of absence of patriarchal nominations, an elaborate system of selection within the *derbhfine*, in which it appears that the actual nomination directly or indirectly lay either with a specific inaugurator, himself usually a hereditary officer, or else by selection at the instance of certain hereditary chieftains within the clan whose joint act supplied the lack of the act of the defunct chief, *e.g.* if the Crown became *de facto* and *de jure* vacant, the Seven Earls of Scotland asserted a right to make a nomination.

If, however, the chief was neither versed in law nor capable of military leadership, in that event either function was delegated to a *judex* (dempster) or *ceann-cath* (war-leader), as the case might be. As representer of the community, he administered for behoof of his clan, the *duthus* and country ; and whilst he was bound by virtue of his position to take measures, and with the assistance of his council to compel the clan itself to take measures, providing for even the least members of the community, it must be borne in mind that the lands— except where expressly conveyed (*e.g.* the Gaelic charters from the

---

[1] A. M. Hocart, *Kingship*, pp. 12–20. (In the coronation of the Holy Roman Empire, *e.g.* Maria Theresa's, the sword is brandished to the four quarters.) I do not by any means accept many of Hocart's theories, but he very rightly says " monarchial government has a psychological value we are not yet in a position to understand " (p. 25). So has hereditary chiefship.

Lords of the Isles), or where a portion had become *duthus*-right by three generations of possession—remained the private property of the chief, which he was entitled to administer by all the various forms of sub-tenure available, whether customary leasehold or feu, the salient point being that in whatever character the land was held, the holder had an obligation to provide for his people upon that land, along with the power to compel them to help themselves in making effective the provisions for their requirements. [Adam had added, " It can thus be understood that the relation of landlord and tenant, which prevailed under the feudal system, had no place under the clan economy." This was an extraordinary statement where tacksmen were an outstanding feature of the clan organisation !]

2. Next to the chief was the *Tanist*, *i.e.* the person (male or female) who, whether at Common Law or in virtue of a nomination or tailzie, was the next heir to the chiefship. He was usually nominated by the reigning chief, and bore the title of tanist during the lifetime of that chief. The tanist, whether heir apparent or heir presumptive, was regarded as *eadem persona* with the chief, is often styled " the young chief," and was semi-inaugurated at the same time with the chief himself. The Masters in the Scottish peerage are simply the tanists of these great feudo-tribal dignities.

3. The " Commander " of the clan, *Ceann-Cath*, was the " war-leader " or commander-in-chief under the *Ceann-Cinnidh*. Robertson [1] points out that whilst the chief was hereditary, and inaugurated, the " leader of the host," whom he says was elected,[2] was not " inaugurated." He summarises the position thus : " The head of the lineage was not necessarily the leader-of-the-host though the offices were not infrequently united in the same person." That is, just as a king used often to, and still sometimes—usually with unfortunate results—takes command himself, so a vigorous chief frequently commanded the clan in person. If he were aged, a youth, or a female, then a *Ceann-Cath* was appointed. The ceremony connected with this differed completely from the solemn inauguration of a *Ceann-Cinnidh*, and consisted in the *Ceann-Cath* being " elevated on the shield of war," when he read his commission.[3] The appointment will normally be by the chief ; whose commission should be read, with the *Ceann-Cath* standing forth,

---

[1] *Scotland Under Her Early Kings*, p. 27.

[2] E. W. Robertson's statement is carefully analysed in *Notes and Queries*, 15th August 1942, p. 96, where it is shown that he errs in thinking the *Toshach* was the " war-leader "—whose Gaelic title is *Ceann-Cath*—for the *Toshach* is correlated with the thane or *tigh-ern* (Macfarlane, *Genealogical Collections*, I., p. 149) and was hereditary and inaugurated. The " leadership of the men " is, moreover, in feudal charters of old Celtic offices such as those of the House of Carrick, related not to the *Kenkynol* or *caput toties progenii*, but to the office of heritable bailie (Great Seal, I., No. 509 ; *Notes and Queries, sup.*, p. 97). This bailiery is quite distinct from the *Kenkynol*.

[3] This ceremony will be recollected in the case of Oliver Sinclair of Pitcairns, as James V.'s Commander-in-Chief (see J. H. Burton, *History of Scotland*, III.; R. St. Clair, *Saint Clairs of the Isles*, p. 462).

with, say, one foot on the supported targe ; but it may (in the chief's absence or incapacity at a crisis) be by selection ; or failing either of these, falls as of right to the " eldest cadet " or, where there is an heir-of-line chief, the heir-male is *Ceann-Cath.* The office was by Skene and some other nineteenth-century writers supposedly anglicis able as " Captain " ; MacBain has shown that " chief " and " captain " mean the same thing—*Ceann-Cinnidh* ; and from the evidence regarding the Jacobites after " the '45 " we find that the accepted term was " Commander of the Clan." [1]

Whilst there is so far no legal finding that a *Ceann-Cath* has any duties or functions save " in battle on land and sea," the close association of the " leading the men " with the office of bailie or maor [2] suggests that as maor or steward under the Representer/Chief of the house he had the oversight of such " peaceful(?) " duties as collecting revenues—*e.g.* the *calps* and *cuddiche*, so that it may well be that (where no other maor-bailie exists) the *Ceann-Cath*/principal cadet has the " function " of organising any formal feast to his *Ceann-Cinnidh* or *Ceann-tighe.*[3]

4. The near kinsmen of the chief who we may define as the *derbhfine* or " true family " of the chief, perhaps in later practice his *gilfine* (*i.e.* descendants of a grandfather-chief), and comprehending : (*a*) the sons entitled to bear by courtesy the chief's arms with temporary marks of cadency ; (*b*) the chief's grandsons, likewise entitled to bear the chief's arms with the appropriate marks of cadency ; (*c*) the chief's daughters and granddaughters, entitled to bear the chief's arms by courtesy ; (*d*) sons of daughters of the chief who had made *mésalliances* with non-armigerous males. (This is a special case referred to in the " courtesy of arms " in the ancient treatise, *Boke of St. Albans.*) In the case of chiefs who are peers, and the Scottish peerages are simply major chiefships, the younger kinsmen are those bearing the courtesy titles of Honourable and Lady.

It is interesting to note that in the British social system the " royal family," the " peerage families," and the above indicated " heraldic families," form a survival of the *gilfine* and *derbhfine* organisation of our ancient British systems of tribality and clanship.[4]

5. The *Ceann-tighes*, or chieftains, the heads of the houses into which the clan was divided. The most powerful among these *ceanntighes* was the " eldest cadet," *e.g.* the second son of this first chief, or, in other words, the first cadet to spring from the stem of the chief's family. This cadet, of course, had usually got the biggest appanage,

---

[1] *Historical Papers*, II., New Spalding Club, pp. 357, 358, 363, 368.

[2] *E.g.* in the Kenkynol charter the " leading " is connected with the bailery of Carrick, and set forth separately and quite distinct from the " *caput toties progenii* " grant.

[3] See Vol. 183 *Notes and Queries*, 15th August 1942, p. 99.

[4] Innes of Learney, *Law of Succession in Ensigns Armorial*, p. 35 ; also *Notes and Queries*, 2nd September 1939, p. 164 ; 9th September 1939, p. 185 ; 24th February 1940, p. 132 ; 27th April 1940, p. 296.

had the longest time to accumulate estates and influence, and is usually heraldically indicated by bearing the chief's arms with a gold bordure. Where the chiefship has passed in the female line, the heir-male of the original chief is treated as eldest cadet, and consequently the principal cadet in the clan. This eldest cadet enjoys the highest dignity inside the clan, with a post at the right hand of the chief, also the principal post of honour in time of war. It appears (according to Skene) that this subsidiary leader was designated by the title *Cure-tuise*,[1] which *tuise* must not be confused with *toshach*. If competent, and no *ad hoc* commission had been otherwise assumed, he led the van during the march, and in battle occupied the right of the line when the chief was present. In the absence of the chief he commanded the whole clan. Another of the offices he often held was that of maor, or steward, in which capacity he collected the revenues of the chief. When for any reason the chief was incapacitated from assuming the leadership of his clan, these duties were undertaken by one of the chieftains appointed specially for that occasion. On such occasions these latterly were given the title of " Commander of the Clan," but in early times *capitanus* and " chief " were synonymous titles.

6. Next to the *ceann-tighes*, or heads of houses, followed in rank the *Daoin'-uasail*, or gentry of the clan. These constituted the only gradation subsisting between the chief and the actual body of the clan, forming a sort of link by which they were united. They were all cadets of the house of the chief, and could invariably trace their connection step by step with his family ; their position is established by matriculation of arms.

7. The subordinate members of the clan, above alluded to—the *Duthaig-n'daoine*.

8. Dependents of the chief, not of the same blood or name, but descendants of more ancient occupiers of the soil, or " broken men " from other clans, or ancient followers who " came in " with the chief. They are styled the *sencliathe*.

The inauguration of a chief involved two, indeed three, distinct ceremonies, which sometimes took place at different times and in different localities, and which survived, with many elaborations, in the Scottish coronation ceremonial,

which is of special interest because, although it combined the ritual of the Picts and Scots with contemporary religious ceremonial, its outstanding characteristic was that it preserved the ancient features of the formal inauguration of a Celtic chief.[2]

The " third " element—the religious ordination ceremonial—in the Dalriad ceremonial sometimes took place at Iona, on other occasions it was embodied in the tribal " inauguration." Of this the first part

---

[1] *Celtic Scotland*, III., p. 145.

[2] *Crown and Empire* (*The Times*, published 1937), p. 89 ; Marquis of Bute, *Scottish Coronations*, p. 33.

was the ascertainment of the heir's right, the second, his inauguration with the ancestral insignia—essentially the White Rod, of patriarchal sway,[1] and the ancestral sword. The Pictish symbols seem to have included a diadem (the future crown) ; it was the foundation of the heraldic " crest coronet " attributed by Nisbet to those who were " Chiefs of Name and Arms." [2]

The first step in the procedure was that six members of the clan council [3] waited on the tanist, or heir-at-law (the " appearand heir " of feudalism) to put two questions : Was he lawful successor ? and Was he willing to accept the Crown chiefship ? [4]

Clearly, what he had to assure them was, (a) that he was the heir, either by law or tanistry, and (b) that he was disposed to " enter heir "—taking on himself or herself the rights and duties of the office.[5]

We can perceive that this stage of the proceedings could have included the *derbhfine* selection, in the conditions prior to the law of Malcolm MacKenneth, in the circumstance of the deceased patriarch having failed in his last duty of appointing—and blessing—his heir, the tanist.[6]

The clan sennachie was now called in, and in the later practice " sworn " by the principal priest (the clan chaplain, say, the *co-arb* of the " clan-saint," no doubt). In the case of the Dalriad kings, this was the Abbot of Iona ; of the Pictish kings, the (Arch)Bishop of St. Andrews, in the case of the Lord of the Isles, the Bishop of the Isles, and in the case of the Lords of Lorn, probably the Baron of the Bachuil.

Clearly, the sennachie's oath was not of " allegiance," but of the nature *de fideli administratione* ; for as custodian of the genealogy, it was his function to avouch the pedigree and to perform the inauguration. Sometimes the inaugurator was a sub-chief, like the Earl of Fife in Alba ; but amongst the Dalriad kings, he was the High Sennachie, the " Arch-Druid," as Lord Bute puts it.[7] In a *derbhfine*

---

[1] The fact that the " wand of office in a feudal barony was also white " (that of a " regality " was red and white and that of the sheriff in the " royalty " was red) further corroborates Craig's surmise that the early Scottish feudal barons were chiefs of clans.

[2] Nisbet, *System of Heraldry*, II., iv., 39. This status was that of great chiefs whose name, fief, and coat of arms *nomen-dignitatis* were all the same, *i.e.* " of that Ilk " and " MacX. of MacX " ; Maclachlan, L. R., 35, p. 72.

[3] In the coronation ceremony it was six of each of the divisions of Crown vassals (save that the clergy amounted to twenty-four).

[4] This is quite incompatible with the concept of his being " offered " it—in the modern sense. The question was whether he is the person entitled to it.

[5] What happened if he declined the succession might be an interesting matter for investigation. Did a " vacancy " follow ? or did the next heir entitled to do so enter ? On the principle *non apparentibus non existentibus* (*Gregory Collections Soc. of Ant., Scot.*), it seems the latter would have applied.

[6] Maine and Pollock, *Ancient Law*, p. 266.

[7] *Scottish Coronations*, p. 16 ; Lord Bute had not, when writing this book, perceived that the red-robed sennachie was he who became Lord Lyon—who wore the scarlet robe and performed the functions at all the recorded coronations, and indeed still wears this robe as his judicial robe.

selection (in case of pre-MacKenneth intestacy) he would have had to preside in the conclave, and give forth its selection.[1]

In either event, upon the tanist's or the heir-at-law's " acceptance," the commissioners said, " God bless you, Sir," and the first part of the ceremony concluded. The second—the inauguration—took place after due proclamation ; and for this the whole clan gathered at the sacred spot. In Western custom, this was the stone with the incised footprints, and accompanying carving of the heraldic or totem-animal of the chiefs ; and in the East, a sacred seat, also of stone, on or beside which, the heraldic animal was carved (cf. the " bear " stone, still at Castle Forbes). The two important (tribal) functionaries now were (1) the Inaugurator-Sennachie, (2) the Keeper of the sacred place of inauguration. In the case of the *Ard-righ* these became the King-of-Arms and the Marshal. At the direction of the former, the whole ceremony proceeded, whilst on the latter devolved the function of " marshalling " the procedure along, whilst the sennachie, and the priests, performed their functions.

The chief, attired in white, was now led to the stone,[2] and presented to the assembled clan—in a ceremony somewhat analogous to the " Recognition "—as their " undoubted chief," [3] and it is to be noted that the " undoubted " successor is brought in already wearing [4] the *chapeau*, turned up with ermine ; that is the parental cap underlying, as we have seen, the whole principle of barony and chiefship.[5]

Here, or at the end, followed the Mass and after the Reformation, a sermon ; whilst in the tribal inauguration, an oration upon the exploits of the chief's ancestors, and the grandeur of the clan—probably by one of the recorder-bards, and analogous to the Historiographer-Royal, whose province in the kingdom is rather its general history, as distinct from the King of Arms/High Sennachie's sphere of legal administrator of the genealogical and chiefly records.

The sennachie, as inaugurator, then commanded the insignia (*i.e.* the rod and sword) to be delivered to the new chief, either himself receiving them, and handing them to the chieftains entitled to make the delivery, or himself delivering them, and falling on bended knee,

---

[1] *Scottish Coronations*, p. 33 ; *Sources of Literature of the Law of Scotland*, p. 383 ; *Crown and Empire* (*Times Pub.* 1937).

[2] In the Scottish coronation ceremony the " honours," crown, sword, sceptre, and also the Great Seal, were carried before the king and placed on a table. The presence of the seal, whereby legal authority was to be exercised, is exceedingly interesting. No doubt, in the case of a chief, after sealing came in, " the family seal of arms " was likewise brought to the ceremony as the Court of Session has held that the seal of the defunct chieftain was " ane sufficient seal " for his heir (see A. Agnew, *Hereditary Sheriffs of Galloway*, p. 111) ; *Mure* v. *Agnew*, *Proc. of the Soc. of Ant. Scot.* vol. 77, p. 171, n. 3.

[3] Form of phraseology found in a number of eighteenth-century *Diplomæ Stemmatis* in the Public Register of Genealogies in Lyon Court.

[4] In the coronation up to the moment for preparation to receive the crown.

[5] This is to be distinguished from the diced bonnet of the military " commander."

declaimed the genealogy in Gaelic back to the founder of the race, *Benach Dhe Ceann Cinnidh, Alastair Mac Sheumas mac. . . .*[1]

Immediately following the sennachie's declamation, " Blessing of God on thee, etc.," followed by the pedigree back to the eponymus, whom the new chief represents, the whole assembly then cried, " God bless him," and then, sitting in state, vested with all his insignia, the chief gave the oath " to be a loving father to the people," which thus most pointedly emphasises the parental aspect of the clan-tribe concept.[2]

Whilst the Royal coronation here involved a ceremony in which the crown was removed, set on a cushion, and, after the homage, " touched " by peers and baronage, whilst the king had his " hat " replaced, we can see in the earlier and patriarchal ceremony (where there was, of course, no crown—that being appropriate only to the *Ard-righ*), that the chief sitting in his parental cap of familial jurisdiction, received the promise of devotion from the clan " Sua mote God helpe me, as I shall supporte thee."

The proceedings ended by a feast—which, in the case of the Lordship of the Isles, lasted a week.

Whilst this then represents the primitive and allodial installation, we find that it lay with the high chiefs (*Righ*) or *Ard-righ*, in any case of difficulty, or dispute, about succession amongst district chiefs to intervene, and by their super-patriarchal authority, to cause the claimant whom, in the exercise of their *jus familiare*, they adjudged proper, to be invested, and the investiture as we have seen carried the *Kaimes*, and principal hearth, with the ancestral insignia and weapons —shield, banner, and, as noticed, even in the Royal coronation, " the seal," whereby in illiterate days, documents were executed.

Next we see the development of the less spectacular and more " legal " forms of feudal investiture ; applicable to succession-at-law where there had been no resettlement *nominatim* by propulsion of fee, or a procuratory of resignation *in favorem* left in a " Disposition and Settlement " of some sort.

The heir in this case took the initiative, craved brieve of inquest, and was " retoured " by a jury before the King's Sheriff—and *judex*— and then, on a " precept " (or *Clare Constat* from the superior where the *duthus* was held under an Earl), was " revested " in the chymmes

---

[1] In the official accounts of the coronation the declamation of the Royal genealogy was apparently—but this may be a slip—made before the crowning and immediately after Lyon had given the Marischall (custodian of the sacred place and executant of the various orders) the command to proceed. The old picture, however, shows this declamation being made after the crowning, which seems more correct. There were, in fact, two stages : the one before investiture of insignia and the other (the declamation) immediately afterwards.

[2] For this ancient oath was subsequently substituted—in the Royal corona- tion—the parliamentary oath, and in the British coronation that oath is admin- istered and taken before investiture with the regal insignia. The Scottish form, wherein it followed investiture, emphasises the hereditary character of Scottish chiefship and that the investiture was not conditional on the oath.

and heirship moveables, including the seal and shield. Here again custom was that the ceremony terminated with a feast in celebration of " the heir served and retoured." [1]

In the growing organisation of the realm, we can see how this form became applicable in those charters of chiefship—such as that of Neil, Earl of Carrick, of the *Ken-kynie* ; and the various charters of chiefship of clans, issued in the reigns of David II. and Robert II.

In the following age, the organisation of heraldry, and its being committed to the jurisdiction of the High Sennachie—Lyon King of Arms—" as belonging to my sphere of duty," the adjudication, and revesting, of " family representation " and the ancestral insignia, rendered Great Seal " gifts of chieftainry " no longer necessary, and the administration of such matters continued to flow and grow in the old Celtic court of the High Sennachie ; whose function of heraldic and genealogical " Visitation " is now recognised as a survival and development of the sennachhiedal *cuairt*.

Often the *duthus* had vanished, and the " subject of succession " was the clan itself as a heritable subject, and that concomitant form of " incorporeal property," the armorial bearings which descended from chief to chief. Where, however, the *duthus* remained " in the name and blood " by any form of devolution which could be construed as carrying the " representation," every effort has always been made to keep the chiefship and arms, in conjunction with the chymmes,[2] the " hearth of the race." The Lord Lyon's Patent, of confirmation, rematriculation, or *Diplomæ Stemmatis*, thus became the writ determining right of succession and representation, amongst the " honourable communities " (clans whose chiefs had been recognised and recorded as amongst the nobles of the realm ; and consequently as noble communities) ; such certificates being sent out " To all concerned whether of the foresaid names or others," and it being a subject for nobiliary reproof for a claimant to have " represented himself as chief " or " designed himself " so " without having got leave from Us." [3] Publication of the *Armorial Diploma* thus became the important formal step in the succession to chiefship.[4]

Ceremonies similar to those observed in the inauguration of a chief were used at the appointment of a tanist, with this difference, that whereas the chief stood upon the stone of inauguration, the tanist

---

[1] Cosmo Innes, *Scottish Legal Antiquities*, p. 91—the " sasine ox."

[2] *Heraldry in Scotland*, p. 353. Reference in a matriculation of arms to their having been borne by ancestors " as proprietor of " a *duthus* would, by Lord Jamieson, evidently be construed, if need be, as directing the insignia in the line of destination of the chymmes (1941 S.C. 767–768).

[3] The *Ard-righ's* " supreme officer of honour " (see p. 11, and Nisbet, *System of Heraldry*, II., iv. p. 172). The point of Lyon being careful about devolution of the *duthus*, where possible, was, moreover, that an intruding claimant like *Ian Muydertach* of Clan Ranald, got his status made effective by Crown charter of the *duthus*, and such charter indeed often contained a " name and arms clause."

[4] See Appendix X.

stood beside the stone with one foot upon it. In the heraldic counterpart, we find the matriculations, such as Chisholm of Chisholm (Lyon
Register, 33, 12) wherein the heir is mentioned, and others where a
matriculation is made *qua* heir, in virtue of an " appointment and
designation " by the chief regarding the chief-arms, such as that by
Gilbert, 12th Earl of Errol.

The appointment of a " commander of the clan " (*ceann-cath*),
i.e. military leader, differed from the foregoing. He was " raised on
a shield " and his commission from the *ceann-cinnidh* was read, after
sound of trumpet (see p. 110).

The emphasis upon genealogy, already so frequently noticed, and
commented on by all observers, was not confined to the inauguration
of the chiefs, but Mackenzie, in his *Defence of the Antiquity of the Royal
Line of Scotland*, refers to these formal recitals of the genealogy as
" also being ordinary in our Highland Families to this very day, not
only at burials, but at baptisms and marriages," [1] and thus (Sir G.
Mackenzie adds) :

but in most of the Considerable Families, like ours, not only the Succession,
but the chief Accidents which befel the Family, are remembered for two
or three hundred years, by many hundreds of the Family, tho' there be
no written history of such families, so far does Interest and Affection
prompt and help Memory and Tradition to supply Letters.[2]

Amongst Highlanders—even at the present day—

the verbal repetition of entire genealogical tables dating back several
centuries, was looked upon not as an unusual feat of memory, but as a
piece of everyday knowledge. All clansmen worthy of the name strove to
acquaint themselves with the lineage of their chieftain, as also with their
own descent ; and shame upon him who exhibited uncertainty on matters
of clan genealogy. . . . I know a number of old people in Lewis who can
trace descent back ten or twelve generations with the utmost ease and
assurance.[3]

Wives were similarly expected to be at pains to acquire knowledge
of the clan or family into which they married, Lady Borthwick (1762)
commenting that her husband

was much attached to his race and family and did pay very particular
attention to his pedigree in all its branches, and she herself being very
young and also very clannish paid particular attention to what she heard
her husband say on these subjects.[4]

---

[1] *Works*, II., p. 363. This is a custom our clan families should take note of
and keep up. [2] *Ibid*. p. 416.

[3] A. Alpin MacGregor, *Summer Days Among the Western Isles*, p. 79. Similarly,
South Sea Islanders can trace back their chief's pedigrees some thirty-nine
generations (*Scottish Geographical Magazine*, October 1943, s.v. " Tonga.")

[4] House of Lords, Borthwick Case, 1812, Minutes of Evidence, p. 9.

Thus not only did Sennachies preserve, and narrate on formal occasions but wives and children were regularly inculcated in the clan genealogy, knowledge of which became a treasured memory of every member of the clan or branch and its *sencliathe*, or ancient followers.

I would stress the importance of this on the modern mothers in the clans. It is their duty to acquaint themselves with the history, traditions, and genealogy of their husband's forebears, and to hand these down to their children, making the traditions of the clan whereinto they have married, as of old, the fireside tale. Nor should they neglect to bring in their own maternal traditions.

The household of the chief included a number of important officers, many of which were hereditary, and supported by farms or crofts which descended along with the office, the lore and skill of which were imparted from generation to generation.

The chief was also accompanied by his *leuchd-crios*, or bodyguard, his "fighting tail," usually more numerous than the four to six halberders of the Lowland laird. These assisted the chief or chieftain in maintaining order and defending the clan against casual marauders.[1]

When travelling, the chief was accompanied by a numerous escort as well as a retinue,[2] consisting of piper, bard, henchman, gillie, etc. When the chief went hunting or upon any expedition, the clansman who lived nearest the halting-place furnished his chief and the chief's followers with a night's entertainment, and also provided brawn for the dogs. This form of tribute was termed "*Cuid Oidhche*"—a night's provision.

Besides the obligation of military service incumbent on every able-bodied member of the clan, two other obligations were due from the clansmen to their chief. One of these was the *calpa*, a species of first-fruits of their cattle or produce ; the other was denominated *herezeld*, and was exigible if the clansman happened to occupy more than the eighth part of a davach of land. The *calpa* was due by the clansman to his chief even although the clansman might not be living on clan territory and was the token of whose group he belonged to. Unless under explicit contract to give *calp* to someone else as chief, the occupier of land was a follower of the " chieftane of the cuntrie " where he dwelt.

The judicial system of the clan was delegated to a *breitheamh*, or brieve, or judge, who administered justice according to the Brehon law. The principle of this primitive law appears to have had for its object the reparation rather than the prevention of crime. The fine inflicted under Brehon law was termed *éirig* ; each form of injury was assessed at a certain rate, named *crò*. The office of *breitheamh* was usually hereditary, and besides a certain proportion of the fines which were imposed, the judge obtained a piece of arable land for his support.

In Scottish history he is known as the dempster, of which the

---

[1] The *leuchd-crios* of Rothiemurchus numbered twenty-four (*Memoirs of a Highland Lady*, p. 186).
[2] See Appendix IV

highest was the hereditary Dempster of Parliament, an office which descended in the old family of Dempster of Auchterless and Pitliver.

The clan military arrangements were fixed on a regular basis. Every clan regiment was commanded by the chief, if he were of sufficient age, and his position was that of colonel, or honorary colonel, and so to say, like a sovereign, head of the clan forces. The eldest cadet, if suitable, or an appointed *ceann-cath*, was lieutenant-colonel and actual " commander of the clan " forces under the chief—the next cadet was major. Each company had two captains, two lieutenants, and two ensigns, and the front ranks were composed of gentlemen (*daoine-uasail*), who were all provided with targets, and were otherwise better armed than the rear ranks. During the battle each company furnished two of their best men as a guard to the chief, and in their choice consanguinity was always considered. The chief was posted in the centre of the column beside the colours, and he stood between two brothers, cousins-german, or other relations. The clansmen were also disposed with regard to their relatives, the father, the son, and the brother standing beside each other. Every head of a distinct house was captain of his own tribe. Every chief had a standard-bearer, which office was at first conferred on someone who had behaved gallantly ; and usually the office became hereditary in his family, and was rewarded with a gratuity or a small annual salary.

Each clan had a stated place of rendezvous, where the members assembled at the summons of their chief. The manner of convoking the clan on a sudden emergency was by means of the *Crois* or *Crann-tàra*, or fiery-cross. This signal consisted of two pieces of wood placed in the form of a cross. One of the ends of the horizontal piece was either burnt or burning, and a piece of linen or white cloth stained with blood was suspended from the other end. Two men, each with a cross in his hand, were despatched by the chief in different directions, who ran shouting the slogan or war-cry of the clan, and naming the place of rendezvous. The cross was delivered from hand to hand, and as each fresh bearer ran at full speed, the clan assembled with great celerity. Stewart of Garth states that one of the most recent instances of the fiery-cross being used was in 1745 by Lord Breadalbane, when it went round Loch Tay, a distance of thirty-two miles, in three hours, to raise his people and prevent their joining Prince Charles. In 1715, however, the cross had gone the same round, but with a different effect, for five hundred men assembled the same evening, under the Laird of Glenlyon, and marched off to join the Earl of Mar, who had unfurled the banner of King James VIII.

Probably the last occasion on which Highlanders were summoned by means of the fiery-cross was in Canada in the winter 1812–1813, when the chief of the Highlanders, who were settled in Glengarry (Canada), sent it round to summon his men to repel an American raid. We are told that these Glengarry men (descendants of the old Glengarry Fencibles) became so proficient in the art of wood fighting, that when, at the end of the Peninsular War, a large number of Wellington's soldiers were despatched to Quebec to fight the Americans, the men of Glengarry (Canada) were detailed to teach the Peninsular veterans how to skirmish in the backwoods of Canada.

Each clan had its own war-cry, or slogan, and also its badge of pine, heather, or some such plant. The sett, or pattern, of the tartan enabled each clan to distinguish friend from foe.

As regards domestic customs, the usages among the Highlanders were in many respects very different from those of the Lowland Scots. The custom denominated "hand-fasting" was maintained among the Highlanders until a comparatively recent period. It consisted of a species of contract between two chiefs, by which it was agreed that the heir of the one should live with the daughter of the other as her husband for twelve months and a day. It was frequently completed with a "right-hand" permanent marriage. Such "left-hand" contracts, which were considered perfectly honourable, were often entered into where the chieftain's "right-hand" marriage had proved unfruitful, or its children died off. Indeed even in a full marriage the early tribal rule apparently was that if within a year and a day there was no child nor was there any appearance of issue, the contract was considered at an end, and each party was at liberty to marry or handfast with any other. Strange though this custom may appear in the light of modern society, it seems to have worked quite well, as most practical customs do ; prevented grievances about childless wives, did much to ensure the direct lineal succession of the chiefs, and to avoid succession disputes and the break of continuity of tradition, so liable to occur in collateral successions when the heir is not brought up in the ancestral home. Another remarkable custom was that of fosterage, which consisted in the mutual change by different families of their children, for the purpose of being nursed and bred. Even the son of the chief was so entrusted during pupilarity to an inferior member of the clan. An adequate reward was either given or accepted in every case, and the lower orders, when the trust was committed to them, regarded it as an honour rather than a service. In this way a strong attachment was created, not only between foster-brothers, but between the child and his foster-parents. Numerous instances are on record of clan devotion in this respect. No surer mode could have been devised for binding the members of one clan to each other, and for ensuring the loyalty of the people to their chief and his family. In every respect the chief was regarded by the members of his clan not as a master or landlord, but as a friend and the father of his people. To quote the description of the similar organisation in olden France :

He commanded the group surrounding him, and, in the words of ancient documents, " he reigned." The family became a fatherland designed in ancient documents by the word *patria*, and was loved with the more affection because it was a living fact under the eyes of everyone.[1]

---

[1] Brentano, *Old Regime in France*, pp. 3, 4

Social life concentrated around the family hearth, and in the little clachans, or " fire-houses," to use the old Scottish term, each with its *tighearn*, or *chef du feu*, as the old Lorraine expression has it : the principal hearth passed with the chiefship and formed the hearth of the race, above which hung the arms and in due course the armorial shield which descended from chief to chief, and was present as a permanent entity carved in stone above this hearth of the Hall or Ha' Hoose.[1]

The clanspeople looked upon the chief's interests as their own, and in return expected him to care for their interests. As an instance of this custom Martin's *Description of the Western Islands of Scotland* (1703) gives the practice in Barra :

When a Tenant's wife dies, he then addresses himself to MacKneil of Barray, representing his Loss, and at the same time desires that he would be pleas'd to recommend a Wife to him, without which he cannot manage his Affairs, nor beget Followers to MacKneil, which would prove a publick Loss to him. Upon this Representation, MacKneil finds out a suitable Match for him ; and the Woman's Name being told him, immediately he goes to her, carrying with him a Bottle of strong Waters for their Entertainment at Marriage, which is then consummated. When a Tenant dies, the Widow addresseth her self to MacKneil in the same manner, who likewise provides her with a Husband, and they are marry'd without any further Courtship. . . . If a Tenant chance to lose his Milk-Cows by the Severity of the Season, or any other Misfortune ; in this Case MacKneil of Barray supplies him with the like Number that he lost. When any of these Tenants are so far advanc'd in Years that they are uncapable to till the Ground, MacKneil takes such old Men into his own Family, and maintains them all their Life after.

Though perhaps more noticed in Barra than elsewhere, in their primitive purity, the foregoing gives a good idea of what the functions of a chief covered in the Scottish Highlands in the Middle Ages. The letter from Glenorchy to Gregor McKane, his Keeper of Kilchurn, in 1570, shows the same kindly relationship between chief and clansman in Breadalbane.[2]

Whilst the supreme, and parental, power lay in the chief, as hereditary and reigning *ceann-cinnidh* (subject, of course, to superior chief, or *Ard-righ*, in matters " wherein these stood patriarchally " in relation to him), he was entitled to, and fortified by, the advice of his council. A chief was no tyrant—for an hereditary monarchy always tends to be in practice " constitutional," however absolute it may seem in theory. As Mrs. Grant of Laggan says :

Nothing can be more erroneous than the prevalent idea that a Highland chief was an ignorant and unprincipled tyrant. . . . If ferocious in disposition, or weak in understanding, he was curbed and directed by the elders of his tribe who by inviolable custom were his standing councillors without whose advice no measure of any kind was decided.

[1] Brentano, *Old Regime in France*, pp. 3, 13.
[2] *Social and Economic Development of Scotland*, p. 518.

If he was not " ferocious " or feeble, he was allowed a good deal of his own way, so long as the results were proving for the weal of the clan, but (whilst treating the chief or parent with every respect) a clan or family has a community opinion which, dutifully expressed, carries weight with every considerate chief (whose strength lies in not merely the devotion but the confidence of his people).

The Clan Mackenzie possessed such influence over their chief that they prevented him from demolishing Brahan Castle, the principal seat of the family (*i.e.* the clan realised that no new building, however gorgeous, could have the traditional significance of the old racial home) ; and in the case of Clan Donnachy Campbells, the councillors of the House of Glenorchy effected a change of site from that proposed by their chieftain when Taymouth Castle was projected.[1]

The chiefs of Grant and Innes, we have noticed, were placed in custody to prevent them squandering the ancestral inheritance ; and Ross of Balnagowan was with less success exhorted by fourteen of his councillors—the principal gentry of the clan—not to " tyne the riggs that his elders wan." [2]

Bachelor chiefs were by their council exhorted to marry—marriage being, of course, a matter of duty. Chiefs whose heirs made *mésalliances*, were advised in council to disinherit the progeny of such union ; whilst in other instances, the council advised divorce and remarriage.[3] The purpose of the council was in every case not so much the interest of the individual as to " confer upon the lasting weal of his house." [4]

In examining the working of what Miss Grant calls a " but little explored yet most vitally important subject," we must first look at its composition. We at once find that it did not consist of the whole family or branch, but of certain persons of weight, and that there " was always a distinction between the *daoine-uasail* and the lesser folk " and that a " generall meeting of the leading men of Fraser " consisted of five named country-gentlemen (*i.e.* lairds) and " some of the Houses of Farrelin and Relick," [5] and seems, as regards " landed men " to have been a five-person (*i.e. gilfine*) group ; whilst the Council of the Isles, sixteen persons, and the Lord of the Isles makes seventeen, that is, an *ind-fine* number.[6] I fancy the normal was either a *gilfine* or a *derbhfine* (nine persons), and it is significant that

[1] *Sketches of the Highlanders*, p. 59.
[2] *Social and Economic Development of Scotland*, p. 518.
[3] *Lordship of the Isles*, p. 176.
[4] *Social and Economic Development of Scotland*, p. 518.
[5] *Ibid.* pp. 521–522.
[6] This council consisted of four thanes, four armins (described as sub-thanes or lords), four " bastards " or " squires " (described as freeholders), and, I perceive, four " factors " or " tacksmen " (for unless the " or " be read as the next " four " the sixteen is not completed, and persons holding land in " factory " are not freeholders). I think, however, it is not wholly clear what this fourth tenure was. It looks like a " representative council " and the first four would evidently include the persons who, in heraldic MSS., are entered as quasi-peers, Maclean, Macleod of Lewis, Cameron of Lochiel.

Skene regards the individuals forming these as capable of including not the five or nine nearest individuals, but nearest heads of houses (or stirps)—where issue existed of whom these were " representers " (the child would not be counted so long as *in potestate parentis*). In the *Maclean of Ardgour* case 1937 *dicta*, (which as regards effect, were overset by the evidence in the 1938 proof) about " recognition " and so forth being matter for " the clan " and in lesser cases " the branch " were in later *dicta* modified, and Lord Mackay—realising the historical and practical aspect—corrects himself to " the principal landed gentlemen within the clan." [1] This would include both actual free-holders (who should have had seals of arms) and the *armigeri* who, in the form of arms, had " incorporeal fiefs " constituting them " gentlemen " ; and in feudal courts ladies likewise sat, if invested in the fief. Two points would seem to emerge : the council was limited in size, and responsible in character, which prevented it degenerating into an unruly assembly such as the local courts of France sometimes became,[2] thus again showing the peculiar genius of Scottish clanship. These freeholders and tacksmen had each to deal with their own " council "—still less formal—which helped them regarding adminis-tration of their own affairs.

The function of these councils was to give advice and assistance, for the chief ruled as well as reigned. As Sir George Mackenzie points out of our Scottish parliaments, their " consent " applied essentially to measures involving contributions of property, which was the " vassal " or clansman's own, and which the chief was bound (along with the rest of the group) to defend, and could not be affected without that owner's own consent, or to making rules and ordinances affecting the internal affairs of these lesser families. This, as regards matters within the branch *patria potestas*, could not be done without the branch-chief's consent.

The most formalised variety of these councils was the Baron Court ; and this, as we should expect, is found taking a direct part in the administration of the clan system—even relating to the tartan.

This close relationship of the feudal barony (*i.e.* the organised " family ") to the clan system and the tartan is well illustrated from the *Court Book of the Regality of Grant* :

Court of the Lordship of the parochine of Duthell holden at Duthell the 20 July 1704 be Duncan Grant of Mullochard, baillie constitute be the Right Honoll. Alexr. Grant of that Ilk, your bailie-principall of the Regalitie of Grant, David Blair notar and clerk to the said Regalitie Court of the Dustrict of Duthell ; suits called and the Court lawfullie fenced and affirmed.[3]

---

[1] 1941 S.C. 646. (These *dicta* were *obiter*.)

[2] *Old Regime in France*, pp. 262–263.

[3] This means that there was a sufficient quorum of the people of the regality, Duthell district, present, to insure genuine self-government. The fencing of the court meant a public declaration of its basis and authority—just as Parliament was " fenced " by the Lord Lyon King of Arms.

This reminds us that by its nature the Baron Court (as Craig explained, our first barons were *Capitani tribuum*) was a council for " the publique weal, rule, and government " of the barony [1] for administering the " common weill and profit " of " a communal community," [2] and that even non-baronial lands had their popular court, the next recorded extract, wherein we shall see the details of the Grant tartan dealt with :

Court of the landes of Tulchine and Skeir-advey, holden at Delay upon the 27 July 1704 be William Grant of Delay, bailie of the saids lands, constitute be the Right Honll. the Laird of Grant, heretor of the saidis landis, David Blair notar and clerk ; James Grant, officer. Suites called and the court lawfully fenced and affirmed :

The said day by ordor from the Laird of Grant, younger, the said bailie ordanes and enacts the haill tenantes cottars (&c.) within the saidis landis of Skear-advie Tulchine and Calendar that are fencible men shall provyd and have in readieness against the eight day of August nixt ilk ane of thame Heighland coates, trewes, and shorthose of tartan of red and greine sett broad-springed and also with gun sword and durk and to present themselves to ane rendezvouze upon 48 hours advertisement, within the country of Strathspey for the said Laird of Grant or his father their hosting and hunting, And this under failie of twenty poundis Scots ilk ane that shall faill in the premisses, And the Master to outrig the servants in the said coates trewes and hose out of their fees.[3]

It will be noticed how the Grant tartan—which is defined in such general terms as would not preclude individual detail in weaving, and clearly local weaving is contemplated—is to be worn not merely by " Grants " but by the " haill " tenants, cottars, and their servants, though as Miss I. F. Grant has shown in *Social and Economic Development of Scotland*, pp. 501–502, many of these had been persuaded to take the name of Grant, and so build up the " organised family "—the clan—and give it strength of unity of name.[4] The entry is only an excerpt of a longer diet, and presumably the enactment is in usual form by the court. On the other hand, in a matter of " honour " it may be the recording of an Act of the chief, who in a matter of insignia such as tartan is, of course, the ultimate clan authority, as parental patriarch, since the tartan is still quasi-allodial possession and not one held " of and under " the *Ard-righ*, like the arms and seal.[5] We are here reminded of the Gallic " family laws, made by the *chefs de familles* for the preservation of their . . . names and distinguishing marks." [6]

[1] A.P.S., VI., ii., p. 816 ; Dickinson, *Baron Court Book of Carnwath*, p. xlvi.
[2] Dickinson, *ibid.* pp. lxiv., lxiii.
[3] D. W. Stewart, *Old and Rare Scottish Tartans*, p. 28.
[4] Cf. M. G. B. Westermarck, *History of Human Marriage*, II., p. 110, on the immense force attributed in tribal communities to this " taking the name."
[5] In this matter the early history of *arms* has been repeating itself in *tartans*. Faced with weaving-trade confusion, chiefs have been getting " the proper tartan " of their clan embodied where possible in some Lyon Register matriculation and so given statutory definition.
[6] Brentano, *Old Regime in France*, p. 21.

In "matters of honour," the settlement of family property, its insignia, etc., we find the chief made the laws, and that the bailie, in terms of an order from the chief "ordains and enacts." The function of the court or council is here to record, or become witnesses of, what the patriarch has, in virtue of his patriarchal authority, been pleased to do. The proceedings are somewhat analogous to the *lit de justice* of the old French monarchy.

Naturally, neither the chief nor his council could affect matters in the prerogative of the Crown, such as the destination of honours including chiefship and its insignia, nor could clan or council prevent the chief and *Ard-righ* effecting a rearrangement of these. An interested member of the family sometimes made representations to the Crown that the rearrangement be stopped or modified.[1] In a matter relating in principle to the "blessing" and transmission of patriarchal personality, the Crown normally gave effect to the chief's wish.[2]

The annals of Clan Grant provide us, moreover, with a documented account of the abdication of an aged chief, Ludovick Grant of Grant, who died in November 1716, having six years previously resigned the estates and chiefship of the clan to his son Alexander. This ceremony took place at the clan's trysting-place at Ballintomb, where they all appeared in full dress. The chief's speech, made to his son before the assembled clan, was as follows :

My dear Sandy : I make you this day a very great present, namely the honour of commanding the Clan Grant, who, while I have commanded them, though in troublous times, yet they never misbehaved, so that you have them this day without spot or blemish. . . . God Bless you all.[3]

There is here no suggestion that the clan's "consent" was required ; nay, they are handed over as a "present" and "so that you have them," and the proceedings terminate patriarchally with the chief's "blessing." The solemn and stately proceeding was thus in the due traditional form of a verbal delivery and blessing,[4] and delivery of a "heritable subject" analogous to the deliveries by the Lords of the Isles and the Irish kings, "by the witnessing of these men who are near and hear my speech."[5]

Whilst the chief, or chieftain, "was the law," as Lord Aitchison has expressed it, he derived his patriarchal authority not from his

---

[1] Earldom of Airth, 1679, *Scots Peerage*, I., p. 141.
[2] *Tartans of the Clans and Families*, pp. 40, 44, quoting Mackenzie and Nisbet.
[3] C. Rampini, *History of Moray*, p. 210 ; *Scots Peerage*, VII., p. 477.
[4] Cf. Maine and Pollock, *Ancient Law*, pp. 266, 211–215.
[5] Grant, *Lordship of the Isles*, p. 144, which illustrates the force of Bruce's verbal nomination by Alexander III. The Celtic system certainly proceeded largely on oral pronouncement and transmission, while the business-like feudal system of the Normans insisted that writ was essential to create or transfer property. Of course, the Normans were right. How much we have to regret that more of the Gaelic proceedings were not reduced to writing—the more so from the few but beautiful examples of it that remain—and that more care was not taken of such priceless Gaelic MSS. as once existed.

children but from the parental relationship to the community, as Sir George Mackenzie so emphatically illustrated in his treatise on the Scottish monarchy.[1]

Nevertheless we have in Scotland, as in Old France and elsewhere to bear in mind the ever-present power and influence of the " family council." In the greater continental houses, such as those of the princely and countly families of Poland, etc., these " councils " not long ago were formal and stately gatherings—in the full panoply of a " family parliament " which deals with the administration of the family estates, trust funds, investments, and so forth, including arranging matrimonial and testamentary affairs, and occupations of members of the family. Indeed, in Scotland, such family councils operated in many such matters at any rate well into the nineteenth century ; and in the annals of county families transactions are recorded as decided on, and careers of children settled by deliberation of, and decision in, such family councils well into the middle of the century. Whilst the ultimate " family laws " were made by the chieftain, be it observed that (as Mrs. Grant pointed out) if he were " prodigious and misguidit " it was competent for the family councillors to resort to the next higher chief, or to the *Ard-righ*, to have the incompetent *chef de famille* put under " interdiction," or, if necessary, in ward.[2]

This was done either by Decree of Council or, where incarceration was the soundest course, by Letters under the Privy Seal, the precise Scottish equivalent of the old French *Lettres de Cachet*.[3]

So late as the eighteenth century, the councillors of Clan Grant, as Garth records,[4] caused the young laird of Grant to be imprisoned on account of his misbehaviour and prodigality, which would have imperilled the Grant estates—a matter affecting the whole clan.

The concept of the " country " or " family property " being the possession of " the family " as a corporation, to be preserved " intact in the hands of its head and strong in its patrimony to be handed on in its integrity to the next heir " [5] is very analogous to the theory of a common clan property, advanced by Adam and other popular writers, who declaim of this as a distinction from feudalism, whereas we find the modern scientific historian describing the same thing as of the essence of feudalism ! Brentano observes that " he who dissipates his patrimony commits a frightful robbery," *i.e.* a robbery against " his race," since the lands belonging to the family must be preserved

---

[1] This treatise was really written to oppose the Exclusion Bill and, accordingly, in some respects is extravagantly argued—as political questions tend to be—and runs away with itself and from the author's more detached juridical writings.

[2] In 1522 the Laird of Innes was consigned to Girniegoe Castle on the ground that " he hes wastit his lands and gudis," and at the instance of some of his principal kinsmen (*Familie of Innes*, p. 98).

[3] These for the most part were issued not for political purposes, but for dealing with family difficulties.

[4] *Sketches of the Highlanders*, p. 58.   [5] *Old Regime in France*, p. 39.

intact, and amongst the principal duties of a *chef de famille* were the maintenance of the splendour of his name, and the integrity of his domain formed his constant preoccupation.[1] This, of course, in no selfish spirit, but because he was responsible for maintaining the integrity of the property of the family *communitas*. The first duty of the chief is to look after the preservation of the family and family property of which he is the representative. " The head of the family was permeated with the feeling that he was directly responsible not only for his own destiny, but also for that of his kinsfolk." [2] This was precisely the position of the clan chief, and what his clan-council had to see that he never forgot.

Whilst it lay with the *Ard-righ* as *Pater Patriæ* and " Chief of Chiefs " to intervene in case of misrule by his vassal-chiefs, analogous constitutional principles covered misrule by an *Ard-righ* himself. In medieval theory, Sovereign Crowns, being held " under God " (hence kings referred to each other as " Our brother of . . ." just as they referred to their own great-chief-magnates as " Our cousin "), the appropriate course of outraged lieges was resort to God the Father, who intervened—as in the case of the oppressions of King John of England—very effectively through the Vice-Regent, the Pope, and the Cardinal-Legates. In more independent, and later instances as well, we find the Head of the Church, *e.g.* St. Columba, and the Archbishops of St. Andrews and Canterbury, exercising a very effective authority, both as regards inauguration and subsequent ethical conduct—constitutionally a most important aspect of the monarchial-clan family system. By its annual change of Moderator, however, the Church of Scotland disenabled itself from either acquiring or exercising just this sort of influence in the manner the Celtic Church and others had done. Not a small part of the conflict of the Church with the Crown and clans during the seventeenth century seems due to this failure of the higher Church organisation to provide a proper continuity and experience in its Principal, such as would have made for close, smooth, and skilful co-relation with the governance of the Realm.

What is here observed had repercussions, not only on the nation as a whole, but also, as will be seen, on several aspects of the clan system and its vicissitudes.

Enough proof has been adduced, we think, to show that the nature of and benefits from the system of clanship were not the wealth which a chief or chieftain might possess, but the number of households comprehended in his little principality. When a clan or a sept was too small or weak to stand by itself, it strengthened itself by entering—through its chief—into a bond or treaty with friendly neighbours against the attacks or encroachments of mutual enemies or rivals. Such bonds were styled bonds of manrent or manred. By the terms of these bonds, the subscribing parties pledged themselves to assist each other. However general their internal insurrections and disputes might be, and

---

[1] *Old Regime in France*, p. 40.   [2] *Ibid.* p. 58.

however extended their cause of quarrel with rivals or neighbours, the subscribers generally bound themselves to be loyal and true to their sovereign. " Always, excepting my duty to our Lord the King," was a usual clause.

When the clan system had become fully organised in the Highlands, there existed no person, family, or tribe who did not owe or profess allegiance to a chief of a clan. The natural tendency to family organisation was indeed strengthened by a statute requiring every man to find himself a lord (*i.e.* chief) for the whole concept of government was based on the plan that the Crown and magnates dealt with groups, not individuals, and that each representer was responsible for the hereditary or adopted members of his clan, family, or branch. A Highlander was considered disgraced when he could not name his chief and claim the protection of his clan. The most glaring insult that could be offered to a clan was to speak disrespectfully of its chief, an offence which was considered as a personal affront by all his followers, and was resented accordingly.

As the wealth of the Highlanders consisted chiefly in flocks and herds, the usual mode of commencing attacks or of making reprisals was by an incursion for carrying off the cattle of the hostile clan. These expeditions were termed *creachs*. They were conducted with systematic order, and were considered perfectly justifiable. If lives were lost in these forays, revenge full and ample was taken. In general, however, personal hostilities were avoided in such incursions, whether they were directed against the Lowlanders or rival clans.

Those unacquainted with the nature and evolution of the clan system have too often imagined and described the clans as communities of marauders. There is little difficulty, however, in disproving such charges, for the Highlanders in that respect were more sinned against than sinning. In the report of General Wade made to the Government in 1724 (to which we shall later on have again occasion to refer), regarding the state of the Highlands at that time, occurs the following paragraph :

Their (the Highlanders) Notions of Virtue and Vice are very different from the more civilised part of Mankind. They think it a most Sublime Virtue to pay a Servile and Abject Obedience to the Commands of their Chieftains, altho' in opposition to their Sovereign and the Laws of the Kingdom, and to encourage this, their Fidelity, they are treated by their Chiefs with great Familiarity, they partake with them in their Diversions, and shake them by the Hand wherever they meet them.

General Wade being a middle-class Englishman, though a kindly and well-meaning one, was evidently astonished that Scotsmen were in the habit of obeying their own " family laws " and those of their immediate chieftains and chiefs in preference to the centralised laws enacted by the Parliament in Edinburgh. Wade was accustomed to the strongly centralised Government of London, which by means of its executive authority had created such havoc and ill-feeling amongst

PLATE IV.

ARMS OF ALEXANDER SKENE OF THAT ILK, 16TH LAIRD BARONOF SKENE,
IMPALING THE ARMS OF HIS SPOUSE, GILES ADIE, THE LADY SKENE

This is a drawing (W. R. Skene, Hist, Roy., *Family of Skene of Skene*, 1887) of the original stone, in the south gable of Skene House, which, consequent on an addition, has long been in a corridor, so that the carving is in excellent and unweathered condition, but is in a situation difficult to photograph.

As a 17th century, and almost contemporary (1692) rendering of the text of the matriculation of arms (1672–7) in Lyon Register, Vol. 2, p. 211, this an especially interesting representation of 17th century highland dress.

The Official blazon of the supporters runs:—Dexter, a highlandman in his proper garb holding a skene in his right hand in a guarding posture; Sinister, another highlandman in a servile habit, his target on the left arm and the darlach by the right side, all proper.

The dexter supporter is, as will be seen, in plaid and trews, the dress worn by those riding on horseback, whilst the sinister supporter is shown in the *breacan-feile*.

PLATE V.

THE LAIRD OF CLUNY-MACPHERSON, *c.* 1700.

From the Portrait belonging to Capt. Cheyne-Macpherson of Dalchully, showing Chief's Dress of
Doublet and Trews, with Plaid.

the Irish tribes, and he was unable to grasp the motives and organisation of the feudo-family system in its ascending pyramidal groups. It was a fundamental principle of the " organised family "—whether in the clan or its formalised equivalent, the feudal barony—that the chief or baron who was actually and officially *chef de famille* (being representer of the common ancestor) was *in loco parentis,* and his wishes were in the ordinary course obeyed without question, as sacred commands emanating from the person who was himself the " sacred embodiment of the race " to which his people belonged. Moreover, under the highly organised feudo-clanship system which obtained in Scotland, the first duty was towards the immediate chieftain and, according to his will, to the highest chieftains, and, consequently, through the great chiefs to the *Ard-righ.* The clan system accordingly strictly embodied the corresponding feudal organisation, so that if a great chief for some reason quarrelled with the king or his advisers, the result was that all the chieftain's branches and clansmen depending on him felt primarily bound to follow and take the part of their immediate chief, even against the more ultimate authority of the *Ard-righ.* Similarly, within the clan, a dispute between two branches almost invariably involved all the dependents of each being involved in an obligation to support their own immediate chieftain, whether right or wrong, and if two powerful cadets quarrelled it was sometimes difficult for the high-chief or *Ard-righ* to prevent internecine war. The clan battle on the North Inch of Perth between, it is said, distinguished branches of the Clan Chattan, is an illustration. This " weakness," as it is usually called, of the central government in Scotland, led in the Middle Ages to an immense amount of minor turbulence, but we ought also to recollect that it contributed to independence and the survivance of local government and personal liberty ; for a Crown, or central government, which claims and successfully enforces immediate authority (and, so to say, " goes past " the chiefs and chieftains, in fact goes past the clan organisation, to rule the clansmen directly, irrespective of the clan system) necessarily becomes sooner or later a tyranny, because it is replacing the natural system of the family by the artificial system of bureaucracy.

It is now well recognised [1] that those who in the early nineteenth century paraded a theory of supposed antagonism between " clan system " and " feudal system," were merely spreading political propaganda for the suppression of clanship as a living force in Scotland.

The real conflict regarding tenures between the chiefs and the Crown arose when kings, following the English practice of the later Plantagenets, endeavoured to cut across the development of pure feudalism (which was the natural and popular machinery for preserving the clan and family systems), by making grants to cadets of " Crown "

---

[1] *E.g.* Professor Rait, *Making of Scotland* ; Professor Trevelyan, *Ramilles* ; I. F. Grant, *Social and Economic Development of Scotland,* pp. 52, 198 ; and other *authorities.*

F

holdings with direct obligations to the Crown, which were liable to cut across the tribal loyalty to chiefs and chieftains.[1] Accordingly the chiefs and clansmen were always endeavouring to preserve the feudal system. The Crown and its ministers in Edinburgh were too often endeavouring to replace that feudalism by administrative tyranny. There is no doubt, partly through the change of language which took place between the Highlands and the Lowlands, and the well-founded knowledge that the Lowlands had also been originally Gaelic-speaking, and therefore orally homogeneous, that the Highlanders adopted the convenient theory that they had a right to make *creaghs* or raids upon the Lowland cattle, similar to those which the Borderers made on either side of the march, and the practice was ultimately more or less regularised between the Highlanders and Lowlanders by the system of " blackmail," whereby certain chiefs and chieftains were financed either in money or in livestock, to the effect that they should themselves refrain from cattle-lifting and stop others from doing so upon the lands of those who paid the levy. Although harsh and improper, the system was really a primitive form of " subsidising " the less productive Highlands.

Professor Rait emphasises that " medieval Scotland was racially homogeneous and conscious of its unity," [2] and " centuries had to pass before the Scottish Highlanders were taught to speak of their Lowland countrymen as Saxons and the story of the Bruce's wars is not the story of a country divided against itself." [3] The " fake " of a " divided Scotland " and a " Celticism v. Feudalism," which caught the imagination of uncritical writers of the past generation or two, is something much more sinister ; the propaganda for dividing Scotland against itself, and to induce the nation to turn against the system whereby its tribality and independence had been preserved.

The persistent attempts of sovereigns such as James I. (acting on his unfortunate English " education ") and the evil ministers in the childhood of James V., and towards the close of the sixteenth century the greedy ministers of James VI., to suppress the highly organised system of feudo-clanship by the English system of centralised and non-feudal government, and as a means of this, by granting superiorities to chiefs of other clans and families than those to which the soil had traditionally belonged, and with the express purpose of fomenting, rather than endeavouring to allay clan differences, naturally made the Highland clans somewhat suspicious of the Royal ministers. Nevertheless, so effectively had the Scottish magnates embodied the tribe-guarding principles of feudalism in the Scottish constitution, that the system of clanship was preserved and remained in full force until after the Rising of " the '45 " when, in order to destroy the clan and

---

[1] For example, when Maclean of Coll got a charter of free barony he, on one occasion, declined on that ground to follow Duart in 1561 (*Glasgow Archæological Society*, X., p. 29).

[2] Professor Rait, *Making of Scotland*, Preface.　　　　[3] *Ibid.* p. 94.

family organism in Scotland, the Government shrewdly struck at the feudal organisation by which the clan system was held together.

For example, the Duke of Gordon, though feudal superior of the lands and estates held by the Camerons, MacPhersons, MacDonells of Keppoch, and others, had no command whatever over these clans. They acknowledged a different authority, and always followed the orders of their patriarchal chiefs. In Duncan Forbes's report of 1745 the above fact is commented upon as follows :

The Duke of Gordon is no Claned familie.[1] Although a Chieften [2] of a Very Considerable and powerfull Name in the Low Countries, besides that he has a great Posse of Gentlemen on horse back in Enzie and Strath-bogie, but he is only placed here upon the Account of his followings of Highlanders in Strathavin and Glenlivet, which will be about 300 Men. His extensive Superiorities and Jurisdictions in the Highlands, Viz., in Badenoch and Lochaber, does not yield him Any followers, the possessions of his own very property, as well as these whole Countreys, follow their Naturall Chieftens, of whom they are Descended, and have no Manner of Regard either to Masters or Superiors.

Duncan Forbes concludes his report with the following somewhat unwilling tribute to the bond which united chief and clansman :

They [the chiefs] have an Inherent Attractive Virtue, which makes their people follow as Iron Claps to the Loadstone.

The alleged relationship between feudal superiors and alien chiefs on the one hand, and the " native men," or original inhabitants [3] of a district, on the other, is described by Skene in his *Highlanders of Scotland* : [4]

When a Norman baron obtained by succession, or otherwise, a Highland

---

[1] Yet Sir James Melville had so early as Mary Queen of Scots' reign described the Gordons as a clan ; and in 1727 (eighteen years previously), Lord Lyon Brodie, who presumably knew, took Melville's and not Forbes's point of view ruling them ! The term " Claned familie " is evidently used of those in which the Reporter considered the rank and file were of the same name and kin as the commander.

[2] This alone might have shown those who in *Maclean of Ardgour* tried to maintain that " chieftain " was a purely " clan " title, that in the eighteenth century as in the fifteenth it had no such restriction.

[3] Not a happy definition, for many contracts provide that a person shall become " native man " to a new chieftain.

[4] In view of Adam's many references to Skene's *Highlanders of Scotland* (a good many of which I have superseded by reference to modern works) it is proper to quote an observation by the late A. M. Mackintosh (historian of his clan) in *Scottish Notes and Queries*, 3rd series, IX., p. 71 : " W. F. Skene—especially in his *Highlanders of Scotland*—and F. Adam are unsafe guides through the intricacies of Highland clan lore . . . and as regards the former, I may mention that in 1874 Skene wrote to me as follows : ' My work on the Highlanders was a juvenile work written nearly forty years ago and, of course, additional information and more matured consideration has led me to modify many of my views.' The result of this modification is apparent in *Celtic Scotland* (1874) where much of what he wrote in 1837 is either reversed or omitted." Still *Highlanders* is only too often the work cited.

property, the Gaelic *nativi* remained in actual possession of the soil under him, but at the same time paid their *calpas* to the natural chief of their clan, and followed him in war. When a Highland chief, however, acquired by the operation of the feudal succession an additional property which had not been previously in the possession of his clan, he found it possessed by the *nativi* of another race. If these *nativi* belonged to another clan which still existed in independence, and if they chose to remain on the property, they did so at the risk of being placed in a perilous situation should a feud arise between the two clans. But if they belonged to no other independent clan, and the stranger chief had acquired the whole possession of their race, the custom seems to have been for them to give a bond of manrent to their new lord, by which they bound themselves to follow him as their chief, and make him the customary acknowledgment of the *calpa*. They thus became a dependent sept upon a clan of a different race, while they were not considered as forming part of that clan.

This is largely speculative rubbish and should be compared with scientific accounts from actual documents, such as those cited in Miss I. F. Grant's *Social and Economic Development of Scotland*, p. 502, where one is shown how chiefs, Norman or Celtic, on acquiring fresh estates, took precisely the same courses to consolidate the inhabitants so far as possible, into a " clan " of their own. Constitutional means had to be used—and a boll of meal was a helpful inducement—but Cameron [1] cites medieval ceremonial used in old Scottish adoptions ; whilst there are numerous specific deeds receiving persons (and chieftains with their own whole followings) into another clan.[2] Frequently, of course, these remained a distinct branch-clan within the greater, sometimes they were quite " merged." It all depended on the intention and the form of the arrangement.

An instance of a clan losing its chief and following an alien leader is that of the Stewarts of Atholl, who ranged themselves under the banner of the Dukes of Atholl (Murray).[3] The Macqueens (of Corryborough) and the Macleans of Dochgarroch and Glen Urquhart, who both joined the Clan Chattan, are instances of branches of clans

---

[1] *Celtic Law*, p. 220.

[2] Cf. I. F. Grant, *Social and Economic Development of Scotland*, pp. 503–504.

[3] A very bad instance, for there were plenty of " male " Stewart chieftains in Atholl to have " elected " a leader from, had that been the practice. What happened instead was that the *duthus* and dignity of the Stewart Earls of Atholl devolved through the heiress of line on the Murray Earl of Tullibardine, who promptly resettled his Tullibardine honours on a cousin, and assumed the position of " chieftain of the country " of Atholl, whereof he had inherited the earldom. He did not, however, immediately take up the Stewart name, which led to the criticism in *Loyall Dissuasive*, viz. : that had he done this he had certainly been chief of the Stewarts in Atholl, but not of the whole Stewart clan. Atholl took the hint and assumed the surname " Stewart-Murray," and has since endeavoured, like some other magnates, a double role to fulfil, for the honours of Tullibardine returned to the Atholl line and under modern English advice the Crown would not be advised to sunder them again to Stewart and Murray lines respectively, as was the older sensible Scottish practice.

who migrated from their own clan territory to other districts, and who placed themselves under a chief of other blood to their own.

How little the status of clanship had altered in the Highlands, and how little even eighteenth-century Englishmen could understand, or sympathise with it, the following extracts from a book written about 1730, entitled *Letters from an Officer of Engineers to his Friend in London*, will show.[1] This officer culled a good deal of his information from General Wade's Report of 1724 to the Government.

The Highlanders are divided into tribes or clans, under chiefs or chieftains, and each clan is again divided into branches from the main stock, who have chieftains over them. These are subdivided into smaller branches of fifty or sixty men, who deduce their original from their particular chieftains, and rely upon them as their more immediate protectors and defenders. The ordinary Highlanders esteem it the most sublime degree of virtue to love their chief and pay him a blind obedience, although it be in opposition to the Government. Next to this love of their chief is that of the particular branch whence they sprang, and, in a third degree, to those of the whole clan or name whom they will assist, right or wrong, against those of any other tribe with which they are at variance. They likewise owe goodwill to such clans as they esteem to be their particular well-wishers. And, lastly, they have an adherence to one another as Highlanders in opposition to the people of the low country, whom they despise as inferior to them in courage, and believe they have a right to plunder them whenever it is in their power. This last arises from a tradition that the Lowlands in old times were the possessions of their ancestors. The chief exercises an arbitrary authority over his vassals, determines all differences and disputes that happen among them (1), and levies taxes (2) upon extraordinary occasions, such as the marriage of a daughter (3), building a house (4), or some pretence for his support (5) or the honour of his name (6) ; and if any one should refuse to contribute to the best of his ability, he is sure of severe treatment, and if he persists in his obstinacy, he would be cast out of his tribe by general consent (7). This power of the chief is not supported by interest, as they are landlords (8), but by consanguinity, as lineally descended from the old patriarchs or fathers of the families, for they hold the same authority when they have lost their estates, as may appear from several instances, and particularly that of one (Lord Lovat) who commands his clan, though at the same time they maintain him, having nothing left of his own. On the other hand, the chief, even against the laws, is bound to protect his followers, as they are sometimes called, be they never so criminal (9). He is their leader in clan quarrels, must free the necessitous from their arrears of rent, and maintain such who by accidents are fallen to total decay. Some of the chiefs have not only personal dislikes and enmity to each other, but there are also hereditary feuds between clan and clan, which have been handed down from one

---

[1] Burt, as Dr. Mackay Mackenzie observed in evidence in the *Ardgour* case proof, July 1938, was neither a captain nor an engineer. Moreover, as Lord Mackay very pertinently commented during the debate, the writings of Burt and Wade were by enemies of the Highlanders, whose purpose was to make out a case for drastic action against the clan system.

generation to another for several ages. These quarrels descend to the meanest vassals, and thus sometimes an innocent person suffers for crimes committed by his tribe, at a vast distance of time, before his being began.

The following notes are here appended in explication of Edward Burt's observations, and the numbers refer back to those points (so numbered) in his account :

(1) This was the patriarchal jurisdiction—the *patria potestas*, the family " judge." [1] " All disputes were settled by his decision." This was the " family tribunal " of similar old French tribes, " they had their tribunal, the tribunal of the seigneur, that is of the head of the family," [2] and far from the people wishing them abolished, they demanded they should be made legally final. [3] In cases of major disputes, Macpherson indicates the chief should appoint a body of nine to hear and report the proper decision, *i.e.* the creation of an *ad hoc derbhfine* council. [4]

(2) What Burt conceived as " taxes " were evidently the " calps of kenkynnie " [5] and the Cain cuddiche and conveth, or " presents " of provisions which were given in addition to the rent, and which represented the family contributions to maintaining the family organisation. In south-west Scotland, after " calps " had been abolished by statute, it appears the contributions were made *sub voce* " presents." The modern analogy is assuredly the contributions made by many Highlanders in business to their parent or relative in the tiny croft in glen or isle, and by which the old home is kept together, and some modern amenities added to the bare croft produce. [6]

(3) The " extraordinary occasions " are analogous to the " feudal aids," where the vassals made standardised contributions on just such occasions as the knighting of the heir, or marriage of the eldest daughter —illustrating even in a great and formalised realm, the dominating " family spirit."

(4) The real significance of this was charmingly illustrated so recently as 1941, when Miss Forbes of Rothiemay married Captain Ramsay Traquair. War " rationing " precluded the Laird of Rothiemay, a chieftain of Clan Forbes, attempting to give the ordinary entertainments, but the tenants were determined the olden gaiety connected with the marriage of a chieftain's daughter should not be abandoned ; and everyone contributed a chicken, some eggs, butter or cheese, from which all enjoyed (probably far more than usual) the clan feast which resulted. I wonder if they realised they were perpetuating in a most practical manner, a most ancient Celtic practice, without which such entertainments would in the Middle Ages have been impossible. The very fact of all contributing is, however, what made the vital family character.

(5) One must recollect that the rebuilding or embellishing of the chief's house was a labour of love, for it is the " Home of the Race " whose turrets were a source of pride to all—emblem of the chief and

---

[1] *Sketches of the Highlanders*, pp. 27, 49.
[2] Brentano, *Old Regime in France*, p. 5.
[3] *Ibid.* p. 133.   [4] *Loyall Dissuasive*, p. 86.
[5] Grant, *Social and Economic Development of Scotland*, p. 503.
[6] Cf. *Sketches of the Highlanders*, p. 92.

clans importance.[1] Here the chief kept " open house " for the members of the clan. Of Lovat's menage at Castle Dounie, Sir Walter Scott records : " His table was filled with Frasers, all of whom he called his cousins, but he took care that the fare with which they were regaled was adapted not to the supposed equality, but to the importance of his guests. The claret did not pass below a particular mark on the table . . . and the clansmen at the extremity of the board were served with single ale. Still, it was drunk at the table of their chief and that made amends for all." With deference to Sir Walter, the principle was practical, and Lovat a most popular chief ; he gave each rank of clansmen the victuals they were used to, and likely to enjoy. None thought any more about it than where, at a large family table, the younger children don't get certain dishes. It was also " the custom of the clan," not any meanness on Lovat's part, *vide* the regime at Castle Grant, sixty years later, in 1803, viz. :

Generally about fifty people sat down to dinner there in the great hall . . . of all ranks. There was not exactly a " below the salt " division so marked on the table, but the company at the lower end was of a very different description from those at the top, and treated accordingly with whisky-punch instead of wine. . . . Sir James Grant was hospitable in the feudal style ; his house open to all ; to each and all he bade a hearty welcome, and he was glad to see his table filled and scrupulous to pay fit attention to every individual present ; but, in spite of much cordiality, it was all somewhat in the king style, the chief condescending to the clan, above the best of whom he considered himself extremely. It was a rough royalty too, plenty, but rude plenty, a footman in the gorgeous green and scarlet livery behind every chair ; but they were mere gillies, lads quite untutored, sons of small tenants, brought in for the occasion, the autumn gathering, and fitted into the suit they best filled.[2]

This description merits some examination ; it emphasises what Stewart of Garth had remarked of Scottish chiefs, and Brentano of French ones, that the character is that of a miniature sovereignty, wherein the chief— as old documents expressed it—" reigned," and, as Burt also found, the chief behaved as if he imagined himself a sovereign. And the principle of the royal power is therefore a family one : " the king is the head of the family." [3] The distinction indeed between our Scottish chieftains and the French (even peasant) *chefs de familles*, is that in " condescending " to the " family " the Highland chiefs were graciously pleasant and not the harsh and taciturn *paterfamilias* of the lesser French families.[4] What Miss Grant of Rothiemurchus, then fresh from England, forgot was that a king, or the chief of a great clan, must behave as such. Remember he is the " Representative " of the community—the community *sees itself in him* and expects him to behave accordingly.[5] By this I do not mean that

[1] *Scots Heraldry*, p. 3 ; *Old Regime in France*, p. 75.
[2] *Memoirs of a Highland Lady*, p. 27.
[3] *Old Regime in France*, p. 145.   [4] Cf. *ibid*. pp. 15–17.
[5] The gathering at Rothiemurchus in 1803 (*Memoirs of a Highland Lady*, p. 23), was only after a long absence, or on a special " arrival " (amongst the great chiefs and *Ard-righ*) and at a chieftain's " home-coming." Whilst thus loving appropriate stateliness " in progress," none more than the Scots recognised the chiefly privacy—as evidence the expeditions of James V., as " the Gudeman o' Ballingeich," and the incognito driving-tours of Queen Victoria and the Prince Consort. The Highlander had no difficulty in equating this informality in private matters with a concurrent daily stateliness of feudal ceremonial.

Highland chiefs continually maintained an extravagant " state " which they could never have afforded [1] and it was just as possible to be " the chieftain " in a tower of three rooms and a store-cellar, like Coxton or Lochbuie (less accommodation than a modern labourer's cottage), or the three-apartment Ha'hoose ; the glamour has lain in it being—great or small—the official seat of " the family " ; the armorial bearings and ceremonial deference to the *Cean-tighe* were the essentials.[2]

The " condescension," be it observed, was not to the remoter clansmen, but likewise to " the best " of his chieftains ; let us remember all were his clan, *i.e.* " children," and that " honour thy father and mother " applied and was literally carried out by all ; whilst, though regally gracious, a Highland chief behaved, and is expected to behave, with patriarchal dignity.[3]

---

[1] The great mansions of Scotland were " opened out " only for a few weeks in autumn, when the clan and neighbours had the leisure before harvest to preen themselves in a pleasant and legitimate peacock glory. The rest of the year the chiefly household, like that of every clansman, was given over to hard work, the treasures and ceremonial garments laid past, though the gracious manners and customs were, of course, maintained, these being essentially similar from palace to cottage.

[2] It will be recollected that the 1st Earl of Strathmore, who so beautified Glamis, started life on a debt-encumbered heritage, with an old bedstead and some pots and pans for his " plenishing," whilst the 21st Baron of Balquhain, a chieftain in Clan Leslie and a count of the empire, finding his resources inadequate to maintain his Castle of Balquhain or Palace of Fetternear, retired with Lady Balquhain and a single maid to the three-roomed House of Tullos until he and the family had reorganised their resources.

[3] There is no place for the degenerate comic father in tribalism or the clan system, nor will you find such in a Highland ploughman's cottage ; a Highland bairn would be ashamed to be the child of " comic " or uncourtly parents.

EXAMPLES OF CRESTS AND BADGES.

| MACKAY. | McNEILL OF COLONSAY. | CLAN CAMERON BADGE. |
| (Cap Badge of Chief Peer.) | (Cap Badge of a Chieftain.) | (Cap Badge of a Clansman —Chief's Crest.) |

All clansmen (even Dukes' brothers) except Chieftains and those with individually matriculated crests as *heads* of houses, and all clanswomen except Chieftainesses wear the " clansman " type of badge.

Heraldic bonnet-badges derive from the 15th century (H. Norris, *Costume*, Vol. 1.) and worn by special followers of Magnates by the 16–17th century. (*Scots Heraldry*, 2nd ed. 180). For economic reasons ordinary clansman wore cockades of their Chief's " colour " (Pl. VI, p. 192) but Highland Regiment practice, and mechanical reproduction, led by the early 19th century to the extension of the old 15th century practice in the chiefs' authorised clan-badges.

The stately "household" of a Speyside clan chief, such as that at Castle Grant, has been described (p. 135) both as regards the chief and his officers, and the *ban-tighearna* and her bevy of twenty-two ladies and maids —of whom the younger were being " educated." Yet, as instancing the corresponding simplicity of life in even the greatest households, some generations back, we find the Ban-Jiarla, of Orkney and Caithness, had a household of seventy-five gentlewomen (dressed in silk and velvet), many of whom were evidently the maids [1] and the castle got burned through one of the seventy-five using a candle to get out a bitch and puppies, which had been born beneath the Princess's straw-mattressed bed. A great mixture of homeliness and state—eighty torches by night, and two hundred riders. This was the chief who had the friendly discussion with MacDonald, when it was proudly explained that " there was nothing but wax burned before MacDonald " in whose Household of the Isles we find a stateliness rivalling in earlier centuries that of seventeenth-century Versailles. In the ceremonious Celtic household, the Lady of the Isles and her daughters, like the queens of France, were attended by those daughters of different houses of the *noblesse* of the Isles who, as Scott records,[2] performed the dressing and undressing as their right.

The ceremonial at Kisimull Castle, under the sway of MacNeil of Barra, has likewise been referred to, with dinner proclaimed by trumpet from the battlements, and, as in most Highland castles, the meals marshalled by hereditary seneschal and marischal, with silver staves. Let us, however, bear ever in mind that all this was the stateliness of the family ceremony which raised a glow of pride in all, impressing on themselves—justifiably so !—(and of course their guests and neighbours) what a fine clan they were ! Beauty, colour, and rhythm, rude though the surroundings might be, cast a happy glow of the fullness of Highland life throughout the whole of this communal, and hereditary, tribal civilisation.

(6) By " support " Burt presumably referred to the cuddiche and conveth already mentioned, but in difficulty, the clan, as many instances record, rallied around their chief or chieftain, maintaining (even after paying their rent to a Government factor) their own forfeited chief, or taking mutual steps to save the *duthus* where misfortune led to foreclosure by creditors. All this emphasises the solidarity of the clan, and the sense that the interests of the whole kin were one.

(7) The honour of the clan was a common property of all, and one of which every member was jealously proud. As one observer in 1640 says, " The meanest fellow among them is as tenacious of his honour as the best nobleman." [3] The aim, as Bishop Leslie expresses it, is to " shawe thameselfes worthie of the hous they are cum off " and by their own efforts " to decore their hous." [4] A breach of trust or disgracing the honour of the clan, led to the culprit being despised or expelled from the clan [5] or

---

[1] Valued, no doubt, for their pedigrees, like Bailie Nicol Jarvie's " Leebie," who was a cousin of the Laird o' Limmerfield (Scott, *Rob Roy*).

[2] He got most of such information from chiefs like Glengarry and MacNab, well versed in the lore of Celtic households.

[3] *Sketches of the Highlanders*, p. xxvi.

[4] Hume Brown, *Scotland Before* 1700, p. 179.

[5] *Sketches of the Highlanders*, pp. 55, 61, 108.

F*

measures concerted for his imprisonment to save the honour of the race.[1] This, indeed, was the cause of so many of the feuds and incursions. The chief and clan were, as a community, responsible for the act of any member, and bound also to protect their members—as Burt notices a sentence farther on.

(8) The distinction here is that the mere ownership of land—as by a bond-holding wadsetter—was not the *nexus*. To be a chieftain—*seigneur-chevetaigne*, " Chiftane of the cuntrie," and *chef de famille* in the sense of " Head of the Fief," *Cap d'Hostal* or *Ceann-Tighe*—one must be more than a " landlord," in fact be a " laird " in the sense of " Head of the Fief " and ruling over a *feudo-familia* (as described on p. 143). Such a group could indeed carry on apart from the land (for a time), and was itself, as we have seen, an incorporeal heritable subject, capable of being the subject of a feudal charter, but the *duthus* was the centre around which the whole clan was built ; its loss a tragedy, as the wailing gathering song of Clan Gregor reminds us.

(9) *Sketches of the Highlanders*, p. 32 ; *Social and Economic Development of Scotland*, pp. 183, 195, 514. When, however, Miss Grant says " the undue power of the nobles prevented the increase of centralised authority, such as took place in England especially during the Tudor period ; it was therefore a fundamental factor in the development, or rather lack of development, of Scotland " (*ibid.* p. 193), one perceives in the light of subsequent " totalitarian " examples that the nation which sang " A ! Fredome is ane nobile thing " realised only too well where " centralised authority " leads ! The *jus familiare* was to a strong and independent race the better alternative.

The seat of the chief, or chieftain, was thus a miniature court in which the whole clan learnt to model itself on the principles of aristocracy, and the liveried gillies behind the chairs at Castle Grant were not " flunkeys " in the English sense, but akin rather to the medieval squires who likewise served at table in the days of chivalry and wore the knightly livery of their masters. Indeed, Rose of Montcoffer, ultimately representer of the old House of Ballivat, commenced his career as such a gillie in the household of Lord Fife. The *ban-tighearna* was surrounded by a bevy of maids of honour, daughters of chieftains, sent to be " educated," all learning and maintaining the standards and ritual of a stately little court. Indeed, as Montaigne observed :

There is nothing more royal than the suite, the subjects, the officers and occupations, and attendance and ceremony of a retired *seigneur* living in his own home.

In Scotland, however, the clan system gave these little courts a broader significance, because they had fully retained the *family*/clan relationship.

At the castle every individual (of the clan) was made welcome, and was treated according to his station, with a degree of courtesy and regard to his feelings unknown in many other countries. This raised the clansman in his

---

[1] *Sketches of the Highlanders*, p. 59 n. Cf. the similar principles of family honour in Brentano's *Old Regime in France*, p. 59. Everyone's duty centred on " preserving the honour of the house."

own estimation and drew closer the ties between him and his chief (and he) was taught to respect himself in the respect which he showed to his chief (and) that he was supporting his own honour in . . . duty to the head of his family.[1]

Hence, says Dalrymple in his *Memoirs*, the Highlanders

carried in the outward expression of their manners the politeness of courts without their vices, and in their bosoms the high point of honour without its follies.

This pride of ancestry, when directed as it was among the people, produced very beneficial effects on their character and conduct. It formed strong attachments, led to the performance of laudable and heroic actions, and enabled the poorest Highlander to support his hardships without a murmur (*ibid.* p. 50).

Burt duly observed that the people " have a pride in their family, as almost everyone is a genealogist," [2] and that his informant said, " the love of our chief, so strongly is it inculcated to us in our infancy " was thereby made a dominant influence. Garth adds that

A Highlander was accustomed to stand before his superior with his bonnet in his (left) hand [3] and his plaid thrown over his left shoulder, with his right arm in full action, adding strength to his expressions, while he preserved perfect command of his mind, words and manners.

Where " superior " means chieftain or chief, this was the proper and reverent, yet " free " and noble deportment.[4] As Garth points out, a most picturesque and " effective " attitude. In the conversation :

If the individual was a man of landed property, or a tacksman, he was addressed by the name of his estate or farm, if otherwise, by his Christian name or patronymic.[5]

Whilst I have, in illustration, had much useful comparison to make with the feudo-tribal equivalents of the " Auld Alliance," in Gaul, in the later history of their social organisation there is the marked

[1] *Sketches of the Highlanders*, p. 51.
[2] E. Burt, Letters, No. 19.
[3] He adds, " if so permitted, which was rarely the case, as few superiors chose to be outdone in politeness by the people " (*Sketches of the Highlanders*, p. 100). This requires explanation. It is accurate as regards " strangers," even of much lesser rank, but when *in loco paternis* the chief was expected to remain covered, as Huntly was at Strathbogie, whilst everyone else uncovered ; so that when the Marquis forgot to uncover at Holyrood he had to explain—and perhaps hardly " improved matters " by the allusion—that where he came from he alone wore his hat !
[4] A servant or an officer on duty keeps his hat on and salutes. A slave or clown, being " unknown," slinks by or does nothing !
[5] *Sketches of the Highlanders*, p. 100. Garth thus indicates the use of the territorial style, where it exists, in priority to a patronymic—as we address the chief of Clan Cameron as " Lochiel." Yet the chief of a clan, or *chef de nom et d'armes*," would be addressed by his simple patronymic, in preference to a non-baronical territorial title, the patriarchal status of these being (as the right to supporters *qua* " chief " denotes) virtually equivalent to barony. Where a chief is also baron, the question of which style is employed depends on his pleasure and the tenor of his registration in the Lyon Register.

distinction that in Scotland, we require no allusion to what in France became noticed as " The Arrogance of the Nobility." [1]

The Scottish chieftains and *daoine-uasail* never forgot that the clan were their kinsmen, and that is precisely why the clan system, and the grandeur of Scottish titles, dignities, and heraldry survived, where so many of those in Europe were to fall in ruins. The clan ideal, so well expressed by Lord Lovat, a good chief though a bad man,[2] is what has made the Highland clan system a subject of such never-failing enthusiasm.

The Highland clan system, which continued unchanged through nearly six centuries, has something inherently grand about it. Primitive it may have been, but it is a primitive organisation which has steadily fulfilled the aspirations of humanity and the system was most admirably adapted to the needs of the communities it controlled. Never in the history of the world has a system of government developed such instances of paternal attachment by the rulers to their subjects, or of devotion of the people to their chiefs.

[1] Brentano, *Old Regime in France*, p. 138.   [2] See p. 219.

VI

The Law of the Clan

THE word " clan " or *clanna* simply means children,[1] *i.e.* the descendants of the actual or mythical ancestor from whom the community
claims descent,[2] in so far as these remain within a tribal group which,
as a social, legal, and economic entity, is treated as a unit. In the
Middle Ages, law and custom did not treat of individuals, but of
groups.[3] The earliest groups were personal and pastoral, but as soon
as a group settled, the territorial influence of the land which it had
occupied affected its structure.[4] Both the group and the land were
called after the chief, who in theory was actually owner of the whole
group and of the land of the group, with absolute power over every
member,[5] though in practice along with a " family council " ; for
hereditary and familial rule (*i.e.* monarchial and clan systems) are
always more " constitutional " and free than the sway of republican
electees of any description. In some forms of tribality, the land
belonged to the tribe as a unit, or to branch families of the tribe as
small communal units, but in Scotland, as Miss Grant points out,[6]
there was never communal, or in that sense " tribal " ownership. The
Celto-Pictish principle emphasised the patriarchal chiefly element in
which the chief was the parent, ruler, landowner, and proprietor on
behalf of his *clanna* or children. This parental aspect is implicit in
the very term *clanna*, which strikes at the root of the modern *canard*
of " elected chiefs." The clan was in fact a " mixture of tribal

---

[1] J. Cameron, *Celtic Law*, p. 79. See also Appendix XXX. regarding the
evidence of Cameron, W. Mackay Mackenzie, and Maclean Watt, to the effect
that " clan and family mean exactly the same thing." Also the Belgian Professor, F. F. Brentano, on the nature of the medieval *familia* and *chef de famille*,
corroborating the Scottish experts.

[2] Skene, *Celtic Scotland*, 1880, III., p. 331 ; J. Cameron, *Celtic Law*, 1937,
p. 79 ; *Macrae* v. *Macrae*, 1909 ; Lyon Court, Typed Report, p. 17.

[3] Misapprehension on this point perplexed witnesses in *Macrae*, p. 85, regarding
the band for the " haill remnant gentles and others of the said name of Ra "
(A. Macrae, *The Clan Macrae*, 1899, p. 341). Such terminology was normal,
e.g. in " Letters of Slaines " (cf. " Barclay of Towie," *Familie of Innes*, 1864,
p. 161).

[4] Sir Henry Maine, *Early History of Institutions*, pp. 64, 72.

[5] Maine and Pollock, *Ancient Law*, p. 211.

[6] *Social and Economic Development of Scotland*, pp. 79, 487.

tradition clustering round the *ipso facto* landholder of the soil "—the chief " fulfilling the functions of the tribal leader." [1]

The clan, however, was actually a tribal organisation in the transitional stage where it is modified by territorial settlement, and before the influence of property in a commercial sense has destroyed the tribal element.[2] The perfect feudalisation, *i.e.* " family organisation," of Scotland provided exactly the legal background which made possible the relatively perfect balance of racial and territorial tradition, in process of steady growth until the fifteenth to sixteenth century, and enabled this not only to develop during several centuries, but also to be projected, with all its grandeur of conception and practical social value, into the modern world. This combination of pride of race with pride of soil comes to form in clanship perhaps the most exalted and powerful relationship of people to soil and chief to people which has ever been evolved as a social system ; one in which " the hail people, noct onlie the nobilitie," take an intense pride in clan grandeur— " Gentility is of all things esteemed the most valuable in the notions of those people." [3] " Clannish ties of relationship ran through every rank of society uniting folk in a homely heart-warm way that the abstract tenets of democracy can never achieve." [4]

The clan, namely, children or family, was thus essentially analogous to the early feudo-familia of ancient Gaul, of which one of the best modern European historians has said :

[1] Miss Grant notices in the *Evolution of the Highlander* the existence of " four distinct and [she thinks] largely conflicting sets of ideas." After comparison with the works of Maine and Pollock and of Brentano, it will be seen they are not so conflicting after all. They are as follows :

(1) " This clan idea, the theory of a social group united by blood ties to the leader or chief." (That is the " family " idea.)

(2) " There was a strongly felt right to the possession of the land that was occupied. This may have been dimly connected with some very ancient tribal ideas." (Possession was the fundamental basis of title to land, as explained by Grotius, and the " tribal ideas " are those connected with the occupying of the land by the issue of the eponymus.)

(3) " There were traditions of the Gaelic laws with regard to landholding, partly derived from Ireland, partly perhaps from the laws of Scotland of the period before Malcolm Canmore. One finds, for instance, the tanister (*i.e.* chosen) successor." (These, we see, were the beginnings of organised rules of succession and tanistry was directly related to the primitive patriarchal rule.)

(4) " The conventional feudal ideas of primogeniture, landholding of the king, and charter rights." (This, we shall see, was simply the formalised organisation of all the foregoing and the building up out of the three earlier ideas of the " tribal state " under a patriarchal high-king, fulfilling as " Father of his People " the functions of tribal sovereignty. As Retif de la Bretonne so well expressed it, " The State is a large family, composed of all the private families, and the prince is the father of all the fathers." Our own Sir George Mackenzie said the same thing at more length. See p. 168.)

[2] Maine, *Early History of Institutions*, pp. 72, 85, 96, 112, 120.

[3] E. Burt, Letters, No. 22.

[4] I. F. Grant, *In the Tracks of Montrose*, p. 208 ; E. Crawford, *Lives of the Lindsays*, p. 117.

First comes family, or, to speak more exactly, feudalism, for in defining as accurately as possible the real meaning of this word, and giving to it its historical sense, we should call it the development, the extension of the family.[1]

The enlarged family, which embraced the younger sons and their children, their cousins, the servants, and workmen attached to the house, took the name of *mesne* from the Latin *mansionata* or house. The *mesne* comprised the family ; the relations assembled round the head of the principal branch, the servants, and all of those living round, maintained for the service of the house and supported by it. At the head of the *mesne* was the Seigneur, invested with a patronal and paternal character. The members of this large family were united like a corporation.[2] They gave each other mutual assistance. They possessed their tribunal, the tribunal of the Seigneur, that is, of the head of the family. They had their own customs, manners, and traditions, and they had their standard and their battle-cry. They had their banner on its staff with gilded point. . . . To bring honour or advantage to the family is the sole ruling sentiment.[3] The fief made its appearance in the eleventh century, in the form of a greatly enlarged family over which the father was suzerain, and so in order to designate the entire agglomeration of all persons united under the governance of a feudal chief, contemporary writers made use of the word familia. The baron at the head of the fief was in reality the *chef de famille*.[4]

The *mesnie* sprang from the family, the fief from the *mesnie*, the smaller fiefs produced the large fiefs, and from the latter the royal power took its rise, carrying to the highest point in a great nation, the character and traditions of one large family.

In Scotland, similarly, this is the history of the *Ard-righ*, King of Scots, rising above the *morairs* and the barons, chieftains of countries, and the lesser *tighearn*. The feudo-clannish Scottish nation was one great social pyramid based on a concept of family blood relationship, or again, to quote Brentano, " the State is a large family composed of all the private families, and the principal is the ' father of all the fathers '."[5] This has been described as the truest definition of the medieval French monarchy and it is likewise the precise definition of the *Ard-righ Albainn* and the tribal sovereignty. It was a fact recognised in Scotland over a century ago, when George IV. was toasted in 1822 as " Chief of Chiefs—The King."[6] These descriptions are, of course, equally applicable to the patriarchal organisation of the clan-family upon the *duthus* in Scotland, namely, the " chieftain of the country," expressly described in the Statute 1592 cap. 59 sec. 11.[7]

---

[1] F. Brentano, *Old Regime in France*, p. 7.
[2] Cf. Maine, *Ancient Law*, 1930, pp. 205, 211, likening the family to a corporation.
[3] *Ibid.* p. 5 ; cf. *Scots Heraldry*, p. 67.
[4] *Old Regime in France*, p. 6 ; cf. Craig, *Jus Feudale*, I., 8, 2 expressing the view that our Scottish barons were originally *capitani tribuum*.
[5] *Ibid.* p. 11.
[6] *Account of the Royal Visit of 1822*, p. 242.　　　　'A.P.S. III. 464.

Another statute of five years later, for the enforcement of the foregoing one, further describes the clan organisation as comprehending

Chiftanis and chieffis of all clannis and the principallis of the brancheis [1] of the saidis clannis duelland in the hielands or bordouris upon the landis of divers landislordis and depending upoun the directionis of the saidis capitanis, chieffis and chiftanis be pretence [2] of blude or place of thare duelling.[3]

This makes it clear that the clan, like the French feudo-familia, might have a territorial nexus, and comprehended the " native men " so often mentioned in the old Scots feudal charters, and illustrates the legal recognition for the process of building up a clan on acquired territory, described by Miss Grant.[4]

Like other tribal bodies, a clan was capable of recruitment by adoption,[5] which took place with elaborate ceremonial,[6] and which is also a recognised feature of heraldic law [7] and of the nobiliary and feudal law on the Continent, though not found in the Common Law of Scotland. This has led to a confusion of ideas, when the clan has come before the courts of Scotland, whose jurisprudence is so largely established upon Lord Stair that our older native jurisprudence is " discarded or ignored." [8] He nevertheless clearly lays down the principle and order of succession to our old Scottish dignities, and observes that, with us, heirs male only take where the grant or investiture specially so provides.[9] Sir George Mackenzie of Rosehaugh, a native Highlander, who treated of our Laws of Arms and precedence, is necessarily a useful guide [10] in any points which our more conventional jurists have ignored or touched with hesitation. During the past century the clan as an institution has been thrice discussed in the Court of Session, where in 1862 [11] Lord Ardmillan in the Outer House delivered himself of a peroration upon clanship and feudalism,[12] disfigured by

[1] Contrary to Lord Mackay's ideas the term " branch " is well known in heraldry and was actually used in the Court of Session in regard to the competing families of Cunningham Lamburgton (11 Dunlop 1139), cf. pp. 1143–4–6 ; Lord Jeffrey, pp. 1151–3; and as elements of a social unit denoted by the heraldic differencing.

[2] This includes not merely actual affiliation, but descent claimed, viz. " indeterminate cadets."

[3] A.P.S. IV. 40.   [4] Social and Economic Development of Scotland, p. 503.

[5] Sir Henry Maine and Sir Frederick Pollock, Ancient Law, p. 146 ; Sir Henry Maine, Early History of Institutions, p. 69 ; J. Cameron, Celtic Law, p. 220.

[6] Black Book of Taymouth, p. 182.

[7] Nisbet, System of Heraldry, II., iii., p. 58, and Lord Aitchison, 1941 S.C. 887.

[8] Sources and Literature of the Law of Scotland, p. 77 ; per Rt. Hon. T. M. Cooper, K.C.   [9] Stair, III., 5, 8 ; III., 5, 11.

[10] It has indeed been laid down, per Lord Aitchison, that he is authoritative, save, of course, when, as in some transient political writings, he is barely consistent with his impartial legal treatises or where an opinion expressed has been superseded by subsequent legislation.   [11] MacGillivray v. Souter, 25 Dunlop 772.

[12] He did realise and state two facts : (a) that clanship is inextricably bound up with feudalism, (b) that clans are corporations—just like the " noble family " (cf. Maine, Ancient Law, p. 205, and Erskine's juristic allusion to " the family seal of arms," Principles of the Law of Scotland, V., 8, 18).

really glaring errors in elementary legal history. He concluded that " clans are not corporations which law sustains, nor societies which law recognises or acknowledges." [1] The Inner House, Lord Colonsay presiding, by no means endorsed this rash assumption that clanship was illegal and confined themselves to holding that they did not find any such distinct statement of any practical qualification for membership of the clan as to exclude the heir-at-law. They were thus cautious, and far less dogmatic than the Lord Ordinary had been. Lord Curriehill observed :

" It is perfectly competent to make it a condition that an heir be a member of a known and legal association, *e.g.* the Highland Society, and if the Clan Chattan were a body of that kind I am not prepared to say that it might not be a lawful condition. Two and a half centuries ago, bodies under the denomination of clans were distinctly recognised by the legislature," and he adds, after referring to the Clan Acts, that " these changes are such as made the continued subsistence of the clan scarcely consistent with law." " I do not say that they are expressly abolished, but that subsequent legislation was of a kind with which the existence of the clans was inconsistent."

His Lordship, it appears, formed the erroneous impression that clanship was of a purely " military character." Lord Deas merely considered the condition insufficiently defined :

I am still left in the dark as to what constitutes membership of the clan. Is it regulated by law ? If so, by what law ? By charter or statute ? If so, what charter or what statute ? By agreement ? If so, by what deed ? By immemorial custom ? and if so, what is the precise nature and effect of the custom alleged ?

Accordingly, the Court held that nothing had been shown to overrule the ordinary descent of heritage in a claim to an estate restricted to " members of the Clan Chattan." Unfortunately, neither in *MacGillivray* v. *Souter* nor in the preliminary pleas in *Maclean of Ardgour* v. *Maclean* (1937) [2] did the Court consider it requisite to order a proof [3]

---

[1] For an acid comment on this by the late Sheriff Macphail, see Typed Report *Macrae* v. *Macrae*, Lyon Court, 1909, p. 352.

[2] 1938 S.L.T. 49. The *Ardgour* petition (1936) did not raise the subject of " clans " directly ; it dealt with the " stem family." *Clan* was introduced, and a judgement pronounced on " chieftain " solely on the assumption that (*a*) the French word " chieftain " necessarily related to " clans," whereas it may apply to any territorial family ; (*b*) the term " branch " referred to " clans," whereas it is equally applicable to families (11 Dunlop 1139). The writer, moreover, is perfectly clear (*infra*) what chiefs and chieftains are, but (*re* S.L.T. 65) can find no legal or definable character " *Highland* chief." Any chief or chieftain anywhere is just a chief or chieftain (*i.e.* representer) of the group concerned. If Highland domicile were the criterion, many Sassenachs would be " Highland chiefs," and, if ancestry, what ancestry ? Jane Porter's term " Scottish chiefs " seems the only " quality " cognisable in Scottish law and the Law of Arms in Scotland. [3] Lord Mackay advised *proof before answer* (1941 S.C., p. 653).

on the nature of a clan [1] and its chiefship, before pronouncing upon these subjects. In the latter case, however, the Court of Session made the important advance (the House of Lords had gone much further in 1921) of conceding what amounts to—or ultimately involves—an answer to Lord Deas's question : " Is it regulated by law ? If so, by what law ? " It was conceded that at any rate the chiefship of a clan is cognisable in " law " for one purpose, a right to armorial supporters.[2] Had they stopped to ask Lord Deas's question, " What law ? " the only answer must have been, " a right which, of course, is regulated by the Law of Arms," [3] which is the law governing " honourable (*i.e.* noble) communities "—which are " distinguished " by arms [4] as both Nisbet [5] and Mackenzie [6] lay down that clans are.

By what charter or statute ? Of old by Crown Charters *quod sit capitani* of sundry clans [7] and later under statues 1592 c. 125 and 1672 c. 47, whereby Lyon is required to give out and difference arms for distinguishing " stok and linage," " chief," and " cadet " of families—clan and family being now recognised as " exactly the same " [8] and the chief or representative of the family identical with the head of the clan.[9]

By what deed ? The armorial confirmation establishing the arms of the head of the clan, thus constituting the banner and standard to be followed, and the badge to be worn by the clansmen of the chief, as members of a noble incorporation.

What is the precise nature and effect of the custom alleged ? The Law and Custom of Arms ; the code governing the distinguishing marks and conduct of noble families in nobiliary matters and assemblies, that is, in the family and amongst other noble families.

---

[1] In *MacGillivray* v. *Souter* a remit for report on this was recalled, much to the regret of historians.

[2] Prior to the nineteenth century supporters, however, were never assigned to, or referred to, as of right pertaining to chiefs of clans as such. Nisbet and Mackenzie both say " chief of families," and it is *qua* chiefs of " families " and " names " that supporters were awarded—as Stevenson points out, *Heraldry in Scotland*, p. 323. Indeed, the term " clan " does not even occur on the page cited as authority at S.L.T. 67 (viz. Stevenson, *Heraldry in Scotland*, pp. 87–89), and the Macnaughton award, 1819 (Lyon Register, II., p. 172), seems the earliest example. The reason is that the medieval attitude was, to paraphrase a well-known phrase, " Show me the chief of the stem family, and I will show you the chief of the clan "—or " name."

[3] This right to supporters being a " dignity " (1938 S.L.T. 67, 70) such right is excluded from the jurisdiction of the Court of Session (*Lauderdale* v. *Scrymgeour Wedderburn*, 1910 S.C. (H.L.) 44).

[4] Nisbet, *System of Heraldry*, I., pp. 283, 424, II., iv., pp. 22, 24.

[5] *Ibid.*

[6] Mackenzie, *Works*, II., pp. 614 and 633.

[7] R.M.S., I., App. ii., 912–914, 982.

[8] Evidence of Lachlan Maclean Watt in *Maclean of Ardgour* v. *Maclean*, 1938, see Appendix XXX.

[9] Mackenzie, *Works*, II., p. 618.

Anyhow the admission in both House of Lords and Court of Session, that clanship is cognisable in law is a gratifying advance which recognises clanship as definitely within the scope of *law*, supersedes Lord Ardmillan's rash generalities in *MacGillivray* v. *Souter*, and obviously involves a closer examination than has hitherto been made of the relations of clanship to heraldry and the Laws of Arms.[1] Since their lordships agreed that a " right " exists—moreover, a heritable right (for supporters are heritable)—it is an axiom of law that such right must be justiciable somewhere, and the great jurist, Lord Dunedin, who chanced to be present to hear the Ardgour judgement of 16th July 1937, immediately afterwards pointed out that their lordships' other *obiter* opinions—that clan chiefship was not determinable in a court of law—must from the very terms of their own opinion necessarily be wrong. The " right " being one existent only in " the law of arms," must moreover necessarily be justiciable in a court of the " law of arms." Even apart from the fact that chiefship of a clan, (like the rights of junior heirs-portioners) was not *sub judice*, any opinions about it being mere *obiter dicta*, the 1937 judgement proved (as Lord Dunedin had indicated) a mistake, was flatly contradicted by the evidence in the proof, and had in 1941 to be quietly departed from (*infra*). As in 1863, so in *Maclean of Ardgour* v. *Maclean*, 1937 the Court had not allowed itself opportunity to be informed by proof of such points as that the clan as a community was expressly recognised by the Imperial Parliament in 1775[2] when the proscription of the surname " Macgregor " was rescinded in favour of members of the Clan Gregor : " so far as respects the clan Gregour or MacGregors shall be and stand repealed " are the actual words of the statute—thus disposing of Lord Curriehill's difficulty. A " clan," it will be observed, is dealt with as a well-recognised entity ; and the word clan is thus, even in modern Imperial Law, clearly a *nomen juris*. Here, moreover, as in the case of " supporters," the subject-matter (Name) is one falling within the Law of Arms and jurisdiction of the Lord Lyon.[3] The clan and chief are thus subjects necessarily cognisable in Lyon Court and involving rights under the branch of Nobiliary Law (*i.e.* the law of dignities and insignia) denominated the " Law of Arms," which is excluded from ordinary courts of law and cognisable

---

[1] Lord Ardmillan's *dicta* were disposed of by the *Dunstaffnage* case : *Argyll* v. *Campbell*, 1912 S.C. 458. This important case settled that the " Clan Acts " did no so completely destroy non-military feudo-Celtic institutions as had been supposed, and shows how feudalism kept alive the ancient offices, whilst the other " chiefship " and armorial cases are necessarily *res noviter* further modifying *MacGillivray* v. *Souter*. Many of the statements in this chapter are, moreover, *res noviter*, bearing upon the recent *dicta* in *Maclean of Ardgour* v. *Maclean*.

[2] 15 George III. cap. 29, *Statutes at Large*, XII., 299.

[3] *Forlong*, 1880, 7 Rettie 910. In view of the terms of the statute, if anyone applies to Lyon for official recognition of assumption of the name Macgregor, obviously Lyon must require proof that the petitioner is a member of the Clan Gregor.

only in Courts of Chivalry.[1] Lord Mackay's surmise proves in fact well founded :

(Supposing the Clan and Disarming Acts) " had as it were eliminated clanship from ordinary civil or statutory law, I am unable to think that can be true of the Law of Honours." [2]

What the Division overlooked in 1937 was that the Lyon Court, unlike our other courts, is a Court of Chivalry, which exists precisely for trying these matters cognisable " by the Law of Arms," and out-with the jurisdiction of other Courts.[3] If this were not so, there would be no point in the existence of Lyon Court.

The next year the evidence of the expert witnesses on both sides established that the clan and the family are exactly the same thing, and consequently that Lyon having been entitled to consider and determine the history, status, and chiefship of the " noble and armigerous family," is necessarily upon the evidence thereby obliged, actually or inferentially, to find and determine the chiefship of the clan. On this ground Lord Lyon Grant, in order to avoid contravening the Division's judgement of 1937 and to extricate himself from a difficulty, declined to declare anyone chief of the family in question, but on the further appeal the Lord Justice-Clerk laid down that there was nothing to prevent Lyon from affirming the successful petitioner to be Representer of the Family, the Court directing him to " proceed as accords." [4] There was nothing further for Lyon to do, except to make this affirmation, and on this point Sir George Mackenzie had laid down the legal synonymity : " The chief, for so we call the representative of the family, and in the Irish (Gaelic with us) the representative of the family is called the chief of the clan." So the result agreed with this great institutionalist whose writings were declared authoritative, the Lord Lyon's historic jurisdiction that has come down from Celtic times was effectually reaffirmed, and some of the further difficulties raised in *MacGillivray* v. *Souter* are accordingly dissipated ; for if clans did not appear to the court in 1862 as " corporations which the law recognised," families—at all events noble and armigerous families—are definitely corporations which the law does recognise ; for the family in this continuing sense of a community with stem, branches, and individual members, and cognisable in the Laws of Honour, e.g. 1672 cap. 47, is, and through its Representative (called " Chief "), the subject of another of our great Scottish jurist's definitions, and regarding

[1] 1937 S.L.T. 156 ; *Herald and Genealogist,* II., 13 (*Grey* v. *Hastings*) ; *Repor on title of " Rt. Hon."* of *Lord Provost of Edinburgh* (1938) ; *Lawson,* 1863, Lyon Register, VI., p. 71, and judgement.

[2] *Maclean of Ardgour* v. *Maclean,* 1938 S.L.T. 65. On this assumption the subject is cognisable in Lyon Court, but not in the Court of Session, since it would be matter not capable (per Lord Aitchison) of being brought to appeal before " us " (Court of Session) " as a question of (civil) law."

[3] W. Cruise, *On Dignities,* p. 251 ; A. C. Fox-Davies, *Right to Bear Arms,* p. 147.

[4] 1941 S.C. 714.

the very " family seal of arms," which, along with the furnishings of the hall and the cushion of the seat in church, passes by the Common Law of Succession, *i.e.* the law of Malcolm MacKenneth, to the senior heir of line.[1] The family seal of arms is thus the seal of the community incorporated by Lyon's Letters Patent, and descendable, like the banner, as an indivisible piece of the machinery of administration to the successive " Representers of the family," and of the eponymus to whom the family, as an heritable subject, belonged. This is " the family as an incorporeal fatherland " ; [2] as an incorporeal subject capable of conveyance by Crown Charter under the Great Seal [3] and ultimately as a subject passing down to and through an heretrix as officially declared, 10th September 1672, in Lord Lyon Erskine's Clan Chattan Declaration,[4] for, be it observed, if a person can be heir or heretrix of a clan, the clan itself is thereby recognised as an incorporeal heritable subject, just like Brentano's early Gaulish family,[5] and that is in all its aspects treated of, and provided for, in the Laws of Arms.

" Arms," says Nisbet, " are hereditary marks of honour regularly composed of certain tinctures and figures granted or authorised by sovereigns for distinguishing, differencing, and illustrating persons, families, and communities," and the first of their uses is the distinction of the nobility.[6]

" The family," in its wider and heraldic sense, is a statutory [7] group including all persons actually affiliated, or even adopted, to a central " stem " deriving from the founder of the race. In its broader sense, however, the " Law of Arms " includes, as

Effigy of Maclean of Ross of Mull, showing *leine croich*, or saffron shirt ; early use by " Highland chieftain " of an armorial shield (*Soc. of Antiq. of Scot.*).

---

[1] Erskine, *Principles of the Law of Scotland*, III., 8, 18.

[2] F. Brentano, *Old Regime in France*, p. 4.

[3] Cf. Kenkynol charter and the charters of clan chiefship in the fourteenth century (R.M.S., I., No. 509, and Appendix I., Nos. 912, 914, 982).

[4] See page 151 *infra*.

[5] Although the subject of conveyance for " grave and weighty considerations," we find, consistently with the " laws of honour," that unlike ancient Rome, we admit no *familiæ emptor*.

[6] Nisbet, *System of Heraldry*, II., pp. 1 and 2.   [7] 1672 cap. 47, A.P.S. VIII. 95.

we have seen, the whole group of vassals, tenants, servants, and all those living around, and maintained for, the house.[1] It is, moreover, synonymous with the two groups of such wide interest and recognised features of Scottish heraldic law, the Clan and the Name, which are grouped in medieval Scottish statute law.[2] Both these groups consist of aggregates of families,[3] comprising not only determinate but also indeterminate or presumed cadet branches of the central stem.[4] In the Lowlands and on the Continent, such a group is distinguished by all its members bearing the same basic surname. In the Highlands, only the chief and his immediate family used the surname at all. Most names were genealogical strings, such as " Alister MacIan MacSheumas MacIan Beg." Accordingly, where the members of the group were not bearers of the same name, the community was denominated a " clan."

Now, all *noblesse* or hereditary gentility flows—in legal theory at any rate—from the Sovereign,[5] or *Ard-righ*,[6] the tribal " Father of all the Fathers " (*i.e.* chiefly patriarchs) from whom, as the " Fountain of Honour," all rank and titular distinctions flow, and even under feudalism they flow—at least indirectly—from the Sovereign as ultimate superior, though some titles are held *in vavasoria* of subject-superiors.[7] Only by the sovereign directly or, since the fifteenth century, in titles and honours of *nobilitas minor* (*i.e.* gentility) by H.M. Commissioner—His King of Arms, to whom this branch of the Royal prerogative is delegated,[8] can any person be confirmed in, elevated to, or received into the *noblesse* as an order in the public life of the realm.[9]

Early grants or confirmations of arms expressly state that the patentee and his descendants (or other specified group) are received into, and henceforth to be " taken and numbered amongst the ancient

[1] Brentano, *Old Regime in France*, pp. 5, 73.

[2] 1594, cap 37, A.P.S. IV. 71

[3] For the various modified implications of the flexible term " family," see Innes of Learney, *Laws of Succession in Ensigns Armorial*, pp. 32–35.

[4] J. H. Stevenson, *Heraldry in Scotland*, p. 408.

[5] Nisbet, *System of Heraldry*, I., p. 9 ; J. H. Stevenson, *Heraldry in Scotland*, XII., n. 1 ; A. C. Fox-Davies, *Heraldry Explained*, 1907, pp. 7 and 8 ; *Right to Bear Arms*, 1900, pp. 26–50 ; *Art of Heraldry*, 1905, p. 10.

[6] In early times it could flow from provincial *Righ* or *Mormaers* and from the Counts Palatine—*e.g.* Chester—in England.

[7] J. R. N. Macphail, *Highland Papers*, II., p. 241 ; W. C. Dickinson, *Court Book of the Barony of Carnwath*, 1937, p. xvi.

[8] *Macdonnell* v. *Macdonald*, 4 Shaw 371, per Lord Robertson ; *Heraldry in Scotland*, p. 72. Where a chief or chieftain, in exercise of the *jus familiare*, adopts someone into his clan, branch, or family by a deed or " name and arms clause " this is completed by confirmation by the *Ard-righ* through Lyon.

[9] J. W. Woodward, *Heraldry, British and Foreign*, pp. 6–12 ; *Privy Council*, 2nd series, III., p. 156.

nobles " of the realm,[1] and that the arms are " tokens of this nobility." [2]

In Scotland amongst the " communities " so taken cognisance of are not only definitely affiliated families, but the broader groups with unaffiliated branches of the Clans and Names. This is the import of the " Clan Chattan Declaration," 10th September 1672,[3] wherein Lord Lyon Sir Charles Erskine of Cambo declares that the Clan Chattan comprehends Macphersons, MacGillivrays, Farquharsons, McQuins, Macphails, MacBains, and others :

And that I have given, and will give, none of these families any arms, but as cadets of the Laird of Mackintosh's family, whose predecessor married the heretrix of the Clan Chattan.[4]

The 1672 Declaration was immediately sent north for the information of all concerned,[5] and was acted upon in future transactions before Lord Lyon Brodie.[6] The fact impressed is that the Crown, through Lyon, had received these families as all forming a " community," viz. the " Clan Chattan," which community was to be distinguished in the military, civil, and social life of the realm by the award of certain basic insignia [7] differenced according to the circumstances of each case. Perhaps the most salient phrase in Lyon's 1672 Declaration is " Heretrix of Clan Chattan," for it officially defines the clan as a heritable subject, and thus in one word sweeps away the whole idea of " elected chiefs." The clan, or noble family, is thus officially an incorporeal heritable subject, and as we see from the charters of David II, one capable of being the subject of feudal grant and re-settlement. Such groups, officially recognised by the Crown, are denominated " honourable communities," [8] and the specified families forming the branches of the honourable community are each armorially

---

[1] Webbe, 1550, *Miscellanea Genealogica et Heraldica*, 3rd series, II., p. 156. Statute 1592 cap. 125 refers to arms as for distinguishing those of " noble stok and linage," *i.e.* chiefs and cadets of noble communities.

[2] Gerard Legh, *Accidens of Armory*, 1576, f. 16 ; A. C. Fox-Davies, *Right to Bear Arms*, 1900, p. 50 ; *Juridical Review*, September 1940, pp. 193–196, 206, 218.

[3] A. M. Mackintosh, *The Mackintoshes and Clan Chattan*, p. 32.

[4] Such certificates were not merely *pro bona memoria*, but are directed to " all nobles and persons competent by whatever eminence and authority, to take cognisance of titles " (*Cumming*, Register of Genealogies, I., p. 1), and anyone who ignores them thereby stamps himself as ignoble.

[5] Macfarlane's *Genealogical Collections*, Scottish History Society Edition, I., p. 393.

[6] C. Fraser Mackintosh, *Dunauchtan*, p. 29.

[7] Cf. the " armigerous name " basis of arms design perceived by Lord Sands (1920 S.C. 802).

[8] " Honourable House of Mowbray " (R. R. Stoddart, *Scottish Arms*, II., p. 185) ; " Honourable Family of Clan Chattan," 1672 (*supra*) ; " Honourable Clan MacBrayne," 1770 (Lyon Register, I., p. 130) ; " Honourable Clan M'Sween," 1773 (*ibid.* I., p. 489) ; " Honourable House of Dick-Cunningham," 1850 (*ibid.* V., p. 16).

treated upon their merits as regards their own branch-members, *i.e.* the " absolute arms " of the branch-chiefs are cadet arms *quoad* the chief of the ruling family of the whole clan. Thus the family of Mac-Bean is (conform to the Declaration) recorded in 1672 as " a branch of Clan Chattan,"[1] whilst the Clan MacBrayne is itself recorded as a branch of the great Irish tribe of O'Brien, and the name of Maxwell as of the Clan MacSween. How far these descents are historically or scientifically true is not the question.[2] Constitutionally the position is that the Crown, in exercise of its prerogative, was pleased, through Lyon, to receive them as such, and to devise differences, and award armorial bearings on that basis. So much is this the case, that I recollect noticing a case where the Lyon Depute even declined, as contrary to Scottish armorial practice, to give a member of an " armigerous name " arms which would not infer dependency on the chief whose name he bears.[3]

The " armorial significance " of the clan as a community is referred to by Mackenzie, Nisbet, and Seton.[4] A clan, whether " Highland " or other, can thus be defined in the law of Scotland, and in particular in the Law of Arms in Scotland,[5] in these terms :

A clan is a social group consisting of an aggregate of distinct erected families[6] actually descended, or accepting themselves as descendants of a common ancestor, and which group has been received by the Sovereign through his supreme Officer of Honour, the Lord Lyon[7] as an honourable community, with its " family seal of arms " held by its chief or Representative,[8] whereof all the members, on establishing right to, or receiving fresh grants of, personal hereditary nobility, will be awarded arms as determinate or indeterminate cadets,

---

[1] Lyon Register, I., p. 359.

[2] Just as one may question how far old women were really guilty of witchcraft ; but in 1672 the sorcery and the pedigrees were both subjects of " conclusive " legal decision !

[3] An *obiter dictum* regarding this in *Maclean of Ardgour* v. *Maclean*, 1938 S.L.T. 62, misapprehending this heraldic aspect of the point, suggested that Lyon's undertaking " as regards the future, went beyond any legitimate legal act." Its nature, however, is really that of a contract between the Crown and the clan, that the heraldic authority would not countenance what we may call the " armorial blackleg " who seeks to obtain arms inconsistent with his place or membership in the clan community under Scottish heraldic law.

[4] Mackenzie, *Works*, II., p. 614 ; XII., p. 618, line 13 ; Nisbet, *System of Heraldry*, 1722, I., pp. 268 and 425 ; Seton, *Law and Practice of Heraldry*, p. 9.

[5] The Law of Arms is regarded as really in the nature of an international law, and in early times was identical in France, England, and Scotland (*Heraldry in Scotland*, p. 131), but in detail is modified by the customs of each realm (Sir John Ferne, *Glorie of Generositie*, 1586, p. 297).

[6] Nisbet, *System of Heraldry*, II., iii., pp. 15, 17. It also includes the *sencliathe* native men, and the tenants and servants forming the following (*Loyall Dissuasive*, p. 56 n. 1 ; *Privy Council*, 3rd series, III., p. 75).

[7] *Ibid.* II., iv., p. 172.

[8] Erskine, *Principles of the Law of Scotland*, V., 8, 18.

both as may be of the chief family of the clan.[1] If such community comprehends only families of one surname, *i.e.* that of the chief family, then the community is or may be termed a " Name."

It will be observed I adopt the evolutionary theory of clanship, which in a primitive form must have been inherent in Pictish Alba as well as in Dalriada.[2] Clanship was not " ignored " in the twelfth to thirteenth centuries. Rather was it in process of organised development under the feudal system, by the machinery of which it was to be strengthened and preserved in Scotland, instead of withering as in other lands. It has been suggested that " clans " organised, as we understand the term, first appear in the fifteenth century. That is indeed a period at which most of our national organisations become more definite and apparent, and with these the clan, for a patriarchalism in the picturesque but effective form of feudalism was by then leavening in its more organised mould. It is, however, significant, and has been entirely overlooked, that it is just prior to this period (*i.e.* in the later fourteenth century) that we find not one but a batch of Royal Charters assuming that the clan—like the noble family—is a community whose representership or chiefship was held not by election but directly of, and under, the Crown [3] as a heritable fief and with an heritable destination.[4]

Such a group may, and in most cases would, have existed, anterior to the recognition or confirmation by the *Ard-righ*,[5] but the constitutional theory is that, even assuming prior noble existence, confirmation by, or on behalf of, the *Ard-righ* as the Fountain of Honour is indispensable to affirm the position of the community as an " honourable clan " in place of a mere gang of *ignobiles* or " lawless limmaris." How many clan communities were officially recognised through their representatives, the loss of the ancient *Liber Insigniorum* [6] prevents our knowing, but although no medieval administration was exhaustive

---

[1] If the claim is to be a branch of a " branch family " there will be double or treble differencing as the case requires.

[2] Cf. I. F. Grant, *Social and Economic Development of Scotland*, pp. 51–52.

[3] Great Seal, I., App. II., Nos. 912–914 and 982. The position of such a community could hardly be better expressed than in the nomination by R. A. Macneil of Barra, 9th October 1913 : " His Britannic Majesty, the Superior of the Chief and the Clan of Macneil." This is entirely consistent with the fourteenth-century charters of chiefship, and the theory of " honours."

[4] Great Seal, II., p. 509, Kenkynol of Carrick ; see *Notes and Queries*, 15th August 1943, pp. 92 and 96 *et seq.*, regarding chiefship in relation to " war leadership " (*ceann cath*).

[5] The groups were then allodial and the chiefs held their *duthus* " under God," but even so, the family organisation was present and the *Ri* or provincial *Morair* was the local *Pater Patriae* (cf. " Duncan, by the Grace of God, Earl of Fife," *Scots Peerage*, IV., p. 6). The process of feudal organisation involved the *Ard-righ* inducing these allodial chiefs to accept feudal charters of their *duthus*, which " cuntries " never belonged to the Crown at all (*Juridical Review*, September 1940, p. 196 ; Sir A. Agnew, *Hereditary Sheriffs of Galloway*, p. 51 ; Hume Brown, *History of Scotland*, I., p. 71). No more does *Udal* land in the Orkneys to-day.

[6] Great Seal, V., p. 262. Scottish armorial patents as early as 1503 are known.

or perfect, the military importance of the clans and their leaders must have rendered the usual record of their titles and insignia [1] a necessary as well as a normal branch of the matters which were made of record under the Law of Arms.

THE CHIEF

The clan being a community cognisable in the Law of Arms, and recognised by the Imperial Parliament,[2] it is next necessary to define its chief. As already indicated, all tribal groups and all subdivisions of these are conceived, by the men who compose them, as descended from a single male ancestor,[3] or sometimes a matriarch.[4] Not only was the tribe or sept named after this eponymus, but the territory it occupied derived from him the name by which it was most commonly known.[5] Upon the death of the eponymus, one of his descendants became the " representer " of him and of the group which was " his," *i.e.* within his patriarchal *potestas*. The successive chiefs were the judges,[6] public officers, and representers of the group,[7] and the very name king or *könig* means the head of the kindred,[8] and a chief is in old documents described as " reigning." [9] Chief succeeds chief in his hereditary honours, says Sir George Mackenzie, " as they would succeed to a crown," [10] whilst Burt observed that a chief " imagines himself to be a sovereign prince " [11]—an assumption for which we see there is the soundest historical authority. Stewart of Garth describes chiefships very correctly as little sovereignties.[12] This chief or primitive " king " formed the centre and sacred embodiment of the race, *i.e.* the supreme individual of the race giving to its race-ideal the coherence and endurance of personality.[13] Whilst the chief's influence was personal and tribal,[14] *i.e.* as the living embodiment of the eponymus,

[1] Nisbet, *System of Heraldry*, II., iv., p. 172.
[2] Clan Gregor Act, 15 Geo. III. cap. 29.
[3] Sir H. S .Maine, *Early History of Institutions* (1875), p. 78.
[4] R. A. M. Macalister, *Ireland in pre-Celtic Times*, p. 242.
[5] *Scottish Notes and Queries*, 15th August 1942, p. 96 and *op. cit.* ; cf. such titles as " Laird of Mackintosh," " Laird of Macfarlane " (A.P.S. and P.C. Register). " Laird " is indeed the colloquial Scots style for chiefs and chieftains.
[6] *Celtic Scotland*, III., p. 145 ; D. Stewart, *Sketches of the Highlanders*, 2nd edition, p. 49.
[7] Maine and Pollock, *Ancient Law* (1930), p. 258.
[8] *Scotland under her Early Kings*, p. 27 ; Maine and Pollock, *Ancient Law*, p. 23.
[9] *Old Regime in France*, pp. 4,14.
[10] Mackenzie, *Works*, II. ,p. 615. As instancing the continuance of the ancient and authoritative pronouncement of the Lord Advocate, we find, in 1938, an old Highlander answering in cross-examination " What is the Crown more than an estate ? " (*Maclean of Ardgour Evidence*, p. 296).
[11] E. Burt, Letters, No. 22, 1876 edition, p. 167.
[12] *Sketches of the Highlanders*, 1825, p. 32.
[13] A. E. A. Joliffe, *Constitutional History of Mediæval England*, *s.v.* " Tribal Kingship," pp. 42, 47.
[14] *Sources and Literature of the Law in Scotland*, p. 427.

he owned an official estate or *earbsa* which descended only along with the chiefly office,[1] in order that the race shall have its retirance [2] to which the whole " children "—the clansmen—can look as their home—as the " hearth of the race," [3] the " principal hearth " above which hung the hereditary weapons of the chief—the sword, crests, and (heraldically emblazoned) " buckler " [4] and later on, symbolically, the carven coat-of-arms. For these chiefs and chieftains of a race with a settled tribal " cuntrie," to achieve the rank of *aire deisa* it was necessary to be " the son of an *Aire* and the grandson of an *Aire*," and to hold " the property of his house," or at all events the principal dwelling-place.[5] " To all," says Garth, " the chief stood in the several relations of landlord, leader, and judge." [6] Sir George Mackenzie explains that :

By the term " chief," we call the representative of the family from the French word *chef* or head, and in the Irish (Gaelic), with us the chief of the family is called the head of the clan.[7]

The *ceann-cinnidh* or clan chief—or more properly the " Head of the Clan "—is thus in nature precisely the same as the chief of the family. Both titles simply denote *the living individual who represents the founder of the tribe, and who is the sacred embodiment of the tribe itself.*

Heraldry, as already explained, is a science for distinguishing persons, families, and communities.

Heraldry (says Fox-Davies) from its earliest infancy possessed two essential qualities. It was the definite sign of hereditary nobility and rank, and it was practically an integral part of warfare, but also from its earliest infancy it formed a means of decoration.[8]

Firstly, it was for distinguishing noble groups, and secondly, for distinguishing the chief of each noble group from the subordinate descendants thereof.[9] The basic, or absolute, shield and flag (for banners are older than shields and coats of arms) [10] exist for the

[1] *Celtic Scotland*, II., pp. 145, 176. *Aire* means " lord " or " chieftain."
[2] *Old Regime in France*, p. 44.
[3] Cf. title " *chef du feu* " (*Old Regime in France*, p. 13), which is relateable to the old Scots " fire house," *i.e.* house with a " lum," and which takes us back to the prehistoric " hearths," and to the allodial claim to ownership of land from being the representative of him who " first raised smoke and boiled water on that land " (*Sketches of the Highlanders*, p. 26).
[4] Balfour's *Practics*, p. 235.
[5] C. N. Starcke, *The Primitive Family*, pp. 47, 164 ; H. G. B. Westermarck, *History of Human Marriage* (1901), p. 110.
[6] *Sketches of the Highlanders*, 1825, p. 26.
[7] Mackenzie, *Works*, II., p. 618, line 13.
[8] *Complete Guide to Heraldry*, 1925, p. 24.
[9] Nisbet, *System of Heraldry*, I., i., p. 2 ; II., iii., p. 2.
[10] Innes of Learney, *Scots Heraldry*, p. 14.

practical purpose of distinguishing the leaders of family or tribe or feudal units, in the military, civil, public, and nobiliary life of the kingdom.

Leaders wore their own devices . . . that they might be distinguished by their particular followers, hence the actual use in battle . . . of personal armorial bearings . . . and even yet the practice is not wholly extinguished, for the tartans . . . are a relic of the usage of former days.[1]

The cap-badges of our Highland regiments, moreover, still display the crests of the chiefs who first raised the regiments,[2] so that actual heraldry has come down via clanship into modern military uniform. There was no such thing in the Middle Ages as " representation in arms," apart from representation in national life [3]—nor is there now. It was part of the everyday machinery of that organised daily life— military and civil, Highland and Lowland.[4] Heraldry was a practical subject in an illiterate age, and had to be strictly controlled, since mistakes could lead to defeat in war,[5] or fraud in business.[6] Chiefs, being directly, or through their *ceann-cath*,[7] persons vested with high military authority, were, in consequence of that status, the very persons to whom ensigns armorial—especially armorial banners—were indispensable,[8] and whose " enseinzies " were controlled under the Law of Arms. At the same time, heraldry " had no necessary connection with fighting." [9] It was primarily the machinery of family administration and the occular evidence of chiefly authority—the rallying-point of the race, beneath the parental banner.

Amongst the other armorial insignia of chiefship of " clans " and of " potent families " [10] is the slogan which was shouted by the followers not only in battle but at tournaments and other honourable gatherings.[11] These are " allowed " by Lyon, *i.e.*, in the Middle Ages,

---

[1] *Complete Guide to Heraldry*, p. 25.

[2] A Hanoverian warrant of 1748 forebade the use of any colonel's arms or device, being used in military badges or uniforms. In Scotland this proved a dead letter. Had it been applied the historic badges of our Highland and Lowland regiments would not have been permitted ! In England the foolish rule, still applied to English regiments, has led to a lot of debased badge-heraldry and meaningless, not to say absurd, devices. Some of those issued during the recent war, *e.g.*, Pioneer Corps, are bad examples of bastard-armory.

[3] Cf. Fox-Davies, *Art of Heraldry*, 1905, p. 10 ; *Complete Guide to Heraldry*, 1925, p. 20 ; J. Woodward, *Heraldry, British and Foreign*, I., pp. 6–15.

[4] The tombstones at Iona and elsewhere show the early use of armorial shields by chiefs and chieftains (see fig. on p. 149).

[5] Battle of Barnet, see *Heraldry in Scotland*, p. 224.   [6] *Ibid.* p. 31.

[7] *Scottish Notes and Queries*, 15th August 1943, p. 96.

[8] Nisbet, *System of Heraldry*, 1722, I., p. 3, line 12 ; A. C. Fox-Davies, *Art of Heraldry*, p. 10 ; *Heraldry in Scotland*, p. 31.

[9] *Heraldry in Scotland*, p. 31 ; *Scots Heraldry*, p. 14.

[10] Mackenzie, *Works*, II., p. 633 ; Nisbet, *System of Heraldry*, II., iv., p. 24.

[11] At a Highland Gathering the slogan should be shouted on the arrival of the chief.

slogan-shouting was prohibited save with Lyon's sanction.[1] Such slogans are recorded, often as a second motto, or as a " woord," [2] and, when short, are displayed running along the standard, or, as the motto should be, and usually is, depicted across it in transverse bands, as is the slogan if it be a long one.

The chief, then, from his representing the founder of the race, succeeded, upon his predecessor's death, to the insignia of the eponymus (or what was heraldically appropriate to the eponymus), his banner, his weapons, his helmet, his surcoat, and his emblazoned shield and his rallying-flag or standard. In the Middle Ages he succeeded to the actual accoutrements which formed part of the " Heirship Moveables " which descended with the mansion to the heir,[3] and which included

The Bellendaine standard of the Earl of Buccleuch with Scott slughorn.

the furnishings of the hall, where the arms and banner normally hung.[4] The succeeding " representer," and he alone, was entitled to bear the undifferenced shield of arms.[5] That is to say, when arms are

[1] The term is that slogans were not " allowed to any but to the chiefs of clans and to great men who had many followers, vassals, and dependers " (*Works*, II., p. 633).

[2] *Macfarlane of that Ilk*, Lyon Register, I., p. 377.

[3] *Law of Succession in Ensigns Armorial*, p. 48.

[4] Erskine, *Principles of the Law of Scotland*, III., 8, 18 ; Balfour's *Practics*, p. 235.

[5] The principle underlying the *Ardgour* (preliminary) judgement of 16th July 1937 was both historically and legally wrong. Consequently, when the evidence in the subsequent proof established that " chief of the family " and " head of the clan " were the same thing, Lyon felt himself precluded from describing the successful party as either " chief " or its synonym " representer " (as the Division had held him entitled to do). Faced with the *impasse* thus created by their precipitate error of 1937 the Division, in 1941 (Lord Aitchison declaring there was now nothing to prevent Lyon making such affirmation), authorised Lyon to " proceed as accords," whereupon Lyon duly, on 26th February 1943, recorded the successful claimant to the " old family arms " as the " representer of the family," which, as we have seen, Sir G. Mackenzie authoritatively laid down as equivalent to the Celtic *ceann-cinnidh*. The heir male who had not been found to be representer was decreed not entitled to the " old family arms " without addition of " a brisure or mark of cadency " (1941 S.C. 714).

assigned to a community,[1] only the representer, *i.e.* chief, is entitled to these arms undifferenced. Any other course would have wrecked the whole value of heraldry, and in warfare would have rendered it a national danger. Its military value involved the immediate recognition of the leader of each group from his cadets, and this came from the leader displaying the undifferenced ensigns. Even if the chief was a kilted Highlander, the chief's banner (*i.e.* the undifferenced banner which had belonged to, or was scientifically appropriate to, the eponymus) and the " old family seal of arms " devolved upon the successive representers of the community.*

Chiefship of an honourable community is thus a title and dignity (related to a " noble fief " (corporeal or incorporeal) and technically represented by its undifferenced arms), even though of no higher rank than esquire,[2] held of the Crown and indicated by armorial bearings in terms of the Commissions of Visitation (" Visite " is a technical term in the Law of Arms),[3] and anyone who " challenges forth any name of tytle or honour or dignitie as Esquire or Gentleman or other [4] must ' justify the same by the Law of Arms ' " ;[5] and Lyon, in 1672, held that an assumption of chiefship without his permission was unlawful.[6] The requisite proof is " by pedigrees, deeds, and such other evidence and matter of record and credit if need requires, as may justify the same." [7] Originally, under tribal custom, the chief was inaugurated like the *Ard-righ* in a solemn ceremony. The account of the form of inauguration of the High Chief of O'Neill by the hereditary inaugurator, The O'Cahan, is as follows :

---

[1] And presumably to " all descendants " of its eponymus (Nisbet, *System of Heraldry*, I., p. 71, line 48) who can prove their descent, *i.e.* the *duine-uasail*.

[2] Highest category of the modern Precedency List, 1905, under which a chief could be grouped, cf. Macpherson : Chiefship " setts you in the front of the first gentlemen of the Kingdome " (*Loyall Dissuasive*, p. 26), *i.e.* confers the rank of Esquire—which descends only to the heir of each person so hereditarily recognised by the King of Arms.

[3] 1592 cap. 25, as interpreted by Lord Constable in *Macrae's Trustees* v. *Lord Lyon*, 1927 S.L.T. 292.

[4] A man may acquire gentility by office, but this dies with him. Only the chief of each family or branch is an " Esquire " by descent, *i.e.* the cadets are merely " Gentlemen " unless or until received by the King of Arms as *ecuyer*—feminine *ecuyere* (*Encyclopædia of Laws of Scotland*, s.v. Precedence, par. 33, 34). Hereditary nobility can only be established by patent or confirmation from the Fountain of Honour, through a King of Arms (Nisbet, *System of Heraldry*, I., p. 2 ; Ferne, *Glorie of Generositie*, p. 67).

[5] *Ipsissima verba* of the Royal Warrant, *Right to Bear Arms*, p. 123 ; *Shrewsbury Peerage*, 1857, Minute of Evidence, pp. 16, 18, 215 (Signet Library).

[6] Letter to Cluny-Macpherson (Macfarlane's *Genealogical Collections*, I., p. 393), consistent with the jurisdiction over " titles and designations " comprehended in the statutory term " visite " (1592 cap. 29) ; cf. Gwillim, *Display of Heraldry*, 1724, p. 29.

[7] *Ibid.* p. 127.   * Agnew, *Her. She iffs of Galloway*, p. 111 (cp. p. 114).

If any will take upon him to be O'Neill, being not named or [1] chosen by O'Cahan, he is not to be obeyed nor taken for O'Neill, for if any undertake the name of O'Neill, not appointed by O'Cahan, the people will think themselves not bound in conscience to obey him. (Hogan, *Irish Law of Kingship*, p. 199.) [2]

It will be observed there is no suggestion that O'Neill's status as chief depended on election or recognition by the tribe. Indeed, we find in the case of the Lord of the Isles, that it might even be contrary to what the clan would have wished, as when " Good John of Isla " settled the chiefship of Clan Donald upon the son of his second marriage, passing over Ranald (1st of Clanranald), son of the first marriage, though the latter had been governing for his father and become popular. Yet, faithful to his duty to the parental direction, Ranald

assembled the gentry of the Isles, brought the sceptre from Kildonan in Eig, and delivered it to his brother Donald, who was thereupon called M'Donald, and Donald, Lord of the Isles, contrary to the opinion of the men of the Isles. [3]

The vital feature was (*a*) designation by the last patriarch, (*b*) proper inauguration—revestiture in the ancestral insignia, and by the proper inaugurator. The right flowed from the patriarchate, and the revestiture was completed by the religio-legal channels.

On pp. 172–175 will be found the various courses adopted for dealing with emergency situations which were capable of being constitutionally resolved in ways still consonant with the parental character of chiefship.

Like the Royal Coronation, this ceremony of a chief's inauguration included three features : (*a*) the ascertainment or determination, *i.e.* ascertainment of the candidates' right to the office [4] by succession,

---

[1] This word " or " is important, for " named " evidently refers to the inaugural ceremony, whilst " or chosen " indicates that if the defunct O'Neill had failed in the last duty of a patriarch, viz. to nominate his tanist, then it lay with O'Cahan to do this on his behalf. As regards the O'Neills the whole passage is a complete negation of any electoral idea.

[2] The hereditary inaugurator of the Pictish kings was the Earl of Fife, who set the king upon the Stone of Scone, whilst the functions of the High Sennachie and official inaugurator of the Dalriad kings devolved, along with the red robe of the Sennachie and duty of declaiming the genealogy, upon the Lord Lyon King of Arms. (The Scottish Coronation, *Crown and Empire* (*Times'* publication), 1937, p. 89 ; J. Sobieski Stuart, *Costumes of the Clans*, 1892, pp. 43–45 (notes) ; *Scots Heraldry*, p. 8.)

[3] Another version of the translation of McVurich is translated as giving the equivalent word " nobles " for " gentry," and " nominated Macdonald " instead of " thereupon called M'Donald." The translation given in the text is obviously the correct one, and " nominate " in the other means " officially named " ; cf. " *nominari scribi et intitulari* " in a peerage investiture, and the Irish " named by O'Cahan," *i.e.* inaugurated.

[4] In the case of the Crown the " destination " is now contained in the Act of Settlement.

nomination, or selection, as the case might be,[1] (b) the " Presentation " as distinct from the English " Recognition," (c) the Inauguration.

Even the English " Recognition " must not be confused with the antecedent determination of title to succeed, which is set forth in the Presentation, and depends on the ruling " destination " of the office. The Recognition comes from the " following "—the people of the " country "—including tenants and " broken " men who had been taken on to the lands by " commendation," of whom much is heard in medieval law—and who might withdraw, or support a rival claimant.

At the coronation its modern English form is :

Sirs, I here present unto you King George, your undoubted [2] king ; wherefore all you who are come this day to do your homage and service, are you willing to do the same ?

The question at this juncture is not "Who is the rightful king/chief?" but whether those present are going to do their " homage and service " as they ought, and presumably will. If the " undoubted " heir be a very unsuitable or incapable person, there may be good reason why the family or following should use their influence to get him to resign in favour of a more suitable nominee, e.g. the resignation of Ferquhard Mackintosh of Mackintosh in favour of his uncle.[3]

In Scotland the " analogous " part of the coronation ceremonial was altogether different :

The Marischall desyred [4] the Lyone to show the kinge's pleasur, quhosayes alloud to the People : " That the King is villinge to accept the Croune." [5]

The people's reply was : " Bring him to us, God blesse him and us for his caus." [6]

Here there is no question of even stating whether he is the " undoubted king," much less asking the people whether they will do

[1] See below, Appendix X.

[2] Compare the term " undoubted chief " which appears in a number of eighteenth-century Lyon Register matriculations (e.g. Brisbane of Brisbane, II., p. 179—an heir female about whose rights the heir male had in 1771 been making inquiries). After the " inaugurator " (Keeper of the Genealogies) had given his " conclusive testimony " (as birthbrieves so significantly express it) the title of the heir was " undoubted." He was then the ascertained " representer " of the defunct chief. Yet, for the " weil of the houss " there might still be good reason for getting him to " renounce " in favour of a fitter member of the kin : Athol, 1609 (P.C. viii., p. 220), when the king put the earl in prison to bring home to him how unfit he was for the position to which he was born.

[3] Macfarlane, Genealogical Collections, p. 182.

[4] Although the Marischall acted in some respects as a Master of Ceremonies the Lord Lyon was the " commanding " element throughout the ceremony. Here, accordingly, he does not, like Lyon, " command," but merely " desyres."

[5] Balfour, Heraldic Tracts, p. 36.

[6] Privy Council, 2nd series, II., p. 393, per Lindsay of Annatland.

what they ought to their *Pater Patriæ.* His right having been ascertained, the only question is whether he will " enter on his inheritance " —whether as heir-at-law or heir-of-tailzie and nomination ; the concept is tribal and feudal, that of the " organised family," viz. the clan.

Just as the king/chief was primarily nominated by his predecessor, the patriarch's last earthly function, as we have pointed out, so in ecclesiastical affairs, in the Celtic Church-tribal, the Abbot it was who named his *co-arb* :

> The power of St. Columba was absolute, and he himself chose Baithene his cousin to be his successor. At Iona, as in Ireland, the hereditary principle was observed, and of the first eleven abbots, nine are known to have been of the same family as St. Columba.[1]

The practice was thus the same in Church and State, and in the latter alike as regards ordinary chiefs and chieftains, and the " Chief of Chiefs," the *Ard-righ Albainn.*

Even in Scottish burghs the same tribo-parental feature became evident in the retiring council, or Provost, naming the new. All was modelled on the clan, the biological tribe-family.

As regards succession under any power delegated from, or expressly recognised by, the *Ard-righ,* the chief with a Crown-title or land-charter was in a far stronger position than the allodial chief, being, in case of dispute, entitled to the *Ard-righ's* assistance. In any event the *Ard-righ* as *Pater Patriæ* and Fountain of Justice and Honour, had ultimate power to intervene if necessary, as did the Irish High King in settling the chiefships of the Burkes.[2]

Any " Recognition," in fact, related to the " power " and membership, not to the Authority and Representation, of the community.

In days when the Royal power was none too strong and communications were difficult, the Crown no doubt found convenient formulæ for giving constitutional appearance to hard facts, but where a title *de Rege* existed, the Crown was bound to support the representative entitled thereunder to lands or chiefly insignia.

Reverting to the ceremony of the inauguration : The new chief's genealogy was declaimed by the clan sennachie, and the insignia of rule, the sword [3] and a white wand,[4] were formally delivered.[5] Such a ceremony is still appropriate, but (as in the case where the *Ard-righ* personally intervened to exercise his prerogative of inaugurating chiefs), if there be any doubt regarding the succession to the " representership " and relative armorial insignia, the effective " inauguration " is now a

---

[1] *Lordship of the Isles,* p. 104.
[2] Hogan, *Irish Law of Kingship,* p. 199.
[3] R. Macleod of Macleod, *The MacLeods of Dunvegan,* p. xiv.
[4] The official wand of a baron is also white (W. C. Dickinson, *Baron Court Book of Carnwath,* p. lxxxvi.), which corroborates the connection of chiefship with the earliest baronial jurisdictions (Craig, *Jus Feudale,* I., 8, 2).
[5] Marquis of Bute, *Scottish Coronations,* p. 16.

G

matriculation of arms in the Lyon Register, *i.e.* a constructive delivery [1] *de Rege* by a picture on parchment, symbolising the actual shield, crest, and helmet of the former *ceann-cinnidh*, which ensigns of honour for distinguishing the group, the chief (as its representer) holds of and under the *Ard-righ* as the Fountain of Honour at the hands of his Commissioner the Lord Lyon—*Qui facit per alium facit per se* [2]—who embodies, and has performed the duties of,[3] the high sennachie and official inaugurator of the ancient Kings of Scots. Indeed, so that Lyon should be invested, to the extent of his Commission, with the full nobiliary prerogative of the King of Scots, he was summoned to dine at Holyroodhouse on the evening of his inauguration, when the Royal Crown of Scotland was set on his head.[4]

> Whom royal James himself had crowned
> And on his temples placed the round
> Of Scotland's ancient diadem. (*Marmion*, iv., l. 159)

The Crown's recognition—direct or through the Supreme Officer of Honour—alone can qualify a chief to be received as such in state or public ceremonial in Scotland, " whereof Lyon hath the management " [5] ; and for any person to submit to, or assist at an inauguration in opposition to a holder under the *Ard-righ's* protection and a destination of chiefly insignia held *de Rege* must necessarily be not only a nullity in effect, but an affront to the Fountain of Honour, and in the nature of treason. In such a matter, says Sheriff Sir Æneas Macpherson, " No subject could *vi et armis* maintain his right against the king *jure et impune.*" [6] In private life, bogus chiefs, like a bogus peer or baronet, or the soi-disant " Countess Cowley," may impose on humble neighbours, but they cannot be officially received by or accorded such titles, and are liable to be publicly denounced as infamous impostors,[7] or " interlopers and upstarts," [8] and public documents in which they are described as chiefs without the King of Arms' permission, are liable to be rejected as irregular—*e.g.* the bonds of

---

[1] A nobiliary " retour " and revesting (see *Law of Succession in Ensigns Armorial*, p. 45, and 1941 S.C. 673).

[2] Mackenzie, *Works*, II., p. 563 Sir John Ferne, *Glorie of Generositie*, p. 67.

[3] *Sources and Literature of the Law of Scotland*, p. 382.

[4] Sir J. B. Paul, *Heraldry in Relation to Scots History and Art*, p. 85 ; Sir W. Scott, *Marmion*, canto iv., line 159.

[5] *Scots Heraldry*, p. 9, n. 2.   [6] *Loyall Dissuasive* , p. 117.

[7] J. Dallaway, *Heraldic Enquiries*, p. 313 ; Boutell's *Heraldry*, 1891, p. 345 ; Macfarlane's *Genealogical Collections* (Scottish History Society), I., p. 393. This was the " sentence " of the old Celtic Druid bards who passed from castle to castle on their sennachiedal *cuairt*, the precursor of the heraldic " visitation " (A. R. Wagner, *Heralds and Heraldry*, p. 3 ; Kings of Arms went, like the bards, says Garter Dugdale, " to the houses of chiefs of familys ") and who " declared infamous " those who failed to establish or maintain their chiefly status (P. W. Joyce, *Social Life in Ancient Ireland*, pp. 45, 449 ; *Sources and Literature of the Law of Scotland* (Stair Society), p. 382).

[8] J. Gwillim, *Display of Heraldry*, 1724, s.v. Honour Civil, p. 49.

Cluny-Macpherson as " Chief of Clan Chattan " were rejected after Lyon had pronounced in favour of Mackintosh. This would be an effective and sufficient enforcement of Lyon's decision [1] for all practical purposes ; if a " more efficient sanction " had been thought requisite in the Middle Ages, it would have been found in the executorial known as " Letters of Fire and Sword." [2]

CHIEFTAIN

Whilst chief and chieftain, chiefship and chieftainry, are used promiscuously in Scottish records, the term " chief " normally does connote a greater chief, and consequently branch-chiefs have in later times come to be designated " chieftains " as being lesser chiefs. The word, originally French, was anciently applied to the head of a terri-torial house,[3] but at a time when, in the " glorious epoch " of French tribo-feudalism, the feudal barons were *chefs de famille* in the true clan sense, " the groups surrounding him not bearing his name." [4] In Scotland the term is not confined to " clan " groups, indeed is largely associated with feudal houses, which, however, are now recognised as essentially clannish.[5] Since the Ardgour hearing, when it was sug-gested the term " Chieftain of Ardgour " was without precedent in the Lyon Registers, such a term—viz. " Chieftain of Innermeath "— has actually transpired to be of record in the Public Register of Genealogies.[6] Chieftain is really a territorial title.[7]

Indeed, the definition and the corresponding term, " *chevetainrie— propriété d'un chevetain, d'un seigneur,*" compared with the Scots term " chiftane of the cuntrie " [8] and the normal use of the title as annexed to a *locus, e.g.* " Chieftain of X——," obviously correlate the title with the *aire deisa,* territorial nobles of the Celtic polity.[9] The chieftain thus appears, in this sense (*i.e.* of a country), as a personage combining

---

[1] This, it happens, is the practical sanction against bogus baronets (Royal Warrant, 1910, sec. II.), and this hereditary dignity is determined either directly by the Crown, on advice of the Secretary of State (under secs. IV., VI., VIII.) or by the Kings of Arms, whose jurisdiction therein is (to prevent the warrant infringing the Declaration of Right, 1695) saved by sec. XIII., whereunder Lyon's certificate was the authority on which the Lord Chamberlain received a man as baronet (*Scottish Offices Inquiry Commission,* 1870, Evidence, par. 1984), and under which Lyon still adjudicates on Nova Scotia Baronetcies, since the right to these under the Act of Union could not be affected by the warrant, when a claimant invokes Lyon Court (*Strathspey,* 1950 S.L.T. 17).

[2] *Social and Economic Development of Scotland,* pp. 512, 530. For some modern enforcements, see p. 177.

[3] Frederick Godefroy, *Lexique de L'Ancien Français,* 1901, p. 83.

[4] *Old Regime in France,* pp. 3, 5, 73.

[5] A. Mure Mackenzie, *History of Scotland,* p. 41.

[6] A. Cameron, *Juridical Review,* I., p. 72 (March 1938), " Diploma of Nobility of Thomas Cumming, 1727." *Cuthbert of Castlehill,* Register of Genealogies, I., p. 182.

[7] Letters patent erecting chieftaincy of Dalkilry, Lyon Register, XXXVIII., p. 35 ; *Hay of Leys,* April 1954, *ib.* XXXIX., p. 153.

[8] A.P.S. III. 464.   [9] Skene, *Celtic Scotland,* III., pp. 145, 176.

the dual character of representer of a family (or branch family) and leading person (as proprietor, tacksman, or occupier) in relation to the inhabitants of a specific district—" be place of thare duelling " [1]— as his *sencliathe*, vassals, and tenantry.[2] In short, he is a laird whose relations to the occupiers of his domain is quasi-tribal as well as economic, *i.e.* closer than " landlord and tenant," who might become themselves armigerous.[3] Any " Recognition," as indicated farther on, relates neither to the title nor right of succession, but to membership of the " community " forming such a following. It is comparable rather to the early British " commendation," [4] which without the permanent bases of the clan/tribe and feudal connections proved evanescent. The strength of the clan system lies—as Stewart of Garth pointed out—in the hereditary tribal bond [5] around the " stem " or central family.[6]

In any case, *grad flaith* or other, the branch-chief or chieftain— and the term " branch " is in heraldry just as applicable to a family as to a clan [7] (these, moreover, being now received, per Sir George Mac- kenzie, as synonymous and interchangeable)—bears precisely the same relation to the members (*i.e.* actual and assumed descendants of the branch) as " The Chief " does to the whole clan or family group. The chieftain is simply " representer " of the " first raiser " [8] of the branch. An interesting question is : when is a branch so raised or erected that it becomes cognisable as a " distinct house " ? In this there is a consensus of Celtic custom [9] with heraldic law, that three generations, or apparently conventionally eighty-one years,[10] was neces-

---

[1] A.P.S. IV. 40.

[2] Cf. *Privy Council*, 3rd series, III., p. 75 ; *Loyall Dissuasive*, p. 56 n.

[3] Cf. Arms of " Clientage " and " Patronage," Nisbet's *System of Heraldry*, II., iii., p. 60 ; II., iv., p. 22 ; I., p. 268 ; *Heraldry in Scotland*, pp. 273, 275.

[4] A. E. F. Jolliffe, *op. cit.* pp. 80, 99.

[5] The importance of the ultimate settlement by the *Ard-righ*—through his Court of Arms or by *Diploma Stemmatis* (a chiefship-birthbrief) from his King of Arms—of chiefly and chieftainly succession disputes is obvious, since if this lay with " the clan " and not, as a determination of representership, with the Fountain of Honour, the result would be dissension and weakness, *e.g. Macrae*, where rivals simply founded opposing " clan societies."

[6] The " Recognition," moreover, would seem to lie with the in-brought tenants, dependers and " broken men " who could resile from the new chieftain, as distinct from the *sencliathe* and " native men " who by three generations (conventionally eighty-one years or maybe three tacks of nineteen years) had become (by comple- ment to the resultant fixity of tenure) hereditary adherents whose membership would be implicit, whereas recently " inbrocht " dependers—unless they had been specifically adopted (see p. 19), were on a " commendation " basis until elapse of the requisite time when they automatically became *sencliathe*.

[7] *Cunyham* v. *Cunyham*, 11 Dunlop 113[9], for use of the term *re* " family."

[8] Nisbet, *System of Heraldry*, I., p. 176, line 51 ; II., iii., p. 17, line 41 ; cf. *Mackenzie of Coull*, Lyon Register, I., p. 190.

[9] Skene, *Celtic Scotland*, III., p. 175.

[10] This seems the conventional three generations when applied to the *sencliathe* (*ibid.* III., p. 173), who then became " native men "—hereditary followers.

sary to perfect a coat of arms,[1] and it would seem on comparison of these analogies that a branch is not perfectly established until it has stood for three generations,[2] in fact until it has produced what in Celtic law was termed a *gilfine*, or five households.[3] Far from the title "chief" being a rare one in Celtic civilisation, the popular unit was evidently the *gilfine* group under a "*gilfine*-chief,"[4] whom we to-day would conveniently term a "chieftain," if "of" an estate or *aire deisa* house.

The question whether chieftain in a clan has any "armorial significance," is illustrated in the patent erecting the Chieftaincy of Dalkilry (L.R., XXXVIII.). Seton[5] had evidently no doubt it had such a significance. An hereditary chieftain,[6] in the sense of a "branch-chief," would—in the heraldic view—be entitled to the arms of his "branch-eponymus," without further brisure.[7] The term *chevtaine* is definitely employed in early heraldic literature,[8] and "A cheivetayn's hedd chappelled embattled Or" appears in an heraldic badge in 1562.[9] This is the same principle, though the restriction is unfortunately not so close that it is not occasionally assigned to people who can claim to be neither chieftains nor military leaders.[10] It seems not unlikely that this

Achievement of Campbell of Inverneil, Chief of Clan Chearleich of Ardeonaig.

[1] Nisbet, *System of Heraldry*, II., iv., pp. 125, 147 ; *Heraldry in Scotland*, p. 79.

[2] In Hungary, a decidedly "clannish" realm, the *praedicatum*, or territorial designation, legally an additional surname, does not "perfect" and become hereditary, apart from the fief, until it has been borne for four generations (Ruvigny, *Titled Nobilities of Europe*, 1910, p. 107). This is the same principle.

[3] *Celtic Scotland*, III., p. 179 ; J. Cameron, *Celtic Law*, pp. 109, 111.

[4] *Celtic Scotland*, III., pp. 180, 182.

[5] *Law and Practice of Heraldry*, p. 9.

[6] We are not here concerned with "chieftains" of (a) Highland Gatherings, (b) Clan Societies, but with "chieftain" as a title and status of gentility—social, feudal, and military rank.

[7] *Hamilton of Binning*, 1886, Lyon Register, I., p. 329 ; *Scott of Sinton*, 1700, *ibid.* II., 189 ; *Grant of Auchernach*, 1777, *ibid.* I., p. 515 ; R. R. Stoddart, *Scottish Arms*, p. 306.

[8] *Book of St. Albans*, 1486 ; J. Dallaway, *Heraldic Enquiries*, p. lxxv.

[9] Gerard Legh, *Accidens of Armory*, 1562 edition, f. 101 (see *Tartans of the Clans and Families of Scotland*, p. 34).

[10] *Leadbetter*, 1900, Lyon Register, XVI., p. 23 ; *Beveridge, ibid.* XXIII., p. 31 ; *Morris*, 1917, *ibid.* XXIII., p. 60. It would be within Lyon's prerogative to confer (or rather to restrict conference of) such a mural circlet of some colour on "chieftains," but many crests would not be improved by such circlets, so chieftain's caps may preferably, following 1562 precedent, be allowed in the badge—which with standard, is an "additament" of arms (*Stewart of Inchmahome, ibid.* XXI., p. 74), allowed to those deemed to have "followings."

medieval chieftain's bonnet survives not merely in the mural crown of heraldry,[1] but in the diced borders of Highland bonnets. In its more primitive form this border was a broad surround of very large checks, a noticeable feature of the bonnet in which the Duchess of Gordon went recruiting.[2] The chieftaincy of a "branch" has actually been specifically taken cognisance of by Lyon Court in at any rate one case [3]—viz. Campbell of Inverneil,[4] who matriculated expressly *to establish his position as* chief of the Clan Chearleich [5] or "old branch or tribe of the family of Craignish," *i.e.* a branch of the great Clan Campbell. What Lyon awarded is illuminating : The arms of Argyll, with a difference of immediacy from the stem of Lochaw, viz. a plain bordure Azure. The ground of the award was an acknowledgement, 6th October 1795, by the "heads of families of the clan," including the "Clan Kater-Campbells in Breadalbane," the "Clan Tearlach Campbells," and the "Clan Iner of Ichtellegherne," who as the "representatives of the above five clans, bind themselves, their heirs, and successors to acknowledge Inverneil and his heirs and successors," on the ground of a traditional pedigree handed down, that Inverneil represented the eldest son, of whom he, according to their tradition, was (they narrate) lineal heir male and representative, and the purpose of the declaration was to put on record their belief in the pedigree.[6] On this declaration, Lyon accepted the "pedigree" from a clan aspect, there being no documentary proof, and awarded the above chieftainly insignia, with destination to "descendants" (not, as in many patents, "heirs male"), conform to the legal implication of the term "heirs and successors." An interesting feature is the existence of branch-clans subsidiary to Clan Chearleich (itself a branch of Clan Campbell), and, co-relating the number five with the *gilfine* number,[7] it may be assumed that Clan Chearleich was head of five sub-clans, whose sub-chiefs must each at least have been *gilfine*,

[1] Fox-Davies, *Art of Heraldry*, p. 284. The true mural crown, as used on the Continent and shown in our older text-books, is embellished with three or five towers, thus distinguishing it from the "chieftain's cap" pattern.

[2] The provenance and development of the diced border accordingly deserves research, since its allocation to privates seems to have been a meaningless copying by regimental tailors of what had originally been an ornament restricted to chieftains' bonnets (p. 114).

[3] Owing to Lyon Register, now existent since 1672, not being printed, it is difficult to say what may not, on a full analysis, be discovered in its voluminous pages.

[4] Lyon Register, IX., p. 88, 18th November 1875.

[5] Letter from Inverneil (younger), 27th October 1875, that he and his father are "quite satisfied if it be proved that we are the chief of the race, tribe, or Clan Chearleich of Ardeonaig, without going to further expense" than £45. Inverneil omitted so to designate himself in the instances of his petition, though the chiefship is referred to *in gremio* of the matriculation, which was sought expressly to prove the chiefship.

[6] Cf. Welsh declaration of the Hoby pedigree accepted by Garter and Clarencieux, 1598, *Misc. Gen. et Her.*, 1st series (1868), I., p. 142.

[7] J. Cameron, *Celtic Law*, p. 111.

i.e. chiefs of five houses.[1] The galley " cottise," [2] or compartment, is evidently a *reddendo* galley.

The development of branch-clans is illustrated amongst the Grants, *e.g.* Clan Allan (Grant of Auchernack) ; Clan Donachie (Grant of Gartenbeg) ; Clan Chiaran (Grant of Dellachapple) ; Clan Phadrick (Grant of Tullochgorum) [3]—again making, curiously enough, with the " stem family " of Freuchie, the *gilfine* number of five.

The expanding nature of the clan-groups of the later historical organisation is thus shown repeating what was evidently assumed to have occurred in the earlier development of the *mortuath*, and the *gilfine*-chief, rising to the status of " chieftain " and then chief/chieftain of a branch-clan.[4]

SUCCESSION TO CHIEFSHIP

The word " clan," meaning " children " and being proved synonymous with " family," necessarily connotes a biological and hereditary group, clustered round an hereditary stem, the " noble stok " of the Lyon Court Act 1592, cap. 125.[5] Lord Lyon Erskine's Declaration, 10th September 1672, anent the heretrix of Clan Chattan also officially emphasises that the clan itself is an incorporeal heritable subject, just like the ancient tribal *familia*.[6]

A chiefless clan, like an orphan family, is an imperfect group. Continuity under the bond of kin embodied in the perpetuation of the parental tie is the whole basis of the clan concept. A clan without

---

[1] It must not be assumed that Lyon will forthwith launch an unlimited fleet of such galleys upon the sea of heraldry.

[2] Mackenzie, *Works*, II., p. 630.

[3] L. Shaw, *History of the Province of Moray*; J. F. S. Gordon, 1882 edition, I., p. 93.

[4] Similarly the Macnabs claim to be a branch of Clan Mackinnon ; the Farquharsons are a branch of Clan Shaw, itself a branch of Clan Mackintosh, stem family of Clan Chattan.

[5] " Stem or stock is a good word perfectly understandable in dealing with Highland matters," L. Maclean Watt, *Ardgour Evidence*, p. 526.

[6] In the heir-males " argument " (S.C. 667) it was suggested that of " Highland chiefship " (a subject which at that stage had been excluded from the Court's consideration), " the Lord Lyon had held, could never pass to a woman." No reference was cited, and Lyon had held nothing of the sort ! He had, in his " note," remarked that evidence had been led on what he supposed was the then excluded point, and which naturally no attempt was even made to " prove " at that juncture ; and he (Grant) had not seen any actual evidence of Eva's existence, meaning apparently contemporary documents. The Lyon's *official* declaration, 10th September 1672 (over his official seal), that he was satisfied she existed and was heretrix of the clan, from evidence then extant, including Lyon's " own registers " (many of these, like other original documents, have since been lost), forms, however, " conclusive testimony," which must be received as authoritative (which the casual remark in a " note " is not) ; and, indeed, the contrary has since been laid down by Lord Lyon Grant himself in the birth-brief of 26th February 1943 when this is compared with Sir George Mackenzie's definitions. The matter has since been decided in *Maclachan of Maclachlan*, 1946, Lyon Register, XXXV., p. 72, and *Rose of Kilravock, ibid.* 36, p. 8.

an hereditary chief is a sorry organisation, alien to the whole idea of Celtic civilisation, wherein the chief is the sacred embodiment of the race. The question of succession to chiefship of, and chieftaincy in, clans, is therefore necessarily of the utmost importance and widest interest to Scotsmen.

The clan is a patriarchal community, based on the assumption of heredity and a " parent and child " *nexus*, and received, as has been shown, by and under the Crown, as an " honourable community," through and under its " representer."

Royal and judicial determination of its chiefship was accordingly not regarded as " grotesque " in the Middle Ages.[1] Such determinations were the very essence of the *jus familiare* vested in the successively ascendant hierarchy of " parental " rulers. The Lord Justice-Clerk rightly said, " The Chief was the Law "—but that " his authority was derived from his own people " is quite unreconcilable with the circumstances. His power, no doubt, depended on the number and loyalty of his people, but his constitutional authority over them was derived from his " representing " the eponymus.[2] The *patria potestas* is not derived from the " children " ; no more is the chief's derived from his *clanna*.

The nature of this succession is, that what passed from patriarch to patriarch was " the community " as a " going concern," namely, " the public responsibility comprehended in the term family," [3] and that in many tribal communities it lay with the patriarch to determine which member of the family, natural or adopted, should succeed to the public office of the patriarchate.[4] The early Celtic system belonged to the type in which the succession was hereditary in the group, but failing an effective nomination, prior to 1034, selective in the individual. It was nevertheless strictly " hereditary," and by whatever means ascertained, as Stewart of Garth explains, the " head of the central or stem family was the chief " of the clan.[5] The system, actually a most complicated one, was that upon the death of the patriarch— without having nominated an heir (*tanist*)—his successor was selected from a group called the *derbhfine*, consisting of his nine nearest kins- men.[6] They were apparently the chiefs of the other *derbhfines* within

---

[1] *Loyall Dissuasive*, pp. 58, 116.

[2] As Mackenzie says, " Every man is subject to his own parents, who (he thus includes the mother as capable of *potestas*), if they were not likewise subject to a higher power (*i.e.* in so far as not subject to a higher *potestas*), might judge . . . lead them out to war, and do all other things that a king could do, as we see the patriarchs did in their own families " (*Works*, II., p. 446).

[3] Maine, *Ancient Law*, pp. 205, 211.   [4] *Ibid.* p. 266; *Old Regime in France*, pp. 21, 42.

[5] D. Stewart of Garth, *Sketches of the Highlanders of Scotland*, 1825, p. 24.

[6] It also appears that after the Royal demise the High-Sennachie/Inaugurator presided in the *derbhfine* conclave (making up, I suppose, the complete number) and directed the inaugural proceedings up to the moment when the new chief was set on the inaugural seat, when he removed his official circlet and, placing it at the king's feet, said, " I surrender and command the king to be crowned " (*Privy Council*, 2nd Ser., p. 394).

the clan, *e.g.* in the case of the Crown, the " Seven Earls of Scotland " traditionally representing the " Seven Sons of Cruithne the Pict," were the functionaries on whom devolved the duty of making the selection which the dying represener ought to have made [1] of the *Ard-righ Albainn* when the Crown *de facto* and fell *de jure* vacant. The nearest modern equivalent of a *derbhfine* is the official " Royal Family " as entitled to special coronets as grandchildren of the Sovereign, and to the prefix " Royal Highness." [2] If we imagined the sovereignty selective at an intestate Royal demise from amongst all the living Royal Highnesses, and assume the selectors were, let us say, the twenty-eight Dukes, and that these twenty-eight Dukes were each selected to their dukedom (in case of intestacy) from amongst the persons who happened to have the courtesy title of " Lord " at the last Duke's death, we should roughly have an idea of what the system was like. The *derbhfine* was, generally speaking, a body of nine people descended from a great-grandfather, and in Ireland it was confined to persons connected by males, *i.e.* was of Salic form. In Scotland, upon Pictish precedent, the *derbhfines* were evidently not so restricted. The membership—that is, the electors and candidates—might be connected by females, and might even be females, because females succeeded to the Celtic mormaerships which in their original nature were the chiefships of *mortuaths*.[3] " The Law Clan Macduff," whereby certain privileges attached to individuals " within nine degrees of kin to Macduff, Earl of Fife," is regarded as really a privilege which belonged to Macduff's *derbhfine*.[4] Now, this group included persons connected through females,[5] so of course must have done the Royal *derbhfine*, from which the *Rex Pictorum* and later the *Ard-righ Albainn* was selected.

The *fine* system, of which the most recent description is by Dr. Cameron,[6] was one of the most important social features of the clan system, not indeed as a means of succession, but from the emphasis it gave to the concept of expanding branches, and the manner in which

[1] For the importance attached to his making the nomination see Maine and Pollock, *Ancient Law*, p. 266. Cameron describes tanistry as " testate succession without writing " (*Ardgour Evidence*, p. 15), which gives point to Bruce's claim to verbal nomination by Alexander III.

[2] In the reigns of Queen Victoria and Edward VII. grandchildren of the sovereign, through daughters, were included in these privileges, which happen to correspond with what is found in early Scottish *derbhfines*.

[3] Skene, *Celtic Scotland*, III., p. 212 ; J. Cameron, *Celtic Law*, p. 237.

[4] *Celtic Scotland*, III., p. 306. The survival of the Picto-tribal basis of the clan in Scotland is illustrated by the surviving assertion that a man may " wear a plaid of his mother's tartan," and the membership condition of certain Clan Associations : " Persons bearing a surname other than Mac . . . but whose maternal parent or grandparent bore either the name Mac . . . or one of the said Septnames." This provision is analogous to a *gilfine* structure admitting, like the Law Clan Macduff, female connections.

[5] Skene, *De Verborum Significatione*, s.v. Law Clan Macduff ; E. W. Robertson, *Scotland under her Early Kings*, I., p. 255 ; *Scots Peerage*, I., p. 274.

[6] *Celtic Law*, pp. 111–114.

G*

it developed biological communities within the clan community, keeping the "pyramid" always of manageable proportions. The *gilfine* consisted of a number of related households and was the minimum family commune. It was composed of "five persons," by which we understand not five individuals but five heads. It represented the descendants of a grandfather as "an actual working unit."

The *derbhfine* (or "true family" commune) consisted of nine conventional heads, or persons, "of which the sons, grandsons, and great-grandsons of one father were members."[1] That is to say, it was the community descended of a great-grandfather ; and that ancestor's "representer" was the "*derbhfine*-chief." Within this group there were several *gilfine*, each with its "*gilfine*-chief," which were the "working units." In each case the principle was that the small unit managed its own affairs, and its representer was a functionary in the greater unit.

Beyond the *derbhfine* came the *iarfine* and the *indfine*, beyond which persons passed into the *duthaig-n'daoine* (*i.e.* "the men of the cuntrie ") as distinct from the "chiefly family " ; but be it remembered they were still all organised in *gilfines* and *derbhfines* of their own, and if the chief of one of these had acquired (by charter or three generations of allodial possession) a *duthus* of his own, one had a "distinct erected branch " of the type which later came to be erected by armorial constitution of a "cadet-coat-of-arms," as Nisbet explains ; for in most ways heraldry was machinery for illustrating and preserving such "family systems." (See diagram, p. 412.)

So long as the patriarch duly "nominated," the system worked all right as regards succession ; though as regards division its students think it must have been next to unworkable. When intestacy supervened, its consequences were disastrous, and this system of *derbhfine*-succession has been described as the "weakest feature of Irish polity." It led to perpetual intrigue and strife, and to lack of continuity in rule, and Professor Hogan concludes that :

Even from the native standpoint, probably the best thing that could have happened would have been the complete success of the attempts to establish primogeniture, or at least to fix a succession more strict and efficient than the traditional kingship by election.[2]

This seems precisely what the Scottish kings (who in nature were the "Chief of Chiefs,"[3] just as the King of France was "Father of

[1] *Celtic Law*, p. 112. Cameron remarks that Dr. MacNeil thinks the *derbhfine* "had no existence " as a social community and "was merely ascertained from time to time for legal purposes." No doubt he was faced with the fact that great-grandfathers are usually past governance. I think MacNeil evidently overlooked the aspect of "representership " and that the very name "true family " shows it was the real administrative unit. Representer, of course, means the descendant who was (primarily by nomination) the re-embodiment of the root of that *fine*.

[2] *Irish Law of Kingship*, p. 249 ; Cameron, *Celtic Law*, p. 120.

[3] *Account of the Royal Visit*, 1822, p. 242.

all the Fathers" whose *familles* made up the realm) [1] achieved, from a combination of the Pictish order of succession, the Hebraic code,[2] and the Roman *gens*. This evolution is attributed to King Malcolm MacKenneth, 1005-1034,[3] who is said to have laid down that the order of succession should be :

by whichever was at the time being the next descendant, that is, a son or a daughter, a nephew or a niece,[4] the nearest then living.[5] Failing these, however, the next heir begotten of the Royal or a collateral stock.

The last provision seems to have evolved into our common law order of succession,[6] which soon came to ignore the " clan " or tribal element entirely.[7] The petition of the Seven Earls in 1292 submitted :

By the laws and customs of Scotland, from time whereof the memory of man was not, it pertained to the right, privilege, and members of the Seven Earls and *communitas* of the said kingdom, whenever the said Royal Seat should be vacant *de facto* and *de jure*, to constitute the King and to place him in the Royal Seat, and to yield up to him the Honours pertaining to the Government of Scotland.[8]

By " Royal or a collateral stock," the Earls apparently sought to argue that, if no heir existed within the degrees of the Royal *derbhfine*, and no tanist had been designated, the succession was then open for selection from the chiefs of the collateral *derbhfines*.[9] The claim was rejected on the ground that the order of succession by next of blood (Malcolm MacKenneth's law) already applied to earldoms, baronies, and other " impartable tenures," and that the Scottish Crown devolved on similar principles. The earldoms (*mormaerships*) were really

---

[1] *Old Regime in France*, p. 51.

[2] Numbers xxvii. 4 and 8, xxxvi. 3.

[3] Skene, *Fordun*, II., p. 136.

[4] Perhaps *nepos aut neptis* meant grandson or granddaughter. If so, the first heads of Mackenneth's law of succession exclude sisters and their issue, which Stair adverts to in commenting on the case of Zelophahad's daughters (Stair, *Institutions*, III., pp. 4-8). Sisters had usually married into other tribes already.

[5] Was this part of the rule the basis of the Bruce's argument for the Crown ?

[6] *Additional Case for Countess of Sutherland*, 1771, pp. 6 and 12.

[7] Cf. decision in *Bruce* v. *Baliol*, 1292, *Scotland under her Early Kings*, p. 21.

[8] *Mar Peerage Case*, 1875, Earl of Kellie's case, p. 99.

[9] Of course there were *derbhfines* beyond *derbhfines*, and apparently any *derbhfine* which had contributed a sovereign within three generations was eligible to provide a candidate—an appalling state of muddle (*Irish Law of Kingship*, pp. 191, 193, 249 ; A. O. Anderson in *Scottish Historical Review*, XXV., p. 383). There was, of course, no suggestion whatever that the office was " spent " or had " reverted " to any " community." The proposition was simply that it had become the function of the Seven Earls—and chiefs—to appoint the heir in the circumstance of the defunct king having failed to make an appointment.

high-chiefships,[1] and the early barons were rightly surmised to have been *capitani tribuum*,[2] *i.e.* clan chiefs.

Cameron has pointed out that whilst tanistry was the equivalent of testate succession, the *derbhfine*-selection was the equivalent of intestate succession.[3] That is, something had to be done because the deceased chief had not nominated, as was his chiefly duty to do.

Strictly, then, the system was never "elective" in Alba in the sense in which it is supposed to have been (but it will now appear less so) in Ireland.

The Picto-Scots evidently saw, what modern historians point out, that the *derbhfine* system "would soon have reduced itself to an impossibility."[4] Rather, the characteristic tendency in Scotland was to make everything as hereditary as possible. Indeed, *derbhfine*-selection in Scotland, as Cameron has pointed out, was only a form of intestate succession, as tanistry was of testamentary settlement. We must remember it was for the patriarch to determine which of his family should be his successor,[5] and that in primitive days this was effected by the blessing of the dying chief.[6] It was his last solemn duty. To die intestate (that is, according to Dr. Cameron, without appointing a tanist) was a disgrace, and as we can readily see, a family tragedy, leading, as it so often did, to disputes. Tanistry was therefore the rule, *derbhfine*-selection the exception. Accordingly two practical measures modified the inefficiency of the *derbhfine* system and incidentally of primogeniture :

(1) By tanistry, the ruling chief—like the Hebraic patriarchs—could nominate his successor, and thus interregnum and dispute were avoided. This was the practice in Roman and Hebraic law,[7] and in days of strife the tanist or *designatus* [8] was usually selected well in

---

[1] *Scotland under her Early Kings*, p. 87.

[2] Craig, *Jus Feudale*, I., 8, 2 (Clyde edition, I., p. 107). Skene thought "captains" were leaders subsidiary to "chiefs," but A. McBain (*Highlanders of Scotland*, 1902, pp. 406, 413) holds *toisach*, captain and chief, as synonymous, and that *capitanus* was the fourteenth- to fifteenth-century translation of *toisach* or *ceann-cinnidh*. Comparison of the terms (Gaelic, French, and English) and the manner of their official usage, confirms this. The idea of "captain" as a subsidiary term is evidently a late one based on its use for an under-officer in the post-feudal and post-tribal Royal Army. The subsidiary "war leader," *ceann-cath*, was in eighteenth-century Scotland translated "Commander of the Clan" (as distinct from the chief). See *Historical Papers* (New Spalding Club), II., pp. 357, 358, 362, 368.   [3] *Maclean of Ardgour Evidence*, p. 15.

[4] A. O. Anderson, S.H.R., XXV., p. 283 ; J. Hogan, *Irish Law of Kingship*, pp. 191, 249.

[5] Sir H. Maine, *Ancient Law*, pp. 211–215, 266.

[6] *Ibid.* p. 266, citing Abraham and Jacob, Genesis xxvii. 29, where the tanistic nomination was reinforced by a patriarchal curse ; cf. C. Knight, *Early Christianising of Scotland*, p. 50.

[7] Maine (*Ancient Law*, pp. 211, 215, 238, 266) and Pollock points out the similarity of the Roman settlement to the Scottish Trust Disposition (*Ancient Law*, p. 238).

[8] John Riddell, *Peerage Law*, p. 210 ; S.H.R., XXV., p. 10.

advance. Tanists are still traceable in the "Masters" as heirs to Scottish peerages.[1] Besides resignations and regrants of honours, Scots peerage law abounds with powers of "nomination" whereby peers had licence to appoint heirs to their dignities,[2] and in other cases a settlement by the peer himself has been given posthumous effect by Royal Warrant.[3] Similar practices in chiefship, family representation and arms ("private rights" saved by Art. 18 of the Treaty of Union) subsist. There are innumerable instances of Lyon giving effect as Crown Commissioner[4] to armorial settlements executed by will, tailzie, or *inter vivos* deed, and several involving chiefship specifically.[5] These are simply developments of the law of tanistry. Where properly executed, Lord Justice-Clerk Aitchison has laid down, and in the authority of Mackenzie, that they are incontrovertible.[6]

The idea of an immutable descent of dignities is a mere reflection of late English peerage-law formulated for preventing voting corruption in the seventeenth/eighteenth-century House of Lords. As regards arms and chiefship it is contrary to the Act of Union,[7] and opposed to Scots common sense, which has naturally favoured passing over ne'er-do-weels, criminals, and fools, and also apportioning cumulated inheritances instead of merging them in one bloated line,[8] and selecting in each case for chief the most suitable son. Our institutional heraldic writers and now the Court of Session recognise the right to "adopt" and "settle"[9]—even upon a natural son[10] or a complete stranger,[11] though settlement outwith the blood on a "stranger" is not approved by Scottish sentiment, and not being in any sense a settlement *in familia*, requires "the Prince's consent," given by a patent from his King of Arms.[12] Those who, when a settlement is made, within the tribe, talk of "disinherited rightful chiefs" are merely vapouring

---

[1] *Sources and Literature of the Law of Scotland*, 1936, p. 433.

[2] Stair Society, *Sources and Literature of the Law of Scotland*, p. 429.

[3] Lord Sinclair, *Scots Heraldry*, p. 87.

[4] *Scots Heraldry*, p. 87 ; J. Ferne, *Glorie of Generositie*, p. 67.

[5] *Grant of Auchernack, Chief of Clan Allan*, 1777, Lyon Register, I., p. 512 ; *Scott of Harden*, 1700, *ibid.* p. 189 ; *Scottish Notes and Queries*, 27th April 1940, p. 293.

[6] 1941 S.C. 684–685.

[7] Lord Sands delivered some *dicta* favouring this English (he didn't realise how alien !) doctrine in *Seaforth* v. *Allangrange*, 1920 S.C. 801—giving no authorities ; whereas principles, precedents and the constant practice of Lyon Court are opposed to this English absurdity.

[8] *Stirling-Maxwell of Pollok* and *Stirling of Keir* ; and the separation of the chiefships of *Grant* and *Colquhoun*, and of the *Earldom of Rothes* from *Haddington*.

[9] Sir George Mackenzie and Nisbet, and Macfarlane's *Genealogical Collections*, I., p. 125.

[10] *Lord of the Isles*, A.P.S. II. 189 ; *Maclean*, 1496 R.M.S. II., No. 2329.

[11] *Ross of Balnagowan*, 1732, Lyon Register, I., p .208 ; *Heraldry in Scotland*, p. 353.

[12] Mackenzie, *Works*, II., p. 615, line 33 ; *Notes and Queries*, Vol. 181, 5th July 1941, p. 3.

Anglo-Saxon nonsense.[1] Tanistry is still a recognised feature of our heraldic and clan law, and modern thought [2] would rather extend it to British peerages than restrict [3] the exercise, where occasion indicates, and subject to official approval, of a useful and age-old patriarchal principle. Mackenzie and Nisbet distinguish settlement within the blood, which they regard as a matter of right,[4] from settlement on a stranger. Careful reading shows it is only in the latter contingency that they consider Royal veto upon the transaction competent.[5] This explains the idea that Lyon is somehow bound to give effect to entail clauses to " enable the heir to take." Feudally, that cannot be, since (a) it would imply the subject could force the Crown's hand, (b) if Lyon refused, the condition would be " impossible " and void. Obviously the true explanation is survival in our Scottish family-law, and the Scottish Law of Arms which deals therewith, of the principle of tanistry—the right of each patriarch to settle his successor (within the family), and only if he makes a settlement outwith the group, or seeks to alter an existing specific destination, would a question of Royal veto or need for Letters Patent arise.[6] Otherwise the heir or nominee makes up his title by matriculation.[7] Unless the antecedent matriculation contains a specific destination, arms in Scotland thus pass by succession or nomination *in familia*, the former admitting of possession on apparency, the latter necessarily involving immediate

[1] Very likely thinking of the Jacobites and our " rightful king," but forgetting the proposition was that the Stuarts had been evicted by foreign force, and that the Hanoverian kings were considered interlopers until Cardinal York settled his " St. Andrew " and the Coronation Ring on George III., making him heir by tanistry. These were heirship jewels, *quae non recipiunt functionem*.

[2] *Hansard*, December 1933, vol. 283, col. 374.

[3] Lord Sands groundless *dicta* have not been followed in *e.g. Macleod of Macleod*, 1935, Lyon Register, XXXI., p. 74, and *Macgregor of Inneregny*, 1935, *ibid*. XXXII., p. 22, and, as in the old precedents of the seventeenth and eighteenth centuries, divertion of arms in the line of expediency or with the *duthus*, has continued. The correct difference of a superseded " heir " is a label, cf. *Duke of Windsor* ; *Lindsay of Spynie, ibid*. XXXIII., p. 17 ; Mackintosh of Clan Chattan, 9th April 1947, *ibid*. XXXVI., p. 36.

[4] Nisbet, *System of Heraldry*, II., iii., pp. 56–60; also p. 33, lines 21 and 42 ; p. 34, line 29 ; and p. 70, line 24 ; referring to those who have not and those who " have right to dispose of the arms by way of testament or disposition."

[5] A person " assumed or adopted by one of his own predecessors or family, for these surely may bear the arms " (Mackenzie, *Works*, II., p. 616, line 23) : " If lands were disponed to a mere stranger not upon condition that he should marry a daughter, but that he should bear the name and arms . . . the receiver of the disposition cannot bear the arms (for that was not within the disponer's power to bestow) except the prince consent " (*ibid*. line 30). See *Notes and Queries*, Vol. 181, July 1942, p. 2.

[6] Although even an alteration of destination may (within the group, I assume) be made in a matriculation (*Heraldry in Scotland*, p. 127) ; no doubt a patent has often been craved in such circumstances, particularly if some ministerial declaration is desired in the deed ; and a patent is appropriate if a resignation has been formally made. Resignation has, however, not been insisted on to be necessary for the changing of a destination *within the blood*, which as we see is often done by simple rematriculation with the terms of the chief's new settlement thereon made of record and *effect*.

[7] *Stewart-Mackenzie of Seaforth*, 1935, Lyon Register, XXXI., p. 56.

rematriculation, which is technically requisite in every case,[1] to make up title to the arms and to establish the gentility and chiefship or chieftaincy denoted by the armorial achievement.

(2) The *Ard-righ*—even the Irish High-King—as part of his pre-rogative, could step in and settle troubles over chiefship, by deter-mining the succession and causing one or other of the claimants to be inaugurated.[2] Similar power certainly came to be exercised by the *Ard-righ Albainn* in the thirteenth century,[3] when, upon the chivalric principle of the " Fountain of Honour," the position was taken that chiefship—a " high social dignity " [4]—flowed from the Crown, and thus in the reign of David II. is found a series of charters confirming the office and diverting the order of succession of the *Kenkynol* of Carrick,[5] *i.e.* the chiefship of the Carrick and Kennedy " clans " and others ; determining who shall be " Captain of " such communities as Clan Muntercasduff, Clan MacGowan, Clan Connan, and Clan Kennelman.[6] The very fact of the charters, not to add the termin-ology used, denotes the Crown's determination of a question.[7]

By the thirteenth to fourteenth century the clans (*parentela*) were thus being held, like " noble families," to be " communities " whose status in public life flowed from the Crown (just as the " Seven Earls " were deemed to flow from the sons of Cruithne) and whereof the chief-ships were dignities held of, and under, the Fountain of Honour.[8] The fifteenth century saw the development of armorial jurisdiction and the Court of Chivalry, *i.e.* Law of Arms ; also of the delegation of the Crown's prerogative regarding *nobilitas minor* (*i.e.* gentility as distinct from peerage) to the Kings of Arms—in Scotland to an officer already vested with the genealogical jurisdiction of the High Sennachie [9] —and consequently no more Royal " gifts of chieftaincy " pass the Great Seal. The " dignities " of Esquire and Gentleman were hence-forth determined in, and matters of record in, the courts of the Law of Arms,[10] and it was there that claimants had to justify the same

---

[1] Innes of Learney, *Law of Succession in Ensigns Armorial*, p. 45.

[2] *Chiefship of Burkes*, 1595, *Irish Law of Kingship*, p. 199 (Royal Irish Acad.).

[3] If this period opened a new and " organised " basis of clanship, obviously that organisation was based on the supremacy of the Crown.

[4] Per Lord Justice-Clerk in *Maclean of Ardgour* v. *Maclean*, 1937.

[5] Great Seal, I., 509 ; II., 379.   [6] *Ibid.* I., Appendix II., Nos. 912, 913, 914, 982.

[7] See evidence of Dr. John Cameron and W. Mackay Mackenzie, Appendix xxx.

[8] The Scottish nobiliary system has always differed from that of England in that whilst it appreciates the value of heredity, it also realises the inexpediency of immutable primogeniture. Tanistry was perpetuated in the regrants, nomina-tions, tailzies, and other expedients whereby honours of every description could, as chiefship and arms still can, be diverted into whatever channel from time to time seems most expedient (*Scots Heraldry*, p. 86), provided resort is made to the Fountain of Honour, and a satisfactory ground for the diversion shown by one having right to the honour to be diverted (Nisbet, *System of Heraldry*, II., iii., pp. 33, 34 ; *Scots Heraldry*, p. 86).

[9] *Juridical Review*, September 1940, p. 194 n.

[10] 1937 S.L.T. 156 ; J. Dallaway, *Heraldic Enquiries*, p. 309 ; Hailsbury's *Laws of England*, 1912 edition, XXII., p. 289, par. 632.

" by the Law of Arms." [1] The King of Arms, commissioned to " visite," inquired not merely into the armorial charges—which are a mere branch of heraldic duty [2]—but as judge inquired into all relevant matters of nobility including " pedigrees, titles or designations," taking cognisance of all and " degrading interlopers and upstarts." [3]

The clan has become the " honourable community," whose chief, as its " representer," is " received and numbered amongst the ancient nobles of the realm," and distinguished by ensigns armorial, over which the Crown, for purposes of national safety, exercises a close control under the " Law of Arms." The chiefship has become a recognised social dignity, but of what rank ? A glance at the Precedency List, and at the degree of " helmets befitting their degree " assigned to chiefs in armorial patents, will show that the degree of this dignity is that of Esquire.[4] This exactly coincides with Macpherson's assertion that chiefship gave its holder precedence before " the first gentlemen of the Kingdom " [5] and the relative helmet.[6]

Now, it is entirely within the prerogative of the Crown whether a person or a community is to be received as a noble person or community amongst the nobles and noble groups of the realm or not.[7] If it be the Crown's pleasure to receive such community, the order of succession is absolutely dependent on the Crown's pleasure in making the grant or confirmation of *noblesse*, and any modification of the succession must be sought from the Crown by seeking a diversion of the order of descent of the insignia conferred by the Crown for distinguishing this dignity.[8] As regards the descent of, and claims to, chiefship, this was a subject which, in the seventeenth century, it was not doubted was capable of legal determination, when the chiefship

---

[1] *Right to Bear Arms*, 1900, p. 123. Shrewsbury Peerage, 1857, Minute of Evidence, pp. 16, 18, 215.

[2] Sir J. Anstis, *Order of the Garter*, p. 326.

[3] J. Gwillim, *Display of Heraldry*, 1724, Honour Civil, p. 49.

[4] This and Gentleman may be relatively low in rank, but they are none the less hereditary honours, flowing only from the Fountain of Honour as the royal commissions affirm, and a degree in the nobility as laid down in the Scottish statute, 1592, cap. 125, and the Baronetcy Warrants of Charles I. wherein the order of precedency is : (1) Baronets ; (2) Equites, *lie* Knights ; (3) Barones, *lie* Lairds ; (4) Armigeri, *lie* Esquires ; (5) et Generosis quibuscunque, *lie* Gentlemen. (Sir R. Douglas, *Baronage of Scotland*, p. 11 ; *Sources and Literature of the Law of Scotland* (Stair Society), p. 431, where Barones, marked for italics, was instead accidentally deleted !)

[5] *Loyall Dissuasive*, p. 26.

[6] *Scots Heraldry*, p. 22, n. 1 ; Denmiln MSS., 34–4–16.

[7] Whilst individual " nobility " depends on creation or proved descent, the Law of Arms has always recognised the existence of " noble " groups (" houses," " families," or " clans," cf. the patrician *gentes* of Rome) and persons are officially described as *e.g.* " of an auld honourable house " (A.P.S. II. 520 ; Lyon Register, V., p. 16), and similarly of an " honourable clan "—which governs the basis of the arms—(*tesseræ nobilitatis*) which they will be awarded on receiving, by grant or confirmation, personal hereditary nobility, *i.e. duine-uasail*.

[8] Sir George Mackenzie, *Works*, II., p. 616. Approved by Lords Aitchison and Jamieson as an authoritative passage.

of Clan Chattan was for five days debated in the Privy Council,[1] and was then understood to have been previously argued before the Lord of the Isles,[2] and not only was decree upon such a subject regarded as enforceable,[3] but Macpherson was of opinion that there was no safe appeal from a Royal determination.[4] Only the party adjudged chief " by the Law of Arms " (by which honours and dignities are alone determinable) [5] could be received as chief [6] by the Crown and public officials.[7] Throughout the *Loyall Dissuasive* there is no suggestion that clan chiefship was elective, any more than there is in the charters of David II. or the patents of chiefly achievements in Lyon Register. If chiefship had been considered elective the " ornaments " (and arms) would, as in the case of corporations, have been limited to " successors in office," not to various series of heirs. No claimant such as John Moydertach of Clanranald could have any security until his status had been acknowledged by the Crown.[8] In constitutional principle, the only occasion where election has been admitted is, where an " honourable community " exists, but the line of chiefly succession has fallen into doubt or cannot be established.[9]

[1] Sir Æneas Macpherson, *Loyall Dissuasive*, p. 58.

[2] *Ibid.* pp. 54, 115.   [3] *Ibid.* p. 115.   [4] *Ibid.* p. 117.

[5] W. Cruise, *Treatise on Dignities*, p. 251.

[6] *O.g.* if chiefs were ever again to be reviewed by the king as in 1822,* or summoned *qua* chiefs to Holyroodhouse, obviously only chiefs of whom there is official record would be summoned, and the dignities of Esquire and Gentleman, within which chiefship falls, are " of record " only in the Registers of a King of Arms (Halsbury's *Laws of England*, 1912, XXII., p. 289, par. 632 ; 1552, cap. 53, A.P.S. VII. 458). It is from Lyon alone that a list of chiefs could be obtained. A list of chiefs in their order of precedence (for the precedence of clans is simply that of their reigning chiefs) was promptly supplied for the Festival of Britain Clan Rally, 1951.

[7] Accordingly, at the Lord High Commissioner's Holyrood State dinner in May 1947, The Mackintosh, after his chiefship-decree, 18th March 1947, was placed much higher than *qua* naval officer in 1946. At the Society of Antiquaries Scot., when a *Raymond Wallace of Wallace* was put up for election as F.S.A on 9th October 1950 (whereas *Col. Robert F. H. Wallace of Wallace* had got Lyon Court decree as chief, 15th March 1950), upon objection from Lyon Office the candidate's name was publicly withdrawn from ballot. Only on resubmission as *Raymond Wallace* was he elected F.S.A. on 30th November 1950. (He is Marquis of Lagos abroad, but not Chief of the Wallaces.)

[8] Moydertach's line was confirmed in the *earbsa* lands by the Crown before Lyon accepted them as " chiefs."

[9] Cf. " *de facto* and *de jure* vacant," of the " Seven Earls' " Petition. Mackenzie expressed himself, " As long as it is known who is the root of the family, or who represents it (this may be by tanistry settlement) there is no place for election " (*Works*, II., p. 446, see remarks on p. 174 n. 5). In 1938 Dr. L. Maclean Watt's evidence was : *Q.* Do you consider that in the case of a clan or family group, where the chiefship is lost as in the case of the Macgregors, it would be reasonable for the Crown to allow the clan or family to elect a chief ? *A.* Yes. . . . *Q.* If the family exists and you cannot trace the chief line, that is an occasion where election is the only way ? *A.* They agree on the man and submit him to the Lord Lyon (*Ardgour Evidence*, p. 549).

* In 1953, when nine chiefs were invited to the State Service in St. Giles' Cathedral, only chiefs of whom the Lord Lyon had approved were invited.

In such a contingency, when the chiefship must otherwise have remained dormant, and the " honourable community " without a head, the Lord Lyon—acting in accordance with the old tribal principle—and exercising the delegated sovereign authority of the *Ard-righ*, has awarded (heritably) the armorial achievement of the chief [1] to the person suggested by the clan.[2] On this subject Mr. J. H. Stevenson, K.C., stated in the Macrae case :

Nothing could be more erroneous than the opinion, or more inconsistent with the character of the Highlanders, than to suppose that they ever in any degree admitted of election.[3]

W. Mackay Mackenzie, LL.D., in 1938 expressed the same view :

Q. It has been suggested that the office of chiefship of a clan or headship of a family was elective ? *A.* No. *Q.* Have you come across any examples of elected heads or chiefs ? *A.* No. How could they draw up clan genealogies if they are going to be interrupted by general election.[4]

It is inconceivable that the Crown, through Lyon, could be compelled to award a chief's achievement and supporters to an electee,[5] in the face of another heir under specific destination to these honours from the Crown, unless the chief, under the existing destination, made a demission of the insignia in Lyon's hands *in favorem*,[6] for although the Crown of Scotland can accept resignations and implement entails or settlements,[7] it cannot derogate from a right already conferred, without the actual holder's initiative, nor can he on his part complete a diversion without the King of Arms' consent *pro Rege*. The disinherited " heir," moreover, cannot " misken " the deed by which his ancestor initiated the diversion ;[8] though, as above indicated, it appears that where

[1] Such confirmation was deemed to confer hereditary right on the line of the electee, see A. Murray Macgregor, *History of Clan Gregor*, II., p. 271 ; *Campbell of Inverneil* (Chief of Clan Chearleich), 1875, Lyon Register, IX., p. 88.

[2] *Macnaughton*, 1818, Lyon Register, II., p. 172 ; *Macgregor*, 1795, *ibid*. I., p. 565 ; A. M. Macgregor, *History of Clan Gregor*, p. 273.

[3] *Macrae* v. *Macrae*, 1909, Lyon Court, Report, p. 104.

[4] See *Tartans of the Clans and Families of Scotland*, 1952 ed., p. 44, n. 2, on nature of elected *pseudo*-chiefs, who are of no legal or social value, and analogous only to the "Lord Justice Clerks," etc., of early nineteenth-century drinking clubs !

[5] This fact was settled 27th March 1941 by the Court's affirmation of Lord Lyon Grant's refusal to give supporters to a person in respect of " recognition " as a chieftain (unless Lyon wished to do so *ex gratia*).

[6] Cf. *Grant of Auchernach, Chief of the Clan Allan*, 1777, Lyon Register, I., p. 515 ; *Scott of Sinton*, 1700, *ibid*. II., p. 189.

[7] 8 & 9 Vict. cap. 23, sec. 21 ; *Scots Heraldry*, p. 86 ; *MacNeil of Barra*, 1915, Lyon Register, XXII., p. 60. The principle involved was laid down as regards dignities in *Oliphant* v. *Oliphant*, 1633, Morrison, *Dictionary of Decisions*, 10027 ; and the same held as regards the validity of " name and arms " clauses regarding arms in *Stevenson* v. *Stevenson*, 1677, *ibid*. 15475.

[8] *Oliphant* v. *Oliphant*, Morrison, *Dictionary of Decisions*, 10027.

nomination within the blood is concerned, the Scottish heraldic view is that the settler has the " right " to divert the representation (*i.e.* chiefship) and relative insignia.[1]

In conclusion, it may be observed that in the limited contingencies when an election is competent, namely where the group has the misfortune to find itself with no ascertainable heir and its chiefship is *de facto* and *de jure* vacant, the selectors will in the case of a chief be the landed armigerous magnates of the whole clan, and in the case of a branch-chieftain, those of the branch.[2] It appears, however, a corollary of the chiefship being a dignity, at least in the case of honourable (*i.e.* armigerous) communities, that only in the above-mentioned contingency could an election be contemplated without involving *purpresture* and treason. An ignoble community could elect whom it liked. Not being *notilis* or known, such " limmers " would have no public status, and their " chief " no dignity.[3] As Sir Æneas puts it : If a person was " of no family her father could not be a Cheefe " ;[4] and, says Nisbet,[5] the " first raiser " of a family is he who first obtains a coat of arms, *i.e.* the *indiciæ* of *noblesse* which brings the community

---

[1] Lord Aitchison says " a destination with a name and arms clause, whether in entail, marriage contract, or testament, appears to me to be incontrovertible " (1941 S.C. 685) ; and in *Oliphant* it was certainly laid down that the disinherited heir " behoved to warrant " the diversion. This agrees with Nisbet's allusion to those who " have right to dispose of the arms " (*System of Heraldry*, II., iii., pp. 33, 34), and points to the great power of the chief in regard to nominating his heir ; yet, if the diversion be not completed representation against it might be conducted by Lyon ministerially, since the function is prerogatival.

[2] Lord Justice-Clerk in *Maclean of Ardgour* v. *Maclean*, 1938 S.L.T. 57, and per Lord Mackay, by the principal landed men of the clan or branch (a significant admission of the territorial character of chieftaincy ; cf. p. 163, *supra*).

[3] There is this great distinction between noble and ignoble communities: in noble groups succession is hereditary, in ignoble groups it is elective. The fundamental reason is that inheritance depended on tribal (ceremonial) marriage, and in primitive communities only the patrician-free class could contract ceremonial marriage, and have a " family." The issue of slave unions were *sequelæ*, and, unlike a free family, there could amongst *sequelæ* be no heirship. Accordingly, the representer of an un-free group could only be ascertained electorally. Thus the ignoble peasant communities in France have an elected " master " and " mistress " (who were not husband and wife), and having no " arms " the flag of such a community bore only the national badge (Brentano, *Old Regime in France*, p. 48). Noble families, on the contrary, had hereditary chiefs and liveries. In Scotland the greatest significance and pride was attached to nobility (*Scots Heraldry*, pp. 4, 16). " Gentility is of all things esteemed the most valuable in the notions of these people " (Burt's Letters, No. 22, cf. W. C. Mackenzie, *Highlands and Isles of Scotland*, p. 89). Accordingly, we find everything in Scotland tended to be hereditary (G. G. Coulton, *Abbeys and Social Life in Scotland*, p. 16). Accordingly, for a group to assert that it elects its chief is tantamount to confessing it is, or was, an ignoble litter ! To deny or repudiate the jurisdiction and authority of the Court of Honour is simply to assert oneself and one's clan to be a base and ignoble community.

[4] *Loyall Dissuasive*, p. 35. That is, to be chief of a clan one must, in Macpherson's view, be the chief of the stem family as recognised by the Crown's officer of honour. [5] *System of Heraldry*, 1722, I., p. 3.

(clan or other) within the cognisance of the Court and Social Life of the Realm—and consequently of the Law of Arms.

ORDER OF SUCCESSION

The Scottish order of succession was derived from a Pictish basis, whose evolution is attributed to Malcolm MacKenneth. Salic law has never obtained in Scotland, and any attempt to introduce it has been repudiated as alien to our tradition and custom,[1] and in numerous clan traditions a fresh eponymus (really an " Incoming Husband ") is made to marry the heiress of an older Gaelic race.[2] It was not because they were women that the clans objected to Mary Macleod and Anne Macpherson. There was a far graver reason—they married Campbells. The tribes had seen what happened with Muriel of Cawdor, and feared that two fresh branches of Clan Diarmid would arise on the ruins of Macpherson and Macleod. This indeed was explicitly pointed out by Nisbet :

> After the marriage Sir John Campbell continued his own surname and did not assume that of Calder, as is frequently done by those who marry heiresses, whereby he seemed rather to found a new family than to continue an old one, which so exasperated the heirs male and relations of the name of Calder that they had constant feuds and skirmishes with the Campbells.[3]

What angered the heir male was not the succession of the heiress, but the conversion of the old Cawdor lairdship into a cadetship in the Clan Campbell, in place of carrying on the House of Cawdor of that Ilk.

In the great Clan Chattan controversy, so strenuously argued in the seventeenth century, there is not a suggestion of Salic law.[4] The Salic theory in the Scottish Highlands (argued, of course, from cases of tailzied nomination, etc.) appears to have been first propounded [5] by the notorious Simon, Lord Lovat, and the theory only occurred to him when he had failed to secure the chiefship by the abduction of either the heiress or the widow of his predecessor.

As regards the Clan Chattan, it was, again, Lovat who, in 1744, stirred up his son-in-law, Cluny-Macpherson, to renew the controversy (settled in 1672 by Lyon's Diploma), for the political reason that Mackintosh was not prepared to raise the clan for Prince Charles, whilst Cluny was ready to go " out."

---

[1] W. Angus, Keeper of the Register and Records, *Sources and Literature of the Law of Scotland*, p. 268.

[2] *Social and Economic Development of Scotland*, pp. 521, 580.

[3] Nisbet, *System of Heraldry*, II., Appendix, p. 239.

[4] *Loyall Dissuasive*, Scottish History Society edition, pp. 29, 33, 34, 35, 39, 48, 55, 59, 71, 114, 116.

[5] Saving, perhaps, William Macpherson of Nuid who was also *auctor in rem suam*, but who admitted the power of his chief to tailzie the succession unless God prevented.

The principle laid down by Macpherson—a lawyer and sheriff—and reiterated through his book,[1] is, in his own words :

Both from law and reason, we have the constant custome and practice of all the families of the Kingdome of our side to plead for us in this point, so much, That if you can instance us one familie in the whole Kingdome that owns one for their Cheefe for his being married to a daughter of the familie or ane heiress, without his assuming the name and bearing (*i.e.* the arms) of the family, we shall forthwith submitt (p. 34).

It must needs follow that being himself M'Pherson, upon the same foot with us, that is, in memory of his predicissors office, his daughter was so,[2] and all that are come of her (if she was ane heiress), should be likewayes called M'Pherson, without which M'Intoshe do or say what he will, can never pretend to be our Cheefe ; for if he should to-morrow, or any time hereafter, assume the name of Cathone, that gives him no more title to be Cheefe of the M'Phersons than if he hade been married to the heiress of Struan, should think to be Cheefe of the Robertsons by calling himself M'Donell (p. 48).[3]

Other high authorities took the same view as Macpherson. The destination of the *Ceann-cinnidh* of Carrick was *heredibus*, and through heirs female it can be shown to have descended ; Walter Macfarlane of that Ilk, the great antiquary and chief of his clan, took the destination of his arms and chiefly insignia—including the slogan—to " heirs," not heirs male,[4] and Maconnochie of Meadowbank, the Lord Advocate in 1819, likewise took the destination of the supporters granted him as chief of the clan, to " the heirs whatsoever of the patentee's body." [5] None of these high authorities believed in Salic law, or applied it to the succession awarded to their own houses.

Another significant point is that not only male heirs-apparent but an eldest daughter (being heiress-apparent) was put out in fosterage,[6] and under the statutes of Iona the eldest daughter of a West Highland chief was, when the chief had no son, to be sent to be educated in law (see p. 56). The point of this was that she was the heir-at-law to the *Ceann-cinnidh* chiefship, and its judicial functions (see p. 108). This,

[1] *Loyall Dissuasive*, p. 33. " M'Intoshe, his marrying (the heiress) without taking the name and bearing of the family could never make him Cheefe. That was *conditio sine qua non*," failing which, the chiefship and following devolved upon the heir male.

[2] Macpherson here recognises that the succession devolves on the heiress herself, and that the patronymic M'Pherson as a title would also devolve on her.

[3] Sir Æneas is silent concerning the Lord Lyon's Declaration, 10th September 1672, and evades the point that neither Macpherson nor Mackintosh bore the name " Chattan," and that Lyon's decision was confined to (a) the aggregate community of " Clan Chattan," (b) the " name of Mackintosh "—one of the components. Lyon never affirmed that Mackintosh was chief of " the Macphersons " as a unit within the honourable community, " the hail kin " of Clan Chattan.

[4] Lyon Register, I., p. 377 (heirs include females).   [5] *Ibid.* II., p. 184.

[6] Mary Bisset, per Wardlaw MSS., p. 3 ; cited in *Macrae* v. *Macrae*, 1909, Lyon Court ; Proof, p. 79.

and the label-differencing of an heiress-apparent's arms *vita patris*,[1] show how natural it was to treat the heiress exactly on the same footing as a male heir, and in France, under the laws of Anjou, Maine, and Brittany, she could, in default of a son, inherit the representation of the family.[2] When she did succeed, Scottish heraldry—and Macpherson talks of " good " and " bad herauldrie " in relation to clanship [3]—treated the heiress exactly as if the succession were uninterrupted, allowing her shield and crest [4] and even a " helmet befitting her degree," [5] so that the representation of the house continued heraldically—as genealogically—uninterrupted.

It will not escape the reader that Macpherson's principle, although it recognises the right being in the heiress herself—as the Royal and Lyon documents likewise expressly do [6]—treats the son-in-law as " chief " *jure uxoris*.[7]

This " incoming husband " is a feature of other tribal countries as well as Scotland.[8] A recent authority writes :

It was recognised that whilst the actual muscle must be that of a man, the man held office by right of his descent or connection with a woman.[9]

The Queen, through whom the Royal Rank and Blood came,[10] must have enjoyed an esteem which, when she knew how to use it, gave her considerable authority.[11]

There are, however, numerous instances of females taking command in their own right, even in the Middle Ages,[12] whereof Boadicea

---

[1] Janet Fenton of Bakie, *Scottish Armorial Seals*, No. 915.

[2] *Old Regime in France*, p. 43.   [3] *Loyall Dissuasive*, pp. 49, 63, 72.

[4] *Buccleuch*, Lyon Register, I., p. 34 ; *Robertson of Lawers*, ibid. II., p. 117 ; *Gibsone of Pentland*, ibid. II., p. 52 ; *Farquharson of Invercauld*, 1815, ibid. II., p. 130 ; 1936, ibid. XXXII., p. 34.

[5] *Buccleuch, supra* ; *Cunningham*, ibid. I., p. 275 ; *Conti-White*, 1778, Register of Genealogies, I. Lyon has since declined to allow women a helmet as not " befitting " (though we find they received them from Lyon in the Middle Ages) and has avoided any debate on the subject, a helmet not being part of the armorial "estate of inheritance," and merely a variable personal adjunct to the arms.

[6] *Loyall Dissuasive*, p. 48. Cf. Lord Royston (W. Fraser, *Earls of Cromartie*, II., p. 179). The original announcement of the northern meeting, 11th June 1788, refers (4) to " Every Gentleman or Lady being Head of a Family " (Sir I. Colquhoun, *Highland Gatherings*, p. 111).

[7] *Lundin of Lundin* (see *Notes and Queries*, CLXXIX., p. 362) ; Lyon Register, I., p. 180 ; Nisbet, *System of Heraldry*, I., p. 66 ; *Loyall Dissuasive*, p. 114 ; *Notes and Queries*, CLXXIX., p. 362 ; *Maclachlan of Maclachlan* (Lyon Court), *Edinburgh Gazette*, 1949.

[8] Sir E. B. Tayler, *The Nineteenth Century*, XL., p. 94 ; H. B. G. Westermarck, *History of Human Marriage*, 1901, p. 110.

[9] R. A. M. Macalister, *Ireland in Pre-Celtic Times*, p. 242. Our Scoto-Pictish customs may thus be " pre-Celtic " and indigenous to the realm of Scotland.

[10] As already pointed out, the " King " and " Mormaer " were just the highest variety of chiefs. The same principles were, *e.g.* in Bruce v. Baliol, held applicable to both.   [11] Henri Hubert, *The Rise of the Celts*, p. 210.

[12] J. Cameron, *Celtic Law*, p. 93, cites primitive instances of them going to battle in an inferior capacity which will hardly be admired, *non constat* that a *Ban-Flaith* or *Ban-Mormaer* did not go in a very different category.

and Cartismandua of the Brigantes are instances, and medieval heraldry even provided rules regarding the cut of armorial tabards to be worn by women commanding in the field.[1] That heraldry may relevantly be referred to in clan matters is evidenced by Sir Æneas Macpherson, who refers to " good " or " bad herauldrie." He appreciated that chiefship was a subject to be " justified by the Law of Arms."[2] In her father or husband's absence, a *ban-tighearna* had no doubt not infrequently to take the role of a " Black Agnes " or a " Helen Macgregor."

Indeed it will not be forgotten that during " the '45 " it was the Lady Mackintosh who organised " the Rout of Moy " and that at the siege of Blair Castle it was the Lady Freda (old Lord Nairne's daughter) who personally fired the first cannon shot.[3]

In the Middle Ages an heiress was usually married or put in a convent at the age of fourteen (in Celtic Scotland), so the independent chieftainess[4] seldom emerged in practice. If the heir was under fourteen, an acting-chief was chosen, who held office, or anyway title, for life, but on the direct heir attaining full age they ruled jointly.[5] This explains the " joint reigns " found in our early history, and similarly Macpherson of Nuid was appointed " chief," pending the majority of his nephew ; but by 1609, this tutor-like office apparently terminated at the heir's majority.[6]

Lady Erroll was, in her obituary notice, described as " Chief of the Noble Family of Hay,"[7] and Lady Kilravock as " Representative " of that ancient family.

The express right of a woman to be *Ceann-cinnidh* and hold

---

[1] G. Legh, *Accidens of Armory* (1562), fol. 96 ; E. J. Millington, *Heraldry in History, Poetry, and Romance* (1858), p. 296 ; Rymour, *Foedera*, II., pp. 200, 525.

[2] *Loyall Dissuasive*, pp. 49, 63, 72, reference to " bearings."

[3] Tullibardine, *Military History of Perthshire*, p. 329.

[4] This term, which appears in the fifteenth century, is sanctioned by Sir Walter Scott (*New Oxford Dictionary*) and is considered unnecessary by the Court of Session, on the ground that a female chairman is not called a " chairwoman." But in the more punctilious and chivalric atmosphere of the Law of Arms, the title of a dignitated female is normally feminised. One does not call a queen regnant a " king," nor a countess in her own right an " earl." The Gaelic dictionary provides feminines of almost every rank in Scotland. The Lord Justice-Clerk's view that chief is a term applicable to either sex is, however, borne out by Trevoux's French Dictionary (1743) : " *Il se dit aussi au feminin* " ; see also *La Dictionaire de L'Academie Française*, s.v. *Dame chevetaigne*. The position —and what Lord Aitchison evidently had in view—is that a number of descriptive titles, *e.g.* "Sovereign," "*Ceann Cinnidh*," and "*Ceann Tighe*," are as applicable to one sex as to another.

[5] W. F. Skene, *Highlanders of Scotland*, 1902 edition, p. 105.

[6] It has been suggested that for convenience such an *ad hoc* " chief " or " chieftain " should be styled " Chieftain-Wardatour," as the term " Sheriff-Wardatour " was used in hereditary sheriffdoms. Chiefship being a feudalised heritable estate, cf. the Great Seal Charters of *Kenkynol*, the term " Wardatour " is legally apposite.

[7] *The Roses of Kilravock*, p. 507.

" chiefship " personally, which is recognised in the armorial patents such as Lord Advocate MacConnochie's and the destination of the *Kenkynol*, however, was necessarily and formally recognised in the case of the Crown, or highest " chiefship " of all, when the " Maid of Norway " [1] was received as Queen. For the Scottish coronation involved receiving the *Ard-righ* as " chief," [2] and though the " Maid " died before her coronation, Mary Queen of Scots was crowned, and must, according to the usual ceremony, have (*omnia rite acta esse presumunter*) been installed " chief."

The principle enunciated by Sir Æneas was re-stated in Council in November 1672 by the Earl Marischal,[3] and so confident of its correctness was Macpherson, that he applies it in favour of Glengarry's claim, through the heiress of Lochalsh, to the chiefship of Clan Donald,[4] on which the Privy Council had already taken the same view.[5] The principle thus laid down by a distinguished seventeenth-century lawyer (whose party-interest was assuredly to propound the Salic law— if anything of the sort had existed in the Scottish Highlands) explains not only many clan successions, but much armorial practice of the Lyon Court, and the terms of the Royal Charters, *e.g.* of *Kenkynol*.

The principle of transmitting the chiefship of an ancient family both through an heiress and to her husband, on his taking the name, were well illustrated—and with the highest authority—in the case of Lundin of that Ilk. About 1648, Margaret Lundin of Lundin married Robert Maitland, second son of the 1st Earl of Lauderdale. He died early, but the children bore the maternal name of Lundin, and the son having died young, the elder daughter, Sophia Lundin of Lundin, married 30th April 1670 the Hon. John Drummond, second son of the 3rd Earl of Perth. On his marriage he took his wife's name, and by 1679 had become so proud of his wife's descent (from a bastard son of William the Lion, who had married an early heiress of Lundin) that he took steps to alter the ancient arms of the Lundin family for a bastardised version of the Scottish Royal Arms.

Since it is a fixed rule of Heraldic law that no part of the Royal Arms can be granted without the Sovereign's Warrant, the aspiration was beyond Lyon's power, though he laid the application before H.M. and, on 27th October 1679, Charles II. issued a Royal Warrant authorising " the present laird of Lundin, and his lawful successors of the

---

[1] Titles of this description are incidentally matter of record in Lyon Register cf. *Fair Maid of Moray*, Lyon Register, I., p. 528, being, of course, factual, " pedigree matter."

[2] Nisbet, *System of Heraldry*, II., iv., p. 155.

[3] *Loyall Dissuasive*, p. 59.

[4] *Ibid.* p. 118. Many complicated considerations are, however, involved in Clan Donald's chiefship. See " Heraldic Legitimation," *Notes and Queries*, CLXXIX., p. 362.

[5] *Privy Council*, 3rd series, III., p. 552.

name of Lundin, and descending from that family " to bear the tressured lion within a bastard bordure,[1] and these arms were duly matriculated by Lyon in name of " The Honourable John Lundin of that Ilk, descended of, and representing, Robert of Lundin, natural son to William the Lion." [2]

Whether, or how, he was " descended of " the bastard I know not, but I suspect the theory was that by marriage he had become *eadem persona* with the fair Sophia of Lundin his wife. His only title to " represent " Robert was *jure uxoris*, having taken the " name and bearing " of her family, whereinto, with due formality, and under the highest auspices, he indigenated himself, with the " higher " right of attiring himself in the coat-armorial of a Royal bastard! We thus see the theory of " adoption " carried to its extreme logical conclusion with the full authority of Lyon and the Crown, and since a legitimate Drummond thus became " in right of his wife " a " representer of a Royal bastard " we can readily understand Macpherson's proposition that, one of Mackintosh's ancestors having been forfeited for treason, Mackintosh :

> Must rest satisfied to be the successor of a forfaulted traitor and without rehabiliation not pretend to be a gentleman, but as come of the heiress of the Clan Chattan, which he seems also to have lost for not taking the name.[3]

He recognises, as in reference to the Clan Donald, at p. 118, that heirship of a clan would pass down provided the name be taken—which is the whole burden of his book.

This interesting principle—so well illustrated by Macpherson's arguments and by the Lundin case—was fully adopted in *Maclean of Ardgour* v. *Maclean*, by Lord Justice-Clerk Aitchison, who observes :

> The question whether the heiress can transmit the family arms undifferenced to her descendants where the husband belongs to another family and has not become a member of the heiress's family by adoption or the assumption of her family name is not necessarily the same question as whether the heiress has the sole right to bear the family arms undifferenced.[4]

Where the name is taken he regards the descent as a foregone conclusion, and the arms descend *in familia*, as indeed Lord Jamieson explains at p. 702, where the heiress has a right to the arms as " heiress," her children " certainly may bear the arms " since they take as heir and not as " disponee " under a name and arms clause—when the succession is conditional on Lyon implementing the transaction. Lord Jamieson had indeed already—in an entail case—formulated in modern language, the principle in matters of name, viz. that where the heir

---

[1] Nisbet, *System of Heraldry*, I., p. 66. [2] Lyon Register, I., p 180.
[3] *Loyall Dissuasive*, p. 114. [4] 1941 S.C. 684.

does not take, or drops, " the name," then he or she becomes " conventionally dead "—in the case in question, " dead " as a Munro.[1]

The principles thus laid down are entirely in accord with what we find in ancient clan-treatises like the *Loyall Dissuasive*, and in the practice of Lyon Court ; so that many clans at present chiefless may ere long be able to establish an heir in the direct line of blood, in accordance with our ancient nobiliary laws.

Sir George Mackenzie considers that a husband who marries the heiress of an armigerous house ought to drop his own name and arms entirely,[2] and when any possibility of confusion exists, that is the only safe course,[3] as it is in any event the only proper course, unless two " houses " are merged in one line.[4] In the Clan Chattan case (whereof Macpherson makes so much, but of Lyon says little—since he had decided against Macpherson), Sir Charles Erskine's decision was

[1] *Munro* v. *Gascoigne*, 1939, see *Scottish Notes and Queries*, 24th February 1940, p. 131, and cf. H. G. B. Westermarck, *History of Human Marriage*, p. 111. *The Scotsman* 22/3/1939 p. 10.

[2] *Works*, II., pp. 490, 616 ; cf. *Scots Heraldry*, p. 107 (non-armigerous husband). The status of the " double-barrelled surname " is one which requires further careful consideration, not only as regards whether it should be indexed under the first or the last of its components, but as to its actual legal character. The tendency—in such lengthy mouthfuls—is to use the last of a double- (or triple-) barrelled surname, and, accordingly, testators sometimes specify that their name shall be the " last name " (*Heraldry in Scotland*, p. 380). On such grounds Debrett's *Baronetage*, for example, indexes per the last name. Technically, however, if the whole be treated as one, then the first name should rule, though it is less liable to be that ordinarily used. Armorially an important point (now becoming clarified) is how far a double-barrelled name is sufficient to retain chiefship, or representation, and, if so, whether use of " the name," first or last, matters. Mackenzie, as we have seen, says (*Works*, II., p. 490) that the name of the family to be represented should be taken alone and that a combined one " is not sufficient." Where a second son (*Stirling of Keir*, 1903) has taken " the name " alone, whilst his elder brother has kept both (*Stirling-Maxwell of Pollok*), the (in this instance) supporters and undifferenced arms have been awarded to the second son bearing " the name " (*Stirling of Keir*) alone. The practice seems thus to be that Lyon Court, in a competition between a senior " hyphenee " and a junior " plain " perpetuator of a name, held the bearer of the " plain name," though junior, is to be preferred as true representer and heir in the insignia—which would agree with Sir George Mackenzie's view as that which would prevail if necessary. Possession of the fief or seal, might, however, bear on such a situation. It is now decided that a person with double-barrelled name cannot be officially recognised as " Chief " of the " Name " of either part of the double surname and the supporters of *Lockhart of Lee* were not allowed to *Macdonald-Lockhart* (Lyon Court, 1948) ; and Campbell-Gray, 22nd Lord Gray, was not recognised as Chief of the Name of Gray, nor allowed the Gray arms undifferenced (1950, Lyon Register, XXVIII., p. 56) which agrees with Lord Jamieson in *Munro* v. *Gascoigne*, 1939, and Lord Aitchison in *Maclean of Ardgour*, 1941 S.C. p. 684.

[3] Cf. Nisbet, *System of Heraldry*, II., iii., p. 48. Nisbet failed to perceive what the chiefs evidently realised. Had the later chiefs of Clan Mackenzie, founding on their ancestress's matriculation, 1815, refrained from quartering Stewart, the great Seaforth litigation, 1920–22, need never have arisen.

[4] Innes of Learney, *Scots Heraldry*, p. 88.

obviously based on the principle that since neither Mackintoshes nor Macphersons bore the name " Chattan," that chiefship passed to the eldest flow of the blood within the clan, nor did the Privy Council overturn Lyon's decision.[1] Cluny-Macpherson's matriculation was of date the day following.[2] Whatever procedure was then preliminary to the issue of a Declaration from the Lord Lyon King of Arms,[3] its official value was such that it was received and acted on by the Crown, to the extent of even awarding differenced versions of the Royal Arms.[4] Since the succession to " clan chiefship " is—save where competently diverted by tailzie or settlement, with consent of the Crown through its King of Arms (*i.e.* in a matriculation of arms or supporters), or where the Crown has similarly received as chief some particular or nominated member of the group—to be in " the eldest line of the eldest blood " bearing the name, it only remains to observe that where such chiefship devolves upon a female, then on her marriage, or within due time,[5] her husband must also take the clan name, and that the heir male has, as principal cadet,[6] a prominent status at the immediate right hand of the heir female chief [7] who is the " premier head " of the race.[8] Until a break occurs in lineal male succession this post of honour belongs to the eldest cadet. Indeed, in many clan cases the so-called " eldest cadet " now appears to be actually the collateral heir male where the name, arms, and chiefship have passed to an heir female.

---

[1] Naturally not—having applied same principle to Clan Donald on 18th July ! The Clan Donald chiefship was decided in Lyon Court, 11th April 1947, see Appendix XXXI and 1950 S.L.T., p. 8.

[2] Cluny's matriculation of 12th March 1672 was necessarily reduced prior to 10th September 1672, at least *quoad* the description and supporters, and evidently *in foro*. Cluny, for example, was not a " baron " as he had averred, but, as a new matriculation followed, he presumably did defend. The declaration was promptly sent north for publication (Macfarlane's *Geneaolgi. Coll.*, I., p. 393).

[3] And these are directed to " all persons of eminence having power and authority to take cognisance of titles " (*Familie of Innes*, p. 45 ; *Cumming*, 1727, Register of Genealogies, I., p. 1).

[4] *Lundin of Lundin*, 1679, Nisbet, *System of Heraldry*, I., p. 66 ; Warrant, John (formerly Drummond) Lundin of that Ilk, " incoming husband " of the heiress Sophia Lundin of Lundin (see *Notes and Queries*, 1941, clxxix., p. 362). See p. 185 *supra*.

[5] *Loyall Dissuasive*, p. 39 ; presumably within *anno deliberandi* (year and day) unless she (Matheson of Achary, *Scots Heraldry*, p. 152) and her child keep her name independently.

[6] *Maclean of Ardgour* v. *Maclean*, 18th July 1941 ; the heir male was found not to be entitled to the " old family (seal of) arms " and only to get a version of them with a " brisure or mark of cadency," *i.e.* the heir male is in such circumstances a cadet.

[7] *Loyall Dissuasive*, p. 52 ; *Notes and Queries*, 15th August 1942, p. 97.

[8] *Clan Cochrane*, Lyon Ct., Register of Gen., I., p. 2 (Earl of Dundonald).

The foregoing has been the view of all our great jurists.[1] Its basis was expediency, and alike in Crown, peerage, and chiefships, this Scots order of succession has in practice proved itself expedient. It is always a matter for regret if continuity of the sacred race embodiment be interrupted, or confusion and discord supervene, or the racial representation be separated from the *earbsa*-land. In the present age of smaller families and high death-duties, we must recognise that perpetuation of male succession is deplorably likely to become progressively rarer. It has therefore seemed a matter of practical importance to demonstrate conclusively that, as in the case of our highest chiefship, the Crown, the dignity of a clan chief or chieftain duly passes in the old Pictish order of the directest succession—the basis of our common law succession—provided the heiress, at least, and her husband retain, or take, the name and title of the clan—a *sine qua non*, legally a " resolutive condition." Owing to the modern English predilection for double-barrelled surnames, Sir George Mackenzie's emphasis upon the advisability of taking the heiress's name and arms alone, requires to be reiterated.

For the succession of the heir of line, we have the considered opinions of Scots Privy Council, the Earl Marischal, the Lord Advocate, five Lords of Session, six Lord Lyons, Nisbet the Herald, and Sir Æneas Macpherson. Riddell, the celebrated peerage lawyer, has pointed out " the constant devolution of all our older peerages to heirs general besides the later female descents," and the nineteenth-century conception of Salic ideas, when applied to Scotland, has recently been described as " a perversion of the facts and misconstruction of the ancient law of the country." [2]

DETERMINATION OF CHIEFSHIP

Since a clan is a community, which it has now been shown has been recognised by the Imperial Parliament as a legal entity,[3] and it has been established by legal proof that " clan and family mean exactly the same thing," [4] and that the Celtic *Ceann-cinnidh*/head of the clan is, as authoritatively laid down by Sir George Mackenzie,[5] synonymous with chief/representative of the family, and that these identical offices are distinguished from the other members of such communities by the arms of all such cadets being heraldically " differenced " by one or other of the various systems of armorial differencing, chiefship of clans is (as our historians have always indicated) necessarily determinable by the Lord Lyon King of Arms in the Scottish

---

[1] Earl of Crawford, *Earldom of Mar in Sunshine and Shade*, pp. 106–135 ; Lord Lyon G. Burnett, *Red Book of Menteith Reviewed*, p. 49 ; *Notes and Queries*, CLXXIX., p. 308, s.v. Erskine of Linlathen.

[2] H. Doubleday, *Complete Peerage*, VIII., p. 854.

[3] Clan Gregor, 15 Geo. III. cap. 29.

[4] *Maclean of Ardgour Evidence*, p. 517. See p. 190 *infra*.

[5] *Works*, II., p. 618, line 15.

Court of Chivalry, and, like other such ancient social dignities, chief-ship is " justiciable by the Law of Arms " and, as we have seen, determinable according to the principles of our Scottish feudal law, that is the law of the " organised family."

In such a cause, the " property " to be adjudicated upon is the hereditary armorial insignia constituting the " old family arms " of the " noble stok " (1592 cap. 125), *i.e.* the insignia borne on banner, surcoat, and shield, by the successive representers of the clan/family, and by the use of which on banner, garments, and seal the chiefly authority was, and is, shown forth and exercised, and the " noble community " (the honourable clan) takes—through its chief/representer —its share in the social and public life of the realm. Having deter-mined the right to this chiefly " property " (which under 1672 cap. 47 can belong to none but the chief), the Lord Lyon is entitled to set forth in the matriculation, or in a birthbrief [1] (normally in such cases of the form intituled *Diploma Stemmatis*), the character in which the arms have been awarded, and to denote and record the successful claimant as " representer " of the noble community,[2] and where the person is chief of the whole name, " Chief of the Name and Arms " or, as in other instances, " chief of the clan."

A clan is similarly an incorporeal nobiliary " fief," and a heritable subject—of which there can be an " heir " or " heretrix "—and a heritable destination, like a " family " as above mentioned ; and in the Ardgour proof in July 1938 the whole basis of the Division's pre-liminary (1937) opinions [3] (which were inappropriate, as clan-chiefship

---

[1] A ministerial Letter-patent with which the Appellate courts " cannot interfere." Admitted by 2nd Div. in *Maclean of Ardgour* v. *Maclean*, 1937, see 1941 S.C. 638 ; the qualification, " which can be brought before *us* as a question of law," left the subject of nobiliary descriptions—such as hereditary chiefships of all " honourable communities "—in Lyon's exclusive jurisdiction, agreeably to Sir Charles Erskine's Clan Chattan letter (see p. 53 *infra*, and also *Juridical Review*, September 1940, pp. 182, 194, 204, 208). A Birthbrief, being Ministerial (admitted by Lord Mackay, 1941 S.C. 642), is immediately placed completely outwith the appellate jurisdiction of the Courts ; just like the Scottish Secretary's " Letter " in *Royal College of Surgeons, Etc.*, which, as an expression of *his* official opinion, and the manner in which *he* would act, could not be muzzled, or varied (save by the Sovereign). The same applies to Lyon's *Diplomae*, so it was outwith the jurisdiction or sphere of the Court, as Lord Aitchison perceived, S.C. 638, to say what Lyon might or might not put in it !— as was laid down of Ministerial Writs in the words " cannot interfere " ; per Lord Robertson in *MacDonell* v. *Macdonald*, 1826, 4 Shaw 371 (see *Heraldry in Scotland*, p. 73).

[2] 1941 S.C. 638, line 21 ; 687, line 10.

[3] Lord Aitchison said at the 1941 hearing, " We went too far in 1937." As to selectors : though applying to the general case what, following the proof and 1941 decision, we know applies only to submissions for regal confirma-tion through Lyon in the special contingency of " *de facto* and *de jure* vacant " from the line being lost (see p. 177), Lord Mackay (who did not suggest Clan Societies or Councils as selectors, whereof see *Tartans of the Clans and Families*, 1950, p. 44, n. 2) gave in his second alternative (1938 S.L.T. 63) what now appears a well-founded and useful indication of the selectors in such a contingency :

was not before the court, and " chieftainship " had been amended out, so that the rights of chiefs of clans and chieftains could not competently or effectively be adjudicated on (1950 S.L.T., p. 16), and the *dicta* were necessarily *obiter*) was overturned by the expert witnesses, including Dr. L. Maclean Watt's evidence :

> Clan and Family mean exactly the same thing. . . . Yes, Clan and Family are the same. . . . Stem or stock [1] is a good word perfectly understandable in dealing with Highland matters.[2]

Indeed, the more so when related to Sir George Mackenzie's pronouncement (subsequently declared authoritative by Lord Aitchison) about undifferenced arms and heraldic differencing, viz.

> such differences or brisure as might . . . distinguish their families from that of their *Chief, for so we call the Representative of the Family,* from the French word *chef* or Head, and in the Irish (Gaelic) with us *the Chief of the Family is called the Head of the Clan.*[3]

This completely equates the Highland clan, and its *ceann-cinnidh*, with the " noble armigerous family " and its chief ; and with the Law of Arms, and heraldic differencing, pursuant to the statutes 1592 cap. 125 and 1672 cap. 47, and with the unanimous opinions of the Lords of Appeal (the operative decisions in the *Seaforth* case, where the question whether there was infringement of the chief's arms was involved) in the House of Lords, 17th December 1921 :

> Lord Dunedin : " If it was undifferenced as head of the clan." [4]
> Lord Shaw : " The chief of the Mackenzies coat which is Azure, a deer's head cabossed Or." [5]
> Lord Sumner : " As the chieftain he could have matriculated the ancient Seaforth arms . . . without any differencing." [6]

The House of Lords (by whose decisions not only Lyon, but the Court of Session is bound) thus unanimously held the " chief of the arms " identical with the " chief of the clan," in short, held the same view as Sir George Mackenzie.

Even without having that before them (since clan chiefship was not *sub judice*) the Court of Session, in 1941, after the Ardgour proof,

---

viz. " the principal landed gentlemen within the clan." As to the inaptitude of general clan conclaves (cf. p. 159 and Lord Clyde on mere acclamation of general assemblages in *A.D.C. in Civil Causes,* p. xxi, Stair Soc.), the word " gentleman " has a legal meaning, but " principal " will require definition. It presumably excludes what I might call " sub-cadets " of the unaffiliated (" indeterminate") armigerous cadets (see p. 578, n. 3) unless any holding *in baroniam.*

[1] The purpose of Arms for distinguishing those of " noble stok " is set forth in 1592 cap. 125.

[2] *Ardgour Evidence,* p. 517.   [3] Mackenzie, *Works,* II. p. 618, line 18.

[4] 1922 S.C. (H.L.) 44, line 42.   [5] *Ibid.,* 47, line 54.

[6] *Ibid.,* 49, line 50. He said " as heir-male," whilst Dunedin and Shaw hold it some (open) form of feudal succession, thus *unanimously* ruling out any form of *electoral* devolution of *clan chiefship.*

had quietly to extricate itself from the position mistakenly adopted without evidence in 1937, before the proof. They had already, in 1937, acknowledged the right to undifferenced arms (which they held descendible by law), as coincident with chiefship, and had remitted back to Lyon as proper for decision *in foro* (Finding 19) :

That the Petitioner bearing the name X . . . and being entitled to substantive possession of the chief arms of X . . . is representative, head, or chief . . . of the family of X.

and now, in 1941, faced with the result of the proof (identity of *clan/ family*) they admitted " chieftaincy " evidence (jettisoning that part of the 1937 interlocutor), and decided—thus reaffirming the competency of crave 19 (*supra*) [1]—there was nothing to prevent Lyon Court affirming that the heir in the estate and arms, is the Representer of the Family—which Mackenzie had authoritatively declared synonymus with " Head of the Clan." Lyon Court has continued in this to exercise jurisdiction conforming to the principle that undifferenced arms have, in relation to clan-chiefship, the character attributed to them by the House of Lords, and in accordance with this a number of important clan-chiefships have been determined,[2] and are, in abbreviated form, reported in 1950 S.L.T.

The only " clans " which are not governed by " the Law of Arms " are a few ignoble groups, whose representers have never obtained *tesseræ gentilitatis,* and who are, or remain, in the status of servile, or *ignobilis,* communities still " unknown," and who can but slink about under a St. Andrew's Cross flag without any honourable ensign evincing themselves to be a " known "/*nobilis* clan, rallying around and under the gallant banner of a " noble stok " in the person of an armigerous chief representing an eponymus in which the clan shares a common pride and of whom they are officially received as the determinate and indeterminate *clanna* ramifying in branches and twigs around the noble parent stem.[3]

When the kindred and followers of the chief saw him thus surrounded by a body so numerous, faithful and brave, they could conceive no power superior to his, and how far they looked back into the history of their tribe, they found his progenitors at their head. Their tales, their traditions and songs continually referred to the exploits or transactions of the same line of kindred and friends living under the same line of chiefs, and the transmission of command and obedience from one generation to another,

---

[1] Lord Lyon Grant had, 19th December 1938, declined to deal with " representation " in light of the inconsistency in the 1937 interlocutor as shown by the evidence, but, following that of 18th July 1941, duly found and described the Petitioner Representer on 26th February 1943 and 11th July 1944 (Lyon Register XXXV., p. 23.)

[2] *Maclachlan,* 1946, Lyon Register, XXXV., p. 72 ; *Rose,* 1946, *ibid.,* XXXVI., p. 8 ; *Clan Chattan, ibid.,* 9th April 1947, XXXVI., p. 36 ; *Macdonald,* 1947, *ibid.,* XXXVI., p. 44 ; *Farquharson,* 1950 S.L.T., p. 13.

[3] Stewart, *Sketches of the Highlanders,* p. 31.

thus became, in the eye of a Highlander, as natural as the transmission
of blood, or the regular laws of descent. The long, unbroken line of chiefs
is as great a proof of the mildness of their sway as of the fidelity of their
followers.[1]

Garth, at pp. 28–29, refers to the clans being often called " tribes "
and, as such, in the *Diploma Stemmatis* of Lord Lyon Sir Alexr.
Erskine, December 1698, we find in the certificate declaring Sir Henry
Innes of that Ilk and Sir James Innes of that Ilk his son, *Phylarchus/*
chiefs of the " tribe "[2] the petition on which the proof and deliverance followed, and which was prepared by Duncan Forbes of Culloden,
Advocate, and Sir David Forbes of Newhall, afterwards a judge, as
Lord Newhall, prays (for defeating the claim to the chiefship by a
" co-rivall ") to adduce evidence " upon such authentick grounds
as may induce those to whom judgment in the lyke cases is competent,
such as the Lyon and Lyon Clerk,"[3] and Lyon, in his official certificate,
declared the foregoing statement to be correct, and narrates having
taken proof and made a *Finding*—the desiderated judgement. Whilst
therefore the publication was made ministerially (see below) we find it
affirmed that Lyon had, as has since followed from the ultimate proceedings in *Maclean of Ardgour* v. *Maclean* (27th March 1941 and 26th
February 1943), jurisdiction to deal judicially with the chiefly titles as
incidental both to pedigree and to the award of the " chiefly " armorial
property, acknowledging that in 1672 the Lord Lyon made a declaration of chiefship of Clan Chattan, and of the " Innes tribe " in 1698.
Lyon's olden jurisdiction to dispose of this matter judicially was thus,
of necessity, recognised in 1941, as little as possible being said about the
unfortunate muddle of 1937 ; and there are many cases in which
judicial decision on such controversies is more expedient than ministerial ruling. Naturally the Court did not, and could not, lay down that
Lyon as a Great Officer of the Crown[4] might not investigate and forthwith make such a " declaration." Their Lordships, however, had,
even in 1937, to admit that Lyon had exercised a ministerial jurisdiction in chiefship, just as in 1910 no one, either on Bench or Bar,
suggested that a Great Officer might not ministerially issue his
official declaration of what he would do about a controversy on
precedence between two persons in any ceremony whereof he had the
management as Lyon has of Scottish Public Ceremonial.

---

[1] Stewart, *Sketches of the Highlanders*, pp. 28–30, where Rose of Kilravock,
which passed through an heiress, is cited as " an instance of uninterrupted linial
descent."

[2] That is the old chief and the young chief—the tanister. The " tribe "
had been recognised as a " clan " by the Privy Council in 1579 (Vol. III., p. 267),
so the instance is apposite.

[3] In 1698 the Lyon Clerk was also Lyon Depute and, therefore, in Lyon's
absence, a judge-competent. The Lyon Clerk-Depute then acted as Clerk of
Court

[4] Cf. Scottish Secretary's intimation regarding *Royal College of Physicians*,
1911 S.C. 1054.

PLATE VI.

PIPER OF THE LAIRD OF GRANT.

From the portrait by R. Waite at Castle Grant, *c.* 1714.

(*By permission of the Countess of Seafield.*)

Here the pipe banner with full achievement—including supporters. Also the red (Grant livery colour) cockade used in times before reasonably cheap crest badges became available. (The Regiments equipped with government-issue badges led to the wide use of the heraldic cap badges which had existed since the fifteenth century.)

PLATE VII.

[*Block : Spalding Club.*

JOHN GORDON OF GLENBUCKET.

Showing elaborately laced Doublet, 1730–1740 period.

As regards the effect of a declaration by Lyon, regarding a hereditary dignity : until the institution of the Roll of Baronets, Lyon's certificate was (see p. 163) the normal evidence accepted by the Lord Chamberlain regarding a claimant's right to the dignity of Baronet.[1] The Lord Lyon's declarations and certificates of genealogy, including that of the type of birthbrief termed a *Diploma Stemmatis* (" Certificate of Chiefship "), etc., are frequently in the form of patents, and therefore are ministerial acts of the King's representative, and as such, outwith any judicial review.[2] In this connection, Lord Lyon Erskine's letter to Cluny-Macpherson, after the pronouncement of the Clan Chattan declaration, indicates the situation and Lyon's official authority in such matters :

> You, without having got leave from Us, have represented yourself as chief of the Macphersons, and moreover without my permission . . . have designed yourself chief of the old Clan Chattans.

Two points are noticeable : (1) Sir Charles Erskine drops into the regal or vice-regal " us " of a King of Arms' most formal documents.[3] (2) Insistence that the dignity of chiefship must not be assumed without leave or permission from the Crown through its armorial representative in *nobilitas minor*, the King of Arms.[4] It was not until 1873 that by decree of Lord Lyon Burnett, Cluny-Macpherson was allowed the chiefship of the Macpherson clan, and awarded the incident armorial ornaments.[5]

---

[1] *Scottish Offices Inquiry Commission*, 1870, Minute of Evidence, par. 1984 ; Baronetage Warrant, 11th February 1910, see XIII. In this Warrant, 11th February 1910, the Crown acknowledges—as Lord Dunedin says it may (1911 S.C. 1060)—the existence of the Kings of Arms' (including Lyon's) jurisdiction in the higher hereditary dignity of baronet. In the preamble of the Warrant the phrase " without any just right " is significantly similar to Lyon's phraseology in the letter to Cluny-Macpherson concerning the chiefships.

[2] *Macdonnell* v. *Macdonald*, 4 Shaw 374. Unless the Crown has infringed any existing right (a right of property) which (per Lord Justice-Clerk in *Maclean of Ardgour* v. *Maclean*) could be raised before a civil court as a question of law. As regards this, allusion may be made to the Lord Chancellor's ruling in *Lauderdale* v. *Scrymgeour-Wedderburn*, 1910 S.C. (H.L.) 44 :

" In respect of the office or dignity now in question, the decree is wholly outside the jurisdiction of the Court of Session of that day, or of any day, and to that extent a nullity."

Not only chiefship but arms are " in the nature of dignities," and the foregoing view may in some future cause terminate the appellate jurisdiction of the Court of Session in *causa armarum*, which includes matter in nature of dignities (cf. A. C. Fox-Davies, *The Right to Bear Arms*, 1900, p. 147), unless where *e.g.* interpretation of a statute arises, or right to the arms conferred is decided as in *Seaforth* (1922) by the House of Lords.

[3] *Heraldry in Scotland*, 121. " We Schir Lord Lyon Forman of Luthrie," 1567.

[4] Cf. Gwillim's *Display of Heraldry*, 1724, Honor Civil, II., p. 49, regarding King of Arms prerogative in " visitation."

[5] Lyon Register, IX., p. 45. Supporters are incidents of chiefship and other high positions. They are not *indiciæ* of anything. They are " exterior ornaments." A chief was distinguished by his shield, surcoat, and banner, not by

H

The text of the Clan Chattan declaration is, for students of clanship, also an instructive document. Proceedings (judicial, " departmental," or other) must have preceded it,[1] but the certificate is not this deliverance itself ; it is the " Letters Patent " [2] following thereon, and making known " to all concerned " the Lord Lyon's decision :

I, Sir Charles Areskine of Cambo, Knight Baronet, Lord Lyon King of Arms, having perused and seen sufficient evidents and testimonies from our histories, my own registers, and bonds of manrent, do hereby declare that I find the Laird of Mackintosh to be

(a) the only undoubted chief of the name of Mackintosh, and
(b) to be the chief of the Clan Chattan, comprehending the Macphersons, Macgillivrays, Farquharsons, MacQueens, Macfaills, Macbeans, and others, and
(c) that I have given and will give none of these families any arms but as cadents of the Laird of Mackintosh's family, whose predecessor married the heretrix of the Clan Chattan, anno 1291,

and that in particular I declare,

(d) that I have given Duncan Macpherson of Cluny a coat of arms as a cadent of the foresaid family,
(e) and that this may remain to posterity,
(f) and may be known to all concerned, whether of the foresaid names or others.

I have subscribed these presents with my hand at Edinburgh the tenth day of September 1672, and have caused append my seal of office hereto.[3]

The document falls into three sections : (a) and (b) are two declarations of chiefship ; (c) and (d) declarations of the armorial consequences ; (e) and (f) the purpose and consequences of the document.

The Lord Justice-Clerk and Lord Mackay both agreed that such official documents were " certificates," not " judgements." This, of course, is consistent with the title *Diploma Stemmatis*, a " diploma " in this sense being essentially a " Letter Patent " and rendering the

---

" supporters." No chief went into battle with a stuffed dog and a gollywog nailed to the corners of his shield to show he was chief—the idea is ludicrous. No, the chief in the field was known to his followers, and amongst his cadets, by the plain arms of the eponymus he represented, and the armigerous cadets springing from that eponymus bore the same arms with brisures. Nevertheless an award *qua* chief of supporters by Lyon, whether by patent or in a matriculation, involves the acknowledgement by Lyon as H.M. "Supreme Officer of Honour" of such person as " chief " of the community in question. An award of these incidents of chiefship can thus be a conclusive determination of chiefship, and resolve any question which might exist as to whether the shield bore " chief arms "—and in some families the shield charges have varied in successive ages.

[1] The Innes of that Ilk birthbrief of 14th December 1698 is more precise ; it describes the taking of a proof, wherein documents were examined ; and officially transcribes the memorial wherein it is averred that Lyon was " judge competent in the lyke cases " and declares the correctness of that statement (*Familie of Innes*, 1864, pp. 1, 46).

[2] Cf. *Campbell*, 1762, Register of Genealogies, I., p. 82.

[3] H. Paton, *The Mackintosh Muniments*, 1903, p. 549 ; A. M. Mackintosh, *The Mackintoshes and Clan Chattan*, p. 32.

document similar to those by which rights in peerage were clarified or confirmed.[1] The effect of such a ruling, by diploma, is, moreover, to make them, what their terms assert, conclusive determinations, issued prerogatively, on behalf of the *Ard-righ* [2] as Fountain of Honour.

The Lord Justice-Clerk, after saying of the Clan Chattan declaration that it was " in no sense a finding pronounced in a *lis* or contested process," [3] proceeds : " It vouches nothing beyond that in this particular case Lyon made a declaration of chiefship." [4]

That, however, as above explained, is vouching just " everything," for this *official* writ contains not one but *two* declarations of chiefship —one of these being the chiefship of a " clan." The important and necessary deduction from Lord Aitchison's opinion is that since it was not judicial, it was a competent ministerial declaration. The parties mentioned therein were assuredly " contestants " for this chiefship of Clan Chattan, which was here declared to be in Mackintosh —a pronouncement officially fatal to his opponent. A matriculation of 12th March preceding in favour of Cluny had just been rescinded, and a fresh matriculation agreeable to this " declaration " was issued 26th November.[5] Moreover, amongst the evidence cited is the Lyon's registers, which accordingly must (*a*) have contained evidence of chiefship, (*b*) have been evidence of the rightful tenure of this dignity, just as they were registers in which other dignities were of record.[6]

Judicial determination of chiefship is, however, a natural corollary of chiefship being a feudalised subject conveyed in Great Seal Charters, and accordingly we find Macpherson emphasising there had been

a Decreet of the Great M'donells, to whom it (the Clan Chattan chiefship) was then submitted, and not by compact or agreement (adding that the chief of Clan Chattan would not have submitted to such a determination) without the force of a Decree pronounced by one who had power as well as authority to back it.[7]

---

[1] J. Riddell, *Peerage Law*, p. 51.   [2] Cf. *Burke*, Chiefship, p. 175, n. 2.

[3] Quite so, but what of the " interlocutor authorising the Lyon Clerk to prepare " this declaration ?—which *omnia rite acta esse* must have preceded the declaration itself. We know these were written on the petitions, and not preserved (*Heraldry in Scotland*, p. 458, line 16). Since both the parties mentioned in the declaration (Mackintosh and Cluny) were claimants to the chiefship, and Cluny's matriculation (or that part of it certifying the chiefship) was reduced, and another (recd. 26th November) followed, it seems evident Lyon heard both and that the extracts from " my own registers " and the " histories " were put before him as evidence. Certainly Lyon was not likely to find the bonds of manrent for himself—they could only be produced from the parties' charter chests. The Declaration was clearly preceded by a litigation *in foro*.

[4] *Ibid.* p. 58.   [5] A. Macpherson, *Glimpses of Church Life*, pp. 432–433.

[6] Peerage, baronetcy, knighthood, and feudal baronies were all matter of nobiliary record in the Lyon Registers (see J. Riddell, *Peerage Law*, p. 629).

[7] *Loyall Dissuasive*, pp. 115–116. Macpherson readily admitted the litigation, and even that it was Mackintosh who appeared therein as chief of Clan Chattan, but (and this, not the Salic law, is the whole burden of his treatise) " urged against M'Intoshes having or pleading the benefits of that Decree from his not

Medieval jurists had thus no doubt about the competency of judicial determination of the social and tribal fact (of chiefship), which is ocularly demonstrated by the display of the armorial insignia of the eponymus ; and it is a mere detail whether one says that this fact is itself " judicially determinable," or whether it is ministerially set forth after judicial determination of the right to the insignia demonstrating the fact. Since chiefship then had extensive daily responsibilities, its judicial determination, and descending therewith, did not appear " grotesque " to anybody.

The final direction of the Court of Session in *Maclean of Ardgour* (18th July 1941) to " proceed as accords " in Miss Catriona's petition, *i.e.* to deal with the outstanding matters therein, arising from the 1909 arms being the " old family arms " and their owner being " representer," acknowledged Lyon Court's judicial functions agreeably to the evidence that " clan and family mean exactly the same thing." Judicial determination of chiefship [1] is (save in certain genealogical petitions) normally only possible in connection with arms, since (as Macpherson aptly pointed out of an heiress—if her father was " a plebian " and " of no family " he " could not be a chief " [2]) arms being the *tesseræ gentilitatis*, it follows that a claimant to chiefship *must claim arms*, and the arms *of*, or appropriate *to*, the eponymus of whom the claimant maintains representership.[3]

The whole subject of " chiefship " or, as the statute 1592 cap. 125 expresses it, " noble stok " (a term which Dr. MacLean Watt pointed out is " a good word perfectly understandable in dealing with Highland matters ") [4] is thus completely related to " the Law of Arms," which in Scotland has always been so closely bound up with clan and name.

We have thus the high judicial authority of the Lord Justice-Clerk that " chiefship " is not only judicially, under the now better understood jurisdiction in arms and family, already referred to, and, moreover, as " titles or designations " under Lyon's judicial function

---

taking the name upon his marrying the heiress." Tradition apparently was that it was Eva's husband who, before the Lord of the Isles, successfully claimed the chiefship, *jure uxoris*. Evidently there had been a series of litigations, which turned, not on Salic law, but on points regarding name, chymmes, and the sacred pebble of St. Chattan.

[1] This, Lord Mackay, more effectively than he probably imagined, had in 1937 pointed out, is synonymous with possession of the undifferenced arms, which literally means the right to assume the coat and personality (*universitas* per Nisbet) of the defunct chief—for Lord Mackay had then no idea of the social and legal import of this armorial succession.

[2] *Loyall Dissuasive*, p. 35.

[3] This, as pointed out in *Scots Heraldry*, p. 16, is no reflection on clansmen in general. It is merely consistent with the doctrine that nobility is a status which must be proved by every claimant.

[4] *Ardgour Evidence*, p. 525, see Appendix XXX. In 1937 the Court of Session had made its premature pronouncement before the proof in which such depositions correlating with the Lyon Court Acts became available, hence the change-over by the Division in 1941.

of " Visitation," [1] but also ministerially determinable by Lyon, H.M. Supreme Officer of Honour,[2] whose " permission " for such an assumption was regarded as necessary and whose testimony is " conclusive," since the Court of Session regards such ministerial matter as beyond review in a " Court of Law," and so preventing expensive appeals.

The ministerial determination by *Diploma Stemmatis* is actually an exercise, through Lyon, of H.M. prerogative as *Pater Patriæ* and High Chief, analogous to that we have seen exercised by the High Kings in ancient Ireland.

The determination of chiefship, whether ministerially or judicially is a matter of much more than academic importance and one which is really the basis of Scottish heraldry. Most Lyon Court litigations have been directly or indirectly connected with this.[3] Not only from its social importance as a binding-force in the community, but for the prevention of discord and uncertainty as well as the importance the subject gives to Scottish heraldry, it is manifestly expedient that such disputes should be capable of the conclusive settlement so effectively provided by a Court and Office of Honour deriving from the High Sennachie and embodying the relative nobiliary *corpus juris* of the Law of Arms.

CLAN SOCIETIES

The past century has seen the development of numerous clan societies and associations, whose services in maintaining the existence of clanship and identity of the clans has been invaluable, though it is unfortunate that few of them have yet gone beyond the sphere of dinners, whist-drives, and bursaries, in place of the wider and more permanent scope of acquiring heritage in the clan country, and starting, even in a small way with a few crofts, to resettle the clan races

---

[1] 1592 cap. 29, A.P.S. III. 554 ; interpreted by Lord Constable, 1927 S.L.T. 292 : " Visitations are in the nature of the circuits of our judges " wherein the Kings of Arms " enquire into all matters concerning nobility and gentility such as arms, crests, pedigrees, titles or designations, and taking still as they go cognisance of all, and degrading interlopers and upstarts " (J. Gwillim, *Display of Heraldry*, 1724, Honour Civil, p. 49). The Court of Session has no jurisdiction in " pedigrees " and remitted such to the Macers—who, it happens, were the nearest available officers of arms ! (A.P.S. III. 449)—procedure consistent with the original jurisdiction of these in pedigrees (1937 S.L.T. 156, n. 1). Far from being precluded from determination of nobiliary descent, or bound by Retours (as surmised by Lord Mackay, 1938 S.L.T. 61), Retours and Judgements of Civil Courts (cf. case of *Earl of Banbury*), however effective for civil purposes, are not conclusive in honours, and require, as in Spain, to be presented as evidence for a confirming nobiliary decree by the Chronicler King of Arms in the case of *nobilitas minor* (dignities of baronetcy and gentility) and of the House of Lords in a peerage case.

[2] Nisbet, *System of Heraldry*, 1742, II., iv., p. 172.

[3] It was most significantly indicated in the *Ardgour* case that if the dispute were limited to a mere matter of " arms " money would not be wasted on such proceedings (*Aberdeen Press and Journal*, 6th January 1937).

upon the soil of their native districts. It seems now important to define the relationship of the clan society to the " clan," the more so as a number of clan societies [1] have recorded armorial bearings. It will be noticed that in each case the arms are a differenced version of the chief's, and that the association is treated as a corporate *persona*. In other words, the clan society is—according to the Law of Arms, wherein the " clan " is nowadays mainly cognisable [2]—simply a " corporate clansman," though no doubt a very important one—in fact, when it becomes armigerous, a corporate *duine-uasail*—an " indeterminate cadet." But the position of chief or president of the clan society and chief of the clan, although they may concur (as in the Stewart Society) in the same individual, are not necessarily synonymous, for the chief, chairman, or convener of the clan society is simply the " representer," for the time being, of the corporate *duine-uasail*, and is—like a branch chief (chieftain)—subordinate to the hereditary chief of the clan, as denoted by the chiefly insignia, holder of the hereditary " high social dignity " of representership of the eponymus and " his " clan as a noble community under the *Ard-righ* as Fountain of Honour. *Convener*, not " president," is the proper style.

Since corporations never die, the clan society as a corporate *duine-uasail* certainly can, or will, become one of the most important members of the clan, and is the " clansman " on whom will fall many of the duties which formerly were, roughly, inherent in the clan council. The " sacred embodiment of the race," however, must (from the nature of the clan and of the Law of Arms, wherein it is cognisable) remain in the line of hereditary chiefs, even if it is occasionally necessary for the society to take steps (from a chief's business abroad, etc.) to recommend the chief to appoint a " commander " of the clan at home.[3]

The clan society is thus, as above indicated, by the Law of Arms, a most important member or branch of the clan organisation, but equally it is not " the clan." This was made evident in recent litigation when the Lyon Court and Court of Session both rejected the plea that resolutions of a clan society or its council should be received in determining the right to arms and other chiefly honours.

Such " resolutions " were in matters of honours, to be disregarded,[4] and fortunately so, since otherwise clan societies would have been placed in the preposterous position of controlling administration of

[1] *Stewart Society*, 1919, Lyon Register, XXIV., p. 1 ; *Clan Buchanan Society*, *ibid*. XXIII., p. 27 ; *Clan Dhai (Davidson) Association*, 1935, *ibid*. XXX. p. 80.

[2] *I.e.* in regard to arms—Nisbet, *System of Heraldry*, I., pp. 268, 425 ; supporters —Lord Justice-Clerk, *Maclean of Ardgour v. Maclean* ; " name "—the Macgregor Act, 1775 cap. 29, and Lyon Court Act, 1867, Schedule B.

[3] *Historical Papers* (New Spalding Club), pp. 357–358, 362, 368 ; *Notes and Queries*, 15th August 1942, p. 96. He may do this of his own prerogative, and the post should not be coincident with that of convener of the society.

[4] *Maclean of Ardgour v. Maclean*, 1941 S.C. 666, 675 and per Lord Jamieson, at p. 707.

justice and exercise of H.M. prerogative. The duties of the societies
as corporate *daoine-uasail* are of a different, but most important,
character.

The society can, and should, become the repository of clan-treasures
and muniments, which might otherwise go amissing, or pass from
possession of the clan. A fund should always exist for the acquisition
or recovery of such objects, and by these means and by its records the
clan association can become the Record Department—the repository
of much evidence which would otherwise be lost to the clan ; and in
effect the " Civil Service " of the clan (let it beware it does not attempt
to become a " clan bureaucracy " !). Its annual report should include
—even if in a small way—the means for publication of clan muniments,
topography, illustrations, and genealogical deductions (the latter only
to be admitted where vouched by evidence ; for publication of loose
unvouched ramblings will only prejudice the association's records if
they have later to be referred to in Lyon Court). The issue of original
matter and actual illustration is of far more value.

Such activities presume the clan society will have some permanent
home, not merely its secretary's office, and every such association
should establish a fund to acquire, and as soon as it can do so, actually
acquire, both a part of the clan territory, at least as a rallying ground,
and also some house associated with the clan or chief, either in the
duthus, the county town, or in Edinburgh or Glasgow. A " MacX——
House " in this or that city could not only house the records but be
let out commercially in so far as not immediately required by the clan.
In the *duthus* there should at least be a cottage ha'-hoose (kept by
some aged member of the clan, and where clansmen may repair for
tea or meeting). The chief's arms over the fireplace and a few prints
or portraits in the ha', and beside the " chimney " the chief's chair
(duly corded across and only used when he is personally present),[1]
armorial glass in the windows, and tea-set, of course, emblazoned with
the arms and crest, would, in quite a small way and within the reach
of almost every clan society's means, lay the foundations of greater
achievement and provide a cheerful clan-welcome not only for clansmen at home but for clansmen from across the seas. If there have
been any particular artistic, architectural, or furnishing features in
the chiefly castle, to give a key-motif in the decoration, these should
be employed ; and clan branches overseas should endeavour to repro-
duce such small clan-quarters, also with copies of the chiefly portraits,
thus bringing alive in distant lands the very spirit of the clan home
in Scotland.[2]

[1] On any occasion when the chief has sent a message to a meeting, and is not
present in person, " the Chair " should be occupied by his plaid, claymore, and
crested bonnet, just as Queen Victoria's " train " effected, for some years after her
bereavement, her presence in Parliament.

[2] It would not be good taste to attempt an exact replica of the chief's baronial
hall (unless his seat has passed out of the clan), because it is never likely to be
convincing and would, in any event, detract from the pleasure and interest of

Amongst important duties which must presently devolve upon these associations, must be the compilation and maintenance of a Roll of the Clan.

MEMBERSHIP OF THE CLAN

Since the clan has now been shown to be a subsisting group recognised by the Imperial Parliament, 15 George III. cap. 29, and whose representative is entitled to legal rights under the Law of Arms, it becomes of definite importance to determine the extent and membership of the organisation, and to indicate at least what privilege such membership confers, points which were raised from the Bench in *MacGillivray* v. *Souter*, but apparently were not answered. By the custom of the Law of Arms, members of the clan, like other dependers of the chief of a noble group, enjoyed the privilege of displaying their chief's livery, but in a peculiarly Scoto-Highland form, namely, the wearing upon their person of the chief's crest and motto, within the well-known strap and buckle,[1] the origin whereof is, that chiefs distributed to their dependers a silver plate engraved with their crest, which was attached to the arm of the doublet, or bonnet, by a short strap, as still seen in porters' number plates. This, in a conventional form, has become the armorial badge of clanship, and is a valuable privilege, because to use the crest without (*a*) the strap and buckle, or (*b*) without being a member of the clan, involves a statutory offence in Scotland, penalty £8, 6s. 8d. sterling.[2] Everyone except the chief (even a Duke's younger brother) wears the strap-and-buckle form of badge.

Now, who are members of the clan, and as such, entitled to enjoy these armorial privileges ? The statutes indicate [3] persons depending upon the *capitanis*, *chieffis*, *chiftanis*, by "pretence of blude or place of their dwelling." The former of these are the actual and indeterminate cadets cognisable in the Law of Arms, and the second category, as appears from the Privy Council's bonds,[4] are the vassals, tenants, and occupiers of land under a territorial, or *grad flaith*, chief and include the *sencliathe* or ancient adherents, *i.e.* those who have followed the chief for over three generations.[5] Not all tenants and vassals were followers of their laird as his clansmen. Often, they depended on a patriarchal chief of their own, and similarly all blood-

---

seeing the original. Just, however, as the towers of clan chieftains often carry through the motif of the chief's castle, so the atmosphere of each clan's domestic architecture should be maintained.

[1] *Scots Heraldry*, p. 132. The plain crest, without strap and buckle, is worn on servants' liveries.

[2] The statutory penalty is in force, and the penalty has been recently exacted (*Fiscal of Lyon Court* v. *Macrae*, 1925 ; *Warrantholders and Fiscal of Lyon Court* v. *Alexander & Co.*, 1933).

[3] 1587 cap. 59, A.P.S. III. 464 ; 1593, A.P.S. IV. 40.

[4] *Privy Council*, 3rd series, III., 75.

[5] *Celtic Scotland* III., p. 145.

descendants are not necessarily members of their " biological " clan. Since surnames came in, bearing the chief's race-name, or one of the approved sept-names, has been the normal criterion of clan member-ship, and the statutory phrase, " depending upon the directions " of the chiefs, may equally, and can now only, apply to " peaceful pageantry "—though whenever a war breaks out, the War Office is thoughtful to exploit the clan spirit ! The power of even French families to exclude pretended members [1] and the bonds of adoption,[2] and specific instances of adoption of clansmen by a chief, e.g. " to be Gordons depending upon the noble House of Huntly," [3] indicate that, apart from descent within the name or sept-names, the consent of the chief, although it has been only occasionally applied for solemnly,[4] was the requisite step to acquire membership of the clan. Indeed, most chiefs endeavoured to persuade their tenantry to join their clan.[5] Similarly in armorial administration—e.g. in doubtful pedigrees—the chief may be invoked to give a certificate that he accepts the party as a member, even if indeterminate, of his community.[6]

With the development of the permanent clan association and modern availability of records and filing, business methods must gradu-ally develop, and the Clan Cameron is compiling an official Roll of Membership, with numbered certificates signed by Lochiel, the chief. It will only be a further, and natural step, to make such a roll definite, and a certificate of membership the evidence of right to wear the strap-and-buckle crest, and for a permanent clan association acting under the chief to institute prosecution of individuals infringing the armorial privilege without having become sanctioned members of the clan as an organised and honourable community.[7] To these senti-mental and armorial privileges, which thus form the cognisable and legal basis of clan membership under the chief of the clan as a statu-torily recognised community,[8] material advantages of country club membership, etc., may render clanship a valuable social privilege.

[1] Seton, *Law and Practice of Heraldry*, p. 421.
[2] Cameron, *Celtic Law*, p. 220.   [3] Spalding Club, Misc. III. 234.
[4] Most chiefs were delighted to accept any adherent who would till land and could wield a claymore ; cf. references cited in process in *Macgregor of Inneregny*, Lyon Register, XXXII., p. 22.
[5] *Social and Economic Development of Scotland*, pp. 500–505.
[6] E.g. *Carstairs*, Lyon Register, II., p. 147 ; *Colquhoun* (Cahun), 1781, *ibid*. I., p. 528 ; *McLeod*, 1948, Lyon Register, XXXVII., p. 36.
[7] Tartans also have been (incidentally) recorded in Lyon Register, and are clearly " cognisances." See pp. 525, 614.
[8] What is constituted and confirmed as a *Family, Name,* or *Clan* by Lyon or in Lyon Court is not a " private family " ; it is a *public tribo-familial* nobiliary *incorporation,* " known " in the public life of the Realm through its *chief*.

H*

VII

The Clans of the Scottish Highlands

BRODIE

THIS name is derived from the Barony of Brodie, in Gaelic *Brothach*, and they are one of the original tribes of Morayshire, who held their lands beyond all human memory. Their ancient charters were destroyed when Lord Lewis Gordon burnt Brodie House in 1645, but Malcolm was Thane of Brodie in the time of Alexander III., and Michael, son of Malcolm, Thane of Brodie, had a charter about 1311 from Robert the Bruce, erecting the old Celtic thaneage into a barony. Alexander Brodie of Brodie, who was appointed a Lord of Session as Lord Brodie in 1649, was one of the Commissioners sent from Scotland to Charles II. during his exile at The Hague. His son and successor, James Brodie of Brodie, married Lady Mary Ker, daughter of William, 3rd Earl of Lothian. Leaving nine daughters but no son, he was succeeded as heir of entail by George, son of Joseph Brodie of Asliesk, younger brother of Lord Brodie. This George married Emily, fifth daughter and co-heiress of his predecessor, and died in 1716. He left three sons and two daughters. James Brodie of Brodie the elder died young in 1720, and was succeeded by his brother, Alexander Brodie of Brodie, Lord Lyon King of Arms, 1727–1754.

The Lord Lyon's son, Alexander Brodie of Brodie, having died early, the chiefship and estate passed to his second cousin James, son of James Brodie of Spynie, Sheriff-Depute of Moray. This chief was Lord Lieutenant of the County of Nairn, and married Lady Margaret Duff, youngest daughter of William, 1st Earl of Fife. He was succeeded by his grandson, William Brodie of Brodie, also Lord Lieutenant of Nairnshire, from whom are descended the subsequent and present chiefs of the Brodie clan. Brodie Castle, near Forres, which has thus been uninterruptedly the seat of Brodie of Brodie, from time immemorial to the present day, is a handsome example of Scottish architecture, being in its present form a Z-shaped castle erected by Alexander Brodie of Brodie in 1609, one of the towers incorporating the older fortalice, whilst a fourth tower was added by Lord Brodie. The principal branches of this clan are : Brodie of Lethen, descending from a son of Lord Brodie ; Brodie of Idvies in Angus ; and a baronetical branch deriving from Sir Benjamin Brodie, Surgeon to the Royal Family, 1834.

BUCHANAN [1]

The Clan Buchanan was formerly a powerful one, whose territory was in Stirlingshire, on the east side of Loch Lomond. They had also considerable possessions in the Lennox. Buchanan of Auchmar (the clan historian) maintains that the progenitor of the family was an Irishman (which in old diction means no more than a *Gael*), named Anselan o' Kyan, who settled in the Lennox in the early part of the eleventh century ; and that the family acquired the lands of " Buchanan," from which the clan took its name.

Skene derives the origin of both the Buchanans and the Macmillans from the *Siol o' Cain*, one of the ancient tribes of north Moray. It would seem that Anselan o' Cain (or o' Kyan) acquired the Barony of " Buchanan " (from which he acquired his surname) by marriage with its heiress and thus perpetuated the tribal chiefship of the old " tribe of the land," which was one of those in the ancient province of the Lennox, and the *duthus* of Buchanan, instead of being made a Crown fief, was according to the true tribal principle *sub-infeudated*, as a fief in the baronage of the Earldom of the Lennox, as appears from a charter in the reign of David II., by which Donald, Earl of Lennox, confirmed to Maurice Buchanan " that pleugh of land called commonly Buchanan."

The Clan Buchanan produced two characters of whom it cannot be proud : George Buchanan, the filthy minded historian who traduced Mary Queen of Scots even to her son James VI., who (whilst his tutor) he malused mentally and physically. In " the '45," Buchanan of Drumnakill earned the curses of all Jacobites and upright people by basely betraying the gallant Lord Tullibardine.

Nisbet (*System of Heraldry*) says :

Macoum de Buquhanan, that is, as I take it, Buchanan, the root of that ancient family. Gilbert, his father, was Senescallus Comitis de Levenax, and the first who got the *carrucatam terrae de Buchanan*, and from it took his name. The principal family failed in the last (eighteenth) century, and the estate is in the possession of the Duke of Montrose. The latest cadet of the House of Buchanan is Buchanan of Auchmar, and as such, is reputed the chief family of the name, though a great many others have better estates. But chiefship goes by blood, not by wealth and riches.

Since Nisbet wrote this (in 1804), the Auchmar branch and its successors, Buchanan of Leny, have also become extinct and the chiefship is now dormant. The seat of the old chiefs, with much of the clan territory, is now owned by the Duke of Montrose.

The clan is thus chiefless and almost landless ; though the Clan Buchanan Society is understood to possess considerable moveable property. A devoted clansman, however, recently recovered and presented to the society the Clareinch in Loch Lomond, whence was derived the slogan of the Buchanan chiefs.

[1] See Appendix V.

CAMERON [1]

The Camerons are said to have their surname from the *Cam-shron* or " wry nose " of an early chief. Tradition says he was a distinguished knight who became chief of the clan by marriage with the heiress of the old line. The first chief of the clan definitely found in historical records is Donald Dhu (*cir.* 1411) (reckoned 11th Chief). He married an heiress of MacMartin of Letterfinlay and left two sons—Allan, Constable of Strone Castle, who succeeded him, and Ewen, who is generally regarded as the progenitor of the Camerons of Strone. Allan left two sons, Ewen and John.

The clan territory has been ever in Lochaber. Prior to the forfeiture of the Lord of the Isles the Camerons were among the vassals of the Isles. According to tradition the Clan Cameron is said to have once formed a branch of the Clan Chattan, but to have broken away from that confederacy after the celebrated battle of the North Inch of Perth.

The defection in 1429 of the Clan Cameron and the Clan Chattan from the Lord of the Isles during his struggle with James I. materially contributed to the Lord of the Isles' overthrow by the Royal forces.

The Clan Cameron consisted originally of three main branches, viz., the MacMartins of Letterfinlay, the MacGillonies of Strone, and the MacSorlies of Glen Nevis. Up to the time of the battle of the North Inch of Perth the MacMartins appear to have been the chiefs of the clan. Since then, however, and since the erection of the Barony of Lochiel gave them Royal recognition and jurisdiction, the Lochiel family (who belong to the Strone branch) have held the chiefship, and in a litigation with Cameron of Erracht in 1795, Lochiel was declared by decree of Lyon Court to be Chief of the Name and of Clan Cameron.

For Ewen, 13th Chief, who first took the title " of Lochiel," the estates of the chiefly line were erected into a Barony of Lochiel in 1528. His eldest son and heir, Donald, died before his father, between the years 1536 and 1539. He married secondly, Marjory, daughter of Lachlan, second son of Malcolm Mackintosh of Mackintosh, by whom he had Ewen, the progenitor of the family of Erracht, and John, progenitor of the Camerons of Kin-Lochiel. Ewen was succeeded by his grandson, *Eoghan Beag*—Little Ewen—who was the father of a natural son, the famous Black Tailor of the Axe.

He was succeeded by his brother, Donald, father of Allan, 16th Chief, who fought under Huntly at Glenlivet, and was grandfather of the famous Sir Ewen Cameron of Lochiel, 17th Chief, born in 1629, the celebrated Highland supporter of King Charles I.

During all the struggles of the Stuart kings with Parliament, Commonwealth, Dutchmen, and Hanoverians, the Camerons were ever on the Stuart side. Lochiel was one of the few chiefs whom Cromwell utterly failed to subdue. The chief of the clan materially contributed

[1] See Appendix VI.

by his energy and example to Dundee's victory at Killiecrankie, while, Donald, " The gentle Lochiel," one of the heroes of " the '45," will long remain green in Highland memories.

After " the '45 " the Cameron lands were forfeited, and the chief died in exile. Later, however, these territories were restored to the family. The chief's ancestral seat is still at Achnacarry.

CAMPBELL

The original and Celtic name of Clan Campbell was the *Clan Duibhne*, which derived its name from Diarmid O' Duin, from whom descended a long line of chiefs, Lords of Lochow. Of these Duncan McDuine is (in a charter of 1368) referred to as an ancestor of the then reigning chief. Paul O' Duine, called *Pol an Sporain*, the king's treasurer, left in the 13th century a daughter, Eva O' Duine, heiress of Lochow and heretrix of Clan Duine, who married Gillespic Cambel, and from them descended Sir Colin Mór Campbell of Lochow, called *Cailein Mór*, from whom the successive chiefs derive the patronymic *MacCailein Mór*. This great chief was killed in 1294 at the *Ath-dearg* (red ford) of Lorn. His son, Sir Neil, one of the earliest and most devoted of the Bruce's supporters, married Lady Marjorie Bruce, and for his son, Sir Colin, the *duthus* of Lochow was in 1315 erected into a free barony. His grandson, *Cailein Iongantach*, got the ancestral lands settled in tail male, with obligation to bear the name and arms of Campbell, in 1409. His son, Sir Duncan Campbell de Ergadia, Lord of Lochow, was created " The Lord Campbell " prior to 1427. At his death in 1453 he was succeeded as 2nd Lord Campbell by his son, Colin, who was created Earl of Argyll, 1457, Justiciar and Chamberlain of Cowal, 1472, founded the Highland burgh of Inverary, 1474, and was Lord High Chancellor of Scotland, 1483. Archibald, 2nd Earl, commanded the right wing of the Scottish army at Flodden, and fell on that tragic day. Colin, 3rd Earl, was in 1528 created hereditary Lord Justice-General and Master of the Royal Household in Scotland, and to the insignia of these great offices, placed saltireways behind MacCailean's shield, relate the motto, " I scarce call these things our own." Archibald, 4th Earl, supported the Reformation, and his eldest son, Archibald, 5th Earl, proved the ruin of Mary Queen of Scots by (having been appointed her Lieutenant-General), at Langside, " fainting " on the field of battle. His brother Colin succeeded as 6th Earl, and was father of Archibald, 7th Earl, who having been sent to seize " the Popish earls " (Huntly, Erroll, and Angus) was signally defeated at Glenlivet, 1594, left the field in tears, and on returning to report his defeat, the pawky James VI. observed of Huntly, " Fair fa' ye, Geordie Gordon, for sending him back lookin' sae like a subject." He subsequently rendered himself hateful to the other clans by ruthless persecution of the Macgregors, and the execution, under trust, of Macgregor of Glenstrae and seven of his clan in 1604. His brutality to Clan Gregor led to a similar commission against Clan Donald, supported by English ships-of-war, in 1613, soon after which he slunk abroad and, overcome by remorse, joined the Church of Rome. It was he who laid the foundation of the hatred of Campbells amongst so many other Highlanders, augmented by his son Archibald, 8th Earl, who was created Marquis of Argyll, 1641, having become the commander of the Covenanters' army during the civil war, for which he has been termed " the Master-fiend Argyll." Actually, though a reluctant Covenanter and cautious politician, he appears to have been at heart a Royalist, was instrumental in bringing Charles II. to Scotland, placed the crown on his head, and helped to bring about the Restoration. He had, however, been too prominent in the councils and armies during the rebellion, and, through the influence of Lord High Commissioner Middleton, he was beheaded in 1661. His son was restored as 9th Earl in 1663, on the fall of Middleton's government, but was condemned, 1681. He escaped dressed as the page of Lady Sophia Lindsay, his step-daughter, but having been caught supporting Monmouth's rebellion, was beheaded 1685, behaving with marked calmness, the subject of the celebrated painting, " Argyll's Last Sleep." His eldest son, Archibald, 10th Earl, was (having been found the most courageous and truthful statesman in Scotland) created Duke of Argyll to him and his heirs male whatsoever, 1701. Dying 1603, his eldest son John, 2nd Duke of Argyll and Greenwich (cr. 1719), was the celebrated Field-Marshal and statesman who indeed brought about the accession of George I.

> Argyll, the State's whole thunder born to wield,
> And shake alike the senate and the field.

His brother and heir, Archibald, 3rd Duke, who had long been a distinguished judge as Lord Islay, was succeeded by his cousin, John Campbell of Mamore, as 4th Duke, from whom descend the subsequent dukes, including George, 8th Duke, the historian, and the 9th Duke, who married Princess Louise, Queen Victoria's daughter. The present chief of the clan is the 11th Duke of Argyll. The seat of the Duke of Argyll is Inveraray Castle, Loch Fyne.

The ramifications of the families of Campbell are so great that it is impossible to go into them. Stewart of Garth quotes these interesting customs amongst them, viz. :

The attachment and friendship of kindred, families and clans were confirmed by many ties. It has been a uniform practice in the families of the Campbells of Melford, Duntroon, and Dunstaffnage that when the head of either family died the chief mourners should be the other two lairds, one of whom supporting the head to the grave, while the other walked before the corpse. In this manner friendship took the place of the nearest consanguinity, for even the eldest sons of the deceased were not permitted to interfere with this arrangement. The first progenitors of these families were three of the sons of the family of Argyle, who took this method of preserving the friendship and securing the support of their posterity to one another.

The Breadalbane branch is, next to the House of Argyll, the most important. It was founded by Black Colin of Glenorchy, second son of Duncan, 1st Lord Campbell, Baron of Lochow. Hence the patronymic of the chiefs of the House of Glenorchy, *Mac-Chailein-Mhic-Dhonnachaidh.* In 1432 Sir Colin received Glenorchy from his father, and by his second wife Margaret Stewart, co-heiress of John, Lord of Lorn, he obtained a third of the land of Lorn. He built the famous castle of Kaolchurn in Glenorchy. The history and crude but interesting portraits of the chiefs of Glenorchy are preserved in the celebrated *Black Book of Taymouth.* Sir Colin, 3rd Baron, was " ane great justiciare all his tyme " and " cuait execute many notable lymarris, he behiddit the laird of Macgregor himself," and in presence of " sundrie nobilmen," whilst he naturally " sustenit the deidlie fied of the Clan Gregor." Colin, 6th Baron, built Taymouth Castle, whilst Sir Duncan, 7th, called " Duncan of the Castles," built five fortalices in his wide domains, and was created a Baronet, 1625. Sir John, 4th Baronet and 11th Chief of Glenorchy, was created Earl of Breadalbane, 1677. A strong Royalist, he contributed to the Restoration ; whilst, after the landing of William of Orange, he adjusted the settlement with the Jacobite chiefs and distributed (it is believed, less a considerable discount) the money supplied to bribe them into quietness. In 1715 he sent a force to support the Chevalier. John, 4th Earl and 15th Chief of Glenorchy, succeeded as lineal descendant of Colin Campbell of Mochastir, second son of Sir Robert, 2nd Baronet.

Cawdor Castle.

He was created Marquis of Breadalbane, 1831, but, the 2nd Marquis dying unmarried, the earldom passed to John, 6th Earl, and Chieftain of Glenfalloch, 17th of Glenorchy. A re-creation of the Marquessate, 1885, for the 7th Earl expired in 1922, since when the Earldom of Breadalbane has passed to the House of Stuckaple and Borland, now Earls of Breadalbane. The most celebrated of the cadets has been Campbell of Glenlyon, deriving from Archibald, second son of the 2nd Chief of Glenorchy. It was Captain Robert Campbell of Glenlyon who perpetrated the massacre of Glencoe in 1692. The Baronets of Aberuchill and Barcaldine and the House of Achallader also spring from Glenorchy.

The Campbells of Calder or Cawdor spring from Sir John Campbell of Inverliver, third son of the 2nd Earl of Argyll, who married Muriel, heiress of the last Thane of Calder in 1510. She was carried off under romantic circumstances. Her relations being in hot pursuit, Inverliver posted six of his seven sons round a sheaf dressed in little Muriel's cloak. All were slain, but Inverliver and the remaining son escaped with the heiress. " What a loss," said his friends, " suppose she were to die ? " But grimly replied Inverliver, " Muriel can never die as long as there is a red-haired lassie on the shores of Loch Awe ! " The Laird of Calder was in 1786 created Baron Cawdor, and Earl Cawdor in 1827. Cawdor Castle, one of the most splendid feudal castles in the Highlands, is built over a hawthorn bush, which still flourishes in the dungeon, and on which tradition avers the fortunes of the house depend.

The Campbells of Loudoun derive their origin from Sir Duncan, the second son of the first MacCailein Mór. He married the heiress of Crauford of Loudoun and their descendant was created Lord Campbell of Loudoun in 1601, and Earl of Loudoun in 1633.

The Earldom (which descends in the female line) has passed to the Hastings family. The heir male of the 1st Earl is Campbell of Aberuchil and Kilbryde, Baronet, 1667, descended from the second son of Sir John Campbell of Lawers. Their seat is Kilbryde Castle.

Campbell of Strachur, an early branch of Argyll, who bears the arms with a mantlet for difference, is styled *MacArtair*.

CLAN CHATTAN

This clan derives its name from the title of its chief, *Gilliechattan Mór* (the Great Servant of St. Catan), and is deduced by modern historians from the *co-arb*, or bailie, of the Abbey of Kilchattan, in Bute. The chiefs later acquired the lands of Glenlui and Loch Arkaig, and others, including Gellovie, in Lochaber and Badenoch, probably by Pictish succession, and about this time *Gilliechattan Mor O'Gualave* appears as the first named chief. The 4th Chief from him, Muriach, Celtic Prior of Kingussie, *Macgilliechattan Clearach*, married the Thane of Cawdor's daughter and had with other issue, (1) *Gilliechattan-Patrick*, 5th Chief, and (2) *Ewan Ban*, ancestor of the Clan Macpherson. The 5th Chief's son, *Dougal Dall*, left an only daughter, Eva, by whose marriage in 1291 to Angus Mackintosh, 6th Chief of Clan Mackintosh, Angus became in right of his heiress-wife 7th Chief of Clan Chattan.

The " Hail kin of Clann Chattan " thus came to include seventeen tribes :

  (1) *The Clan Mackintosh* itself, thenceforth until
      1938 the stem-family.
  (2) *Clan Vurich* (Macphersons).
  (3) *Clan Gillivray* (Macgillivrays).
  (4) *Clan Vean* (Macbeans).
  (5) *Clan Dhai* (Davidsons).
  (6) *Clan Tarrell*.
  (7) *Clan vic Gorries*.
  (8) *Clan Cheandhui of Glenbeg*.
  (9) *Slioch Gow Chruim* (Smiths).
  (10) *Clan Tearlaich* (Macleans of Dochgarroch).
  (11) *Clan Revan* (MacQueens).
  (12) *Clan vic Gillandris na Connage*.
  (13) *Clan Clerich* (Clarks).

(14) *Slioch Illvorvic Innish.*
(15) *Clan Phail* (Macphails).
(16) *Clan Fionlaigh Cheir.*
(17) *Clan Inteir.*

In addition to these there were the " Nine tribes of Clan Mackintosh " of whom the three major ones were : Clan Farquharson, the Shaws, and the Toshachs ; the whole forming what was known as *Fuil vic' an Toisach agus Clanni Chattan,* also the *Cattanachs.*

A tribal community of this magnitude was a source of apprehension both to the Lords of the Isles, and (still more) to the Kings of Scots ; and, when the Macdonalds' island power had been broken, we find in the records machinations for " crying doon the Clan Chattan," which, however, was effected by rendering it powerless by fomenting internal dissension, and not by oppression like the " danting of the Isles."

Ultimately the plan resorted to (by both political parties) was to incite rebellions by the Macphersons, and to misrepresent a former dispute between these and Clan Dhai about the leadership of the right wing of Clan Chattan's 2,000-man army.

This, however, was disposed of by Lyon Court, 10th September 1672 (see p. 194), when Mackintosh was adjudged Chief of the Name of Mackintosh and Chief of the Clan Chattan—expressly on descent from Eva the " Heretrix of Clan Chattan." Thenceforth the chiefship passed in tailzie, along with the Lochaber lands, until the death of Alfred Donald Mackintosh of Mackintosh, 28th of Mackintosh and 29th Chief of Clan Chattan, when the Mackintosh estates and chiefship passed under special settlement, and the final dispersal of the Clan Chattan lands left the chiefship of Clan Chattan to descend again to heirs-general, first, as 30th Chief, to Arbell Mackintosh of Mackintosh, Lady of Dalcross, on whose marriage to Anthony Warre (a non Clan Chattan name) it devolved on Alfred Donald's next heir-of-line (and incidentally heir-male), Duncan Alexander Mackintosh of Clan Chattan, owner of the estate of Fairburn, Felixburg, S. Rhodesia now 31st Chief and *Gilliechattan Mór, Ceann Cinnidh* of this seventeen-tribe community, which by re-emergence of an independent hereditary chief, and recognition of the *Clan Chattan tartan,* now finds itself the second greatest Celtic community (next to Clan Donald) in the life and history of the Highlands.

CHISHOLM

The Chisholms in Scotland are first found on the Borders, in Roxburghshire. This clan is of Norman origin, and the name was originally spelt De Cheseholm. Their original Border seat was the Barony of Chiesholme in Roxburghshire, which long continued in the House of Chisholme, afterwards Scott-Chisholme of Chisholme. In the fourteenth century, Sir Robert de Chisholme, a scion of the De Chisholme line, was Constable of Urquhart Castle, and his son, Alexander de Chisholme, having married Margaret, Lady of Erchless, daughter and heiress of Weyland of the Aird, had a son, Thomas de Chisholm, 1403, from whom the Chisholms of Comer and Strathglass descend. In accordance with the Clan Chattan decision of 1672, the Chisholms would have become chiefs of Margaret's "clan," if no "del Aird" surname was in use—and at that period and locality it was no doubt only a designation. The Chisholms are therefore quite properly chiefs of a Highland clan. For John Chisholm, great-grandson of Thomas Chisholm, the lands of Erchless and Comer were erected into baronies, 1538–1539. The direct line terminated with Alexander Chisholm, 1793, whose daughter Mary, married James Gooden. She is celebrated in the Highlands for her opposition to the "clearances." The chiefship and estates passed under entail to his brother William, whose two sons, Alexander and Duncan, died without issue, leaving a sister Jemima, Mrs. Chisholm-Batten, while the estates passed to a cadet, James Sutherland Chisholm, great-grandson of Alexander Chisholm of Muckerach, whose son, Roderick Chisholm, The Chisholm, died without issue,

Erchless Castle.

1887, and was succeeded in Erchless by his sisters, at whose death Erchless passed to Edmund Chisholm-Batten (grandson of Jemima), by whose son this picturesque fortalice in Strathglass, for centuries the seat of the race, was sold. In 1887, Roderick, the last chief in the male line by possession of the estates, having died, and Jemima's descendants having taken the principal name and arms of Batten, James Gooden-Chisholm, eldest son of Mary, Mrs. Gooden-Chisholm, heiress of the direct line, claimed and was awarded the undifferenced arms of the race, with supporters, and was thereafter designated *An Siosalach*, and received as Chief of the Clan Chisholm. The name of "Gooden" was subsequently dropped and the title "Chisholm of Chisholm" officially recognised in Lyon Court. The representative of this line is now chief of the clan.

COLQUHOUN

Colquhoun is a territorial name, and is derived from the Barony of Colquhoun, in the parish of West Kilpatrick, Dunbartonshire. The chief of the clan is Colquhoun of Luss, and the clan's territories are on Lochlomondside, where their slogan, *Cnoc Ealachain*, is taken from a well-known mountain.

The founder of the family of Colquhoun of Luss was Humphrey de Kilpatrick or Kirkpatrick, who obtained from Malcolm, Earl of Lennox, during the reign of King Alexander II., a grant of the lands of Colquhoun, *pro servitio unius militis*. Ingram, the son of

Humphrey Kilpatrick, was the first who assumed the name of Colquhoun.

The lands of Luss were acquired during the reign of King Robert II. by marriage with the " Fair Maid of Luss," heiress of the House of Luss of that Ilk, descending Maldwin, Dean of the Lennox, 1150.

Sir John Colquhoun of Luss was Governor of Dumbarton Castle under James II., and Luss was erected into a barony in 1457 for his grandson, another Sir John.

Sir Humphry Colquhoun, 12th Laird of Luss, acquired the Heritable Coronership of Dunbartonshire in 1583. From his brother and heir, Sir Alexander, descended Sir Humphrey, 17th Laird of Luss, who married a daughter of Houston of that Ilk, by whom he had only a daughter, Anne, who in 1702 married James Grant of Pluscardine, second son of Grant of that Ilk ; and being resolved that the young couple should succeed him in his whole estate and honours, in 1704 he resigned his baronetcy to the Crown, and obtained a new grant— to himself in life rent, to his daughter and son-in-law in fee, providing that their heirs should adopt the name and arms of Colquhoun, and that the estates of Grant and Luss should never be conjoined. Sir Humphry died in 1715. James Grant succeeded as Sir James Colquhoun of Luss ; but his elder brother dying without issue in 1719, he succeeded to the estates of Grant, and resuming that name, was succeeded in the chiefship of Colquhoun and the Luss estates by his second son, Sir Ludovick. He, on the death of his elder brother, unmarried, also succeeded to the estates of Grant, and that of Luss went to his younger brother, James, who was officially recognised by Lyon as chief of the name of Colquhoun in 1781. He was created a baronet in 1786, and from him descend the present line of chiefs of whom Sir Iain Colquhoun of Luss, 7th Baronet, and 28th Chief, was created a Knight of the Thistle. The seat of the chiefs is Rossdhu House, Luss, Dunbartonshire.

CUMMING

This Scottish family of Norman origin migrated from England to Scotland in the reign of David I. Richard Cumyn was high in the service of William the Lion. He owned the lands of Northallerton, in England, and from the Scottish king received grants of estates in Roxburghshire, which were the Cumming family's first possessions in Scotland.

William, son of the above Richard, married Marjory, Countess of Buchan, and by his marriage obtained possessions in the north. The family, thus founded, including " The Lords of Badenoch," became very powerful. In the reign of Alexander III. there were three earls of the name of Cumming (those of Buchan, Menteith, and Atholl), besides a baron, the Lord of Strathbogie.

The chief of the family wedded Marjory, sister of King John Baliol, and by that marriage as well as his Royal descent (by the daughter of Donald Bane, son of King Duncan), the next representative of the Cumming clan, John, Lord of Badenoch, styled the " Red Cumyn," acquired formidable claims to the Scottish Crown when the succession was in abeyance, before King Robert the Bruce eventually became King of Scotland. The death of the " Red Cumyn " by the dagger of Robert the Bruce, in the church of the Minorites, Dumfries, is an event which marks a well-known epoch in Scottish history.

From the advent to power of King Robert the Bruce, the power of the Cummings commenced to decline, and they never regained the influence which was then lost.

The House of Altyre, on whom the undifferenced arms and chiefship devolved, claims descent from Robert, younger brother of the Black Comyn, whose son Thomas was exempted from the proscription of the clan in 1320 ; and his son Sir Richard Cumming, Hereditary Forester of Darnaway, in the days of King David II., established the House of Altyre which has continued to hold that estate for five centuries. Robert Cumming of Altyre, 13th Chief of his line, married Lucy, daughter of Sir Ludovic Gordon of Gordonstown, and his great-grandson, Sir Alexander Cumming of Altyre, was created a Baronet in 1804, and took the name of Gordon-Cumming on succeeding to the estates of Gordon of Gordonstown—thus compromising his chiefship.

Fort Augustus, on Loch Ness, used to bear the Gaelic name of *Cill-Chuimein* (Church of St. Cumine), St. Cumine being 7th Abbot of Iona, A.D. 669.

DAVIDSON

This is one of the principal branch clans of the great Clan Chattan. The traditional descent of the Davidsons, or *Clan Dhài*, is from David Dhu, fourth son of Muiriach of Kingussie, chief of Clan Chattan. From David Dhu are descended the Davidsons or *MacDhàis*, the principal family of whom were the Davidsons of Invernahavon, who are now represented by the Davidsons of Tulloch. Invernahavon was sold about the middle of the eighteenth century, and the estate of Tulloch in Ross-shire was purchased by the Davidsons from the Baynes in 1753. The chief of the Clan Davidson was hereditary keeper of the Royal castle of Dingwall.

The Davidsons are supposed to have been the Clan " Quhele," or " Yha," or " Kay," one of the two clans which fought the celebrated battle of the North Inch of Perth in 1396 ; the opposing clan having been the Macphersons. The subject of dispute was apparently whether Davidson of Invernahavon, Chief of Clan Dhai, as eldest cadet of Clan Chattan, or Cluny-Macpherson, as heir-male thereof, should command the right wing of Clan Chattan under Mackintosh, as its chief.

The leading families are the Davidsons of Cantray, in Inverness, and the Davidsons of Tulloch, in Ross-shire.

About the year 1700 Alexander Davidson of Davidson, in Cromarty, married Miss Bayne of Tulloch, and purchased the estate from his father-in-law.   His representative is now Davidson of Davidson.   The Baynes had great influence in Ross-shire.   Tulloch Castle is of ancient date, the keep having been built in 1466, and other parts of it in 1665. A branch of this family entered the service of France in the seventeenth century, having proved their descent to be noble for six generations prior to July 1629, as shown by the *Livre d'Or* in the imperial archives of France.

DRUMMOND

This clan's name is evidently a territorial one, from the lands of Drummond or Drymen, in Stirlingshire.

Malcolm Beg, so called from his low stature, Steward of the Earldom of Strathearn, 1225, is the first of the line on record and his son Sir Malcolm first assumed the name of Drummond.

Sir Malcolm de Drymen (or Drummond) was one of the chiefs who fought on the side of King Robert the Bruce at Bannockburn, and to his action in strewing the field with the caltrops or spikes, which had the effect of disabling a large proportion of the English cavalry, much of the success of the battle was due.   The caltrops, on which the savages (which form the supporters of the arms of the chief of Clan Drummond) stand, as well as the chief's motto, " Gang warily," are in allusion to this.

At an early period the Drummonds became allied to royalty.   King David II. espoused in 1369 Margaret Drummond, and Annabella Drummond became the queen of King Robert III.

The Barony of Drummond was created in 1488 in favour of Sir John Drummond.   The fourth Lord was in 1605 created Earl of Perth. In 1609 James, the younger brother of Patrick, 3rd Lord Drummond, was created Lord Madderty.   From him descended the Viscount of Strathallan.   In 1686 the Earldom of Melfort was created in favour of John, younger brother of the 4th Earl of Perth.   When the revolution of 1688 cost the Stuart dynasty their throne, the Earls of Perth and Melfort as well as the Viscount Strathallan cast in their lot with the family of their ancient kings.   They pursued the same course during the Risings of 1715 and 1745.   The consequence was attainder and forfeiture of the ancestral Drummond estates.   The 4th Viscount Strathallan fell at Culloden.   The Earls of Perth and of Melfort were both created Dukes by King James VII. after his flight to France.

The 9th titular Earl and " Duke " of Perth died without issue when the chiefship passed to his cousin, eldest son of the Duke of Melfort, who had been made a duke by Louis XIV. in 1692.

The Drummond estates remained in the possession of the Crown until the General Act of Restoration of Forfeited Highland Estates. James Drummond-Lundin, of Lundin, grandson of John, 1st Earl and Duke of Melfort (second son of James, 3rd Earl of Perth), claimed the chiefship, and was in Edinburgh in 1766 served heir-male-general to the last Earl, whereupon he assumed the name of Drummond only. To his son James (created Lord Perth, 1797, Peerage of the United Kingdom), the Drummond estates were restored in 1785 by the Court of Session and by Parliament. On his demise in 1800 the estates passed to his only child, Lady Clementina, who married Lord Willoughby de Eresby, ancestor of the Earls of Ancaster. The chiefship of Clan Drummond passed to James, 4th titular Duke of Melfort, a general in the French army, and *de jure*, 12th Earl of Perth. The Duke died without issue so his honours passed to his brother Charles Edward, a Roman Catholic prelate. He died in Rome, 1840, succeeded by his nephew, George, who established, before the Conseil d'Etat and the Tribunal de la Seine, his right to the French honours of Duke of Melfort, Comte de Lussan, and Baron de Valrose. In 1853 an Act of Parliament restored to him the Scottish titles of Earl of Perth and of Melfort as 14th Earl. In 1868 he instituted legal proceedings against the Willoughbys for recovery of the ancestral estates, but failed.

On his death in 1902, the Earldom of Melfort apparently passed *de jure* to Lady Marie Drummond, the 12th Earl's only surviving child. The Earldom of Perth and the chiefship of the Clan Drummond passed to William, 11th Viscount of Strathallan, whose nephew, John 17th Earl and Chief of Clan Drummond, was by arrangement restored the ancient seat, Stobhall in Perthshire.

DUNBAR

The connection of the Dunbars with Moray and its earldom during the greater part of Scottish history and their recognition as a Moray-shire clan by the Privy Council in 1579 entitle them to a place amongst the Highland clans.

Crinan the Thane and Seneschal of the Isles, born about A.D. 975, was father of King Duncan I., and of Maldred, whose son, Gospatric, was confirmed in the Earldom of Northumbria by William the Conqueror in 1067. In 1072 he was deprived of that earldom, and, flying to Scotland, was given Dunbar and the adjacent lands by King Malcolm III., thus becoming Earl of Dunbar. Patrick, 9th Earl, married Agnes Randolph, daughter of Thomas Randolph, 1st Earl of Moray, and companion of Bruce. She is celebrated in history as "Black Agnes," and when the English forces under Salisbury besieged Dunbar Castle in 1337, she successfully defended it for some months. In 1346, on the death of her brother John, 3rd Earl of Moray, she became Countess of Moray, but dying in 1368 without surviving issue, the Earldom of Dunbar devolved on his grand-nephew, George, whose brother, John, became Earl of Moray in 1372, their mother being Isabelle Randolph, sister of "Black Agnes." John Dunbar, Earl of Moray, married

Marjorie, daughter of King Robert II., and had a son Thomas, 2nd Earl, who first married the heiress of Frendraught, by whom he had Thomas, 3rd, and James, 4th Earl, who was murdered at Frendraught, having by his first wife two daughters successively Countesses of Moray. By Isobel Innes, who died before the dispensation for their marriage arrived from Rome, he left a son, Sir Alexander Dunbar of Westfield, ancestor of the hereditary Sheriffs of Moray. The Dunbars, Baronets of Mochrum, created Baronet in 1694, as the line of Cumnock and Mochrum, whose seat is Mochrum Park, Wigtonshire, are the present Chiefs of the Name of Dunbar. The Baronets of Durn, 1698, and of Northfield, 1700, are cadets of Westfield. So also are the Baronets of Hempriggs, in Caithness, whose dignity, like the Baronetcy of Dunbar of Baldoon, passes to heirs female.

Of the Mochrum family was Gavin Dunbar, Archbishop of Glasgow and Lord Chancellor of Scotland in the reign of King James V. William Dunbar, born about 1460, is one of the most celebrated of ancient Scottish poets. Gavin Dunbar, of the Westfield family, was appointed Bishop of Aberdeen in 1518.

ERSKINE

The name is derived from the Barony of Erskine, in Renfrewshire, held by Henry de Erskine, in the reign of Alexander II. The Erskines' connection with the Highlands arose from the marriage of Sir Thomas de Erskine with Janet Keith, granddaughter of Lady Elyne of Mar, and their son Robert, de jure Earl of Mar, was created Lord Erskine. Through his mother, however, he had inherited the representation and dignity of the oldest Celtic earldom and chiefship of the " tribe of the land " of Mar. Her ancestors had been Earls of Mar ab initio, and in 1014 Donald MacEmin, Mormaer of Mar, already held the dignity by succession through a Pictish heiress.

Robert, 4th Lord Erskine (and de jure Earl of Mar), was killed at Flodden, and his son, James, 5th Lord, was father of the Regent, John, 6th Lord, restored as 18th Earl of Mar by Queen Mary, and also in 1565—perhaps in case of the Crown ever cancelling the restoration—granted a new Earldom of Mar, of which the seat was Alloa. John, 23rd and 6th Earl, raised the Royal Standard for King James at Braemar, in 1715, and was created " Duke of Mar." His descendant John Francis Miller, 28th and 9th Earl, successfully claimed the Earldom of Kellie on the extinction of a junior branch of the family ; but, dying without issue, 1866, his cousin, Walter Coningsby, succeeded as 12th Earl of Kellie, and in 1875 his son, Walter Henry, 13th Earl of Kellie, made out his claim to the Earldom of Mar, dated 1565. The Earl of Mar and Kellie, Lord Erskine, whose seats are at Alloa and Kellie Castle in Fife, is chief of the Erskines. The ancient earldom, originally Mormaership of Mar, was confirmed to John Francis Goodeve-Erskine (nephew of the 28th) as 29th Earl, and has devolved on the heir-general of this line, now 35th Earl from Gillocher, Mormaer of Mar in the days of King David I. and chief of "the tribe of Mar." The seats of these earls were at Migvie and Kildrummy Castle, in Mar. Branches of Erskines have also inherited the Earldom of Buchan, and a Lordship of Erskine of Restormell, Sir John, Lord Erskine of Rerrick became Governor of N. Ireland. Sir Thomas Erskine of Cambo represents the line of Sir Charles and Sir Alexander Erskine of Cambo, the celebrated Lord Lyon Kings of Arms.

FARQUHARSON

The Clan Farquharson derives from Farquhar, fourth son of Alexander Ciar, the 3rd Shaw of Rothiemurchus, a branch of Clan Chattan. Taking up their residence in Aberdeenshire, the descendants of this Farquhar were called Farquharsons. Farquhar's son, Donald, married Isobel Stewart, heiress of Invercauld, and their son was Finlay Mór, 1st of the House of Farquharson of Invercauld. In their early history the name of this Finlay Mór, deputy royal standard-bearer at Pinkie, where he fell, 1547, stands prominent, and from and after him the Farquharsons are termed *Clann Fhionnlaigh*, or descendants of Finlay.

In the Rising of 1715 John Farquharson of Invercauld, with four officers and a hundred and forty men, joined the Clan Chattan Regiment, in which he was Lieutenant-Colonel, and accompanying it to England, was taken prisoner at Preston, where he remained for ten months. At Culloden, the Farquharsons were led by Francis Farquharson of Monaltrie, the "Baron Ban." They mustered three hundred men, and were in the centre of the front line.

James Farquharson of Invercauld died in 1750, and was succeeded by his son, also named James, a Captain of Foot in the Hanoverian army, who died in 1806, after having held the estates for fifty-six years. His only surviving child, Catherine Farquharson of Invercauld, who, in virtue of the Lyon Court Decree, 1815, assigning the chief arms and supporters, was the head of the central or "stem family" of Farquharson of Invercauld, and so chief of the clan, married Captain James Ross, R.N. (second son of Sir John Lockhart-Ross of Balnagowan), who took the name of Farquharson of Invercauld. She was succeeded by her son, James, on the death of whose descendant, Alexander Haldane Farquharson of Invercauld, in 1936, the crest, arms, and supporters were by Lyon Court Decree, 3rd December 1936, confirmed to his daughter, Mrs. Myrtle Farquharson of Invercauld, who was killed in an air-raid in 1940. This succession passed to her nephew, now Captain A. A. C. Farquharson of Invercauld, who was by Lyon Court in 1949 confirmed as MacFionnlaigh.

The principal branches of the name and clan of Farquharson have been Monaltrie, Whitehouse, and Haughton, Allargue, Breda, and Finzean. In Aberdeenshire, Joseph Farquharson of Finzean, R.A., the celebrated artist, was chieftain of the Finzean branch until his death in 1935. The Farquharsons of Inverey were a celebrated Jacobite branch, of whom the " Black Colonel " (John, 3rd Laird of Inverey) lives in Deeside legend and ballads and to escape from the Hanoverians rode his horse up the precipitous side of the Pass of Ballater.

FERGUSON OR FERGUSSON

The Fergusons appear to have been of Scoto-Dalriadic descent, and to have had their first settlement in Scotland in Kintyre. As regards Fergussons in the strictly Highland area : in Argyll the chiefs of *Clannfhearghuis of Stra-chur* long held the estate of Glenshellich (the valley of the willows) and with it the office of hereditary *maer* of Strachur on Loch Fyne, their seat being *Caisteal Dubh* on Beinn Bheula.

As some corroboration of the theory as to Kintyre having been the original seat of the Fergusons in Scotland, Kilkerran, the seat of the chief of the Fergusons, in Ayrshire, is the modern form of the Gaelic name of what is now Campbeltown. St. Ciaran, one of the Twelve Apostles of Ireland, landed, in the sixth century, at Dalruadhain, where there is a cave, still known as *Uaimh-a-Chiarain*, and the name of the place *Ceann Loch Chille-Chiarain*, is, in modernised form, Kilkerran. It passed into the possession of the MacDonalds. When the Campbells became owners it received the name which it now bears, viz., Campbeltown. The Fergussons of Kilkerran (named after St. Ciaran), descending from Fergus, son of Fergus, in the time of Robert the Bruce, may have been Keepers of the Cross of St. Ciaran. Sir John of Kilkerran was created a Baronet in 1703, and the line has been celebrated as judges and statesmen.

From Fergus, Prince of Galloway, whom we find ruling in 1165, and whose wife was a daughter of Henry I. of England, the Fergusons of Craigdarroch, in Dumfriesshire, claim descent. Alan, Lord of Galloway, a descendant and successor of Fergus, and Fergus of Glencairn witnessed Alexander II.'s charter to the monks of Melrose.

Craigdarroch, Dumfries, was the possession of the Fergusons for many centuries. " Bonnie Annie Laurie," so enshrined in Scottish hearts and song, was the wife of Alexander Ferguson of Craigdarroch.

The Fergussons of Atholl descend from Adam, son of Fergus, styled *Adamh-na-Cainbe*, who lived in the time of Baliol, and claimed descent from the Lords of Galloway. Adam obtained the barony of Derculich in Atholl, and later, by murdering the *Baron Maol* and his sons at the *clach dearg Dunfallandaigh*, made their sister an heiress, whom his son married ; hence the baronial house of Fergusson of Dunfallandy, which still holds that estate and the style of *Baran Dunfallandaigh* and Chief of the *Clan-vic-Fergus-na-Derculich-Athfodhla*.

Fergusons have been settled in Balquhidder, according to tradition, for about six centuries. Their origin is lost in antiquity. The oldest families of the Balquhidder Fergusons would appear to have been those of Ardandamh (in Laggan of Strathyre, on Loch Lubnaig), and Immervoulin. The Balquhidder branch of the clan wore a sett of tartan different from that worn by the Atholl families.

A branch of the Fergusons existed in Aberdeenshire and probably sprang from issue of one of the Ferguses who appear as younger sons of the Earls of Buchan. The head of this branch appears to have been Ferguson of Badifurrow. All cadet families of Badifurrow are believed to be extinct, except two, viz., Pitfour and Kinmundy.

FORBES

Tradition derives the chiefs and clan of Forbes from Ochonochar, who slew a savage bear by which part of Donside, the braes of Forbes, in Aberdeenshire, was rendered uninhabitable. He and his family then settled on the district he had won from the wild animal, and this became the *duthus* of Forbes which was altered from allodial to feudal

Castle Forbes.

tenure by charter in 1271 and part of which still belongs to the chiefs of Forbes, the Lord Forbes.

Alexander de Forbes was one of the most strenuous opponents of King Edward I. of England, when that monarch sought to subvert the liberties of the kingdom of Scotland. Alexander de Forbes lost his life when defending the castle of Urquhart against the English king. Sir John Forbes of Forbes, who lived during the reigns of King Robert II. and III., had four sons. From the three younger sprang the families of Pitsligo, Culloden, Waterton, and Foveran. His eldest son, Sir Alexander, was in 1442 raised to the peerage by King James I.. as Lord Forbes. That title is still in existence, and the holder of it is premier baron of Scotland. The first Lord Forbes married Elizabeth, daughter of the Earl of Angus by Princess Margaret, daughter of King Robert II.

James, 2nd Lord Forbes, had three sons, viz., William, the eldest, who succeeded his father as 3rd Baron ; Duncan, the ancestor of the families of Corsindae and Monymusk ; and Patrick, the ancestor of the Forbeses, Baronets of Craigievar, as well as of the Earls of Granard. Sir William Forbes, 8th Baronet of Craigievar, succeeded in 1884 to the title of Baron Sempill.

Alexander, 4th Lord Pitsligo, was attainted for his share in the events of " '45," and the peerage is now dormant.

To the head of the Forbeses of Culloden at the time of the events of " the '45 " (Lord-President Forbes) it may be said that the Hanoverian sovereign was indebted for the retention of his throne. For, owing to the great influence which the Lord-President possessed with the Highland chiefs, many of them who were on the point of throwing in their lot with Prince Charlie were induced by Lord-President Forbes to hold aloof from the struggle. The Lord-President freely employed his private means in furthering the interests of George II., but was by that monarch treated with the greatest ingratitude.

FRASER

Simon, Udard, and Gilbert Frasers (whose name derives from *La Fresiliere*, in Anjou, France) were in Scotland by 1160, and whilst some of their issue held Olivercastle in Tweedale, the main line was by Sir Gilbert (died by 1263) established at Touch-Fraser, Stirlingshire. The line continued, in the styles of Touch, Durris, and Philorth, where Sir Alexander, 8th of Philorth, got into financial difficulty expanding his town and university of Fraserburgh, and having, before 1620, disposed by an unclarified transaction " the Old Manorplace of Philorth " so that Fraser of Muchal by then got the undifferenced arms, and his estate named " Castle-Fraser," and was in 1633 created " Lord Fraser," the chiefship of Name and Arms thence held to Lord Fraser, a dignity now dormant, whereto the Lord Saltoun seems now entitled (and again holds Cairnbulg Castle), and is reckoned presumably chief of the Name of Fraser.

Simon Fraser, a younger brother of Sir Alexander, who fought for Bruce, is reckoned founder of the branch that by marriage acquired the Lordship of Lovat—which belonged to the Bissets of whom John died (1268) leaving three co-heiresses through one of whom Lovat came, before 1367, to Hugh Fraser, 1st recorded of the house of Lovat, but evidently son or grandson of the above Simon, from whom each succeeding Chief of Clan Fraser of Lovat is styled *MacShimi* (son of simon). Sir Hugh Fraser of Lovat, Sheriff of Inverness in 1431, was raised to the Peerage as Lord Fraser of Lovat.

The Lovat Peerage was attainted after Culloden, and Simon, Lord Lovat, beheaded for his share in the Rising of " '45." In 1815 the direct line of Fraser of Lovat became extinct, and Fraser of Strichen, a cadet (descended from a second son of the 4th Lord Lovat), became chief of the Highland clan Fraser of Lovat.

Thomas Alexander Fraser of Strichen was in 1837 created Baron Lovat in the United Kingdom Peerage. The present Lord Lovat is the 4th of this creation.

Several other petty clans in the district of the Aird adopted the surname of Fraser between 1730 and 1740, owing to the influence of the notorious Lord Lovat, who was none the less a chief most zealous for the good of his clan of whom he said they were his " glory and honour " and that " there is nothing I place in balance with my kindred."

GORDON

This is a name derived from the parish of Gordon in Berwickshire. The progenitors of the powerful clan of the name were Anglo-Norman and settled in the south of Scotland in the twelfth century. Adam de Gordon was one of the Scots barons who joined King Louis XI. of France in the Crusade of 1270.

In the reign of King Robert the Bruce, Sir Adam, Lord of Gordon, obtained a grant of the Lordship of Strathbogie in Aberdeenshire. He proved of the greatest service to the cause of Scottish freedom, for as Ambassador to Rome it was he who effected a reconciliation between the Bruce and the Pope. He was slain at the Battle of Halidon Hill in 1333. His great-grandson, also Sir Adam, fell at the Battle of Homildon in 1402, leaving an only child and heiress, Elizabeth, who inherited all her father's possessions.

Elizabeth de Gordon married Alexander, second son of Sir William Seton of Seton. Her only son, Alexander, was created in 1449 Earl of Huntly, with limitation to the issue of his third wife, such heirs assuming the surname and bearing the name of Gordon. (The Earl had no children by his first wife; his only son, by his second wife, carried on the name of " Seton.")

Huntly Castle.

George, 2nd Earl, left four sons. The second, Adam, married Elizabeth, Countess (and heiress) of Sutherland.

The 4th Earl was celebrated as the magnate whom the Regent Moray induced Mary Queen of Scots to attack and defeat at Corrichie after which his great castle of Strathbogie, which still contained the spoils of Bannockburn, was sacked.

George, 6th Earl of Huntly who, along with Lord Erroll, defeated Argyll in 1592 at the Battle of Glenlivet, was created Marquis in 1599. The 2nd Marquis, who was beheaded by the Scots Parliament in 1649, was survived by two sons—Lewis, 3rd Marquis, and Charles, created Earl of Aboyne in 1660. Their father, the 2nd Marquess, had been one of Charles I.'s staunchest supporters and before his execution declared, " You may take my head from my shoulders, but not my heart from my sovereign." George, 4th Marquis, was in 1684 created Duke of Gordon. The 4th Duke married the celebrated Jane Maxwell, and they raised the Gordon Highlanders.

In 1836 the 5th and last Duke of Gordon died without issue, when George, 5th Earl of Aboyne, succeeded as 9th Marquis of Huntly and chief of the clan and " Cock o' the North." Aboyne Castle is still the seat of the Marquis of Huntly, and on the " green of Aboyne " is annually held the celebrated Aboyne Highland Gathering.

There are many distinguished cadets of the Gordon clan. The Marquis of Aberdeen is descended from John Gordon of Essie, a scion of the original male line of Strathbogie. The 1st Earl was President of the Court of Session and Chancellor of Scotland. He received his Peerage in 1682 in reward for the service of his father, Sir John Gordon of Haddo, a celebrated cavalier.

Gordon of Kenmure descends from the second son of Sir Adam of Gordon, who flourished in the fourteenth century. Of this house Sir John, in 1633, was made Viscount of Kenmure and Lord Lochinvar, peerages which, however, became dormant in 1847.

So powerful was Clan Gordon in the Highlands that the chief is known as " The Cock of the North," and was jocularly termed " Gudeman of the Bog " (from the Bog of Gight, now Gordon Castle, near the mouth of the Spey), because this estate was held in feu from the Earls of Moray. This joke led to a long feud, and the burning of the " Bonny Earl of Moray " in 1592. Huntly Castle, now a ruin, was their most magnificent seat.

GRAHAM

Tradition traces the Grahams from an alleged " Gramus," demolisher of the wall or line of defence built by direction of the Roman Emperor, Antoninus, betwixt the Clyde and the Forth, in order to keep back the Caledonians, and which came to be called " Graeme's Dyke." Whether or not the overthrower of the Wall of Antoninus was ancestor of the noble House of Graham is another matter !

The first authentic Graham seems to have been William de Graham, who witnessed the charter of the Abbey of Holyrood by King David I. in 1128, and who obtained from the same Prince the lands of Abercorn and Dalkeith in Midlothian. The Grahams of Dalkeith appear to have acquired northern property during the reign of King William the Lion, when Sir David, a descendant of the first Graham of Dalkeith, obtained Dundaff, still held by the Dukes of Montrose, in 1237, and his descendant, another Sir David, got the Lordship of Kinnaber and Old Montrose in Angus from the Bruce in 1325, as well as other properties near Montrose. Sir John de Graham, who was termed " the right hand " of the patriot Wallace, and who fell in 1298 at the Battle of Falkirk, was the second son of the then chief of the Grahams. Sir William Graham, who lived during the reign of King James I., married, as his second wife, Mary Stewart, second daughter of King Robert III. By the sons of this second marriage various distinguished cadet branches of the Grahams were founded, including Balgowan (ancestors of Lord Lynedoch) and Claverhouse (ancestors of Viscount Dundee, the hero of Killiecrankie and the " Bonnie Dundee " of Sir Walter Scott's ballad). Patrick, the eldest grandson of Sir William, was in 1445 raised to the Peerage as Lord Graham, in recognition of his gallantry in the field and his services as a Lord of Regency during the minority of James III. William, 3rd Lord Graham, was in 1504 created Earl of Montrose, the title being derived from the lands of " Auld Montrose."

James, 5th Earl, born in 1612, was the celebrated Marquis of Montrose, the great Royalist whose gallant career is part of Scotland's history. The Marquisate was created in 1644. James, 4th Marquis, was in 1707 created Duke of Montrose, and from him is descended the present Duke of Montrose, Chief of the Clan Graham.

From the second son of Sir Patrick, Chief of the Grahams during the reign of King David II., descended the Earls of Stratherne, Menteith, and Airth. This Sir Patrick married Euphemia, sole heiress of Prince David Stewart (son of Robert II.), who was Countess of Stratherne in her own right. Their son succeeded his mother as Earl of Stratherne. Of this, however, he was deprived by King James I., the reason assigned for this deprivation being that the Earldom was a male fee. In compensation the monarch bestowed on Earl Malise (late of Stratherne) the Earldom of Menteith.

In 1630, William, 7th Earl of Menteith, was restored by King Charles I. to the Earldom of Stratherne, but mischief having been made out of some chance remarks, this revival of the Stratherne Earldom was withdrawn by the King, and the Earl of Menteith received instead the additional title of Earl of Airth. On the death in 1694 of William, Earl of Airth and Menteith without male heirs, these titles became dormant. The descendants of the last Earl's sister then became heirs of line and repeated efforts have been made by these— the line of Barclay Allardice of Urie and Allardice—to get the old dignities revived. The Grahams of Esk, Netherby, and Norton-Conyers (in England) are descended from Sir John Graham of Kilbride, near Dunblane, who was second son of Malise, 1st Earl of Stratherne. Sir John, having fallen into disfavour at the Scottish Court, retired along with a considerable following, to the " Debateable Land " on the Borders, and settled on lands on the bank of the River Esk, during the reign of Henry IV. of England.

Highlanders owe a deep debt of gratitude to the noble House of Graham since it was through the Marquis of Graham (afterwards Duke of Montrose) that in 1782 the statute repealing the disgraceful Act of 1747 (which abolished and made penal the use of the Highland garb) was passed.

GRANT

This clan is one of the principal branches of the " Siol Alpine," of which the " Clan Gregor " is the chief.

The Grants are said to derive their origin from Gregor Mór MacGregor, who lived in the twelfth century. The territory of Clan Grant is Strathspey, where an extensive moor called *Griantach*, otherwise *Sliabh-Griantais*, or " Plain of the Sun," may be the origin of the clan name. Sir Lawrence Grant, Sheriff of Inverness 1263, is the first authentic ancestor, and whilst a number of others of the name, such as Patrick Grant of Stratherrick and Inverallan, and Sir John le Grant, Forester of Darnaway, are mentioned 1331–1371, *Ian Ruadh* Grant, Knight, and Sheriff of Inverness in 1434, is the 1st Chief from whom an uninterrupted succession by documentary evidence is deducible, though there is, of course, no doubt about the subsequent chiefs being of the same race as the earlier chiefs. He married Matilda, daughter of Gilbert of Glencairnie, a descendant of the Earls of Strathearn, and whilst his younger son is claimed as ancestor of Clan *Phadruig* (Tullochgorum), the elder became Sir Duncan Le Grant of Freuchie, first chief to be so designated, and this was erected into a Barony for his grandson, John Grant, *Am Bard Ruadh*, Keeper of the Castle of Urquhart. His son and successor, *Seumas nan Creach*, was one of those who as an adherent of Mary Queen of Scots, signed the bond against " Our auld enymyies of Ingland." His successor, John " the Gentle," was with the Queen at Holyrood when Rizzio was murdered, and his grandson is said to have been offered a peerage of Strathspey by James VI. but politely declined it with the query : " And wha'll

be Laird o' Grant ? " This had been the style of the chief from the fifteenth century, and in 1694 when the 8th Laird had his whole lands erected into a Regality of Grant. James, 7th of Freuchie, was to have been created Earl of Strathspey in 1663, but died before the warrant was signed.

Castle Grant.

Alexander, 18th Chief, died without issue, and was succeeded by his brother James (of Pluscarden), who had married the heiress of the Colquhouns, and in the following generation family arrangements consistent with the old principles of tanistry arranged the respective successions of the Houses of Grant of Grant and Colquhoun of Luss. Sir Ludovic Grant of Grant, 20th Chief, was twice married. By his first wife, he had one daughter, who died young. Sir Ludovic married secondly Lady Margaret Ogilvie, eldest daughter of James, Earl of Findlater and Seafield. Their grandson, Sir Lewis, succeeded as 5th Earl of Seafield on the death of the Earl of Findlater and Seafield in 1811 and took the name " Grant Ogilvie." Ian Charles, 8th Earl, died without issue, when the honours and chiefship of the Clan Grant were inherited by a kinsman in New Zealand. The late Earl of Seafield was killed in action during the War of 1914–1918. His Ogilvie honours were inherited by his only child, Nina, Countess of Seafield in her own right, whilst his brother succeeded to the Barony of Strathspey and chiefship of Clan Grant, of which the Lords Strathspey are now chiefs, and bear the surname Grant of Grant.

Castle Grant, the *Balla-Chasteil* of Freuchie, on Speyside, contains one of the finest collections of Highland portraits in Scotland. The oldest part, Babbette's Tower, contains the haunted tapestry room, decorated by the embroidery of twenty-two of the Lady of Grant's maids of honour.

The Clan Grant is divided into five branch-clans, those surrounding the parent stem of Freuchie being Clan Allan (Grant of Auchernack), Clan *Phadraig* (Grant of Tullochgorum), Clan Donnachie (Grant of Gartenbeg), and Clan Chiaran (Grant of Dellachapple). The baronial branches of Corrimony and of Ballindalloch were respectively represented by Sir F. J. Grant, Lord Lyon King of Arms, and Sir George Macpherson-Grant; whilst the Chieftain of the Clan Donnachie Grants is the Baronet of Dalvey. Glenmoriston, on Loch Ness, and on Speyside, the great Forest of Rothiemurchus, belong to other historic branches of the clan. Craigellachie is the clan gathering-place, its rock the crest symbol, with the slogan, " Stand Fast."

GUNN

This clan is of Norse origin. They claim descent from Guinn, second son of Olave the Black, King of Man and the Isles, who died 1237, and their ancient seats were at Hallburg and Kilearnan. The Gunns were a warlike clan of Caithness and Sutherland.

The Gunns and the Keiths were for ever at enmity. Lachlan Gunn of Braemor had an only daughter, Helen, who was famous for her beauty, and the day of her marriage with her cousin Alexander was fixed; but Dugald Keith, a retainer of Keith of Ackergill, whose advances she had repelled, surrounded her father's house with a body of armed Keiths, slew many of the Gunns, who were unprepared for an attack, and carried off the girl to Ackergill, where she became the victim of her abductor, and eventually threw herself from the summit of the tower.

About the middle of the fifteenth century the chief of the clan was George, who lived in what the dismal jimmies of modern degeneracy have termed barbaric pomp in his castle at Clyth. Actually he maintained the colourful culture of a Celtic chieftain's home. From his office of Coroner of Caithness he was known as Crouner Gunn, but by the natives as *Am Bràisteach Mór*, from a large silver brooch which fastened his plaid and was the badge of his coronership. Weary of the feud, he and the chief of the Keiths agreed in 1464 to meet with twelve horsemen a-side at the Chapel of St. Tears and settle it amicably. The Keiths came with twenty-four men—two on each horse. The Gunns fought desperately, but were cut to pieces. George Gunn was slain and stripped of his arms, armour, and brooch. Soon after William MacKames, a kinsman of the Gunns, killed George Keith of Ackergill and his son, with ten men, at Drummoy.

The patronymic of Gunn of Kilearnan is *Mac-Sheumais-Chataich*.

The chiefship is now before Lyon Court at the instance of three or four competing petitioners.

PLATE VIII.

[*Photo: Ideal Studio, Edinburgh.*

THE BARON OF MACDONALD'S CHILDREN, *c.* 1745.

From the portrait at Armadale Castle, showing (a) Gartered Trews, (b) *Feileadh-beag*.

(*By permission of Lord Macdonald.*)

PLATE IX.

FLORA MACDONALD.

After Allan Ramsay, from a contemporary copy of the portrait in the Bodleian Library, Oxford, showing mid-eighteenth-century Woman's Highland Dress.

(*By courtesy of the Board of Trustees of the National Gallery of Scotland.*)

The *arisaid*, which could be worn belted round the waist below the lower edge of the corsage, is seen brooched up to the *right* shoulder leaving the loose floating portion to be (here) gracefully gathered over the left arm. This plaid-use of the *arisaid* is an important, picturesque and graceful part of the dress (see Pl. XIV, p. 384).

INNES

This clan springs from Berowald, to whom in 1160 Malcolm IV. gave the Barony of Innes, in Moray, which comprehends all the lands along the seashore from the Spey to the Lossie, and he seems to have acquired, by marriage with a daughter of its former chieftain, descent from the native Moravienses. The shiel of Edder-Innes is held by the Innes Clan Trust, which thus holds part of the *duthus*. The tall white mansion of Innes was built in 1646 by Sir Robert, 1st Baronet.

The name means *greens* and is derived from the broad plain contained between Innes House and the River Lossie. In 1579, the Privy Council recognised the Inneses as a " clan." Sir Alexander, 9th of that Ilk, married Janet, daughter of the last Thane of Aberchirder, and their son Sir Walter, 10th Chief, built the great Tower of Kincairdy Castle. Sir James, 12th Chief, was Esquire to James III. and entertained James IV. at Innes in 1490. William, 15th Baron of Innes, sat in the Reformation Parliament 1560. His elder son, Alexander, 16th Chief, was beheaded by the Regent Morton ; his brother John, 17th, resigned his chiefship to Alexander Innes of Crommey, grand-nephew of the 13th Chief. Robert, 19th Chief, founded the burgh of Garmoch (Garmouth) on Spey, 1587, and in 1598 had the " Queen of Elphin " riding about in the Parks of Innes. His son, Sir Robert, 20th Chief, M.P. for Moray, a prominent Covenanter, but a faithful supporter of Charles II., whom he received at Speymouth in 1650, was made a Baronet, 1625. Sir James, 3rd Bt., married Lady Margaret Ker and his descendant, Sir James, 6th Bt. and 25th Chief, succeeded as 5th Duke of Roxburghe, 1805. His son was created Earl Innes, 1836. George, 9th Duke, is 4th Earl Innes, 10th Bt., and 29th from Berowald. On Scots practice his second son, Lord Robert Anthony, would take up the arms and chiefship as Innes of that Ilk.

The Baronets of Balvenie, created 1628, descend from Walter Innes of Innermarkie, second son of Sir Robert Innes, 11th of that Ilk. Robert, 2nd of Innermarkie, was made hereditary Constable of Redcastle. Sir Robert, 6th Baronet, enlisted in the Scots Greys and romantically married the Colonel's daughter. Sir William, 8th Baronet, who fought at Dettingen and Culloden, was succeeded by Sir John, 9th Baronet, and 9th of Edingight, whose father, the 8th of Edingight, was " out " with Prince Charles. Sir Walter, 15th Baronet of Balvenie and Edingight, represents this line.

Innes of Coxton (Baronet, 1686), a branch of Innermarkie, were in all the Jacobite Risings, and built the remarkable tower of Coxton, near Elgin. Sir Alexander, 1st Baronet, organised a Jacobite attempt in 1708, and Sir George, 2nd Baronet, died of wounds after Sheriffmuir. Father Lewis Innes, Jacobite Secretary for Scotland, 1690, descended from Robert Innes of Drainie, third son of the 11th Chief, and from Innes of Toux sprang George Innes of Stow, the millionaire, whose fortune passed to the Mitchell-Inneses.

I

LAMONT OR LAMOND

The Lamonts once owned the greater part of Cowal, but, to quote Skene, " their great antiquity could not protect the Lamonts from the encroachments of the Campbells, by whom they were soon reduced to as small a portion of their original possessions in Lower Cowal as the other Argyllshire clans had been of theirs."

The Clan Lamont was, traditionally, founded by Ferchar, who lived about the time of 1200. Ferchar left three sons, Murdoch, Malcolm, and Duncan. About the year 1238 we find Duncan, son of Ferchar, and Lauman, son of Malcolm, son of Ferchar, granting to the monks of Paisley the Church of Kilfinan with its patronage, as well as " those three-halfpenny lands which they and their ancestors had at Kilmun," also some land, with a chapel at Kilmory, on Loch-gilp. Previous to this time the clan was known as *Chlann 'ic Fhear-chair*. They afterwards assumed the name of " Lauman," after the ancestor Lauman referred to above. At the end of the twelfth century the clan possessed all Cowal as well as part of Argyll proper, from a point on Lochawe to Braeleckan on Lochfyne.

The chiefs of the clan were styled Lamont of Inveryne, but have latterly borne the more characteristic chiefly title of " Lamont of Lamont." In 1539 John Lamont of Inveryne was knighted. He had the honour of entertaining Queen Mary at Toward and Strone.

The family seat of Toward having been utterly destroyed by the Campbells, Ardlamont became the residence of the chief of the clan who was reinstated in his possessions in 1663, and remained so until sold by the chief, who died in 1929, when the chiefship passed to his cousin Ronald in Australia as 24th Chief. He was succeeded by his daughter, who renounced in favour of her cousin Keith John Lamont, 26th of that Ilk, on whose resignation 1953 in favour of his cousin, Alfred G. Lamont, 27th of that Ilk, the Lord Lyon confirmed to him the arms and chiefship.

In the eighteenth century the chiefship passed through Margaret, daughter and heiress of Donald Lamont of Lamont, to the heir of line, her son, Archibald Lamont of Lamont, to whose descendant, John Henry Lamont of Lamont, the chief arms and supporters were awarded by Lyon Court in 1909, as heir of line.

Of the Lamonts, although by no means a powerful clan, the chiefs' genealogy can be proved by charters at a time when most other Highland families are obliged to have recourse to the uncertain lights of tradition, and the genealogies of their ancient sennachies.

LESLIE

This Aberdeenshire clan, which take their name from the Barony of Leslie in the Garioch, claim descent from Bartolf, an Hungarian noble in the suite of Eadgar the Atheling, and his sister St. Margaret (queen to Malcolm Canmore), who landed at Queensferry and Bartolf, as Chamberlain to the Queen, had the duty of carrying her on pillion, hence the blue baldric and gold buckles (by which she held on) in the Leslie arms. They claimed their lands by " first occupation of vacant ground ' *between the les-ley and the mair, my horse wis tired and stoppit there* '; " a century later, this *allod* was feudalised by charter, for protection against boundary-claims by the Bishop of Aberdeen, in the time of Malcolm, son of Bartolf, constable of the Royal castle of Inverurie. By subsequent marriages the Barons of Leslie acquired, (1) by the heiress of " Wat-son," (of the line of Pollock) Rothes; (2) Fythkill, by a Fifeshire heiress ; and (3) Ballinbriech, by Mary, daughter of Alexander de Abernethy, spouse of Sir Andrew Leslie of that Ilk. Sir Andrew was one of the Scottish barons who in 1320 signed the memorable letter to the Pope asserting the independence of Scotland. The second son of Sir Andrew married the daughter and heiress of the Earl of Ross, and in his wife's right became Earl. How, as a result of this marriage, was fought the Battle of Harlaw, belongs to a page of " Clan Donald " history.

George Leslie of Rothes and Fytekill, a great-grandson of Sir Andrew Leslie of that Ilk, was in 1437 created Earl of Rothes. John, the 6th Earl, was created Duke of Rothes by Charles II. in 1680. On the death of the Duke, without male issue, the Dukedom became extinct, while the Earldom of Rothes was inherited by his elder daughter Margaret, who married the Earl of Haddington. Her eldest son, John, inherited his mother's Earldom of Rothes, took the name of Leslie, and handed down the Leslie chiefship, while the second son, under a practical arrangement, took up his father's Earldom of Haddington. The Earls of Rothes still own the ancient Castle of Rothes, on Speyside.

Besides the Rothes honours the Leslie family in its cadet branches have been honoured with the peerages of Newark, Leven, and Lindores. Sir Alexander Leslie, 1st Earl of Leven, 1641, is celebrated as one of the great generals in the civil wars of the 17th century.

The most distinguished cadet is Leslie, Baron of Balquhain in the Garioch, from whom sprang Count Leslie in Austria (who killed Wallenstein), and the Baronets of Wardis, 1625, and Leslie of Warthill, a son of whom became Prince Bishop of Laibach.

LENNOX

The territory of Levenach, comprehending much of Dunbartonshire, originally belonged to a race of Celtic chiefs, of whom the first was Alwin MacMuredach, Mac Maldouen, Mormaer of the Levenach. This earl lived about 1180. Alwin, 2nd Earl, had several sons, of whom the fifth, Aulay de Faslane, was ancestor of Allan de Faslane, who, as the nearest male branch, was created heritable Bailie of the Lennox. Gilchrist, the seventh, founded the Clan Macfarlane. Corc, the eighth, was ancestor of Leckie of that Ilk. Malcolm, 4th Earl, was one of those who acknowledged the Maid of Norway, supported Wallace, and opposed the hated English Treasurer, Cressingham. Malcolm, 5th Earl, was one of the Bruce's staunchest supporters. Many of the patriot king's adventures are connected with the Lennox. Donald, 6th Earl's only daughter Margaret, Countess of Lennox, married Walter de Faslane, the heir male, and hereditary Bailie. She was careful to see that he only used the title " Lord of the Lennox "—not Earl. Their son Duncan, 8th Earl, had a resettlement of the Earldom in 1392, was foully beheaded by James I., and that this was mere murder is shown from the Lennox not having been forfeited. The Earl left, with a son—whom the Regent alleged and historians proved was illegitimate—Donald, ancestor of Lennox of Woodhead, three daughters of whom Elizabeth married Sir John Stewart of Darnley.

Owing to dispute regarding the seniority of the co-heiresses, it was not until 1473 that Sir John Stewart of Darnley, grandson of the Lady Elizabeth, was retoured heir and became the 1st Stewart Earl of Lennox. Matthew, 4th Earl of the Stewart line, married Lady Margaret Douglas, daughter of the Earl of Angus by Queen Margaret Tudor. She is the Countess of Lennox whose portrait in the tartan cloak is extant. They had two sons, Henry, Lord Darnley, husband of Mary Queen of Scots and ancestor of our Royal line, and Charles, on whom Lennox was conferred in 1572 and whose only daughter was the unhappy Lady Arabella Stewart. In 1581 a Dukedom of Lennox was created for Esmé Stewart d'Aubigny, a junior grandson of John, 3rd Earl ; a line is now represented by the English Earls of Darnley. The Dukedom, however, expired in 1673, the widow of Charles, 6th Duke, being Frances Stuart, of the House of Blantyre— an intimate friend of Charles II.—celebrated as " La Belle Stuart," the model of Britannia on our coinage. King Charles subsequently conferred the title on his natural son by the Duchess of Portsmouth. Lennox Castle, in Stirlingshire, belonged, until 1927, to the House of Lennox of Woodhead, Baron of Antermony whom Lyon Court has always regarded as Chief of the Name. For a time it recently took the name " Peareth-Kincaid-Lennox " but has now resumed the title Lennox of Woodhead, and rematriculated the undifferenced arms, and Kincaid of Kincaid has been established in a collateral, as chief of that name.

LINDSAY

The country of the Lindsays in the Braes of Angus and their chief having been first commander of the first Highland regiment *Am Freicedan Dubh*, entitles them to place among the Highland clans.

Baldric de Lindesay, a Norman, is the first recorded member of this illustrious race. In 1120 Sir Walter Lindsay was a member of the Council of Prince David, and in 1180 William de Lindsay was Baron of Luffness and Laird of Crawford. Sir David Lindsay of Crawford, living about 1340, acquired Glenesk, in Angus, by marriage with Maria Abernethy, one of the heiresses of the Earldom of Angus.

He had two sons : (1) Alexander of Glenesk, father of David, a celebrated knight, created Earl of Crawford 1398 ; and (2) Sir William of the Byres. The grandson of the 1st Earl—David, 3rd Earl—left two sons—Alexander, 4th Earl, and Walter of Edzell. On the death of the 16th Earl the title [1] went by settlement to the Lindsays of the Byres, passing over the Edzell family.

The 4th, or " Tiger Earl," or " Earl Beardie," made a " band " with the Earl of Douglas which imperilled the Crown, but Crawford was defeated by Huntly at Brechin in 1452, and eventually pardoned. Alexander, " The Wicked Master," son and heir of the 8th Earl, was so evil that, having been convicted of attempt to kill his father, the Earl, he was disinherited, and the dignity devolved on his cousin, the Laird of Edzell as David, 9th Earl of Crawford (at whose death the dignity reverted to the son of the Wicked Master). He left two sons : (1) Sir David of Edzell, whose line failed in 1744 ; and (2) John of Balcarres, father of David, created Lord Lindsay of Balcarres 1633, whose son, Alexander, was created Earl of Balcarres 1651. This Earl's grandson was James, 5th Earl of Balcarres. His elder son, Alexander, 6th Earl, became 23rd Earl of Crawford 1808, and Chief on the failure of the direct line of Lindsay of Byres on whom the Earldom of Crawford had devolved under a regrant obtained by the 16th Earl. The seat of the Earl of Crawford and Balcarres, Chief of the Clan Lindsay, is Balcarres, in Fife. John, 20th Earl of Crawford, " The Gallant Earl," is celebrated as first colonel of the Black Watch, and for his romantic marriage with Lady Jean Murray, daughter of the 2nd Duke of Atholl.

Sir William, fourth son of the 6th Baron of Crawford, was created Lord Lindsay of the Byres, 1366, and John, 10th Lord, was created Earl of Lindsay, 1633. Sir David Lindsay of the Mount, poet and Lord Lyon King of Arms, was a cadet of this line. This house was celebrated in the heraldic annals of Scotland as it produced three Kings of Arms—two Sir Davids of the Mount and Sir David Lindsay of Rathillet.

The well-known song, " Auld Robin Gray," was composed by Lady Anne Lindsay, born 1750, eldest daughter of James Lindsay, 5th Earl of Balcarres.

The Lindsays, known as " The Lightsome Lindsays," formed a Clan Association in 1897.

MACALISTER

The MacAlisters, one of the principal branches of Clan Donald, trace their descent from Alexander, brother of Angus Mor, son of Donald, *eponymus* of Clan Donald and grandson of Somerled of Argyll.

The territory of the clan was in South Knapdale (Kintyre), and the

---

[1] Title, undifferenced arms, and chiefship went to the genealogically junior heir of Tailzie, whilst the heirmale—Spynie and Edzell—bore the arms only differenced by a label. In 1868 the arms and chiefship came back to the heirmale—the 6th Earl of Balcarres.

ancient seat of the chief was at *Ard Phàdruig*, on the north of West Loch Tarbert. Later, the residence of the chief of the clan was at Loup, and the chief title was MacAlister of Loup. In 1618 the chief was one of the twenty who were to be held responsible for the good rule of Argyllshire during the absence of the Marquis of Argyll.

The later seat of the Chief of the MacAlisters was Kennox, near Stewarton, in Ayrshire. In 1805 Charles MacAlester of Loup assumed the name and arms of Somervill in addition to his own, in right of his wife, Janet Somervill, the heiress of the entailed estates of Kennox.

MACALPIN OR MACALPINE

This clan is one of the chief branches of the Royal clan, " Alpin." The seat of the chief of the clan is said to have been at Dunstaffnage, in Argyllshire.

The clan is now, however, what their relations, the MacGregors, once were, " landless," and the family of their chief has been lost sight of.

MACARTHUR

The Clan Arthur is one of the oldest of the clans of Argyll, and its *duthus* was on the shores of Loch Awe where its chief also held Innestrarynich. This particular clan was known from others of the name of Arthur as the *Clann-Artair-na-Tir-a-chladich* (*i.e.* " of the shore-land.") So long had they been seated there that even in Celtic days they gave rise to the celebrated couplet :

> *Cruic 'is uillt 'is Ailpeinich*
> *Ach cuin a thaning Artairich ?*
>
> The hills and streams and MacAlpine
> But whence came forth MacArthur ?

The title *Mac-ic-Artair* suggests that the Clan Arthur of Tirracladich were originally a branch of a major line (which, of course, would be the case if their ancestor was a son of the " King Arthur " of romance, as they duly claim !). Their slogan was *O eisd, O eisd !* (" Listen ! Listen ! "). Ian, Chief of the Clan Artair of Tirracladich, was one of the chiefs of Argyll who was put to death by James I., and from this disaster they never recovered.

Staunch supporter of the Bruce, *Mac-ic-Artair* was rewarded with grants of lands forfeited by the Macdougalls, but a century later this influential position was lost.

There has been a good deal of confusion between the foregoing Clan Arthur and another of the same patronymic—the MacArthur-Campbells, one of the branch-clans of the Clan Campbell. (See p. 208.)

A family of MacArthurs were hereditary pipers to the MacDonalds of the Isles, and, as such, held the lands of Peingowen, in Skye.

Stewart of Garth says : " There is a very ancient clan of this name (MacArthur), quite distinct from the branch of the Campbells ; the chief's estate lay on the side of Loch Awe, in Argyllshire."

MACAULAY

The Ardencaple MacAulays are a minor branch of the great " Clan Alpin." Their name appears in the " Ragman Roll " of 1296. In 1591 a bond of manrent was executed between the Chief of the MacAulays and the Chief of the Clan MacGregor, in which the chief of the former clan acknowledged himself to be a cadet of the MacGregors. He agrees, in that character, to pay MacGregor of Glenstrae the Calp, which was a tribute of cattle given in acknowledgement of superiority. In 1694 a similar bond was given to Sir Duncan Campbell of Achanbreac, where the MacAulays again professed themselves to be MacGregors.

The last portion of the clan territory passed out of the hands of the 12th Chief in 1767, when Ardencaple was sold to the Duke of Argyll.

Another and quite different tribe of MacAulays had their territory at Uig, in the south-west of the Island of Lewis. They appear to have been followers of the MacLeods of Lewis, and they had no connection with the MacAulays of " Clan Alpin." These Lewis MacAulays are said to be descended from Aula, Olla, or Olave " the Black," brother of Magnus, the last King of Man and the Isles. Lord Macaulay, the historian who so traduced the Highlanders, belonged to the Lewis MacAulays. The MacAulays and the Morrisons of Lewis used to be inveterate foes.

MACBEAN OR MACBAIN

Tradition records that the MacBeans as a branch of the Clan Chattan, and so recognised by Lyon Court in 1672, came north with Eva the heretrix on her marriage to Angus Mackintosh of that Ilk ; and from the Sword prominent by itself in the third quarter of MacBean's shield it is at least inferable that Milmor MacBean was *An Gille Mor*, the Swordbearer or *Somotophilax* of the chiefs of Clan Chattan. Other traditions represent them as a Morayshire clan akin to the MacBeaths but there may have been more than one race so named.[1] A more or less consecutive number of MacBean chiefs are traced through the 14th and 15th centuries and in 1609 Angus MacBean, then chief, acquired a territorial duthus getting a charter of Kinchyle from Campbell of Cawdor.

According to Lachlan Shaw (historian of " The Province of Moray "), the first MacBean came from Lochaber, in the suite of Eva, heir of line of the Chief of the Clan Chattan, and settled near Inverness.

Kinchyle was lost to the clan in the 18th century but the main line continued in Canada to be represented by MacBean of Glen Bean in Saskatchewan, who in 1958 resigned his chiefship in favour of his junior cousin Hughston M. MacBean, a celebrated American business magnate, who accordingly was by decree of Lyon Court 1959 invested in the chiefly arms of the race as MacBean of MacBean and who has recovered part of Kinchyle.

[1] Of the name " MacBean," Dr. MacBain says : " The clan name MacBheathain or MacBean represents what in older times would have been Mac-'ic-Bheatha or MacBeath."

Dr. Fraser-Mackintosh in *Minor Septs of Clan Chattan,* says :

The MacBean territory lay chiefly in the parish of Dores (Inverness shire), as may be seen from the preponderance of the name on the tomb-stones in the churchyard, represented by Kinchyle and Drummond as heritors. They were represented in Strathnairn by MacBean of Faillie, and in Strathdearn by MacBean of Tomatin. Kinchyle was undoubted head, and signs the Bond of Union among the Clan Chattan in 1609 ; the Bond of Maintenance of 1664 ; and, finally, in 1756, the Letter of Authority from the clan to Mackintosh to redeem the Loch Laggan estate.

MACDONALD (CLAN DONALD) [1]

No clan has exercised such a powerful influence in early Highland history as the MacDonalds, Kings of the Isles and of Man, Lords of the Isles, and Earls of Ross. At one period of their history their power rivalled and indeed threatened to eclipse that of the Scottish king. In fact, the early history of the MacDonalds is the early history of not only the Western Isles but also of the greater part of the Highlands.

The founder of the clan was Somerled, son of Gillebride. The history of Gillebride, who lived about the end of the tenth and begin-ning of the eleventh century, is involved in obscurity. Apparently through some political misfortune, Gillebride had been deprived of his possessions and forced to seek concealment with his son, Somerled, in Morvern. About this time the Norwegians held the inhabitants of the Western Isles and western mainland seaboard in terror by their piratical incursions. Somerled put himself at the head of the inhabitants of Morvern, expelled the Norwegians, and made himself master of the whole of Morvern, Lochaber, and North Argyll. He later reconquered southern Argyll. About 1135 King David I. reconquered from the Norwegians the islands of Man, Arran, and Bute. These islands seem to have been conferred on Somerled by King David. Though Somerled was now very powerful, he could not hope to cope with the strength of the Norwegian King of the Isles. He therefore effected by policy what he feared not to be able to effect by strategy. He obtained in marriage Ragnhildis, daughter of the Norwegian King of the Isles. The issue of this marriage were three sons, Dugall, Reginald (or Ranald), and Angus.

Olave the Red, Norwegian King of the Isles, was murdered in the Isle of Man by his nephews, and succeeded by his son, Godred the Black, who, at the time of his father's death, was in Norway. Godred promptly arrested and executed his cousins, the murderers of his father. Godred had not been long on the throne of Man and the Isles before his tyranical conduct estranged the affections of many of his subjects. A number of these, headed by a powerful noble named Thorfinn, approached Somerled, who had now assumed the title of Lord of Argyll, and asked that his son Dugall be proclaimed King of the Isles, in room of his uncle, Godred. Somerled readily agreed. Thorfinn accordingly took Dugall through the isles, with the

---

[1] See Appendices VII. and VIII.

exception of Man, and forced the inhabitants to acknowledge Dugall as their King. Godred, alarmed by the intelligence of this revolt, sailed north with a powerful fleet but was met by Somerled with a fleet of eighty galleys. A bloody but indecisive naval battle was fought in 1156, resulting in a treaty, according to which Godred conceded to the sons of Somerled the South Isles, reserving for himself the North Isles and Man. The North Isles were those north of the point of Ardna-murchan, while among the South Isles was included the peninsula of Kintyre. Despite the treaty, Somerled invaded Man two years later, and routed Godred who fled to Norway, where he remained until the death of Somerled. Up to this time all the isles appear to have acknowledged their allegiance to Norway.

Somerled was now able to wage war with the Scottish king, Malcolm IV., but their contests were for the time ended in 1159 by treaty. Fresh disputes arose, however, and in 1164 Somerled landed a large force on the Clyde, near Renfrew. Here he was met by an army under the High Steward of Scotland, and utterly defeated, both Somerled and his son Gillecolum (by his first marriage) being slain.

After the death of Somerled, Man returned to its allegiance to Godred. Mull, Coll, Tiree, and Jura seem to have fallen to Dugall, Somerled's eldest son by his second marriage ; Islay, Kintyre, and part of Arran were the portion of Reginald, the second son by the same marriage ; while the remainder of Arran as well as Bute came under the sway of Angus, the youngest of the three brothers. All three brothers were then styled Kings of the Isles, while their cousin, Reginald, son of Godred, had the title of King of Man and the Isles. Dugall, besides the territories which he received by right of his mother, on the death of Somerled, obtained among other possessions the important district of Lorn as his paternal heritage.

The principal portion of the mainland possessions of Somerled, 1st Lord of Argyll, appear to have fallen to Somerled, his grandson, and son of Gillecolum, the first Somerled's son, by his first marriage.

In 1221 Somerled, the son of Gillecolum, was defeated in Argyll by Alexander II., King of Scots, and forced to fly to the Isles, where he died.

Events finally reduced immediate descendants of the first Somerled, Lord of Argyll, to the families of Dugall and Reginald, his two eldest sons by his second marriage.

From Dugall sprung the Clan Dougall or MacDougalls of Argyll and Lorn.

Reginald, second son of the first Somerled by his second marriage, founded two families. Donald, the elder son, was progenitor of the Clan Donald or MacDonalds of Islay ; while his brother Roderick, or Ruari, founded the Clan Ruari or the Macrories of Bute.

In consequence of the famous Battle of Largs, 1263, when Haco, King of Norway, was defeated by Alexander III., King of Scots, a

I*

treaty was effected by Magnus, King of Norway, the successor of Haco, and Alexander III., in 1266, whereby the overlordship of all the Western Isles was transferred from the Norwegian Crown to that of Scotland.

After this there seems to have been a rearrangement of the possessions of some of the descendants of the great Somerled. The islands of Skye and Lewis were conferred on the Earl of Ross, and Somerled's descendants were also deprived of Man, Arran, and Bute. The Clan Ruari of Bute, however, obtained compensation by the grant of lands in the North Isles. The progenitor of the Clan Ruari left two sons, Dugal, who died without issue, and Allan, who left one son, Roderic. This Roderic was succeeded by his only son, Ranald, who was assassinated at Perth in 1346 by the Earl of Ross. With Ranald expired the male line of the chiefs of the Clan Ruari. Ranald's only sister, Amy, was married to John, Chief of Clan Donald.

During the wars of succession for the Scottish throne between the Baliol and Comyn faction on the one side, and that of Bruce on the other, Alexander, Chief of Clan Dougall, and Alexander, Chief of Clan Donald, supported the former party. Consequently, when Bruce vanquished his opponents, both those chiefs were forfeited.

MacDougall, however, retained a portion of his once wide domains, including Dunolly, which still remains the seat of the Chief of the Clan Dougall.

Alexander, Chief of the Clan Donald, was imprisoned by Robert the Bruce in Dundonald Castle, where he died. His possessions were for the most part conferred on his brother, Angus Og, who had been a steady supporter of Bruce from the beginning. Angus Og, with a large number of his clan, was with Bruce at Bannockburn.

Angus died early in the fourteenth century, leaving two sons, John, who succeeded him as Chief of Clan Donald, and John Og, progenitor of the MacIans or MacDonalds of Glencoe.

After the death of Robert the Bruce and whilst Edward Baliol held the Scottish throne, John, Chief of Clan Donald, forsook the Bruces and adhered to Baliol. On the return of King David II. from France (where he had fled from Edward Baliol), and the final defeat of the Baliol faction, MacDonald fared badly and lost many of his possessions.

In 1344, however, David II., in order to secure the support of the powerful MacDonalds, pardoned both John, Chief of Clan Donald, and his kinsman, Ranald, Chief of Clan Ruari, whose father, Roderic, had been forfeited by Robert the Bruce. John, Chief of the Clan Donald, was confirmed in possession of Islay, Jura, Gigha, Scarba, Colonsay, Mull, Coll, Tiree, and Lewis, as well as the districts of Morvern, Lochaber, Duror, and Glencoe; Ranald was confirmed in the original northern territories of his clan, namely, Uist, Barra, Eigg, and Rum, and the lordship of Garmoran, Kintyre, Knapdale, and Skye reverted to their former owners, whilst Ardnamurchan was given to Angus MacIan, one of the relations of John of the Isles, who thus became founder of Clan MacIan of Ardnamurchan. This branch of the MacDonalds appears to have become extinct in Ardnamurchan during the seventeenth century, whence they were forced to seek other homes, in consequence of the hostility of the Government and of neighbouring clans (notably the MacLeans and Campbells). Its representation has, however, recently been claimed by a family, named MacKain, hailing from Elgin.

Ranald, Chief of the " Clan Ruari " (whose only sister, Amy, was married to John, Chief of " Clan Donald "), having been killed at Perth in 1346, John, Chief of " Clan Donald," succeeded in his wife's right to the possessions of Ranald MacRuari. He then assumed the title of " Lord of the Isles."

By Amy MacRuari the Lord of the Isles had issue, three sons, John, Godfrey (or Gorrie), and Ranald. John and his young son predeceased his father. Prior to the death of David II. and the accession to the Scottish throne of the Steward of Scotland, by the title of Robert II., the Lord of the Isles divorced his wife, Amy, and married Margaret, daughter of Robert, the High Steward. By his second wife John had also three sons, Donald, John, and Alexander.

By arrangement between the King and the Lord of the Isles, the Macdonald chiefship and Lordship of the Isles were (in accordance with the principles of the Law of Tanistry), so altered as to descend after John's death to the children of his Royal second marriage. Godfrey, the eldest surviving son of the Lord of the Isles by his first marriage, dutifully accepted his father's patriarchal resettlement, and carried on only the representation of his mother's line. Ranald, the younger brother of Godfrey, received as his appanage the North Isles, Garmoran, and other properties, to hold of John, Lord of the Isles, and his heirs.

On the death in 1380 of John, Lord of the Isles, his eldest son by his second marriage (Donald) became, according to the principles of tanistry inherent in Scottish peerages, 2nd Lord of the Isles. Donald's wife was Mary (or Margaret) Leslie, only daughter of the Countess of Ross and of her husband, Sir Andrew Leslie. Margaret had an only brother, Alexander, who at his mother's death succeeded her as Earl of Ross. Alexander, Earl of Ross, by his marriage with Isabel, daughter of the Regent Albany, left an only child, a daughter, Euphemia, who was put into a convent and forced to resign her possessions and title to the Regent Albany and his direct male heirs. This was resisted by the Lord of the Isles, who claimed the Earldom of Ross in right of his wife. Donald took up arms in order to assert his claims. The result of the struggle was the historical but indecisive Battle of Harlaw in 1411, owing to which, however, the Earldom of Ross was vested for a brief period in the Albany family.

Donald, 2nd Lord of the Isles, was liberal to his full brothers, John and Alexander, and enfefted them both in territories, to be held by them as his vassals. John (called " John Mór " or " The Tanister "), founded " The Clan Ian Vhor " or " Clan Donald " of Islay and Kintyre ; while from Alexander (or Alister Carrach), who was styled Lord of Lochaber, are descended the MacDonells of Keppoch or Clan Ranald of Lochaber. John, Chief of the Clan Donald of Islay, further increased his possessions and influence by marrying Marjory Bissett, heiress of the " Glens " in Antrim in Ireland.

Ranald, second surviving son of the 1st Lord of the Isles by his first marriage, did not long survive his father. On Ranald's death his children were dispossessed by their uncle, Godfrey, Ranald's elder brother, Lord of Uist, and head of the " Siol Gorrie." After Godfrey's death feuds were frequent between the " Siol Gorrie " and the " Clan Ranald." Godfrey's grandson, Alister MacGorrie, died in 1460, and afterwards the " Siol Gorrie " seem to have fallen into decay.

Donald, 2nd Lord of the Isles, died in 1420, leaving two sons, Alexander, his successor, and Angus, afterwards Bishop of the Isles. In 1424 the Earldom of Ross was confirmed by King James I. to the mother of the Lord of the Isles. Notwithstanding this proof of Royal favour, we find the 3rd Lord of the Isles in opposition to the King in 1427, and finally a prisoner at Inverness, though eventually he was liberated. In 1429, by the death of his mother, Alexander, Lord of the Isles became Earl of Ross. Smarting on account of his imprisonment he and his vassals, both of the Isles and of Ross, wasted the Crown lands, near Inverness, and burned Inverness. James I. promptly collected an army, and in person attacked and defeated the forces of the Lord of the Isles, who were then in Lochaber. The life of the Lord of the Isles was only spared by an abject submission to the Royal clemency, and he was thereafter imprisoned in Tantallon Castle. During his imprisonment a rising headed by his cousin, Donald Balloch of Islay, was suppressed. In connection with this rebellion, the Earl's uncle, Alexander of Lochaber, was deprived of his lands in Lochaber, which were bestowed on Mackintosh. Alexander, Earl of Ross, was released from prison in a couple of years. He died in 1449, and was succeeded by his eldest son, John, 4th Lord of the Isles and 2nd Earl of Ross (of the MacDonald blood). His other children were Celestine of Lochalsh, and Hugh of Sleat.

The reign of the 4th Lord of the Isles, who had no legitimate issue, was a stormy one, in consequence of the rebellions against Royal authority of his nephew and heir-apparent, Alexander (son of his brother, Celestine), and of his bastard son, Angus. In 1476 the Earldom of Ross was annexed to the Crown, and in 1493 the Lordship of the Isles was also finally absorbed, and the arms and chiefship of Macdonald fell, leaving the branches as independent clans. John, last Lord of the Isles, died in 1503.

Since then the disputes regarding seniority, legitimacy, and extent to which tanistry was applicable, have, needless to say, been prolonged and extensive. Eventually Charles II., at the Restoration conferred the dignity of *Lord Macdonnel and Aros* upon Glengarry, the heir of line of Celestine of Lochalsh, on the ordinary principle of Royal and Common Law succession ; and his Lordship was forthwith officially treated as Chief, being duly, as " Chief of the Name and Clan of Macdonald," ordered to exhibit the unruly members of the Clan Donald, 18th July 1672. The dignity of Lord Macdonnel, with which the chiefship was thus connected was, however, limited to heirs male of his body, and on his death in 1680 the chiefship of Clan Donald again fell dormant, whilst the chiefship of Glengarry passed to the Laird of Scotus.[1]

Sir James Macdonald of Sleate, Chief of Clan Huisdean, held the island estates of Skye and a baronetcy which had been conferred on Sir Donald Gorm Macdonald of Sleate in 1625. The Crown approved the line of Donald Gorm being the stem of Clan Donald and the Sleate estates seem to have been accordingly united in a territorial lairdship of " Macdonald "—giving the Chief of Clan Huisdean the old status of Macdonald of Macdonald (*cf.* the old grant, " I Donald of Donald, sitting on Dun-Donald give to you . . .") and in the charter erecting the Barony of Barra, 1688, that island is stated to have been then part of the " Barony of Macdonald." In 1727 there was a further grant of this feudal barony in favour of the heir-male of Clan Huisdean as *Macdonald of Macdonald* ; and in 1776 his son, Sir Alexander Macdonald of Macdonald, 9th Baronet of Sleate, was created Lord Macdonald in the peerage of Ireland (a dodge to prevent Scotsmen getting votes

Eilean Tirrim.

in the House of Lords even when elevated to the peerage !). Difficulties arose in connection with the marriage of Godfrey, 3rd Lord Macdonald, whose mother was heiress of the English Bosvilles of Thorpe. For technical reasons the first ceremony (in England) was not effective, and in the event, his eldest son, Alexander, though believed to be technically illegitimate, was really legitimate under Scots law, and in relation to the Scottish baronetcy, but under English and Irish law, in relation to the peerage, only the " lawfully begotten " son born after the later ceremony was competent to succeed to heritage and

---

[1] Sir Æneas Macpherson makes the position (and his own views on the principle of succession to chiefship) clear in *Loyall Dissuasive*, p. 118 : " If I were to give my judgement or opinion of all the three competitors for the chiftanrie. Glengerrie seems to me to have the best pretensions, having married the heiress of Ross, *i.e.* Lochalsh (supposing him a bastard which you know is objected against the other two as well as him) became legittimated by that match, a benefit the other competitors never yet pleaded." I examined the most interesting heraldic import of this (at first sight peculiar) statement in 1941 in *Notes and Queries*, CLXXIX., p. 362, and the principle laid down by Macpherson is not only perfectly clear when it is examined, but also one which is found applied in practice in other seventeenth-century cases, such as Lundin of Lundin.

honours there. His Lordship had moreover to settle two inheritances, and in the circumstances, exercising as he wisely believed, the powers of settlement analogous to tanistry, he settled the Bosville estates in England on his first-born son (who accordingly took the name of Bosville of Thorpe), whilst he settled the Macdonald estates in Skye on his son born after the marriage, who inherited the peerage of Lord Macdonald, and (it was supposed) the baronetcy, then masked by the peerage. In 1910, Bosville, anxious to remove the reflection of bastardy [1] was successful in this, and naturally in obtaining the baronetcy. He then assumed the name of Bosville-Macdonald, and was recognised in Lyon Court in the chiefship of Sleate. Soon after this, Sleate, Glengarry, and Clan Ranald made an agreement to waive their respective claims on the chiefship of Clan Donald, and to toss a coin for settling who should pose as chief on any occasion they met ; [2] but Sir Somerled, 16th Baronet and Chief of Clan Huistean, in 1952 abrogated that indignity, taking his historic hereditary status as Chief of Sleate, as confirmed by Lyon Court in 1910.

Lord Macdonald was indisposed in and after 1910, so his " claims " or his views were not considered (Appendix XXXI).

On his death, however, the right to Macdonald chiefship was brought by his grandson and heir before Lyon Court, who, after careful examination of the rights established by the other claimants in their several matriculations, found that the chiefship had fallen under the attainder of the fifteenth century, and that under the last restoration (1727) and devolution of the Barony of Macdonald in Skye, Alexander, 7th Lord Macdonald, was entitled to restoration of the undifferenced arms of Macdonald of Macdonald, Chief of the Name and Arms, and Head of Clan Macdonald.

Prior to the forfeiture the Lords of the Isles were followed not only by MacDonalds, MacDonells, MacIans, MacAlisters, Macintyres, etc., but also as vassals by the following clans, not descended from " Clan Donald," viz. Macleans, MacLeods, Camerons, Clan Chattan, MacNeils, Mackinnons, Macquarries, Macfies, MacEacherns of Killellan, Mackays of the Rhinns of Islay. After the forfeiture these clans became independent. The MacKenzies, Rosses, Urquharts and Roses of Kilravock, as vassals of the Earls of Ross, were for half a century followers of MacDonald.

Ranald, 1st Chief of Clanranald (third son of John MacAngus Og, 1st of the Isles), had five sons of whom three left issue : (1) Allan, 2nd of Clanranald, and Laird of Moidart, from whom descended the House of Clanranald ; (2) Donald of Knoydart, founder of the

---

[1] As Bosville of Thorpe there was no suggestion of bastardy, for they became " heraldically legitimate " (cf. *Notes and Queries*, 179, p. 362), but this aspect of the Law of Arms was not noticed in 1910.

[2] To what depths of ignominy had clanship fallen ! What the old Lords of the Isles would think about playing " pitch and toss " for the chance of pretending to " represent " them, one hesitates to contemplate.

House of Glengarry ; and (3) Dugal, of Sunart, ancestor of the *Siol Dhughall.*

Of these the two elder lines engaged in feuds and disputes regarding legitimacy (an easy source of wrangling in view of the reluctance of Church and Crown to recognise handfast marriages).

The story of Allan's line is briefly that Allan, 4th of Clanranald, had three sons : (1) Ranald Bane, 5th of Clanranald, whose only son, Dugall, 6th Chief, was slain by the clan on account of his cruelties, and his five sons excluded from the succession ; (2) Alastair, who " became " 7th Chief after the murder of his nephew, and was father of the celebrated Ian Muydertach, 8th of Clanranald ; (3) Ranald Galda, who with the assistance of Lord Lovat, endeavoured to seize the chiefship during Ian Muydertach's imprisonment, but who was defeated and slain at the Battle of Loch Lochy, 1544. Although heir-male, the *Ard-righ's* confirmation of Muydertach had divested him of the Clanranald chiefship, and he was thus a mere pretender at the time of his death.

Ian Muydertach, issue of Alastair by a handfast marriage, and who instead of the old title MacAllan, was tactfully denominated *Mac mhic Alein* (for none knew who really was to be MacAllan), got letters of legitimation from James V., and in 1531 had a Crown charter of the Clanranald estates, and Castle of Eilean Tirrim. He thus established himself as 8th Chief of Clanranald, and was supported loyally by the clan. From him descends the celebrated House of Macdonald of Clanranald, of whom Ranald, 17th of Clanranald and 5th of Benbecula, was the devoted adherent of Prince Charles in 1745.

It may be observed that whilst the 7th and subsequent chiefs of Clanranald have been heirs by tanistry, they have not been heirs male of Clanranald ; this position (*pariente major* as it is termed in Spanish families—where chiefship may likewise be diverted to junior lines),[1] having devolved on the House of Morar, eldest son of Dugall, 6th of Clanranald, from whom spring the branches of Knockiltaig, Rhetland, Genheil, Dumore, and Bornish.

Donald, of Knoydart, second son of the 1st Clanranald, founded the House of Glengarry, of whom Alasdair, 6th of Glengarry, married Margaret, daughter and co-heiress of Sir Alexander of Lochalsh, by which he acquired great influence, and his issue their claim to be lawful heirs of line of the early Lords of the Isles. (Glengarry also claimed to be *jure sanguinis* lawful heir of the line of Clanranald, but as both sides hurled charges of bastardy at one another much may be discounted. Neither house bears bastardised arms. It was this sort of claim which was at the root of the armorial lawsuit *Macdonell* v. *Macdonald*, 1826). Donald, 8th of Glengarry, had his lands erected into a barony, 1627, and his son, being created Lord

---

[1] *Juridical Review,* September 1940, p. 219, and France, cf. F. F. Brentano, *Old Regime in France,* p. 42.

Macdonell and Aros, 1660,[1] became Chief of Clan Donald, but this again expired with him,[2] whilst the chiefship of Glengarry passed to his uncle, Donald. Alasdair, 15th of Glengarry, was the friend of Sir Walter Scott and subject of Raeburn's portrait. On the death in 1868 of his grandson, Charles, 18th Chief of Glengarry, that chief's sister, Rebecca, Mrs. Cuninghame of Balgownie, became " heir of line," but being " conventionally dead " (as a Macdonell), the chiefship of Glengarry passed to Aeneas, 7th of Scotus, as 19th of Glengarry.

The MacDonalds of Staffa were a cadet of Clanranald, who got merged in the Steuart-Setons of Allanton.

The Macdonnells of Antrim (Ireland), and the Clanranaldbane, or Macdonalds of Largie (Kintyre), are cadets of Macdonald of Islay.

Gregory divides " Clan Donald " into nine main branches :

(1) *The House of Lochalsh*, whose heirship passed to Glengarry.

(2) *The House of Sleate (Clann Uistein)*, now represented by Sir Somerled Bosville Macdonald of Sleate and of Thorpe, Yorkshire, in the baronetcy, and by Lord Macdonald in estates in Skye and the High Chiefship of Macdonald as *Macdonald of Macdonald*.

(3) *The Clan Ian Vor* or *Clan Donald of Islay and Kintyre*.

(4) *The Clan Ranald of Lochaber*, the MacDonnells of Keppoch.

(5) *The Siol Gorrie*, Lords of North Uist, now long extinct.

(6) *The Clan Ranald of Garmoran*, comprehending the families of Knoydart, Glengarry, Moidart, and Morar. This clan is represented, *de facto*, by MacDonald of Clanranald.

(7) *The Clan Ian Abrach of Glencoe* or *MacIan MacDonalds of Glencoe*, victims of the cruel Massacre of Glencoe.

(8) *The Clan Ian of Ardnamurchan* (MacDonalds or MacIans of Ardnamurchan), who apparently became extinct in the 17th century.

(9) *Clan Alister of Kintyre*, represented by MacAlister of Loup.

Lord Macdonald, holder of the territorial Barony of Macdonald in Skye and whose seat there is Armadale Castle, is now, as above mentioned, *High Chief of Clan Donald*, whilst each of the other historic chiefships subsists under him.

This is a résumé of the present position of the others :

(1) The senior descendant is, without doubt, MacDougall of that Ilk and Dunolly, descendant of Dougall, son of Somerled, King of the Isles, but he forms a separate " name " and clan.

(2) MacDonnell of Glengarry, lineal descendant of Reginald, Dougall's younger brother (whose eldest son, Donald, was the founder of the " Clan Donald "), also heir of line (in the name) through Celestine of Lochalsh, of Alexander, 3rd of the Isles, but only chief of *Glengarry*.

---

[1] See Appendix IX.   [2] By reason of the limited destination.

(3) The heir male of Hugh of Sleate, third son of the said Alexander, 3rd of the Isles (and junior half-brother of Celestine) is Sir Ian Bosville-Macdonald, 17th Baronet of Sleate, whose predecessors were " Bosvilles of Thorpe " from 1832–1910, when the 13th became Chief of Sleate and Clan Huisdean under Lyon Court Decree.

(4) Reginald Macdonald of Castle Tirrim, 1st Chief of Clanranald, is represented (following disinheritance of the heirs of Dugall, 6th of Clanranald, *i.e.* Morar and its branches, of whom several were extant late in the 19th century), by the Muydertach line of the chiefs of Clanranald.

In 1957, in competing claims by Macdonalds of Waternish and of Inchkenneth, the Lord Lyon held that the latter as representer of Boisdale had made out his claim to be 24th chief of Clanranald and was accordingly revested in the Clanranald arms. Waternish established his position as chieftain of Belfinlay.

MACDOUGALL

The early history of this once powerful clan has been told under that of Clan Donald. The chroniclers of King Alexander II.'s Highland expeditions describe Ewen, then Chief of Macdougall, as " a very comely knight," which illustrates that West Highland chiefs, far from being uncouth barbarians, were equals of any in the courteous code of chivalry.

MacDougall of Lorn was on the losing side in the contest for the Scottish throne between Bruce and Baliol. An episode in that contest is the story of the Brooch of Lorn, won by MacDougall of Lorn from Bruce at the Pass of Brander. After Bruce's accession to the throne the MacDougalls were deprived of the greater part of their lands. The chief of the clan appears, however, during the reign of David II., Bruce's successor, to have married a grand-daughter of Robert the Bruce, and thereafter to have had his lands restored. On the death of Ewen, Lord of Lorn, without male issue, his estates passed to the Stewarts of Innermeath, John Stewart of Innermeath and his brother, Robert, having married the two daughters and co-heiresses of Ewen. As the heir of line, Stewart, did not continue the name MacDougall, the chiefship of the clan passed to MacDougall of Dunolly, the next male heir. His descendant is now the Chief of the Clan Dougall, and Baron of Dunolly. In 1715 MacDougall of that Ilk joined the Earl of Mar, and his estates were forfeited. They were, however, restored just before the Rising of " the '45," so the MacDougalls did not go out for Prince Charles. The ancient castle of Dunolly, on its crag above Oban, stands above Dunolly House the seat of the chief. The eldest daughter of a MacDougall chief bears, whilst unmarried, the old title " Maid of Lorn." Madam MacDougall of MacDougall and Dunolly succeeded to the chiefship in 1952.

MACDUFF

The kings of Fife, chiefs of a race intituled the " Clan MacDuff," claimed descent from Connall Cerr, a son of Eochaid Buidhe, King of the Picts. Their provincial kingdom was from about 1100 styled an earldom, which they set forth as held " By the grace of God " (*i.e.* allodially) and not from the King of Scots. Traditionally, " the Great MacDuff " was vanquisher of MacBeth and probably was a supporter of Malcolm Ceann-Mhor, and he is said to have given name to the clan. Anyhow, Constantine MacDuff was Earl of Fife by 1107 (and probably succeeded a cousin or niece, spouse of Prince Ethelred, apparently in her right—since *he* could himself have had none—Earl of Fife), and Gillemichael MacDuff, Constantine's brother and heir, was Earl by about 1127. His son Duncan was Earl by 1136, whilst Hugo, his second son was ancestor of the family of Wemyss.

On the death in 1353 of Duncan, last Earl, his sister, Isabella, Countess of Fife was forced to resign the Earldom.

Wemyss of Wemyss, whose ancient *duthus* and castle stands on the southern shore of Fife, was in 1757 recognised by Lyon Court as the representative of the race of the old Earls of Fife.

The titles, Earl Fife and Viscount MacDuff, were conferred, in 1759, on William Duff of Braco, created Lord Braco 1735. His descendant, the Duke of Fife, married the Princess Royal, eldest daughter of Edward VII.

As the hereditary inaugurator of the Pictish kings, the Chief of Clan MacDuff had the duty of crowning the king. At the coronation of King Robert the Bruce at Scone in 1306 the Earl of Fife, having joined the English party, Bruce was crowned by Isabel, Countess of Buchan, sister of Duncan, Earl of Fife. Though this courageous lady's husband was John Comyn, one of Bruce's bitterest opponents, the Countess did not let this deter her from performing a ceremony and exercising a function which she deemed it a duty to her country to undertake. Shortly after, the Countess fell into the hands of Edward I. of England, who imprisoned her in a cage on one of the towers of Berwick Castle. Here she remained for seven years, until liberated by King Edward II. The " Law of Clan MacDuff " is one of the interesting survivals of Celtic law in medieval Scotland, and shows the structure of the *derbhfine* groups in Alba. It was invoked in 1421 when Hugh Arbuthnott of that Ilk and his accomplices seized, boiled and " suppressed " the Sheriff of Kincardineshire but got a royal pardon under " the Law of Clan MacDuff ".

MACFARLANE

Of this old but most unfortunate clan Skene writes :

This clan is the only one, with the exception perhaps of the Clan Donnachie (Robertsons), whose descent from the ancient earls of the district in which their possessions lay, can be proved by charter, and it can be shewn in the clearest manner that their ancestor was Gilchrist, brother of Maldowen, the third Earl of Lennox. (W. F. Skene.)

The clan appear to have derived their name from the chief, Parlan (or Bartholomew), who lived during the reign of King David Bruce. Their territory was at the head of Loch Lomond, between that loch and Loch Long, and the seat of the Chief was at Inveruglas ; then afterwards, at Tarbert, and lastly, at Arrochar.

On the death in 1373 of Donald, last of the old Earls of Lennox, without male issue, it is claimed that MacFarlane became heir male. The Earldom, however, was confirmed to Sir John Stewart of Darnley, who married Elizabeth, one of the daughters of the last Earl of Lennox of the old line. The resistance of the MacFarlanes to the Stewart Earls of Lennox appears to have led to loss of their own lands. That the MacFarlanes were not entirely deprived of their territory was in consequence of the marriage of Andrew, head of one of the cadet branches, to the daughter of John Stewart, Earl of Lennox. By this marriage Andrew MacFarlane obtained possession of the *duthus* territory of Arrochar. His son, Sir John MacFarlane, assumed in 1493 the designation of Captain of the Clan MacFarlane, which at that period was synonymous with " Chief." Sir John, 11th Chief, fell at Flodden, and his grandson, Duncan, 13th of MacFarlane, at Pinkie, 1547.

The Clan MacFarlane became one of the broken clans towards the end of the sixteenth century. They appear to have been as turbulent as their neighbours, the Clan Gregor, and, like them, were proscribed and deprived of lands and of name. By Act of the Estates of 1587 the MacFarlanes were declared one of the clans for whom the chief was held responsible and by Act of 1594, were denounced as committing theft, robbery, and oppression. In 1624 many were tried and convicted of theft and robbery. Thereafter there was a general deportation of MacFarlanes to different parts of the kingdom, where they assumed various surnames. Many settled, under different names, in Aberdeenshire and Banffshire. Buchanan of Auchmar observes :

There is a vast number of descendants from and dependants of the surname of MacFarlane, of which those of most account are a sept termed Allans or MacAllans, who are so called from Allan MacFarlane their predecessor, a younger son of one of the lairds of MacFarlane, who went to the north and settled there. They reside mostly in Mar, Strathdon, and other northern counties.

Not an acre of MacFarlane clan territory now remains in MacFarlane possession. The last MacFarlane of MacFarlane emigrated to America during the eighteenth century.

The limitations of the chiefly honours is to " heirs " (general) (Lyon Register), so the chief is probably to be sought in the female line, but it now appears a nomination was made by the daughter and heretrix of the last chief in favour of a scion of the line of Macfarlane of Keithton and a claim to chiefship is pending in Lyon Court.

Besides the Castle of Arrochar (Loch Long), the Castles of Ellanbui and Inveruglas, on islands of Loch Lomond, were seats of the clan.

MACFIE (OR MACDUFFIE)

This is another of the branches of the Clan Alpin. Skene writes :

The MacDuffies or Macphees are the most ancient inhabitants of Colonsay, and their genealogy which is preserved in the manuscript of 1450 evinces their connection by descent with the MacGregors and Mackinnons. Of their early history nothing is known, and the only notice regarding their chiefs at that period is one which strongly confirms the genealogy contained in the manuscript.

Donald MacDuffie is witness to a charter by John, Earl of Ross, and Lord of the Isles, dated at the Earl's Castle of Dingwall, 12th April 1463.

Macfie of Colonsay was the Hereditary Keeper of the Records of the Isles in the time of the old Lords of the Isles.

After the forfeiture of the Lord of the Isles the Macfies followed the MacDonalds of Islay.

The Macfies appear to have remained in the possession of Colonsay till the middle of the seventeenth century. The island then passed into the hands of the MacDonalds, and, later, became the property of the McNeills. From them it was purchased by Lord Strathcona. After the Clan Macfie had lost their ancestral territory some of them settled in Lochaber and followed Cameron of Lochiel.

MACGILLIVRAY

The MacGillivrays have been for centuries one of the branches of Clan Chattan. All old chroniclers agree that the original home of the Clan Gillivray was in Morvern and Lochaber, and that they were intimately associated with the MacInneses, the MacMasters, and the MacEacherns. Browne (*History of the Highlands and Clans*) says :

Besides the MacDonalds and the MacDougalls, various other clans in Argyllshire appear to have sprung from the original stock of the " Siol Cuinn." From the manuscript of 1450 we learn that in the twelfth century there lived a certain Gillebride, surnamed King of the Isles, who derived his descent from a brother of Suibhne, the ancestor of the MacDonalds, who was slain in the year 1034. [But he admits] The genealogy by which this Gilbride is derived from an ancestor of the MacDonalds in the beginning of the eleventh century is, perhaps, of questionable authority ; [and continues] The original seat of the race appears to have been Lochaber.

It has received the name of Siol Gillebride or Gillivray from the circumstances mentioned by an old sennachie of the MacDonalds, that, in the
time of Somerled, the principal surnames in that country were MacInnes
and MacGillivray, which is the same as MacInnes. The different branches
of this tribe, therefore, probably formed but one clan under the denomination of the Clan Gillivray. But in the conquest of Argyle by Alexander II.
they were involved in the ruin which overtook all the adherents of Somerled,
with the exception of the MacNeills, who consented to hold their lands of
the Crown, and the MacLachlans.

The " Siol Gillebride " theory, however, is now largely discredited.
Skene (*Highlanders of Scotland*) says :

> The oldest inhabitants of Morvern, Ardgour, and Lochaber consisted
> of two clans, the MacGillevrays and the Macinnes, who were of the same
> race ; and as there is a very old traditionary connection between the
> *Clann-a'-Mhaighstir* (MacMaster) or Macinnes of Ardgour, and several of
> the clans descended from Anradan MacGillebride, it seems to establish
> the identity of this tribe with the old MacGillevrays of Morvern.

A MS. *History of the MacDonalds* written in the reign of Charles II.
(Gregory collection) says the principal surnames in the country of
Morvern were Macinnes and MacGilvray, who are the same as the
Macinneses. These seem to have been the original Dalriadic tribes of
Morvern, akin to the Campbells rather than to the Macdonalds. There
seems no basis for the alleged " dispersal " either—they just spread
naturally in their native area. Logan says :

> There is a very respectable branch of the MacGillivrays in the island
> of Mull, designated from the residence of the *Ceann-tighe*, or head of the
> house, as of *Beinn-nan-gall*, the mountain of the stranger. They are
> probably descended from those in Lochaber and Morvern, who were
> dispersed on the discomfiture of Somerled by Alexander II., and seem to
> have been otherwise called *MacAonghais* or Macinnes.

In *Collectanea de rebus Albanacis* it is stated that " Mac Ilvora or
MacGilvra of Pennygail in Mull was the name of an ancient family of
small property, who followed the Macleans."

Though a small portion of the MacGillevrays, after they had
ceased to be vassals of the Lord of the Isles, followed the Macleans,
the larger portion of the clan became members of Clan Chattan.

Alexander of Dunmaglas was the Commander of Clan Chattan
during the Rising of 1745, and fell at Culloden when gallantly rallying
his clan for Prince Charles. On that occasion Clan Chattan regiment
by the fierceness of its attack almost annihilated the left wing of
Cumberland's army.

The seat of the Chief of the MacGillivrays was at Dun-ma-glas, in
Strathnairn ; but since the sale of the estate and extinction of the
direct line, the chiefship has been dormant.

MACGREGOR

'S rioghail mo dhream (Royal is my Race) is the motto of this ancient clan, the senior one of the Clan Alpin, and the most unfortunate. The clan claims descent from Griogar, third son of King Alpin, who ascended the Celtic Scottish throne about 787 ; but this is mere tradition, and in history it seems that it is from *Aodh Urchaidh*, a native ruler of Glenorchy, that the Chiefs of the Clan Gregor were descended.

Though Glenurchy was the original seat of the Clan Gregor, they, in their halcyon days, possessed much territory on the borders of Perthshire and Argyll, Glenstrae and Glenlochy, lands in Glenlyon, and (later) Glengyle being at one time MacGregor territory. These broad acres, however, were held allodially by right of first occupation. They had, therefore, no title deeds ; and when the MacGregors' neighbours, the Campbells, began to wax powerful they got Crown charters for lands which had been in the possession of the Clan Gregor for years. Harassed and deprived by powerful neighbours of the territories which, rightly or wrongly, they looked upon as their own, is it to be wondered at that the Clan Gregor adopted lawless and desperate courses, and endeavoured to hold by the sword what their ancestors appear to have held by immemorial possession ?

> Glenorchy's proud mountains, Caolchurn and her towers,
> Glenstrae and Glenlyon no longer are ours !
> We're landless, landless, Gregalach !

In early days their chiefs bore a territorial style. John of Glenorchy was the chief in 1292 ; and the name MacGregor was not apparently used until the clan lost possession of Glenorchy through the marriage of an heiress, Mariota, to John Campbell, a son of Lochawe. For a time the junior branch of the clan, who succeeded to the chiefship, remained in Glenorchy as tenants of the Campbells ; but when their main line also seems to have become extinct, even the tenancy of Glenorchy was lost to the clan. The chiefship passed to a junior line of that branch, the MacGregors of Glenstrae, with their seat at Stronmelochan ; and even in Glenstrae they were only tenants of the Campbells.

While they were in that precarious situation Duncan Ladasach ("the lordly") of Ardchoille, whose father was probably Tutor of Glenstrae during the minority of Alasdair, the young chief (and who himself became Tutor for Gregor Roy, Alasdair's heir), acquired for the clan by his lawlessness an evil reputation that they could never shake off. The Campbells of Glenorchy accordingly tried to evict first Gregor Roy, then his son Alasdair, from their tenancy of Glenstrae ; and the Clan Gregor were driven into conflicts with the authority of the Crown which culminated in their victory in 1603 at Glen Fruin over the Colquhouns, who held the King's commission. This was the final fatal event which decided the Government to exterminate the clan.

Those who had fought at Glen Fruin became outlaws, any of whom being captured were tried and executed, as was Alasdair, the Chief. Innocent MacGregors had to change their name, under pain of death. They were prohibited from carrying arms, except a pointless knife for use at their meals ; no more than four of the clan were permitted to meet together. In 1606 it was ordained that the change of name should apply not only to the rising generation, but also to the unborn children of themselves and their parents. Various members of the Clan Gregor

sweir that in all tyme cumin that they sall call thaimselffs and thair bairnis already procreat or to be procreat of thair bodyis efter the surnames respective abone written and use the samyn in all thair doingis under the paine of deid to be execute upoun them without favour or ony of theme in caice thay failyie in the premissis.

In consequence members of the Clan Gregor adopted various names, such as Campbell, Cunynghame, Dougall, Drummond, Gordon, Graham, Grant, Murray, Ramsay, Stewart, etc. In 1643 it was re-enacted that it was unlawful for any man to bear the name of MacGregor. No signature bearing that name, and no agreement entered into with a MacGregor, was legal ; and to kill a man of that name was not punishable ; no minister was to baptise any male child of a MacGregor.

Although the MacGregors had thus no reason for gratitude to the Stuart Kings, yet when Montrose raised King Charles I.'s standard in the Highlands the Laird of MacGregor (as the Chiefs styled themselves after losing Glenstrae) brought out his people in 1644 to join Montrose, hoping to recover his ancestral lands from the King's enemies, the Campbells ; and till the Restoration, Clan Gregor consistently upheld the Stuarts' cause. Charles II. in 1661 was not indeed sufficiently grateful for their support to give the MacGregors back their lands, but at least he restored to them their Name by repealing the Act of 1633 which made its use unlawful,

considering [to quote this Act of Repeal] that those who were formerly designed by the name of Macgregor had, during the troubles, carried themselves with such loyalty and affection to his Majesty as might justly wipe off all memory of their former miscarriages, and take off all mark of reproach put upon them for the same.

For thirty-two years the MacGregors enjoyed the benefits of the restoration of their Name and their civil rights. The Revolution of 1688, however, gave the Crown to William III. and Mary instead of James VII. ; Clan Gregor took arms in support of King James ; and in 1693 the penal statutes against them were reimposed. Nevertheless, in 1714 an attempt was made to restore the clan. This failed, partly because Queen Anne died, to be succeeded by George I., partly because the chief put forward was MacGregor of Balhaldie, who had no just right to the chiefship. Thereafter MacGregors fought for the Stuarts in three Jacobite Risings, in 1715 under Balhaldie, Glengyle and his uncle Rob Roy, in 1719 under Rob Roy, in 1745 under Glengyle and MacGregor of Glencarnaig.

At last, in 1775, by Act of Parliament the Name of MacGregor was restored to the clan—a clan being thus statutorily recognised by *the Imperial Parliament*; and John MacGregor Murray of Lanrick, nephew of Glencarnaig of the '45, was, by 856 MacGregors endorsing his pedigree, submitted to the Lord Lyon. Lanrick's claim to the chiefship had been disputed by the MacGregors of Glengyle and of Balhadie. But in 1795 the Lord Lyon, in exercise of the Royal prerogative, was pleased to give effect to this by confirming to Sir John the chief arms of MacGregor of MacGregor, and the line of baronets, of Lanrick and Balquhidder, have accordingly since been the hereditary chiefs of the clan. Auchmar says of the MacGregors :

> The surname is now divided into four principal families. The first is that of the laird of MacGregor, being in a manner extinct, there being few or none of any account of the same. The next family to that of MacGregor is Dugald Keir's family, so named from their ancestor, Dugal Keir, a son of the laird of MacGregor ; the principal person of that family is MacGregor of Glengyle, whose residence and interest is at the head of Lochcattern, in the parish of Callander, in the shire of Perth. The third family is that of Rora in Rannoch, in the shire of Perth. The fourth family is that of Brackly.

The famous Rob Roy was a son of MacGregor of Glengyle by a sister of the notorious Captain Robert Campbell of Glenlyon. Rob Roy, deprived of his lands by quarrels with the House of Montrose, became a prominent Jacobite and his exploits form a vivid chapter in Highland romance.

In 1624 about 300 MacGregors from the Earl of Moray's estates in Menteith had been brought north to oppose the Mackintoshes. Many of these settled in Aberdeenshire. In 1715 Rob Roy was sent by the Earl of Mar to raise them for the Chevalier, seeing these MacGregors were of the same stock as his own family.

During the time of the proscription of the MacGregors in 1748 a conference was held at Blair Atholl of the Clan Alpin (Grants, Mackinnons, Macnabs, etc.), for assuming a common name. If reversal of the proscription of the Macgregors could be obtained, the name of MacGregor might be adopted by all the branches of Clan Alpin ; but if it were found impossible to obtain such reversal, then some other name should be adopted. Two matters caused the conference to break up without any result : (1) the question of the chiefship, (2) the name to be adopted.

MACINNES

Remarkably little of this clan's history is recorded. Lt.-Col. J. Macinnes (author of *Brave Sons of Skye*) derives them from one, Angus, whom he says " was succeeded by his son Murchad, and this is all we know of his descendents for hundreds of years "—a statement which presents problems for the genealogist. The real position seems to be that MacGillivrays and Macinneses were of the original Dalriads, akin to the O'Duine, though they held castleward under the Macdonald regime in its day of power.

An old tradition has it that, after returning from an expedition, in which the Macinneses had borne themselves very bravely, the chief of the clan was addressed thus by the Lord of the Isles : *Mo bheannachd ort Fhir Chinn-Lochalainn ! fhad's a bhios MacDòhmnuill a stigh, cha bhi MacAonghais a muigh*—" My blessing on you, Chief of Kinlochaline ! while MacDonald is in power, Macinnes shall be in favour." This is another instance of the territorial tendency which is so strongly present in clan history and in the customs of the Lordship of the Isles.

Kinlochaline Castle.

A later Chief of Clan Macinnes was apparently Keeper of the Castle of Kinlochaline in Morvern, and seems to have held it for Roderick MacKenzie of Coigeach, the celebrated " Tutor of Kintail," when the castle was burnt about 1645 by young Colkitto the Royalist.

Logan seems to connect Macinnes with the siege, and the castle in a Macinnes coat of arms suggests keepership.

A family of the Macinneses were hereditary bowmen to the Chief of the Clan Mackinnon. Tradition deduces this line from a second son of the Keeper, and from it descended the Macinneses of Rickerby, who (illegally) bore without registration the gyrony and castle coat of arms. Arms of a scion of the Malagawatch branch have been recorded in Lyon Court.

MACKINTOSH

The Mackintoshes are supposed to derive their name from the Gaelic word *Toisach*, and from the Thaneage of Petty in Moray, and were styled *Princeps Regionum*, or " Chief of the Country," well illustrating the territorial *duthus*—base of the clan system. They were later on held to have inherited, as heir of line, the chiefship of Clan Chattan, and both designations thereafter descended with the estates by entail and tanistry.

According to Nisbet (who states that he got the narrative from the Laird of Mackintosh), the 1st Chief of Mackintosh was Shaw, second son to Duncan, the second of that name, Earl of Fife, who accompanied King Malcolm IV. in his expedition in suppressing the rebels in Moray in 1160 ; and was rewarded with many lands in the north, and made Constable of the Castle of Inverness. " He was commonly called *Mac-an-Tòisich mhic Duibh,* that is to say, Thane MacDuff's son, from which the name Mackintosh became a surname to posterity."

In the seventeenth century the chiefship of the Clan Chattan was a disputed point between the Mackintoshes and the Macphersons. However, a full discussion of the controversy (which, in the seventeenth century, both parties regarded as a litigateable subject, and related to heraldry) lies beyond the scope of this article,[1] where we are only concerned with what was decided ; namely by Lyon, 10th September 1672, that Mackintosh was " Chief of the Name of Mackintosh " and " Chief of the Clan Chattan," and that the " Laird of Mackintosh's " (as he officially describes him) " predecessor married the heretrix of the Clan Chattan, *anno* 1291." The Privy Council accepted Lyon's decision, and disallowed Cluny-Macpherson's bonds as " Chief of the Clan." It has been observed (*Proc. of Soc. of Antiquaries,* XV., 126–127) that " In whatever else they differ, the Macphersons and the Mackintoshes seem always to agree as to the fact of the marriage." Lyon, moreover, (officially) declares that his pronouncement proceeded on evidence *inter alia* in " my registers," and many of the older Lyon Court registers have vanished since 1672.

There is, however, independent evidence of the structure of the Clan Chattan, before and after the matrimonial alliance. There is noticeably no lion (Mackintosh emblem) in the arms of Macpherson, Gillies, Gillespie, MacGillivray, McIntyre ; and these, with the galley —emblems, probably represent pre-1291 Clan Chattan branches, and the " incorporeal heritage " which passed down to and through Eva along with the undifferenced galley-quartering, whilst Cluny-Macpherson, the heir male, retained the galley differenced by " parting per fess."

[1] In this momentous controversy the modern (anglicised) idea that a woman could not take or transmit a " Highland chiefship " was never even raised ; as a doctrine it was unknown to Scotland, Highland or Lowland. The argument was that the Mackintosh line, not having taken the name Macpherson, could neither inherit nor hold the chiefship of Clan Chattan. To this Mackintosh retorted that since the chiefship of this community could be, and had been, held by one named Macpherson, " name " was not an essential to chiefship of that particular group, and that " Chattan " would, if any, be the essential name (derived from the eponymus *Gilliechattan-Mhor*)—which, if need be, he would assume. The decision—to summarise it in brief—was that in a community comprehending various names, and as a group called after the eponymus Chattan, the name Chattan had not been indispensable, and that of Macpherson could not be indispensable ; so that there was nothing to prevent a person named Mackintosh being a chief of Clan Chattan, or in other words that the " son of the thane " was no less eligible than the " son of the parson," provided there was heirship at law or by tailzie ! Lyon's decision was pretty much on the true thread of opinion in *MacGillivray* v. *Souter,* 1862, with the difference that Lord Lyon understood both families, clans, and armorial law, whereas the Lords of Session understood the principles of neither, and made many incongruous and anti-Celtic utterances. In 1672 *Mackintosh* became the *chief-name.*

The Clan Chattan were among the vassals of the Lord of the Isles. But when in 1429 Alexander, Lord of the Isles and Earl of Ross, defied the Royal authority and advanced against James I. into Lochaber at the head of a large army, the Clan Chattan and the Clan Cameron deserted the Lord of the Isles and went over to the Royal army. The result was a total defeat of the Lord of the Isles. The downfall of the Lord of the Isles resulted in the advancement of the Mackintoshes, for in 1431 Malcolm Mackintosh, Captain of the Clan Chattan, received a grant of the territories of Alexander of Lochaber, uncle of the Lord of the Isles. In 1466 the Lord of the Isles granted to Duncan Mackintosh the lands of Moymore and others in Lochaber. In 1493 Royal charters were given to the same Duncan of the lands which the Mackintoshes had previously held from the Lord of the Isles, among the rest the lands of Keppoch and of Innerorgan. William, 13th Chief of Mackintosh, married in 1497 Isabel, daughter of MacNiven of Dunnachton, and thereby added still further to his territorial influence.

During the Revolution of 1688, which drove the Stuarts from the throne, the Mackintoshes were on the side of the new government. In 1715, however, Lachlan, 20th Mackintosh, was active on the side of the Jacobites. On the outbreak of the Rising of " the '45," Angus, 22nd Chief, was in command of one of the companies of The Black Watch, and did not therefore raise his clan for Prince Charles. His wife, the Lady Mackintosh, however (a daughter of Farquharson of Invercauld), took a prominent part on the Jacobite side ; raised the Clan Chattan for the young chevalier, and placed the Chief of the MacGillivrays at their head. The famous episode of the " Rout of Moy," when Lord Loudon's force was routed by a handful of Lady Mackintosh's retainers, was due to the boldness and stratagem of that brave lady.

The principal cadet family of the clan was Kyllachy, which derived from the issue of Ferquhard, 9th Chief, who abdicated, c. 1409, and whose issue were called *Slioch Ferchar vich Lachlan*.

The ancient seat of the Chief of Mackintosh was on an island in Loch Moy, and subsequently nearby at Moy Hall, near Inverness ; and on its descent on tailzie of Alfred Donald, 28th Chief (who died 1938), Lyon Court in 1947 held that Rear-Admiral Lachlan Mackintosh of Mackintosh had become by tanistry The Mackintosh and Chief of the Clan.

MACINTYRE

The *Clan-an-Teir*, otherwise *Clan-an-t-saor*, meaning " children of the carpenter," traditionally came to Lorn from the Hebrides in a galley with a white cow (which may have some traditional significance), and established themselves as a small but independent clan, claiming to have been settled in Glen Oe (Glen Noe), near Bonawe, Argyll, by 1300, though other chronological indications suggest that the " 1st Chief of Glen-oe " flourished somewhat later, about 1400. The Macintyre chiefs are said to have been hereditary foresters to the Stewarts of Lorn, and to have retained that office under the Campbells, so their " Macdonald " connection (which is also alleged) was probably earlier and related to the Lordship of Lorn. In 1556 Clan Teir gave bond for good behaviour to Campbell of Glenurchy over the slaughter of one MacGillenlag. From Glenorchy they held Glen Oe by *reddendo* of a snowball, and were ruined by consenting to have this changed to a money-rent. The first chief from whom a continuous affiliation can be deduced (since the loss of the " Black Book of Glenoe ") is Duncan (*d.* 1695), who married Mary, daughter of *Para Beag* Campbell of Barcaldine. His son Donald, " 2nd " of Glenoe, had by his second wife, Catherine Macdonald of Dalness, a son James, 3rd of Glenoe, who married Anne, daughter of Duncan Campbell of Barcaldine. His third son, Capt. Donald, apparently acquired Glenoe from his elder brother but died in London 1808, and Glenoe was lost 1806–1810. James's eldest son, Donald, M.D., and Chief of Macintyre, emigrated to New York 1783, where he married Esther Haines. Dying 1792, he was succeeded by his eldest son, James, born at Newburgh, Orange Co., N.Y., 1785, who returned to Scotland 1806 and married Anne, daughter of Peter Campbell of Corries. Failing to retain Glenoe, he returned to the U.S.A., settling at Fulton Co., N.Y., and died 1887, leaving by his wife Phoebe Shepherd, a family of whom the eldest son, James, next Chief of the Clan, was born 1864. He and his brothers are said to have flourished in business ; and a claim is pending in Lyon Court but the chiefship has not yet been legally established, so that the clan is chiefless, and, except for the branch of Sorn, represented by the Hon. Lord Macintyre, also landless. The most ancient cadet, Macintyre of *Camus-na-h-Eireadh*, deduced descent through eleven generations from the " first chief of Glenoe," who must have lived about 1400 ; and this branch came to be represented in the early nineteenth century by the Rev. John Macintyre, D.D., of Kilmonivaig. The 16th chieftain of *Camus-na-h-Eireadh* is Alastair Macintyre (Edinburgh). The Macintyres have been famous as Highland pipers ; and around the '45 *Duncan Ban Macintyre* was one of Scotland's most celebrated Gaelic bards.

MACKAY

The Clan Mackay claim descent from the old Royal House of Moray ; and this was evidently through a junior line springing from Morgund of Pluscarden, from which the Clan Aodh derives the patronymic description *Clann Vich Morgainn* (the form in which this is handed down by Sir R. Gordon). They were evidently amongst the Moraymen removed in 1160 by Malcolm IV., and given lands elsewhere, apparently in Ross, whence they migrated to Sutherland under the auspices of the Bishop of Caithness.

The rise of the clan took place about the beginning of the thirteenth century. The ancient territory of the clan, which rapidly became a very powerful one, was about eighty miles in length and about eighteen miles in breadth in the north-west extremity of Scotland, known by the name of Lord Reay's or Mackay's country, from Drimholisten, which divides it from Caithness on the north-east to Kylescow, an arm of the sea dividing it from Assynt on the south-west.

Magnus, the great-grandson of Alexander, who lived in the reign of William the Lion, fought on the side of King Robert the Bruce at Bannockburn. He was succeeded by his son Morgan. Donald, son of Morgan, was succeeded again by his son, Aoidh or Ye, who gave the clan the designation which they now bear, viz., *MacAoidh* or Mackay.

In 1427 the leader of the Clan Mackay (Angus Dow) could muster 4000 men, which shows the powerful position to which this clan had by that time attained. The *Clan Aberigh* (so called from their territories in Strathnaver), deriving their descent from Farquhar, the brother of Morgan, Chief of the Mackays, and great-great-grandson of Alexander, the progenitor of the clan, also attained to much power and influence.

Sir Donald Mackay of Strathnaver (chief of the clan in the reign of King Charles I.) greatly distinguished himself in the service of Gustavus Adolphus, King of Sweden, for whom he raised a large body of men in the north of Scotland, bearing principally the names of Mackay, Sinclair, Gordon, Munro, and Gunn. Sir Donald was raised to the peerage in 1628 by King Charles I., under the title of Lord Reay, with destination to " his heirs male bearing the name and arms of Mackay," thus tailzieing the chiefship with the dignity of Lord Reay.

Reay's military services to the Swedish king, coupled with the losses which he sustained during the time of the struggles of his own king with the Parliament (when Lord Reay was on the side of the king), were the cause of pecuniary difficulties.

During the Revolution of 1688 and the Risings of 1715 and 1745, the Mackays were on the Whig side. During the time of Eric, 7th Lord Reay, the pecuniary difficulties of the chief had reached such a pitch that he was forced to dispose of the Reay country to the Earl of Sutherland.

MACKENZIE

There are two versions of the origin of the Clan Kenneth or MacKenzies. One account derives them from a Colin Fitzgerald, of the Geraldine family in Ireland, who was present on the side of King Alexander at the Battle of Largs, in command of a body of Irish auxiliaries, and who was rewarded by the king with a grant of lands in Kintail.

But modern genealogists and early traditions derive the Mac-Kenzies from Gilleon Og, a younger son of *Gilleon na h-Airde*, the ancestor of Anrias, progenitor of the O'Beolans, the old Earls of Ross.

The first ancestor of the *Chlann Choinnich* of whom there is authentic charter evidence is " Murdo filius Kennethi de Kintail," who was, in 1362, granted a charter by King David II., and the stag with motto *Cuiddiche an Righ* evidently represents the *cuiddiche* done by the Chief of Clan Kenneth to the *Ard-righ* as High Chief.

In 1427 the chief of the clan is mentioned as having a following of 2000 men.

After the final forfeiture of the Lord of the Isles (Earl of Ross) the MacKenzies rapidly increased their influence, and acquired large possessions in Ross-shire. Kenneth MacKenzie of Kintail was a *persona grata* with King James IV., by whom he was knighted. Colin of Kintail was a member of the Privy Council of James VI. His son and successor, Kenneth, was, in 1609, raised to the peerage as Lord MacKenzie of Kintail. Colin, 2nd Lord, was created Earl of Seaforth in 1623. The Earls of Seaforth were loyal supporters of the Stuart cause, and the 2nd and 3rd Earls suffered much for their devotion to Charles I. and his successor. The 4th Earl adhered to James VII. at the time of the Revolution of 1688. He was created Marquis of Seaforth by that unfortunate monarch. As, however, the honour was conferred after the Revolution, it never proved more than a mere nominal title. During the reigns of William and Mary and of Anne, the Earl of Seaforth remained quiet and unmolested.

Lord Seaforth took a prominent part in the Rising of 1715 on the Jacobite side. This involved the attainder of the Earldom. Seaforth received a pardon in 1726, granted on recommendation of General Wade, and in spite of the determined opposition of the Duke of Argyll. The General, however, threatened to throw up his command of the forces in Scotland if the pardon was not granted. He based his recommendation on the policy of maintaining the balance of power in the Highlands, by dividing the influence of the four most powerful chiefs—viz., the Dukes of Argyll, Atholl, and Gordon, and the Earl of Seaforth. An Act of 1733 enabled him to inherit and hold real or personal estate. Thereafter Seaforth had a large portion of his ancestral possessions, though not his title, restored. He died in 1740.

In 1766 Kenneth, grandson of the last Earl of Seaforth, having held aloof from the Rising of " the '45," was created Viscount Fortrose and Baron Ardelve in the peerage of Ireland, and in 1771, Earl of Seaforth, in the same peerage, but he died in 1784 without male issue, when the peerages expired. The estates and chiefship passed to his cousin, Colonel Thomas Frederick Humberston MacKenzie, great-grandson of the 3rd Earl of Seaforth.

This chief fell at the Battle of Gheriah, in India, while in command of the Bombay army. He was succeeded by his brother, Francis Humberston MacKenzie, who was, in 1797, created Lord Seaforth and Baron MacKenzie of Kintail. The reign of this chief was a particularly sad and unfortunate one. Lord Seaforth's sons all pre-deceased him without issue, while he himself was obliged to dispose of a large portion of the MacKenzie property. He died in 1815, the last male representative of the Seaforths, Lords of Kintail. The chiefship of the clan then devolved on his elder daughter, Fredericka, widow of Admiral Hood, who was officially recognised in Lyon Court as Lady Fredericka Hood-Mackenzie of Seaforth, re-vested in the undifferenced Seaforth arms, and hailed as *Caberfeidh*. From her descend the Stewart-Mackenzies of Seaforth, of whom James Frances Alex. was created Lord Seaforth in 1921. Meantime the character of " heir male," and in the circumstances principal cadet, passed to MacKenzie of Allangrange (who only got an " Allangrange " coat of arms) a descendant of Kenneth, 1st Lord MacKenzie of Kintail,[1] and, this line having expired, is now claimed by Mackenzie of Ord, though Scatwell seems obviously to intervene.

The MacKenzies, Earls of Cromartie, Viscounts Tarbat, and Barons MacLeod of Castlehaven, are descended from Sir Roderick MacKenzie of Coigeach, second son of Colin, father of Kenneth, 1st Lord MacKenzie of Kintail. Sir Roderick married the daughter and heiress of Torquil MacLeod of Lewis, and added the arms of MacLeod to his own. George, 1st Earl of Cromartie, had his whole landed property in Scotland erected into one county, called the County of Cromarty. This accounts for the scattered portions of Cromartyshire found throughout Ross-shire.

The Earldom was forfeited in consequence of the share which the Earl took in " the '45." In 1861, however, the Cromartie honours were revived in favour of Anne, only child of John Hay MacKenzie of Cromartie and Newhall. The Countess of Cromartie (Mistress of the Robes to Queen Victoria) married the Duke of Sutherland. On the death of the Duchess the Cromartie honours and estates devolved on her second son, who, during his mother's lifetime, bore the courtesy title of Viscount Tarbat.

The MacKenzies of Scatwell (Baronet) appear now to be heir male of the House of MacKenzie of Kintail.

The Kintail and Cromarty families are both distinguished on account of the number of regiments which they raised for the service of their country. In 1745 the effective strength of the Clan MacKenzie was estimated at 2500 men.

Since the death of Lord Seaforth of Brahan, 1923, no one has effectively taken up the chiefship, which Madam Stewart-Mackenzie of Seaforth seems to disclaim, and the nearest heirs of line in the name of Mackenzie are Lady Cromartie and her son Viscount Tarbat.

MACKINNON

The Mackinnon Clan is a branch of Clan Alpin, and their traditional descent is from Fingon, grandson of Gregor, son of Kenneth MacAlpin, King of the Scots. A fanciful rendering of the name is *Mac Ionmhuinn* (Love-son).

The Mackinnons were vassals of the Lord of the Isles, and it is recorded that they were hereditary custodians of the standards of weights and measures in the Lordship of the Isles.

A family of Mackinnons held, for many generations, the post of

[1] See Appendix XI.

hereditary standard-bearers to the MacDonalds of Sleat, and had the township of Duisdalebeg, near Isleoronsay, Sleat, as the reward of their services.

Gregory says that

The first authentic notice of this ancient tribe is in an indenture between the Lord of the Isles and the Lord of Lorn. The latter stipulates, in surrendering to the Lord of the Isles the island of Mull and other lands, that the keeping of the Castle of Kerneburg, in the Treshnish Isles, is not to be given to any of the race of Clan Finnon.

The Mackinnons originally possessed the district of Griban, in the island of Mull, but exchanged it for the district of Mishnish, in the same island. The clan also possessed the lands of Strathordell, in the island of Skye, and the chief was usually designated as " of Strathordell."

It is interesting to record, as showing the ancient belief of the various branches of the Clan Alpin in their common origin, two bonds of fellowship executed by the Chief of the Clan Mackinnon. One is, in 1606, between " Lauchlan Mackinnon of Strathardil and Finlay Macnabb of Bowaine." The other bond is one, in 1671, " betwixt the honourable persons underwritten, to wit, James MacGregor of that Ilk on the ane part, and Lauchlan MacFingon of Strathardil on the other part." Both bonds set forth the acknowledgement of the common origin of the clans of the subscribing parties.

After the forfeiture of the Lords of the Isles the Mackinnons usually followed the Macleans of Duart, and sometimes, too, they took part with the MacDonalds of Skye in their feuds against the MacLeods.

The clan was out for the Stuarts in 1715 and also in " the '45." Lord-President Forbes, in 1745, estimated the effective following of the chief as 200 men. The aged Chief of the Clan Mackinnon, who was out in " the '45," was afterwards arrested and imprisoned. He was confined for nearly a year in Tilbury Fort, but was ultimately released on account of his advanced age, and was permitted to return home. At the time of the chief's release he was reminded by Sir Dudley Ryder, who was then Attorney-General, of the King's clemency. Whereupon Mackinnon quaintly [1] rejoined, " Had I the King in *my* power, as I am in *his*, I would return him the compliment, by sending him back to his own country."

The ancient possessions of the clan were numerous. These comprised lands in the islands of Mull, Skye, Arran, Tiree, Pabay, and Scalpa. Now, however, the Mackinnons are landless in the old clan territory. Strathordell, which was acquired in 1354, had to be parted with in 1765, as a sequel to the troubles which followed Culloden. The last chief of the main line died, in 1808, in humble circumstances. It was then that the chiefship of the Clan Mackinnon was confirmed to the family of the present chief by decree of Lyon Court.

[1] This " quaint " rejoinder is really a polite assertion of allodial right, (by first occupancy) of the duthus, see pp. 46, 97.

MACLACHLAN

According to a Gaelic MS., dated 1450, the MacLachlans, the McNeills, and the MacEwans are all descended from one common ancestor, who was related to the progenitor of the MacDonalds, Lords of the Isles. The original seat of the first-named appears to have been in Lochaber ; and tradition has it that the MacLachlans acquired their Cowal possessions in consequence of the marriage of one of their Chiefs to a Lamont heiress. This is doubtful, but it is certain that in the year 1292 the lands of Gileskil MacLachlan were included in the sheriffdom of Argyll or Lorn, erected in that year by King John Baliol, and that the King granted him a charter of his lands. He also received a charter of his lands from King Robert Bruce.

Buchanan of Auchmar, writing of the Lochaber MacLachlans, says :

There is another numerous sept of the MacLachlans residing in Morven and Lochaber, the principal person of these being MacLachlan of Corryuanan, in Lochaber. Of this family is MacLachlan of Drumblane, in Monteith, with others of that surname there. Those of this sept residing in Lochaber depend upon the Laird of Lochiel.

These MacLachlans of Coire-uanan, to whom Buchanan refers, held the hereditary position of standard-bearers to the Camerons of Lochiel.

The MacLachlans of Cowal formerly possessed broad lands lying between Loch Long and Loch Fyne, and generally followed the Campbells. At the time of " the '45 " their strength was estimated at 300 men. The clan territory is now reduced to a strip bordering the eastern side of Loch Fyne. The seat of MacLachlan of that Ilk is Castle Lachlan, Strathlachlan, near Strachur, Loch Fyne.

It was long the custom, when either the Laird of Strathlachlan or the Laird of Strachur died, that the survivor laid his late neighbour's head in the grave. This observance is traditionally connected with the time of the Crusades, when it is said that the heads of these two families accompanied each other to the Holy War, each solemnly engaging with the other to lay him in his family burying-place if he should fall in battle. On the death of John MacLachlan of that Ilk, his daughter, Marjorie MacLachlan of MacLachlan, was in 1946 confirmed by Lyon Court as chief of the clan.

MACLAREN

The MacLarens in the Gaelic genealogy of 1450 " are deduced from an Abbot of Achtus, by which no doubt Achtow in Balquhidder, where the clan had its seat, is meant " (W. F. Skene, *Celtic Scotland*, III., p. 344).

K

There appear to be two quite distinct races of this name (*a*) The Maclarens of Perthshire, to whom most Maclarens and members of the organised clan pertain ; (*b*) Maclaurins alleged to have owned the isle of Tiree (where there seems next to no trace of such) as claimed by Maclaurins of Dreghorn, which line however expired and the Clan Laurin of Tiree [1] is now landless and chiefless.

The Clan Maclaren of Perthshire has been more flourishing. It survives in stem and several branches. Its native country is in Strathearn and Balquhidder where three brothers are mentioned as having received the lands of Auchleskine, Stank, and Druach, whilst another branch held Ardveche on Lochearnside. The Maclaren chiefs as indicated by their arms were apparently a junior branch of the native lords, afterwards earls, of Strathearn, and the Maclarens may have been the *Lavernani*, who in 1138 fought under Malise Earl of Strathearn at the Battle of the Standard. The Maclaren chiefs were apparently Hereditary Celtic Abbots of Achtow in Balquhidder and derived their Patronymic from Abbot Lawrence. In 1957 Robert Maclaren, of the house of Auchleskine, established in Lyon Court, his chiefship, as Robert Maclaren of Maclaren, and holds the ancient rallying ground of the clan—Craig-an-Turk, in Balquhidder.

In the Roll of Submission to Edward I. in 1296, includes Maurice of Tiree, Conan of Balquhidder, and Laurin of Ardveche, in Strathearn, all said to have been cadets of the Earl of Strathearn.

When the Earldom of Strathearn was seized by the Crown in 1370, the MacLarens were then reduced from allodial proprietors to tenants. The clan appears in the Rolls of the Clans, 1587 and 1594 as having a chief of its own. During the sixteenth century Clan Laurin (West) appear to have followed the Stewarts of Lorn and Appin. John, 3rd Lord Lorn, had an illegitimate son, Dugall (by a daughter of a Perthshire MacLaren), from which Dugall descend the Stewarts of Appin.

The MacLarens engaged in frequent feuds with their neighbours, the MacGregors. In 1558 the latter clan slaughtered no fewer than eighteen whole families of MacLarens, and seized the lands of their victims.

In 1745 the MacLarens were out under Appin. In the list of killed and wounded of Appin's following MacLarens come third, the first, Stewarts, and second, MacColls.

John Maclaren of Dreghorn, raised to the bench in 1787 as Lord Dreghorn, like his colleague, Lord Meadowbank, recognising Lord Lyon's jurisdiction in such matters, invoked this ancient jurisdiction and established in Lyon Court his claim to the chiefship of the " Tiree " Clan MacLauren. These, from their arms, seem a different race from the MacLaurens of Strathearn.

[1] Wherever it was, the Perthshire Tyrie seems to have belonged to a family named Tyrie.

MACLEAN

One of the traditionary accounts of the origin of the Clan Gillean derives them from a race situated in the neighbourhood of Scone. According to Skene (*Highlanders of Scotland*) the Macleans were one of the tribes transplanted from the old province of Moray by Malcolm IV. in 1160. The eponymus of the clan is Gillean (surnamed *Gilleathain na Tuaidh*, or Gillean of the Battle-axe, from his proverbial dexterity with that weapon), who lived during the reign of Alexander III., and fought at the Battle of Largs. Most of the branches of the Clan Maclean bear as their crest or one of their armorial badges a battle-axe, in memory of their famed ancestor.

The son of Gillean of the Battle-axe appears to have settled in Lorn, and he is one of the subscribers to the Ragman's Roll, in 1296, as " Gillemoir Macilyn." His son, Malise, supported the Bruce, and was father of Gillecullum, who fought at Bannockburn, and whose son, Ian Dhu Maclean, settled in Mull. He had two sons—Lachlan Lubanach, progenitor of the Macleans of Duart ; and Eachin Reganach, progenitor of the Maclaines of Lochbuie. These two brothers lived during the reign of King Robert II., and appear to have been, at first, followers of MacDougall, Lord of Lorn. However, in consequence of some dispute with the Lord of Lorn, the two brothers left him and became followers of MacDonald, Lord of the Isles. They rose to such distinction in the service of the Lord of the Isles that, by him, the Macleans were rewarded by large grants of land in Mull. These grants brought the Macleans into conflict with the Mackinnons, who were settled in Mull before the advent of the brothers Lachlan and Eachin. Lachlan married Margaret, daughter of the Lord of the Isles, and his son, Hector, *Eachan Ruad nan Cath* (Red Hector of the Battles), acted as Lieutenant-General of the Lord of the Isles' army at the Battle of Harlaw and was slain there.

The Lochbuie Maclaines disputed the chiefship of the Clan Gillean with the Duart Macleans, alleging that of the two sons of Ian Dhu MacGillemoir MacLean, Eachin Reganach was elder to Lachlan Lubanach. The point is immaterial as the chief was entitled to settle his succession by tanistry, and the Crown recognised Duart as chief of the clan and " Laird of Maclean."

Charles, son of Eachin Reganach, settled in " Glen Urquhart," and was the founder of the *Clann Thearlaich of Glen Urquhart and Dochgarroch*, known also as " The Macleans of the North." The Clan Thearlaich, according to Mr. Fraser-Mackintosh, joined the Clan Chattan about 1460. The Macleans of Glen Urquhart, on being oppressed by the Chisholms, appealed to Maclean of Duart, as their hereditary chief (although they themselves were under the Clan Chattan) for protection. Duart recognised the right of these clansmen, and forced the Chisholms to desist from their oppression.

At the date of the forfeiture of the last Lord of the Isles in 1493 the Macleans had attained great power and large territories comprising the larger part of the islands of Mull and of Tiree, with lands in Islay, Jura, Scarba, and in Morvern, Lochaber, and Knapdale. The Macleans were then divided into four branch-clans where chieftains held great estates under direct charters from the Lord of the Isles, which charters were confirmed and continued by the Crown. These four branch-clans were : (1) Macleans of Duart, descended from Lachlan Lubanach ; (2) Macleans of Ardgour, cadets of Duart ; (3) Macleans of Coll, also cadets of the same house ; (4) Maclaines of Lochbuie, descended from Eachin Reganach.

Duart Castle, a massive fortress in Mull, became the seat of the chiefs, and this, along with the ensigns armorial of the chiefs, was settled on a series of heirs male and female, by a charter of 1496. In 1632 Lachlan Maclean of Morvern, brother and heir of Hector Maclean of Duart, was created a Baronet. He was a zealous Royalist, and died in 1649. Sir Hector, 2nd Baronet, fell at Inverkeithing fighting for King Charles, and thence derives the battle cry *Fear eile airson*

Duart Castle.

Eachainn. Sir John, 4th Baronet, raised the clan for James VII. in 1689. The direct line expired in 1750 on the death of Sir Hector, 5th Baronet (who during " the '45 " was retained a political prisoner in London), when the honours and chiefship devolved, according to the provisions of the charter of 1496 and the patent of baronetcy, on Sir Alan Maclean of Brolas, as 6th Baronet. Sir Fitzroy Maclean of Duart, 10th Baronet, succeeded in recovering Duart Castle in 1910, and restored it as the home of the chiefs. There, within its massive walls above the lofty cliff, he lived to be a centenarian, and it remains the seat of the chief of the clan.

The House of Ardgour was established by Donald, younger son of Lachlan Maclean of Duart, who, about 1432, was directed by the Lord of the Isles *Leum a balla far as ishle,* and accordingly slew Macmaster of Ardgour and was given Ardgour by Macdonald. This still belongs to the head of *Clan Eoghainn of Ardgour,* for Catriona Maclean of Ardgour, heretrix of race, was, in 1943, declared " Representer " (*i.e.* chief) of Maclean of Ardgour.

The Macleans of Coll retained their baronial fief and Castle of Breachacha until 1848, when Alexander Maclean of Coll emigrated to Natal where he died unmarried. Maclean of Achnasul is the senior cadet of Coll.

Maclean of Drimnin was a Jacobite branch, and he, as Commander of the Clan (*Ceann Cath*), led 500 Macleans in support of Prince Charles in 1745 ; the chief was then in custody.

Maclaine of Lochbuie was expropriated by an English bond-holder soon after the war of 1914–1918. The tower of Lochbuie is still intact, and understood to remain his property.

MACLENNAN OR LOGAN

This clan, though a small one and followers of the MacKenzies of Kintail, Earls of Seaforth, played a distinguished part in the history of the MacKenzies, whose standard-bearers the Maclennans were.

It is difficult to trace the history of the *Siol Ghillinnein* to an earlier period than the fourteenth century. They appear to have derived their descent from Logan, or Loban, who hailed from Easter Ross. Gilliegorm, the head of the Logans, appears to have had a very serious quarrel with Hugh, the second Lord Lovat, one of whose relatives Gilliegorm had married. The dispute culminated in a sanguinary battle between the Frasers and the Logans near Kessock. In this battle Gilliegorm and most of his following were slain. Logan's wife was captured by Lovat. She was enceinte at the time. Lovat's intention was to destroy the child of Logan's wife should it be a male. In due time the lady gave birth to a male child. It was, however, so stunted and deformed that the child was suffered to live. The boy received the appellation of " Crotach," or hump-backed, from his deformed appearance. He was educated by the monks of Beauly, took Holy Orders, and founded the churches of Kilmor in Skye and Kilchrinan in Glenelg. Logan, like many medieval Scottish priests, left several children. One of these became a devotee of the Saint Finnan, and his descendants were known by the appellation of Mac-Ghille Fhinnein, or Maclennan.

The Maclennans inhabited the district of Kintail ; a river which flows into Loch Duich having been the boundary between them and their neighbours, the Macraes. The residence of the chief was on a hill, named originally Druic-na-Clavan, and afterwards, Drumderfit.

MACLEOD

Some authorities represent the Clan MacLeod as having a Celtic origin, but the larger number favour the tradition of a Norse ancestry. The latter theory seems to us as by far the most likely one, and the names of the two great branches of the clan (*Siol Tormod* [or Norman] and *Siol Torquil*) would seem to bear out the theory of their Norse descent.

According to their officially certified descent (and the ministerial decision of the Lord Lyon in such *Diplomæ Stemmatis* is, according to their preamble, " conclusive "—and is so received in all Courts of Honour and Ancestry), the progenitor of the MacLeods was Leod, son of Olave, brother of Magnus, the last King of Man. The present Dame Flora MacLeod of MacLeod, is reckoned 28th from Leod and 35th from Godfred, surnamed Crovan, son of Harold the Black, of the Nor-wegian Royal Family, in the year 1066. The Macleods thus rank as a " Royal race " amongst the princely houses of Europe.

Leod, the progenitor of the clan, left two sons—Tormod, the founder of the *Siol Tormod*, or MacLeods of MacLeod and Harris, and Torquil, the founder of the *Siol Torquil*, or MacLeods of Lewis. These two main branches of the clan were, from an early period, quite independent of each other. There has for long been a contention as to which was the senior family, but the consensus of opinion is in favour of the seniority of Tormod to his brother, Torquil.

By Leod's marriage with the daughter and heiress of Macarailt, Armuin of Dunvegan, Tormod inherited also the famous stronghold on the northern coast of Skye.

Glenelg seems to have been the earliest possession of the MacLeods, and tradition seems to suggest that it, like Dunvegan, was acquired through an heiress, and that it was an allodial " country "—only feudalised by a charter of 1342. The original chieftain of Glenelg, whoever he was, is stated to have acquired it by killing a black bull,

Dunvegan Castle.

still commemorated in MacLeod's crest. Tormod, son of the first Tormod, was a staunch adherent of Robert the Bruce, and his son, Malcolm, obtained from David II. a charter of two-thirds of Glenelg (being part of the forfeited lands of the Bissets) on condition of providing a galley of thirty-six oars for the King's use, whenever it should be required. Later on, the MacLeods of Glenelg acquired lands in Harris from the MacRories of Garmoran. The Skye possessions of the *Siol Tormod* comprised the districts of Dunvegan, Duirinish, Bracadale, Lyndale, Trouterness, and Minginish. The original possessions of the *Siol Tormod* were held under charters from the Crown, while they held their Harris lands as vassals of the Lord of the Isles.

Of the historic line of Macleod chiefs, the 8th, Alasdair Crottach, built the " Fairy Tower " of Dunvegan, and in 1547 was buried in an elaborate tomb erected in St. Clement's at Rodill. Sir Rory Mor Macleod of Macleod, celebrated as 16th Chief in the reign of James VI., built the long portion of the castle between the ancient keep and the Fairy Tower, whilst Ian Breac, 19th Chief, added further to the fortress in 1686. Alasdair Crottach's sword, Rory Mor's horn and " the Fairy Flag " are, along with many other treasures, still found in this historic castle, whose muniment room is amongst the richest in the West Highlands. Under Roderick, 18th Chief, Clan MacLeod fought for Charles I. at Worcester, but the later chiefs were cautious in avoiding political warfare. The clan was out for King James in 1715, but, during the Rising of " the '45," the Chief, who was influenced by Lord President Forbes of Culloden, remained inactive, though many of his clan fought for Prince Charles. Norman, 23rd Chief, entertained Boswell and Johnson during their tour in the Hebrides, and became a famous soldier.

The first charter to the *Siol Torquil* is one by King David II. to Torquil MacLeod, of the Barony of Assynt. The lands of Assynt are supposed to have been previously acquired by Torquil by his marriage with the daughter of the Chief of the Clan Nicol or MacNicols. The lands of the *Siol Torquil* in Lewis were held by them as vassals of the Earl of Ross and Lord of the Isles. The territories of the *Siol Torquil* were at one time very extensive. They comprehended the islands of Lewis and Raasay, the district of Waterness in Skye, and the lands of Assynt, Coigeach, and Gairloch on the mainland.

The Lewis MacLeods (or *Siol Torquil*) became extinct in the direct line in the sixteenth century. The heiress of that branch was wedded to one of the MacKenzies of Seaforth, who founded the House of Cromarty, and whose second title, when the Cromarty peerage became an earldom, was Lord MacLeod, and this was held to carry the chief-ship of this branch of the clan. The senior cadet of the *Siol Torquil*, MacLeod or *MacGillechaluim* of Raasay, who was descended from Malcolm *Garbh MacGillechaluim*, second son of Malcolm, 9th Chief of Lewis accordingly received from Lyon only the arms of " chiefest cadet " of the *Siol Torquil*. From a branch of the *Siol Torquil* derived MacLeod of Assynt, the renegade cavalier, who sold Montrose to the Roundheads for 400 bolls of meal, the " deed of deathless shame," after which the House of Assynt withered to extinction.

The Raasay estates were sold in 1846, when the chieftain emigrated to Australia.

The old MacLeod lands in the Lewis passed from the MacKenzies to the Mathesons by purchase. At the present day, therefore, the *Siol Torquil* are landless as well as chiefless.

The *Siol Tormod*, though no longer owners of the large territories of bygone days, still retain part of the old lands of their clan. The seat of the chief is, as of yore, Dunvegan Castle (in Skye), the " hearth of the race," and the chief's title is " MacLeod of MacLeod." On the death of Sir Reginald MacLeod of MacLeod, 27th Chief, his daughter, Flora, Mrs. MacLeod of MacLeod, 28th Chief, was duly revested in the arms, crest and insignia of the Chief of MacLeod.

MACMILLAN

One tradition ascribes the origin of this clan to the *Siol O'Cain*, a tribe of the Mormaorship of Moray, before the evolution of the clan system in the thirteenth century. The *Siol O'Cain* again derived its origin from the ancient tribe of the *Kanteai* (referred to by Ptolemy, the Egyptian geographer, in the first half of the second century of our era), one of the subdivisions of the Northern Picts.

Investigation does not support a connection between the Clan Buchanan and the Clan Macmillan, suggested by Buchanan of Auchmar, the historian of the former clan, who deduced the descent of the Macmillans from Methlan, second son of an Anselan, Chief of the Buchanans.

Whatever origin is to be attributed to the Clan Macmillan, in the thirteenth century they held lands on Tayside, where in 1263 Gilleonan MacMolan appears on an assize. The clan was, however, established as a powerful community some three generations later, when by 1360 Malcolm Mor Macmillan received from the Lord of the Isles Knapdale in knight-service (the " bastards " of the Council of the Isles seem a version of *Bachards*—lesser knighthood, later termed Esquires), his charter being inscribed on a rock, the *Crag Mhic Maolain*, at Knap Point, thus :

> Macmillan's right to Knap shall be
> As long as this rock withstands the sea—

as it did until 1615, when Campbell of Cawdor, on Argyll's order, hurled the stone into the sea. Malcolm's grandson, Lachlan Macmillan of Knap, fell at Harlaw 1411. His grandson, Allan Macmillan of Knap, married Eva McNeill, heiress of Castle Sween, and erected the present cross at Kilmory Knap. Knap was, however, lost at the time of the fall of the Lordship of the Isles, but the family managed to retain the adjoining lands of Tireteaghan. On the extinction of the direct line of the Knap family, about 1665, Macmillan of Dunmore (on the north side of West Loch Tarbert), whose descent is deduced from John, a grandson of Alexander, last chief of Knap, inherited the chiefship, and Duncan Macmillan of Dunmore, having been confirmed by Lyon Court in arms for, and representation of, Knap, assumed the designation of Macmillan of Macmillan.

Alexander Macmillan of Macmillan and Dunmore, Deputy Keeper of the Signet, in 1767 settled the estate and representation on his cousin Duncan, youngest son of Macmillan of Lagalgarve, who thus became chief, but who, with his next brothers, dying unmarried, the chiefship passed to the issue of Lagalgarve's second son, whose representative, Lieut.-Gen. Sir Gordon Macmillan of Macmillan and Knap, Commander-in-Chief, Scottish Command, Governor of Edinburgh Castle, was by Lyon Court in 1951 revested as Chief of the Clan Macmillan.

Some of the clan found their way to Lochaber, where they became adherents of Lochiel. One of these afterwards settled in Argyllshire, and was progenitor of the family of Glen Shira. The Macmillans of Urquhart and Glenmoriston were followers of Grant of Glenmoriston.

The verse inscribed on the rock at Knap, which was, of course, in Gaelic,

> *Fhad's a ruitheas sruth is goath*
> *Bidh coir Mhic Mhaoilein air a' Chnap*

illustrates the strong Celtic love of *territoriality* and *inheritance*. The great Celtic cross of the Macmillans of Knap is one of the celebrated stones of the Highlands.

In some parts of Argyllshire the Macmillans are known as *Na Belich* (the Bells). In Gaelic a Macmillan is called *Mac-Mhaoilean* or *Mac-Gille-Mhaoil*, that is, son of the tonsured one, and the clan is regarded as of ecclesiastical origin, so the original line of chiefs may have been a race of hereditary abbots, so usual in the Celtic Church. The Clan Buchanan Society seek to recognise Macmillan as a sept of Buchanan, but this is repudiated by the Clan Macmillan, who have their own independent chief, organisation, and society.

MACNAB

The Macnabs derive from the hereditary Celtic Abbot of Glendochart in the reign of David I. Hence the name, *Clann-an-Aba*— descendants of the Abbot. There was a bond of fellowship between the chiefs of the Clan Macnab and the Clan Mackinnon in 1606.

The early possessions of Clan Macnab lay on the shores (principally the western ones) of Loch Tay, and in Strathfillan and Glen Dochart. The residence of the chief was at Kinnell, on the banks of the Dochart.

The Macnabs were on the losing side during the struggle of King Robert the Bruce for the Scottish Crown, as they then espoused the cause of the Bruce's bitterest enemy, MacDougall of Lorn. As might have been expected, when Bruce's party became the victors the Macnabs lost a large slice of their lands. The only possessions which were then left to them were the lands of Bovain, in Glendochart. It appears the senior line—*MacNab Oire*—of Innishewan was dispossessed by the Bruce, and thereafter subsisted only as a cadet, while the House of Bovain was elevated to the chiefship, and in 1336 Gilbert Macnab of Bovain had a charter-title from David II.

During the wars between King and Parliament in the 17th century, the Macnabs, under Iain Min, " Smooth John," yr. of Bovain, were faithful to the Royal cause, and suffered in consequence. Their estates were, however, restored under Charles II. Francis MacNab of that Ilk, 16th Laird of MacNab, is the subject of Raeburn's celebrated portrait, " The MacNab." He died in 1815, and was succeeded by his nephew, Archibald MacNab of MacNab, 17th Chief. The fortunes of the family continued to decay, and in 1832 this chief was forced to dispose of what remained of the clan territory. He and many of his clan emigrated to Canada, where he strove to resettle the clan, but good intentions were marred by other failings, and his schemes, good in themselves, were brought to nought by a treacherous clansman, who, bad though his chief may have been, ought to have supported the clan effort. Disloyalty to one's chief is always inexcusable and ugly. They should have placed his affairs in trust. The chief returned to Europe in 1853,

K*

and in 1860 died in France. His daughter, Miss Macnab of Macnab, bore the chiefly title until her death in 1894 ; thereafter it was dormant. The family burying-place is Innis Buie, in the River Dochart just before it issues into Loch Tay. Kinnell, the old seat of the chiefs, has recently been recovered by A. C. Macnabb (whose wife on this event renounced the tanistry of Macleod) ; and in 1954 he was (on abdication of his nephew the heir male and 21st chief) confirmed as Archibald Macnab of Macnab, 22nd chief of the clan, *The Macnab*, by decree of Lyon Court.

MACNAUGHTEN

The earliest authentic reference to the Clan MacNaughten connects them with Argyll, where in the thirteenth century we find them possessing the upper part of Lochawe, Glenara, Glenshira, and Loch Fyne. Their strongholds were " Dubh-Loch " in Glenshira, and the picturesque Castle of Dundarave on Loch Fyne, the " Castle of the Two Oars." Above the entrance to the old castle of Dunderave is inscribed the following, viz. : " I . Behold . The . End . Be . Nocht . Vyser . Nor . The . Hiestest . I . Hoip . in . God . 1598."

Alexander III. in 1267 granted to *Gillichrist MacNachdan* the keeping of his castle of Frechelen, on an island in Loch Awe, so that he should cause it to be built and repaired at the king's expense, as often as needful, and keep it safely for the king's necessity ; and that as often as he should come to it, the castle, well furnished, should be delivered to him to lodge and dwell there at his pleasure. Between the years 1390 and 1406 Robert III. confirmed Maurice MacNaughtane a grant by Colin Campbell of Lochow, in heritage, of various lands in Over-Lochow.

Donald, the chief of the clan in the beginning of the fourteenth century, being nearly related to the MacDougalls of Lorn, joined that clan against King Robert the Bruce. As a consequence of this, when the star of the Bruce was in the ascendant, some of the MacNaughten lands were given to the Campbells.

Duncan, son and successor of Donald, was, however, a staunch adherent of King David II. That monarch conferred on Alexander, Duncan's son and successor, lands in the Island of Lewis, which formed a part of the forfeited possessions of John of the Isles.

Sir Alexander, the chief of the clan during the reign of King James IV., fell with his sovereign at the Battle of Flodden.

During the wars between King Charles I. and the Parliament, and also during the Revolution of 1688, which drove King James VII. from the throne, MacNaughten remained unswervingly loyal to the Stuarts, so in 1691 the MacNaughton estates were forfeited. The last of the MacNaughtens of Dundarave was John, who, after too much refreshment, married c. 1700 a daughter of Sir James Campbell of Ardkinglass, and next morning found himself married to the eldest daughter instead of the second. Upon this MacNaughten and the second daughter fled, leaving his wife to bear a daughter, whom Ardkinglass drowned in the river, after which he got escheat of MacNaughten's lands as those of an absconding adulterer. According to the genealogy addressed in Lyon Court, John Dhu MacNaughten, brother to the Laird of Dundarave, settled in Antrim about 1580 and from him is descended the present line of chiefs. In 1818, on this petition, Edmund A. MacNaughten of Bushmills, Antrim, whose genealogy was attested by 400 of the clan, was confirmed by Lyon Court in the chief arms of MacNaughten, and his line became hereditary chiefs of the clan.

Sir Francis Edmund MacNaughten of Dunderave, son of the applicant to whom Lyon had conferred the arms, was created a Baronet, and the later chiefs have borne this designation.

The name is spelt in many forms ; but since MacNaughten is the spelling wherein the chiefs have been officially recognised, this is necessarily the legal spelling of the name of their clan.

MACNEIL

The Clan MacNeil derives its descent through forty-five generations from Niall of the Nine Hostages, *Oir-righ Eireann*, through the line of sub-kings of Ailech and Ulster. Niall, 21st in descent, came, it is claimed, to Barra in 1049, the date given in the " Barra Register," and founded the Clan Niall in Scotland. Ninth in descent from him, Gilleonan Roderick Murchaid MacNeil received from Alexander, Lord of the Isles, a charter of the island of Barra in 1427. This was confirmed in favour of Gilleonan MacNeil of Barra by King James IV. at Stirling in 1495, after the power of the Lords of the Isles had been broken. The seat of the chief is the island castle of Kismull, in Barra.

After the forfeiture of the Lords of the Isles in 1493, the MacNeils of Barra and those of Gigha acted quite independently of each other— the Barra clan became allies of Maclean of Duart, while those of Gigha followed the MacDonalds of Islay and Kintyre.

The chiefs of Barra maintained high state in Kismull, and after the daily feast, MacNeil's trumpeter sounded a fanfare from the battlements of the tower and proclamation was made, " Hear, O ye people, and listen, O ye nations ! The great MacNeil of Barra, having finished his meal, the princes of the earth may dine."

Rory the Turbulent, whose galleys pirated amongst English shipping, excused himself to James VI., on the plea that he felt such conduct against those who had killed Queen Mary, would please the king. Black Roderick, reckoned 18th Chief of the clan, obtained a fresh baronial charter from James VII. in 1688, and a year later fought for his Royal Master under Dundee at Killiecrankie. His son Roderick, " Dove of the West," was imprisoned for his part in the Rising of 1745.

Lieutenant-General Roderick MacNeil of Barra died in England in 1863, leaving one child, a daughter. General MacNeil had, in 1838, to sell the island of Barra, which was purchased by Colonel John Gordon of Cluny, and thus for a couple of generations the chiefs were landless until the beloved isle was recovered for the clan by Robert, 45th in descent and 25th Chief of Barra and his second wife, the late Marie, Madam MacNeil of Barra.

After the death, in 1863, of General Roderick MacNeil, the chiefship of the Barra MacNeils passed to the lineal representative of James MacNeil, youngest son of Roderick Dhu ; of this line Roderick Ambrose MacNeil of Barra died in 1914, having, in exercise of tanistry, settled the chiefship on his second son, Robert Lister MacNeil of Barra, who established his position as chief by decree of Lyon Court in 1915. He and his wife repurchased the greater part of Barra including Kismull Castle, on a rocky island at Castle-bay. MacNeil of Brevaig claims descent from a first-born son of Roderick Dhu, and thus to be an elder line than that of the General's or Ersary. (Such diversions from direct line have, however, been frequent in Highland history, *e.g.* Clan Ranald, Mackintosh, Macdonald, and Maclean.)

The original seat of the McNeills of Gigha would appear to have

Kismull Castle.

been in Knapdale, where the chief was hereditary keeper of Castle Sween. The direct line of the chiefs appears to have become extinct in the fifteenth century, and the Knapdale possessions of the clan to have then passed to the Macmillans by the marriage of one of them to a McNeill heiress. In 1478 Malcolm McNeill was Chief of the Gigha family. His younger brother, Hector, was the progenitor of the McNeills of Taynish.

Gigha has had a chequered history. Neil, the last chief, was killed in battle in 1530, and left one child, a daughter, Annabella, who made over the lands of Gigha to her natural brother, Neil. Neil, in 1544, sold the island to James MacDonald of Islay. After the death of Neil, who was killed in 1530, the chiefship of the Gigha McNeills passed to Neil McNeill of Taynish. His descendant, Hector, purchased in 1590 the island of Gigha from Campbell of Calder, who had bought it from MacDonald of Islay. Later, the estates of Gigha and Taynish were sold, the former passing into the possession of the McNeills of Colonsay, who are descended from a cadet branch of the Taynish family.

The Chief of the McNeills of Gigha married the daughter of Hamilton Price, Esq., of Raploch, Lanarkshire, and assumed the name of Hamilton. His descendants are now designated as " of Raploch."

Many cadet branches of the McNeills settled in north Ireland. The MacNeills, a celebrated race of bards, were the hereditary harpers to the Macleans of Duart ; and MacNeills were also hereditary pipers to the Macleans of Duart.

MACPHERSON

This clan derives its name, Macpherson—denoting " son of the Parson "—from Duncan, Parson of Kingussie (1438), who was descended from Kenneth, son of Ewan Ban, second son of Muriach, Chief of Clan Chattan, 1173. Kenneth was presumably (on chronological grounds) father of another Muriach, *eponymus* of the *Clan Vurich*, and father of the " tribe of the three brothers," (1) Kenneth, who fought at Invernahavon, 1376, and was ancestor of Cluny, (2) John, ancestor of Pitmain, (3) Gillies, ancestor of Invereshie.

The earlier history of both Clan Vurich and Clan Chattan has been the subject of much speculation ; and it has been suggested that Clan Vurich was a small tribe in the Badenoch area, whilst it certainly appears the Clan Chattan originated further west, and that its name and status derive from keepership of a relic of St. Catan—a sacred stone, which was duly transmitted through Eva to the Mackintoshes, and in Martin's time was still held as Keeper of the *Baul Muluy* by a Mackintosh in Balliminich, Arran.

The arms, a galley, suggest a western origin, whilst the " cat " crest, though a play on the name, pertains rather to the mountains of Badenoch. Whilst the stone and the simple coat of Clan Chattan descended to The Mackintosh, as for the Chief of Clan Chattan (as Sir George Mackenzie records in his *Herauldrie*), the coat assigned to the line of Macpherson chiefs descending from Kenneth is " party per fess," and as such " differenced "—as the Lord Lyon declared—from the plain arms of Clan Chattan. From Kenneth the warrior of Invernahavon, through Donald Mor Macpherson (son of the 1438 parson), descended Andrew Macpherson in Cluny, who also held Banffshire lands in Strathisla, and this Macpherson of Cluny fought under the Earl of Huntly at Glenlivet. Dying about 1660, he was succeeded by the son of his only son, Ewen Macpherson of Cluny.

This Ewen's sons, Andrew and Duncan, successively chiefs of Cluny-Macpherson, left no male issue, and Duncan proposed settling (as by tanistry he was entitled to do) the chiefship of the Macphersons on his daughter Anne, and her husband Sir Duncan Campbell. William of Nuid, the heir male, and others, bound themselves to dissuade him — in which they succeeded — so upon Cluny's death, 1722, Lachlan, 4th of Nuid, succeeded as Chief of Cluny-Macpherson, dying in 1746. His son Ewen Macpherson of Cluny (son-in-law of the notorious Lord Lovat) became one of the most

Breacan-feile, back view, with targe hung on shoulder.

distinguished Highland leaders in the Rising of 1745. Cluny-Macpherson hid in Badenoch for nine years after Culloden, during which he was faithfully supported by his clan and tenantry, and to his son Duncan, Cluny was restored in 1784. His son, Ewen Macpherson of Cluny, was recognised in Lyon Court as Chief of the Clan Macpherson in 1873, and picturesquely maintained the state of a Highland chief until his death in 1885. On the death of his youngest son, Albert Cameron Macpherson of Cluny (by tanistry 17th Chief), the estate passed to a judicial factor, whilst the arms and chiefship devolved on his nephew in Australia, Ewen George Macpherson of Cluny-Macpherson, as 18th Chief of the Clan Macpherson.

The Cluny estate eventually meant most of Laggan, and is one of the most romantic of the clan country. Several acres of it have now been settled in perpetuity as a rallying-ground for the Clan Vurich by means of a Trust.

In 1688, when the Mackintoshes were defeated by MacDonnell of Keppoch at the Battle of Mulroy and Mackintosh was taken prisoner, although the Macphersons had taken no part in the conflict, after the battle they confronted the victorious MacDonells and compelled them to deliver up the Chief of Mackintosh to them and then escorted Mackintosh in safety to his own castle.

Duncan, Chief of the Macphersons in 1672, obtained from the Lord Lyon the matriculation of his arms as " Laird of Clunie Macpherson, and the only true representative of ancient family of the Clan Chattan." Against this matriculation, however, Mackintosh successfully sued a reduction and Lyon apparently charged Cluny with adding supporters which had not been really granted in the text of the parchment. Under the Clan Security Act the Privy Council further ordered Cluny Macpherson to give bond only for those of his name descended of his house and the Chief of Mackintosh to give security for the peaceable behaviour of the clan. Mackintosh was thus held Chief of the Clan Chattan and of the name of Mackintosh, and Lyon's decision was upheld.

The seat of the chief was Cluny Castle, near Kingussie. Among the many cadet branches of the Clan Macpherson, the oldest are those of Pitmain and of Invereshie (the *Slioch Gillies*). George Macpherson of Invereshie inherited in 1806 the estate of Ballindalloch from his father's maternal uncle, General James Grant, and then assumed the additional surname of " Grant." He was created a baronet in 1838.

MACQUARRIE

This small clan possessed as their territory the little island of Ulva, lying opposite to the west coast of Mull, and also owned a small portion of the island of Mull. They form one of the branches of the " Clan Alpin," and are, according to tradition, descended from Guaire, a brother of Fingon, who was the ancestor of the Mackinnons.

In 1249 Cormac Mór, chief of the clan, is said to have joined in the expedition of King Alexander II., against the Western Isles. Hector Macquarrie of Ulva is said to have fought with his clan at the Battle of Bannockburn on the side of King Robert the Bruce. The first chief, however, of whom there is any notice in the public records, was John Macquarrie of Ulva, who died in 1473. Mr. Smibert (*Clans of Scotland*) says : " Most of the family papers of the Macquarries' house were consumed by fire in 1688, leaving early annals more dubious than they might have otherwise been."

Prior to the forfeiture of the Lord of the Isles in 1493, the Macquarries were followers of the MacDonalds. Subsequent to that period, however, they followed the Macleans of Duart.

Lauchlan, Chief of the Macquarries, and the proprietor of Ulva at the time of the visit of Dr. Johnson and Mr. Boswell to that island in 1773, was in 1778, owing to financial embarrassments, compelled to part with his estate. He entered the army at the age of sixty-three, obtaining a commission in the old 74th Regiment (or " Argyllshire Highlanders "), and died at Glenforsa (Mull) in 1818 at the age of 103. This chief was the last of his line. He left no male issue, and with him the chiefship became dormant, but was claimed by a line of Macquarries, the representative of which was for a time beadle of a church in Knapdale. No effort, however, was made to establish the right to chiefly insignia.

The MacGuires of Ireland are said to derive their descent from Gregor, second son of Cormac Mór, Chief of the Macquarries, who was slain by the Norwegians during the reign of King Alexander II. The Chief of the Irish MacGuires was raised to the peerage by King Charles I. in 1627, under the title of Lord Enniskillen.

MACQUEEN

The Macqueens, or Macsweyns, come of the same stock as the MacDonalds, both being of the race of Conn, or Cuinn, " of the hundred battles."

The Macqueens of Garafad, in Skye, held the lands of Garafad for many centuries free, on the condition of giving a certain number of salmon yearly at a fixed price to the proprietor. It is said that they lost the above lands by getting into arrears with this rent.

During the fifteenth century we find a branch of the Macqueens among the followers of the MacDonalds of Clanranald. Malcolm Beg Mackintosh, 10th Chief of Mackintosh, married Mora MacDonald of Moidart. When the bride went to the Mackintosh country, several of her kinsmen accompanied her, including Revan-Mac-Mulmor Mac-Angus Macqueen. This same Revan fought under Mackintosh of Mackintosh at the Battle of Harlaw in 1411. His descendants settled in Strathdearn, where they acquired the lands of Corryborough, and became members of Clan Chattan. They were known as the " Clan

Revan," from the name of their progenitor. Cadet branches of the Clan Revan came in time to occupy a good deal of territory in the valley of the Findhorn. The Corryborough lands appear to have passed from the Macqueens during the latter half of the eighteenth century. The line which claims to be now that of the chief is resident in New Zealand, and no effort has been made to establish the claim. The MacSweens were received in Lyon Court as a distinct honourable clan, and do not fall under the MacQueen chiefship.

When, in 1778, Lord MacDonald of Sleate raised a Highland regiment, he conferred a lieutenancy in it upon a son of Donald Macqueen of Corryborough. In the letter to old Corryborough intimating the granting of a commission to Corryborough's son, Lord MacDonald wrote to the former as follows, viz. : " It does me great honour to have the sons of chieftains in the regiment, and as the Macqueens have been invariably attached to our family, to whom we believe we owe our existence, I am proud of the nomination." Lord MacDonald, when making the above observations, doubtless intended to emphasise the fact that before his clan became known as the " Clan Donald," they had borne the designation of the *Siol Cuinn* (the race of Conn of the Hundred Battles).

MACRAE

Owing to the Macraes having for centuries occupied the position of a clan subordinate to the Clan MacKenzie, but little is known of their early history and origin. The name has been spelt variously, Macrae, Macra, Macrach, Maccraw, Macraith, etc.

The Macraes are said to have settled in Kintail early in the fourteenth century. Before that time they are supposed to have lived at Clunes, on the Lordship of Lovat, near the southern shore of the Beauly Firth. Like the Maclennans, the Macraes were staunch followers of the Mac-Kenzies of Kintail (afterwards Earls of Seaforth). The Mac-lennans were standard-bearers to the Lords of Kintail ; while the Macraes would appear to have formed the bodyguard of the Chief of the Clan MacKenzie (for they were known as " MacKenzie's Shirt of Mail ! ").

Eilean-Donan Castle.

The Macraes were chamberlains of Kintail for many generations, and frequently vicars of the parish and, from 1520 onwards, constables of Eilean-Donan Castle. The late Constable of Eilean-Donan Castle, Lieutenant-Colonel John Macrae-Gilstrap of Balliemore, recently restored the ancient stronghold, one of the most picturesque in the Highlands.

Rev. Farquhar Macrae (1508–1662) was Vicar of Kintail for forty-four years. One of his sons, Rev. John Macrae of Dingwall (1614–1673), was progenitor of the Macraes of Conchra, a family that has been honourably represented in the British army for several generations.

Macrae of Inverinate claimed the chiefship of the clan, and Sir Colin Macrae, representative of that house, petitioned Lyon Court 1909, but the claim was opposed by a descendant of Conchra, who alleged there was no Chief of the Clan Macrae. The chiefship of this clan has not yet been settled, but that there is *no* " representer " of the first Macrae is an untenable proposition.

In 1778 the Earl of Seaforth raised " the 78th Regiment," or " Seaforth's Highlanders " (afterwards the 72nd Regiment). So strong did the Macraes muster in its ranks that, during a rising of the regiment the same year (caused by the apprehension of the soldiers that the Government did not mean to treat them fairly), the emeute was styled " The Affair of the Wild Macraes ! "

The Macraes of Clunes would seem to have stood in high favour with the Frasers of Lovat. Mary, daughter of the last Lord Bisset, who carried the estates of Lovat to the Frasers, was fostered with Macrae of Clunes, for whom she naturally entertained the highest respect, in which feeling her husband cordially participated, and a firm alliance continued long afterwards to subsist between their descendants. It is said that a stone was erected at the door of Lord Lovat's castle, intimating that no Macrae should lodge without while a Fraser resided within :

Fhad 'sa bhitheas Frisealach a stigh, Na bitheadh Macrath a muigh.

MALCOLM

This small Argyllshire clan, whose territory lies in the Lochawe district, are traditionally reported to be an offshot of the MacGhille-Challums (or MacLeods) of Raasay, and to have settled in Argyllshire at an early date. The arms of the family, however, do not suggest any connection with Clan MacLeod. They took protection of the Campbells of Lochow ; and we find in 1414 Sir Duncan Campbell of Lochow granting to Reginald MacCallum of Corbarron certain lands of Craignish, and on the banks of Loch Avich, in Nether Lorn, with the office of hereditary constable of the castles of Lochaffy and Craignish. This branch of the MacCallums, or Malcolms, appears to have become extinct during the latter half of the seventeenth century, when Corbarron, or Corran, was inherited by Zachary MacCallum of Poltalloch.

Dugald MacCallum of Poltalloch, who inherited the estate in 1779, appears to have been the first to adopt " Malcolm " permanently as the family patronymic, and received arms with supporters from the Lord Lyon in 1818. Of this surname there is, however, more definite historical fact ; in 1562 Donald M'Gillespie vic O'Challum was seized in the lands of Poltalloch. He was the lineal ancestor of Neil Malcolm of Poltalloch, who succeeded his cousin, Dugald, in 1787 and died in 1802. John Wingfield, 15th Laird, was created Lord Malcolm of Poltalloch in 1896 and died in 1902. He was succeeded in the estate by his brother.

Malcolm of Poltalloch is the Chief of the Clan Malcolm.

MATHESON

Investigation shows that the Mathesons were an early upshoot of the ancient Celtic Earls of Ross ; but the early history of this clan is obscure. Clan historians have tried to identify them with the Mac-Mathews, whose chief was one of the Highland chiefs seized by James I. at Inverness in 1427. Bower mentions MacMaken, leader of two thousand men, but it has not been proved that he was a Matheson. Of their fate as a clan, Skene says :

this circumstance affords a most striking instance of the rise and fall of different families ; for while the Mathison appears at that early period as the leader of two thousand men, the MacKenzie has the same number only, and we now see the Clan of MacKenzie extending their numberless branches over an extent of territory of which few families can exhibit a parallel, while the once powerful clan of the Mathisons has disappeared, and their name become nearly forgotten.

Kermac MacMaghan of Ross-shire is mentioned in the " Public Accounts " of Lawrence le Grant, Sheriff of Inverness, about 1263, in the reign of King Alexander III.

The country of the clan appears to have been in the district of Lochalsh. Some writers derive the Mathesons from the same stock as the MacKenzies, while others maintain their origin to have been a Norse one. They appear a cadet, and as vassals of the old Earls of Ross. After 1427, for a period of about two hundred years, there seem no records of the history of the clan. They seem, in the interval, to have become followers of MacKenzie, and to have had many feuds with the MacDonnells of Glengarry, their neighbours in Lochalsh.

The Clan Matheson became divided into two great branches, those of Lochalsh, of which the House of Bennetsfield became Chief, and from whom descended the Mathesons of Attadale and Ardross, and those of Shiness (Sutherlandshire).

In later days the wealthiest family of the name has been the House of Matheson of Attadale, an estate held from about 1730.

In 1851 Alexander Matheson of Ardross and Attadale, purchased the estate of Lochalsh, which had been forfeited by his ancestor in 1427. About the same time James Matheson, Esq. (one of the Mathesons of Shiness), owner of the estate of Achany, acquired the island of Lewis. Matheson of Attadale became M.P. for the counties of Ross and Cromarty, and was, in 1850, created a Baronet.

Logan (*Clans of the Scottish Highlands*) says :

By the MS. history of this clan in our possession, it appears that Alexander MacMhatain, who lived in Sallachie 1822, was the representative, in lineal descent, of the eldest branch of the ancient house of Lochalsh.

According to the *Old Statistical Account of Ross-shire*, the chiefship of the Clan Matheson was in the representative of the Mathesons of Bennetsfield who descend from Roderick Matheson of Fernaig, elder son of Murdoch Buidh Matheson, Constable of Eilean-Donan in 1570, whose other son was Dougal of Balmacara. Messrs. MacKenzie and MacBain, the historians of the clan, adopt the same view, and a claim to the appropriate arms and chiefship was in 1963 sustained by Lyon Court finding Col. Bertram Matheson of that Ilk hereditary Chief, and according a Tanistry remainder-over to the Baronets of Lochalsh.

MENZIES

According to Robertson (*Historical Proofs on the Highlanders*) though the clan is descended from a Gaelic-speaking race, the chiefs are of Lowland origin. Robertson's opinion is shared by Skene. The grant of the lands to the first *de Meeners* included the " following," and according to tribal principle he became *in loco paternis* to the people, and ere long true blood bonds were created by the spreading amongst these of the younger children of the chief.

The name occurs in charters during the reigns of William the Lion and Alexander II. About 1250 Robert de Meyners, Knight, was Lord High Chamberlain of Scotland. His son, Alexander, held Weem, Aberfeldy, and Fortingal, in Atholl, Glendochart, in Breadalbane, as well as Durisdeer, in Nithsdale. Sir Robert de Mengues, Knight, had his lands erected into the Barony of Menzies in 1487. His descendant, Sir Alexander Menzies of Castle Menzies, was in 1665 created a Baronet of Nova Scotia. From him descended Sir Neil Menzies, who died in 1910, when the baronetcy expired, and his sister, Miss Egidia Menzies of Menzies became chieftainess of the clan until her death.

A distinguished cadet was Menzies of Pitfoddels, who branched off the stock in the fourteenth century. Its last chieftain settled his estate of Blairs on the Roman Catholic Church, and at Blairs' College near Aberdeen, the surviving muniments of the old Scots College of Paris are now preserved.

Clan Menzies fought for The Bruce at Bannockburn. In 1688, when the Stuarts were driven from the throne, the Chief of Clan Menzies favoured the new Government. However at the Rising of 1715, the Menzies were out for the Chevalier. In " the '45," the chief took no part, but the clan was out under Menzies of Shian.

To a Menzies Scotland is indebted for introduction of the larch tree, which now flourishes all over the Highlands. The first larch saplings were raised from seven seedlings brought in 1738 from the Tyrol by Menzies of Culdares.

The house of Culdares, whose seat was latterly Arndilly on Spey-side, regarded as nearest line to the chiefship was by Lyon Court in 1958 in the person of Ronald Menzies of that Ilk revested as *The Menzies* in the chiefly arms and Castle Menzies which had been sold by Sir Neil's creditors has been re-acquired by the clan to become the headquarters of Clan Menzies.

MORRISON

The *Chlann Mhic-Gille-Mhoire* or Morrison Clan is said to be of Scandinavian extraction. Tradition says that their founder was a natural son of the King of Norway, who, along with his wife and child, was cast ashore on the island of Lewis on a piece of driftwood. The clan's badge is *sgoid cladach*, or driftwood, in memory of the above circumstances.

Morrison of Habost and Barvas, their chief, had his castle at Dun Eystein and from the chief holding the office of brieve, the clan was also known as *Chlann-na Breitheamh*. Sir Robert Gordon (*Earldom of Sutherland*) writes :

What the office of a Brieve is among the islanders ; the Brieve is a kind of judge who hath an absolute judicatorie, unto whose authoritie and censure they willinglie submit themselves when he determineth any debateable question between partie and partie.

The Morrisons held the hereditary brieveship of Lewis until 1613, when they lost in the "Evil Troubles of the Lewis," and by the nineteenth century it became impossible to trace the line. They and the Lewis MacAulays were deadly foes. With the MacDonells of Glengarry, however, the Morrisons were friendly. The main line is by others said to have been the Morrisons in Pabbay of Harris, whose seat was the Dun there, and from these as part of the *Siol an-t-hearrchdfhear* is handed down the genealogy of the Morrisons of Ruchdi, a cadet of whom was in 1959 created Viscount Dunrossil. Dun Eystein in North Lewis has been reckoned the principal fortress. The chiefship has not yet been settled.

About sixty families of Morrisons are said to have been brought to the vicinity of Durness, in the "Mackay Country," by one of their chiefs, who married a daughter of one of the Bishops of Caithness, whose dowry was territory in the district above alluded to.

There is an island on the coast of Eddrachyllis, which is called *Eilean a' Breitheamh*, or Judge's Island. In 1861 the Morrisons numbered 1402, or about one-seventeenth of the whole population of Lewis. Morrison of Islay has (1964) been created Lord Margadale, a glen in Islay.

The arms usually presented as those of " its chief " are those of the prominent Aberdeenshire family of Morison of Bognie, which attained a great addition to its estates by marriage with the widow of a Viscount of Frendraught.

MUNRO

The Munros, the seat of whose chief is at Foulis, in the east of Ross-shire, were anciently vassals of the Earls of Ross. There has been a great deal of conjecture with regard to the origin of their name. Smibert (*Clans of Scotland*) says their first designation was *Monrosse*, and is of opinion that the Munroes were so designated as being the Hill-men, or Mountaineers, of Ross. Their traditionary origin is from the *Siol o' Cain* of North Moray, from whom, also, have been deduced the Buchanans and the Macmillans.

The first chief of the clan, styled " of Foulis," was Hugh, who lived in the twelfth century. We find George, Chief of the Munros, obtaining charters from King Alexander II. ; and Robert, the chief, fighting at Bannockburn for King Robert the Bruce. Robert, 8th Baron of Foulis, married a niece of Euphame, daughter of the Earl of Ross and Queen of Robert II. Though Robert Mór Munro, the 15th Chief, was a staunch Protestant, he was a loyal supporter of Mary Queen of Scots.

Robert, the 18th Chief of Munro, went to Sweden with Sir Donald Mackay, 1st Lord Reay, in 1626, and joined the army of King Gustavus Adolphus. He achieved such distinction in the service of the Swedish King that he was at one time colonel of two regiments, one of foot and one of cavalry. It is related that about the same time there were in the service of the King of Sweden no less than three generals, eight colonels, five lieutenant-colonels, eleven majors, and above thirty captains, as well as many subalterns, all named Munro.

The 18th Chief died from his wounds at Ulm in 1633, and was succeeded by his brother, Hector, also a distinguished soldier, who, in 1634, was created a baronet by Charles I. On the death of Sir Hector's son and heir, the direct line of the chiefs became extinct. The title and property then passed to Robert Munro of Opisdale, grandson of George, third son of the 15th Chief of Foulis. Sir John, 4th Baronet, and chief of the clan at the Revolution of 1688, espoused the side of the new government. Sir Robert, 5th Baronet, though blind, became Sheriff of Ross.

In 1740, when the independent companies of the " Black Watch " were formed into the 43rd (afterwards 42nd) Regiment, Sir Robert Munro, 6th Baronet, had the honour of being appointed its Lieutenant-Colonel, John, Earl of Crawford, being the Colonel. Sir Robert's next brother, George, was one of the captains, while his youngest brother, James, became surgeon of the regiment.

During the Rising of "the '45," Sir Robert and his clan fought on the Hanoverian side, and Sir Robert and his brother, Duncan, both fell at the Battle of Falkirk.

On the death of Sir Hector, 11th Baronet, his daughter, Mrs. Gascoigne, became heiress of tailzie, and for a few years became "Munro of Foulis," but desiring to propel the estate, resumed the name of Gascoigne, and was declared "conventionally dead" as a Munro, by the Court of Session in 1939, whereupon her son, Patrick G. Munro of Foulis, became Baron of Foulis and recorded arms as Chief of the Munros in Lyon Court, whilst the heir male and Baronet is styled "of Foulis-Obsdale."

MURRAY

The ancestor of this powerful family was Freskin de Moravia, who acquired from David I. the lands of Strabrock, in West Lothian, and held Duffus, in Moray. He was evidently chieftain of the Duffus branch of the Royal House of Moray, and secured the chiefship by allying with the King of Scots. Freskin was succeeded by his elder son, William, and William was succeeded by his son, also William, who assumed the designation of "de Moravia," which indicates that he was then regarded as the Chief and Representer of the old Pictish Mormaers of Moray. William de Moravia married the daughter and heiress of Bothwell and Drumsargard in Lanarkshire and Smailholm, in Berwickshire. Besides Sir Walter, his heir, William de Moravia left other sons, from one being descended the Murrays of Tullibardine, progenitors of the Dukes of Atholl and chiefs of the Clan Murray of Atholl.

Two other branches also claim the chiefship of the name of Murray, viz. : Murray of Polmaise and Moray of Abercairney.

These houses were lineally descended from Sir Walter, eldest son of William of Moravia, one of their ancestors having been the celebrated patriot, Sir Andrew Moray of Bothwell, who was one of the first to join Sir William Wallace when Wallace raised the Scottish standard of independence against the pretensions of King Edward I. of England.

It has, moreover, also been claimed that the Murrays of Pulrossie and Skelbo were a senior branch of the clan. These respective claims have not apparently been so far exhaustively examined.

William, son of Malcolmus de Moravia, miles, Vicecomes de Perth (1284), obtained (by marriage with Ada, daughter of Malise, Seneschal of Strathearn) the lands of Tullibardine.

Sir John Murray, 12th feudal Baron of Tullibardine, was, by James VI. in 1606, created Earl of Tullibardine. William, 2nd Earl, married Lady Dorothea Stewart, eldest daughter and heir of line of the 5th Earl of Atholl (of the first Stewart creation) who died in

1594 without male issue. His son, John Murray, as heir of line of the Stewart Earls of Atholl was in 1629 confirmed in the Earldom by King Charles I. The 2nd Earl was raised to Marquis of Atholl, while the 2nd Marquis became in 1703 Duke of Atholl. The Duke of Atholl took no part in the events of 1715, and died in 1724. His eldest surviving son, the Marquis of Tullibardine, having, with two of his brothers, been out in 1715, was attainted for his share in that rising. The Dukedom of Atholl, and other family honours, therefore, were settled by a private Act of Parliament (1 Geo. I., cap. 34) upon his immediate younger brother, James, who became the 2nd Duke of Atholl. This is an interesting instance of a divertion of a Scottish peerage *after* the Union, and that it was done by a private Act shows that Scottish peerages must be amongst the private rights protected by the Treaty of Union, and of which resettlement by tanistry ought to be held competent. The attainted Marquis of Tullibardine and his talented brother, Lord George Murray, took a prominent part in the Rising of " the '45." The Marquis unfurled Prince Charles's standard in Glenfinnan, while Lord George Murray acted with great ability as generalissimo of the Prince's forces. Lord Tullibardine was taken prisoner after Culloden, and died in the Tower of London, 1746. Lord George Murray escaped to the Continent.

The 2nd Duke, in right of his mother, succeeded to the Sovereignty of the Isle of Man, as heir-general of the Stanleys at the death of the 10th Earl of Derby. The 2nd Duke died in 1764, leaving a daughter, Charlotte, who married her cousin, John, eldest son of Lord George Murray, Prince Charles's general. Charlotte succeeded in her own right to the Sovereignty of Man and the Barony of Strange. Though her husband's father had been attainted, John Murray of Strowan succeeded under statute 6 Geo. II., cap. 14, to the Dukedom of Atholl. In him and his wife, therefore, were concentrated again all the Murray dignities. John, 3rd Duke, and his Duchess ceded in 1765 to the British Crown their sovereign rights over the Isle of Man, those only excepted which pertain to ordinary Crown vassals, and received £70,000, with a life annuity of £2,000 each.

The 8th Duke was originator of the Scottish National War Memorial Scheme. The ducal seat is Blair Castle, Perthshire.

There are numerous distinguished cadet branches of Tullibardine, and among these the Earls of Dunmore, descended from Lord Charles Murray, second son of the 1st Marquis of Atholl ; also the Viscounts of Stormont, afterwards Earls of Mansfield, descended from Sir Andrew Murray, third son of Sir William of Tullibardine, who lived during the end of the seventeenth century.

The Tullibardine or Atholl Murrays were chiefs of a large district following, and in that respect resembled the Gordons and the Suther-lands. In his memorial to Government (1745) Forbes of Culloden said (with what meaning is not over clear) : " The Murrays is no clan family, though the Duke of Atholl is chief and head of a number of barons and gentlemen of the name of Murray in the Lowlands ; but he is deservedly placed here on account of his extensive following of about 3,000 Highlanders, a good many of them out of his own property, but most of them from the estates of the barons and gentlemen who hold their land of him on account of his great superiorities in Atholl, Glenalmond, and Balquidder. The most numerous of these and the readiest to turn out on all occasions are the Stewarts of Atholl, in number more than 1,000 men, as also 500 Robertsons, who do not follow their chief ; likewise the Fergussons, Smalls, Spaldings, Rattrays, Mackintoshes in Atholl, and MacLarens in Balquidder, with other broken names in Atholl, are followers of the Duke of Atholl."

The technical position was that at that stage Atholl was neither Chief of the Murrays nor had he taken the name and chiefship of the Stewarts of Atholl. He was *Princeps Regionum*, but had not consolidated its varied tribes into a specific clan.

In 1958, however, the Duke of Atholl, having dropped the surname of *Stewart*, was—as Marquis of Tullibardine—adjudged chief of the Name and Arms of Murray.

NICOLSON

In modern Gaelic the name of this clan takes the form " MacNeacail " ; while in old documents we have " M'Nicail." In Argyll the surname invariably takes the form MacNicol ; while in Skye and the North generally Nicolson is the approved designation. The Nicolsons held the lands of Scorrybreac, Skye, as principal tenants. " MacNicol of Portree," was, it is said, one of the sixteen men who formed the Council of the Lord of the Isles. Son succeeded father in the chiefship, and there is a local tradition to the effect that over one hundred chiefs of the clan were borne to their last resting-place in Snizort Churchyard from the old house of Scorrybreac. On 12th February 1813 (press of the day), " there died at Scorrybreac, in the Isle of Skye, in the eighty-seventh year of his age, Malcolm Nicolson, Esq., who, with his predecessors, lineally and without interruption, possessed that farm for many centuries back." Norman Nicolson of Scorrybreac, emigrated to New Zealand. He was a Gaelic bard of some repute, and his successor in the chiefship of the Nicolsons of Scorrybreac matriculated arms with a chevron between the eagles' heads. He holds a large estate at Scorrybrec, near Campbelltown, Tasmania.

MacNicols are numerous in Argyll. The Rev. Donald MacNicol

was minister of Lismore. He made a collection of Gaelic Ossianic poetry in 1755, and published in 1779 *Remarks on Dr. Samuel Johnson's Journey to the Hebrides*, at which the great moralist " growled hideously."

The lowland line of Nicolsons of Lasswade, descended from the Dean of Brechin, in Angus, has been officially recognised under the chiefly designation Nicolson of that Ilk, and was accordingly received as chief of the whole name, though Scorrybreac is Chief of the Highland Nicolsons. The seat of the now dormant Nicolsons Baronets of that Ilk was Grimista, Shetland.

Another branch, that of Sir George Nicolson of Cluny, a judge as Lord Kemnay, received a baronetcy in the person of his son, Sir Thomas, 1700. Sir William, 2nd Baronet, who married the widow of Thomas Burnett of Glenbervie, acquired that estate, which, on the death of the 3rd Baronet, passed in the female line to the Badenach-Nicolsons of Glenbervie.

OGILVY

The chiefs of this clan derive their origin from Gillibride, second son of Ghillechriost, Earl of Angus. The Barony of Ogilvy, in the parish of Glamis, in Angus, was bestowed on this Gillibride by King William the Lion about 1163, and Gillibride assumed the name of Ogilvy, from the name of his property. The lion passant on the arms of the chief of the clan (the Earl of Airlie) is to denote his descent from the old Earls of Angus, who also bore the lion on their arms. Smibert (*Clans of the Highlands of Scotland*), says : " The Ogilvies merit well a notice here, as a family intermingled with, if not derived from, the true Gael of northern Britain."

Patrick de Ogilvy figures in the Ragman Roll. He left two sons, both adherents of King Robert the Bruce. Sir Patrick obtained for his services the Kettins lands in Angus. Sir Walter, a descendant of Sir Patrick, having wedded Isabel, the heiress of the Ramsays of Auchterhouse, obtained with her that barony, as well as the hereditary sheriffship of Angus. He was succeeded by his son, Alexander, whose sole issue was a daughter, who married the Earl of Buchan, and who carried the Barony of Auchterhouse into that family.

On the death of Sir Alexander, the chiefship of the clan passed to his younger brother, Sir Walter, who married Isobel Durward, the heiress of Lintrathan. Sir John, 8th Baron, obtained in 1458 a charter of the lands of Airlie. His brother, Walter, was the progenitor of the Lords Banff and Earls of Findlater. The Viscounts (afterwards Earls) of Seafield were descended from the second son of the third Earl of Findlater.

Sir James Ogilvy, eldest son and successor of Sir John of Lintrathan, was, in 1491, elevated to the peerage by James IV., as Lord Ogilvy of Airlie. James, 8th Lord Ogilvy of Airlie, was created Earl of

Airlie by Charles I. in 1639, and was officially recognised by His Majesty as chief of the clan.

During all the troubles of the House of Stuart, the Ogilvies of Airlie adhered loyally to the cause of the ancient monarchy, David, 2nd Earl of Airlie, being one of the most distinguished of the Scottish Cavaliers who supported Charles I. The House of Airlie suffered, of course, in consequence. James, Lord Ogilvy, son of David, 3rd Earl of Airlie, was attainted for his participation in the Rising of 1715, though he was afterwards pardoned. His brother, John, succeeded as 4th Earl in 1731. At the time of the Rising of " the '45," David, Lord Ogilvy, son of the 4th Earl, had barely reached the age of twenty when he joined Prince Charles. For this he was attainted. He fled to France, where he entered the French military service, and rose to the rank of lieutenant-general. Lord Ogilvy's father, the Earl of Airlie, died in 1761, when the title fell on passing to the attainted heir. In 1778 a pardon was granted in consideration of his extreme youth at the time of " the '45 " ; the Earldom was restored in 1826.

That devotion to sovereign and country is perpetuated in the Airlie family was proved by the death of the 8th Earl on the field of battle in South Africa. The family seats are Cortachy Castle and the " Bonnie Hoose o' Airlie."

The title of Lord Banff, held by a cadet of the Ogilvies, became dormant in 1803 on the death of the 8th Baron.

James, second son of the 3rd Earl of Findlater, was created Viscount of Seafield in 1698 and Earl of Seafield in 1701. This Earl took a leading (and not altogether a creditable part) in consummating the parliamentary union of England and Scotland. When the Act of Union was finally passed he made the heartless remark, " There is the end o' an auld sang ! " but his brother—who dealt in cattle—having been chaffed by the anglicised Earl about his rustic occupation, tersely observed, " I sell nowt (cattle) ; ye sell nations." In 1711 the Earl of Seafield succeeded his father as 4th Earl of Findlater, his elder brother having predeceased his father without issue.

On the death of James, 7th Earl of Findlater and 4th Earl of Seafield in 1811 without issue, the Earldom of Findlater became dormant. The Earldom of Seafield, however, was inherited by the late Earl's cousin, Sir Lewis Alexander Grant of Grant, Bart., who, when he succeeded to the Seafield honours, with the name of " Grant-Ogilvie." On the death of the 11th Earl, the Ogilvie honour of Seafield and Deskford again passed to an heir female, his daughter, the present Countess of Seafield.

ROBERTSON (CLAN DONNACHIE)

The clan historians derive the Robertsons from the Old Earls of Atholl, as the early chiefs of Clan Donnachie were designated " de Atholia."

The chief, who gave the clan the patronymic of " Donnachie," appears to have been Donnchadh or Duncan Reamhar, who led the clan at the Battle of Bannockburn. From a later chief, Robert, who lived in the reign of James I., the clan took its appellation of " Robertson."

Duncan Reamhar left two sons, Robert, ancestor of the Robertsons of Struan, chiefs of the clan, and Patrick, of the Robertsons of Lude.

Besides the lands of Struan, the chiefs had at one time wide possessions on the banks of Loch Tay and of Loch Rannoch. These, however, they lost bit by bit, until now but a small portion remains of the clan's once broad acres.

The Robertsons were ever most loyal supporters of the House of Stuart. It was by the chief of the clan that the assassins of the ill-fated James I. were brought to justice, and as a reward was granted the armorial augmentation of a " wild man in chains " beneath the shield of the chief.

In the sixteenth century the Earl of Atholl profiting by a mortgage over the lands of Strowan, seized nearly half the estate, which the Robertsons were never able to recover. At the time of the Revolution of 1688 Struan, then under age, joined Lord Dundee, and as a consequence was attainted, and his estates forfeited. He was granted a remission by Queen Anne in 1703, and he returned to Scotland, but through some informality the remission was not complete. Struan was again in arms with 500 of his clan for King James in 1715, was taken prisoner at Sheriffmuir, rescued, and again captured. Finally, by the assistance of his only sister, Margaret, he escaped to France. In 1723 the Government restored the estate of Struan to Margaret Robertson, the only sister of the chief, who conveyed it in trust for the behoof of her brother, or, failing him, the next male heir. Margaret, who was then for a time the legal chief, died unmarried in 1727. Struan, having obtained a remission, had, previous to the death of his sister, returned to Scotland. He died at Carie, in Rannoch, in 1749.

In 1745, when Prince Charles arrived in Perthshire, Struan marshalled part of his clan for the Stuarts. He was, however, too advanced in years to take a personal part in the Rising, and to that may be ascribed the action of the Government in taking no cognisance of the old chief's action.

On the death of old Struan, the estate and chiefship devolved upon Duncan Robertson of Drumachine, but as his name was excluded from the Act of Indemnity, he was dispossessed of the estate in 1752, and retired to France. His son, Colonel Alexander Robertson, however, obtained a restitution of the estate in 1784.

The ancient residence of the chiefs of Clan Donnachie was at Dun-Alister, at the east end of Loch Rannoch. Later, however, the residence was transferred to Rannoch Barracks, Rannoch. These barracks were built by the Hanoverian Government in 1746 to over-awe the Robertson clan, but by a strange irony of circumstances became the residence of the chief whose clan they were meant to hold in check.

The Clan Donnachie has branches in the north Highlands. The principal offshoots are the Robertsons of Inshes (Inverness-shire), descended from Duncan, second son of the grandson in the direct line of Duncan de Atholia. The Robertsons of Kindeace descend from William, third son of one of the Robertsons of Inshes. Kindeace appears to have been acquired about 1639.

ROSE

This small Nairnshire clan were, before the forfeiture of the last Lord of the Isles, vassals of the old Earls of Ross. The family of the chief of the clan, Rose of Kilravock, settled in the county of Nairn in the reign of David I., but their first designation appears to have been that " of Geddes." In the beginning of the reign of Alexander II., Hugh Rose of Geddes was witness to the foundation charter of the Priory of Beauly by Sir John Bisset of Lovat. His son and successor, also Hugh, acquired the lands of Kilravock by his marriage with Mary, daughter of Sir Andrew de Bosco by Elizabeth, his wife (who was daughter and co-heiress of Sir John Bisset of Lovat). On the forfeiture of John, Earl of Ross, in 1474, Hugh Rose of Kilravock was confirmed by King James III. in the lands of Kilravock and Geddes, " to be holden immediately of the King," and subsequent lairds were addressed by the Crown as " Baron of Kilravock."

The Rev. Lachlan Shaw, in his *History of the Province of Moray* (Elgin, 1775), says of the Roses : " Had not the writings of the family been destroyed in the burning of the Cathedral of Moray in 1390, few families could have better demonstrated their antiquity, and, even with that misfortune, few can exceed it." In the *Statistical Account of Inverness-shire* (1845) it is (quite correctly) stated that the succession in the Rose family did not once diverge to a collateral branch for upwards of 600 years.

We find the Roses, at an early date, executing bonds of friendship with their powerful neighbours, the Mackintoshes. By an Act of Council, dated 28th July 1643, the broken men of the name of Rose were bound upon Mackintosh, who was ordained to be accountable for them.

During the Revolution of 1688, and the Risings of 1715 and 1745, the Roses were on the side of the new Government. Two days before the Battle of Culloden, Hugh Rose of Kilravock had an unexpected visit from Prince Charles, whom he entertained to dinner, when the Prince, history relates, behaved most agreeably.

The seat of the chief of the clan is still the Castle of Kilravock (which has been the residence of the Roses since 1460), picturesquely situated on the banks of the River Nairn, and the chief is always styled the Baron of Kilravock.

ROSS

An old account of the origin of the Rosses (quoted by Buchanan of Auchmar) gives them a Norse origin. The other and more probable account, which the best authorities have adopted, is, that the progenitor of the old Earls of Ross was the eldest son of Gilleon na h-àirde, the ancestor of Anrias, who, again, was the progenitor of the O'Beolans or Gillanders, the old Celtic Earls of Ross.

The first of the O'Beolan Earls of Ross was Fearcher MacinTagart, grandson of Gillianrias, and son of the *Sagart*, or priest, who was the *co-arb*, or hereditary abbot, of the old monastery founded by the Irish St. Maelrubha at Applecross in the seventh century.

Fearchar rendered great assistance to King Alexander II. in helping the king to crush a rebellion in the province of Moray in 1215. In recognition of these services Fearchar was knighted by the king, and in 1234 recognised as Earl of Ross. The dignity had evidently been inherited by the O'Beolan line through marriage with the heiress of line of Malcolm, Earl in 1160.

The 5th Earl of Ross (William) died in 1372, leaving no sons. His daughter, Euphemia, married to Sir Walter Leslie, then inherited the title as Countess of Ross in her own right. As we have seen, the Earldom of Ross passed to the Lord of the Isles by the marriage of that chief to Margaret, daughter of the Countess of Ross and Sir Andrew Leslie.

On the death of William, 5th Earl, chiefship of the Name and Clan of Ross passed to Hugh of Rariches, his brother. Hugh was the progenitor of the Rosses of Balnagowan. Of the Balnagowan Rosses Sir Robert Gordon (*Earldom of Sutherland*) says :

From the second son of the Earl of Ross the lairds of Balnagowan are descended, and had by inheritance the lands of Rarieches and Coulleigh, where you may observe that the laird of Balnagowan's surname should not be Ross, seeing that there was never any Earl of Ross of that surname ; but the Earls of Ross were first of the surname of Beolan, then they were Leslies, and last of all that earldom fell by inheritance to the Lords of the Isles, who resigned the same into King James the Third's hands in the year of God 1477. So I do think that the lairds of Balnagowan, perceiving the Earls of Ross decayed, and that earldom fallen into the Lord of the Isles' hands, they called themselves Ross, thereby to testify their descent from the Earls of Ross. Besides, all the Rosses in that province are unto this day called in the Irish (Gaelic) language Clan Leandries, which by their own tradition is sprung from another stock.

Nisbet (*System of Heraldry*) tells us :

Hugh Ross of Rariches, son of Hugh, Earl of Ross, who was killed in the Battle of Halidon Hill, got from his father the lands of Rariches, as also the lands of Easterallan from his brother William, Earl of Ross, 1357 ; and these lands were confirmed by a charter of King David II.

At the beginning of the eighteenth century David Ross of

Balnagowan was the last of his race in the direct line. He therefore entailed the estate to General Charles Ross, brother of Lord Ross of Hawkhead, a family which, however, was in nowise related to his own, but to whom, in accordance with the principle of tanistry, the Lord Lyon confirmed the chief arms and representation of Ross.

Upon the death, in 1711, of David, the male representation of the O'Beolan Rosses passed to Munro-Ross of Pitcalnie.

In 1778 Monro-Ross of Pitcalnie laid claim to the Earldom of Ross, as being lineal male descendant of Hugh Ross of Rariches, first Chief of Balnagowan, 1370, brother of William, Earl of Ross. His petition was laid before the House of Lords, but nothing came of it.

His house was, however, more successful over the chiefship, for, when the Hawkhead line expired, and Balnagowan passed to the Lockhart-Rosses, these omitted to make up title to the arms ; and even before their baronetcy expired (with the inventor of the " Ross rifle "), Miss Ross of Pitcalnie had in 1903 got decree of Lyon Court re-vesting her in the chief arms of Ross, and so became established as Chief of the Clan Ross.

SINCLAIR

The founder of this family was Sir William Saint-Clair, son of Robert de Saint-Clair in Normandy, and Eleanor de Dreux (a granddaughter of the Sire de Coucy). Sir William was guardian of the Prince, and from Alexander III. had a grant of the Barony of Roslin, with which, however, there appears to have been an earlier connection. His son, Sir Henry de Sancto Claro, supported Robert the Bruce, and was one of the Scottish barons who signed the celebrated letter to the Pope asserting the independence of Scotland. Sir William, his son, fell with " Good Sir James Douglas " defending the Bruce's heart in Spain, and his son, Sir Henry, laid the northern foundation of the family by marrying one of the co-heiresses of Malise, Earl of Stratherne, Caithness, and Orkney. The eldest son of this marriage, Henry Sinclair of Roslin, obtained from King Haco VI. of Norway a recognition of his claim to the Earldom of Orkney. William, 3rd Sinclair Earl of Orkney, received in 1455 from the Scottish King, James II., a grant of the Earldom of Caithness. He was the founder of Roslin Chapel, and (as Prince of Orkney) is commemorated in the celebrated " Prince's Pillar " there (to which, in recent years, the hackneyed German " prentice " legend has been applied, which Scottish Masonry should repudiate). In 1470 the Earl of Orkney and Caithness was compelled to resign Orkney to the Scottish Crown in exchange for the Castle of Ravenscraig in Fife. The king was jealous because Orkney was a semi-royal fief, inherited by the Sinclairs from the Norse Jarls or Sea-Kings, who sprang from Rognvald, Jarl of Moeri, also ancestor of Rolf the Ganger, 1st Duke of Normandy. Rognvald was grandson of Ivar, Jarl of the Uplands, a Prince of the Royal House of Norway.

The Earl resettled the Earldom of Caithness on his son by his second wife, Marjory, daughter of Alexander Sutherland of Dunbeath. The direct line of the Sinclair Earls of Caithness came to an end with the death of George, 6th Earl. In 1672 he had executed a disposition to Sir John Campbell of Glenorchy of all his titles, property, and heritable jurisdictions, Sir John being one of his principal creditors. On the death of the Earl, in 1676, Sir John Campbell assumed the title. George Sinclair of Keiss, son of Francis, second son of George, 5th Earl of Caithness, did not tamely submit to the usurpation of his Earldom and inheritance by the Campbells. During the absence of Sir John Campbell in London in 1677, Sinclair of Keiss gathered a strong band of Sinclairs and seized the Caithness estates. Campbell thereupon obtained an order from the Privy Council for Keiss's ejection, and, in 1680, marched north against the Sinclairs. A fierce battle between the Sinclairs and the Campbells was fought at *Allt-nam-meirleach*, near Wick, in which the former were defeated. Still Sinclair of Keiss was not disheartened. What he failed to win by the sword he won, in the long run, by prosecuting his claims before the Privy Council. These claims were at length admitted, and George Sinclair of Keiss took his place, in 1681, among his peers as 7th Earl of Caithness, Campbell of Glenorchy being created Earl of Breadalbane.

At the time of " the '45 " the northern Sinclairs were in arms, and ready, with their men, to join Prince Charles. The result of the Battle of Culloden, however, induced them to disband quietly, and Alexander, 9th Earl, lived until 1765—the last surviving peer, who had sat in the Parliament of Scotland, where he voted against every article in the Treaty of Union. The Earldom then passed to the Sinclairs of Ratter, whose line expired with the 11th Earl in 1789, when Sir James Sinclair of Mey, 8th Baronet, became 12th Earl. His great-grandson, George, 15th Earl, left Barrogill Castle to an English school-friend, whilst the Earldom devolved on James Augustus, 16th Earl, and representative of Sinclair of Durran, a cadet of Mey, of which line James Roderick is 19th Earl and chief of the clan. He holds Girnigoe Castle, the ancient stronghold of the Earls. Vast estates are still enjoyed in Caithness by the Sinclairs of Ulbster. Sir John Sinclair of Ulbster, 1st Baronet, was not only celebrated as an agriculturist, but compiled the great *Statistical Account of Scotland*. The Sinclairs of Roslin (descending from another son of the last Earl of Orkney, and now represented by the Earls of Rosslyn) were long Hereditary Master Masons of Scotland.

The progenitor of Lord Sinclair was " William the Waster," eldest son of William, 3rd Earl of Orkney, by his first wife, Lady Margaret, daughter of the 4th Earl of Douglas, Duke of Touraine. William got from his father the Barony of Newburgh, in Aberdeenshire, in 1450, and his son established his right to the Lordship of Sinclair in 1488. His descendants retained it until they expired in 1677, having resigned their peerage to Sinclair of Herdmanston, and the Earls of Caithness became chiefs of the clan.

SKENE

According to tradition, the progenitor of the Skenes was a younger son of Robertson of Struan, and the wolves' heads in the arms bear this out. For some service to one of the early kings, Malcolm Canmore of course being the one specified, the young Robertson was given the lands and lake of Skene in the Forest of Stocket, Aberdeenshire. The king offered Robertson the choice of two things—as much land as was encompassed by a hound's chase, or what could be covered by a hawk's flight. The latter was chosen by Robertson, and this formed the ancient Barony of Skene, in Aberdeenshire. This " hawk's flight," also noticed in the Hay traditions, is an ancient Gallic symbol which denoted the inalienable area of land surrounding the chief's house.

The armorial bearings of the Skenes, whose Gaelic appellation is *Siol Sgéine, no Clann Donnachaidh Mhàr* (Clan Robertson of Mar) contain the earliest official description of Highland dress.

Robert de Skene, who lived in the reign of King Robert the Bruce, was a firm supporter of that monarch's cause. In 1318 he obtained a charter erecting the *duthus* of Skene into a free barony, and the original dirk with which investiture was given is still in the charter chest of the Duffs.

James Skene of Skene was a loyal supporter of King Charles I. After the Revolution of 1688, however, his successors appear to have adhered to the new Government.

The family of Skene of Skene became extinct, in the direct line, in 1827, when the estates of the family devolved on James, 4th Earl of Fife, nephew of the last Skene of Skene (the Earl's father, Alexander, 3rd Earl of Fife, having married Mary, the daughter and heiress of George, last Skene of Skene), for the Duffs did not take the name.

The representation of the Skenes seems then to have passed to the family of Skene of Hallyards, descended from Andrew of Auchorrie, second son of James Skene, 12th Chief of that Ilk, who died in 1605 and now to be in Skene of Pitlour in Fife.

Next is Skene of Preraw, in Austria, whose progenitor was Patrick, second son of Andrew Skene of Auchorrie, who has already been alluded to above.

Several cadet branches have sprung from the chiefs of Skene ; among the rest, those of Hallyards, Dyce, Cariston, etc., and now the Moncrief-Skenes of Pitlour are the only territorial house of the name in Scotland.

STEWART

This Royal clan, whose history is the history of Scotland, sprung from a scion of the ancient hereditary Stewards of Dol, in Normandy. Of this family Alan Fitz Flaald obtained from Henry I. of England

PLATE X.

Photo: T. & R. Annan & Sons, Glasgow.

ALASDAIR MACDONELL OF GLENGARRY.

Showing *Feileadh-beag* worn with Tartan Doublet and Belted-Plaid.

(*From the Painting by Sir Henry Raeburn, reproduced by permission of the Scottish National Gallery.*)

PLATE XI.

[*Scottish Notes and Queries.*

ALEXANDER, 13TH EARL OF CAITHNESS, 1823–1855, CHIEF OF CLAN SINCLAIR.

Showing Full Dress of a Highland Chief, wearing Tartan Doublet and Shoulder Plaid.

the Barony of Oswestry, in Shropshire. Alan was the father of three sons—William, Walter, and Simon. From Walter, the second son, descended the Scottish Royal Family of Stewart.

Alan's eldest son, William, was the progenitor of the Earls of Arundel, whose title and possessions passed, through an heiress, into the ducal family of Norfolk.

The two younger sons of Alan sought their fortune in Scotland. Simon, the youngest, became the progenitor of the Boyds, his son, Robert, having been designated *Buidhe*, from his yellow hair.

Walter received from King David I. the lands of Paisley, Pollock, Cathcart, etc., and was appointed Steward of the Royal Household. In 1157 Walter's possessions were confirmed by a charter from King Malcolm IV. The Abbey of Paisley was founded by Walter, who was buried there. Walter's son and successor, Alan, left an heir, Walter, who was, by King Alexander II., created Justiciar of Scotland, in addition to his hereditary office of High Steward. He died in 1246, leaving four sons and three daughters. Walter, the third son, became Earl of Menteith. The eldest son, Alexander, was one of the Regents of Scotland during the minority of King Alexander III. He married Jean, heiress of the Lord of Bute, and a descendant of Somerled, Lord of Argyll. Alexander the Steward in his wife's right seized the islands of Arran and Bute.

Alexander had two sons, James (his successor) and John, who was afterwards known as Sir John Stewart of Bonkill, and who fell at the Battle of Falkirk. Sir John Stewart of Bonkill had seven sons. From Alan, the second son, were descended the Stewart Earls of Lennox. Alexander, the eldest, was the progenitor of the Stewart Earls of Angus, which line failed in 1377 ; the third son, Walter, was the ancestor of the present Earl of Galloway ; while the Earls of Atholl, Buchan, and Traquair, as well as the Stewart Lords Lorn and Inner-meath, were descended from James, the fourth son. The Lordship of Lorn was acquired by the 2nd Lord Campbell, ancestor of the Duke of Argyll, in exchange for the lands of Baldoning, Innerdoning, etc., in Perthshire. The exchange was effected during the time of the 5th Lord Innermeath. All the peerages issuing from Sir James, son of Sir John of Bonkill, are extinct, the Earldom of Atholl having become extinct in 1625. The later Stewarts of Atholl were descendants, by his five illegitimate sons, of Sir Alexander Stewart, Earl of Buchan, known as the " Wolf of Badenoch."

Continuing the main line of the Stewarts : James, elder son of Alexander, succeeded his father as hereditary High Steward in 1283. On the death of Alexander III. in 1286 he was chosen as one of the Regents of the kingdom of Scotland. The High Steward fought bravely for Scottish independence under both Wallace and Bruce, and died in 1309. Walter, his son and successor, the 6th High Steward, took a prominent part in the Battle of Bannockburn. Shortly afterwards, King Robert the Bruce bestowed upon him the hand of his

L

daughter, the Princess Marjory, in marriage. From this union were descended the Royal line of Stewart. The 6th High Steward died in 1326, and was succeeded by his son, Robert, 7th High Steward. On the death, without issue, in 1371 of King David II., uncle of the High Steward, the High Steward was proclaimed King of Scots by the title of Robert II.

The direct male line of the Stewarts failed in 1542, on the death of King James V. The representation of the clan, as well as the Crown itself, devolved, however, on his daughter, Mary Queen of Scots, who married her cousin, Lord Darnley, whose father, the Earl of Lennox, was actually the heir male. Darnley himself, however, became, in right of his wife, King (*i.e.* chief) and was so proclaimed and styled in statutes and charter. King James VI. was accordingly both heir of line and heir male of the Clan Stewart. How the hopes of the House of Stewart and the prospects of " Bonnie Prince Charlie " perished on the field of Culloden is a tragic episode of clan history too well known to need repetition here. Henry, Cardinal Duke of York, who died in 1807, was last of the line of Royal Stewarts, and by tanistry he nominated George III. heir in his claim to the throne.

The Lennox peerage was again revived by James VI., for his uncle, Charles, younger brother of Lord Darnley, in 1572 ; and when this creation expired in 1576, the king, in 1578, conferred the earldom on Robert Stuart, second son of John, 3rd Earl of Lennox, who also died without issue.

The third creation of the Earldom of Lennox by King James VI. was in favour of Esmé, Lord of Aubigny, son of John Stuart, Lord of Aubigny, third son of the 3rd Earl. Esmé became Earl in 1579, and Duke, of Lennox in 1581. The 6th Duke of Lennox (who was also 4th Duke of Richmond) died without issue in 1680, when the dukedom devolved upon King Charles II., as nearest collateral heir. The title was later bestowed by Charles II. on his illegitimate son, from whom is descended the present Duke, Richmond and Gordon and Lennox (also Duc d'Aubigny in France).

The Earl of Galloway, descendant of Walter, third son of Sir John Stewart of Bonkill, who was the second son of Alexander, the 4th High Steward, seems nearest lawful heir of the race bearing the name.[1]

The spelling of the name as " Stuart " by the Royal Family appears to have been introduced by Mary Queen of Scots, the lovely but unfortunate daughter of King James V.

The branches of the Stewart Clan are so numerous that it is impossible to refer to them all in detail. The Earls of Moray are descended on the male side from Murdoch, Duke of Albany, cousin of James I.; while on the female side they are derived from the Regent Moray, natural son of James V., through marriage with his daughter and heiress.

---

[1] Yet, Lord Bute's arms (but for the present Crichton (*Dumfries*) conjunction) would seem to potentially vest the heirship of the House of Stewart in the Marquessate of Bute, if Dumfries passes to a daughter.

Smibert (*Clans of Scotland*) remarks :

If the royal house left few legitimate male descendants whose issue was fated to continue, it left, at least, abundance of successors through natural offspring. About forty illegitimate children are mentioned in authentic genealogic works as having sprung from the kings alone.

The Stewarts of Appin and those of Atholl were important branch-clans within " the clan." The former are descended from a son of the last Stewart, Lord of Lorn, by a lady of the Clan MacLaren. This son, by the assistance of his mother's clan, succeeded in seizing and retaining part of his father's possessions. The Appin Stewarts took a prominent part in " the '45 " on the side of Prince Charles, under Stewart of Ardshiel. Some of their lands were forfeited then, but were afterwards restored. The Appin estates have now passed away from the family. There are, however, several representatives of cadet families in the district. Although now landless, the chiefs of the Clan Stewart of Appin still bear the arms and title of Stewart of Appin and Ardshiel.

The last Stewart, Lord Lorn, died in 1469, without any lawful male issue, when his estates passed to his brother and heir male, Walter, Lord Innermeath, whose descendant became Earl of Atholl.

The Stewarts of Grandtully, Perthshire, are descended from Alexander, third son of Sir John Stewart of Innermeath and Lorn, and brother to Robert, 1st Lord Lorn, and the famous " Black Knight of Lorn."

Sir John of Balveny, 1st Stewart Earl of Atholl, was son of Sir James Stewart, the Black Knight of Lorn (second son of Sir John Stewart of Innermeath and Lorn), and Joan, Queen Dowager of Scotland, widow of King James I. About 1457 he was created Earl of Atholl by King James II. This line ended in 1595 by the death of John, 5th Earl of Atholl, whose daughter, Lady Dorothy, married the 2nd Earl of Tullibardine. The title of Earl of Atholl was revived by King James VI. in 1595, in favour of John, Lord Innermeath, whose son, James, Lord Innermeath and Earl of Atholl, died without issue. Lord Tullibardine, Lady Dorothy's son, then claimed the Earldom, of which he got a *novodamus* from James VI. without prejudice to his claim to the dignity also as heir female of the 5th Earl.

The Stewarts of Atholl have long been closely allied with the Robertsons. In 1824 an association of Stewarts and Robertsons of Atholl was formed, styled afterwards " The Association of the Atholl-men." One of the objects was stated to be " for the purpose of promoting and cementing a generous, manly, and brotherly friendship between the two clans, such as subsisted between their ancestors." This association in 1825 adopted the name of " The Atholl Gathering."

The Stuarts of Bute (of whom the Marquis of Bute is the chief) are descended from Sir John Stuart, a natural son of King Robert II., to whom his father granted extensive possessions in the island of Bute, with the heritable sheriffship of that county, wherein he was confirmed by Robert III. The Chief of the Bute Stuarts was created a baronet in 1627, Earl of Bute in 1705, and Marquis of Bute in 1796. The Marquis is Hereditary Keeper of Rothesay Castle.

SUTHERLAND

What is now known as the county of Sutherland was long overrun by the Norsemen. Indeed, " Sutherland " is but a corruption of the Norse *Sudrland.* The name Sutherland (or South Land) was given to that district as being south of Gallaibh, or Caithness. Stewart of Garth writes : " The name of Sutherland is unknown in the Gaelic. The Highlanders call that country Cataibh, and Lord Sutherland Morair Chataibh (*i.e.* Lord of Cataibh)." The same writer also says : " The Highlanders call the country [of Caithness] Gallaibh " (actually this means the peninsula, *cf.* Galloway). " Lord Caithness is called Morair Ghallaibh—Caithness being a word unknown in the Gaelic."

One version of the origin of the Highlanders of Sutherland is that, the original Celts of that country having been altogether driven out or destroyed by the Scandinavian invaders, the Gaelic-speaking population of Sutherland are derived from immigrants, after the expulsion of the Norsemen, from the provinces of Ross and Moray. The other account of the origin of the Celts of Sutherland is that they are descended from the Celtic population who retreated before the Norsemen into the mountainous and inaccessible regions of their district, and a later and quite unfounded story is that the ancestors of these fugitives were the Catti, a tribe who migrated from Germany early in the Christian era. Be this as it may, we have already seen that the old chiefs of the Clan Sutherland were styled Lords of Cataibh (or Catti). In allusion to this the crest of the Sutherland family is a *cat-a-mountain*—the characteristic beast of the province.

So much for the population of Sutherland, many of whom formed part of the clan, bearing the same name. The chiefs of the clan are descended from Freskin, the progenitor of the Murrays. Freskin's eldest son, William de Moravia, became (*vide* remarks about the Clan Murray) the ancestor of the Murrays ; while from a younger son, Hugh, were derived the old Earls of Sutherland. Hugh Freskin received from King William the Lion the southern portion of Caithness after the insurrections of Harold, Earl of Orkney and Caithness, in 1196 and 1197.

William, 3rd Earl, signed the Letter to the Pope 1320. Kenneth, 4th Earl, was one of the leaders of the Scottish army at Halidon Hill, 1333. William, 5th Earl, was father of Robert, 6th Earl, and Kenneth Sutherland of Drumoy, ancestor of the House of Forse. John, 8th Earl, became insane 1494, but had two legitimate children, John, 9th Earl, who suffered from his father's malady, and dying 1514 was succeeded by his sister Elisabeth, Countess of Sutherland, who married

Adam Gordon, second son of the 2nd Earl of Huntly, who in her right became, in Scots law, Earl of Sutherland. The Gordon earls did not take the name of Sutherland, and accordingly, as Sir Æneas Macpherson points out, remained cadets of the House of Huntly. George, 15th Earl, proposed to take the name of Sutherland, but was taken bound by the 1st Duke of Gordon to use the surname of Gordon only. William, 16th Earl, however, did so, and was duly recognised as Chief of the Sutherland Clan. He supported George II. and was almost captured by the Jacobites. William, 17th Earl, left an only daughter, Elisabeth, who, after a celebrated litigation, was in 1771 declared Countess of Sutherland. She married George Granville Leveson-Gower, Marquis of Stafford, who in 1833 was created Duke of Sutherland. The Duke's consort, however, chose to be known as " the Duchess-Countess of Sutherland."

His descendant, the present Countess of Sutherland, is now chief of the clan. Her seat is Dunrobin Castle.

The dormant title of Lord Duffus was derived from the second brother (Nicol) of the Earl of Sutherland, who fell at Halidon Hill in 1333. He got the lands of Torboll from his brother, the Earl, and by marriage with Jean, heiress of Reginald Cheyne, acquired the lands of Duffus. Nicol's descendant was raised to the peerage by King Charles II. in 1650, as Lord Duffus.

URQUHART

This clan, though a small one, is of great antiquity. A late traditional connection with the Clans Mackay and Forbes seems to be quite unsubstantiated. They derive their surname from the lands of Urquhart on the south side of the Cromarty Firth opposite Dingwall.

Logan states that "there are records of the Urquharts, who were chiefs of the name, from the year 1306, when we find William Urquhart of Cromartie sheriff of the county, which office was afterwards made heritable in the family." This William married a daughter of the Earl of Ross. The family estates were later greatly increased by marriages with powerful neighbouring families. Adam, son of William de Urquhart, received from Earl William the lands of Inchrory in 1338 ; and Alexander Urquhart of Cromartie was Sheriff in 1364 as appears from a charter by David II. In 1436 a subsequent sheriff, William Urquhart of Cromartie, was husband of an Isobel Forbes (probably the origin of the connection between the clans) ; and in 1487 a subsequent William Urquhart of Cromartie had licence to build the castle upon the mote of Cromartie. For about half a century the Urquharts, as vassals of the Earldom of Ross, were connected with the Lordship of the Isles.

Sir Thomas Urquhart of Cromarty, chief of the clan during the reigns of Kings Charles I. and II., distinguished himself greatly in the service of his sovereigns, with the consequence that he suffered much loss in property and money. Sir Thomas expired in a fit of joyous laughter upon hearing of the restoration of King Charles II. Sir Thomas was succeeded by his brother, and that brother by a cousin, in whose time Cromarty, which had become much embarrassed by the troubles during the war between King and Parliament, was sold to the MacKenzies, afterwards Earls of Cromarty.

The direct line of the Urquharts ended in 1741, when the representation of the family devolved upon the Urquharts of Meldrum. The Meldrum estates were obtained by that branch of the clan through the marriage of John Urquhart of Craigfintry, Tutor of Cromarty, with Elizabeth Seton, heiress of Meldrum.

In Inverness-shire, Ross-shire, and Morayshire there are parishes of the name of Urquhart.

"The Brahan Seer" (*Coinneach Odhar :* see App. XI) made the following prediction with regard to the "land-grasping" Urquharts of Cromarty, viz. : "That, extensive though their possessions in the Black Isle now are, the day will come—and it is close at hand—when they will not own twenty acres in the district."

Like many of the Seer's other predictions, this one was fulfilled, though at the time it was uttered nothing seemed more improbable ; for the Urquharts, at that time, possessed the estates of Kinbeachie, Braelangwell, Newhall, and Monteagle. These large possessions were, however, later reduced to a small piece of Braelangwell.

The chiefship remained dormant until 1958, when Wilkins F. Urquhart heirmale of Braelangwell (New Orleans, U.S.A.) was by Lyon Court adjudged heirmale and chief as *Urquhart of that Ilk.* He has recovered the ancestral Urquhart fortress of Castlecraig, near Cromarty—a picturesque ruin.

CLAN AND FAMILY HISTORY

Those who wish to study in detail the history of their race, will in many cases find succinct pedigrees of Chiefs and Chieftains in *Burke's Peerage and Baronetage* and *Burke's Landed Gentry* (new editions published every three years or so, and available in most libraries). In Margaret Stuart's *Scottish Family History* (1928) will be found an index of all Clan and family histories issued down to that time, whilst an introduction thereto by Lord Lyon Balfour Paul indicates how to compile your own family tree and history.

Get to *know* the history of your clan—and learn the moral of good and bad actions, the consequences of economic mistakes, and the course of policies which have contributed to its "weil and standing" in successive ages.

VIII

The Septs of the Highland Clans [1]

THIS chapter must be regarded as a rather wonderful effort of imagination. Since Highland nomenclature was, until the eighteenth century, rather in the nature " Iain mac Donald, mac Alistair mac Lachlan," the question of which " clan " Iain ultimately belonged to becomes none too clear. He and his uncles—and their descendants—stand a fair chance of being " attached " to quite different clans, depending on the generation in which they happened to fix a surname. Of course, collateral information may often settle the matter. Apart from such, the matter is one of guess-work.

The very word " sept " is delusive, and no serious attention can now be attached to Skene's theories about " septs " as non-genealogical branches. Sometimes they might be—sometimes not. Professor Cosmo Innes uses the term " sept " as a noun indicating the " whole descendants of " a branch eponymous, as distinct from the main " family " descending from him, *i.e.* as the " stem family " of a " branch " and the distinct branch families off that branch stem. A sept is thus a " house within a house," denoting the branch of a line which is itself a main clan stem, also an unaffiliated in-taken tribe.

CLAN BUCHANAN SEPTS

(1) *Colman, MacCalman, etc. ; Dove, Dow, Murchison, MacMurchie, etc. ; Ruskin.*—The ancestor of the MacCalmans or MacColmans (Dove's sons) was Colman, third son of the 7th Chief of Buchanan.

---

[1] The names grouped under each number are those which are either synonymous or affiliated ones. For example : MacCalman, anglicised Dove, Dow, etc., with names such as Murchison, Ruskin, etc., which are derived from the same stock. It is hoped that the arrangement above indicated may facilitate reference to cognate surnames. Wherever and whenever it has been possible a detailed account of septs in their relation to their clan has been given. In many cases, however, such an account is an impossibility, as only the bare fact of the sept's connection with the parent clan is on record, without the why and wherefore of the connection.

Surnames denoting colour are common to several clans. Clerical names, such as Mac-a'-Chlerich (Mac-Clery), MacNiven, Mac-an-Deoir (Dewar), etc., are also found in more than one clan's list of septs. In the same manner, such names as Leeche or Leitch (meaning doctor or surgeon) and Smith or Gow are the property of several clans.

For further remarks on Highland surnames see Chapter XI.

One of Colman's descendants, named Murcho, migrated to Kintail, hence the names Murchison, MacMurchie, etc. Some of Murcho's descendants were known by the name of *Mac-a'-Mhaighstir* ; whence Masterton, MacMaster, etc., owing, it has been suggested, to their progenitor being a minister, a Master of Arts (M.A.). Another family of the MacCalmans settled at Glen Lonan in Argyllshire. At Bonawe, on Loch Etive, there was an iron-smelting furnace as well as a tannery from a very early date. The MacCalmans supplied the tannery with bark, and, from the nature of their occupation, acquired the appellation of *Na Rùsgain*—the Ruskins—from *rùsg* (peel or bark). The names Murchie, MacMurchie, and Murchison, as well as the name of Murphy, are found in Arran and in Kintyre. They are variations of "Murchad," but do not seem to have any connection with the MacCalman Murchisons of Clan Buchanan. Dove and Dow are but anglicised forms of Calman, and were adopted by MacCalmans who had emigrated to the Lowlands.

(2) *Donleavy, Mackinlay, etc.*—There appears more than ordinary confusion regarding the clan origin of the name " Mackinlay," and the various forms in which it is found (Donleavy, Finlay, Findlay, Finlayson, Macinally, Mackinley, etc.).

The Lennox Mackinlays or Macinallys descended from Finlay, a son of Buchanan of Drumikill. The Mackinleys and Irish MacGinleys, as well as Donleavys (*Mac-don-Leavy*) appear also to have derived their origin from the Buchanan Mackinlays.

(3) *Gilbertson, MacGilbert, etc.*—Descendants of Buchanan of Arduill.

(4) *Harperson, MacChruiter, etc.*—Descendants of one of the harpers to the Chief of Buchanan. Hence the names MacChruiter, etc., from *cruit*, a harp or *clàrsach*.

(5) *Lennie, Lenny.*—Descendants of Buchanan of Lenny.

(6) *MacAslan, MacAuselan, etc.*—Names synonymous with Buchanan, which is a territorial one. The early chiefs of Buchanan were known as MacAnselan, MacCausland, etc., in allusion to their descent from Anselan, progenitor of the family. In the reign of David II., Maurice Macausland, dominus or laird of Buchanan, witnessed a charter by Donald, Earl of Lennox, to Finlay Campsy, of a part of the lands of Campsy. The MacAuslans, however, kept a distinct identity under their own chief, *The Baron Macauslan* (in the Baronage of Argyll and the Isles), and *not* as a sept of the Clan Buchanan.

(7) *MacMaurice.*—One family are descendants of an illegitimate son, Maurice, of 2nd Chief of Buchanan, while a second branch derive their descent from Maurice, an illegitimate son of the 4th Chief of Clan Buchanan.

(8) *MacWattie, Watson, etc.*—The MacWatties are descended from Walter, son of Buchanan, of Lenny. Watson, Watt, etc., are anglicised forms of the name, but these are *Forbes* septs.

(9) *Spittal, Spittel.*—Descendants of Buchanan of Spittel. In the reign of King James V. Walter Buchanan of Spittel is designated brother-german to George Buchanan of that Ilk.

(10) *Yule, Yuill, etc.*—Descendants of a son of Buchanan of Drumikill, who was born on Yule-day.

(11) *MacAldonich.*—Descendants of one of the Buchanans of Lenny, whose Christian name was Muldonich.

(12) *MacAndeoir, MacIndeoir, MacIndoe.*—Descendants of a Buchanan, who migrated to Argyll, when the daughter of Walter, Chief of Buchanan, married Campbell of Ardkinglass, in the reign of James III. As there was no other of the same name in the locality in which Buchanan settled, his posterity were termed the MacAndeoirs, or sons of the sojourner or pilgrim, from the Gaelic *deoradh,* an alien.

(13) *MacCormack.*—In the list (made by Alexander Stewart of Invernahyle, and is still preserved in the Achnacone branch) of killed and wounded followers of Stewart of Appin at Culloden we find five MacCormacks or Buchanans mentioned as " killed," and one as " wounded."

(14) *MacGreusich.*—Are descended from one of the first MacAndeoir whose profession was that of a cordiner, hence his name.

(15) *MacNuyer.*—A family of the MacAndeoirs, who settled on Lochgoilside, were named MacNuyer of Evan Glass, or Gray Hugh's race. The name is now frequently rendered Weir.

(16) *Risk.*—A cadet of Drumikill was born upon the Risks of Drymen, and hence received the name of Risk, which was perpetuated by his descendants.

CLAN CAMERON SEPTS

(1) *Clark, Clarke, etc. ; Mac-a'-Chlerich, MacClery, etc.*—Clark and similar names are but anglicised versions of the Gaelic *Mac-a'-Chlerich,* son of the cleric. The sept is of ecclesiastical origin, as the name denotes. The Mac-a'-Chlerichs or Clerks, as well as the MacPhails, are classified by Buchanan of Auchmar, the historian, as Cameron septs. These septs are, however, also claimed by the Clan Chattan as septs of the latter clan.

(2) *Kennedy, MacUalrig, etc.*—The progenitor of the Kennedys or MacUalrigs or MacWalricks of Lochaber was Ualrig Kennedy of the family of Dunure, in Ayrshire. This Ualrig was involved in some fatal affray, and fled from justice to the wilds of Lochaber during the sixteenth century. His descendants became followers of Clan Cameron, and, later, some of the MacWalricks attached themselves to Mac-Donnell of Keppoch. The name Kennedy is an old one. It appears in Ayr and Galloway as early as 1222. John MacKennedy was Captain of the clan or family of Muintircasduff in the reign of King David II.

L.*

Kennedy is the family name of the Marquis of Ailsa (Earl of Cassilis). The Lochaber Kennedys had a very handsome family tartan reproduced in MacIan's well-known work, and also in D. W. Stewart's *Old and Rare Scottish Tartans.*

(3) *MacGillonie, MacOnie.*—" MacGillonie " was the appellation of the Camerons of Strone, one of the three principal branches of the clan. The name is evidently from the Gaelic *Mac-Gill'-an-fhàidh,* son of the servant of the prophet.

(4) *MacPhail, etc.; Paul.*—MacPhail is one of the septs already alluded to as officially declared a branch of the Clan Chattan. Paul is but an anglicised rendering of the same name. There is also a Mackay sept named MacPhail or Polson, which has no connection with the MacPhails of Lochaber.

(5) *MacMartin, Martin.*—" MacMartin " was the appellation of the Camerons of Letterfinlay, one of the three principal branches of the clan.

(6) *MacSorley, Sorley.*—The MacSorleys of Glen Nevis formed one of the three principal branches of Clan Cameron.

(7) *Chalmers.*—Buchanan of Auchmar states :

> The Camerons contend that the surname of Chalmers is descended of a cadet of their surname, who, having gone into the French service, assumed the name of Camerarius, or Chalmers, for that of Cameron, as more agreeable to the language of that country, . . . another of that name having returned to Scotland was ancestor of the Chalmerses of the shire of Aberdeen and other parts of this kingdom.

(8) *MacIldowie* is derived from the appellation *MacDhòmhnuil duibh,* from *Dòmhnull Dubh,* head of the clan in 1429. In the " Rentaill of the Lordschippe of Huntly " made in 1600 (*Spalding Club Misc. IV.*), appear " Allone Camerone MacOuildowy," and in *Moysie's Memoirs,* " Allane MacKildowie."

(9) *Taylor.*—This sept claim to be descendants of a Clan Cameron warrior named *Taillear dubh na tuaighe* (black tailor of the axe), who lived in the seventeenth century. The progenitor of this sept was a natural son of Ewen Cameron, the 14th of Lochiel, by a daughter of the Chief of MacDougall. Lochiel acknowledged the paternity of the child. He had the boy nursed by a tailor's wife at Lundavra. The boy became a famous warrior, skilled in the wielding of the Lochaber axe, and so came to be known as *An Taillear dubh na tuaighe.* Professor Malcolm Taylor (*Celtic Magazine,* September 1884), remarks that

> In Cowal a group of families, *Mac-an-tàillear*—later, Taylor—by name have always regarded themselves as his (the *tàillear dubh's*) descendants. . . . These Cowal people were wont to regard themselves as Camerons of the Camerons, and to designate themselves, down to the closing years of last (*i.e.* eighteenth) century, as *Clann an Tàillear Dhuibh Chamronach.*

CLAN CAMPBELL OF ARGYLL SEPTS

(1) *Burns, Burnes.*—The Lord Lyon's patent of arms to the family of Burnes of Montrose traces the family's descent from Walter Campbell, the proprietor of a small estate named Burnhouse, near Taynuilt, in Argyllshire, who fled to Kincardineshire during the civil wars of the seventeenth century. There, for purposes of concealment, Campbell assumed the name of Burnhouse in place of his own. This was subsequently modified into Burness, Burnes, and Burns.

(2) *Connochie, MacConnochy, etc.*—The MacConnochies are descendants of Campbell of Inverawe, on Loch Etive, the progenitor of whom was Duncan Campbell, eldest son of Sir Neil Campbell of Lochow by his second wife (a daughter of Sir John Cameron of Lochiel). The eldest son of that marriage (Duncan) obtained a grant of Inverawe and Cruachan from King David II. in 1330. In the Roll of the Clans of 1587 appears the name of " M'Condoquhy of Inneraw."

(3) *Denoon, Denune.*—This sept derives its name from the lands of Dunoon, on the Firth of Clyde. In a charter relating to the monastery of Paisley in 1294 appears Sir Arthur de Denoon. Among the Scots barons, who in 1296 swore fealty to King Edward I. of England, were Sir Arthur de Denune as well as Sir Guy (supposed to be Sir Arthur's brother).

(4) *MacPhedran.*—The name of a small Argyllshire sept, whose ancestor, Dominic MacFederan, was, by the 1st Lord Campbell of Lochow, granted the lands of Port Sonochan on Loch Awe, along with the office of " porter and hereditary *ferrier* " (*i.e.* " Ferryman").

(5) *Macglasrich.*—The Macglasrichs are descendants of a race of pipers, who belonged to the sept of the MacIver Campbells, and who came from the parish of Glassary. These MacIvers migrated to Lochaber, where they became hereditary pipers to the MacDonnells of Keppoch. They assumed the name of Macglasrich, in allusion to the district whence they hailed. The last of these hereditary pipers played at Culloden, and shortly afterwards the family emigrated to Prince Edward Island. The stand of pipes which was used at Culloden is said to be in the possession of one of the descendants of the Keppoch piper, who is resident in Prince Edward Island.

(6) *MacIsaacs.*—These are offshoots of a sept of the MacDonalds of Clanranald, bearing the same name. One of them migrated to the territory of the Campbells of Craignish in the early part of the sixteenth century. On 20th January 1544 John MacIsaac was appointed Sergeant and Mair of Craignish. In a bond of manrent, at Barrichbean 8th April 1592, in favour of Ronald Campbell of Barrichbean, representative of the old Campbells of Craignish, there appear among the " native men of Craignish," as signatories, " Malcolme Moir Makesaig, Donald Bane Makesaig, Duncane Makesaig, and Gilcallum Makesaig his sonnes."

A sept of MacKessocks hail from the shores of the Moray Firth. They are supposed to be the descendants of one of the same name, who accompanied Colin, Earl of Argyll, who married the widow of the Regent Moray, and who had, therefore, much influence in the above district between 1572 and 1583.

(7) *MacIver, MacIvor, MacUre, Ure, Iverach.*—The progenitor of this sept was Ivor, son of Duncan, Lord of Lochow, in the time of Malcolm IV. The original possessions of the MacIvers were Lergach-onzie and Asknish, with certain lands in Cowal. It appears that, several centuries ago, the MacIvers were a separate clan under their own chief. In 1361, Iver MacIver of Lergachonie was Chief of the MacIvers, and, in 1564, another Iver was chief. Still another Iver was chief, in 1685, when he was forfeited for supporting Archibald, 9th Earl of Argyll, in his rebellion. After the Revolution of 1688, Archibald, 10th Earl of Argyll, gave the estates, which had belonged to Iver, to Iver's son, Duncan, but on condition that Duncan and his heirs of the family of MacIver should bear the name and arms of Campbell. The MacIvers held various positions of trust under the Argyll Campbells, among others that of hereditary keepers of Inverary Castle. During the Rising of " the '45," when the Campbells of Argyll espoused the Hanoverian cause, the MacIvers of Asknish went out for Prince Charles under the banner of MacDonnell of Keppoch. At Culloden they were drawn up as a separate body with officers of their own, as they were desirous of being placed in a position where there was no chance of their being opposed to the Argyll militia, who had the same colours, and who wore the same sett of tartan (*see* MacVicars, page 337).

A colony of MacIvers were found in Wester-Ross during the thirteenth century. They became followers of MacKenzie of Seaforth. They were known as *Siol Mhic-Iamhair*, and appear to have settled in the neighbourhood of Loch Broom. The principal family seems to have been that of Leckmelme. The name is common in Lewis. At the census of 1861 there were 1,072 persons of the name in Lewis, chiefly in the Tolsta and Back districts of the parish of Stornoway. The name is from the Norse " Ivarr."

A further offshoot from the MacIvers took place between 1575 and 1585, when a colony of MacIvers, known as " MacIver Buey," settled in Caithness. They there became noted for their feuds with the Gunns. In 1633 we find William, Chieftain of the Caithness MacIvers, involved in a dispute with Lord Berriedale, son of the Earl of Caithness, when MacIver invoked the assistance of Lord Lorn, giving as his reason that he belonged to the same clan as his lordship, and that he was a Campbell.

Robert MacUre, the first of this family, born in 1589, was son lawful to Charles MacUre alias MacIver Campbell of Ballachyle. These MacIver Campbells appear to have settled in Glasgow, where the transmogrification of the name, MacIver, to MacUre appears to have taken place.

(8) *MacTavish, Thompson, etc.*—The MacTavishes, Tawessons, Thompsons, etc., are said to derive their origin from *Taus Coir*, an illegitimate son of one of the Lords of Lochow, who lived in the days of King Alexander II. Henry White (" Fionn ") said :

Many of the Argyllshire MacTavishes now make Thomsons of them selves, while others are known as Tawesons. The surnames, MacLehose and MacLaws, are regarded as corrupted forms of *Mac-Gille-Thomais*— son of the gille or servant of Thomas. There was a strong colony of MacTavishes in Strathglass at an early period.

But these repudiate dependency on Clan Campbell, and MacTavish of Dunardrie is chief of that clan, whilst Thomson of that Ilk on the Border is regarded as a remotely connected or indeterminate connection of the MacTavishes.

(9) *Bannatyne.*—The Bannatynes or MacAmelynes derive their origin from an old Bute family, whose seat was at Kames Castle, Bute, where they seem to have had their residence since the thirteenth century. The name Bannatynes is still perpetuated in the village named Port Bannatyne. In a charter dated 1489, out of seventy-eight feuars in Bute eleven bore the name Bannatyne. The Bannatynes were not of Campbell stock, but became followers of them in 1538. In a bond 10th May 1547, the Chief of the MacAmelynes and Sir John Stuart, ancestor of the Marquis of Bute, engaged to stand by and support each other against all persons except the King and the Earl of Argyll ; this latter reservation being made in order to permit the Chief of the Bannatynes to fulfil the conditions of a bond of manrent, dated 14th April 1538, which he had given to the Earl of Argyll. In the year 1475 King James III. granted to Robert of Bannachtyne, the son of Ninian Bannachtyne of Camys, certain lands in Bute. In 1491 Ninian Stewart, Sheriff of Bute, gave seisin to Alexander Bannatyne in the lands of Kerrylamont.

(10) *MacGibbon*.[1]—This sept hailed from the neighbourhood of Glendaruel. The superiority of their lands was, about 1508, made over to Colin, Earl of Argyll.

(11) *MacKellar.*—The name appears to be derived from the Latin " Hilarius." As far back as 1470 the MacKellars owned Ardare, in Glassary. Duncan MacKellar of Trochan signs a bond of manrent, as witness, at Ardchattan, 27th January 1519 ; and on 25th May 1520 Duncan MacKellar of Ardare is witness to another.

(12) *MacOran.*—This was the name assumed by one of the Campbells of Melfort, who got into trouble and fled to Menteith, where he was befriended by the Earl of Menteith, who about the middle of the seventeenth century bestowed upon Campbell the farm of Inchannoch.

(13) *MacOwen* was the name of the family who were the sennachies to the Campbells of Argyll.

(14) *MacNichol.*—" According to the Red Book of Argyle, they

[1] *Vide* Appendix V.

(the MacNichols) spring from a younger son of that house, and were entirely distinct from the MacNichols or MacRiculs of Ross-shire. The head of the Lochawe MacNichols was MacNichol of Succoth in Glenurcha."—(*Vestiarium Scoticum*).

(15) *MacPhun.*—A small sept bearing this name appears to have been located in Cowal since a remote time. Of these MacPhuns, the Duke of Argyll remarks in a letter to the *Oban Times*, 18th February 1917 :

Original charters show this family as flourishing in Cowal chiefly in the parish of Kilmalaish, alias Strachur, at least as early as 1525. . . . The main branch of the MacPhuns were those designated of Invernaodan, and those called of Driep were an offshoot.

CLAN CAMPBELL OF BREADALBANE SEPTS

(1) *MacDiarmid, MacDermid.*—This sept derives its name from the progenitor of the House of Lochow, Diarmid O'Duine, the Ossianic hero and slayer of the wild boar. The MacDiarmids belong to Breadalbane and are said to be the oldest family in Glenlyon. Their ancient cemetery is Morenish churchyard near Killin.

CLAN CAMPBELL OF CAWDOR SEPTS

Caddell, Calder.—Caddell and Calder are versions of the name Cawdor. In old documents the Campbells of Cawdor are frequently described " de Cadella."

CLAN CHATTAN SEPTS

(1) *Cattanach* is, as the name signifies, one of the oldest septs of the Clan Chattan.

(2) *Keith, MacKeith.*—The Keiths are *not* of Clan Chattan but a distinct noble *Name*. Sir William Keith, Hereditary Great Marischal of Scotland, was by King James II. created Earl Marischal. Shaw's *History of the Province of Moray* says : " The MacBains, MacPhails, Catteighs are branches of the old Clan Chattan, and the Keiths are likewise said to have descended from them." In the fourteenth century one of the Keiths, by marriage with the heiress of the Cheynes of Akergill, settled near the territory of Clan Gunn. This gave rise to feuds between the Gunns and the Keiths.

> Sinclair, Sutherland, Keith, and Clan Gunn,
> Never was peace where these four were in.

The castle of Akergill, the seat of the Keiths, afterwards passed into the hands of the Earl of Caithness, then of Lord Glenorchy, from whom the estate was purchased by Dunbar of Hempriggs.

Nisbet (*System of Heraldry*) says :

The surname of Dickson as descended of one Richard Keith, said to be a son of the family of Keith Marischal, took their name from Richard (called in the south country Dick), and to show themselves descended of Keith, Earl Marischal, they carry the Chief of Keith.

Austins : D. W. Stewart (*Old and Rare Scottish Tartans*) remarks :

In 1587 . . . Alexander Ousteane, burgess of Edinburgh, as one of the cautioners for George Keith, Earl Marshall, in an action raised against him by Margaret Erskine, Lady Pitcarie.

(3) *MacPhail, MacFall, Paul, MacVail.*—All forms of " Paul." The name is of clerical origin. In the Kinrara *History of the Mac-Kintoshes* it is said that in the time of Duncan, 11th Chief (1464–1496) lived " Paul Gow good sir of Sir Andrew MacPhail the priest, of whom the Clan Phail had their beginning." The head of this sept had his residence at Inverarnie on the water of Nairn.

(4) *Tarrill.*—Clan Tarrill are believed to hail from Ross where in 1449 Thomas Tarrill occupied Skibo. The Tarrills settled in Petty under Mackintosh. Their burial ground was at Dalarossie.

(5) *Elder.*—Mentioned by Logan (*Scottish Gael*) as a Clan Chattan sept. On page 353 will be found an extract from a letter regarding the Highlanders, written in 1543 to King Henry VIII. of England by John Elder.

(6) *Dallas, Doles.*—Is derived from the Barony of Dallas in Moray. William of Doleys, knight, witnessed Hugh Herock's gift of Daldeleyth to the Holy Trinity of Elgin in 1286. Dallas of Cantray followed the banner of Mackintosh.

CLAN COLQUHOUN SEPTS

(1) *Cowan* and *MacCowan* are names assumed by the Colquhouns in the Lowlands. Buchanan of Auchmar mentions Cowan of Corstoun in Fife as the principal family of the name. *Mac-a-chounich* was the name assumed by some Colquhouns who migrated to Lorn and Appin. Cowan and MacCowan are names of ecclesiastical origin, from St. Comgan a brother of St. Kentigerna (*see* Clan MacDougall).

(2) *Kilpatrick, Kirkpatrick.*—This seems a debateable sept. It is disputed by the Clan Colquhoun Society, that the above names are Colquhoun septs. However, the fact remains that the ancestor of the Colquhouns, before they became possessors of the property by whose name they are now known was Humphrey Kilpatrick or Kirkpatrick, in whose favour Malduin, Earl of Lennox, granted the charter of the lands of Colquhoun in the reign of King Alexander II.

CLAN CUMMING SEPTS

(1) *Buchan.*—The Buchans consider themselves a *clan* not a sept. They are the old " tribe of the land " of the province of Buchan, and since the Comyns, on marrying the heiress, did not take her name and arms, the tribe continued as a clan under their own chief. They wear (and claim) the " old " so-called " Comyn " tartan (D. C. Stewart, *Setts of the Scottish Tartans*, No. 34) as distinct from the regular Cumming setts. In 1830 the family and name of Buchan were received in Lyon Court as descendants of the ancient Celtic Earls of Buchan prior to the marriage of the heiress to Comyn, and Buchan of Auchmacoy in Aberdeenshire, as being the Chief of the name of Buchan. The family has held that estate (part of the old earldom lands) from the dawn of history, and tradition says that the Buchans, unlike the Comyns, were loyal to the Bruce, and therefore allowed to retain their patrimony.

(2) *Macniven, Niven.*—The Macnivens of Breachachie were a sept of the Cummings of Badenoch, who were almost annihilated by their neighbours the Macphersons, as the result of a clan feud. The name Macniven is from *Gille-naomh* or *Naoimhein*—servant of the saint.

CLAN DAVIDSON SEPTS

All the names under this head are, in their various forms, modifications of the original clan name (Clan Dài or Kay).

CLAN DRUMMOND SEPTS

(1) *Macgrowther, Macgruder, Macgruther.*—*Vide* Clan Gregor Septs.

(2) *MacRobbie.*—In the days of James IV., MacRobbies inhabited Balloch, near Crieff, and, though a sept of the Clan Donnachie, appear to have followed the Drummonds of whom they were tenants. Allied with the Drummonds, the MacRobbies signally defeated the Murrays at the Battle of Knock Mary. In consideration of the help rendered by the MacRobbies to the Drummonds, the latter granted them an aisle in Muthil Church for the burial of their slain.

CLAN FARQUHARSON SEPTS

(1) *Coutts.*—The earliest notice of the bearers of this name appear to be that of the proprietors of a small estate in Cromar called Auchtercoul, now Wester Coull. In the Invercauld papers the Couttses are named as dependents of the Farquharsons.

(2) *Finlay, Mackinlay, etc.*—(a) Descendants of *Findla Mór* (Farquharson of Braemar), sixteenth century, and (b) Finlaysons or *MacFhionnlaighs* of Lochalsh and Kintail.

(3) *Hardy, Machardy, MacCardney, etc.*—The Machardies of Strathdon followed the banner of Mackintosh, while those of Braemar were dependents of the Farquharsons. The Machardies appear to have been in great favour with the Earls of Mar. MacCardney is but another form of Machardy. Invercauld was acquired by the Farquharsons through marriage with the heiress of Machardy of Invercauld.

(4) *Farquhar, MacFarquhar, MacEarachar, etc.*, are but other forms of the name Farquharson or *MacEarachair*, the race of Fearchar, the founder of the clan.

(5) *MacCaig ;* (6) *Greusach ;* (7) *Lyon ;* (8) *Reoch*, are all mentioned by MacIan (*Costumes of the Clans*) as septs of Clan Farquharson.

(6) *Brebner.*—There are a number of small families of this name in North-East Scotland.

CLAN FERGUSON SEPTS

(1) *Fergus and MacFergus* are but other forms of Ferguson or Fergusson.

(2) *MacKerras, MacKersey,* are forms of the name Ferguson (*MacFhearghuis*) which are found in Kintyre.

(3) *Ferries.*—" In more than one case the names of early ministers of the Scottish Church have been handed down alternately as ' Ferries ' or ' Ferguson '."—*Records of the Clan Ferguson.*

(4) *MacAdie.*—" Balmacruchie Fergusons, and those who left Strathardle and settled in the vale of Athole under Dunfallandie, were always known as MacAdies (Clan Aid)."—*Ibid.*

CLAN FORBES SEPTS

(1) The *Bannermans* were hereditary standard-bearers of the city of Aberdeen. The Bannermans intermarried largely with the Forbeses, whose followers they became.

(2) *Fordyce* is an Aberdeenshire name, and is said to be a corruption of the name Forbes.

(3) *Michie.*—The name Michie appears for the first time about 1530 in Morayshire. Thence the Michies spread into Strathdon, in Aberdeenshire. In the latter district they acquired considerable influence through their intermarriages with the Forbeses, whose followers they became.

(4) *Watt.*—Many of this name hail from the Aberdeenshire Highlands (Strathdon, Cromar, Glenbucket, Glenesk, and Glenisla). The great bulk of the Watts, however, appear to have remained on the Forbes's lands, especially in the parish of Innernochty, Strathdon, and to have been intimately connected with the Forbes Clan. Macouat, MacQuattie, MacWatt, MacWattie, Walters, and Watson are all varieties of the name Watt.

CLAN FRASER SEPTS

(1) *Frissell or Frizell.*—The chiefs of Clan Fraser were of Norman origin, their original name having been " de Frisell." Simon, Lord Lovat, one of the victims of " the '45," entered into a formal league of amity with the French Marquis de la Frezeliere, the representative of a noble family of great antiquity in Touraine, named Frereau de la Frezeliere. This record acknowledged the relationship between the Frasers and the Frezelieres, and declared an alliance between them. The deed was executed on the one part by the Marquis de la Frezeliere, the Duc de Luxembourg, the Duc de Chatillon, and the Prince de Tingrie ; while on the other side the subscribers were Lord Lovat, his brother John Fraser with George Henry Fraser, Major of the Irish Regiment of Bourke in the French service.

We find the name Frisell in fifteenth-, sixteenth-, and seventeenth-century charters.

(2) *MacShimis, MacKimmie, Simpson, etc.*—Simon has always been a favourite Fraser name. It was that of the founder of the old Frasers of Lovat, and the head of the clan was known by the appellation of " MacShimi," or the son of Simon. The names are modifications of " Simon's son."

(3) *Tweedie.*—Before the Frasers became clan chiefs in the north, they were important landholders in Tweeddale, in the south of Scotland. The Tweedies are believed to be offshoots of the Frasers of Tweeddale.

(4) *MacGruer.*—The MacGruers were hereditary standard-bearers to the chiefs of Clan Fraser.

CLAN GORDON SEPTS

(1) *Adam, Adie, Edie.*—Adam, as being the name of the founder of the clan, has always been a favourite one with the Gordons, in the same manner as Simon is a favourite name with the Frasers. Adie and Edie are diminutives. MacAdies are claimed by the Fergusons.

(2) *Huntly.*—A place name derived from the place from which the Chief of the Gordons (the Marquis of Huntly) takes his title.

(3) *Todd.*

CLAN GRAHAM (OF MENTEITH) SEPTS

(1) *Allardice.*—The male line of the Grahams of Menteith terminated in 1694 on the death without issue of William, 2nd Earl of Airth and Menteith. The heir of line, however, was the earl's eldest sister who had married Sir John Allardice of Allardice by whose descendants the dignities have long been claimed.

(2) *Menteith, Monteith,* are place names derived from the district from which the Grahams, Earls of Menteith, took their title.

(3) *MacGrime.*—This is also believed to be a Graham sept. One of the witnesses to the Blackmail Contract of 1741 was James Mac-Grime, who signs in company of other dependents of the Menteith Grahams.

(4) *Bontein, etc.*—The Bonteins are a family of antiquity. The Bonteins of Ardoch have been most intimately connected with the Grahams of Gartmore (a branch of the Grahams of Menteith) by marriage and otherwise. " Bontein " was the form of name adopted by Sir James Bontein of Balglas in 1782. " Nicolas Buntyng, son and heir of John Buntyng of Ardoch," was among the witnesses to a charter at Edinburgh, 2nd August 1452, which granted to Alexander Conyngham of Kilmaurs the lands of Kilmaurs etc.

A charter by King James VI., 24th February 1603, granted James Buntene of Succoth in right of his wife Margaret Smollet, the lands of Kirktoun and Clerkhill in Dunbartonshire. In the famous Black Mail Contract for " keeping watch on the borders of the Highlands " (1741) Robert Bontein of Mildovan is the first signatory. He was the nephew of Graham of Gartmore, and was married to the daughter and heiress of Bontein of Balglass.

There are Buntens of Dunalastair in Perthshire, and Buntines of Torbrex in Stirlingshire as well as Buntains at Inverary. The lands between the Gareloch and Loch Lomond granted by King Robert III. in 1398 to Finlay Buntyn, were still in the possession of his descendant, the late R. Bontine Cunningham Graham of Gartmore, the celebrated Scottish Nationalist leader.

(5) *MacGilvernock.*—Sir John Graham, second son of the 1st Earl of Menteith, married a daughter of Campbell of Barbreck. By her he had two sons. From the elder son descended the Grahams of Gartmore and Gallingad ; while, from the younger came the family of the MacGilvernocks. This sept, therefore, branched off from the Grahams of Menteith about the year 1500. The name " MacIlvernoch " also appeared in North Knapdale in 1751, in the Valuation Roll of Argyll. The meaning of the name is *gillie* or servant of St. Mernock—that is St. Ernan or Ferreolus. Donald MacIlvermoik was servitor to the sub-dean of the Isles in 1678.

CLAN GRANT SEPTS

(1) *MacGilroy, MacIlroy, Gilroy.*—These names appear to be derived from that of MacGilderoy or Gilleroy, otherwise known as *Seumas an Tuim* Grant, a famous outlaw who lived in the early part of the seventeenth century. He was the youngest son of John Roy Grant of Carron.

(2) *MacKerron, MacKiaran.*—Said to be of Clan Grant.

CLAN GUNN SEPTS

The majority of the septs of the Clan Gunn are descendants of George Gunn, " the Crowner " (or Coroner of Caithness), who flourished during the fifteenth century, and of his son James. The " Crowner " was also known as *Fear a' Bhraistich mhóir*, on account of the great brooch which he wore as the badge of his office of coroner. From James, the son of the coroner, was derived the patronymic of *Mac-Sheumais-Chataich* (or the MacJames or Jameson of Caithness).

(1) *Jameson, MacKeamish, etc.*—All forms of the name " son of James," derived from James, the son of the Crowner, and Chief of Clan Gunn, above referred to.

(2) *Johnson, MacIan, etc.*—From another son, John, who was slain by the Keiths, are descended the MacIans or Johnsons of Caithness.

(3) The *Hendersons* of the north trace their descent to yet another of the numerous sons of the Crowner, named Henry.

(4) *Robson, MacRob, etc.*—Another son of the Crowner, named Robert, who was slain by the Keiths along with his father, was progenitor of the Robsons. Sir Robert Gordon remarks :

John Robson, chieftain of the Clangun in Catteness, did now of late, the yeir of God 1618, mak his refuge of Southerland, having fallen out with the Earle of Catteness and Macky ; so that this whole surname doth for the present depend altogether upon the house of Southerland.

(5) *Wilson* (of Caithness and Sutherland).—The progenitor of the Wilsons of Caithness was William, another son of the Crowner. The " Clan Gunn Wilsons " are quite distinct from the East Coast Wilsons, who belong to the Innes Clan and have different arms.

(6) The *Williamsons* are descended from a William, son of a later chief.

(7) *Georgeson.*—Quotation from a receipt, 21st November 1623, in Sinclair's book on the Gunns, viz. :

I, Alexander Gunn, alias Georgeson, in Altbraggach, for myself and Christian Gunn, my spouse, eldest lawful daughter of the late John Gunn, alias Robson, in Dunrobin, grant that I have received from the Right Honourable and Worshipful Sir Robert Gordon, Knight Baronet, and Alexander Gunn, alias Jameson, 8 head of old kye, 7 young kye, 4 great mares, and two followers left to the said Christian Gunn by the said John Gunn, her father.

(8) *Gaunson* is another form of " Gunn's son."

(9) *Manson* is a Gunn offshoot, and means the son of Magnus.

(10) *Swanson*, or " Sweyn's son," is a sept said to be descended from Sweyn, a noted Freswick pirate, brother of the first Gunn, who settled in Caithness.

(11) *Nelson.*—The Nelsons (sons of Neil) have no connection with the McNeills of the West Coast.

(12) *Sandison*, another form of " Alexander's son."

(13) *MacCorkill.*—In the feuds between Clan Gunn and the Mackays, the MacCorkills (or *Mac-Thor-Ketils*) are mentioned as belonging to the former.

(14) *Enrick, Eanrig, Eanruig.*—These Caithness names are equated with " Henderson."

CLAN INNES SEPTS

(1) *Innie, Oynie, Yunie* are local Speyside varieties of the name, *Dinnes* (de Innes) being also noticed.

(2) *Ennis*, though also the name of a Cornish family, various Ennises in Britain and U.S.A., including members of the Ennis Association, Utah, claim to be of Clan Innes.

(3) *McTary* and some Middletons appear in record as " *alias* Innes.''

(4) *Marnoch*, as descendants of the tribe of Aberkerder, rank as a Clan Innes sept.

(5) *Mitchell.*—Following the intermarriage with Innes of Rora, the Mitchell-Inneses, of Stow, and Mitchells of the East and North-East, have been reckoned a Clan Innes sept.

(6) *Reidfurd.*—The Inneses of Turtory and Sinnahard were " *alias* Reidfurd,'' a name which relates to the Innes lands of Reidfuird in Aberkerder.

(7) *Wilson*, of around Banffshire and Edinburgh, bear arms as from Wilson of Littlefield, and as early Innes-Aberkerder cadets, they are quite distinct from the Gunn-Wilsons of Caithness and the far North.

(8) *McInnes*, of around lower Speyside, are *alias* Inneses, bore badge as off Innes of Blairton, and were held by Sir Jas. Balfour Paul as an off-shoot of the Moray Inneses.

(9) *Mavor* of Mavorston, which immediately adjoins Innes, bore arms indicative of cadency off Innes.

CLAN LAMONT OR LAMOND SEPTS

(1) *Lambie, Lamondson, MacClymont, Meikleham, etc.*, are all supposed to be forms of Lamont. MacIlwhom is a corruption of Meikleham.

(2) *Landers, Lamb* are descendants of the Chief of Lamont, who lived about the time of King Robert III.

(3) *Bourdon, Burdon.*—The Bourdons trace their descent to a younger son of one of the chiefs of Lamont, who married the heiress of Bourdon of Feddals, whose name he adopted. Nisbet, *System of Heraldry*, says :

By a letter under the subscription of Lamont of that Ilk, of the date the 4th of November 1699, given to the Herald Office by James Bourdon

of Feddel, as descended of a younger son of Lamont, in the reign of King
Robert III. . . . The name of Bourdon is much older than the reign of
Robert III., for I find William de Bourdon a witness in a charter of
King Alexander III. to Hugh Abernethy, and in several other charters
as old.

(4) *Lucas, Luke, MacLucas.*—All offshoots of the Lamonts.

(5) *MacPatrick, Patrick.*—The above are aliases of the Lamonts,
descended from Baron MacPatrick, who was the ancestor of the
Lamonts of Cowstone.

(6) *Black, MacAlduie, MacGilledow, etc.*—All the above are
synonymous names, and are traceable to Blacks, who were originally
Lamonts. William Black, the novelist, traced his descent from a
branch of Clan Lamont, driven from the Lamont country under a
leader called the " black priest." The exiles settled at Carnwath, in
Lanarkshire, and became in process of time noted covenanters. A declaration by Sir James Lamont in 1661 (now among the papers of the
chief) states that those descended from the names " MacIlzegowie,
MacGilligowie, MacGilledow, and MacIlzegui," are offshoots from the
Lamonts of Castletoune of Braemar. Another branch of Blacks are
descended from the Blacks of Garvie, Glendaruel, of the parish of
Kilmodan. The head of the sept was known as *Mac-'Ille-Dhuibh-mor-
na-Garbha.*

(7) *Toward, Towart.*—Lamont aliases, derived from the Castle of
Toward, in Cowal, formerly the seat of the chief of the clan.

(8) *Brown and White.*—Names of Lamonts who changed their
names in troublous times.

(9) *Sorley, MacSorley.*—Aliases adopted by Lamonts named
Samuel.

(10) *Turner.*—The MacTournors or Turners of Luss are descendants
of a fugitive Lamont who settled on Lochlomondside, and engaged in
the business of a turner.

CLAN LESLIE SEPTS

(1) *Lang*, of whom there was a number in the Northern section of
the Garioch, have been erroneously described as a Leslie sept ; they are
by their arms shown to be a branch of Clan MacDuff, the ancient
house of Fife.

(2) *More.*—The Leslies obtained the larger part of their Fife lands
in the thirteenth century, by their chief's marriage with a More heiress.

CLAN LINDSAY SEPTS

(1) *Crawford* is a name which is intimately associated with the Lindsay clan, whose chief bears the title of Earl of Crawford.

(2) *Deuchar.*—The Deuchars of Angus are a very old family, and held the estate of Deuchar in the parish of Ferne under the superiority, first, of the de Montealts or Mowatts, and subsequently the Lindsays. In 1379 Sir Alexander Lindsay of Glenesk granted a charter of the lands to William Deuhqwhyr of that Ilk, as heir to his father.

CLAN MACALISTER SEPT

Alexander.—Alexander, Lord of Lochaber (forfeited 1431) had two sons, Angus, ancestor of MacAlister of Loup, Argyll, and Alexander MacAlister who obtained the lands of Menstrie, Clackmannanshire, in feu from the family of Argyll. He was ancestor of the Earls of Stirling, a title at present dormant. Alexander MacAlister's posterity took the surname of Alexander from the Christian name of their progenitor. Sir William Alexander, 7th Baron of Menstrie, was in 1633 created Earl of Stirling, and was the organiser of the colonisation of Nova Scotia.

CLAN MACALPIN SEPT

Alpin is but an abbreviation of MacAlpin.

CLAN MACAULAY SEPTS

MacPhedron, MacPheidiran.—By both Buchanan the historian, and MacIan, the MacPheidirans are alluded to as a sept of the Mac-Aulays of Ardincaple, Dunbartonshire.

CLAN MACARTHUR SEPTS

Arthur, MacArtair, MacArter.—All forms of the same name.

CLAN MACBEAN SEPTS

See remarks under the heading of the Clan MacBean, page 231.

SEPTS OF THE CLAN DONALD

A detailed account of all the septs and dependents of this powerful clan is all but an impossibility. Not only did the Clan Donald territory extend from the north of North Uist to the south of Kintyre in Scotland, but it also embraced part of Antrim in Ireland. Indeed the present

Earl of Antrim is a cadet of Clan Donald. Especially in Kintyre we find MacDonald dependents with an unmistakably Irish ring of name. These are probably descendants of Irish from Antrim, who left Ireland to follow the fortunes of the MacDonalds. During Prince Charles's wanderings, one of the disguises the Royal fugitive adopted was that of Betty Burke, an Irish servant-maid of Flora MacDonald. Burkes are found in Kintyre to this day.

(1) *Isles.*—In almost all of their early charters the MacDonalds of the Isles were designated " de Insulis," and later " Isles," and we find the chiefs and chieftains of the clan actually signing themselves as " Isles," without the prefix of MacDonald. About the sixteenth century it became the practice to use the territorial title " of the Isles " for the Mac Donalds of the Isles. Hence the former name is now assumed to be as a MacDonald sept one.

(2) *Colson, MacCall, MacColl.*—Though the MacColls were of the Clan Donald race, they were for centuries devoted followers of the Stewarts of Appin. So intimate was the connection between the Stewarts and MacColls, that it was the custom, when a chieftain of the House of Achnacone died, that he should be buried in a spot where a MacColl lay on either side of him. During the Rising of " the '45," when the Stewarts of Appin were out for the Stewarts, the casualties of the Appin regiment amounted to ninety-one killed and sixty-five wounded. Out of the above total, the killed among those of the name of Stewart amounted to twenty-two and the wounded to twenty-five. The balance, viz., sixty-nine killed and forty wounded, consisted of eighteen other names, out of which the MacColls furnished as their quota, eighteen killed and fifteen wounded.

(3) *Connall, Connell, Donald, Donaldson, Donillson, Donnelson, Kinnell, MacDaniell, MacKinnell, MacWhannell, Whannell.*—These names are all identical with MacDonald, for in old days the name of the clan was spelt in a variety of forms, and these are found in old charters and documents. The forms " Donillson," " Donnelson," and " MacDaniell," as well as " Donaldson," are in old charters of MacDonalds settled in the north of Ireland.

(4) *Gorrie, MacGorrie, MacGorry, MacRorie, MacRory, MacRuer, MacRurie, MacRury, Rorison.*—These are forms of the name MacRorie and MacGorrie, having been important subdivisions of Clan Donald. It is said that those of the surname Gorrie or Gowrie are descendants of some MacDonalds or MacGorries, who settled some four centuries ago in the neighbourhood of Logie Almond, Perthshire, but it is far more likely these derive their name from the district of Gowrie.

(5) *Hewison, MacHutcheon, MacQuistan, etc.*—These (forms of the name Huisdean or Hugh), are derived from the name of Hugh, progenitor of the MacDonalds of Sleate, known as Clan Huisdean.

(6) *Gilbride, MacBride, MacIlvride.*—Gillebride was the father of Somerled. Martin (*Description of the Western Isles of Scotland*), when describing the tombs of Iona, says : " In the west end are the

tombs of Gilbrid and Paul Sporran, antient Tribes of the Mack-Donalds."

(7) *MacElheran.*—This appears to be a modification of MacGille-Ciaran (or Kieran), descendant of the disciple of St. Ciaran or Kieran. This seventh-century saint dwelt in a cave near modern Campbeltown.

(8) *Darroch, MacIlreach, MacIlriach, MacIlleriach, Reoch, Riach, MacIlwraith, MacRaith, MacIlrevie, Revie, Bowie.*—These names are all synonyms for *Mac-Gille-Riabhaich* (son of the brindled or freckled man). The Mac-Gille-Riabhaichs were hereditary bards to the Clan Donald North, and in virtue of their office held the land of Baile Mhic Gille-Riabhich in Trotternish. MacIlwraith and MacRaith are forms of the name met with in Ayr and Galloway. MacIlrevie and Revie are the forms in Kintyre. Reoch and Riach are abbreviations adopted by those who settled in the Lowlands. Darroch is a form of the name found in Islay and Jura. In 1794 the Lord Lyon King of Arms officially registered " Duncan Darroch of Gourock, chief of that ancient name, the patronymic of which is M'Iliriach," showing that *Iliriach* was the progenitor of this sept. The bye-name of Darrach, so says tradition, was applied to one of the MacIlleriachs, who, in some clan foray, distinguished himself by the good use he made of an oak staff. The *History of Clan Donald* says :

> In more modern times the island of Jura is the nursery of the Darroch race, and there the name is most frequently met with in its special form of Darroch. In this form it is supposed to be a corruption of the words Dath Riabhach or brindled colour, to distinguish the sept of the Dath Buidhe or yellow colour, there being many of the Clan Bowie also among the inhabitants of Jura.

The Darrochs are officially reckoned a clan of their own.

(9) *MacCook, MacCuag.*—Different forms of the same name peculiar to Arran. MacCuag is not to be confounded with MacCaig or MacCuaig (*Mac-Cuthaig*) the latter being a Hebridean sept name.

(10) *MacCooish, MacCuish.*—Are common in the north of Skye, and said to be from *MacUis.*

(11) *MacCash, MacCaishe.*—In a commission of justiciary, 22nd October 1614, relating to the capture of the Castle of Dunnyvaig, in Islay, we find Hector McCaishe one of the followers of Angus Oig McConeill (MacDonald) of Dunnyvaig.

(12) *MacGoun, MacGown, etc.*, were the Smiths of the MacDonalds.

(13) *MacEachran, MacEachern.*—Alex. MacBain translates this " Horse-lord." Skene's *Highlands of Scotland* :

> The Campbells of Craignish are said to be descended from Dogall, an illegitimate son of one of the ancestors of the Campbells in the twelfth century, but the universal tradition of the country is that their old name was MacEachern, and that they were of the same race with the MacDonalds. This is partly confirmed by their arms being the galley of the Isles, from the mast of which hangs a shield containing the gironé of eight pieces or

and sable of the Campbells, and still more by the manuscript of 1450, which contains a genealogy of the MacEacherns, deducing them, not from the Campbells, but from a certain Nicol MacMurdoch in the twelfth century. When the MacGillevrays and Macinnes of Morvern and Ardgour were dispersed and broken up, we find that many of their septs, especially the Macinnes, although not residing on any of the Craignish properties, acknowledged that family as their chief. Accordingly, as the Mac-Gillevrays and Macinnes were two branches of the same clan, and separate from each other, as early as the twelfth century ; and as the MacEacherns are certainly of the same race, while Murdoch, the first of the clan, is exactly contemporary with Murdoch, the father of Gillebride, the ancestor of the Siol Gillevray, there seems little doubt that the Siol Eachern and the Macinnes were the same clan. . . . There was an old family of Mac-Eachern of Kingerloch, and as Kingerloch marches with Ardgour, the old property of the Macinnes, it strongly confirms the hypothesis that the two clans were of the same race.

MacEachern has long been an Islay name. It is said some Mac-Eacherns, on going to the Lowlands, adopted the name of Cochrane.

(14) *Galbraith.*—The Galbraiths of Macrihanish and Drumore are descendants of the Galbraiths, formerly of Gigha, whose progenitor was a Galbraith of Baldernock. This Baldernock fled from the Lennox with Lord James Stewart, son of Murdoch, Duke of Albany, during the reign of King James I. The Galbraiths, known as *Chlann a' Bhreatannaich* (children of the Britons), held the island of Gigha from the Clan Donald till after 1590.

(15) *MacLardie, MacLaverty, etc.*—These are Arran names, though holders of some of them passed over to Kintyre. Among the papers of the Campbells of Cawdor (who formerly owned Islay), in a deed of remission 1524, appears Johannes Makgillecrist Maklafferdich. The Maclaverties were the " speakers," *i.e.* Heralds of the Lords of the Isles, and were accordingly settled in the neighbourhood of their Court at Islay.

(16) *MacSorley, Sorley.*—Synonymous with MacSomhairle or MacSomerled, Somerled being the name of the progenitor of Clan Donald.

(17) *MacSporran, Sporran, Purcell.*—The MacSporrans were heredi-tary purse-bearers to the Lords of the Isles. Martin (*Description of the Western Islands of Scotland*), *s.v.* Iona, says : " In the west end are the tombs of Gilbrid and Paul Sporran, antient Tribes of the Mack-Donalds." Some of the sept who went to the south changed their names to Purcell.

(18) *MacCodrum.*—A north Uist name, from the Norse Guttormr, and one borne by a celebrated bard, Iain MacCodrum.

(19) *MacCrain.*—Is a Jura name. One of these families was noted for the longevity of its members. In the burying-ground of Ardlussa, in Jura, there is a grave-stone inscribed : " *Mary MacCrain*, Died in 1856, Aged 128. Descendant of Gillouir MacCrain, who kept a Hundred

and Eighty Christmases in His own house, and who died in the reign of Charles I."

(20) *MacCuithein* is a MacDonald name, which is found in Skye.

(21) *MacElfrish*, believed to be a corruption of *Mac-Gille-Bhris*, son of the servant of Saint Bricins or Brice.

(22) *Beton, MacBeth, etc.*—Much confusion exists regarding these names and the forms in which they appear (Beath, Beaton, Beton, Bethune, MacBeth, MacBeath, MacBheath, MacVeagh, MacVey, etc.). These septs may be classed in three categories, viz. :

(*a*) The MacBeths or MacBeaths of the old province of Moray, who are allied to the MacBains or MacBeans of Clan Chattan (*see* Clan MacBain, page 231).

(*b*) The old hereditary physicians to the Lords of the Isles. Tradition says that these physicians were descendants of Beath, who came from Ireland in the train of the widow O'Neill, who married Angus Og of the Isles, friend of Robert the Bruce.

In 1379 Prince Alexander Stewart granted to Ferchard " Leiche " (physician), one of the Islay MacBeths, and the King's physician the lands of Melness and Hope, in Sutherland ; and in 1386 King Robert II. further granted to this Ferchard, who became physician to the Mackays of Farr, all the islands from Rhu Stoer, in Assynt, to Armadale Head, in Farr. In 1511 Donald MacDonachy MacCorrachie, " descendit frae Farquhar Leiche," resigned Melness, Hope, and all his lands in Strathnaver to Mackay. The *Old Statistical Account of the Parish of Eddrachillis* states that this Ferchard was Ferchard Beton a native of Islay.

At one time MacBeaths appear to have owned the island of Ghruaidh, on Loch Maree, the small island on Loch Tolly, and the Dun, at the east end of the Big Sand.

Fergus MacBheth or MacBheatha was Chancellor of the Isles in 1448. In 1609, on the fall of the MacDonalds of Islay, Fergus Mac-Baithe of Balinaby, in Islay, received from James VI. a charter of lands in Islay as " principalis medici intra bondas Insularum." In 1628 John, son of Fergus, succeeded to his father's estates, but resigned them to the Thane of Cawdor in 1629, when MacBeaths seem to have left Islay. However, their skill as physicians was held in as high estimation by the Campbells, the new possessors of Islay, as they were by the old MacDonalds, for among the accounts of the Campbells of Islay in 1638 appear the two following items, viz. :

Item waireit one Doctor Beatoune for his charges in goeing to Illa and coming from Illa home againe to Edinburgh, £178, 8s.

Item givin to Doctor Arnot, Doctor Beatoune, and Doctor Sybbald in ane consultatioun concerneing the Laird his seiknes in Edinburgh, £71, 6s.

A branch of the Islay MacBeths or Beatons settled at Pennycross, in Mull, as physicians to MacLean of Duart, and were also known as MacVeaghs or MacVeys.

(c) The third family of Betons (those of Skye) claimed descent from Archibald Bethune of Pittochy or Capeldray, in Fife, fifth son of John Bethune, 5th Laird of Balfour. One of that family was so renowned as a physician that, in the fifteenth century, he was invited to settle and practise in Argyll. He later received an invitation from the MacDonalds and MacLeods of Skye to settle there. The conditions offered were, that in return for his medical services Bethune should receive, rent free, as much land as he desired. Bethune was to promise that one of his posterity should be educated as a physician so long as any of the family remained in Skye and had a bent for the practice of medicine.

The MacBeths of Angus appear as physicians a century earlier. King David II. granted a charter :

Thome de Rate, terrarum de Balgillachy, in vic. de Forfar, quas Gilbertus medicus, frater et heres Ecctoris medici, apud Monros, 23 Octob. a.d. 1369, coram pluribus regni resignavit ; tenend. sicut quondam Patricius MacBeth pater dicti Gilberti infeodatus fuit in eisdem.

(23) *MacLairish.*—One of the oldest sept names, and described in old genealogies as descended from " Conn of the Hundred Battles," an ancestor of the MacDonalds.

(24) *Martin.*—Those of this sept appear to have originally come from Kilmuir, in Skye, where they were neighbours of the Macqueens.

(25) *MacMurchie, MacMurdoch, Murchison, MacMurphy, Murphy. etc.*—These names are forms of *MacMhurchaidh*, a sept of Clan Donald, found principally in Arran and Kintyre. The above are not to be confounded with the MacMurrichs or MacVurrichs, septs of Clan Ranald and of the MacPhersons. The bond by Ranald MacJames vic Donald, surrendering the isle and fortalice of Illanlochgorme, 24th January 1615, is witnessed by Johne MacMurchie, doctour of medecine, who is further described in the deed itself as " John Oig MacMurquhie, leiche in Islay."

(26) *Drain, MacDrain, O'Drain, Train.*

(27) *Mac O'Shannaig, Mac Shannachan, O'Shaig, O'Shannon, Shannon.*

(28) *Hawthorn, May, O'May.*

(29) *MacKiggan.*—This name is found in North Uist, and also in Harris and Lewis, and appears to be a Clan Donald one.

(30) *Paton.*—This name is equated with *Beaton.*

SEPTS OF THE MACDONALDS OF CLAN RANALD

(1) *MacAllan, etc.*—The Clan Ranald MacDonalds are frequently referred to in old charters as Allanson and their chief as MacAllan. The modern designation of *Mac-'ic-Ailein* dates from the time of a dispute as to who was *MacAllan.* Many cadets of this family came to be known as Allansons and MacAllans when they went to the

Lowlands. A parallel instance is that of some of the Clan Donald MacDonalds assuming the name of *Isles*.

(2) *MacVurrich, MacBurie, Currie, etc.*—These are modifications of the name *MacVurrich*. The MacVurrichs were hereditary bards and sennachies to Clan Ranald. A family of MacVurrichs were also hereditary standard-bearers to the MacGregors of Glen Lyon.

(3) *MacEachan, MacGeachie, MacKechnie, etc.*—All forms of the same name, viz., " Hector " or *Eachann*. This sept of the MacDonalds is descended from Hector (Gaelic *Eachann*), second son of Roderick MacDonald, 3rd of Moydart and Clanranald. Stephen James Mac-Donald, Duke of Tarentum, Napoleon's celebrated marshal, was son of Neil MacEachainn of South Uist, who was out with Prince Charles in 1745, and afterwards accompanied the royal fugitive to France.

(4) *MacIsaac, MacKessock, MacKissock.*—The MacIsaacs are a Clan Ranald sept, and appear to have hailed from Moidart. They are still found in Uist, an old Clan Ranald possession. A family of MacIsaacs entered the service of Campbell of Craignish.

(5) *MacVarish.*—Also a Moidart name, signifying " son of Maurice." John MacWarish from Drumley, Moidart, was one of the surgeons of Prince Charles's army during " the '45."

SEPTS OF THE MACDONALDS (MACIANS) OF ARDNAMURCHAN

MacIans, Johnson, etc.—These names and the Johnsons of Coll are offshoots of the MacIans or MacDonalds of Ardnamurchan.

SEPTS OF THE MACDONALDS (MACIANS) OF GLENCOE

(1) *MacIan, Johnson, etc.*, are all patronymics derived from the founder of the clan, John Og, younger son of Angus, Lord of the Isles, who lived in the fourteenth century.

(2) *Henderson, MacHenry.*—The Hendersons or Clann Eanruig are said to have been in Glencoe for about 300 years before King Robert the Bruce granted to Angus of the Isles lordship over Glencoe and Appin westward to Duror Bridge, in acknowledgement of the support given to Bruce by him and his clansmen at the Battle of Bannockburn. The Hendersons claim descent from Henry Mor, son of Nectan, who came to Kinlochleven in 1011, where his descendants dwelt at Callart, till, during the fifteenth century, they were dispossessed by a sept of the Camerons. In 1314, when John, the founder of the Clan MacIan of Glencoe, arrived there to take possession of his claim, Dugald Henderson or MacHenry was the principal individual in the district. Henderson's daughter became John MacDonald's wife, and from that union descended the Clan Abrach or MacIans of Glencoe.

SEPTS OF THE MACDONELLS OF GLENGARRY

Alexander, Sanderson.—The name Alexander is derived from the designation of *Mac-'ic-Alastair*, or son of Alexander, which was borne by the chief of the clan in allusion to the name of his progenitor. Sanderson is but a Lowland rendering of MacAlexander.

SEPTS OF THE MACDONELLS OF KEPPOCH

(1) *Ronald, Ronaldson.*—These names are derived from that of the designation of the chief of the clan, *Mac-'ic-Raonaill*, in reference to Ronald, the progenitor of the clan.

(2) *MacGilp, MacKillop, etc.*—The MacKillops of Brae-Lochaber were followers of the MacDonnells of Keppoch. A family of MacKillops were standard-bearers to the Campbells of Dunstaffnage.

(3) *MacGillivantic* or *Mac-Gille-Mhanntaich* (the Son of the Stutterer). John, Chief of Keppoch, who succeeded his father Donald about 1498, made himself so obnoxious to his clan by delivering up to Mackintosh as steward of Lochaber one of his clan named MacGillivantic (who, having committed some crime had fled to his chief for protection), that the clan deposed their chief, and elected Donald Glas, the cousin-german of the deposed chief, to be their head.

(4) *MacGlasrich.*—*Vide* under Clan Campbell of Argyll Septs.

CLAN MACDOUGALL SEPTS

(1) *Dougall, MacDowall, MacCoul, etc.*—Are all forms of the name MacDougall. Nisbet (*System of Heraldry*) speaks of the MacDowalls or MacDougalls or MacCouls, "ancient Lords of Lorn." The priory of Ardchattan is said to have been founded about the middle of the thirteenth century by Duncan Makoul or MacDougall. In 1515 Archibald Campbell of Kilmichel gave a bond of manrent to Sir John Campbell of Calder. A young MacCoul or MacDougall was one of the few survivors of the massacre perpetrated by General Leslie after the fall of Dunaverty Castle. MacDowall is the form most frequently met with in Galloway.

(2) *MacDulothe.*—In the list of the clans which were to be raised for King James in 1704, appears "MacDulothes 500 men." Dr. Stewart ("Nether Lochaber"), in a footnote to Logan's *Scottish Gael*, suggests that these MacDulothes were MacDougalls.

(3) *MacCulloch, MacLulich.*—In a MS. "History of the Mac-Donalds," written in the reign of King Charles II. (Gregory collection), Reginald, son of Somerled, is said to have married

MacRandel's daughter, or as some say to a sister of Thomas Randel, Earl of Murray. . . . He had by her Angus, of whom are descended . . . the MacLulichs, who are now called in the low country Pitullichs.

(Actually he married a daughter of Angus, Earl of Moray).   This would point to the MacCullochs or MacLulichs being dependents of the MacDonalds. However, they appear to be identified (as far as the Argyllshire MacCullochs are concerned) with the MacDougall clan. R. C. MacLagan in *Scottish Myths* says :

The lands surrounding Balamhaodan forming the district of Benderloch are alleged to have belonged to Modan, who was the head, so runs the tradition, of the Clan MacLullich, as recorded in the local phrase, *Clann Lulich o thulaich Mhaodain*, the MacLullichs from the hill of Maodan.

Many of the MacCullochs hail from the neighbourhood of Oban and the island of Kerrara. MacCulloch of Colgin, near Oban was regarded as the head of the Argyllshire MacCullochs.

(4) *Conacher, MacConacher.*—The MacConachers or Conachers of Lorn were of Irish origin, and proprietors of Ardorain. Many were buried in Kilbride churchyard, near Oban. They were for centuries hereditary physicians to the MacDougalls of Lorn. The name appears to have been originally O'Conacher, but the Irish " O " was discarded for the Scottish " Mac." In the sixteenth century Dr. John Mac-Conacher was sent from Argyll to Rome, to attend the family of the third son of the Earl of Argyll. In 1560 John MacConacher Stronchor-mich, paid to my Lord forty merks " for ye grassum for office of churgeon." Some of the Gaelic MSS. of the MacConachers are in the Advocates' Library, Edinburgh. One of them bears the inscription of " Leabhar Eoin MacConcobar."

(5) *MacLucas, MacLugash.*—Have been used interchangeably with MacDougall by those bearing them. They are found in Mull and the West Highlands, in some instances corrupted into " Douglas."

(6) *MacKichan.*—This is another form of *Mac-Fhitheachain* or " Son of the Raven " (the raven being the clan bird of the MacDougalls), and quite another origin from the Clan Ranald MacEachan (meaning " the Son of Hector "). When Lorn was devastated by General Leslie, a MacKichan hid the clan charter chest and kept it safely until the return of peace. The chief was so grateful for MacKichan's faithfulness, that he declared that as long as there was a MacDougall at Dunolly, there would be a MacKichan on the estate.

(7) *Cowan, MacCowan.*—Cowans were numerous in Kilchoan (Kill Cowan), Nether Lorn. A family of Cowans or MacCowans followed MacDougall of Reyran, from whom they held lands about Loch Seil.

(8) *MacGougan* or *MacGugan.*—There is some doubt whether the bearers of this name are a sept of the MacDougalls. According to Thos. Robson, *British Herald*, 1830, after describing the coat of arms of the MacGougans, it says the armorial motto is : *Vincere vel mori*, which is also stated in the same book as being that of the MacDowalls, McNeills, and MacNellys. The surname MacGougan is more frequently met with in the McNeill district of Argyll than in Lorn, the seat of the MacDougalls.

(9) *MacNamell.*—A sept of MacDougalls in Jura is known as MacNamells (*Mac-na-Maoile*, Sons of the Bald), and are regarded as outside the real MacDougalls—those of Dunolly.

(10) *Livingstone, Livingston.*—A family of Livingstons were hereditary standard-bearers to the MacDougalls of Lorn.

(11) *Carmichael.*—A family of Carmichaels were hereditary henchmen to the same chiefs.

CLAN MACDUFF SEPTS

(1) *Duff.*—MacDuff means " Son of Duff."

(2) *Fife, Fyfe.*—The name Fife is referred to by both Nisbet (*System of Heraldry*) and Shaw, the historian of the province of Moray, as a MacDuff sept name. The former writer speaks of the Fifes as descended from a younger son of MacDuff, Earl of Fife, and he adds, " from which title they have the name and carry the arms."

(3) *Wemyss.*—Descent of the family of Wemyss from MacDuff, Earl of Fife, was officially declared by Lyon in 1757. Their seat is the historic castle of Wemyss on the rocky shore of Fife. There are extant charters granted to persons named Wemyss by King Robert the Bruce. Charters are granted by the Earl of Fife, as holding his earldom " by the grace of God," and not as a fief from the King of Scots.

Though Wemyss is often classed as a sept of MacDuff, in actual fact the Lord Lyon in 1757 held Wemyss of Wemyss (then the Countess of Wemyss) to be Chief of the race of MacDuff.

Anderson (in *Surnames*) says :

The Scottish surname of Wemyss, from the Gaelic word *uamh*, a cave, was derived from lands now forming the parish of that name in Fifeshire, appropriately so called from the number of caves in the rocks on the seashore there. These lands are said to have been part of the estate of MacDuff, the famous mormaor, or, as Shakespeare styles him, " Thane " of Fife, in the reign of Malcolm Canmore. Gillimichael, the third in descent from MacDuff, gave to his second son, Hugo, with other lands, the lands of Wemyss. Hugo's son, also named Hugo, had a son, John, who was the first to assume, or rather had conferred upon him, the name of Wemyss, being styled *Iain mor nan Uamh*, or Great John of the Caves. He was the ancestor of the Earl of Wemyss.

Buchanan of Auchmar adds :

We have an account of Duncan MacDuff, who was Thane of Fife, in the reign of MacBeath, and is recorded to have been a person of great power and authority, and chief of a numerous and potent surname, as the many considerable branches descended of that family near those times clearly evince, such as the Wemysses, Mackintoshes, and Shaws, with divers others. The first of these derive their surname from caves, with which the sea-coasts of those lands first acquired by the progenitor of that

PLATE XII.

GEORGE, 5TH DUKE OF GORDON, G.C.B., ETC.

In full Highland Dress as worn at the beginning of the nineteenth century.

PLATE XIII.

[Scottish Notes and Queries.

JAMES, 14TH EARL OF CAITHNESS, 1855–1883.

Showing mid-nineteenth-century Full Dress.

name abounds ; caves being termed in Irish Uaimh, which can be no other way rendered in English than Wemyss. The surname of Hume has also the same etymology, all the difference being that the H, or note of aspiration, is more plainly pronounced in the last of these surnames.

(4) *Spence, Spens.*—In Nisbet's *System of Heraldry* we find the following, viz. : " Spence of Wormiston, an ancient family with us, said to be descended of the old Earls of Fife, has been in use to carry the lion of MacDuff, Earls of Fife."

CLAN MACFARLANE SEPTS

Most sept names, not specially alluded to here, are from Buchanan of Auchmar, the clan historian (*see* p. 243).

(1) *Allan, Allanson, MacAllan.*—Descendants of Allan, a younger son of one of the early chiefs of MacFarlane who settled in the north of Scotland ; alluded to by Nisbet (*System of Heraldry*) as of Kirkton, Markinch, Auchorrachan, Balengown, Lismurdie, etc.

(2) *Macause, Thomason, etc.*—Descendants of Thomas, son of the Chief of MacFarlane, in the reign of King Robert III.

(3) *MacWalter.*—Race of Walter MacFarlane of Auchinvenal.

(4) *Bartholomew, Parlane.*—The first is an anglicised, the latter a gaelicised form of MacFarlane, which means " Bartholomew's son."

(5) *Mackinlay.*—Alluded to by Buchanan of Auchmar.

(6) *Galbraith.*—The first known is Gillespick Galbrait, witness in a charter by Malduin, Earl of Lennox, to Humphry Kilpatrick, of the lands of Colquhoun. The same Earl gave a charter of Gartonbenach, in Stirlingshire, to Maurice, son of Gillespick, and in 1238 the same lands (now Baldernock), were conveyed to Arthur Galbraith, son of Maurice, with power to seize and condemn malefactors, on condition that the culprits should be hanged on the Earl's gallows.

In the mid thirteenth century Malduin, Earl of Lennox, granted to Maurice, son of Gillaspic Galbraith, and Arthur, his son, that quarter of land in Auchincloich lying next to Strochelmakessoc (Arochelmakessoc ?) in exchange for Thombothy and Letyrmolyn for a thirty-second part of the service of a man-at-arms. During the same century Malcolm, Earl of Lennox, granted to Arthur Galbraith and his heirs the quarter of Buchmonyn (Balfunning) nearest to Blarnefode, and that half-quarter of Bilgirnane nearest Cartonwene and Tyrwaldonny, for as much service in the king's foreign service as due in Scotch service. Earl Malcolm also granted to Arthur of Galbraith the liberty of making a prison, and holding a court for trial of theft and slaughter in his lands.

(7) *MacNider, MacNiter.*—Alluded to by Buchanan ; rarely met in Scotland, but found in Canada. " MacNider " means *Mac an*

M

Fhigheadair (Son of the weaver). Many whose names have been anglicised to Weaver are of Clan MacFarlane.

(8) *MacNair.*—From *Mac an oighre* (Son of the Heir). This imports the disinherition of a senior grandson.

CLAN MACFIE SEPTS

All these septs bear names which are but variations of the name Macfie. In ancient times the Clan Macfie was known as the Clan Mac-Duffie. The form of the name MacGuffie is one which is peculiar to Galloway, while MacHaffie is the form used in the north of Ireland.

CLAN MACGILLIVRAY SEPTS

The sept names under this heading are but varieties of the spelling of the name MacGillivray. In 1791, one Farquhar MacGillivour, aged eighty-two, who lived on the banks of the River Nairn, was examined in court, and in answer to a query as to what his real name was, said he was called Farquhar MacGillivour in every part of the country, and that the MacGillivours were followers of the MacGillivrays, having come at the same time from the Western Islands.

CLAN MACGREGOR SEPTS

Owing to the MacGregors having been long a " broken " clan, forbidden to use the clan name, they had resort to many surnames to conceal their identity. Not only were " by-names " of Highland origin adopted, but names of other clans were assumed, as well as names, such as Cunninghame, Ramsay, etc. The last two classes cannot be included in a list of sept names.

(1) *Gregor, Gregory, etc.*—All these names are modifications of MacGregor. In 1715, when Rob Roy was sent by the Earl of Mar to raise a body of men in Aberdeenshire from those of his own race (the Ciar Mor), who were located there by the Earl of Moray in 1624, he became acquainted with a relation of his own, Dr. James Gregory, Professor of Medicine in King's College, Aberdeen. In return for the kindness shown to him by the Professor, Rob Roy offered to take to the Highlands with him, and " make a man of him," the Professor's son, also named James, then a boy. This attention was, however, delicately declined by the lad's father. The boy, when he grew up, succeeded his father at King's College.

The Griersons of Lag, in Dumfriesshire, are descended from Gilbert, second son of Malcolm, dominus de MacGregor, who died in 1374.

(2) *MacGrowther, MacGruder, MacGruther, etc.*—Owing to being derived from a profession, " grudair " (*Anglicé*, " brewer "), they may be appropriate to several clans. The names seem, however, to be more closely connected with the MacGregors and the Drummonds than with any other clan. Some of the bearers have, when going south, anglicised their names to " Brewer," much in the same manner as Macintyres have become Wrights ; MacCalmans, Doves or Dows ; Macsporrans, Purcells, etc. The name " Macgrowther " appears in old records in many forms, such as Macgruther, Macgruder, Macgrewar, Grewar, and Gruer.

Alexander MacBain, the well-known authority on Highland names, remarks :

The malster and brewster were represented by the Gaelic names of " *brachadair* " and " *grudair* " respectively. Both were used in personal designations and surnames, but the former disappeared soon. . . . The earliest reference to the name is possibly 1447, when there was a Gillawone M'gruder at Comrie. John M'gruder, servant to Lord Drummond, gives trouble at Bocastle in 1580.

(3) *MacLiver (MacLiomhair)*.—Was the surname of Sir Colin Campbell (Lord Clyde). In deference, however, to the wishes of his maternal uncle, Colonel Campbell, through whose influence young Colin procured a commission in the army, the future Lord Clyde assumed the name of Campbell in lieu of his own name of MacLiver.

(4) *MacAdam*.—descended from Gregor MacGregor, second son of the chief, who, after the outlawry of Clan Gregor, took refuge in Galloway. John Loudoun MacAdam, the well-known improver of the public roads, member of this sept, was born in Ayr 1756.

(5) *Fletcher, MacLeister*.—The *Mac-an-leisdears*, modernised into Fletcher, etc., were arrow-makers to the MacGregors. They were the original inhabitants of the highest and most mountainous parts of Glenorchy, the lands of Achallader and Baravurich. There is a saying current in Glenorchy, *'Se Clann-an-leisdear a thog a chiad smùid a thug goil air uisge 'an Urcha* (The Fletchers were the first to raise smoke to boil water in Glenorchy). The stronghold of the Fletchers was Achallader Castle, the ruins of which are still to be seen on the shores of Loch Tulla. Shortly after " the '45 " the Fletchers of Achallader removed to Dunans, at the head of Glendaruel. They carried with them the door of the old castle of Achallader (made of pine grown in the forest of Crannich), and this door is now that of the private chapel at Dunans House. MacLeister is the form of the name which is found in Islay.

Smibert's *Clans of Scotland* says :

Occasionally Rob Roy suffered disasters, and incurred great personal danger. On one remarkable occasion he was saved by the coolness of his lieutenant, Mac-an-leister, or Fletcher, the *Little John* of his band—a fine, active fellow, of course, and celebrated as a marksman. It happened that MacGregor and his party had been surprised and dispersed by a superior force of horse and foot, and the word was given to " split and squander." Each shifted for himself, but a bold dragoon attached himself to pursuit of Rob, and, overtaking him, struck at him with his broadsword. A plate of iron in his bonnet saved MacGregor from being cut down to the teeth ; but the blow was heavy enough to bear him to the ground, crying, as he fell, " O ! Mac-an-leistear, is there naething in her ? " (*i.e.* in the gun). The trooper, at the same time, exclaiming, " D—n ye, your mother never wrought your nightcap ! " had his arm raised for a second blow, when Mac-an-leister fired, and the ball pierced the dragoon's heart.

(6) *Black, MacIlduy.*—Names assumed by the MacGregors when their own name was proscribed. The name MacIlduy is common in the south-west of Perthshire.

(7) *White, Whyte.*—Names assumed for the same reason.

(8) *MacAra, Macaree, MacNee, King.*—All supposed to be forms of *Mac-an-righ* (or ree), or King's son. Buchanan of Auchmar alludes to the MacCarras as a sept of the MacGregors in north Perthshire. Some changed their name to King.

(9) *MacChoiter.*—" Son of the Cotter," one of the MacGregor sept names mentioned by Auchmar.

(10) *MacNeish, Neish, etc.*—This small sept were all but exterminated during a feud with the Macnabs.

(11) *MacPeter, Peter.*—Assumed by MacGregors after the proscription.

(12) *Malloch.*—Alluded to in Heron's *Tour of Scotland* (1793) as MacGregors who had changed their name when the clan was proscribed. In MacLeay's *Highlanders of Scotland* the Mallochs or Mhallichs are said to be so named owing to the heavy eyebrows of their ancestor.

(13) *Leckie, Lecky.*—The name of an old Dunbartonshire family, the head of which was Leckie of Croy-Leckie. John Leckie, of Croy-Leckie and Balvie, married a daughter of MacGregor of Glengyle by his wife, Campbell of Glenfalloch. He was brother-in-law of Rob Roy whom he joined during the Rising of 1715 and was with Rob Roy at Sheriffmuir.

(14) *Mac-Conachies.*—*Sliochd Dhonnachaidh Abaraich* derive their descent and name from Duncan, 17th Chief of MacGregor by his second lady, a daughter of MacFarlane of that Ilk, by whom he had three sons, whose descendants are known by the same name, viz., the progeny of Lochaber Duncan.

(15) *Dochart.*—According to Dean Ramsay :

A good many families in and around Dunblane rejoice in the patronymic of Dochart. This name, which sounds somewhat Irish, is derived from Loch Dochart, in Argyllshire. The MacGregors, having been proscribed, were subjected to severe penalties, and a group of the clan having been hunted by their superiors, swam the stream which issues from Loch Dochart, and in gratitude to the river they afterwards assumed the family name of Dochart.

Many Docharts are, however, probably of a sept of Clan Macnab.

(16) *Comrie.*—At the time of the proscription of the clan and name of MacGregor, some of that clan settled at Comrie in Strathearn, which name was adopted by the fugitive MacGregors.

(17) *MacPetrie.*—The MacPetries of Marr are MacGregors.

CLAN MACINNES SEPTS

(1) *MacAngus, MacCainsh, MacCansh* are all forms of Macinnes or *MacAonghais.*

(2) *MacMaster.*—*Vide* what is said under the heading of the Clan Macinnes. The original possessions of the MacMasters were situated in Ardgour. The Chief of the MacMasters having given offence to the Lord of the Isles, in the fifteenth century, he sanctioned dispersion of the MacMasters by the Macleans, and the appropriation of the territory of the offending vassl by Donald, first Maclean of Ardgour. MacMaster and his son were killed at Clovullin (*Cladh a' Mhuillinn*), and the rest of the MacMasters fled across Corran Ferry to Inverlochy.

CLAN MACINTYRE SEPTS

(1) *Tyre* is an abbreviation of Macintyre.

(2) *Wright.*—Macintyre signifies " Son of the Wright " (*Mhic-an-t-saoir*).

(3) *MacTear.*—Some Scots MacTears and Irish Mac-a-tears are really Macintyres.

CLAN MACKAY SEPTS

(1) *Bain, Bayne.*—The Bains, or Baynes, are descendants of the son of Neil, brother of Angus Dubh, Chief of the Clan Mackay in the early fifteenth century. Their progenitor was John Bain or Fair. A branch of these Bains settled near Dingwall in the sixteenth century. They acquired Tulloch, afterwards the property of the Davidsons.

(2) *MacPhail, Macvail, Paul, Polson.*—All synonymous names. Paul, another descendant of Neil, the ancestor of the Bains, was the progenitor of the *Siol-Phàil* sept of the Mackays. Paul MacTyre was the name of a famous Sutherlandshire freebooter who lived in the fourteenth century, and was Lord of Strathcarron, Strathoykell, and Westray. His fortress was Dun Creich, commanding the Kyle of Sutherland. The Polsons of Creichmore were said to be descendants of this Paul or Pol. Alex. MacBain, in his notes to Skene's *Highlanders of Scotland* (2nd edition), says : " Tyre was not his father, as usually is supposed, but *Mac-tire* (meaning ' Wolf,' a common name in his day and earlier) ; the name is Paul Mac-'Ic-tire."

(3) *Neilson.*—This sept is descended from Neil MacNeill Mackay. King James I. gave him lands in Creich and Gairloch in 1430.

(4) *Williamson.*—Robert Mackay, historian of the clan, writes (in 1829) : " During the last two centuries there have been a respectable family of Williamsons of Banneskirk, in Caithness, of the *Shiol Thòmais* Mackays, descended from Thomas," brother of Neil Mackay, slain at Drimnacoub.

(5) *MacCay, MacQuey, MacQuoid.*—The name Mackay in another form. The last an anglicised rendering of *Mac-Aoidh.*

(6) *MacKee, MacKie, MacCrie.*—These forms of Mackay are found in the Hebrides and Galloway. The clan historian says :

Alexander (progenitor of the Mackays) was succeeded by his son Walter, and he by his son Martin, who was slain in Lochaber, from whom, it is supposed, the Mackies, MacGhies, and MacCries of Galloway and Ireland, and Mackays of Argyle are descended.

MacGhee/MacGhie are not " Mackays " and the old family of MacGhie of Balmaghie, which for about 600 years possessed estates in Galloway, used completely different arms from any arms of the Chief of the Mackays. They continued in possession of their lands till 1786, and presumably derived from Isle MacGhee in Ulster.

The Mackays of Argyll are frequently alluded to as MacGhees.

CLAN MACKENZIE SEPTS

(1) *Kenneth, Kennethson, MacConnach* are synonyms for MacKenzie (son of Kenneth).

(2) *MacBeolain.*—In a MS. by Dr. George MacKenzie, nephew of the 3rd Earl of Seaforth, relating to a feud between the Earl of Ross and the MacKenzies about 1267, the chief of the latter clan is said to have been joined by the MacIvers, MacAulays, MacBeolans, and Clan Tarlichs, " the ancient inhabitants of Kintail." The territory of the MacBeolains was Glenshiel and the south side of Loch Duich as far as Kylerhea.

(3) *MacKerlich* (or *Mac-Thearlaich* or Charleson) is the Clan Tarlich above referred to. The country of Clan Tarlich was Glenelchaig.

(4) *MacIver* or *MacIvor.*—*Vide* Campbell of Argyll Septs.

(5) *MacMurchie, Murchison, etc.*—*Vide* Clan Buchanan Septs.

The Murchisons were long trusted followers and standard-bearers to MacKenzie of Seaforth, and were made governors of Eilean Donan Castle. Colonel Donald Murchison of Auchtertyre, Lochalsh, commissioner to William, 5th Earl of Seaforth, was, during 1719 to 1726, the leader of the Mackenzies, Maclennans, and Macraes in their opposition to the Hanoverian Government. Of this devoted adherent of the attainted Lord Seaforth, General Wade, in his report (1724) to the Government, wrote :

The (Seaforth) Rents continue to be levied by one Donald Murchieson, a Servant of the late Earl's, who annually remits (or carries) the same to his Master in France. The Tenants when in a Condition are also said to have sent him free Gifts in proportion to their several Circumstances, but are now a year and a half in Arrears of Rent. The Receipts he gives to the Tenants are, as Deputy Factor to the Commissioners of Forfeited Estates, which pretended Power in the year 1721 he extorted from the Factor appointed by the said Commissioners to Collect those Rents for the use of the Publick, whom he attacked with above 400 Arm'd Men as he was going to enter upon the said Estate ; having with him a Body of 30 of Your Majesty's Troops. The last year this Murchison travell'd in a Public manner to Edinburgh to remit £800 to France for his Master's use, and remained there fourteen days unmolested.

Sir Roderick Impey Murchison, the distinguished geologist, was a descendant of the family.

(6) *MacVanish, MacVinish.*—A subordinate sept, dependents of the MacKenzies. Some of the MacVanishes are mentioned in 1600 as followers of the Chief of the MacKenzie clan. Dr. MacBain gives " Son of Magnus " as the probable derivation of MacVinish.

(7) *Charleson, MacThearlaich.*—Equated with Mackerlich.

CLAN MACKINNON SEPTS

(1) *MacKinny, MacKinning, MacKinven, Love.*—The first two are transmogrifications of the name Mackinnon. For the last two, Kintyre is responsible.

(2) *MacMorran.*—The Mackinnons of Mull are known as the " Clan Mhoirein " or MacMorrans, from *Moghron,* meaning " Son of the Seal."

CLAN MACKINTOSH SEPTS

(1) *McKeggie.*

(2) *MacCombie, MacOmie, MacThomas, etc.*—" The son of Thomas " or " Tommie's son." The MacCombies are descended from a younger son of the 6th Chief of Macintosh. They settled in Glen Shee some centuries ago. In the Roll of the Clans of 1587, they appear as the " Clan M'Thomas in Glenesche," the name appears again in the Roll of the Clans of 1594, as " M'Thomas in Glenesche."

(3) *Shaw.*—The chief family of this sept of the MacKintoshes were the Shaws of Rothiemurchus, descended from Shaw, son of Gilchrist, son of John, son of Angus, 6th Chief of MacKintosh. This Shaw, owing to the configuration of his front teeth was called *Corr fiach-lach.* He was granted the lands of Rothiemurchus in 1396. The seat

of the Chief of the Shaws was the beautifully situated castle of Loch-an-eilean, in the loch of that name. In 1536 Allan Shaw, 5th of Rothiemurchus, was owing to pecuniary difficulties compelled to part with the estate to Adam Gordon, reserving only his son's life-rent. The Gordons in 1573 sold the estate to the Grants to whom it now belongs. Loch-an-eilean Castle is now a ruin. The Shaws of Tordarroch are descended from Adam, second son of James Shaw, 2nd of Rothiemurchus. From the Christian name of their progenitor they bear the name of " Clan Ay " (or Clan Adam). The Laird of Tordarroch is their chief.

(4) *MacAy, MacHay.*—Some of the Tordarroch Shaws moved into Ross-shire about the beginning of the seventeenth century, settling in the neighbourhood of Tarradale. They were known as McAy and McHay but no connection with the Mackays of Sutherland.

(5) *Tosh, Toshack, Hossack.*—The Toshes or Toshachs are the oldest cadets of the family of Mackintosh, being descended from Edward, son of Shaw, 2nd Chief of Mackintosh. They settled in Perthshire, where they held lands in Monzievaird, Culcrief, Pittenzie, and Glentilt. In 1599 the Toshes, oppressed by the Drummonds and Murrays, entrusted their title deeds to Mackintosh. MacKeggie (No. 1) is supposed a form of the above names, Tosh or Toshach.

(6) *Adamson, Ayson, and Esson.*

(7) *Hardy, MacHardie, MacCardney.*—*Vide* Farquharson Septs.

James Shaw of Crathinard on Deeside married the daughter and heiress of John Machardy of Crathie.

(8) *Crerar.*—Fraser-MacKintosh (*Minor Septs of Clan Chattan*) writes :

Originally MacKintoshes it is a matter of tradition that the name took its rise in the person of a prominent member owing his safety to concealment from his foes in a manner somewhat similar to that connected with the Lobans of Drumderfit.

A letter regarding the Crerars appeared in the *Celtic Magazine*, May 1880 :

My ancestors were always called Mackintoshes in Gaelic, and my grandfather is so designated, though a Crerar, on his tombstone in the churchyard of his native glen in Perthshire. Before the Breadalbane clearances many families of the name of Crerar resided at Glenquaich and at Loch Tayside, who used to muster at the Kenmore markets arrayed in the genuine Mackintosh tartan, and wearing sprigs of boxwood in their Highland bonnets. There are many on this side of the Atlantic now calling themselves Mackintoshes who were at home known as Crerars.

(9) *Noble.*—Fraser-MacKintosh says :

This name was found chiefly in Strathnairn and Strathdearn dwelling amid the Clan Chattan. Some, particularly tenants of Raigmore, are still to be found in the parish of Moy.

(10) *McConchy*.

(11) *MacAndrew*.—*Sliochd Andrais* are supposed to have come from the West Highlands at the same time as the Macqueens of Corryborough. They took protection from Mackintosh about 1400, and settled in Connage of Petty.

(12) *McKillican*.

(13) *MacGlashan*.—Mentioned by Fraser-MacKintosh (*Minor Septs of Clan Chattan*) as dependent on Mackintosh.

(14) *Glen, Glennie*.—Kennedy's *Annals of Aberdeen*, 1399, mentions suit of Willielmus Gleny, with respect to the wool from certain lands. These lands are still called " Glennie's Parks." Glennies settled in Strathdon and Deeside appear to have followed the banner of Mackintosh.

(15) *Ritchie, Macritchie*.—An offshoot from Mackintosh of Dalmunzie, in which family Richard was a frequent name.

(16) *Macniven, Niven*.—William, Chief of Mackintosh, in the early sixteenth century married Isabel MacNiven, heiress of Dunnachtan.

(17) *Seath, Seth*.—These are said to be Shaws.

CLAN MACLACHLAN SEPTS

(1) *Lachlan, Lauchlan*.—Abbreviations of MacLachlan.

(2) *Ewan, MacEwen, etc.*—An old clan now extinct as such, derived from the same tribe as the MacLachlans and the MacNeills, viz., the Siol Gillivray. The ancient seat of the Chief of Clan Ewen was at Otter Lochfyne, in Cowal. In the twelfth century the Lamonts, MacEwens, and MacLachlans were in possession of the greater part of the district of Cowal, from Toward Point to Strachur. Lamonts were separated from MacEwens by the River Kilfinnan, and MacEwens from MacLachlans by the stream which divides the parishes of Kilfinnan and Strath Lachlan.

In 1432 Swene, son of Ewen, resigned to King James I. the Barony of Ottirinwerane in Cowale, which the King granted to him anew with remainder to Celestine Cambel, the son and heir of Duncan Cambel of Lochaw. By an indenture in the same year at the Ottir it was agreed that when Suffne M'Ewyn, Laird of Ottirinweran, should have an heir he should pay to Gillaspy Cambel, the son and heir of Duncan Cambel, Lord of Lochaw, on one day or otherwise at Gillaspy's pleasure, sixty marks Scots and twenty-five sufficient marks at the Ottirweran, Inchconnil, or Innerayra, or give him the two Larragis and the lands of Killala in the Barony of Ottir for yearly payment of half a mark, and should his heir die before he should have another, that the agreement should remain valid, and Suffne should give Gillaspy the first offer of the land if leased. In this manner the heritage of the Clan Ewen passed into the rapacious grasp of the Campbells. After their extinction as a clan the MacEwens of Cowal appear to have followed their

M*

kinsman MacLachlan of Clan Lachlan. A note to the translation of a Gaelic MS. of 1450 in *Collectanea de Rebus Albanicis* :

On a rocky point on the coast of Lochfyne, about a mile below the church of Kilfinan, is to be seen the vestige of a building called *Caisteal mhic Eoghain,* or M'Ewen's Castle. This M'Ewen was the chief of a clan and proprietor of Otter. From the genealogy this tribe seems to have been a branch of the Clan Lauchlan.

Some of the Clan Ewen, Ewing appear to have settled in Dunbartonshire under the Earl of Lennox about the fifteenth century.

A family of MacEwen were sennachies to the Campbells of Glenurchy.

(3) *Gilchrist, MacGilchrist.*—Derived from Gilchrist, the son of Dedaalan, progenitor of the MacLachlans.

CLAN MACLAINE OF LOCHBUIE SEPTS

(1) *MacFadyen, MacFadzean.*—There are still many families of MacFadyens on the Lochbuie estates. Accounts of the origin of the MacFadyens vary. One version makes them the " nativi " of that part of Mull before it came under Lochbuie. Another says the MacFadyens came from Ireland along with Murchadh Gearr, one of the early Maclaine chiefs, during the sixteenth century.

(2) *MacIlvora, MacGilvra.*—The name of an ancient family of Pennygael, in Mull, followers of the Maclaines. See obligation, 10th August 1631, Murdoch Maclaine of Lochbuie to Martine M'Ilvora, Minister at the churches of Killeane and Killenachin, regarding the payment of salary, etc., to the latter. The minister was either the head of the MacIlvoras or a near relation. These MacGilvras or MacIlvoras appear to have been an offshoot from the old Clan Gillivray, previous to that clan joining Clan Chattan.

(3) *MacCormick.*—One of this sept was the companion of Murdoch Gearr, Chief of Lochbuie, in a daring exploit against the Maclean of Duart. Lochbuie, in acknowledgement of MacCormick's help on the above occasion, had cut on the lintel above the gateway of the castle of Lochbuie the words *Biadh is deoch do MhacCormaig* (Food and Drink to MacCormick).

(4) *Patten* is equated with MacPhadden (*i.e.* MacFadzean).

CLAN MACLAREN SEPTS

(1) *Paterson, MacPatrick.*—In bonds of manrent given by the MacLarens to the Campbells of Glenurchy in 1559, and also in 1573, occur the name of " MacPatrick." Paterson is but a Lowland rendering of the same name. MacPhater and MacFeat are equated with Paterson.

(2) *MacRory* or *MacGrory* of Perth are MacLarens, according to tradition, and some of them have resumed the MacLaren surname.

(3) *Larnach* is said to be a sept of the MacLarens.

CLAN MACLEAN OF DUART SEPTS

(1) *Lean* is but an abbreviation of Maclean.

(2) *Beath, Beaton, MacBeath, MacBeth, Paton, etc.*—*Vide* Septs of Clan Donald.

(3) *Black, MacIlduy.*—The MacIlduys or Blacks inhabited the island of Gometra, off the coast of Mull. At the court held at Aros Castle in 1608 by Lord Ochiltree, the Royal Lieutenant, which was attended by the principal chiefs and gentlemen of the Isles, Neil MacIlduy appeared as one of the followers of Maclean of Duart. A good many of the Mull Blacks appear later to have migrated to the island of Lismore.

(4) *Rankin, Macrankin.*—The Rankins are said to be descendants of Cuduilligh, of Irish origin. They were anciently called " Clan Duille," but later discarded that designation for that of Clan Mhic Raing, which has been anglicised to Rankin or Rankine. The Rankins were hereditary pipers to the Macleans of Duart, and after the chiefs of Duart lost their possessions, the Rankins became pipers to the lairds of Coll. The last of the Rankin hereditary pipers emigrated to Prince Edward Island. John MacCodrum, the Uist bard, who flourished during the eighteenth century, refers to the Clan Duille as among the leading pipers of the day. When Dr. Johnson made his tour of the Hebrides with Boswell, he was entertained by Maclean of Coll, whose piper, one of the Clan Duille, played before the doctor. " The bagpiper played regularly when dinner was served, whose person and dress made a good appearance ; and he brought no disgrace upon the family of Rankine, which has long supplied to the Laird of Coll with hereditary music."

(5) *MacLergain.*—The above name is to be met with in Islay. It is believed to be of Maclean origin, and to be synonymous with *Mac-ghille-Fheargain.*

(6) *Gilzean, Gillan, Gillon.*—These are MacLeans of Dochgarroch.

CLAN MACLENNAN SEPTS

(1) *Logan.*—The Clan Maclennan are also known as the Logans, from the name of the progenitor of their clan (*vide* Clan Maclennan or Logan).

(2) *Lobban.*—MacBain's *Inverness Surnames* says :

Lobban is a Morayshire name to all intents and purposes ; a belt of a few miles along the Moray Firth holds most of them. William Lobane appears in 1564 as tenant in Drumderfit, in the Black Isle, where the family were so long tenants that the local proverb said : " As old as the Lobans of Drumderfit." It (the name Loban) seems to be from the Gaelic *lòban,* a kind of basket peat-cart or sledge, under which the " first original " of them hid—a M'Lennan he was—in terror, and escaped with the nickname as the only detriment.

CLAN MACLEOD OF HARRIS SEPTS

(1) *Beaton, Beton.—Vide* septs of Clan Donald.

(2) *Norman.*—An anglicised form of " Tormod," the MacLeods of Harris being known as the *Siol Thormaid* (or race of Norman).

(3) *MacCaig, MacCuaig.*—Derived from the Gaelic *cuthaig*, or cuckoo. The tradition with regard to the origin of the sept is, that the father of a decaying famly gave his child, in order to ensure long life to it, the name of the first living thing which he met. This happened to be a cuckoo. Hence the name *Mac-cubhaig*, or MacCuaig.

(4) *Mac-clure.*—The name of Mac-clure is derived from the Gaelic *Mac-gille-leabhair* (Son of the Servant of the Book). The Mac-clures are said to have been tutors to the MacLeods in Skye, cf. Boswell's *Tour to the Hebrides with Dr. Johnson* :

Captain Maclure, whom we found here (at the house of Macquarrie of Ulva), was of Scotch extraction, and a MacLeod, being descended of some of the MacLeods who went with Sir Norman of Bernera to the Battle of Worcester ; and after the defeat of the royalists fled to Ireland, and to conceal themselves took a different name. He told me there was a number of them about Londonderry, some of good property.

John Wilfrid Mac-clure, Tralee, says :

With regard to these Galloway Mac-clures, the authentic family tradition is that in early times this MacLeod sept came over to Ulster where the northern Irish pronounced the " d " as " r," and the name thus passed to MacLure. They left Ireland for Galloway as Mac-clures, and returned in the seventeenth century. This tradition has been handed down through a long line of long-lived successors.

(5) *Macraild, MacHarold.*—The Macrailds or MacHarolds were " nativi " of some of the earliest possessions of the *Siol Thormaid*. Leod, the progenitor of the clan, married a daughter of Macraild Armuinn, a Scandinavian knight, whose seat was where now stands the castle of Dunvegan. With his wife, Leod received the lands of Dunvegan, Minginish, Bracadale, Duirinish, Lyndale, and part of Troternish, in the Isle of Skye. There are still families of the name of Macraild living on the MacLeod estates.

(6) *Mac-crimmon.*—The Mac-crimmons were hereditary pipers to MacLeod, and in that capacity had a grant of the farm of Borrevaig, near Dunvegan. There they had a college for pipers, the most celebrated of its kind in the Highlands. Donald Ban Mac-crimmon, piper to MacLeod during the Rising of 1745, was killed during the celebrated " Rout of Moy," when MacLeod (who was on the Hanoverian side) attempted to capture Prince Charles Edward, who was the guest of Lady Mackintosh at Moy. It was Donald Ban Mac-crimmon who composed the famous lament known as *Cumha Mhic-criomain*,

or " Mac-crimmon's Lament." It is said that this was composed by Mac-crimmon shortly before he met his death, of which he had a presentiment. John Dubh Mac-crimmon was the last of the race who held the hereditary office. It is told that in 1795 he had made up his mind to emigrate to America, and that he actually got as far as Greenock. His love for his native island, however, was too strong for him, and he returned to Skye, where he died in 1822 at the age of ninety-one. Logan's *Scottish Gael*, 1831, says that a Captain Mac-crimmon " died lately in Kent at an advanced age, and the descendant of these celebrated pipers is now a respectable farmer in Kent." A monument to the Mac-crimmons has been erected in Skye.

CLAN MACLEOD OF LEWIS SEPTS

(1) *Callum, Mac-callum, Malcolmson.*—*Mac-Gille-Chaluim* is the designation borne by MacLeod of Raasay, the senior cadet of MacLeod of Lewis. It indicates their descent from Malcolm Garve, son of Malcolm, 8th Baron of Lewis. In the " Rentale of the Bishoprick of the Ilis and Abbacie of Ecolmkill " (1561) Dean Munro notes :

The Ile of Raarsay is excellent for fishing, porteining to M'Gyllychallum of Raarsay be the suord, and to the Bischop of the Iles be heritage. This same M'Gyllychallum shuld obey M'Cloyd of the Lewis.

Buchanan of Auchmar writes of Raasay :

Those of other denominations descended of that surname (MacLeod) are the MacGillechollums, the chief of which is MacGillechollum of Raarsa, a considerable island near Skye. He hath a pretty numerous clan, not only in those parts, but also in the shires of Perth and Argyll, though some in the last of these shires term themselves Mac-callums, pretending to be Campbells ; but it is generally thought these are led to do so, more by interest than by justice, there being no satisfying reason given by them of their being a different stem from those others of that name, who own themselves to be MacLeods.

Boswell's *Journal of a Tour to the Hebrides* (1773) says :

There has been an ancient league between the families of MacDonald and Rasay. Whenever the head of either family dies, his sword is given to the head of the other. The present Rasay has the late Sir James MacDonald's sword.

The name Malcolmson is but an anglicised rendering of Mac-Callum and both are of *Clan Malcolm*.

(2) *Lewis, MacLewis.*—Buchanan says MacLewises are a sept of the MacLeods, " some of which (MacLewis) are in the shire of Stirling."

(3) *MacAskill, MacCaskill.*—Information is meagre : their chief habitat was Lewis, the chiefs of which island they followed. The name is Norse.

MacCorquodale, MacCorkindale.—Are forms of " Mac Torquil."

The traditional account of the MacCorquodales makes them of even more ancient origin than the MacLeods. The name of Torquil like many in the Hebrides is of Scandinavian origin, and signifies " Thor's kettle or cauldron." " MacCorquodale of that Ilk " is the first instance in Lyon Register of the application of the honorific title " of that Ilk " to a clan chief. His motto is " Vivat Rex " (May the King Live). The Baron of Fionnt Eilean, on Loch Awe, owned at one time the whole northern shore of Loch Awe from Avich to Ard-an-aiseig. These lands are said to have been granted to Torquil the progenitor of the family, by Kenneth MacAlpin, King of the Scots, under the following circumstances. Alpin, the King of the Scots, was killed in battle and his head carried off by the Picts, who exposed it in their town of Camelon. It was, however, recovered by a soldier named Torquil, and as reward he was invested with the lands on Loch Awe side by King Kenneth, son and successor of Alpin.

There seems no suggestion that this Torquil was of the Clan Leod ; and it is evident, by both habitat and title, that the MacCorquodales *are a distinct clan*, whose chief was the Baron MacCorquodale. His arms were in 1904 confirmed to MacCorquodale of Dalchroy.

(4) *MacAulay.*—The name is not in any way connected with the MacAulays of Ardencaple, a branch of the Clan Alpin. The Lewis MacAulays had their habitat in Uig (Lewis), and derive their name from Olaf, thus Olafson or MacOlaf or MacAulay. It is recorded in the Orkneyinga Saga, that Gunni Olafson, the brother of Swein Gairsay, was expelled from the Orkneys by Earl Harald, and that he fled to the Lewis, by whose chief he was hospitably received. The traditions of the MacKenzies show that the MacAulays once had a settlement on Lochbroom. Ullapool is an old Norse name meaning " the homestead of Olaf."

Between the MacAulays and their neighbours the Morrisons feud succeeded feud. While the MacAulays were assembled at a banquet given by their chief at the place called " An Earrainn," situated between the Reef and Valtos in the parish of Uig, the whole of *Clann Mhic Gille Mhoire* or the Morrisons, accompanied by Tormoid Mor of Bernera, surrounded the building in which the unfortunate MacAulays were assembled, and slaughtered all the company save one young boy who managed to make his escape.

Lord Macaulay, the statesman, historian, and calumniator of the Highlanders, belonged to the Lewis MacAulays.

(5) *Tolmie* is derived from the Gaelic " tolm," a hillock. The name is a Skye one, and was originally Talmach or Tolmach. In the account of a clan conflict in the island of Raasay during the year 1611 between the MacLeods and the MacKenzies, mention is made of John Tolmach, near cousin to the Laird of Raasay.

(6) *MacNicol, Nicolson, etc.*—MacNicols form an independent clan whose progenitor was one Krycul or Crigul. Their first known possessions were in Coigeach, Ross-shire. About the beginning of the

fourteenth century the family of the chief became extinct in the male line. The chief's only child was a daughter, who married Torquil MacLeod of the Lews. Torquil obtained a Crown charter of the district of Assynt and other lands in the west of Ross, apparently in right of his wife. Subsequently to this the MacNicols followed the Lewis MacLeods, and the most of them removed to Skye. One of the chapels, which was attached to the religious establishment at the head of Loch Snisort, of which the ruins still remain, was named *Aiteadhlaic Mhic Neacail* or MacNicol's Aisle. The Nicolsons held the lands of Scorrybreac, Skye, as principal tenants from about the middle of the eleventh century, and were thus distinct from the MacNicols of Coigeach.

CLAN MACMILLAN SEPTS

(1) *Baxter, MacBaxter.*—The sept derived its name from one of Glenshira Macmillans happening to have slain one of the members of a neighbouring clan, who took refuge in the kitchen of Inveraray Castle. He exchanged clothes with the cook and set to work in the kitchen, kneading barley bannocks. From this his children received the designation of " Macbaxter " or Son of the Baker. Their descendants were at one time fairly numerous in Glendaruel, Cowal.

(2) *Bell.*—The name *Mac'Illemhaoil*, or Macmillan, is, in Islay, and also in Kintyre, rendered as " Bell."

(3) *Brown.*—This sept name is recognised by the Clan Macmillan.

CLAN MACNAB SEPTS

(1) *Abbot, Abbotson.*—Anglicised renderings of MacNab.

(2) *Dewar, Macandeoir.*—The Mac-an-deoirs or Dewars of Glendochart were the hereditary custodians of the *Bachuil*, crozier, or *cuigreach* of St. Fillan. This crozier is a relic of the greatest antiquity, and also bore the designation of the *Fearachd*. Hence the Mac-an-deoirs were also known as *Deòraich-na-Fearachd*. Mr. MacLagan (*Scottish Myths*) states, that in the time of King Robert the Bruce the name of Dewar was spelt as *Jore*. The crozier of St. Fillan, of which the Dewars were the hereditary custodians, is one of the most venerable of Scottish relics. It dates back to the seventh century A.D., and is only exceeded in antiquity by the famous Coronation Stone of Destiny of Scone. The custody of the holy relic conferred some very important privileges on its custodians. These were confirmed and added to by King Robert the Bruce after the Battle of Bannockburn. Though on that occasion the Macnabs were opponents of the Bruce, the Dewars were present on the Scottish side and had the crozier along with them. It is traditionally reported that previous to the Battle of Bannockburn King Robert the Bruce and his army received the sacrament, during the administration of which the crozier of St. Fillan was elevated in

full sight of the army. In 1314, as a thank offering for the victory of Bannockburn, King Robert erected a church at Tyndrum in Strathfillan, and dedicated it to St. Fillan. After the Reformation the crozier was faithfully guarded by its hereditary custodians, the Dewars, and was passed on from father to son. At the beginning of the nineteenth century the sept was broken up and left the country. Some of them emigrated to America, among them the custodian of the cuigreach, and so the relic was lost sight of for a time. Some years ago, however, Sir Daniel Wilson, while hunting on the shores of Lake Superior, took refuge in the hut of a Scottish settler named Alexander Dewar. Sir Daniel found that the settler's family had once lived in Inch Buie, that he was the custodian of St. Fillan's crozier, and that he had the relic in the house. It was then exhibited to Sir Daniel, and in 1876 was acquired by the Society of Antiquaries of Scotland, in whose museum at Edinburgh it has now found a resting-place. The hereditary keeper of the cuigreach of St. Fillan duly received, in 1930, armorial insignia indicative of his ancient office (Lyon Register, XXVIII., p. 128), although he no longer holds St. Fillan's crozier. The inquest of 1428 shows that the *Deoir-Cuigreach* was the *Co-arb* (and, as it explains, heir) of St. Fillan, *i.e.* in the Celtic sense, Hereditary Abbot. He and the Baron of the Bachuil (of St. Moluag of Lismore) seem to be the only surviving prelates of the old Celtic Church.

(3) *Gilfillan*, "servant of St. Fillan." *See* D. Mitchell's *History of the Highlands* :

The Macnabs should probably be recognised as the lay abbots of Glendochart. In their genealogy we find the name *Gillefhaolain* or the servant of St. Fillan, a fact which shows their association with the monastery of St. Fillan. In the time of William the Lyon the Abbot of Glendochart was an important individual, and ranked with the neighbouring Earls of Atholl and Menteath.

(He was, of course, not a "lay" abbot, but a hereditary tribal abbot.)

Maclellan, derived from the same source as Gilfillan, is a clan rather than a sept name. A colony of Maclellans is to be found in Morar, Inverness-shire. There are also some MacLellans to be found in the Aberfeldy district of Perthshire. The Clelands of Cleland, who were hereditary foresters to the Earls of Douglas, likewise derive their name from St. Fillan.

CLAN MACNAUGHTEN SEPTS

(1) *MacKendrick, MacHendry, Henry, etc.*—Descendants of one Henry MacNaughton.

(2) *MacBrayne*, "Son of the Brehon" (or judge). So probably the MacBraynes held the position of hereditary judges of Clan MacNaughton.

(3) *MacNair, MacNayer, MacNuir, MacNuyer, Weir.*—The first four of these names are mentioned by old writers as septs of the MacNaughtons. MacNairs of Cowal anglicise their name " Weir."

(4) *MacNiven, Niven.*—MacBain gives as the English equivalent of Macniven, " Holy-man's slave " (*Mac-Gille-Naoimh*).

The Macnivens used to be located about Loch Awe side, and there is an island on Loch More (Craignish) named Macniven Island. Macnivens appeared to have remained in the province of Moray after their chiefs, the MacNaughtons, had removed further south, and to have occupied the old MacNaughton castle of Dunnachtan, in Strathspey.

(5) *MacEol* and also (6) *MacKnight* are referred to by several clan authorities as MacNaughton septs.

(7) *MacVicar,* " Son of the Vicar," is a name found on Loch Fyne. It was formerly a MacNaughton sept name, as the territory of the Clan MacNaughton extended from Loch Fyne to Loch Awe. After the dispersion of the MacNaughtons the MacVicars appear to have followed the Campbells of Argyll. A standing stone on the lawn of the castle of Inveraray was said to mark the old march between MacVicars and MacIvers. *See* Clan Campbell.

CLAN MACNEIL SEPTS

Neal, Neil, and Neill are all abbreviations of MacNeil. MacNeilage, MacNeiledge, and MacNelly are forms of the name to be met with in the Lowlands. In Fairbairn's *Crests of Great Britain and Ireland* those of MacNeil and MacNelly are bracketed together as identical. The MacGougans also have the same arms as the MacNeils. (*See* under MacDougall Septs).

CLAN MACPHERSON SEPTS

(1) *Clark, Mac-a'-Chleric, etc.*—*Vide* remarks under Clan Cameron Septs.

(2) *Clarkson.*

(3) *Currie, MacCurrach, MacMurdoch, MacVurrich, etc.*, are all forms of the name MacMuirich, from Muiriach or Murdoch, the progenitor of the Clan Macpherson (*vide* remarks under the heading of Clan Macpherson, Chap. VII.).

(4) *Gow, MacGowan.*—*Gow* in Gaelic signifies Smith. The Gows of Clan Chattan are said to be descendants of Henry of the Wynd, the bandy-legged smith of Perth, who fought on the side of the Macphersons at the celebrated battle of the North Inch of Perth. This branch of the Clan Chattan has long been known as *Sliochd a' Ghobha Chrom* (the race of the bandy-legged smith). It is possible that a number of families rejoicing in the well-known name of Smith may be descendants of Henry Gow.

(5) *Fersen.*—The Fersens of Sweden are a noble house, whose progenitor was a Macpherson, who settled in Sweden during the Thirty
Years' War. Count Fersen of the above-named family was an attaché
of the Swedish embassy at Paris, at the outbreak of the French
Revolution. Owing to his intrepid exertions the French Royal Family
all but succeeded in effecting their escape from France.

(6) *Gillespie, Gillies, Lees, MacLeish, MacLise.*—These names are
all derived from the *Sliochd Gillies* (Macphersons of Invereshie).
The founder of the sept was Gillies, or Elias Macpherson, 1st of Invereshie, who lived in the reign of Alexander III. He was a younger son
of Ewan, and brother of Kenneth Macpherson, ancestors of the
Macphersons of Cluny, the chiefs of the clan. *Sliochd Gillies* are now
represented by Macpherson-Grant of Ballindalloch. On the death
in 1806 of General James Grant of Ballindalloch without issue, he
was succeeded by his maternal grand-nephew, George MacPherson
of Invereshie, who assumed the additional name of Grant and was
created a baronet in 1838.

(7) *MacLeish, MacLise.*

CLAN MACQUARRIE SEPTS

All the sept names given are but varieties of the name Macquarrie,
which is variously mentioned as MacQuire, MacGuire, MacCorrie.
Of *MacGuaran*, MacIan (*Costumes of the Clans*) remarks :

> The MacGuarans of Ireland have generally called themselves MacGuire,
> but they are an undoubted offspring from the Scottish tribe, and the
> lineage is attested by the identity of their coat armour with that of the
> lairds of Ulva, chiefs of the name.

—which is not recorded !

CLAN MACQUEEN SEPTS

Some of the names of the septs of this clan are regarded as Mac-
Donald ones. The Hebridean MacQueens, though of the same stock
as the MacDonalds, were but a small clan, followers of the MacDonalds.
The name Macqueen is derived from *Suibhne*, or " Sweyn." From
the former the name varies to MacSwyde, Mac-Cunn, and in some
old documents MacQueyn. The latter has varied into MacSwen,
MacSweyn, and MacSwan.

CLAN MACRAE SEPTS

The sept names given under the heading of the above clan are all
variations of the name Macrae. Of Macara, Smibert (*Clans of Scotland*)
remarks : " The gallant Sir Robert Macara, who fell at Waterloo,
was undoubtedly of this house."

CLAN MALCOLM SEPTS

MacCalum is the Gaelic form of Malcolm.

CLAN MATHESON SEPTS

The names given are varieties of Matheson, or MacMakan.

CLAN MENZIES SEPTS

(1) The sept names are all varieties of the name Menzies, which in Gaelic is *Meinn* or *Meinnearach*. All the names are recognised as Menzies ones by the Clan Menzies Society.

(2) *Dewar, MacIndeor.*—The Clan Menzies Society also claim the Dewars as one of their clan septs, as being the custodians of St. Fillan's crozier, which has already been referred to under the heading of Clan Macnab Septs. The Menzies' Dewars seem rather to be the descendants of the custodians of the staff of St. Munn.

CLAN MUNRO SEPTS

(1) *Dingwall* and

(2) *Foulis* are Ross-shire place names, the latter being that of the seat of the Chief of the Clan Munro. The Dingwalls were especially prominent as followers of the Munros, in numerous clan conflicts.

(3) *Vass, Wass.*—These names were originally de Vallibus or Vaux, and derived from a Norman settler, John Vaux or de Vallibus, who witnesses a charter by Alexander III. at Kincardine in 1252. The de Vallibus family appear to have obtained lands in the province of Ross, where they attached themselves to the Munros, who were closely associated with the old Earls of Ross.

In 1500 occurred the Battle of Druim-a'-chait, between the Mac-Kenzies and Munros, when the former were the victors, and a number of the dependents of the Munros were slain. Among the slain was Sir William Munro's sheriff, Alexander Vass of Lochslinn. In 1515 Elizabeth, Countess of Sutherland, was served heir-special to her brother-german, John, last Earl of Sutherland, before the principal barons of the neighbourhood, among them John Vass of Lochline.

(4) *MacCulloch, MacLulich* belong more properly to the Rosses, and are referred to under Clan Ross Septs. After the fall of the Lords of the Isles, Earls of Ross, the MacCullochs followed the Munros. At Druim-a'-chait, aforesaid (when Hector Roy MacKenzie with 140 men defeated Sir William Munro, who had some 700 under his command), nearly every able-bodied man of the Dingwalls and the MacCullochs fell, and the Munros were seriously crippled for many years.

CLAN MORRISON SEPTS

(1) *Brieve, MacBrieve.*—These sept names originate from the Morrisons having been hereditary brieves or judges of Lewis.

(2) *Gilmore* is the Gaelic form of Morrison (*Mac-gille-Mhoire*).

CLAN MURRAY SEPTS

(1) *MacMurray, Moray* are variations of the name Murray.

(2) *Small, Spalding.*—Lord-President Forbes refers to these two names in the memorial regarding the Highland clans, which he prepared for the government at the time of the Rising of 1745, as being followers of the Duke of Atholl. Rattray of Craighall is chief, of his Name and a follower but not a "sept" of Atholl, and Spalding of Ardintully was the leading family of that name.

CLAN OGILVY SEPTS

(1) *Airlie* is a place name, derived from the barony and castle from which the Chief of the Ogilvies (the Earl of Airlie) takes his title.

(2) *Gilchrist, MacGilchrist* are names derived from the progenitor of the clan, the Clan Ogilvy being known in Gaelic as *Siol Ghillechriost*.

(3) *Milns* of Banffshire.

CLAN ROBERTSON OR DONNACHIE SEPTS

(1) *Duncan, Duncanson.*—The progenitor of the Clan Donnachie was Duncan, or *Donnachadh Reamhar* ; the appellation of Robertson having been derived from the name of the chief, Robert, who flourished during the reign of James I. Among the charters granted during the reign of Robert III., is one to Thomas Duncanson of Athol, of the lands of Strathloche or Easter Davache, and Thomcury, Dekarwand, Dalacharmy ; also another charter to the same individual, designated "of Strowane," of "ane ratification of all his lands, with a taillie."

In the reign of David II. Robert, son of "Duncan de Atholia," got a charter of Ferdill.

(2) *MacConachie, MacConnechy,* and *MacDonachie* are Gaelic forms of Duncanson.

(3) *Donachie, Dunnachie, Tonnochy* are forms of the clan name adopted by some of its members in order to conceal their identity after the 1745.

(4) *MacRobert* is but Robertson in another form.

(5) *Collier, Colyear.*—The title of Earl of Portmore (now extinct) was in 1703 conferred on Sir David Colyear, a younger son of the Strowan family. This scion of the Clan Donnachie made a fortune in Holland, and assumed the above name of Colyear or Collier. The tradition regarding the assumption of the name is, that the person who first assumed it had taken refuge, when being pursued, in a coal-pit.

(6) *Inches* was a name assumed after " the '45 " by some of the Clan Donnachie.

(7) *Reid, Roy, MacInroy.*—The Robertsons of Strathloch were descended from the youngest son of Patrick Robertson, the first of Lude. These Robertsons were known as the Barons Ruadh, Roy, or Red, from the fact of the progenitor of the family having had red hair. The member of the family who perpetuated the name of Reid was General John Robertson, or Reid, born 1721, and who was celebrated as a musician. He composed the celebrated tune " In the Garb of Old Gaul," and established the Reid Chair of Music in Edinburgh University. The General chose the name of Reid in preference to that of Robertson, and his descendants adhered to the use of the former name. MacInroy appears to be a form of *Mac Iain Ruaidh.*

(8) *MacIver, MacIvor.*—In *Sketches of the Highlanders,* General Stewart of Garth remarks : " The MacIvors of Athole and Breadalbane are Robertsons."

(9) *MacLagan.*—This Atholl name is alluded to as a Robertson one by R. G. MacLagan (*Scottish Myths*). It seems to have been spelt in a variety of ways : M'Glagane, MakLachlan, M'Claggon, etc.

(10) *MacRobbie.*—Robbie being a diminutive of Robert, the Mac-Robbies are a sept of the Robertsons, or Clan Donnachie.

(11) *Stark.*—This is also claimed as a Robertson sept name.

CLAN ROSS SEPTS

(1) *Anderson, Andrew, Gillanders, MacAndrew.*

(2) *MacTaggart, Taggart.*

(3) *MacTear, MacTier, MacTire.*—The Gaelic name of the Clan Ross is *Siol Aindrea* or *Clann Aindrea,* meaning the " race of Andrew." The three above groups of names derive their origin from one or other of the early progenitors of the Clan Ross. Alexander MacKenzie's *History of the MacKenzies* says :

It has been established that Gillanders and O'Beolan were the names of the ancient and original Earls of Ross, and that they continued to be represented in the male line by the old Rosses of Balnagowan down to the end of the eighteenth century. . . . It will, it is believed, be now admitted with equal certainty that the Rosses and the MacKenzies are descended from the same progenitor, Beolan or Gilleon na h'Airde, the undoubted common ancestor of the old Earls of Ross, the Gillanders, and the Rosses.

Skene (*Highlanders of Scotland*) remarks :

It is well known that the surname of Ross has always been rendered in Gaelic *clan Anrias* or *clan Gille Anrias,* and that they appear under the former of these appellations in all the early Acts of Parliament ; there is also an unvarying tradition in the Highlands that on the death of William, last Earl of Ross of this family, a certain Paul MacTire was for some time chief of the clan, and this tradition is corroborated by the fact that there is a charter by this William, Earl of Ross, to this very Paul MacTire, in which he styles him his cousin.   There appears, however, among the numerous clans contained in the MS. of 1450, one termed Clan Gilleanrias, which commences with Paul MacTire, so that there can be little doubt that this clan is the same [1] with that of the Rosses, and in this MS. they are traced upwards in a direct line to a certain *Gilleon na h'Airde*, or Collin of Aird, who must have lived in the tenth century.

(4) *Vaas, Wass.*—These sept names have already been referred to under Clan Munro Septs.   As the Munros were intimately associated with the Rosses it was only natural that their dependents should also have been found serving the chiefs of the Rosses.   The Vasses or Wasses, indeed, appear to have taken a considerable share of the fighting done by the Rosses.   At the Conflict of Aldicharrish in 1487, when the forces under Alexander Ross of Balnagowan, Chief of the Rosses, were defeated by the combined forces of the Sutherlands and Mackays, many gentlemen of the name of Waus were slain.

In 1512 King James IV. granted anew to John Vaus of Lochslyn lands which he had resigned for yearly payment of one pound of *cucumeris*, or of three pence at Whitsunday.[2]

(5) *MacCulloch, MacLulich.*—Lulach was the name of the King of Scots who succeeded MacBeth (whom Shakespeare has made so notorious).

About the year 1368 John MacCulloch of Tarrell appears in record. In 1458 John of Ile, Earl of Ross, Lord of the Isles, and Sheriff of Innernys, addressed to John MacCulloch, Bailie of the girth of Sanct Duthowis, a letter requiring him to protect the privileges of Innernys in that quarter.   In 1512 King James IV. granted anew to William MacCulloch of Pladdis the lands of Scardy, Pladdis, Petnely, Pettogarty, Balmoduthy (apparently Baile-dhuich or Tain), and Ballecarew, with the office of bailie of the immunity of Tane, in the earldom of Ross and sheriffdom of Innernys which William had resigned, reserving to the king the escheats of the bailie-courts, for the usual services and the yearly payment of five marks to a perpetual chaplain in the cathedral church of Ross.

Among the aristocracy of the earldom of Ross there was no name more respected than that of MacCulloch, whose original designation was of " Plaidis."   Seven generations were so designated, until John Mac-Culloch, Provost of Tain, having acquired the lands of Kindeace from the Munroes of Culnald, in 1612, changed his style to that of Kindeace.—*The Scottish Antiquary*, April 1898.

The MacCullochs' holdings in the province of Ross appear to have been very considerable, for we find them in possession of the lands of Piltoun, Mulderg, Bellnagore, Easter Drumm, etc.   A charter, dated

---

[1] This seems rather inconsequent.   [2] See under Clan Munro Septs.

1649, by Walter Ross of Bellamuckie, conveys to Andrew MacCulloch, Provost of Tain, the two last-named estates. In 1674 the Lyon King of Arms matriculates the coat armour of Sir Hugh MacCulloch as " being descended of the family of Cadboll in Rosse."

Alexander MacCullauch witnesses an obligation of Alexander, Earl of Ross and Lord of the Isles, to Alexander, Earl of Sutherland, husband of Marion, the Earl of Ross's sister, regarding the castle and lands of Dunbeth and lands of Ra, and William MacCulloch of Priorides was one of the barons present when on 3rd October 1514 Elizabeth, Countess of Sutherland, was served heir-in-special to her brother, Earl John.

At the Conflict of Aldicharrish in 1487 Angus MacCulloch of Tarrell, one of the gentlemen of Ross of Balnagowan, was among the slain.

(6) *Dingwall.*—In 1463 John of Yla, Earl of Ross and Lord of the Isles, granted to Thomas, the younger of Dingvale, with remainder in succession to his brother, John of Dingvale, and his heirs, and to the better and more worthy successor of his relatives of the name of Dinguale, the lands of Vsuy in the earldom of Ross and sheriffdom of Innernys with certain reservations in exchange for the third part of the Arkboll and the lands of Inchfure in the mairdom (*maragium*) of Delny for payment of six pennies in the name of blenchferme. In 1464 the grant was confirmed by King James III.[1]

CLAN SINCLAIR SEPTS

(1) *Caird.*—The Cairds (*Clann-na-ceairde*) including both those of that name and the romantic " Romany " Gypsies of Scotland, are reckoned as a sept of the Sinclair Clan. The name signifies (Gaelic, *ceard* or craftsman) worker in metals. The name appeared in various forms such as MacNecaird, MacNokerd, MacIncaird, etc., most frequently on the borders of Argyll and Perthshire.

MacBain remarks of the Cairds (or Sinclairs) :

In the course of inflection the name, Sinclair, when borrowed into Gaelic as it stands, becomes " Tinclair," pronounced like Scotch " tinkler," a caird, and in looking about for a suitable equivalent or translation for M'Na Cearda, popular fancy hit upon what was at once a translation and an equivalent M'Na-Cearda translated into Scotch Tinkler, and passed by a law of Gaelic phonetics into Sinclair (Ma-an-t-Sinclair).

(2) *Clyne.*—As far back as 1561 the Sutherlands of Berriedale were dispossessed by the Earl of Caithness in consequence of their cruel treatment of the Clynes, dependents of the Caithness family, several members of the former having been killed by the Sutherlands.

(3) *Gallie.*—Gunns from Caithness who settled in Ross in the seventeenth century were locally termed *na Gallaich*—the Caithness men. They would appear to be a Sinclair sept according to all normal rules.

[1] See under Clan Munro Septs.

(4) *Linklater.*—As *Erl's-Kin* of the Lord of Orkney, the Linklater's were, with consent of the Earl of Caithness and his acceptance of them as a sept, authorised to wear the green Sinclair tartan.

(5) *Mason.*—Those of this name are received as a sept of Clan Sinclair as Hereditary Protectors of the Masonic Craft in Scotland.

CLAN SKENE SEPTS

The names *Cariston, Dyce,* and *Hallyard* are all alluded to by MacIan (*Costumes of the Clans*) as offshoots of the Skenes.

CLAN STEWART OR STUART SEPTS (ROYAL LINE)

(1) *Lennox* is a place name derived from one of the Stewart titles. *See* remarks under notes on Clan Stewart, Chap. VII.

(2) *Menteith* or *Monteith.*—The same remarks apply to these names.

(3) *Boyd.*—*Vide* remarks under Clan Stewart, Chap. VII.

(4) *Garrow.*—The *Sliochd-Garaidh* was a small sept of the Stuarts in Braemar, said to have been descended from Alexander, Earl of Mar. This Alexander was a natural son of the Earl of Buchan (fourth son of King Robert II.), who was better known as " The Wolf of Badenoch." Donald Mòr MacGaraidh was piper to the Earl of Mar during the Rising of 1715. The name MacGaraidh is now almost lost in the anglicised one of Garrow.

(5) *France.*—Stuart of Logie-Almond, said to have been descended illegitimately from one of the Stuart sovereigns, found it necessary to fly to France during the second half of the seventeenth century, when for purposes of concealment he adopted the name of France, which continued to be borne by his descendants.

CLAN STEWART OF APPIN SEPTS

(1) *Carmichael, MacMichael.*—The Carmichaels of Lismore and Appin are said to be descended from MacMichaels, followers of the Earls of Galloway (Stewarts), who left Galloway and became dependents of the Appin Stewarts, who were kinsmen of the Stewarts of Galloway. In the list of killed and wounded of the followers of the Stewarts of Appin at the Battle of Culloden the Carmichaels rank third, the first two places being taken by the MacColls and the MacLarens respectively.

(2) *Combich, MacCombich.*—General Stewart of Garth refers to these as following the Appin Stewarts. At the Battle of Culloden the MacCombichs were fourth on the list of the followers of Stewart of Appin as regards the number of killed and wounded.

In connection with these MacCombichs or Colquhouns Dr. Stewart (*Nether Lochaber*) remarks :

At the battle of Inverlochy (1645) a young man whose name was David Colquhoun, from Loch Lomond side, performed such prodigies of valour that Stewart of Appin took special notice of him, and soon afterwards took him into his own service. David Colquhoun married, and had lands given him in Duror. In course of time the Colquhouns multiplied, and became an important sept under the banner of MacIain Stiubhart. Seventeen Colquhouns from Appin were at Culloden, where eight of them were killed. They were physically a very fine body of men, being accounted the biggest and heaviest men of the western mainland. Their descendants even at the present day are remarkable for personal strength and size. They are called the " dimpled Colquhouns " from a peculiar dimpling all over the face when they smile, giving them a most pleasing expression. This dimpling is characteristic only of the Appin sept. Other Colquhouns have it not.

(3) *Livingston, MacLay, Mackinlay, etc.*—The Gaelic rendering of these names is *Mac-an-Leigh.* Not unfrequently, therefore, have the Livingstons or MacLays been classed as Mackinlays.

The Livingstons, early followers of the Appin Stewarts, were the hereditary custodians of the crozier (*Bachuil mor*) of St. Moluag. A small freehold in the island of Lismore, originally of twelve acres but latterly of six only, was held on condition that the holder " do keep and take care of the Baculus or pastoral staff of St. Maluaig," the patron saint of the church of that island. The holder of the relic, *Baran a' Bhachuill* [1] in the Baronage of Argyll, is *co-arb*, or " heir," of St. Moluag. In 1544 John Macmachnore vic Ewir, then hereditary keeper thereof, had a confirmation of his rights from Argyll, as Lord of Lorn ; and until about 1870 the Bachuill was kept in Lismore ; since when it has (for safety) been at Inveraray Castle, but the Baron remains its legal custodian. At Culloden, Donald Livingstone saved the clan banner of the Stewarts of Appin. The African explorer, Dr. Livingstone, was a member of this sept.

(4) *Levack.*—The Levacks are offshoots of the Livingstones.

CLAN STEWART OF ATHOLL SEPTS

(1) *Crookshanks, Cruickshanks*, and

(2) *Duilach* are mentioned by Stewart of Garth as Stewart Septs.

(3) *MacGlashan* or *Gray.*—The MacGlashans are a sept said to be descended from the old family Stewart of Ballechin. The founder of the sept was a younger son of that family, and a noted soldier in his day. Owing to some family disagreement these Stewarts renounced their family name, and adopted in place of it that of MacGlashan, by which name they have ever since been known. The MacGlashans appear to have become followers of the Clan Donnachie. Some of them who settled in the south anglicised their names as Gray.

---

[1] This title shows that the office was regarded as an hereditary incorporeal noble fief.

CLAN STEWART OF BUTE SEPTS

(1) *Bannatyne.—Vide* what is said under Clan Campbell of Argyll Septs (9).

(2) *Fullarton, Jameson, MacCamiey, MacCloy, MacLewis.*—Martin (*Western Islands of Scotland*) describes the Fullertons as the " most ancient family " in Arran. He further says : " They own themselves to be descended of *French* parentage. . . . If tradition be true, this little family is said to be of 700 years' standing." The Fullartons appear to have derived the name MacLewis from the Christian name of the progenitor who settled in Arran.

In the *Statistical Account of the County of Bute* (1841) appears the following account of the Fullartons of Kilmichael (Kilbride), Arran :

Traces of Bruce are furnished by grants of land which he made to several of the natives for services rendered him while in the island. Mr. Fullarton of Kilmichael is the lineal descendant of one of these, Feargus Macloy or MacLewis. He still possesses the charter for his lands given to his ancestor, which is signed by Robert II., and dated Arnele, 26th November, in the second year of his reign. The lands granted to others on the same occasion have passed long ago out of the hands of their descendants, and now form parts of the property of the Duke of Hamilton.

Fullarton, or MacLouis, is referred to by Sir Walter Scott in *The Lord of the Isles* under the cognomen of *Fitzlouis*. Among other offices conferred on the Fullartons by King Robert was that of hereditary coroner of the bailliedom of Arran.

The family held the lands of Kilmichael and the crownership of Arran early in the fourteenth century, one of that surname having received a grant of them from King Robert Bruce. In 1464 James III. granted to George of Foularton the lands of Knychtisland, in the Isle of Arane, which he had resigned, with remainder to his brother William and his heirs, and to his own heirs whomsoever, to be held of the King and his successors as Stewards of Scotland.

James, a scion of the family, settled in Bute, and his descendants were known as the MacCamies, or Jamiesons.

The office of Coroner of Bute from the beginning of the fourteenth century or earlier was held in heritage by a family named Jamieson, or Neilson, and latterly in connection with the lands of Over Kilmory and others. Nigel, the son of James, appears as Chamberlain of Bute from 1445 to 1459.

(3) *MacCaw.*—James IV. in 1506 granted the lands of North Garachach, in Kingarth (Bute), to Gilnew MacKaw, and the lands of Garachach equally divided between Gilpatrik and John Mackaw. In 1510 the same king granted the lands of South Garochty in feu to Patrick M'Caw, who, in 1515, appears in record as Patrik Makcaw of Garachty.

(4) *MacKirdy, MacMutrie.*—The following is extracted from Anderson's *Scottish Nation* :

MacKirdy, formerly *Mackurerdy* or *Makwrerdy*, an ancient surname in Bute, Arran, and others of the Western Islands, and derived from their original inhabitants. At a very early period the larger portion of the island of Bute belonged to the MacKurerdys, which was leased to them by James IV. in 1489, and in 1506 feued as crown lands, in one general charter of the 30th parliament. The charter shows that there were a total of 78 feuars, and of these 12 were MacKurerdys, 11 Bannachtynes, and 10 Stewarts. . . . The properties in Bute feued to the MacKurerdys, with others, principally descended to Robert MacKurerdy, baron of Garachty.

These Celtic chieftains held *duthus*-lands allodially ; and after the forfeiture of the Lord of the Isles, the Crown endeavoured to deny their ancient right to their native soil and to make them lessees. This wicked and oppressive policy led to war in the West Highlands and in due course the chieftains were given Crown charters, and were henceforth known as the " Barons of Bute."

Dr. Alexander MacBain makes the name *MacMutrie* synonymous with that of MacKirdie, and assigns the probable derivation of *Muircheartach* (or " sea-ruler ").

(5) *MacMunn, Munn.*—In 1506, a MacKilmon or MacMunn was, by King James IV., granted a feu charter of lands of Kerrymanach, in Bute. His descendants appear to have been dependents of the Stuarts of Bute. In 1646, Angus MacIlmun met his death along with the Lamonts at Toward.

STEWART OF GALLOWAY SEPTS

(1) *Carmichael, MacMichael.*—*Vide* remarks under Stewart of Appin Septs (1).

CLAN SUTHERLAND SEPTS

(1) *Cheyne.*—The Cheynes, or Du Chesynes, were of Norman extraction, and were among the numerous Norman barons domiciled in Scotland by King Malcolm Ceann-mór and his successors. Their seat was the castle of Inverugie, parish of St. Fergus, in the county of Aberdeen. Sir Reynald Cheyne, belonging to the parish of St. Fergus, had two sons, one of whom (Reginald) was Lord Chamberlain of Scotland in 1267, while the other (Henry) became in 1281 Bishop of Aberdeen. In 1296 Sir Reginald Cheyne signed the " Ragman Roll," and swore fealty to King Edward I., but his son, Reginald, who had, in the meantime, succeeded his father, was one of the subscribers to the famous declaration to the Pope, regarding the independence of Scotland, signed in the abbey of Arbroath, 6th April 1320. Sir Reginald's sole issue were two daughters, Marjory and Mariota. The latter

married Nicholas, second son of the Earl of Sutherland whence sprung the Lords Duffus. Marjory became the wife of John de Keith, second son of Edward—the Marischal of Scotland. Sir Reginald divided his estates previous to his death.

King David II. granted the following charters to the Cheynes, viz. : (*a*) to Ronald Chene, Duffus and the fourth part of Kathness, given by William de Federeth, in the county of Innerness ; (*b*) to Marjory Chene, the lands of Strathbrock, etc., and half of Catnes.

Among the charters of King James IV. is one to George Oliphant and Lady Duffus, his spouse, of the lands of Duffus, Berridale, Auldwick, and Strabrock. James V. grants in 1526 to Lord Oliphant the lands of Berridale, Auldwick, etc.

(2) *Federeth.*—Among those who in 1290 joined in recommending marriage between Edward, the son of King Edward I., and the Maid of Norway, grandchild of Alexander III. of Scotland, were John, Earl of Catenes, Ranald le Chen, the father, Ranald le Chen, the son, and Magnus of Fetherith. In 1296 one or both of the Chens, and William, son of William of Federed, of the county of Elgyn in Morref, swore fealty to Edward I. The Chens and Federeths were connected with each other by marriage with the Morays or Sutherlands of Duffus. The lands inherited by the daughters of Ranald Chen were by them carried respectively to the Sutherlands and Keiths, from whom they passed to the Oliphants, and ultimately became the property of the Sinclairs, Earls of Caithness.

(3) *Gray.*—The first of the Grays to come to the north was a son of Lord Gray of Fowlis, who had to fly on account of having killed the Constable of Dundee. The principal possession of the Grays of the north was Skibo, but they also held Sordell and Ardinsh.

(4) *Mowat.*—Originally " de Montealto," one of the early Norman settlers in Scotland. Robert the Bruce gave to Patricius de Montealto of the lands of Losscragy and Culpedauchis. Among the charters, during the regency of Robert, Duke of Albany, is " Con. of a wadset by William de Monte Alto of Losscragy to John his son of the lands of Freswick and Ochyngill, in Caithness." The first on record as the sheriffs of Cromarty was William de Monte Alto in 1263.

(5) *Oliphant.*—The Oliphants of the north are descended from William, second son of the 2nd Lord Oliphant. William Oliphant married the only daughter and heiress of Alexander Sutherland of Duffus (in Moray), Strabrock (in West Lothian), and Berriedale (in Caithness). He took the designation Oliphant of Berriedale. His wife also inherited a fourth part of the earldom of Caithness, of which she was co-heir. Their son, Andrew Oliphant, having no male issue, resigned his estates in Caithness to his kinsman, Lord Oliphant, on condition that his lordship should provide suitable matches and tochers for his three daughters. Most of the northern possessions of the Oliphants ultimately passed into the hands of the Sinclairs, Earls of Caithness.

PART III

Celtic Culture

IX

The Highland Garb [1]

THE origin of the Highland garb in its primitive state is lost in the mists of antiquity. It is a costume which appears to have been evolved to meet the needs and habits of a pastoral and warlike race of mountaineers.

Before the eleventh century, descriptions of the Highland garb are scanty and rare. Its earliest form appears to have been that of a loose tartan garment descending to the knees and buckled at the waist. As late as 1726 the identity of habits between the two Gaelic nations was so familiarly remembered, that this was adduced by Burt (in his *Letters from the North of Scotland*) as an argument for abolishing the dress of the Scottish Highlanders. In his view the reasons which rendered dangerous the wearing of that garb by the Scottish clans, had before occasioned its proscription among the Irish.

Though written testimony as to the Highland garb before the eleventh century is meagre, ancient sculptured evidence proves the dress to have had great antiquity. Skene (*The Highlanders of Scotland*) writes :

From the Dupplin Cross, the date of which can from various circumstances be fixed to have been towards the end of the ninth century, there are a number of figures represented in the Highland garb, armed with the target and long spear . . . they afford complete proof of its having been the ordinary dress of a considerable part of the northern population from the earliest period of their history.

Robertson (*Historical Proofs on the Highlanders*) also says :

In the sculptured stones of Scotland we have most clear and decided evidence of the antiquity of the national garb of the Gael—they bear clear testimony to the dress of the Highlanders. . . . There is a natural representation of the dress of the Gael in the Isle of Skye . . . a rock named *Creag an fhéile*, or the " rock of the kilt " . . . strong proof that the earliest inhabitants wore the Highlanders' dress, and must have brought it with them, and it likewise proves they must have spoken the same Gaelic as the present Gael.

Grant (*Tartans of the Clans of Scotland*) observes : " A sculptured stone at Nigg, thought to be not later than the seventh century, represented a kilted Highlander with a sporran or purse."

[1] See Appendix XVII. for English and Gaelic equivalents for the various parts of the Highland garb and Highland arms.

In the Norwegian saga of Magnus Barefoot, it is said that in 1093 that monarch returned from his great expedition through the Hebrides. He and many of his courtiers had adopted and introduced into Norway the dress worn by the Highlanders of the Western Isles, a mantle and kirtle, the *breacan* and *falluinn* or plaid and tunic of the Highlanders of Scotland and of the Celts of Ireland, the legs, when this costume was worn, being uncovered.

Pennant gives a drawing of a Highland chief from a monumental effigy by a Mr. Fraser. The date is supposed to be 1306. Harrison reproduces it in his work on costumes. The chief is represented as being clothed in tartan trews, kilt, and jacket and skin sporran, and holding a spear in his right hand, and a shield kite-shaped on his left arm ; on the chief of the shield is blazoned a galley with a lion rampant surrounded with a border underneath. The chief has an iron head-piece with horns, similar to those worn by the ancient Celts. This bears out the later evidence that the trews were the normal dress of chiefs, and that they already used shields with armorial bearings—a fact also readily ascertainable from their seals. One of the earliest detailed representations of the trews is the representation of " Malcolm Canmor " in the sixteenth-century Seton armorial.

In 1773 Sir Joseph Ayliffe, F.R.S., read, to the Society of Antiquaries, a paper, " Account of Some Ancient English Historical Paintings at Cowdray in Sussex " (seat of Viscount Montague). These paintings, in oil on stucco, occupied the whole length of each side of the room. The paintings were attributed to Holbein (1494–1543), but Ayliffe thought they were by Theodore Bernardi, 1519. One of the pictures depicted an episode in the siege of Boulogne, and referred to some Scottish auxiliaries of the English army. Ayliffe says :

Between the Duke of Alberquerque's camp and that of the Lord Admiral is a bagpiper playing on his drone, and followed by a number of men dressed in plaids, their hair red, their heads uncovered, and their legs bare. They have pikes in their hands, and broadswords hanging by their sides.

The historian, John Major, wrote (in Latin) in 1512, thus :

Translation.—From the middle of the thigh to the foot they have no covering for the leg, clothing themselves with a mantle instead of an upper garment, and a shirt dyed with saffron. They always carry a bow and arrows, a very broad sword with a small halbert, a large dagger, sharpened on one side only, but very sharp, under the belt. In time of war they cover their whole body with a shirt of mail of iron rings, and fight in that. The common people of the Highland Scots rush into battle, having their body clothed with a linen garment manifoldly sewed and painted or daubed with pitch, with a covering of deerskin.

At the period to which Major alludes, it will be observed that the lower ranks of the Highlanders wore tartan kilts. The habit of the upper ranks was plaid (mantle) and *leine-chroich*, saffron-coloured shirt. This, as its name imports, was dyed yellow, and resembled a very ample belted plaid of saffron-coloured linen, fastened round the middle, and formed of sufficient breadth to fall below the knees when required. The *leine-chroich* usually contained twenty-four yards of material, but sometimes more.

In Ireland, however, the *leine-chroich*, so costly from its profusion of cloth, was the subject of a statute by Henry VIII. prohibiting people from putting in it more than seven yards.[1] Martin (*Western Islands of Scotland*) says that the *leine-chroich* began to be disused by the Scottish Highlanders about the year 1600.

The plaid and the hose (trews) appear to have been from the first the form of dress in tartan worn by Celts of chieftain grade in Scotland ; the belted plaid of tartan later replacing the *leine-chroich*.

A letter written in 1543 by John Elder, a Highland priest, to Henry VIII. of England, shows how Highlanders of that day were clad :

Wherfor they call us in Scotland Redd Shankes, and in your Grace's dominion of England, roghe footide Scottis ; pleas it Your majestie to understande, that we of all people can tollerat, suffir, and away best with cold, for boithe somer and wyntir (excepte when the froest is most vehemente), goynge alwaies bairleggide and bairfootide ; our delite and pleasure is not onely in huntynge of redd deir, wolfes, foxes, and graies, whereof we abounde and have great plentie, but also in rynninge, leapinge, swymmynge, shootynge, and thrawinge of dartis ; therfor in so moche as we use and delite so to go alwaies, the tender, delicatt gentillmen of Scotland call us Reddshankes. And agayne, in wynter, whene the froest is mooste vehement (as I have saide), which we cannot suffir barefootide so weill as snow, which can never hurt us when it cummes to our girdills, we go a huntynge, and after that we have slayne redd deir, we flaye of the skyne bey and bey, and setting of our bair foote on the inside thereof, for neide of cunnynge shoe makers, by Your Grace's pardon, we play the sutters ; compasinge and measuringe so moche thereof as shall retche up to our anclers, pryckynge the upper part thereof also with holis that the water may repas when it entres, and stretchide up with a stronge thwange of the same, meitand above our said ancklers, so, and pleas your noble Grace, we make our shoois ; therefor, usinge such maner of shoois, the roghe hairie side outwart, in your Grace's dominion of England, we be callit roghe footide Scottis ; which maner of shoois (and pleas your Highness in Latyne be called " perones," whereof the poet Virgill makis mentioun, sayinge that the old auncient Latyns in tyme of warrs uside such maner of shoos). And althoughe a great sorte of us Reddshankes go after this maner in our countrethe, yeit never the les, and pleas Your Grace, when we come to the Courte (the Kinge's Grace our great master being alyve) waitinge on our Lordes and maisters, who also for velvetis and silkis be right well araide, we have as good garmentis as some of our fellowis whiche gyve attendance in the Court every daye.

The untanned shoe referred to by the above writer was the *bròg*. The Highlanders made also a higher foot-covering of untanned skin, which was laced up to below the knee and was termed the *cuaran*.

Vide Appendix XVIII.

N

An account of the campaigns of the French auxiliaries in Scotland in 1548–1549, by Monsieur Jean de Beaugué (one of the French officers who accompanied the expedition), *L'Histoire de la Guerre d'Écosse* (Paris, 1556), describes the dress and arms of some Highlanders present at the siege of Haddington in 1549 :

Quelques Sauvages les suyvirent ainsi qu'ils sont nuz fors que de leurs chemises taintes et de certaines couvertures légères faites de laine, de plusieurs couleurs, portans de grands arcs et semblables épées et boucliers que les autres.

Translation.—Several Highlanders (or wild Scots) followed them (the Scottish army) and they were naked except their stained shirts and a certain light covering made of wool of various colours, carrying large bows and similar swords and bucklers to the others (*i.e.* to the Lowlanders).

John Lesley, Bishop of Ross, writes in 1578 :

They made also of linen very large shirts with numerous folds and wide sleeves, which flowed abroad loosely to their knees. These rich coloured with saffron, and others smeared with grease to preserve them longer clean among the toils and exercises of a camp, which they held it of the highest consequence to practice continually. In the manufacture of these, ornament and a certain attention to taste were not altogether neglected, and they joined the different parts of their shirts very neatly with silk threads, chiefly of a green or red colour.

An account was published (Paris, 1583) of the visit to Scotland of Nicolay D'Arfeville, Cosmographer to the King of France. The following is a translation of an extract from this :

Those who inhabit Scotland to the south of the Grampian chain are tolerably civilised and obedient to the laws and speak the English language, but those who inhabit the north are more rude, homely and unruly, and for this reason are called savages (or wild Scots). They wear like the Irish a large and full shirt coloured with saffron, and over this a garment hanging to the knee, of thick wool, after the manner of a cassock. They go with bare heads and allow their hair to grow very long and they wear neither stockings nor shoes, except some who have buskins made in a very old fashion which come as high as their knees. Their arms are the bow and arrow and some darts, which they throw with great dexterity, and a large sword with a single edged dagger.

Commenting on this description of D'Arfeville, the brothers Stuart in *The Costume of the Highland Clans*, observe :

In this brief sketch the French navigator, like Major, has generalised the habits of all ranks among the Highlanders without discriminating that the naked head and feet were the characteristics of the lower orders, and that the higher wore both bonnets and hose, as is sufficiently proved by the representation of the former twenty-one years before in the print of the Highland Chief in the *Recueil des Habits*, and by the mention of the latter as " hoiss of Heland tartane," in the wardrobe accounts of that sovereign under whom D'Arfeville became acquainted with the Highlanders. The buskins mentioned by him under the designation of "botines a l'antique" were the fur or skin boots called by the Highlanders "calpanach," and represented in the woodcut of the Highland Chief in the Recueil des Habits and the portrait of Sir Donald MacDonald of Sleat, in the possession of the Duke of Tarentum.

George Buchanan, in his history (published in 1582), says :

They (the Highlanders) delight in variegated garments especially stripped, and their favourite colours are purple and blue. Their ancestors wore plaids of many different colours and numbers still retain this custom, but the majority now in their dress prefer a dark brown, imitating nearly the leaves of the heather, that when lying upon the heath in the day, they may not be discovered by the appearance of their clothes, in these, wrapped rather than covered, they brave the severest storms in the open air and sometimes lay themselves down to sleep even in the midst of snow. . . . Their defensive armour consists of an iron headpiece and a coat of mail formed of small iron rings and frequently reaching to the heels. Their weapons are, for the most part, a bow and arrows barbed with iron, which cannot be extracted without widely enlarging the orifice of the wound, but a few carry swords or Lochaber axes.

The Lochaber axe, to which the historian refers, was a most deadly weapon. It had a very long haft and was provided with a long hook at the end of the haft above the axe, with which it was possible to pull a mounted man from his horse preparatory to dispatching him with the axe. At the present time when the usefulness of khaki as the colour for a campaigning kit has been so clearly demonstrated, it is interesting to note the adoption in the sixteenth century of a similar colour (brown) as an invisible one.

What Buchanan writes about old Highland defensive armour is borne out by the sculptures on the tombstones of Highland chiefs. The tombstones of the great MacDonald warriors in Saddell Monastery, Kintyre, depict the old soldiers all dressed in armour with the shirt down to below the knee, iron helmet, chain armour tippet over shoulders, and down the arms. The tombstone said to be that of the great Somerled, Lord of the Isles, shows that at the elbow there was a joint in the armour which proves that the arms were also covered by armour.

From about the time of the reign of King James V. the yellow falluinn or leine-chroich began to be disused. In O'Clery's account of the Hebridean auxiliaries, who in 1594 assisted the clans of Ulster against Queen Elizabeth no mention is made of the falluinn. The principal garment of the Islesmen is described as a tartan belted plaid, and for the first time its adjustment is distinctly explained :

Their outward clothing is a mottled garment with numerous colours, hanging in folds to the calf of the leg, with a girdle round the loins over the garment. Some of them (the Highlanders) with horn-hafted swords large and military over their shoulders. A man when he had to strike with them was obliged to apply both hands to the haft.

Highland dress thereafter resolved itself into three main forms :

(1) The *breacan-feile* [1] or " belted plaid." This was a combination of kilt and plaid made of twelve ells of tartan, *i.e.* six ells of double tartan which, being pleated, was fastened round the body with a belt, the lower part forming the kilt and the other half, left fixed to the shoulder by a brooch, hung down behind, and thus formed the plaid. Great neatness was displayed in arranging the pleats so as to show the sett of the tartan. This was a particularly convenient form of the dress : as the plaid hung loosely behind it did not encumber the arms and in wet weather could be thrown over the shoulders, while in the event of camping out at night it could be thrown loose and covered the whole body. It was principally worn on warlike expeditions or when going any distance from home. It was called the belted plaid from the fact of its being simply made of a piece of tartan unsewn and fixed round the body with a belt.

(2) The second form of the Highland garb was the *feileadh-beag* [2] or " little kilt." This was made of six ells of single tartan which, being pleated and sewn was fixed round the waist with a strap : half a yard being unpleated at each end, these ends crossed each other in front. The *feileadh-beag* had much the same appearance as the kilt now worn.

The *feileadh-beag* had developed, at any rate by the beginning of the seventeenth century, and is described by J. Aston, valet to Charles I., who was in Scotland in 1639, as " like a pair of bases," these being the pleated " skirt," usually of some rich brocade, worn along with a suit of plate-armour in the sixteenth century. Examples and patterns of these pleated " bases " are well illustrated in H. Norris, *Costume and Fashion*, III., Part I., pp. 36–40 ; and with such an example, in sixteenth-century chivalry, one can hardly suppose, if the *feileadh-beag* had not been already evolved before then, that it would not have been adopted in the sixteenth century, long before the days of Rawlinson.

It seems, however, that in general, the kilt was worn of the double width, strapped in the middle, thus saving the cloth whole, and that a picturesque use was made of the second " lap," which could also be employed as a short " shoulder plaid." To elaborate Aston's phrase, by example from the portraits :

The " two bases " were thus an inner and outer fold of the *breacan* strapped around the waist ; and the outer " kilting " was left slightly the shorter, and tucked up under the belt on either side, or if worn longer was hitched up to the left shoulder. The former fashions are well shown in Waite's portrait of the late-seventeenth-century " Highland Chieftain," the later in " Lord Duffus," where, the plaid being of a different tartan, the character of the philabeg as a distinct garment is,

---

[1] See Plate No. III.   [2] See Plate No. X.

agreeably to the descriptions of Aston and Kirk, made pictorially evident.[1]

(3) The third form of the Highland garb was that of the *triubhas* or trews. These were always made of tartan. They were cut crossways and worn tight to the skin after the style of breeches. They were often elaborately laced down the seam, sometimes finished with gold braid. It required considerable skill to make a pair of trews as the tartan had to be matched at the seams so as to show the pattern. The setts of tartan for trews were generally smaller than those used for the plaid. The trews were worn principally by chiefs and gentlemen on horseback, and by Highlanders when travelling in the Lowlands.

The following description of the old Highland garb of *breacan-feile*, etc., is given by Stewart of Garth :

The coat or jacket was sometimes of green, blue, or black cloth. The waistcoat and short coat were adorned with silver buttons, tassels, embroidery or lace, according to the fashion of the times or the taste of the wearer. But the arrangements of the belted plaid were of the greatest importance in the toilet of a Highlandman of fashion. This was a piece of tartan two yards in breadth and four in length, which surrounded the waist in large plaits or folds, adjusted with great nicety and confined by a belt buckled tight round the body, and while the lower part came down to the knees the other was drawn up and adjusted to the left shoulder, leaving the right arm uncovered and at full liberty. In wet weather the plaid was thrown loose and covered both shoulders and body, and when the use of both arms was required it was fastened across the breast by a large silver bodkin or circular brooch often enriched with precious stones or imitations of them, having mottoes engraved consisting of allegorical sentences or mottoes of armorial bearings. These were employed to fix the plaid on the left shoulder. A large purse of goat's or badger's skins answering the purpose of a pocket, and ornamented with a silver or brass mouthpiece and many tassels hung before. A dirk with a knife and fork stuck in the side of the sheath, and sometimes a spoon, together with a pair of steel pistols, were essential accompaniments. The bonnet which gentlemen generally wore with one or more feathers completed the national garb. The dress of the common people differed only in the deficiency of finer or brighter colours and of silver ornaments, being otherwise essentially the same, a tuft of heather, pine, holly, oak, etc., supplying the place of feathers in the bonnet. The garters were broad and of rich colours wrought in a small, primitive kind of loom the use of which is now little known, and formed a close texture which was not liable to wrinkle, but which kept the pattern in full display. The silver buttons were frequently found among the better and more provident of the lower ranks, an inheritance often of long descent. The belted plaid, which was generally double or in two folds, formed, when let down so as to envelop the whole person, a shelter from the storm and a covering in which the wearer wrapt himself up in full security when he lay down fearlessly among the heather.

In old days the garters were a prominent part of the Highland

[1] See L. Spence in *Book of the Braemar Gathering*, 1939, p. 189.

dress. The garter measured a yard in length wound repeatedly around the leg, finishing outside the hose in a particular knot called *snaoim gartain* or " garter knot." The Macintyres of Cladich, Loch Awe, carried on for many years an extensive weaving industry in the manufacturing of garters and hose. The Cladich garters were, at one time, very celebrated. The hose were not then as is now the case knitted, but were made out of the tartan web.

While Garth thus describes the full Highland dress of old days in its completeness, it must be remembered that many wore the garb in a far more primitive manner. Many readers will remember having seen, in the Highlands, Highland laddies in their teens to whom the use of shoes, hose, and bonnet was quite unknown. This was also the case in the seventeenth and early eighteenth century, when in daily life Highlanders of humble rank often used no foot or leg covering, or were content to don the *cuaran* (hide shoe of untanned leather).

Besides the green, blue, or black cloth jackets referred to by Garth as forming part of the full Highland garb, the doublet or coat (Gaelic *cota geàrr*) was sometimes made of tartan cloth cut crossways, the size of the checks being less than in the kilt or plaid. This style of coat was called *cota fiaraidh*.

John Taylor (styled the " Water Poet "), who was the guest of the Earl of Mar at a hunting party at Braemar in 1618 (on which occasion the poet was attired in Highland garb by his host) thus describes the costume of the Highlanders of that period :

Their habite is shooes with but one sole apiece ; stockings (which they call short hose) made of a warm stuffe of divers colours, which they call Tartane ; as for breeches, many of them, nor their forefathers, never wore any, but a jerkin of the same stuffe that their hose is of, their garters being bands or wreathes of hay or straw, with a plead about their shoulders, which is a mantle of divers colours, much finer and lighter stuffe than their hose, with blue flat caps on their heads, a handkerchiefe knit with two knots about their necke ; and thus they are attyred. Now, their weapons are long bowes and forked arrowes, swords, and targets, harquebusses, muskets, durks, and Loquhabor-axes. With these armes I found many of them armed for the hunting. As for their attire, any man of what degree soever that comes amongst them must not disdaine to weare it ; for if they doe, then they will disdaine to hunt, or willingly to bring in their dogges ; but if men be kind unto them, and be in their habit, then are they conquered with kindnesse, and the sport will be plentifull. This was the reason that I found so many noblemen and gentlemen in those shapes.

That the Highland costume practically remained the same during seventy years subsequent to the date at which Taylor wrote is evident from the remarks made about it by William Sacheverell, Governor of the Isle of Man. Sacheverell visited the island of Mull and other islands of the Hebrides in 1689 when he was despatched to Mull by the Government to supervise the attempts made to recover guns, etc., from the wreck of the *Florida*, one of the vessels of the Spanish Armada which was said to have been blown up in Tobermory Bay in 1588. In his account of his experiences in the West Highlands Sacheverell wrote :

During my stay I generally observed the men to be large-bodied, stout, subtle, active, patient of cold and hunger. There appeared in all their actions a certain generous air of freedom and contempt of those trifles, luxury and ambition, which we so servilely creep after. They bound their appetites by their necessities, and their happiness consists, not in having much, but in coveting little. The women seem to have the same sentiments with the men, though their habits were mean and they had not our sort of breeding, yet in many of them there was a natural beauty and a graceful modesty, which never fails of attracting. The usual habit of both sexes is the pladd ; the women's much finer, the colours more lively, and the squares larger than the men's, and put me in mind of the ancient Picts. This serves them for a veil, and covers both head and body. The men wear theirs after another manner, especially when designed for ornament it is loose and flowing, like the mantles our painters give their heroes. Their thighs are bare, with brawny muscles. Nature has drawn all her strokes bold and masterly, what is covered is only adapted to necessity—a thin brogue on the foot, a short buskin of various colours on the legg, tied above the calf with a striped pair of garters. What should be concealed is hid with a large shot-pouch, on each side of which hangs a pistol and a dagger, as if they found it necessary to keep these parts well guarded. A round target on their backs, a blew bonnet on their heads, in one hand a broadsword, and a musquet in the other ; perhaps no nation goes better armed, and I assure you they will handle them with bravery and dexterity, especially the sword and target, as our veteran regiments found to their cost at Gille Crankee.

In Donald W. Stewart's *Old and Rare Scottish Tartans* (limited edition, 1893), a rare book, not noticed in former editions of this work, there is an erudite introduction citing a number of little-known references to early Highland dress. Thomas Kirk (1677) makes it clear that the kilt and plaid were already by then known as separate garments.[1] His description is as follows :

Here we may note the habit of a Highlander : . . . their breeches and stockings are either all of a piece, and straight to the plaid colour,[2] or otherwise a sort of breeches not unlike a petticoat, that reaches not so low, by far, as their knees,[3] and their stockings are rolled up about the calves of their legs and tied with a garter, their knee and thigh being naked.

---

[1] Hume Brown, *Travels in Scotland*, 1892, p. 179 ; Stewart, *Old and Rare Scottish Tartans*, p. 19.

[2] This is the trews, which were worn with dirk and sporran ; so Sir John Sinclair of Ulbster's celebrated portrait by Raeburn shows a uniform quite historically " correct " in these details. My ancestor, John Innes, 5th of Edingight (1674), wore " ane whinger with knives " and a small " bag "—obviously a dirk and sporran (see *Transactions of Banffshire Club*, 1937, p. 38).

[3] A glance at Nisbet's plate of the Skene of Skene supporters will confirm this point of the prevailing fashion of the latter seventeenth century.

On their right side they wear a dagger about a foot, or half a yard, long, the back filed like a saw, and several skeans stuck in the sheath of it, in either pocket a case of iron or brass pistols, a sword about a handful broad. . . . Thus accoutred, with a plaid over the left shoulder and under the right arm, and, cap a'cock, he struts like a peacock.[1]

Colonel Cleland, writing of the 1678 campaign, distinguishes the kilt, worn by Highlanders in general, and the trews-and-plaid costume worn by chieftains. Of these, and their right to armorial standards, he says :

> But those who were their chief commanders,
> As such who bore the pirnie standarts,
> Who led the van and drove the rear,
> Were right well mounted of their gear,
> With brogues, trues, and pirnie plaides,
> With good blew bonnets on their heads,
> Which on the one side had a flipe
> Adorned with a tobacco pipe,[2]
> With dirk and snapwork and snuff-mull,
> A bagg [3] which they with onions fill,
> And, as their strick observers say,
> A tupe-horn filled with usquebay,[4]
> A slasht-out coat beneath their plaides
> A targe of timber nails and hide.[5]

The slashed coat is one similar to that seen in the " Lord Duffus " portrait. The distinction is pointedly, and officially laid down, by Lord Lyon Sir Charles Erskine of Cambo, in the matriculation of Skene of that Ilk, 1672, where the supporters are blazoned :

On the dexter by a Highland man in his proper garb holding a skene with his right hand in a guarding posture, and on the sinister by another in a servill habit, his target on the left arm and his darlach by his side.[6]

Nisbet's description reads, " Supported on the dexter by a Highland gentleman in his proper garb . . . " [7] and the accompanying engraving by Robert Wood, 1695–1704, shows the dexter supporter the " Highland gentleman " in trews, and the sinister " Highlandman " in a very obvious kilt, and without a plaid.

[1] *Old and Rare Scottish Tartans*, p. 19, account of Thomas Kirk, 1677. The allusion to the plaid grammatically refers to " accoutred " in *either* form, and thus *does* infer that Kirk saw a philabeg.

[2] This is evidently a sarcastic allusion to the cockade and crest.

[3] I suppose some joke about a sporran or " pock," which does on occasion seem to have been worn with trews, as seen in Sinclair of Ulbster's celebrated portrait.

[4] I was therefore not wrong in suggesting this purpose in *Scottish Clans and Their Tartans*, p. 14.

[5] *Old and Rare Scottish Tartans*, p. 21.

[6] *Public Register of All Arms and Bearings in Scotland*, I.

[7] Andrew Ross edition of Nisbet's *Heraldic Plates*.

Stewart observes :

It is impossible to conceive of evidence of a more conclusive and satisfactory character than that here adduced of the existence of both modes of dress at this period and of the rank of the respective wearers.[1]

In 1672 the philabeg was thus a legally cognisable Scottish variety of " habit," applicable to the ordinary Highlander, whilst the *duine-uasail* wore trews (at least on formal occasions). By 1747, the philabeg, as a *nomen juris*, was proscribed in the " Dress Act." McClintock cites four pre-1745 representations of it, and himself cites two more, to which De Heere's " Highlander " of 1577 might be added.[2]

Now we come to Rawlinson (not a " Major," but a Quaker), whose wood-burning at Glengarry was in the years 1727–1731. It is incredible (as McClintock appreciates, p. 55) that his " invention " spread all over the Highlands by 1745 (inside eighteen years), even if incapacitated " Old Glengarry " had taken it up. The " authority " for fathering the kilt upon our Quaker was Evan Baillie of Abriachan, who we are told " gave much useful information during 1745–1746 "[3] —to the Hanoverian Government, of course. Upon the repeal of the Dress Proscription Act, he unburdened himself of some more[4] by informing Scotsmen, with all the authority of his hoary head, that the dress they had re-acquired the right to wear, had been the quite-recent invention of an Englishman. He could hardly have hit on a

[1] *Old and Rare Scottish Tartans*, p. 22.

[2] McClintock, *Old Highland Dress and Tartan*, pp. 36–44. He is himself, I feel hypercritically sceptical about the philabeg upon grounds deserving observation : (*a*) He seeks to give " bases " not its ordinary meaning, but a specialised and doubtful one of Johnson's. (*b*) On Burnett of Leys' supporters he alludes to what is " said to have been " done in the matriculations (p. 40 n.) ; but, in referring to the contents of a statutory and " Publick " Register of the Kingdom, it would have been possible for the author of this admirably valuable scientific book to make himself acquainted with the contents of such Register. (*c*) He refers (p. 41) to Wood's drawings in Nisbet's *Heraldic Plates* as " drawings made in the early nineteenth century," whereas they are 1694–1704 work. It is a moot point whether the supposed " ragged trews " in that two-and-a-half-centuries-old drawing is not an attempt to reproduce the pleated margin of a philabeg, as one must conclude it was meant to be, since Lyon would not have blazoned another trews " habit " differently from a " gentleman's " simply by being " ragged." Even a so-called " servil habit " could be ragged or not. (*d*) He suggests the Muchalls plaster-cast (showing what he concedes is a " kilt or skirt to the knee "—though why should a Highland huntsman wear a " skirt " ?) is " probably considerably worn." However, in fact it is not, being indoors, painted with whiting. (*e*) The kilted boy in Gordon of Rothiemay's map, he thinks, was not a Scottish figure at all, and presumably drawn by a Dutchman. This would rule out McClintock's French drawings as dress evidence. Anyway, he doesn't show it is a Dutch costume, so we are left with the question : What did the Dutchman draw ?

[3] J. G. Mackay, *Romantic Story of the Highland Garb and Tartan*, p. 207 ; H. F. McClintock, *Old Highland Dress and Tartan*, p. 47.

[4] *Edinburgh Magazine*, 1785, p. 235 ; H. F. McClintock, *op. cit.*, pp. 46, 49.

N*

better story with which to " kill the kilt." Like many another *canard*
it was promptly swallowed, and by 1795 Sir John Sinclair was announc-
ing that it " is well known the philabeg was invented by an Englishman
in Lochaber about sixty years ago," though by 1804 [1] Sir John had
become more cautious, and is said to have regretted dressing his
regiment in trews, of which his uniform was a magnificent
example

The Rawlinson story appears with important detail in *Costumes
of the Clans*,[2] and, like McClintock, I consider Stuart's narrative,
with caution, receivable up to a point, but I do not think it amounts
to invention of the philabeg (though it may have seemed so to those
concerned, and to Stuart, hearing Glengarry's forester). The " hero "
here is not Rawlinson, for whom a garment is made, but Parkinson,
regimental tailor. On learning from a wetted Highlander the nature
of the belted-plaid costume, and

being told that it was plaited under the belt every time it was put on,
and prompted by his trade, he suggested the improvement of *sewing the
folds in the required disposition*, and separating them from the rest of
the plaid, by which the mantle part might be laid aside at pleasure.

The philabeg had hitherto been a belt-on of half-plaid width
material, probably with an overlap above the belt, and, doubtless,
even (like the modern kilt) with loops for the belt—anyway, with loose,
" flounced " folds. The crucial words about Parkinson's invention
are " sewing the folds " ; and as a uniform-maker he doubtless also
ironed the pleats to keep them in the " required disposition," and
accoutred Rawlinson and Glengarry in the first fixed-pleat ironed-
edge philabegs. Parkinson's style, via Glengarry, the Fencibles,
indeed regimentally via the Black Watch, may well have been the
origin of the modern flat-pleated, neatly regimental kilt, which from
1782 passed into civilian fashion with the revival of Highland dress.
That is very different from inventing the philabeg itself, which we see
was a recognised Scottish garment in the preceding (and doubtless
from the late sixteenth) century.

Whether Prince Charles wore the kilt, and when, is a matter of
dispute ; but he undoubtedly wore, at the moment of his re-embarka-
tion for France, " a threadbare coat of coarse black frieze, tartan trews,
and over them a belted plaid." [3]

Burt concurs that this dress " makes an agreeable figure " and that
" few besides gentlemen wear the trews." [4]

It is the form of Highland dress in which most of the eighteenth-
century chiefs are painted. Allan Ramsay's portrait of Norman
Macleod of that Ilk is a splendid example and the garb is perpetuated

[1] *Old Highland Dress and Tartan*, pp. 48–49.
[2] Conveniently available in McClintock, *op. cit.* p. 53.
[3] Letter from Colonel Warren, *ibid.* p. 23.
[4] **Letter 22.**

in the celebrated description of Patrick Grant of Rothiemurchus (*Macalpine*) : [1]

Macalpine " went about with a body of four and twenty picked men gaily dressed, of whom the principal and favourite was his foster-brother Ian Bain of the family of Auchnahatanich. Macalpine was a great man in every sense of the word, tall and strong made, and very handsome and a beau ; his trews (he never wore the kilt) were laced down the sides with gold, the brogues on his beautifully formed feet were lined and trimmed with feathers."

Towards the end of the seventeenth century a journey was made through the Western Highlands by M. Martin to study " the habites and costume " of the Highlanders. From his *Description of the Western Islands of Scotland* the following is extracted :

The first Habit wore by Persons of Distinction in the Islands was the *leine-chroich*, from the Irish word *leine*, which signifies a Shirt, and *chroich* Saffron, because their shirt was dyed with that herb ; the ordinary number of Ells used to make this Robe was twenty-four ; it was the upper Garb, reaching below the Knees, and was tied with a Belt round the middle, but the Islanders have laid it aside about a hundred years ago.

They now generally use Coat, Waistcoat, and Breeches, as elsewhere, and on their heads wear Bonnets made of thick cloth, some blue, some black, and some grey.

Many of the people wear Trowis, some have them very fine woven like stockings of those made of cloth, some are coloured, and others striped ; the latter are as well shaped as the former, lying close to the body from the middle downwards, and tied round with a belt above the haunches. There is a square piece of cloth which hangs down before. The measure for shaping the Trowis is a stick of wood, whose length is a cubit, and that divided into the length of a finger, and half a finger, so that it requires more skill to make it than the ordinary habit.

The Shoes antiently wore were a piece of the hide of a deer, cow, or horse, with the hair on, being tied behind and before with a point of leather. The generality now wear Shoes having one thin sole only, and shaped after the right and left foot, so that what is for one foot will not serve the other.

But persons of distinction wear the garb in fashion in the south of Scotland.

The Plad, wore only by the Men, is made of fine wool, the thred as fine as can be made of that kind ; it consists of divers colours, so as to be agreeable to the nicest fancy. For this reason the women are at great pains, first to give an exact pattern of the Plad upon a piece of wood, having the number of every thred of the stripe on it. The length of it is commonly seven double ells, the one hangs by the middle over the left arm, the other going round the body, hangs by the end over the left arm also, the right hand above it is to be at liberty to do any thing upon occasion. Every Isle differs from each other in their fancy of making Plads as to the stripes in breadth and colours. The humour is as different

---

[1] *Memoirs of a Highland Lady*, p. 186.

thro the main-land of the Highlands, in so far that they who have seen those places are able at the first view of a man's Plad, to guess the place of his residence.[1]

When they travel on foot the Plad is tied on the breast with a bodkin of bone or wood (just as the Spina wore by the Germans, according to the description by C. Tacitus), the Plad is tied round the middle with a leather belt ; it is pleated from the belt to the knee very nicely. This dress for footmen is found much easier and lighter than Breeches or Trowis. . . .

The antient way of fighting was by set battles, and for arms some had broad two-handed swords and head-pieces, and others bows and arrows. When all their arrows were spent, they attacked one another with sword in hand. Since the invention of guns they are very early accustomed to use them, and carry their pieces with them wherever they go. They likewise learn to handle the broad sword and target. The Chief of each tribe advances with his followers within shot of the enemy, having first laid aside their upper garments, and after one general discharge, they attack them with sword in hand, having their target on their left hand (as they did at Kelicranky), which soon brings the matter to an issue, and verifies the observation made of 'em (by) your historians " *Aut Mors cito aut Victoria laeta.*"

In the *Memoirs of Marshall Keith* the Highland costume, as worn in 1715, is thus described, viz. :

At the battle with the Duke of Argyll a number of men lost their clothes. To explain this one must know the habits of the Highlanders and their manner of fighting. Their clothes are composed of two short vests—the one above reaching only to their waist, the other about six inches longer—short stockings, which reaches not quite to their knee, and no breeches ; but above all they have another piece of the same stuff, of about six yards long, which they tie about them in such a manner that it covers their thighs and all their body when they please, but commonly it is fixed on their right shoulder, and leave their right arm free. This kind of mantle they throw away when they are ready to engage, to be lighter and less encumbered.

The *Letters from the Highlands* of Edmund Burt, a truculent English tax-collector at Inverness,[2] to his friend in London (published

---

[1] This important and oft-quoted passage is, in the light of present knowledge, of significance in illustrating the strongly territorialised basis of the clan, duly indicated by the terms of the statute, 1593 (A.P.S. IV. 40). Hitherto, critics like Colonel Haldane have referred to Martin's statement as one which assists them in " demolishing " what they call " the great clan tartan myth." Viewed in the light of modern scientific examination of the clan, it goes, on the contrary, to establish that tartans identified with the " clan cuntrie "—the *duthus* or home-land of each Celtic race—were well recognised in the seventeenth century. It corroborates the expert evidence and documentary record, which show so conclusively that clanship was feudal ; indeed, the most beautiful and long-standing example of the kindly tribo-feudalism radiating from the " hearth of the race," so long as that could be kept as the pivot of the representer of the family community, the clan, or children, grouped as a noble organisation around their chief

[2] J. B. Salmond, *Wade in Scotland*, p. 98.

1726), gives a good description of Highland dress in the years preceding
" the '45," and show how little the costume had changed during the
preceding century :

The Highland dress consists of a bonnet made of thrum, without a
brim, a short coat, a waistcoat (longer by five or six inches), short stockings
and brogues, or pumps without heels—by the way, they cut holes in their
brogues though new made, to let out the water when they have far to go
and rivers to pass, this they do to preserve their feet from galling. Few,
besides gentlemen, wear the trowze, that is, the breeches and stocking
all of one piece and drawn on together ; over this habit they wear a plaid,
which is usually three yards long and two breadths wide, and the whole
garb is made of chequered tartan, or plaiding. This, with the sword and
pistol, is called a full dress, and to a well-proportioned man with any
tolerable air it makes an agreeable figure ; but this you have seen in
London, and it is chiefly their mode of dressing when they are in the
Lowlands, or when they are making a neighbouring visit, or go anywhere
on horseback ; but when those among them travel on foot, and have not
attendants to carry them over the waters, they vary it into the quelt,
which is a manner I am about to describe.

The common habit of the ordinary Highlanders is far from being
acceptable to the eye ; with them a small part of the plaid, which is not
so large as the former, is set in folds and girt round the waist, to make of
it a short petticoat that reaches half-way down the thigh, and the rest is
brought over the shoulders, and then fastened before, below the neck,
often with a fork, and sometimes with a bodkin or sharpened piece of
stick. . . . In this way of wearing the plaid they have sometimes nothing
else to cover them, and are often barefoot, but some I have seen shod with
a kind of pumps, made out of a raw cow-hide with the hair turned outward. . . . These are called quarrants. . . . The stocking rises no higher
than the thick of the calf, and from the middle of the leg is a naked space,
which, being exposed to all weathers, becomes tanned and freckled. This
dress is called the quelt. . . .

It is alleged the dress is most convenient to those who are obliged to
travel from one part to another upon their lawful occasions, viz. that they
would not be so free to skip over the rocks and bogs with breeches as they
are in the short petticoat, that it would be greatly incommodious to those
who are frequently to wade through waters to wear breeches, which must
be taken off upon every such occurrence, or would not only gall the wearer,
but render it very unhealthful and dangerous to their limbs to be constantly
wet in that part of the body, especially in winter-time when they might
be frozen ; and with respect to the plaid in particular, the distance between
one place of shelter and another is often too great to be reached before
night comes on, and, being intercepted by sudden floods, or hindered by
other impediments, they are frequently obliged to lie all night in the hills,
in which case they must perish were it not for the covering they carry
with them. That, even if they should be so fortunate as to reach some
hospitable hut, they must lie upon the ground uncovered, there being
nothing to be spared from the family for that purpose.

And to conclude, a few shillings will buy this dress for an ordinary
Highlander, who, very probably, might hardly ever be in condition to

purchase a Lowland suit, though of the coarsest cloth or stuff, fit to keep him warm in that cold climate. . . . The whole people are fond and tenacious of the Highland clothing.

The kilt, or *feile-beag* (little kilt) appears to have been the dress worn at home (*i.e.* when not travelling), for a considerable time before the date of above letters, and was that which Burt found the chieftain he visited wearing at home, in the presence of the ladies of the family, and at which Burt was duly shocked !

Gough's additions to *Camden's Britannica* (London, 1789, Vol. III.) give the following description of Highland dress and arms in Breadalbane prior to the proscription of the kilt of 1747 :

The dress of the men is the *brechan* or plaid, twelve or thirteen yards of narrow stuff wrapped round the middle, and reaching to the knees, often girt round the waist, and in cold weather covering the whole body, even on the open hills all night, and fastened on the shoulders with a broche ; short stockings tied below the knee ; *truish*, a genteeler kind of breeches, and stockings of one piece ; *cuoranen*, a laced shoe of skin, with the hairy side out, rather disused ; *kelt* or *fillebeg*, *g.d.*, little plaid or short petticoat reaching to the knees, substituted of late to the longer end of the plaid ; and lastly, the pouch of badger or other skins, with tassels hanging before them. The Lochaber axe, used only by the Town Guard of Edinburgh, was a tremendous weapon. Bows and arrows were in use in the middle of the last century, now as well as the broadsword and target laid aside since the disarming act, but the dirk, or ancient *pugio*, is still worn as a dress with the knife and fork.

The women's dress is the *kirch* or white linen pinned round behind like a hood, and over the foreheads of married women, whereas maidens wear only a snood or ribbon round their heads ; the *tanac* or plaid fastened over their shoulders, and drawn over their heads in bad weather ; a plaited long stocking called *ossan* is their high dress.

The following details of the complete equipment of a Highland chief (of the time of " the '45 "), and instructions for belting the plaid, were communicated by a Highland gentleman to Charles Grant, Vicomte de Vaux, etc., by whom they were printed in his *Mémoires de la Maison Grant* in 1796 :

Composition de l'equipment complet d'un Seigneur des Montagnes d'Ecosse.

1. A full-trimmed bonnet.
2. Tartan jacket, vest, kilt, and cross-belt.
3. A tartan belted plaid.
4. Hose made up of cloth.
5. Stockings, do., yellow garters.
6. Two pair of brogs.
7. A silver-mounted purse and belt.
8. A target with spear.
9. A broad-sword.
10. Pair of pistols and bullet-mould.
11. Dirk, knife, fork, and belt.

Method of Belting the Plaid.—Being sewed, and the broad belt within the keepers, the gentleman stands with nothing on but his shirt ; when the servant gets the plaid and belt round, he must hold both ends of the belt till the gentleman adjusts and puts across in a proper manner the two folds or flaps before ; that done, he tightens the belt to the degree wanted ; then the purse and purse-belt is put on loosely ; afterwards, the coat and waistcoat is put on, and the great low part hanging down behind, where a loop is fixed, is to be pinned up to the right shoulder,[1] immediately under the shoulder-strap, to be pinned in such a manner that the corner or low-flyer behind hang as low as the kilt or hough, and no lower ; that properly adjusted, the pointed corner or flap that hangs at the left thigh to be taken through the purse-belt, and to hang, having a cast back very near as low as the belt, putting at the same time an awkward bulky part of the plaid on the left side back from the haunch, stuffed under the purse-belt. When the shoulder or sword-belt is put on, the flyer that hangs behind is to be taken through, and hang over the shoulder-belt.

N.B.—No kilt ought ever to hang lower than the hough or knee— scarcely that far down.

The above notes carry us down to the costume in use in the Highlands at the time of the Rising of " the '45." Before, however, proceeding further, a few remarks regarding the costume anciently worn by the Highland women will not be inappropriate.

The dress of the Celtic women in ancient times differed but little in form from that of the men. The tunic was bound round the waist, and had seldom any sleeves, their arms being left bare, and their bosoms partly uncovered. They wore a sagum, which they fastened like the men with a pin or brooch, as they did other parts of their dress.

Lesley, writing in 1578, describes the costume of the Highland women thus, viz. :

Mulierum autem habitus apud illos decentissimus erat. Nam talari tunicae arte Phrygiâ ut plurimum confectae amplas chlamydes, quas jam diximus, atque illas quidem polymitas superinduerunt. Illarum brachia armillis, ac colla monilibus elegantius ornata maximam habent decoris speciem.

Translation.—Their women's attire was very becoming. Over a gown reaching to the ankles, and generally embroidered, they wore large mantles of the kind already described, and woven of different colours. Their chief ornaments were the bracelets and necklaces with which they decorated their arms and necks.

In the seventeenth and eighteenth centuries, down to about 1740, the arisaid was the dress of the Highland women. Martin, in his *Description of the Western Islands of Scotland*, written at the beginning of the eighteenth century, thus describes the dress :

The ancient dress worn by the women, and which is yet worn by some of the vulgar, called Arisaid, is a white plad, having a few small stripes of black, blue, and red. It reached from the neck to the heels, and was tied before on the breast, with a buckle of silver or brass, according to the quality of the person. I have seen some of the former of a hundred marks value ; it was broad as an ordinary pewter plate, the whole curiously

---

[1] Of course, this should be " left shoulder " of the wearer.

engraven with various animals, etc. There was a lesser buckle, which was worn in the middle of the larger, and above two ounces weight ; it had in the centre a large piece of chrystal, or some finer stone, and this was set all round with several finer stones of a lesser size. The plad, being pleated all round, was tied with a belt below the breast, the belt was of leather, and several pieces of silver intermixed with the leather like a chain. The lower end of the belt has a piece of plate, about 8 inches long and 3 in breadth, curiously engraven, the end of which was adorned with fine stones or pieces of red coral. They wore sleeves of scarlet cloth, closed at the end as men's vests, with gold lace round them, having plate buttons set with fine stones. The head-dress was a fine kerchief of linen straight about the head, hanging down the back taperwise. A large lock of hair hangs down their cheeks above their breast, the lower end tied with a knot of ribands.

This, it will be noticed, is a dress the lavishness and beauty of which vies with any of the folk-costumes of the Continent. Some such examples of our picturesque Highland past have survived ; and the dress is still worn by Highland girls.

The ground of *arisaid* plaids worn by women was frequently white.[1]

Thus, the so-called " dress Stewart " and " Victoria " tartan, which should properly be styled " Arisaid-Royal," are arisaid setts of the Royal tartan, and no doubt the sett worn by the queens when they went a-hunting—as recorded by Fordun and Leslie.

In the seventeenth and eighteenth centuries magnificently designed tartan dresses were worn by Highland women, a number of which still survive. Whilst modelled on the current styles of dress—low-cut bodices and wide sleeves caught up with silver buttons at the elbow, with white frilling and undersleeves—they formed a distinct and picturesque form of dress as perfectly suited for modern wear as the male Highland dress, and have now been resumed for dancing and evening wear (see p. 384). The plaid or arisaid of silk was also worn as an adjunct to ordinary female dress, and portraits of Flora Macdonald show her in both these styles.

Nowadays, for day wear, when rougher garments have become convenient, various forms of tartan skirt, some pleated and some unpleated, have been adapted, and are handsome and practical. Though many are pleated like a kilt they are, in cut, quite different from a male kilt (hideous on a woman) as a woman requires quite a different cut and construction for a graceful result.

The plaid is still frequently seen in use in Scotland, and Burt refers to the fact that by the eighteenth century ministers again encouraged the wearing of it at Church—not, of course, because of its own beauty, but to cover up finery beneath ! Actually, the result was charming, and Burt quotes a description to the effect that these plaids, " striped with green, scarlet, and other colours . . . in the middle of the church on a Sunday look like a *parterre de fleurs*."

[1] Martin, see p. 367, supra.

He thereafter observes that " chequered " would have been a more accurate term than " striped," and then, of course, sneers at the effect. The plaid is actually a most picturesque garment and, either alone, or in various forms of make-up, could be much extended in use. May we hope that Highland women will resume going to Church in the tartan ?—as do other races with pride in their national dress.

In evening wear, the sash is used, worn over the *right* shoulder except by lady chiefs, chieftainesses, and the wives of chiefs and chieftains, or colonels. Those who have left their own clan, *e.g.* by marriage, and not entered another, or *sencliathe* women, wear it over the right shoulder and tied on the left hip. When worn by ladies of " chieftain grade " (see above), it is of more flowing proportions, 108 by 24 inches with 12-inch fringes, and over the left shoulder. Other women wear the lesser-sash or arisaidette, brooch to or over the *right* shoulder only.

It is remarkable that, both in male and female fashions, the tartan has throughout the centuries been capable of being happily combined with and adapted to the successive styles of current dress, from the saffron shirt through the slashed Cavalier dress, the long-skirted, wide-cuffed, eighteenth-century coats, and the broadcloth of the nineteenth century, to modern tweeds, and once more in evening dress, with velvets and corduroys forming the only artistic form of male dress in so-called " civilised " life.

Women in the Highlands before marriage went with the head bare, and after marriage they wore the *currac*, or *bréid*, of linen, which was put over the head and fastened under the chin, falling in a tapering form on the shoulders. A large lock of hair hung down each side of the face to the bosom, the lower end being ornamented with a knot of ribbons. The *Tonnag* is a small square of tartan silk or woollen stuff folded and worn over the shoulders as a mantle. The unmarried women usually wore a snood or ribbon round their heads. The women of lower rank usually went barefoot, but on high occasions wore a plaited long stocking, called *osan*.

Burt (*Letters from the Highlands*, No. VIII.) remarks (1726) :

The plaid is the undress of the ladies, and to a genteel woman, who adjusts it with a good air, it is a becoming veil. But as I am pretty sure you never saw one of them in England, I shall employ a few words to describe it to you. " It is made of silk or fine worsted, chequered with various lively colours, two breadths wide, and three yards in length ; it is brought over the head, and may hide or discover the face, according to the wearer's fancy or occasion ; it reaches to the waist behind ; one corner falls as low as the ankle on one side, and the other part, in folds, hangs down from the opposite arm."

The ordinary girls wear nothing upon their heads until they are married, or have a child, except sometimes a fillet of red or blue coarse cloth, of which they are very proud ; but often their hair hangs down over the forehead like that of a wild colt. If they wear stockings, which is very rare, they lay them in plaits one above another, from their ankle up to the calf, to make their legs appear as near as they can in the form of a cylinder. . . .

I have been told in Edinburgh that the ladies distinguish their political principles, whether Whig or Tory, by the manner of wearing their plaids ; that is, one of the parties reverses the old fashion, but which of them it is I do not remember.

This shows that the plaid or sash was worn by women in different ways, but the old portraits and prints concur in it being normally worn by women on, or brooched to, the *right* shoulder.

MacIan, in *Clans of the Scottish Highlands*, gives a beautiful coloured illustration of a lady in the costume of the early eighteenth century, wearing the Lamont tartan and plaid. The lady is attired in a rich brocade gown and silk quilted petticoat, while the plaid is thrown over the shoulders, crossed over the breast, where it is fastened by a Highland brooch, and the ends are draped in front of the gown. The hair is powdered, curled, and made up in the eighteenth-century style, and in the blue snood binding the hair is fixed her chief's badge.

But dark days came to wearers of the national garb. The Act [1] for the " Abolition and Proscription of the Highland Dress " enacted :

That from and after the first day of August (new style 13th August) one thousand seven hundred and forty-seven, no man or boy within that part of Great Britain called Scotland, other than such as shall be employed as Officers and Soldiers in His Majesty's Forces, shall, on any pretext whatsoever, wear or put on the clothes commonly called Highland clothes (that is to say) the Plaid, Philabeg, or little Kilt, Trowse, Shoulder-belts, or any part whatsoever of what peculiarly belongs to the Highland Garb ; and that no tartan or party-coloured plaid or stuff shall be used for Great Coats or upper Coats, and if any such person shall presume after the said first day of August to wear or put on the aforesaid garments or any part of them, every such person so offending being convicted thereof by the oath of one or more credible witness or witnesses before any Court of Justiciary, or any one or more Justices of the Peace for the Shire or Stewartry or Judge-Ordinary of the place where such offence shall be committed, shall suffer imprisonment without bail during the space of six months and no longer, and being convicted of a second offence before the Court of Justiciary, or at the Circuits, shall be liable to be transported to any of His Majesty's plantations beyond the seas, there to remain for the space of seven years.

The following is an extract from the General Orders to the Army in Scotland, 22nd December 1748, showing that the Whigs selected Christmas day as the date for abolishing the kilt and plaid :

By the Act passed last session of Parliament, the time for the general abolishing the Highland dress is enlarged to the 1st day of August 1749. But that the wearing and use of such parts thereof as are called the plaid, philibeg, or little kilt, is absolutely prohibited and abolished from and

---

[1] 19 George II., cap. 39, sec. 17, 1746.

after the 25th day of this instant December, and as to these particulars the law takes place from that day.

You are to seize all such persons as shall be found offending herein, by wearing the plaid, philibeg, or little kilt, and carry them before a civil magistrate, in the same dress, that he may be convinced with his own eyes of their having offended, in order to their being punished for the same according to law ; in the performance of which let no insult or abuse be offered to the person or persons of those who shall be so taken up and carried before the civil power, who are solely authorised to inflict the punishment as the Act directs ; but in case the magistrate before whom such offenders are carried shall refuse or neglect putting the law in execution, in that case let me know immediately the name of such magistrate, with the reason of his not doing it, that I may acquaint the Duke of Newcastle with it, who will no doubt send immediately orders to the lord advocate of this country to prosecute him to the utmost for his contempt of the said Act, by not putting it in execution.

That the people in the Highlands might have no excuse by pleading ignorance, the lord chief-justice clerk wrote to the sheriffs depute of the Highland counties, ordering them to give notice at every parish church that they must quit the plaid, philibeg, or little kilt on Christmas day, as the Act directs, otherwise they would be carried before the civil magistrate and punished for it accordingly.

I must likewise desire you will let me know from time to time what obedience the people pay to this Act, for they must and shall obey it, with the names of those magistrates who are industrious in putting the laws in execution, that I may take an opportunity in thanking them for performing their duty, and acquainting the Duke of Newcastle with it.

You may acquaint the magistrates and justices of the peace in your neighbourhood with the contents of this letter since it may be the means of inciting them the more readily to perform their duty.

The restrictions of the Proscription Act were suspended in favour of those chiefs who had supported the Hanoverian Government. Against the Jacobite clans, however, the terms of the Act were enforced with a brutal severity. Those who were suspected of evading the obnoxious law were summoned before the local authorities, and compelled to make the following abjuration, viz. :

I swear as I shall answer to God at the great day of judgment, I have not and I shall not have in my possession any gun, sword, or arms whatsoever, and never use tartan, plaid, or any part of the Highland garb, and if I do so may I be accursed in my undertakings, family, and property, may I never see my wife, nor children, nor father, mother, or relations, may I be killed in battle as a fugitive coward, and lie without christian burial in a foreign land, far from the graves of my forefathers and kindred ; may all this come upon me if I break this oath.

Those who evaded this abjuration and disregarded the Act were deemed outlaws, and in the first rigour of the proscription the troops, detached through the country, received orders to " kill upon the spot any person whem they met dressed in the Highland garb."

In the remote glens where people never heard of the Act abolishing the Highland garb, or possessed little or no means to procure a change of dress, grey-headed men and young boys were shot without challenge or inquiry by patrols crossing the country.

Stewart of Garth (*Sketches of the Highlanders*) remarks, with reference to the savage law :

It certainly was not consistent with the boasted freedom of our country (and in that instance, indeed, it was shown that this freedom was only a name) to inflict on a whole people the severest punishment short of death for wearing a particular dress. Had the whole race been decimated, more violent grief, indignation and shame could not have been excited among them, than by being deprived of this long inherited costume. This was an encroachment on the feelings of the people, whose ancient and martial garb had been worn from a period reaching back beyond all history or even tradition. . . . Considering the severity of the law against this garb, nothing but the strong partiality of the people could have prevented its going entirely into disuse. The prohibitory laws were so long in force, that more than two-thirds of the generation who saw it enacted had passed away before the repeal. The youth of the latter period knew it only as an illegal garb, to be worn by stealth under the fear of imprisonment and transportation. Breeches, by force of habit, had become so common that it is remarkable how the plaid and philibeg were resumed at all.

Dr. Johnson (*Journey to the Western Islands*, in 1773) condemns the Act scathingly : " Laws that place the subjects in such a state, contravene the first principles of the compact of authority, they exact obedience and yield no protection."

The opinion of Lord President Forbes of Culloden (who might rightly be termed the saviour of the Hanoverian dynasty) regarding the Act for the abolition of the Highland garb is worthy of record. The Lord President in a letter to the Lord Lyon (Brodie of Brodie, then in London as M.P. for Moray) wrote :

I do not wonder that you, and a great many wise men where you are, who know nothing at all of the matter should incline to it. The garb certainly fits men inured to it, to go through great fatigues, to make very quick marches, to bear out against the inclemency of the weather, to wade through rivers and shelter in huts, woods, and rocks, upon occasions which men dressed in the low country garb could not possibly endure. As the Highlanders are circumstanced at present it is, at least it seems to me, to be an utter impossibility without the advantage of this dress for the inhabitants to tend their cattle and to go through the other parts of their business without which they could not subsist, not to speak of paying rents to their landlords.

Both Act and oath evoked from the Gaelic bard, Duncan Ban Macintyre of Glenorchy, an indignant poem entitled " The Anathema of the Breeks." In this the bard boldly attacked the Government for passing such an Act, equally obnoxious to the clans which favoured the House of Hanover as to the Jacobites. Macintyre declared that the Act was enough to make the whole country turn Jacobite should Prince Charles return to Scotland.

There were many attempts at evasion of the hated Act abolishing the national garb. All infringements of it, however, were punished with rigorous severity. About 1757 the harsh law began to be somewhat relaxed.

About 1778 the Highland Society of London was instituted for promoting objects of advantage to the Highlands generally, and good fellowship with social union, among such of its natives as inhabited the more southern part of the island. The Society had other objects, among which were the restoration of the Highland dress, the preservation of the music, and the cultivation of the Gaelic language. About the same time it would appear that people in the Highlands were beginning to resume use of the national costume, without being punished under the Act of 1746. William Gilpin, Prebendary of Salisbury, in *Observations on the Highlands of Scotland During the Year* A.D. 1776, states :

Nor are the cattle of this wild country more picturesque than its human inhabitants. The Highland dress (which, notwithstanding an Act of Parliament, is still in general use) is greatly more ornamental than the English. I speak of its form not its colour which is checked of different hues, and has a disagreeable appearance. The plaid consists of a simple piece of cloth three yards in length and half that measure in breadth. A common one sells for about ten shillings. The Highlander wears it in two forms. In fine weather he throws it loosely round him and the greater part of it hangs over his shoulder. In rain he wraps the whole close to his body. In both forms it makes elegant drapery, and when he is armed with his pistols and Ferrara (Andrew Ferrara, a Spaniard, was invited into Scotland by James III to teach his countrymen the art of tempering steel ; from him the best broad-swords take their name) has a good effect. Oftener than once we amused ourselves with desiring some Highlander, whom we accidentally met, to perform the exercise of his plaid by changing it from one form to the other. Trifling as the operation seems, it would puzzle any man who had not been long used to it. But to see the plaid in perfection you must see the Highland gentleman on horseback. Such a figure carries you into Roman times, and presents you with the idea of Marcus Aurelius. If the bonnet were laid aside (for the elegance of which but little can be said) the drapery is very nearly Roman. The bonnet is commonly made in the form of a beef-eater's cap which is very ugly. I have sometimes, however, seen the bonnet fit snugger to the head and adorned with a plume of feathers, it is then picturesque. When the common people take a journey on horseback, they often gather up the plaid in a few plaits, and so form it into a cloak. In this shape it is scanty and unpleasing.

What little change three centuries have made in the dress and accoutrements of a Highlander will appear from the following account, written in the time of Henry the Seventh (Latin quotation) :

Translation.—A race of men, much the hardiest and rough, inhabits the other northern and mountainous part, and they are called wild. They are clothed in military cloak (plaid) and inner tunic, and go about with their legs bare to the knees. Their arms are bow and arrows with in addition a sword, somewhat broad and a dagger, sharp only on one side.

If we take away his bow and arrows and stick a couple of pistols in his belt, the Highlander of those days is the very Highlander of these.

Gilpin's remarks, as from one who was not a Scotsman, are valuable because they show how the Highlanders clung to the use of their ancient costume, despite the measures for its suppression. It is, however, apparent from the foregoing—and observations of other travellers (*infra*)—that the proscription was not being enforced in the 1760–1780 period. Indeed, the evidence suggests that this indefensible form of oppression was stopped in 1760 after the accession of George III., a monarch whom we know was much influenced by his Scottish Prime Minister, Lord Bute, a cultured Highlander, however unfit he may have been to deal with the political chicanery of Sassenachs.

Whilst the proscription thus no longer affected the Highlanders in general the existence of the Act virtually precluded chieftains and lairds from wearing the tartan, since in their case a pointed breach of " the law " could scarcely have been overlooked, and it is to this unfortunate aspect of the oppression that we evidently owe the loss of records and confusion regarding tartans, another instance of the signal importance of chieftaincy in any clan-family system of society. It became evident that steps must be taken to restore the legality of the garb so that it could be worn on public and official occasions, and to collect records of its details.

In 1782 the Highland Society of London appointed a committee to have the obnoxious Act for the abolition of the Highland garb repealed. Its executive members were the Hon. General Fraser of Lovat (President), Lord Chief Baron MacDonald, Lord Adam Gordon, Earl of Seaforth, Colonel MacPherson of Cluny, Captain Alan Cameron of Erracht, and John MacKenzie of Temple, Honorary Secretary. One member of the Society, the Marquis of Graham (afterwards Duke of Montrose), was a member of Parliament. To him, therefore, the Society entrusted a Bill for repeal of the Act for abolition of the Highland dress. The Marquis pressed the cause with such earnestness in the House of Commons that his Bill (introduced in May 1782) was passed in both Houses of Parliament without a dissentient note. It is significant that Fraser of Lovat, in seconding Lord Graham's motion for the Bill, stressed that the measure would help " keep such a useful body of subjects on this side of the Atlantic . . . and keep them happy at home "—another instance of the desire of the chiefs to keep their clansmen in the glens, and not to clear them off, as is so often wickedly asserted. The Act [1] repealing that of 1747 was as follows, viz. :

Whereas by an Act made in the nineteenth year of the reign of his late Majesty King George the Second, entitled " An Act for the more

---

[1] 22 George III., cap. 63, 1782.

effectual disarming the Highlands in Scotland and for more effectually securing the peace of the said Highlands and for restraining the use of the Highland dress " [1] . . . it was, among other things enacted that from and after the first day of August one thousand seven hundred and forty-seven no man or boy, within that part of Great Britain called Scotland other than such as shall be employed as officers and soldiers in his Majesty's forces, etc., etc. And whereas it is judged expedient that so much of the Acts above mentioned as restrains the use of the Highland dress should be repealed. Be it therefore enacted by the King's most Excellent Majesty, by and with the advice of the Lords Spiritual and Temporal and Commons in this present Parliament assembled and by the authority of the same. That so much of the Acts above mentioned or any Acts of Parliament as restrains the use of the Highland dress be, and are hereby repealed.

The Marquis of Graham, for his exertions in having been the means of obliterating from the statute book an Act which was an insult to the Highland people, received from all parts of the Highlands addresses which recorded the indebtedness of Highlanders, and the celebrated Highland poet, Duncan Ban Macintyre, tried again to make his voice heard—this time in celebration of the restoration to his fellow Gaels of their cherished national costume.

Robert Heron in *Observations Made in a Journey through the Western Counties of Scotland, in the Autumn of 1792*, remarks about his reception at Kenmore Inn (Loch Tay) : " The servants are Highlanders, and the waiters wear fillibegs, but are not less cheerfully and actively attentive than the supercilious and foppish attendants at the inns and taverns in great cities."

Such observations, and those which follow relating to the years 1782–1790, show that the proscription was nothing like so effective as has been represented, for one cannot re-clothe a whole nation in a few months.

Of this period John Lane Buchanan, Missionary Minister in the Hebrides, records : [2]

The men wear the shortcoat, the feilabeg, and the short hose with bonnets sewed with black ribbons [3] around their rims and with a slit behind with the same ribbon tied in a knot. Their coats are commonly tartan . . . after a pattern made upon a stick . . . their waistcoats are either of the same, or some such stuff, [4] but the *feilabegs* are commonly of *breacan* or fine Stirling plaids, if their money can afford them. [5] The

---

[1] See Act of 1746, already quoted.

[2] *Travels in the Western Hebrides from 1782 to 1790.*

[3] We notice that the Black Ribbon of Hanover had replaced the white cockade. Obviously inclusion of the black ribbon was a necessary precaution if one were to don Highland dress between 1747 and 1782.

[4] It thus appears the *cota-gearr* was still widely worn.

[5] Here I think we perceive the genesis of the subsequent decline of Highland dress in the Highlands. The tendency was to purchase the cloth, instead of weaving it at home ; and as prices rose in the early nineteenth century, whilst the Highlanders remained poor, and on the old " price level," they slipped into buying cheaper non-tartan cloth.

women wear long or short gowns, with a waistcoat and two petticoats mostly of the stripes or tartan . . . except the lower coat [*the flowing under-garment*] which is white. The married wives wear linen muches or caps . . . fastened with ribbons of various colours. . . . All of them wear a small plaid a yard broad called a *guilechan* about their shoulders fastened by a large broach. The broaches are generally round and of silver . . . if poor, of baser metal and modern date. The first kind has been worn time immemorial, even by the ladies.[1] The *arrisads* are quite laid aside in all this country, by the different ranks of women, being the most ancient dress used by that class. It consisted of one large piece of flannel that reached down to the shoe, and fastened with clasps below [2] and the large silver broach at the breast, while the whole arm was entirely naked. The ladies made use of the finer, while common women used coarser kinds.[3] . . . The *bréid*, or *curtah*, a fine linen handkerchief fastened about married women's heads, with a flap hanging behind their backs above the *guilechan*, is mostly laid aside.

The last-mentioned item was the picturesque Scoto-Highland linen and ribboned head-dress, seen in old Highland miniatures.

In 1795, Ramsay of Ochtertyre found amongst the Episcopal congregation at Linshart, in Aberdeenshire, that the dress reminded him of " forty years ago," *i.e.* prior to " the '45," " parti-coloured plaids being frequent," and adds :

In 1747, when I first knew Edinburgh, nine-tenths of the ladies still wore plaids, especially at church. By this time, however, silk or velvet cloaks of one form or another were very much in request among the people of fashion [*or, one imagines, anyone else who didn't want to be shot at sight !*]. And so rapidly did the plaid wear out, that when I returned to Edinburgh in 1752 one could hardly see a lady in that piece of dress.[4]

Considering the terms of the statute, which certainly was bound to be enforced in Edinburgh, one can well believe this ! In the circumstances, " wear out " hardly seems the appropriate phrase. Can we not picture the scramble—amongst those with any money—to buy any available " cloaks " to replace the ancient national dress which had been so brutally suppressed.

Public interest in the Highlands and the Highland garb was powerfully influenced by the writings of Sir Walter Scott at the beginning of the nineteenth century. To Queen Victoria, also, the Highlands and Highlanders owe a deep debt of gratitude for the interest she took

[1] That is to say, they wore inherited silver brooches of the round pattern decorated with " animals," *i.e.* crests (cf. Martin's description).

[2] Was this at the shoulder, or is he referring to the belt which sometimes held it at the waist ? From portraits such as that of Flora Macdonald in the Bodleian Library, it appears an arisaid might be held on the shoulders, necessarily by " clasps " of some sort, *i.e.* brooches.

[3] As elsewhere observed a silk arisaid is again used by Highland ladies with evening dress, and the " most ancient dress " is exceedingly handsome.

[4] *Ramsay of Ochtertyre*, ed. A. Allardyce, I., p. 540 ; II., p. 87.

both in them and in their ancient garb, which is worn regularly by the
Sovereign and Princes of the Royal Family when in Scotland.

It is not too much to say that but for the Royal influence of
George IV. and Queen Victoria (and the survival of the Highland
regiments through that Royal influence and in face of the persistent
efforts at suppression by the military authorities) the Highland dress
would have expired completely in the early nineteenth century.
Looking to the accounts of its continued widespread use amongst the
people during the last twenty years of the eighteenth century, the
interesting question is just why that use declined in spite of the efforts
and encouragement it received.

The answer, I am afraid, is that " progress " and " industrialism "
were attacking the clan system with far more deadly effect than the
saighdeirean-ruadh of the Duke of Cumberland. Military " victory " is a
hollow thing, which more often than not engulfs the " victor " than
the vanquished. It is the economist, the planner, and the industrialist
who " kill " a civilisation, and it is against these and crafty politicians
that nations have ever to beware. Indeed, in the pages of Miss Grant
of Rothiemurchus, one can perceive the waning of the clan-nexus and
the waxing of the cash-nexus.

The " self-made " monster was beginning to show his ugly face
(with sentiments very different from that of clansmen seeking to
" decore their hous " and " shawe thameselfes worthie of the hous
they are cum of "), and " the people " were being encouraged to believe
that " progress " meant money and ugliness. The Lum Hat (with or
without a " croon ") was playing havoc with inward mentality and
outward appearance, and being encouraged (by the smug and " unco
guid ") in every rural parish to replace the *breacan* and the braid
bonnet.

Fortunately for Scotland and the clan system, at this very juncture
Clanship, the Tartan, and the Highland Dress, were saved from
extinction by their resumption, under Royal influence, by the chiefs
and chieftains, who thus again functioned as the pivots on which a
nation's tradition is preserved, and again spread amongst the clansmen [1]
before the wonderful traditions of " the old days and the old ways "
had been submerged by the new materialism.

If a tribal aristocracy is to perform its functions, it must, though
not failing to acquire and exercise the international attributes of
chivalry and *noblesse*, assiduously maintain its own clannish local

---

[1] We must remember that whilst tradition lingers long amongst a rural
population, unless scientifically maintained and supported by such a people's
" natural leaders " (*i.e.* patriarchal chiefs and their experts (sennachies, heralds,
and so forth)), there comes a moment when—usually after a course of degenera-
tion of forms and symbolism into meaningless chaos of the " folk-lore " type
and debased " customs "—the whole civilisation of the race is suddenly, and
within a few years, abandoned, and the people become a deculturalised herd of
dissatisfied (naturally so) and uncouth " masses." (For a most instructive
examination of this " deculturalisation," see *Antiquity*, September 1943.)

dress, character, and traditions—an aspect which in some realms it, with disastrous consequences, has overlooked. It is one of the special features of a monarchy to see that it does not ; and in this George IV., the " First Gentleman in Europe," also showed himself an able tribal sovereign, a true " chief of chiefs," and was followed by his niece Victoria, and by King George VI. and his Scottish Queen.

Plate No. XII. depicts the costume of a Highland chief at the beginning of the nineteenth century. The portrait is that of George, 5th Duke of Gordon, who, whilst Marquis of Huntly, commanded the Gordon Highlanders (92nd Regiment).

With the reintroduction of the Highland costume several changes were evolved in the manner of wearing the garb. The ancient *breacan féile*, or belted plaid (plaid and kilt in one piece, as already described), became almost entirely disused. At the present day that form of the costume is seldom seen. The *breacan féile* has been quite supplanted by the more convenient *feilebeag*, or little kilt ; and the *feilebeag* itself is now made up in ordinary pleats in place of being in the old style of box-pleating. Then, as may be seen by reference to old prints, both kilt and hose are, nowadays, worn of a longer length than formerly. In Logan's *Scottish Gael* there is a Plate showing a piper of the 42nd Regiment, whose kilt is worn considerably above the knee, while his hose do not reach to above the middle of the calf of the leg. As now worn, the hose are fastened above the calf. On kneeling, the kilt should not touch the ground by about two inches, *i.e.* should just reach the middle of the knee-cap when standing. For rough work or hiking, however, the kilt should be (as of old) one and a half inches shorter if of " hard tartan," otherwise the skin behind the knee may be chafed, which does not occur when the kilt is worn at the old length.

The following is a description of the Highland dress as worn at the present day (for everyday wear and for full dress respectively).[1]

In the simplest form the Highland dress consists of *brògan*, hose (plain knitted), garters, *feilebeag* or little kilt, jacket, waistcoat, bonnet with sporran (animal or leather), and *sgian-dubh*. For outdoor use a stouter *bròg* is worn, and sometimes over the *bròg* or shoe, cloth or leather spats or gaiters, reaching to the calf. Though, for everyday use, the plaid has been largely superseded by the Inverness cloak or Highland cape, a plaid is often carried over the shoulder as a protection against the weather. The full plaid is about four yards long by one and a half yards wide, weighs about four pounds, and is generally fringed at the ends. The plaid, before being put on, should be folded twice lengthways, so that it is four times less in width than when spread out. It should then be folded once crossways, and placed once on the left shoulder, with the ends hanging down in front to about the level of the waist, care being taken that the two outer edges of one half of the plaid are placed on the shoulder, and to the right. Having

[1] For illustrations of the garb see Plates Nos. XIV. and XV.

placed the plaid on the shoulder in the manner as described, the top
end is turned back to the rear and passed to the right, round the body,
under the right arm, then across the chest, and over the left shoulder,
until it hangs down the left rear. The kilt is made of tartan, and the
jacket and waistcoat of tweed. The kilt should be belted round the
waist, and the apron fastened by a pin to the under-apron, the pin
being about two inches above the bottom edge of the kilt. The kilt
should never be worn with braces or straps. The *sgian-dubh* is worn in
the stocking, on the outer part of the right leg, in a hollow between
two bones. The bonnet (which bears a silver brooch showing the crest
of the wearer or of the wearer's chief within belt and buckle, see p. 200)
should be cocked, and should just touch the right ear.

For car-driving, as for riding, the kilt is an unsuitable garb, and
common sense indicates a version of the trews, viz. the tartan breeches,
long worn by military field-officers. Worn either with plain stockings
or riding-boots these form a natural evolution of the trews, far more
befitting the chieftain than sloppy " plus fours." For such breeches
the hunting tartan, or a weave in which the reds have been reduced
to beech-brown, are preferable, since the absence of flowing pleats
calls for a less brilliant shade, unless a belted plaid is also worn and
the tartan thereby more distributed. The writer wears either these or
the kilt according to circumstances, which is precisely what old-time
chieftains did (see p. 357).

The full-dress Highland costume is one of the handsomest in the
world, and few who have seen a ball after one of our Northern Gatherings will deny that the varied and waving clan tartan and the display
of Highland jewellery and ornaments are a brilliant sight. The full
dress is, viz. : doublet and waistcoat, with silver buttons of Celtic
pattern. The doublet of velvet, velveteen, or cloth ; the waistcoat of
scarlet or white cloth, or of tartan. Sporran, with tassels, and, if
armigerous, wearer's crest on its silver top. Diced or clan tartan fine
hose, either woven or cut from the web, secured by garters, ornamented
on the outside by tartan streamers. The kilt, worn as already described.
Dress *brògan* with ornamental silver buckles. Claymore and two pistols
worn on the left side ; on the right side is worn the jewelled dirk,
provided with knife and fork ; while the powder-horn, the mouthpiece
to the front, is worn under the right arm ; sword belt over the right
shoulder. The plaid should be the last thing put on and the first to be
taken off, though, when the full plaid is worn it is now often put on
under the shoulder-belt, in order that the latter may be better shown off.
This is really a survival of one manner of carrying the *breacan féile*
across the upper part of the person.

Perhaps the most effective and convenient form of plaid for full
dress is the following, being a modification of the old belted plaid.
It consists of a plaid made up and secured round the waist by a strap,
fastened underneath the waistcoat, the top end being secured to the
left shoulder by a brooch ; this form of plaid does not conceal any

part of the accoutrements, as is the case with the full plaid. This version of the belted plaid is, when cut for use with the coatee, often made fairly narrow at the waist. The effect (particularly with a doublet) is *far finer* and more correct if the plaid is brought farther round the waist at each side (as often seen in even nineteenth-century portraits, *e.g.* Plate XII.). The alternative for full dress is the full plaid, already referred to. The plaid, having first been folded, one end of it is placed on the left shoulder, so as to hang down in front, the rear part is then brought round under the right arm as before, and placed over the left shoulder, but under the other portion of the plaid, with the end hanging to the rear ; the shoulder-strap is then fastened over both, the two pendant parts are brought close together, so as to cover the left arm ; a portion of the rear part is then brought over towards the front, so as to conceal the point of contact, and is secured with a brooch, so that the two ends hang down like one piece of drapery. The bonnet, as already described, with a lace ruffle worn round the neck, complete a most becoming costume.

The tendency in recent years has been to keep abbreviating the doublet, or coatee, and waistcoat on nineteenth-century " mess dress " style, in order to " show more tartan," and disclosing the close-sewn parts round the waistline. The effect is (in my view) to unbalance the figure, making the upper part seem " too small " and the kilt " stiff looking." One need only compare the effect with the older style of doublet and waistcoat to perceive that covering the " tight-belted " waist-portion of the kilt, and allowing the tartan to appear when it commences to flow loosely, makes it catch the eye far better than the larger area of " motionless " tartan.

The Highland feather bonnet is not a modern invention, as many have tried to argue. There is ample evidence to the contrary. The feather bonnet seems always to have been used, not as an article of daily dress but rather one for high occasions. The portrait of the Highland Cavalier, *circa* 1660, by Wright (Plate III.), shows what may be regarded as the early form of the feather bonnet and from which it rapidly developed to its later style. Such feathers were certainly worn by chieftains even in the sixteenth century ; the 6th Laird of Ardgour was, for example, styled *Eoghan-na-hiteach*. The feathered head-dress got, in Gaelic, the name *A' bhoineid-mhor-iteach* (the great feather bonnet). This was the head-dress worn by the great Marquis of Montrose when he and his cousin (Patrick Graham of Inchbrackie) joined the Highland army in Atholl in 1644. There exists a painting said to represent Montrose wearing the feather bonnet and clad in the trews. This is copied from a picture once in the possession of Robert, 1st Lord Nairne, attainted in 1746, and who died in France. Lord Nairne was married to Margaret, daughter of Graham of Inchbrackie, the cousin and friend of the great Marquis.

Lord Archibald Campbell, in the London *Standard* (21st January 1884), wrote :

To speak plainly and to the point, £4,000 would preserve to the Highland regiments a head-dress which is historic and picturesque, which both officers and men like. I have lately caused a picture to be engraved of one of the Earls of Murray, painted by Jamesone, the Scottish Vandyke. He is arrayed in the Highland dress, kilt, and belted plaid ; on his head he wears a broad blue bonnet with ostrich feathers—Jamesone painted in the days of Charles I.[1]

The description of the early uniform of the oldest of our Highland regiments (the famous " Black Watch ") given in the chapter on Highland regiments, shows the rank and file stuck to the use of the great Highland bonnet, even when the cost of the head-dress had to be paid by its wearers.

At the time of the correspondence in both the London as well as the Scottish press in 1884, during one of the many attempts of the War Office to deprive the Highland regiments of the national garb, appeared many letters from Highland officers and others testifying to the popularity of the great Highland bonnet. One apt remark made in the course of the correspondence appeared in a letter signed " Lieutenant-Colonel, late 93rd Highlanders " :

One of the many obvious rejoinders to the arguments used by the opponents of the feather bonnet, " *that it is not suitable for skirmishing, nor for a gale of wind, nor for the African bush*," being the fact that these objections equally apply to the bearskin of the Guards, not *at present* proposed to be abolished !

We have since then come to learn that, as our ancestors well knew, feather bonnets and bearskins are appropriate to " great occasions," not for skirmishing in the bush ! The *boineid-mhor* is, however, just as sacrosanct as the bearskin, and Highland regiments have given ample proofs that they fight no worse through being permitted in peace to preserve their traditional uniform in its entirety.[2]

Of the old 78th (or Fraser's) Highlanders, in America in 1757, General Stewart of Garth says :

When the regiment landed in North America it was proposed to change the uniform, as the Highland garb was said to be unfit for the severe winters and the hot summers of that country. The officers and soldiers vehemently protested against any change, and Colonel Fraser explained to the Commander-in-Chief the strong attachment which the men cherished to their national dress, and the consequences that might be expected to follow if they were deprived of it. This representation was successful. In the words of a veteran who embarked and returned with the regiment, " Thanks to our generous Chief, we were allowed to wear the garb of our fathers, and in the course of six winters showed the doctors that they did not understand our constitutions, for in the coldest winters our men were more healthy than those regiments who wore breeches and warm clothing."

---

[1] This portrait, now in the Scottish National Portrait Gallery, and by J. M. Wright, is of date about 1660.   [2] See Appendix XIX.

In the march through Holland and Westphalia in 1794 and 1795, when the cold was so intense that brandy froze in bottles, the Highlanders, consisting of the 78th, 79th, and the new recruits of the 42nd (very young soldiers) wore their kilts, and yet the loss was out of all comparison less than that sustained by some other corps.

Of the 92nd (Gordon) Highlanders in 1800, Garth relates :

At this time a notion was very prevalent that the Highland garb was highly improper for soldiers in any situation, particularly in hot climates. Colonel Erskine gave in to this opinion, and put his men in trowsers of the strong thick cloth of which the greatcoats are made. In this he was strongly supported by the advice of the surgeon and many others. But this dress was too much for the constitutions of young men who had been recently so thinly clothed even in a cold climate. The increased warmth and confinement were followed by an inflammatory fever, which broke out in the transports of the regiment. Of this malady a number of the finest young men died, and a great many were so debilitated as to be totally unfit for service in Egypt. Their brave commander saw how inadvertently he had followed this advice, and declared he would never again alter the uniform.

In 1804 a letter from the War Office to Colonel (Sir Alan) Cameron, of the 79th Cameron Highlanders, broached one of the many efforts to abolish the kilt in the army :

I am directed to request that you will state for the information of the Adjutant-General your *private* opinion as to the expediency of abolishing the kilt in Highland regiments and substituting the tartan trews, which have been represented to the Commander-in-Chief from respectable authority as an article now become acceptable to your countrymen— easier to be provided, and calculated to preserve the health and promote the comfort of the men on service.

There are always sensible and solicitous grounds for abolishing Scottish, or Irish, customs. The gallant Colonel's reply, 27th October 1804, was forcible :

The Highlander . . . has the exclusive advantage, when halted, of drenching his kilt in the next brook as well as washing his limbs, and drying both, as it were, by constant fanning, without injury to either, but on the contrary, feeling clean and comfortable ; while the buffoon in tartan pantaloon, with all its fringed frippery (as some mongrel Highlanders would have it [1]), sticking wet and dirty to their skin, is not easily pulled off, and less so to get on again *in cases of alarm* or any other hurry, and all this time absorbing both wet and dirt, followed up by rheumatism and fevers, which ultimately make great havoc in hot and cold climates ; while it consists with my knowledge that the Highlander in his native

---

[1] Laced trews were, as we have seen, a most ancient form of Highland dress, that of the chiefs and chieftains who rode. There was nothing " buffoon " or " harlequin " about them, but they were not the fighting garb of the Highlander afoot.

garb always appeared more cleanly and maintained better health in both climates than those who wore even the thick cloth pantaloon. Independent of these circumstances, I feel no hesitation in saying that the proposed alteration must have proceeded from a whimsical idea more than the real comfort of the Highland soldier, and a wish to lay aside the national martial garb, the very sight of which has upon many occasions struck the enemy with terror and confusion. . . . But I sincerely hope that his Royal Highness will never acquiese in so painful and degrading an idea (come from whatever quarter it may) as to strip us of our native garb (admitted hitherto our regimental uniform), and stuff us into a harlequin tartan pantaloon.

An eminent commander (living 1924) stated :

My opinion as to the kilt is that its advantages outweigh its dis-advantages for more reasons than meet the casual eye. It is a unique dress and keeps alive old traditions and the pride of race. It is picturesque and attracts the eye and warms the hearts of a noble race. It confers distinction on the wearer.

At the annual dinner of the Scottish Clans Association in November 1902, Colonel Ewart said that his father had commanded the 93rd Highlanders in the Crimea. The Highland dress had been said to be unsuitable for warfare. His father had told him that in the Crimea the health of the Highland regiments was excellent, owing largely to their dress. He (the speaker) had himself served through three campaigns in the kilt, and had no hesitation in saying that it was the finest campaign-ing dress a man could wear, and not at all cold.

In the 1914–1918 war, the kilt was worn with success even amidst the unfavourable conditions of trench warfare. From a camouflage aspect the tartan was, however, criticised by Whitehall (of course with a view to its abolition), but Highland indignation again resisted, and the kilts were covered by conspicuous ochre-coloured " aprons," far more conspicuous than even the chemico-dyed tartan cloth.

Had the Government ordered cloth of carefully toned vegetable-hued dye, producing a low-tone sett in the style of Burberry linings, the result would have been recognisable as the regimental sett, yet a more perfect camouflage than khaki or any other form of uniform.

When the " War for Freedom " and defence of small nations began in 1939, one of the first steps was an (at last successful) effort to get the national garb of *one* small nation—Scotland—off the military map ! The tartan, however, was retained as a flash on cap or shoulder.

In concluding this chapter one cannot do better than quote the remarks on the Highland garb made by Sir Walter Scott in 1821 :

It is the best dress fitted for the country of the Gael : intersected as it is by rivers and streams from their native hills, and exposed to the severity of a northern climate, they required a dress which united the recom-mendation of lightness and comfort, and *in no other dress are these so completely obtained* as in that which, as a plaid, formed during the day a graceful ornament, and at night a comfortable covering when forced from their pastoral employments to repose upon their native heath. . . . It is an ancient dress, a martial dress, and a becoming dress.

WOMEN'S HIGHLAND FULL DRESS

We have seen that in the past Highland women had picturesque dresses, which were overlooked in the late nineteenth and early twentieth centuries. Public irritation at besporraned girls masquerading in male Highland dress led, however, to re-examination of ancient female Highland dress, which indeed had never ceased to be worn in some upland North-East glens ; and in 1952 the old costume was officially resumed at the Aboyne Highland Gathering.

The dress consists of a full dirndl-gathered, or lightly pleated skirt, of the lightest tartan-material, worn with a low-cut velvet corsage (the " waistcoat " of the somewhat confused 1695 description), flagged on the lower edge, sometimes embellished with gold or silver braid, and with a lacing front, close-laced at the waist but expanding with the bust, the lacing passing round (or through holes under) an ascending row of Celtic silver or jewelled buttons. This corsage is worn over the loose white, or saffron, cambric or silken " undergown," with voluminous elbow-length sleeves (originally detachable), fixed at the shoulders with five bows of tartan ribbon and gathered at the elbow with another such bow and silver button.

From below the corsage flows out (close in front) the *arisaid*, in the picturesque backward sloping " pannier "-effect of eighteenth-century costume, which combines with the narrowing corsage-lacing to create an impression of a very slim waist, whilst this *arisaid*, floating backwards, is (8 inches from the end) brooched up plaid-wise to the right shoulder with a small-sized Celtic brooch, leaving the fringed " end " of the *arisaid* flowing downwards from the right shoulder and swinging picturesquely like the male plaid. The *arisaid*, thus worn, could be gathered round the left forearm when carrying a baby. A snood of tartan ribbon, brooched with a ¾-inch (smallest) badge-brooch, is the head-dress. Flesh-coloured nylon stockings and Celtic-laced dancing shoes complete the traditional dress. The skirt may be as short as, or above the knee for step-dancing, or 3 or 4 inches below for more general dancing, or ankle-length if desired, and in each case is perfect and picturesque for either exhibition or ballroom wear, and a proper counterpart of the man's full-dress Highland garb. I must emphasise that the plaid part is an essential portion of this as female full-dress, plaid and skirt having originally been the unseparated *arisaid*.

The principal plea for the male-masqueraders a year or two earlier was that dancing girls *must* wear full male dress—as picturesqueness required the shoulder plaid ! *Well, the arisaid-plaid is correct*, and a necessary part for securing the full traditional and picturesque effect of the genuine female highland dress. The corsage looks best in black, blue, or darkish green velvet, depending on the colour of the tartan. Celtic bangles may be worn.

PLATE XIV.

[*Photo : Aberdeen Press and Journal.*

THE TRADITIONAL HIGHLAND WOMEN'S DRESS.

(As preserved in the North-East Highlands, and resumed as official dress at
the Aboyne Highland Gathering.)

The skirt may be as short as the knee for step-dances and still retains its graceful and feminine character.

PLATE XV.

THE MacNeil of Barra.

Full-dress Costume of a Highland Chief (present century), showing Shoulder Plaid, Doublet worn with Jabot and Ruffles, Waist and Shoulder Belts (being the Dress as worn at H.M. Levees).

(Reproduced from Alasdair Alpin MacGregor's "Summer Days among the Western Isles," with permission of Messrs. Nelson and the author.)

X

The Tartan

THE name Tartan is unknown amongst the Highlanders. The true Gaelic word is *breacan*, which is derived from *breac*, meaning chequered.

Chequered garments, under the names of " Breach," " Brecan," " Brycan," " Breacan," etc., appear to have been common not only to the Caledonians and the Irish but also to the ancient Britons, as well as to the Celts of Europe.

In the *Æneid* of Virgil we find reference to the chequered garments worn by the Celts :

Virgatis lucent sagalis.
Translation.—Their cloaks are striped and shining.
Æneid, Book VIII., line 660.

The original use of these chequered garments was not, it is said, to show the tribe or clan to which their wearer belonged, but a distinctive emblem of rank or position. There was but one colour in the clothes of servants ; two in the clothes of rent-paying farmers ; three in the clothes of officers ; five in the clothes of chieftains ; six in the garments of Druids or poets ; while the King, *Ard-righ*, or Chief, had right to seven colours.

Breacan, or tartan, is mentioned by Turgot, the Bishop of St. Andrews, in a letter (late eleventh century) in Latin to King Malcolm Ceann-mór, where the Bishop speaks of the wearing of *diversis coloribus vestes*.

The earliest reference in Scottish literature to tartan seems to be in the chartularies of the Episcopal See of Aberdeen, where the statutes or canons of the Scottish Church, in 1242 and in 1249, and the ordinances of the See of Aberdeen, 1256, direct that all ecclesiastics be suitably apparelled, avoiding red, green, striped clothing, and their garments not to be shorter than the middle of the leg. Of the early Scotic Church and the external vestment of the priest, MacGregor says :

Over all was placed a wide, loose, flowing garment, called the Robe of Offering, a square or oval cloth having in the centre a hole through which the head was passed. It was usually striped or chequered with eight colours, to indicate that while officiating the priest was superior to the king, who, according to our ancient Court etiquette, wore seven colours in his tartan, while others wore fewer according to their rank.

The *Leabhar Breac* gives the following as the eight colours : yellow, blue, white, green, brown, red, black, and purple. In the celebration

o   385

of the Eucharist the sacred vessels were covered with two veils, the inner of pure white linen, the outer of chequered silk (*siric brec*).

Was it a tartan silk associated with the clan or district, thereby relating the sacraments to the " tribe of the land " ?

The Reformed Kirk decided to banish tartan from Divine Service, and prohibited

all using of plaids in the Kirk be Reidars or Ministers, namelie in tyme of thair ministry and using thair office. . . . Bot that their habite be of grave colour, black, russet, sad gray, sad brown, or searges. . . .

The clergy had a special, quiet sett of tartan devoted to their use, which was styled *Breacan nan Cléireach*. The sett is a plain blue, black and white one.

Whilst the tartans for ordinary wear were distinctive district setts, bright hued, yet for hunting, and such-like pursuits, it appears there was a general use of brown-hued tartan, of which the portrait of the seventeenth-century " chieftain " by Wright is a good example. The original " hunting setts " were probably, as in the case of Fraser and Mackinnon, effected by largely substituting brown for red.

George Buchanan (1582) remarks that the Highlanders delighted

to wear marled cloaths, specially that have long stripes of divers colours, sundry-ways divided ; and amongst some the same custom is observed to this day, but for the most part now they are brown, most near to the colour of the hadder, to the effect when they lie among the hadder the bright colours of their plaids shall not bewray them.

In some large clans there is a special so-called " chief's tartan," probably worn by his immediate relatives, *i.e.* his *derbhfine*. Chieftains often wore silken plaids. As regards their ordinary wear we find Heron's *History of Scotland* states that : " In Argyle and the Hebudae, before the middle of the fifteenth century, tartan was manufactured of one or two colours for the poor, more varied for the rich."

Among expenses of John, Lord of the Isles, in 1355, occur : " Unum sagulum de panno laneo. Unus caligarum braccatarum de tiretatana. III. ulnae pannus lineus croceus pro tunica." (A vest of woollen cloth ; one pair of tartan truis ; three ells of yellow cloth for a hood ; one tartan plaid ; fourteen ells of yellow linen for a tunic.)

Like other chiefs, the kings of Scots regularly wore the Highland dress, and interesting details of the Highland costume, as worn by James V. on his expedition to the Highlands in 1538, are preserved in the *Lord High Treasurer's Accounts*. The Treasurer, it will be noticed, debits the material, which accordingly was made up by the Royal tailors, who evidently included men skilled in making up the Highland dress.

In the Accounts of the Lord High Treasurer to King James V., in 1538, items relating to Highland dress and tartan for the Royal use appear as follows :

Item, in the first for ij. elnis ane quarter elne of variant cullorit velvet to be the Kingis grace ane schort Heland coit, price of the elne vj. lib. ; summa, XIIJ. lib. Xs.

Item, for iij. elnis quarter elne of grene taffatyis, to lyne the said coit with, price of the elne Xs. ; summa, XXXIJs. VJd.

Item, for iij. elnis of *Heland tartane* to be hoiss to the Kingis grace, price of the elne IIIJs. IIJd. ; summa XIIJs.

Item, for xv. elnis of Holland claith to be syde Heland sarkis to the Kingis grace, price of the elne VIIJs. ; summa VJ. lib.

Item, for sewing and making of the said sarkis IXs.

Item, for twa unce of silk to sew thame Xs.

Item, for iij. elnis of ribanis to the handes of them, IJs.

King James thus wore tartan trews, which would be of the brilliant Royal tartan, a velvet coatee, lined with green taffeta, and under the coat flowing underwear embroidered with silk thread and garnished with ribbons, which, judging from the tradition of ribbons of the Royal tartan worn by Charles II., may well have been of that description. Since there was more lining than cloth, the sleeves, etc., of the coatee may have been doubled of the green lining, which would contrast well with the brilliance of the Royal tartan, and King James must indeed have looked every inch an *Ard-righ* when he landed from the Royal lymphad.[1]

The Accounts do not mention plaid, bonnet, or accoutrements, probably because these were already in existence, whereas coat and trews are garments which call for renewal from time to time.

A few years later, Beaugué, the French historian, describing the Highlanders in the Scottish army at the siege of Haddington, 1548, relates that they wore a woollen covering of many colours (" certaines couvertures légères faites de laine de plusieurs couleurs ").

The remarks of the poet Taylor, who visited Braemar in 1618, with regard to *tartane* are given in the chapter in this work which treats of the Highland garb. The poet appears to have been particularly struck with the universal and undeviating uniformity of costume among the 1,500 persons who had assembled for the hunting party to which Taylor had been invited, for he states that : " Lords, knights, esquires, and their followers, all and every man, in general, were in one habit, as if Lycurgus had been there."

At the time of Taylor's visit the attachment of the Highlanders to their costume was so strong that any one, even though a stranger, who assumed the tartan of the clan was considered as being under the special protection of that clan.

The tartan cloth as worn by the Highlanders was of two descriptions, viz. *breacan*, the finer quality, worn as dress tartan, or by the women ;

---

[1] In the *Seton Armorial* a sixteenth century representation of " Malcolm Ceanmor " is shown in tartan trews ,cut on the cross, the tartan having a yellow ground with red overchecks.

and *cath-dath* (from *cath*, war, and *dath*, colour), the thick, coarse cloth worn by the men when at work, or when engaged in warlike service.

The " setts," or patterns, were many, each clan eventually having its own particular setts. The setts were classified as follows, viz. :

1. The *Chief's Dress Sett*, which was worn by him and by the members of his family only, *i.e.* of his *derbhfine*, one supposes, and where such setts are now in use they would properly be confined to those who are children or grandchildren of a chief, *e.g.* in the case of a peer-chief, those bearing courtesy titles.

2. The *Clan Tartan*, which was worn by the other members of the clan. The early " chiefly-rank " tartan must frequently have broadened into the clan sett, and so developed the *clan tartan* idea.

3. The *Hunting Tartan*, a dark or brown-based sett, worn in the chase by clans whose ordinary tartan was of a brilliant hue. (It may be mentioned parenthetically that clans such as MacKenzie, Gordon, etc., whose ordinary tartan sett is of a dark hue, wear the same sett for dress as is worn for hunting.)

4. *Family Setts.*—By this term I presume is meant tartans used by " families " within the clan, *i.e.* chieftains or their *derbhfine*, and a variant, no doubt by their branch, of the chief's tartan.

5. *Mourning Setts.*—Most of these seem mere imagination. Brown, in *History of the Highlands and Clans*, reproduces a black and white tartan which he noticeably calls the MacFarlane *Clan* sett. Such tartans were probably not " mourning setts."

6. *District Setts.*—These were setts which were common to the inhabitants of certain districts irrespective of clan names. Thus there were setts of tartan peculiar to such districts as Sleat, Glenorchy, Atholl, Strathearn, Badenoch, Huntly, Mar, etc.

7. The *Arisaid Setts* were worn by women, for the plaid used with the ancient dress, and generally white-ground setts, *e.g.* the Stuart tartan on a white ground, nowadays known as Victoria tartan.[1]

8. The *Royal Sett.*—This was the Dress Stewart (so-called " Royal Stewart ") tartan, and being the Royal, not the Stewart sett, it was appropriately enough worn by the regimental pipers of even the Hanoverian kings.

Prior to the Act of 1746 Highlanders were at great pains to perpetuate correctly the various clan and district setts of tartan. Martin, in his account of the Western Isles, alludes to the distinctive setts :

Every isle differs from the other in their fancy of making plaids as to the stripes in breadth and colours. This humour is as different through the mainland of the Highlands in so far that they who have seen those places are able at the first view of a man's plaid to guess the place of his residence.

---

[1] It is incorrect and effeminate for men to wear *arisaid*-setts, and a recent tendency to do this is condemned. Their beauty is seen when worn by women in mixed dances.

This, it will be observed, indicates, *not* that tartans had nothing to do with " clans," but that clans were exceedingly territorial, viz. " feudal," in character,[1] which is precisely what the expert witnesses in the *Ardgour* case (1938) emphasised (see Appendix XXX.). The tartan is thus at once co-related to the " cuntrie " and " chiftane of the cuntrie " in the Statute 1593 cap.[2]

Stewart of Garth writes :

In dyeing and arranging the various colours of their tartans they displayed no small art and taste, preserving at the same time the distinctive patterns (or setts as they were called), of the different clans, tribes, families, and districts. Thus a MacDonald, a Campbell, a MacKenzie, etc., was known by his plaid ; and in like manner the Athole, Glenorchy, and other colours of different districts were easily distinguishable. Besides those general divisions, industrious housewives had patterns distinguished by the sett, superior quality and fineness of the cloth, or brightness and variety of the colours. In those times, when mutual attachment and confidence subsisted between the proprietors and occupiers of lands in the Highlands, the removal of tenants, except in remarkable cases, rarely occurred, and consequently it was easy to preserve and perpetuate any particular sett or pattern, even among the lower orders.

Logan remarks :

The Highlanders had neither cochineal, lac dye, foreign woods, nor other excellent substances to impart various tints to their Breacan ; but their native hills afforded articles with which they had the art of dyeing brilliant, permanent, and pleasing colours. . . . A gentleman assured me that he had seen a garment upwards of 200 years old, the colours in which were still admirable. . . . Every farmer's good wife was competent to dye blue, red, green, yellow, black, brown, and their compounds. When we consider the care with which the Highlanders arranged and preserved the patterns of their different tartans, and the pride which they had in their manufacture, we must believe that the dyers spared no pains to preserve and improve the excellence of their craft. . . . The pattern of the web was not left to the weaver's fancy. He received his instructions by means of a small stick round which the exact number of threads in every bar was shown, a practice in use to this very day.

After the Revolution of 1688, when the Stuarts were driven from the throne, tartan, and the wearing of tartan plaids, became symbols of Royalist and political principles.

During the period immediately subsequent to the Union of the Parliaments of England and Scotland, tartan plaids were worn in the Lowlands of Scotland as a protest against the Union, which was far from popular among all ranks.

Shortly before the Rising of 1715 a special sett of tartan was invented, and was worn by sympathisers of the exiled Royal Family. The sett was known by the name of the " Jacobite Tartan."

[1] Old Regime in France, p. 5.　　　　　　[2] A.P.S. IV. 40.

In the chapter on " Highland Garb " it was noted that, about 1730, Edinburgh ladies used to distinguish their political principles by the method of wearing their tartan plaids. Tartan plaids, down to the time of the proscription of the tartan in 1747, were worn all over the Lowlands as an article of ladies' dress. When we find Ramsay of Ochtertyre stating that " in 1747, when I first came to Edinburgh, nine-tenths of the ladies still wore plaids," it becomes very difficult to believe what Scott says he was " told," viz. " that the use of tartan was never general in Scotland "—that is, " until the Union," he adds, and the use of " tartan screens " by ladies admitted ; but the ancient archery medals (going back to about 1600) show that, amongst archers anyway, tartan was the usual dress, even in the Lowlands.

The first military body to adopt tartan as part of their uniform was not, as might have been expected, a Highland regiment, but a Lowland one. The Royal Company of Archers, whatever they wore previously (and archery medals show that all Scottish archers wore tartan), in 1713 adopted a red tartan sett for their uniform.[1] The Royal Company of Archers were, however, the nearest guard of the *Ard-righ*—a survival of the *Luchd-tighe* (p. 92), and therefore properly wore the Highland dress allusive to the retinue of our monarchy. The first Highland regiment to wear tartan was the Black Watch (42nd), raised in 1739.

The proscription of tartan following " the '45 " led to the methods of preparing tartan, as known to the old Highlanders, becoming all but a lost art.

It is, at the present day, hardly realised what a prejudicial influence the proscription of the Highland dress and tartan had on Highland home industries. Before 1747, when tartan was universally worn, the cloth for the *breacan* was spun and dyed by the women, and woven by the weaver of the clachan. All the men knew how to make their own kilt, hose, and brogues ; while the village smith was an adept not only in manufacturing dirks, sgian-dubhs, and buckles, but could also fabricate the brooches, sporran-tops, etc. All that the inhabitants of the glen required, in the way of clothing and equipment, they were compelled to manufacture themselves, and, in this manner, were quite independent of the towns. The dyes needed for the preparation of the tartan were not, as nowadays, mostly mineral ones, but were derived from vegetable sources.[2] When the hated breeches had to be worn instead of the tartan, and all Highland weapons and ornaments were prohibited, there was then no use for the preparation of dyes by the housewife, for the weaving of the tartan by the village weaver, nor for the manufacture of weapons and ornaments by the smith of the glen. And when a generation had passed away, and the Highlanders were again permitted to wear their national garb, those who knew

[1] M'Clintock, *Old Highland Dress* (per Telfer Dunbar), p. 26.
[2] See Appendix XX. for a detailed list of these vegetable dyes.

the secrets of preparing the dyes for the tartan, spinning and weaving the cloth, and the smith who fabricated the Highland ornaments and weapons, had, too, passed away, leaving no successors behind them. This, at least, was the case in all too many instances. Fortunately, in some Highland glens, one can nowadays again purchase home-made tartan, and the smith of the clachan is starting to furnish us with home-made Highland ornaments and ironwork. Scottish craftsmanship is slowly reviving.

Before the Act for Abolition of Highland Dress and Tartan was repealed, many old setts were lost sight of. The measuring-sticks for the setts had been laid aside as of no value, or the guardians of these sticks had died, and the sett or setts were lost to posterity.

Logan, in his *Scottish Gael*, states that, in the middle of the eighteenth century, " Cloth, if good, and for sale, fetched 1s. per yard ; and tartan, if also good, and of fine colours, 1s. or 1s. 2d." " That industry and simplicity of life," adds Logan, " are now gone."

The people had, as Buchanan observes of the 1790s, taken to buying " Stirling plaids " instead of making their own *breacan* ; and with the rise in prices and scarcity (following on amongst other things, the Napoleonic Wars), and the bad times in the Highlands, people no doubt began buying cheaper non-tartan cloth. Highlanders consequently no longer made, and could no longer buy, the tartan, so took to broadcloth and trousers.

Amongst ordinary Highlanders, the folded plaid on shoulder, and the tartan scarf, were all that, in general, remained of the Highland dress, though the braid bonnet held sway well into the nineteenth century, for informal wear, until the tweed cap of industrialism all but extinguished it.

Fortunately, a few patriotic people, including a number of chiefs and chieftains, staunchly maintained the dress, and were sneered at for doing so, whilst a few of the Highland societies, founded under the ægis of the wave of Highland enthusiasm of the early nineteenth century, also encouraged it. However, Queen Victoria and her sons presently set a fashion which justified the chiefs who had maintained the dress, and soon forced the self-conscious remainder into resuming the garb ; and the tartan was saved as a living, practical, and officially recognised form of dress, which has thus never ceased to be, in one way or another, worn in the daily life of Scotland, and since the beginning of the present century the practice has grown by leaps and bounds.

The tartan of old days was much superior in durability to that of to-day. Its colours, too, of vegetable dye excelled in fineness and in fastness [1] the mineral dyes now employed in tartan manufacture. McIan and Logan, in *Highlanders at Home*, state :

[1] This, I am afraid, was not the case ! Some of the colours, amongst others, *e.g.* blues, were liable to fade ; indeed the irregularity of dyes, and tendency to fade irregularly, sometimes explains the apparent differences in tartans of the same clan.

Tartan, as known in later times, may be indisputably held to be an original Scottish production. . . . The fabrics of these are often exceedingly good in material and design, and the old webs are far from inferior to those of the present day. A plaid of elegant pattern has been obligingly submitted to us by Mrs. Mackintosh of Stephen's Green, Dublin, of the family of Macpherson of Crubin. The colours and texture are very fine, and there is a considerable intermixture of silk. She states that, when it is placed on the shoulders of her grand-daughter, it is the seventh generation by whom it has been worn ; and although thus more than two hundred years old, it is still in good condition, but rather threadbare. It is of the hand manufacture, and believed to have been the veritable tartan worn by her ancestors, the Clan Mhuirich. . . . Several remains of garments worn in 1745 display very fine thread and colours, which are still vivid.

A description of the *Luathadh*, or process of fulling or cleansing cloth, used in the Highlands in old days, is here appropriate. Six or eight, or sometimes even fourteen, women sat down on each side of a long frame of wattled work, or a board ribbed longitudinally for the purpose, and placed on the ground. The cloth, being wet, was then laid on the frame or board, and the women, kneeling, rubbed it with all their strength until their arms became tired, when they sat down, and, applying their bare feet, commenced the " waulking " in good earnest, singing one of the haunting " waulking song " melodies, the notes of which increased in loudness as the work proceeded. The following account of the manner of preparing the plaids, about the middle of the eighteenth century, is given in the " Agricultural Report of Caithness " :

When the web was sent home it was washed in warm water, and, if it was necessary to full it, the door was taken off its hinges and laid on the floor, the web being taken out of the water and laid on it. Four women, with bare legs, having sat down on a little straw at equal distances on each side, on the signal of a song (similar to the " Ranz de Vache " in Switzerland), each applied the soles of her feet to the web, and began pushing and tumbling it about until it was sufficiently done, when it was stretched out to dry.

There has been much controversy as to the antiquity of tartans as clan distinctions. Most responsible historians would now agree with Stewart's conclusion that

The use of specific tartans as cognisances of clans and families developed during the seventeenth and eighteenth centuries, but was never built up into a rigid system. No formal record of the designs, such as we have in heraldry, was kept.[1]

The lack of such " formal record " is indeed the cause of most of the controversy and ensuing problems. During the past few years, however, whenever a person or limb attired in " the proper tartan of

[1] D. C. Stewart, *Setts of the Scottish Tartans*, 1950, p. 16.

[Block by courtesy of the New Spalding Club.

CLOTH-WAULKING AT DUNVEGAN.

O*

the clan X . . . " occurs in armorial bearings, Lyon Court takes evidence, and defines such tartan, the system of definition adopted being (after careful consideration of " threads," etc.) the Logan system of one-eighth inch proportions as the only reliable one.

A record of authentic clan tartans is thus being gradually built up, on legal evidence and statutory authority, in the *Public Register of All Arms and Bearings in Scotland*, one of the National Public Registers of the kingdom.

Things were not, however, so completely haphazard, since records were kept by the " tartan sticks " recorded by Logan in the *Scottish Gael*, 1831. Unfortunately, most of these vanished during the proscription, 1746–1782.

Such a system was as definite as most medieval measurements, as any one can verify by studying castle-building contracts or the measurements of old buildings. By 1700 the chief was laying down what the tartan was, *e.g.* Clan Grant ; the " clan-tartan idea " was becoming a conscious one, though the design was in most cases much older.[1]

Tartans, as we have seen, had both a rank and a district connection. Since " district " often just meant " clan cuntrie," there would, as in other matters, be a local, *i.e.* familial, " pattern," and the more elaborate and distinctive " pattern " worn by the chief, or " chiftane of the cuntrie," and his nearer relatives—the *derbhfine*, or *daoine-uasail*—naturally ended by becoming, first traditionally, and then consciously, " the clan pattern." [2]

By the commencement of the eighteenth century, some clans, *e.g.* the Grants, were being equipped with what were meant to be uniform setts, and the Union gave an impetus to the tartan as a Scottish garb. Its proscription presently gave it an added interest, and in the revival which followed its restoration in 1782 the clan aspect became the dominant one. Now every chief and clan wanted to resume " their " tartan, and the former roughly local or tribal tradition came to have conscious precision, though many mistakes were made and much available portrait and such-like evidence overlooked.

The tartan had, however, now become—and this is the important point—an invaluable clan-livery. The setts, whether of tribal or district origin, were now, along with the ancient " strap-and-buckle " crested cap-badge of the chief, an ideal dress for giving to each clan traditional pride and conscious cohesion. Clan tartans therefore became, in their organised form, invaluable for preserving the clan as a tribal community at the moment when modern and industrial changes were in so many directions tending to minimise tribo-familial activities.

Just as feudalism had in Scotland saved the Celtic social system during the thirteenth to seventeenth centuries, so the tartan came to its rescue in the eighteenth and nineteenth. Thanks to these and to

---

[1] *Tartans of the Clans and Families*, p. 9.
[2] Cf. *Setts of the Scottish Tartans*, p. 32.

its laws of armory, which, along with the tartan, have such an important part in Scottish dress, Scotland has still an age-old and vigorous clan system, functioning effectively within, and along with, modern national developments.[1]

If Stewart of Garth and Sir Walter Scott were " dreamers of dreams who out of a (not so ' fabulous ') story, fashion a nation's glory," but for their vision in recapturing the spirit of clanship at the critical moment, Scotland to-day would have been as shadowy a name as Mercia, Bernicia, or the other lost kingdoms of the heptarchy.

The tartan is not only to the Highlander, but also for at any rate over two and a half centuries to the Lowland Scot, the emblem of his nationality. Any attempt, therefore, to disparage it or abolish the tartan awakes the ire and offends the sentiment of Highlanders and Lowlanders alike. Scottish feeling was stirred to its depths in 1881 when the War Office, in one of its periodic fits of Scoto-phobia, proposed to do away with the distinctive tartans worn by the Scottish regiments, and to substitute, instead, one uniform tartan for all the Highland battalions. The numerous and strong expressions of opinion of the highest to the lowest in Scotland against the proposed innovation caused the abandonment of their disgraceful scheme so contrary to Scottish character and clan instinct.

What does not the tartan mean to exiled Highlanders, and do not their hearts " warm to the tartan " when, on returning home, after many years' absence in a foreign clime, they hear the sounds of the pipes and see the waving tartans of a Highland regiment ? Not only that, but the sight of the tartan reminds us of the days when the kilt and the tartan were our youthful dress, and of happy days spent on the hills or by the loch-side in our loved Highlands—scenes which can be eclipsed by no other land on earth. All my readers of Scottish nationality will agree that, when our " heart does not warm to the tartan, it will be as cold as death can make it ! "

---

[1] D. C. Stewart, *Setts of the Scottish Tartans*, pp. 17, 15 ; Innes of Learney, *Tartans of the Clans and Families of Scotland*, p. 11. Whilst scorn has rightly been hurled at the *Vestiarium* (the inaccuracies—where not imaginations—have lately been checked against some cited portraits), the Ross/" Urquhart " MS (never seen by critics such as Scott) came to light temporarily in a lawyer's office in the 1890s, and was examined by Andrew Ross, Ross Herald, a cautious and reliable antiquary, who held that he could not say that it was not an old MS. It seems not unlikely that " 1721 " (the date written on it) was fairly near its completion ; that its compilation was perhaps under the *aegis* of the Earl of Cromartie (whose Mackenzie *history* contains matter as unconvincing as the " Urquhart " lucubrations) ; that it was framed to crystallise the tartan-conscious concept materialising around 1700–07, and probably did formulate the early eighteenth-century ideas seen developing in the Grant Baron Court and other regulatory steps, as consciously setting about organising old custom into set forms (*Tartans of the Clans*, p. 9). This deserves further investigation. It transpires photographs of pages of the " 1721 " MS. exist (J. Telfer Dunbar, *History of Highland Dress*, p. 138). One wishes these were illustrated for further expert analysis, and that such a contentious MS., extant in a legal firms hands about 1896, might yet be located for *modern* scientific tests.

XI

Highland Surnames and Titles

THE introduction of surnames into Scotland is traditionally said to date from the reign of King Malcolm III. (*Ceann-mór*), in the second half of the eleventh century. The *Chronicles of Scotland* relate that " He was a religious and valiant King, he rewarded his nobles with great lands and offices and commanded that the lands and offices should be called after their names."

Quite possibly the custom of adopting description by " surname " may have made a beginning in his time, such surnames being essentially descriptions identifying great persons—primarily no doubt the " representers " of families patriarchal or allodial ; and it is also quite likely that in Malcolm's time there commenced grants of lands by the *Ard-righ*—probably by verbal gift before witnesses—as the first steps in altering the old allodial tenures. Naturally we cannot learn much about names and surnames until we reach the days of written records, and it is from early charters and contracts that we obtain evidence regarding them.

Surnames being primarily for distinguishing people, early surnames are almost all in some way descriptive. Either they mark out the person from his office, or work, from some individual peculiarity, or from his dwelling-place or property, or from his relationship to some-one else, *i.e.* a description of his pedigree. The Norman was usually distinguished by the name of his lands—his fief, because this was the most important fact. Nobility depended on ownership of " free property " ; moreover each fief had a *caput* or " chief-chymmes," the " hearth of the race," as we have seen, and such a designation was in every way useful as a surname. An early allodial *duthus* usually had no name ; the race had occupied it before that was thought of, and were self-sufficient. Their whole being was bound up in their beloved *duthus*, and accordingly the subject of distinction was their descent from and relationship to the eponymus, and bound up in his name (which became sacred to the tribe) or the name of any great— or sacred—office which he and the successive chiefs held, such as " servant of Saint X . . ." (Gillie X . . .). The *duthus* being name-less, and having no *caput* other than the hearth of the eponymus and his representer, the " cuntrie " came to be called after him also, *e.g. Duthaig MacLauchlan* (MacLachlan's country), and so forth.

It is quite illogical to suppose that a patrimonial name suggests that the tribe had no interest in, or fixed, territory. On the contrary, it may often indicate that they occupied such territory (and therefore that their patriarchal eponymus held it allodially by occupation) before the idea of place-names had evolved, and been given to this and that part of the territory by the tribe. The very fact of a great district being called " MacX's country " implies its possession from the dawn of civilisation. Later on the chief's *Dun*, or Palace, acquired a name ; and under feudalisation became the *caput* of the fief ; or the fief was recorded by some place-name (usually from the chief fortalice) in the Royal Books ; and thus a secondary, and " baronial " name came into existence, often used along with, or in addition to, the chief's patriarchal title.

In the " suit roll " of the king, everyone was called by the name of their fief, and answered to that ; so it naturally became their name. Thus the Lords of the Isles came, from being styled " Macdonald," to be entitled " de Isla " by the monkly scribes who kept the records.

The fief was regarded, as elsewhere pointed out, as the foundation of the *familia*, and the fief name became the family name, where there was no other. Sometimes, however, the old allodial pedigree name of the " Representer of the eponymus " continued ; and became a distinct " family name," covering not only the people of this and that fief, but others settled on other fiefs (creating indeed difficult double loyalties) ; and also fiefs got lost, whilst clans or families subsisted on some other piece of land ; and (as already shown) " the clan " or " family " of an armigerous line of chiefs came to be itself regarded as an incorporeal heritable subject—a " fief " feudally dealt with in Crown charters ; and, as every fief had to have a name, the clan name or chief name, in fact, became the " name " of such a fief, and the " name " of the coat of arms recorded in name of its representer. The " family name " or " clan name " thus became the index of membership of the community. As Stevenson explains :

Roughly speaking, the surname of to-day is taken as the index of the family, and the Christian name the *difference*, to use the heraldic expression, which distinguishes one member of the family from another.[1]

Since a clan is an incorporeal heritable subject, and a " noble " one, we find the chief of a whole clan, or name, described as " The Laird of Maclean," " The Laird of Mackintosh," " The Laird of MacLeod," and so on, even in the Acts of Parliament and Privy Council. In light of what has been said, it will be seen that this was not only strictly correct, but is an acknowledgement of the nobiliary character of the clan—a real compliment to the race. The chief could not have been properly termed " Laird of MacX " unless " MacX " was a noble fief. It therefore implies that the MacX clan is a noble community.

The origin of clan sept names may be traced to a variety of causes. The principal of these were the following, viz. : (1) The names of those

---

[1] *Heraldry in Scotland*, p. 364.

related to the chief by marriage, though not blood relations of his clan. (2) Those who, though unconnected by blood with the clan, had become bound to it by bonds of manrent. (3) Those of the blood of the clan who, in order that they might be better distinguished from their namesakes, adopted (*a*) a pedigree by-name, such as Angus MacRanald, Angus the son of Ranald (though the man's surname might have been not MacRanald but MacDonald) : (*b*) a by-name derived from some profession or hereditary occupation or office—thus we have Macsporran anglicised Purcell, or the son of the hereditary purse-bearer ; Macbrayne, or the son of the judge ; Macintyre anglicised Wright, the son of the carpenter, etc. : (*c*) a by-name given on account of some personal peculiarity or infirmity. In this category we find Macilleriach, or the son of the brindled, or spotted one (really MacDonalds) ; MacGillivantic, or the son of the stutterer, who belong to the MacDonells of Keppoch : (*d*) those of the clan who were originally distinguished by the name of the part of the clan territory occupied by them. In this category we find such names as Toward, who are really Lamonts, Lennys, who are really Buchanans, etc.: (*e*) clan names which have been unaccountably anglicised ; such as Macmillan anglicised Bell, Mackinnon taken phonetically from Gaelic *Mac Fhiongh'uin*, and under the impression that it was derived from *Mac ionmhuinn*, beloved son, later anglicised Love: (*f*) a varied collection of names adopted by members of oppressed and proscribed clans, such as MacGregors, MacFarlanes, and Lamonts. The MacGregors, as already narrated, were compelled by law to change their own name for others : (*g*) names adopted after " the '45 " in order to conceal their owners' identity.

Until comparatively recent times (indeed still—on the Moray Firth coast—as may be verified from its Valuation Rolls) it was quite common in the Highlands for individuals to possess two surnames, one of these being the clan name, while the other is a by-name. To instance this curious custom the following extracts from the works of well-known Celtic writers are of interest.

Skene remarks :

The position of the dependent septs will be best understood by the bonds of manrent or manred which came to be taken by the Chiefs from their dependents, when the relation constituted by usage or traditional custom was relaxed by time, or when a new relationship was constituted at a later period. Of these bonds it was frequently a condition that the name of the superior should be assumed. Thus we find MacGregors binding themselves and their descendants to " call themselves and to be Gordons." [1]

---

[1] Skene, to be quite plain, did not know or understand what modern research (as on examination of Mackenzie's *Works* and Nisbet's *System of Heraldry*) informs us, that this had nothing to do with " septs " but was simply the old tribal custom of " adoption " which Lord Aitchison has now (1941) recognised as part of the heraldic and princely Law of Arms (1941 S.C. 684).

Stewart of Garth writes :

Many families of the same descent had two names, one common to the whole clan, as MacDonald, MacLeod, etc., the other to distinguish a branch, which last was called the *bun sloinne* or genealogical surname, taken from the Christian name or whatever designation marked the first man who branched off from the original family. In this manner Campbell of Strachur is always called Macartair or Macarthur, Campbell of Asknish, MacIvor, and a tribe of the Robertsons in Perthshire, descendants from Strowan, are also called Clanivor, etc.

Robert Mackay, historian of Clan Mackay, in his work (published 1829), observes :

In the Highlands, where there were many of the same name and surname, the manner in all periods to distinguish them was to design them after their forefathers. Thus Sir Robert Gordon usually designs the Highlanders : he calls John Gun, whose father was Robert, *John Robson*, because there were many in one district named John Gun ; and for a similar reason he terms Niel Mackay, *Niel-Mack-Ean-Mack-William*, *i.e.* Niel, son of John, son of William. In this manner, Thomas Mackay and his two brethren are surnamed *Neleson*, in place of Mackay, because their father was Niel ; and in former times the family surname, such as Mac-Donald, Mackay, Mackintosh, MacKenzie, etc., was applied only to the chief of the clan.

The *Statistical Account of Scotland*, 1845, (parish of Tain, in the Synod of Ross) :

Most of the landowners, and in truth most of the people, bore the name of Ross, or, to speak more correctly, almost everybody possessed two surnames, by one of which (in general a patronymic beginning with Mac) he was universally known in conversation, though he deemed himself called upon to change it to Ross, or sometimes to Munro, whenever he acquired any status in society, or became able to write his name. (Easter Ross, it may be observed, was of old divided between these two clans.) . . . From this circumstance of each individual being furnished with two appellations seems partly to have arisen the remark, which has found its way into Encyclopedias, that Tain is famous for nicknames ; but, partly, the remark was once true, for, when the by-names of those who had risen in society were forgotten, it became absolutely necessary to invent others (and those often of the oddest description) to distinguish the multitudes of Rosses and Munroes.

These extracts show the number of sept names (or by-names) which existed among the clans. Many by-names were finally adopted by Highlanders instead of their clan names. Many names lost sight of in the old country, still flourish on the other side of the Atlantic. Stewart of Garth, commenting on extinct sept names, remarks :

It has been alleged that the more ancient names and people must have been removed by violence, or extirpated to make room for the more recent clans. This opinion seems founded on conjecture rather than fact. Such changes often occur from natural causes. The name of Cunnison or Macconich was prevalent in Athole in the fifteenth, sixteenth, and seventeenth centuries, yet not an individual of that name now remains. All died out without violence or expulsion. In the same period there were twenty-four small landed proprietors (or wadsetters, as they were called) of the name of MacCairbre in Breadalbane, but not a man of that name is now to be found, nor is there even a tradition of one of them having ever been extirpated, or their lands taken from them by force. All became extinct by natural causes. One of these MacCairbres, probably their Chief, possessed Finlarig Castle, afterwards one of the principal seats of the family of Glenorchy.[1]

Of sept names seldom heard in Scotland, but met with in the United States and Canada, we may instance MacNider, or MacNiter, from the Gaelic *Mac-an-fhigheadair*, son of the weaver.

Many Highland surnames (both clan and sept) were derived from religious sources. Macpherson, son of the parson ; Mactaggart, son of the priest ; Macvicar, son of the vicar ; Macnab, son of the abbot ; Maclean, son of the servant of St. John ; Gilfillan, the servant of St. Fillan. Many other such examples might be quoted. Not only this, but the place-names of the Highlands abound in reference to churches and saints.

The evolution of clan and of sept names from one common progenitor is an interesting study. For example, there is Macduff, the son of Duff ; Mackintosh, the son of the *toisach* ; Shaw Mackintosh, son of Mackintosh, thus the surname Shaw ; Farquhar Shaw, thus the surname Farquhar ; Farquharson, or Mackerracher, the son of Farquhar ; Findla or Finlay Farquharson, hence the surnames Finlay and Findlay ; Finlayson and Mackinlay, the sons of Finlay, etc.

When we examine Scottish heraldic practice it is interesting to observe the manner in which the cadet families of a clan acknowledge their dependence on their chief. For instance, the motto of the Duke of Argyll, Chief of the Clan Campbell, is " Do not forget." MacIver Campbells reply, with their motto, " I will never forget." Campbell of Auchmannoch, " I byde my time." Breadalbane, as Chief of a branch-clan, cries " Follow me." The answering cries of his cadets are : Campbell of Mochastir, " I follow " ; Lochdochart, " I follow straight " ; Barcaldine, " I am ready " ; Achallader, " Without fear " ; Lawers, " Do and hope " ; and Aberuchill, " Victory follows the brave." The motto of the Chief of Clan Grant is " Stand fast " or " Stand sure." The answer of the Grants of Corrimony is " I'll stand sure." This, as Stevenson remarks (*Heraldry in Scotland*, p. 207), is one of the finest things in clan heraldry, and care should be taken by cadets on matriculation to observe it.

In the United States of America, Highland names are rapidly undergoing a process of transmogrification. Thus, we have Urghad

---

[1] See Appendix XIII.

for Urquhart, McCollister for MacAllister, Furguson for Ferguson, Cahoun for Colquhoun, McCloud for MacLeod, MacGuilvery for Mac-Gillivray, McCullom for MacCallum, Chissim for Chisholm, McKlemin for MacLamont, McGlauflin for MacLauchlan, MacCray for Macrae, McCawley for MacAulay, etc.

TITLES OF CHIEFS AND CHIEFTAINS

Scottish law and nobiliary practice, like those of many other European realms, recognise a number of special titles, some of which relate to chiefship and chieftaincy of families and groups as such, others being in respect of territorial lairdship. These form part of the Law of Name which falls under the jurisdiction of the Lord Lyon King of Arms, and are recognised by the Crown.[1] At the instance of the Lord Advocate they have even been subject of important legal decision involving estates, and also entail disputes.[2] As regards these chiefly, clan, and territorial titles, by Scots law each proprietor of an estate is entitled to add the name of his property to his surname, and if he does this consistently, to treat the whole as a title or name, and under Statute 1672 cap. 47, to subscribe himself so.[3]

Whilst the heads of Highland tribes and clans were, briefly, or simply known at home as " Maclachlan," " Mackintosh," etc., the chiefs of Lowland families took their surnames from their lands, e.g. " Sir Andrew de Leslie," or " Lord of Leslie," but were subsequently also designated " of " the same, hence titles such as " Udny of that Ilk," and " Dundas of that Ilk," whilst cadets were designated, e.g. " Dundas of Duddingston," or " Udny of Auchterellon." Highland chiefs had also to be designated in land charters, and accordingly were styled, e.g. " Cameron of Lochiel," " Macleod of Dunvegan," or " Macdougall of Dunollie." Outside the Highlands, such titles suggested cadetship rather than chiefship, and the simple patronymics such as " Maclachlan " or " Macnab " were found insufficient designation when the chief was at a distance from his own neighbourhood. Therefore, in order to make their status clear at Court and amongst the Lowland lairds " of that ilk,"—a style which had come to be recognised as an " honorific title indicating that the man is head of his family," and which " might or might not imply ownership of land," [4] many Highland chiefs adopted the same style (" MacLachlan of that Ilk " in 1573 is probably the earliest), were, like " M'Corquodale

---

[1] Sir R. Douglas, *Baronage of Scotland*, p. 11 ; Prestonfield Act, 8 & 9 Vict. cap. 23, sec. 20.

[2] See Innes of Learney, *Scots Heraldry*, chapter XV.

[3] Stevenson, *Heraldry in Scotland*, p. 441, e.g. " Jas. Campbell of Glenfalloch." Only peers and bishops are allowed to sign without prefixing Christian name or initial. Wife and daughters, of course, similarly use the territorial chiefly title in signatures.

[4] Gordon Peerage Case, pp. 246–247.

of that Ilk," so recorded in the Lyon Register, and were—alike in Crown charters and Acts of Parliament—referred to as " The Laird of Mackintosh," or " The Laird of Macfarlane," although no such place existed.[1]

This, however, was a technically correct description, because the clan itself, or family if such community had been recognised by the Crown and its High Sennachie, the Lord Lyon, as one of the honourable communities of the kingdom, was regarded as an incorporeal heritable incorporation passing from chief to chief successively as " noble heritage," and accordingly the description " Laird of Macfarlane " recognised the Macfarlanes as being a corporate community to which each successive chief was heir or heretrix—to use the phraseology of Lord Lyon Erskine in 1672. The same principle was recognised in the fact that a clan and its chiefship could be the subject of a Crown charter.

Burt duly notices these Scoto-Celtic titles in *Letter* XII., p. 153 :

One thing which I take to be exclusively in its kind [2] . . . a single enclosed field adjoining . . . this town, as near as I can guess about 5 or 6 acres, called Fairfield. This to the owner gives the title of Laird of Fairfield, and it must be a neglect or kind of affront to call him by his proper surname, but only " Fairfield." For those they call " Lairds " in Scotland do not go by their surname, but—as in France—by the name of their House, Estate, or part of it.[3]

The practice is also found in other clannish lands, such as Hungary, the social organisation of which is of a particularly clannish character, and has many affinities with the Scottish clan system ; the great estates belonging to the " original tribes " being held on a title of *primae occupationis*.[4] As in Scotland many, but not all, of these were converted into feus [5] and the notion of nobility is associated with the ownership of free real-property ; [6] subsequently, as in Scotland, grants of nobility, apart from corporeal land, were effected by *litterae armoriales*, conferring a grant of arms.[7] Their practice regarding tribal and *noblesse* titles is just like that in Scotland :

[1] Buchanan of Auchmar, on " Surnames."
[2] This shows Burt's English insularity ; we shall see the custom is used in all tribo-feudal countries.
[3] He adds : " But if the lairdship be sold the title goes along with it to the purchaser and nothing can continue the name of it to the first proprietor but mere courtesy." This was maybe an effort of Burt's to deprecate the perpetuance of such titles, but, as we shall see, he was wrong—and it was indeed expressly so decided in the instance of the Crown [8] in various cases where attainder under *surnoms terriens* depended on whether the " title " was or was not part of the name (see *Scots Heraldry*, p. 149). He was right enough as to the purchaser acquiring a right to the title by the same law under which the vendor had himself so acquired it (unless expressly excluded) (*ibid.* p. 150).
[4] Ruvigny, *Titled Nobility of Europe*, 1910, pp. 108, 112.   [5] *Ibid.* p. 109.
[6] *Ibid.* p. 105.   [7] *Ibid.* p. 112.   [8] (See p. 404, *infra*.)

Either a land-name or a patriarchal name became permanent and to it were added the estate name. . . . If this " second surname " is held for four generations or so [1] it also becomes permanent and is termed the *prædicatum*, and this name of the property is likewise added and perpetuated . . . it making no difference whether they were, or were not, really in possession of the land in question. Some families used, and even now use, two, three, or even more, *prædicatum*.[2]

Such is the explanation of names such as " Lazlo de Lombos," and the practice it will be observed is exactly similar to that obtaining in Scots law, as determined alike in the Lyon Court and Court of Session, where the matter was fully debated *in foro* at the instance of the Lord Advocate in the Jacobite Attainder Cases, where the forfeitures' effects depended precisely on whether the " territorial designation " was really part of the name. The Court held that if adopted as such, and so used, it was. On this ground these titles are, as names, recorded in birth, death, and marriage registrations, but unless the person registering is actual owner of the estate, or the wife or child of such, the Registrar requires a certificate of matriculation from Lyon Court, vouching that it *is* the person's name duly recognised in the Scottish nobiliary registers, where it is a *nomen dignitatis* of *nobilitas minor*.[3]

In Spain and the Celto-Basque provinces the same custom is found as law, and thus explained officially by the Spanish Kings of Arms :

Before the time that importance was attached to lineage, families were known only by their patronymics. . . . Then later, in order to be distinguished from each other there was added to the patronymic, either the name of the castle fortress and tower that they conquered, or the name of the place where they were born. . . . In the year 1384 lived Sancho Martinez—Lord of Leyba. He was father of Ladron Martinez de Leyba who took this second name.[4]

It has been desirable to be somewhat explicit about the foregoing and to cite the Continental analogies, since Counsel are aware that a foreign authority, or decision, often impresses metropolitan departments and jurisdictions, where citation of a Scottish authority or decision is politely but firmly " pooh-poohed " and since in London the tendency some twenty or more years ago was [5] (whilst admitting

---

[1] Here we have the concept of " perfect nobility " achieved by tenure for three generations (Nisbet, *System of Heraldry*, I., p. 176), and the similar Celtic law that he who held land or heritage for three generations acquired an indefeasable right of property therein (*Tartans of the Clans and Families of Scotland*, p. 33 ; Skene, *Celtic Scotland*, III., p. 176).

[2] Ruvigny, *Titled Nobility of Europe*, p. 107.

[3] *Juridical Review*, September 1940, p. 214.

[4] Innes of Learney, *Law of Succession in Ensigns Armorial*, p. 44.

[5] The War Office and other State Departments, however, duly recognise them, on production of Lyon's Warrant, which is satisfactory. They also (*e.g.* Passport Officers) will not accept such names without production of authority from the Lord Lyon.

the Irish titles, such as " The MacDermott of Coolaven " and " The MacGillicuddy of the Reeks ") to deprecate any Scottish titles ; or indicate bluntly that " they don't recognise Scotch titles." The blow to this attitude (which had been adopted in several departments shortly after the 1914–1918 War), came when it was established that in Scots law, they were *part of the name*, and had been so held, at the instance of the Crown (!) and to secure convictions under an English treason law. The English authorities " could not have it both ways " and had no right to disregard peoples' lawful names, or apply other names to people ; so the old Scoto-Celtic titles survive—where their holders are thick-skinned enough to stand out for their rights. The legal point is also of some importance to Scots in U.S.A., etc., where " titles " are (it is understood) not admitted. Here, although the " name " itself enshrines a very high social " title," it is in law a name (consisting of the words employed, neither more nor less) and must therefore be registered as it stands.[1]

The point was indeed raised, by the heirs of some Highland chiefs whose predecessors had been forfeited after " the '15 " and the Lord Advocate, on behalf of the Crown, maintained, successfully, that the attainders were effective because the designations " of Lochiel," " of Clanranald " etc., were *part of the name* :

Lord Advocate : He was properly enough called, according to the use of speech, " of Lochiel," and having been attainted by that name, if he had got a pardon, must have been pardoned by the same. . . . People lose their rights by forfeiture, but not their ordinary names,[2] and these names do not necessarily imply either the property nor right of apparency in the estates.[3] Gentlemen are named of their estates, and retain the same titles after they have sold them, which are also given to their eldest sons.[4]

In the cases where the Crown confers a name, *e.g.* " Heraldic Names " (such as those of the Heralds and Kings of Arms), the phraseology is instructive ; the appointee being by the Commission

[1] The Crown, as Secretary of State Grey explained in the *Jones of Clytha* case, is not bound to recognise capricious assumptions of name, or changes not connected with " descent or rights of property," and that is just the point ; " chieftainly " names are " officially recognised " by Lyon only in favour of those entitled substantively, or by the courtesy—*e.g.* the heir and younger daughters—to the arms " of that description," undifferenced, or with the heir's label (*Law of Succession in Ensigns Armorial*, p. 44). The arms *are* property (*MacDonell* v. *Macdonald*, 1826), and property which is " of that description," *e.g.* the description " Moir of Leckie," as was held in the Leckie entail case (*Moir* v. *Graham*, M. 15538). The arms being an indivisible right (*Maclean or Ardgour* v. *Maclean*, 1941) the ambit of those who get " recognised " in chiefly and territorial title names is quite well protected, and quite clear—in fact the chiefly or chieftainly *gilfine*.

[2] Here compare the case of the divorced Countess Cowley, who, although she ceased to be a peeress, did not lose the " name " she had lawfully acquired —" Violet, Countess Cowley " (1901 A.C.)

[3] Lochiel Case, Morrison's *Dictionary of Decisions*, 4161.

[4] Cluny-Macpherson Case, *ibid.*

commanded to be " named, written, and intitulat ' Sir Jerome Lindsay of Annatland, Knight, Lyon King of His Heiness Armes'." [1] The prefix " Sir " being, it will be noticed, also " part of the name."

These chiefly and territorial names are, however, each a *nomen dignitatis* of *nobilitas minor*, and the Representer of the House is declared to be " Known " (*nobilis* means " known ") " and publicly Recognised and Recorded " in the Registers of Honour of Lyon, as H.M. Supreme Officer of Honour, and the " name " is likewise the recorded title of the incorporeal armorial fief ; therefore mere assumption is not sufficient to warrant these territorial and chiefly names (though they are possessible by inheritance-apparency along with the arms). Their constitution, or any change of them, requires to be made by warrant in the Lord Lyon's Registers, and as explained, the right to them goes with the right of what in Moir of Leckie's case was well termed, the " arms of that description," [2] again emphasising the close relation of heraldry to the clan system and its titles.

Early in the nineteenth century, the Highland chiefs appear to have resolved to distinguish themselves from the Lowland lairds of that ilk, by substituting a re-duplication of the patronymic, hence titles such as " Macgregor of Macgregor." Since a territorial designation was, as in legal proceedings, also necessary or convenient, [3] others styled themselves, *e.g.* " Macdougall of Macdougall and Dunollie." There is nothing illegal in these somewhat ponderous descriptions, so they have been duly recorded in the Lyon Registers ; indeed continental families often have far longer surnames, *e.g.* " Boucher-de Crèvecoeur-de Perthes," and Englishmen who complain that such surnames are " too long " should recollect such mouthfuls as " Temple-Nugent-Brydges-Chandos-Morgan-Grenville."

Whilst a number of them have latterly preferred to reduplicate the patronymic, *e.g.* Macleod of Macleod, yet the ancient practice was for all chiefs to use the form " of that ilk," which is the more characteristically Scottish form of title, and Lamont of that Ilk was officially recognised under that title in 1909. [4] Even where no land estate existed, chiefs were styled, *e.g.* Laird of Macleod and Laird of Mackinnon, meaning high chief of the Macleods and Mackinnons, and of the clan country. For Scottish rank in both Gaelic and Scots was characteristically associated with land—the *earbsa* or *duthus*.

[1] Stevenson, *Heraldry in Scotland*, p. 451.
[2] Innes of Learney, *Law of Succession in Ensigns Armorial*, p. 44. *Notes and Queries*, 3rd February 1940, p. 76 n. 5 ; 24th February 1940, p. 132.
[3] I have already explained that a chief is correctly styled " The Laird of MacSporran," because the Clan MacSporran is an incorporeal noble fief. Being " incorporeal," however, one cannot serve a summons at " MacSporran," hence the importance, in sueing an action (other than in the Court of Chivalry), of having a corporeo-territorial designation where writs can be served, for if the place is on the map of Scotland and the title thereof be used, then writs served there operate from the date of service. [4] Lyon Register, XX., p. 24.

In the fourteenth century, chiefs of Lowland families, and principally those of Norman origin, for a time distinguished themselves as " Le Graham," " Le Lindsay," " The Bruce," and this was carried to the Highlands by " The Chisholm," " The MacNab," and " The Mackintosh." Such titles briefly and usefully denote a chief.[1] In *full* description the title " of that ilk "—so characteristically Scottish— is almost invariably the form used, whether by Highland or Lowland chiefs, until the nineteenth century.[2]

Chiefly styles and territorial designations of chieftains and lairds are, where ordinarily used, legally regarded as an adjected portion of the surname, and the precise form of signature for those using them is laid down in the Statute 1672 cap. 47.[3] A similar custom developed amongst the French *noblesse*,[4] from the seventeenth century onwards, and is still recognised even in modern French law.

Whilst in Lowland Scotland the colloquial title, even for those of baronial rank, tended to be " the Laird of ", in the Highlands and along the Highland border, the more definite title of " Baron," *An Baran*, and *Ban-Baran*, tended to be employed ; for the Highlander's courtliness tended to love correctness in titular appellation and ceremonial. Actually (I am informed), the title of " Baron " is of great moment abroad, as compared with " Laird " and " Baronet " which are not understood. Baron, like Knight/Chevalier is immediately understood in society all over Europe. Not only were the Baronages of Argyll, and of the Isles " Orders " recognised by the Scottish Parliament (A.P.S. Vol. I.), but we find right down to the nineteenth century (and still) numbers of such titles ordinarily used[5] : " The Baron of Kilravock " ; the (various) " Bisset Barons " in the Aird ; the divided " Barons of Moniack " ; " The Baron of Kinchardin " (Stewart) on Speyside ; " The Baron of Towie-Clatt " ; and the celebrated *Baran Ban* (Farquharson of Monaltrie—who led Clan Farquharson in " the '45 "), in Aberdeenshire ; " The Baron o' Leys " (Burnett) was well known on middle Deeside, but though baronial, " The Laird o' Drum " became the title of that great (Irvine) house near Aberdeen. Across the Grampians, on the borders of Breadalbane, Reid-Robertson of Strathloch was *An Baran Ruadh*, and in the West the Barons of Argyll included " The Baron MacCorquodale " and others ; whilst of interest in the West was " The Baron of the

---

[1] " The " is here *not* a translation of Gaelic *an*, but rather of the affix *Mor*. Since it is often erroneously stated that " The Mackintosh " did not himself use it, I may say that he always so wrote it himself in the celebrated Moy Game Book, beside H.M. and other great names.

[2] See Appendix XXXI.

[3] *Encyclopaedia of the Laws of Scotland*, s.v. Name and change of Name.

[4] Of the complete " ordinary use " of feudal fief names and titles as the " ordinary name," even in great supposed " democrats," I would remind readers that the surname of Voltaire was Arouet—therefore, in full, Monsieur Arouet de Voltaire—and that of Le Marquis de Mirabeau was Riqueti.

[5] *Proceedings of Soc. of Antiquaries of Scot.*, Vol. 79, p. 157.

Bachuil," hereditary keeper of the *Bachuil Mor*, the pastoral staff of St. Moluag,[1] an office equivalent to the *Deoir Cuigreach* of the Dewars, hereditary keepers of the Crozier of St. Fillan—an office duly recognised by grant of armorial insignia in Lyon Court.[2]

Sir Walter Scott was thus strictly correct with his " Baron of Bradwardine " ; but it *is* instructive to emphasise the marked use of the baronial title throughout the Highlands, and that custody of such sacred emblems, constituted a " baronial fief." Of course the title is carefully employed in Lyon Court whenever a matriculation or birthbrief is wanted for use abroad (for the Lyon Court recognised its social importance). That the rank and title of Feudal Baron is fully recognised, even in ordinary statute law, is indicated by 1672 cap. 47, whereunder the " Barons " were grouped in a special section of Lyon Register, and now in the consecutive continuation are carefully so styled, and allowed the " cap of dignity," where craved. The disuse " in society " of the title has led to a very serious abuse. A Scottish Barony—like the chiefly *capitani tribuum* from which it derives—descends indivisibly to " the heir " (and even the landless " Representer " of the " baronial race " inherits the title and baronial quality, getting the *cap* doubled *contre-ermine*). On the continent the title often passes to " all descendants." This, and the considerable disuse of the title in " British " social life, has led to a serious abuse, most detrimental to our Scottish and Highland houses. A younger son of a younger branch of some quite modern continental family comes to Scotland ; and immediately " Le Baron Auguste de St. Jude," or whatever he may be, and his wife, " La Baronne Auguste de St. J.," are forthwith given place of honour and to this couple of negligible " cadets," people such as a " Mr. Stewart of Grantully " or " Mrs. Udny of Udny " will, as a sort of honour, be " introduced," whereas *they* are *chefs de famille* in actual possession of baronial fiefs on which " the high justice, the middle and the low " was ratified some five centuries back. On the Continent (the moment their baronial status is disclosed—and avouched by Lyon's Birth-brief) they are received as of equivalent rank amongst the chiefs of the great baronial houses of the Continent. Being " modest and unassuming " is one thing—and a rather " English " one at that !—but " letting down " one's Order and one's country is quite another. The late Lord Lyon Burnett emphasised that it is the *duty* of our baronial chiefs (and most of the Highland chiefs are such) to *assert* their position. This, of course, involves using their title, and making their position clear *vis-a-vis* foreign cadets whom any Highland *Marischall Tighe* would promptly have put in their proper place twenty feet or so down the table, amongst their " equivalents "—the cadets of Scottish baronial families. In this connection, it should be noted that a number of our Highland chiefly families are of, technically, " Princely," and

---

[1] *Lordship of the Isles*, p. 315 ; Lyon Register, XXXVIII., p. 86.
[2] Lyon Register, XXVII., p. 78.

some of " Royal," rank—having the " equality of birth " entitling them to contract effectual, as distinct from morganatic, marriages, with holders of " sovereign " fiefs abroad. The same, of course, applies to a number of the old Irish houses.

The wives and unmarried daughters [1] of chiefs, chieftains, and lairds are all entitled to use these titles, and the heir-apparent prefixes the word " younger " (or " ygr.") to the title. In formal deeds or columns where surname has to be inserted, he should put the complete name and title, affixing the word " younger " afterwards, e.g. " Ian MacSporran of Glenbrachan, younger." The reason is that Southern officials might otherwise suppose " younger " to be a surname.[2] In speech, etc., he is " MacSporran younger of Glenbrachan " or " Young Glenbrachan." Only the actual head of the house, his wife, and heir, normally use the style " of that ilk," e.g. Mactavish of that Ilk ; Mrs. Mactavish of that Ilk ; Ian Mactavish, younger of that Ilk ; but his sister would be, Miss Jean Mactavish of Mactavish.

All unmarried daughters bear these titles, but younger sons, younger brothers, and collaterals do *not* bear the designation of the house. According to Scottish principle, they have to make their way, and found houses of their own.[3]

Observe that the ambit of these titles in Scottish practice corresponds exactly with the persons who are by the Law of Arms entitled to bear substantively or derivatively the undifferenced arms of the house—and the heir of course with his temporary label *brisure*.

Celtic chiefly and territorial titles should be supplied and carefully used on all official occasions and in official documents. They, of course, regularly appear in the Scottish Registers of the Great Seal, as an examination of the printed volumes will show, and without them these registers would be valueless to the historian and genealogist. Unless, however, (a) the succession is by immediate descent, or (b) the person is actual owner of the estate, officials usually require production a of Lyon Court matriculation of arms, or statutory certificate of recognition by the Lord Lyon as a voucher. This is consistent with the King of Arms' jurisdiction in matters of name [4] and designations and titles,[5] and the fact that Lyon's permission or declaration is necessary for the assumption of chiefly titles.[6] In France, where

[1] As in France, since the eighteenth century, even the daughters of peers being styled, e.g. " Lady Mary Stewart of Traquair " in Lyon Court Birthbrieves.

[2] Nevertheless Malcolm Alfred Laing, younger of Crook, appears—and quite properly---in a Royal Commission, 1892, Great Seal, Lib. 46, No. 211.

[3] On the Continent, it is the practice for younger male branches to continue the designation of the house, and to add the designation of their own property, thus forming long-stringed surnames, e.g. " Boucher-de Crèvecœur-de Perthes." The practice in Scotland is to add the cadet's own estate title direct to the basic name.

[4] Forlong, 1870, II. Rettie 910.

[5] J. Gwillim, *Display of Heraldry*, 1724, Honour Civil, 49 ; *Right to Bear Arms*, 123.

[6] Macfarlane, *Genealogical Collections*, I., 393 ; Lyon's letter to Cluny.

similar conditions obtain and the laws of nomenclature are stricter than in Scotland, a celebrated French lawyer, editor of the *Annuaire de la Noblesse de la France*, observes :

In your interests and those of your children, if you possess or can vindicate a nobiliary title or territorial name, *surnom terrien*, you should be careful that these are regularly employed in all registrations of Births, Marriages, or Deaths.

As in France, however, you are likely to be asked to produce official evidence that you have been recognised by the proper department (in Scotland, the Lord Lyon)—unless you actually own the property. Care upon such points, in regard to vital registration, commissions, etc., is just as requisite in Scotland as in France, if Celtic and chiefly titles are to be preserved unquestioned. It need hardly be pointed out that official recognition is only accorded where such titles are ordinarily used, and that officials cannot be expected to accept an alias which has been assumed for the night of the Caledonian Ball, or the day of some Highland Gathering, and is thereafter dropped for the remainder of the year ! Signature on cheques is a good test !

The words Chief, Chieftain, Laird, and Baron (in the feudal sense) are each a statutory *nomen juris* found in use both by the Kings of Scots and in the records of Parliament ; and—as indicated—a chief is often referred to as " The Laird of Mackintosh." It is simply an affront to a laird to describe him as a " proprietor " or a " landlord " (which is technically a publican !), and " The Laird " or " The Laird of Glenbracken " or " The Baron of Bradwardine " are the proper Scottish terms in which to refer to our *grad flaith* (territorial houses). " The Laird " is the popular Scottish description. *An Baran* or *An Tighearn*, or in either case the place name as patronymic, are the other colloquial terms employed.[1]

In personal address, the title alone is used,[2] *e.g.* " Lochiel," " Glengarry," " Monaltrie "—no " Mr."—or in Gaelic the patronymic, if any, *e.g. Mac Cailein Mor*,[3] *Mac Mhic Alein*.[4] It is characteristic of our tribally democratic custom that such address is used by all ranks. It is rude,[5] not " respectful," to address Clanranald as " Mr. Macdonald " or the Laird of Keir as " Mr. Stirling."

[1] In Scottish peerage practice, the chief alone is created, *e.g.* Lord Forbes, a cadet of surname title, *e.g.* Lord Forbes of Pitsligo. On this principle, from regard for Cluny as *The Macpherson*, his cadet was in 1953 only created *Lord Macpherson of Drumochter*.

[2] I have been asked, " Is it correct for a lady to address a gentleman by his feudo-Celtic title, *e.g.* ' Lochiel ' ? " The answer is certainly. In early nineteenth-century Aberdeenshire we find the Laird of Craigmyle's wife addressed him as " Craigmyle," and when the Laird of Skene (Skene of that Ilk) was introduced —and, characteristically, as a person of very ancient descent !—to the Countess of Dundonald, she immediately asked, " But, Skene, I would gladly know what you can produce to instruct your antiquity ? " This not only indicates form of address, but how to start conversation ! [3] Duke of Argyll.

[4] Clanranald (*Ian Muydertach*) ; titles like *Mac Mhic X——* do not denote the chief of X——'s line (*Loyall Dissuasive*, p. 102) ; but—as examination shows—a prominent cadet. [5] Even Burt realised this, see p. 402 *supra*.

In address writing, or in lists, " Esquire " is not normally added, the designation being taken to infer it.   Where esquire is used, and that is usual in deeds and useful on the Continent when the laird or chief is not a baron, the word follows the territorial or chiefly designation, Alexander Irvine of Tulloch, Esquire.[1]   Similarly, where the title Baronet, C.M.G., D.S.O., are used, these honours follow *after* the territorial or chiefly title, *e.g.* " Colonel Hugh Rose of Kilravock, C.B." ; " Sir James Burnett of Leys, Bt., C.B., C.M.G." [2]

In personal letters, a Scottish laird or chief, *e.g.* " Campbell of Glenfalloch," is addressed " Dear Glenfalloch," not " Dear Campbell," which would be as rude to Glenfalloch as to Lord Breadalbane, for the laird or chieftain of Glenfalloch has just as much a " title " as the earl.   The old prefix of a laird or chief was " The Much Honoured," and letters should be and still sometimes are addressed, *e.g.* " The Much Honoured, the Laird of Glenfalloch," [3] or if a baron, " The Much Honoured, the Baron of Dunfallandy " [4]—they arrive quite safely.   A clansman in writing to his chief may, of course, commence "Dear Chief."

Where husband and wife are referred to, the correct styles are, *e.g.* " Glenfalloch and Lady Jean Campbell of Glenfalloch," or " Mr. and Mrs. Gordon of Cluny," but more correctly, " Monaltrie and the Lady Monaltrie."   A form of description such as " Mr. Mactavish of Dunardrie and Mrs. Mactavish " is *wrong*, and suggests that the unfortunate lady is not his wife ; any respectable hotel would be justified in turning them out ! Under Scots law, a wife or widow has certain rights in her husband's estate, and in our law of families and titles she has corresponding rights in the name and title of her husband.

Territorial and chiefly titles are, of course, used upon visiting-cards, where they may (and strictly should) be on the same line as the name, but, in nineteenth-century practice, were placed slightly below :

| GENERAL LEITH | MRS. LEITH | MISS FYFFE-DUFF |
| OF FREEFIELD | OF FREEFIELD | OF CORSINDAE |

In nobiliary practice, titles are normally feminised,[5] *i.e.* when an earldom devolves upon a female in her own right, she is designated a " countess," and a female baronet is a " baronetess."   Certain descriptive titles, *e.g.* Sovereign, Monarch, Chief, *Ceann-Cinnidh*, and

---

[1] " Alexander Irvine, Esquire, of Drum Castle," would be doubly wrong, since one does not use the word " castle " as part of one's title, for one presumably owns the whole lairdship (or superiority) of which a castle is the *caput*.   Drum is, of course, colloquially called " Drum," or " The Laird of Drum " (his wife " The Lady Drum "), and on the Continent, as deeds for production, then " The Baron of Drum."

[2] *Encyclopædia of the Laws of Scotland*, *s.v.* Name and Change of Name ; *Scots Heraldry*, Oliver & Boyd, 1934, Chapter XV.

[3] Cf. J. Stirton, *Crathie and Braemar*, p. 96.

[4] This style should invariably be employed if *An Baran* is on the Continent. The baronial title is carefully set forth in Lyon Court Birthbrieves for production at foreign courts.

[5] So are surnames—in Germany and in the Gaelic.

Ceann-tighe,[1] are equally applicable to either sex. Where there *is* a proper feminine one does not invent a new one ; *e.g.* there is no such thing as a " woman laird." [2] When a lairdship devolves upon a female, she has been, in Scottish official documents and judicial proceedings, normally, formally, and officially described as, *e.g.* " Lady Invercauld " if proprietrix, and similarly in the case of wives, *e.g.* Lady Invergelly (wife of Robert Lumisden of Invergelly),[3] Lady Craigcaffie (wife of Gilbert Neilson of Craigcaffie).[4] This feudal title of " lady " is not a " courtesy " but a proper legal description of the female. The wife of a knight or baronet was invariably described as " Dame." In modern practice, the latter have, by courtesy, been accorded the title of " Lady " properly belonging to the wives of lairds, and a laird's wife is now ordinarily known as " Mrs. Neilson of Craigcaffie," in formal documents, " Madam Neilson of Craigcaffie " ; but " Lady Craigcaffie " is a style still used, *e.g.* Lyon Court record narrative. " Laird and leddy " (*e.g.* " Leddy Glensnooks ")—is still the normal and correct (also legal) way of addressing a laird's or chief's wife in rural Scotland.[5] Away from home it is, under modern conditions, simpler to use the form—well recognised since the eighteenth century—" Mrs. Snooks of Glensnooks "—but the designation should be carefully insisted on by those entitled thereto.

The terms " chief," " head," and " representative " (*Ceann-Cinnidh* and *Ceann-tighe*) are of course grammatical terms as applicable to a female as to a male, and there has been no occasion to feminise such ; but " Chieftain," which more commonly indicates the representer of a territorial or *grad flaith* house, has—like other such titles—been where necessary feminised since the fifteenth century in the recognised form of " Chieftainess," and this is the normal equivalent of the Gaelic *Ban Flaith* and *Ban Tighearna*—which last is the proper form of Gaelic address for a chieftainess or for the wife of a laird or chieftain.

The principles and practice regarding these titles has been dealt with at some length, since their preservation and correct use is important in preserving the structure and spirit of our native Scottish social system, and the courtly manners of the Highlanders.

It was the custom in Highland families for the children to be taught their genealogy on Sunday mornings, *backwards* (just like the

---

[1] The sex-distinct versions are *Fear-Tighe* and *Ban-Tighe*, but *Tighearn* (Lord of a House) is feminised *Ban Tighearna*, the correct Celtic title for " Lady " when the descriptive titles of *Ceann-Cinnidh* and *Ceann-tighe* are not used and one does not colloquially address a king or queen as " sovereign " nor a chief as *Ceann-Cinnidh*.

[2] This horrible description appeared in one or two instances in the Press—autumn, 1937.

[3] Morrison's *Dictionary of Decisions*, 5944.

[4] *Ibid.* 5922.

[5] " The Lady Mackintosh," " The Lady Dunstaffage," " The Lady Wathill," " The Lady Learney," and " The Lady Invercauld," are examples of such titles which down to the past few years have been regularly used by the people of the countryside.

declaimed Royal pedigree) to the founder of the " house," and then, in the cases of branches, the chief's lineage downwards from the eponymus to the reigning chief.[1]

The bairns thus learnt not only their own descent, but also how to answer the test of the true clansman : " Name your chief." [2]

The descent and exploits were also the subject of evening fireside tale, and had to be repeated by each child in turn, *word-perfect*, and any slip was noted by a light tap with a hazel-wand-twig.[3] Thus was tradition handed down accurately, and the names and titles of chief and chieftains correctly learnt, along with the history of the race. Nowadays, the branch-genealogy, so far as known, should likewise be taught, but *also* this ought to be written up, in the Family Bible, or back pages of a copy of the Clan History, *or of your copy of this book.*

[1] This was the practice in the house of McNeill of Gigha and others ; and in other cases the inculcation was in the form of a catechism, commencing " Who are you ? "

[2] Burt's *Letters*, p. 219. At a clan dinner the chief's health is given (with his title and " Our Chief ") immediately after the Royal Toast.

[3] Inf. Reg. Fairlie of Myres, R.S.A.

The Scottish System of Heraldic Cadency
for organising the leaders of the family

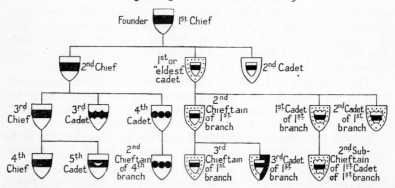

This scheme shows you how the *undifferenced shield* passes down from chief to chief, and always indicates the reigning chief. Also, how the various " differences " indicate the cadet houses in their order ; how the shield differenced for each cadet descends to, and indicates, the successive chieftains of that branch ; and how the cadets within each branch are also sub-differenced.

XII

Highland Music

No book on Highland clan matters would be complete without some reference to Highland music and its kindred subject, the ballad, or poem ; for the olden poem-sagas were created for singing, words and tune together forming a composition which was more easily remembered, more effective in delivery, and more readily remembered by the hearers. The poet-bard sometimes accompanied himself on the small harp, but frequently the poet declaimed and the harper played an accompaniment. So song and poem must be considered together, just as they were delivered in the hall of the chieftain, where bard and harpist were honoured and hereditary executants ; though it is characteristic of medieval culture that everyone took part in these evening entertainments—the *ceilidh*—and that many of the poetic compositions were alternatively narrative and chorus, so that all could join in the latter.

As Garth says : " Recitation of their traditional poetry was a favourite pastime of the Highlanders collected round their evening fire and ' *Bheil dud agud air na Fian ?* ' (' Can you speak of the days of Fionn ? ') the interrogation likely to be put to the guest." The character of our Scottish poetry, whether historical or faerie, merits attention, and as D. P. Bliss has aptly observed of the latter :

The old Scots ballads, whatever their origin, were essentially aristocratic in character. The folk of Elphin are radiantly apparelled in green and blue, and girdled with gold . . . and bear themselves like children of princes and earls.

Similarly the historical sagas of the Highlanders were such as to :

raise the feelings and energies of the hearers by songs and narratives in which the exploits of their ancestors and kinsmen were recorded. . . . By connecting the past with the present, by showing the warlike hero, the honoured chief, or the respected parent, who, though no longer present to his friends, could not die in their memory, and that though dead he still survived in fame, and might sympathise with those whom he had left behind . . . it has become a singular and characteristic feature of Highland sentiment to contemplate with easy familiarity the prospect of death, which is considered as merely a passage from this to another state of existence, enlivened with the assured hope of meeting their friends and kindred who had gone before them, and of being followed by those whom they should leave behind.[1]

---

[1] *Sketches of the Highlanders*, p. 85.

The powers of memory and fancy thus acquired a strength unexampled . . . where recitation is not practiced in a similar way. . . . It is owing to this custom that we still meet with Highlanders who can give a connected and minutely accurate detail of the history, genealogy, feuds, and battles of all tribes and families in every district or glen, for many miles around [1] and, as Burt observed, " They have a pride in their family so almost everyone is a genealogist."

Nothing indeed is more remarkable in old Scottish mansions than the way in which the ancestral chieftains, and the portraits on the dining-room wall, seem a living part of " the household " cheerfully alluded to in conversation, as if they were to all intents and purposes alive—as indeed their deeds are imperishable in " the family," which, as we have seen, extends to all around and connected with " the house." In a Scottish castle you will not find the caretaker, like the one who disgusted Horace Walpole at Knole, describing the Sackville portraits as " old frights." On the contrary, the housekeeper, often herself of kin to the clan or " hous," shows a lively pride in, and knowledge of, each of them ; and one's experience is not so much of being " shown the pictures " as being successively " presented " to a series of *Tighearn* and *Ban-tighearna*, each of whom is, in some charming remark, made seem a living part of the venerable building.

This may seem a digression ; but it is an inseparable part of the relationship of Highland song and music to " the clan " and " hous " ; all part of a whole which the song and ballad have helped to perpetuate.

Since the first edition of this book appeared, earnest collectors, such as Marjory and Patuffa Kennedy-Fraser, the Laird of Inverneil, younger, and others, have, by gramophone-recording and dictation, made invaluable records of many old Highland songs and much Celtic music which would otherwise have perished. Amongst these are the numerous working songs, rowing, cloth-waulking, milking, spinning, and others, along with those in praise of the Lords of the Isles and other chieftains, their castles, galleys, and romances ; forming a " living treasure-house of living folk-tradition," and Mrs. Kennedy-Fraser emphasises that " the special characteristics of Scots music are found in their purest form in the West Highland folk-music." [2]

It has been said that the ballads of Scotland, and no less the Gaelic songs, are all suffused with a weird fey element of tragedy ; and this indeed is so present in many that during the nineteenth century fresh insipid rhymes were invented to replace the stark beauty and pathos of the original ballads. In later times we have come to realise that the old, and often sad, lays were the essential concomitants of a country, and of districts, which had so often to defend their integrity and survivance against the play of fierce passions and foreign aggression, and that though maybe often tinged with a wistful sadness

---

[1] *Sketches of the Highlanders*, p. 99.
[2] See I. F. Grant, *Lordship of the Isles*, " Ancient Gaelic Culture," pp. 411–419 and *op. cit.* therein.

or shattering surge of passion, they reflect the vicissitudes of age-old races.

There is, however, about these Gaelic songs, born of the Highland surroundings, and with a vein of sadness running through many of the melodies, always a love of country which is passionate in its expression. And, withal, when listening to the songs of the Gael one is insensibly carried back in thought to the straths and the glens, and " the everlasting hills." National songs of various nations exist which fire the blood and excite the national feelings of their hearers. The Gaelic melodies, however, go far deeper than this. They appeal to the innermost feelings of the Gael who hears them. Demonstrativeness is not a character of the Scottish Celt. Watch, however, the faces of a Gaelic audience when the chorus of such songs as *Hó-ró! mo nighean donn bhòidheach* (" Ho-ro! my nut-brown maiden ") or *Mo rùn geal dìleas!* (" My faithful fair one! ") is being sung and you will be able to form an idea of how the songs are felt by the audience.

The most ancient Celtic musical instruments seem to have been the *cornu* or horn, and this was used by the Druids for sacred purposes. After the introduction of Christianity, however, the use of the sacred horn was discontinued, save in its survival in the horn of the Messenger-at-Arms, and the trumpet of the trumpeter who accompanies a herald —these officers being the medieval survivals of the Druidic sennachies.[1] Horns continued to be employed for purposes of war, in the chase, law and amusement. Many of these horns answered a double purpose, that of a musical instrument and of a drinking-vessel. Such horns had a kind of stopper for screwing in when the instrument of music was used at table. After the introduction of gunpowder, not a few of the horns were converted into powder-horns. The ornamental horn is still a beautiful and not unuseful adjunct worn with full Highland dress.

The harp for long held an equal place with the bagpipes in Gaelic circles ; and each chief had a hereditary harper as well as a piper. One of the earliest writers on Celtic instrumental music was a Welshman, Giraldus Cambrensis, who wrote, about the year 1187 :

In Ireland they use for their delight only two musical instruments— the harp and the tabor. In Scotland we find three—the harp, the tabor, and the choro. . . . It is the opinion of many at this day that Scotland has not only equalled her mistress, Ireland, in musical skill but has far excelled her, so that good judges are accustomed to consider that country as the fountainhead of the art.

The " choro " is supposed to mean the bagpipes.

At the court of James I., " both after soper and ynto quarter of the nyght," the court engaged " yn syngyng and pypyng, yn harpyng

---

[1] A. R. Wagner, *Heralds and Heraldry*, quoting Garter Dugdale, *Sources and Literature of the Law of Scotland* (Stair Soc.), p. 382.

and in other honest solaces of grete plesance." [1]   James IV. had at least three harpers, Patrick Sinclair, James Mylson, and Alexander.[2] Many of the chiefs kept harpers—usually hereditary, as instruction commenced about the age of ten ; and amongst those of whom there is public and documentary record, are the harpers of the Laird of Balnagowan, the Thane of Cawdor, Countess of Crawford, and the Bishops of Ross and Caithness.   The Earl of Argyll and the Laird of Maclean are specifically recorded as having *clarsachs*,[3] that is, the smaller Highland harp, and for songs to the accompaniment of the harp, Highland bards " seldom chose any other subject than the praises of brave men."

Of these Highland *clarsachs* two splendid examples survive in the National Museum of Antiquities, Edinburgh, the Lamont Harp, and the more elaborate one called the Queen Mary Harp, both of which belonged to John Robertson, 11th of Lude, and which were eventually secured for the National Museum by Stewart of Dalguise.   Lude was a noted harpist, and, of these now worm-eaten instruments, the Queen Mary Harp was last strung and played to the Society of Antiquaries, after its presentation to them, in 1807.[4]

In 1594 Argyll took his harper with him in the Glenlivet campaign, and Rory Dall was the celebrated harper of Macleod, at Dunvegan. The cultivation of the *clarsach*, like so many other aspects of Gaelic culture, suddenly lapsed in the middle of the eighteenth century.

The harp for many centuries was the favourite instrument of the Irish and the Welsh, as well as the Highlanders of Scotland.   For long the first-named nation held the pre-eminence as harpers.   However, as we have already seen, they were ultimately surpassed by their pupils, the Scottish Gaels.   The ancient harp holds to this day the place of honour in the Irish Coat of Arms.   The Celtic harp is known as the *clarsach*, though, in some ancient records, it is alluded to as the *clarischoe*.   Logan remarks :

The Caledonian harp has thirty strings, and has this peculiarity that the front arm is not perpendicular to the sounding-board, but is turned considerably towards the left to afford a greater opening for the voice of the performer, and this construction shows that the accompaniment of the voice was a chief province of the harper. Giraldus Cambrensis describes the harp as containing twenty-eight strings, but they were afterwards increased to thirty-three, and Mysut, a Jesuit, is said to have introduced double strings in the fifteenth century. The old Welsh harp is said to have had nine strings, and that of the Caledonians only four. . . . It was first intended to string the above two harps with brass wire, according to the old Scots and Irish manner, but as it would have been necessary, in order to bring out the proper sound, for one to allow the finger nails to grow to a certain length, that method was abandoned. A fine clear tone was produced by the finger nails from the wire, and it is related of O'Kane,

---

[1] R. B. Armstrong, *The Irish and Highland Harps*, p. 140.
[2] *Ibid*. p. 143.   [3] *Ibid*. p. 146.   [4] *Ibid*. p. 182.

PLATE XVI.

HIGHLAND DANCING AT CRATHES CASTLE ON DEESIDE, 1834.

PLATE XVII.

CONFIRMATION AND MATRICULATION OF THE NAME, ARMS AND CHIEFSHIP OF MACKINTOSH.
Court of the Lord Lyon, 9 April 1947, Lyon Register, xxxvi, p. 40.

the Irish harper, who frequented the Highlands about thirty years ago, that, inheriting a bardic spirit of arrogance, he was often punished by being turned from the houses of his patrons with his nails cut. The strings were also sometimes struck by a plectrum, or bit of crooked iron. The Highlanders, Irish and Welsh held their harp on the left side, and a remarkable peculiarity in the construction of the Caledonian one, as represented by Gunn, is that it is bent to accommodate the arm.

Many of the early Scottish sovereigns were proficient harp-players. King James I. excelled all his contemporaries in this respect. Mary Queen of Scots was also a good harpist. George Buchanan, in his *History* (1582), writes :

Instead of a trumpet they (the Highlanders of Scotland) use a bagpipe. They are exceedingly fond of music, and employ harps of a peculiar kind, some of which are strung with brass and some with catgut. In playing they strike the wires either with a quill or with their nails, suffered to grow long for the purpose ; but their grand ambition is to adorn their harps with great quantities of silver and gems, those who are too poor to afford jewels substituting crystals in their stead. Their songs are not inelegant, and, in general, celebrate the praises of brave men, their bards seldom choosing any other subject.

Many of the harps, above described, were handed down as family heirlooms, and were studded with jewels and cairngorms.

Attempts have been made at various times to revive clàrsach music, and there is no more graceful instrument, but it requires much skill and practice. It is, however, again a feature at the Gaelic Mod, and its popularity was much increased by the beautiful playing of Miss Patuffa Kennedy-Fraser.

The violin has long held a place in the Highlands, but as an instrument for dancing-tunes and by no means a rival of the pipes. The violin, owing to its greater compass, is admirably adapted for playing reels, strathspeys, and light dance-music, for some of which the bagpipes are not adapted. The genius of Neil Gow, James Marshall, and others has made Highland violin dance-music justly celebrated. Such a tune, for example, as " The Marquis of Huntly's Farewell," which makes one's feet tingle when it is played by a good performer, is quite unsuited, owing to its compass, for the bagpipes. Those who have not listened to Highland dance-music as performed on the violin, should take the first possible opportunity of listening to a performance of the Edinburgh Highland Reel and Strathspey Society. What they then will hear will be a revelation to them !

As comparison between the different forms of Gaelic instrumental music the following is quoted from an article by A. MacAonghuis, in the *Celtic Monthly*, June 1902 :

As an interesting and pretty representative example of the respective degrees of popular estimation in which the pipe, the harp, and the fiddle were held at one time in the Highlands, let us quote the following from the

P

very instructive notes to Captain Fraser of Knockie's *Collection of Highland Music*, new edition, 1874, which says : " Grant of Sheugly, in Glenurquhart, supposed composer only of the verses to this beautiful ancient air *Màiri Nighean Deòrsa* (' Mary, George's Daughter '), was himself a performer on the violin, pipe, and harp, and it would appear, a poet in like manner. In appreciating the qualities of each instrument, he supposes they had quarrelled, and that he was called upon to decide the contest. In addressing a verse to his pipes, he observes, ' how it would delight him, on hearing the sound of war, to listen to her notes in striking up the *Gathering*, to rally round the chief, on a frosty spring morning, whilst the hard earth reverberated all her notes, so as to be heard by the most distant person interested.' To the harp he says, ' The pleasure which thy tones afford are doubled whilst accompanying a sweet female voice, or round the festive board, inspired by love or wine, I reach beyond my ordinary capacity, and feel the pleasure of pleasing.' But to his violin, which he calls by the literal name of the air, ' Mary, George's Daughter,' and seems to have been his favourite, though held cheap by the other combatants, he says, ' I love thee for the sake of those who do—the sprightly youth and bonnie lasses—all of whom declare that at a wedding, dance,[1] or ball, thou with thy bass in attendance can have no competitor, thy music having the effect of electricity on those who listen to it ' ; and on thus receiving their due share of praise, their reconciliation is convivally celebrated."

Nevertheless, it is the *Piob-mhòr*, the Great Highland Bagpipe, which is pre-eminently the national instrument, not only of the Gael, but of all Scotland. This was recognised by Government when in 1881 the territorial re-organisation of the British army took place.

---

[1] At marriages (when the genealogies of the two families were recited), the wedding favours were of the livery colours of the families of the bride and bridegroom (*i.e.* the colours of the heraldic wreath of the chief's or chieftain's crest), the guests of each being supplied respectively with those of each party, which created a pleasant diversity. The bridal wreath was often of the badge-plant of the bride's clan ; and after the ceremony, and before she set off home in the attire of a married woman, this was flung among the guests, bringing luck to the one on whom it fell or who first picked it up. In a stately and ceremonious people such as the Highlanders—and Scots in general prior to the recent debasement—there were, of course, no such undignified antics as breaking bannocks over brides' heads (food was not so plentiful as to be thus wasted), nor carrying brides over thresholds. A garland of flowers was indeed " broke " over the bride's head—apparently at her away-going ; and the party was " convoyed " home (for there were no honeymoons in those practical days) ; and, on arriving at the green before the bridegroom's home, they assembled for a formal dance with which the home-coming was celebrated, and which, in picturesque old French, was entitled " the *Chez-mez* Reel." For this the bride called the tune, and led off the reel with the best man, as recorded by Sheriff Rampini (*History of Moray and Nairn*,), as " The Shamit Reel," which, ignorant of the Gallic terms that we derived from the " Auld Alliance," he supposes had something to do with being " ashamed " ! Nothing of the sort ! The *chez-mez*, chymmes, (*chez-mez* reel) is a well-known term, found even in the Scots Statutes ; and the " Home-coming reel " (a national dance), falls into place with other gracious medieval customs, just as the *pavanne* was danced by councillors, and the minuet was the height of stateliness. Let us always remember that dignity, colour, and ceremony are the *motifs* we find underlying our national customs.

Then all Scottish regiments, whether Highland or Lowland, were provided with pipe bands.

The pipes appear to have been used by the Celts, who colonised the greater part of the European continent. It is, however, to the Highlanders of Scotland that the evolution of the bagpipes in their present form is due, and after having been in early times used throughout Scotland, and later banned, first by the Reformers in the Lowlands, then by the Whigs after Culloden, the pipes again, through their use in the Highland regiments became once more the national musical instrument of Scotland, besides having identified many of the military triumphs of the British nation with the inspiriting encouragement on the field of battle to the strains of the *piob-mhòr*.

There are frequent allusions to the use of the pipes in England during the fourteenth century, and there were pipers in the English navy about that time. Both Chaucer and Shakespeare make reference to the pipes in their poems. In the Lowlands of Scotland the pipes flourished until the Reformation, when not only the pipes but also all musical instruments were classified as sinful by the Calvinistic divines. The Exchequer Rolls record a payment to the King's pipers in 1362, and it is also on record that pipers formed part of the municipal institutions of all the large Scottish towns. In some burghs, as Aberdeen, Banff, and Jedburgh, for instance (till the eighteenth century), the office of burgh piper was a hereditary one, and the pipe-banner displayed the city arms.

In Europe there were various forms of the bagpipes in use, but in the British Isles the forms of pipes used were of three varieties : (1) the Lowland or Northumbrian Bagpipe ; (2) the Irish Union (or *Uilleann*) Pipes ; (3) the *Piob-mhòr*, or Great Highland Bagpipe.

Of these three, the Highland bagpipes are the only ones blown by mouth. The wind for the other two kinds is supplied by a bellows fastened underneath the arm of the performer. The ancient Northumbrian pipes had three drones in one stoc, while the modern have four drones. These pipes, however, are nowadays rarely or never seen. The Irish Union pipes have four drones. Their tone is so sweet that, though they are not so powerful as the great Highland pipes, the Irish ones are sometimes known as the " Irish Organ." The Irish type was occasionally used by Scottish chieftains, and the Jacobite Inneses of Balnacraig had a fine pipe embellished with heraldic silver mountings. In 1912 a new kind of bagpipe was designed for use by the pipe bands of Irish regiments—the " Brian Boru " pipe. The instrument consists of a wooden pillow, from which issued three drones, and this wooden pillow again was fastened to the upper part of the bag, the lower part of which was provided with a blowpipe and a chanter. The chanter had a much greater compass than that of the Great Highland Bagpipe. In appearance it resembled a cornopean. The tones of all these pipes, however, lack the stirring and warlike sound of the *piob-mhòr*.

The form of the Great Highland Bagpipe first used had apparently chanter and blow-piece. The next evolution was the addition of one drone, thus giving pipes with chanter, blow-piece, and one drone. Such a set of pipes, belonging to MacDonald of Kinloch-Moidart, is shown in MacIntyre North's *Book of the Club of True Highlanders*. In a letter to the *Celtic Magazine*, 13th February 1880, Kinloch-Moidart says :

It was given in the end of last century to my maternal uncle, Donald MacDonald of Kinlochmoidart, Colonel of the Royals (whom I now represent), by the Macintyres, who were the hereditary pipers to the Clanranald branch of the MacDonalds, as they were on the point of emigrating to America. They told him the MacDonalds had followed its inspiriting strains into the battle of Bannockburn, and that it had never been played at any lost battle.

By the commencement of the fifteenth century the bagpipes developed a second drone. In the possession of J. & R. Glen, Edinburgh, is a set of pipes with two drones, both proceeding in a bifurcated manner from one stoc, and with blow-pipe and chanter. The drone-stoc bears the letters " R. McD.," below them a lymphad or galley, and below the lymphad the date 1409 in Roman letters (" M : CCCC : IX "). The next development was two drones, each proceeding from a separate stoc.

Authorities on Highland matters are at variance as to when the third or large bass drone was added to the bagpipes, some maintaining that this took place during the eighteenth century, while others say that it was not till the commencement of the nineteenth century. For some time before a third drone was added to the bagpipes, they had, in addition to the two drone stocs, a third stoc, which carried a long unpierced rod, from which was suspended the banner of the chief.[1] Later on this rod was pierced and grooved and fitted with the large drone. In this manner was evolved the *piob-mhòr*, or Great

---

[1] The pipe-banner appears in most old representations of the Highland bagpipes, and its use was very ancient, being referred to in Hume Brown, *Early Travellers in Scotland*, p. 265. A pipe-banner is an armorial flag, subject to the laws of arms, its misuse a statutory offence. In the army, Company-Officers are those who have pipe-banners. The details vary according to the tradition of each regiment. Usually the regimental crest is on one side and either the arms or crest of the Company-Officer (if armigerous) on the other. In civil life, lairds, chieftains, and chiefs are those entitled to pipe-banners, which either display their arms over the whole area (sometimes with a tartan fringe) or the whole coat of arms with crest and supporters. The former is the older form. A chief has three pipers, a chieftain two, and other lairds one. Only the senior of two or three pipers bears the *Tighearn's* pipe-banner, and they are not permissible by professional pipers as a piece of meaningless show, *i.e.* when not appearing *for* a person entitled to a pipe-banner. A Lord Provost's or Provost's piper, or that of the head of an armigerous corporation entitled to supporters, may have a pipe-banner of the corporation's arms. The Captain of Dunstaffnage and one or two other chiefs have special grants of a long thin pipe-pennant, matter of most special historic right.

Highland Military Bagpipe, of the present day. The addition of the leather valve to the blow-pipe was coincident with the addition of the large third drone. Previous to that time most pipers appear to have stopped the blow-pipe with the tongue.[1]

The drones, drone-stocs, chanter, and blow-pipe of the Highland bagpipes are made of ebony or cocoa-wood, mounted with ivory or silver ; the drone and chanter-reeds being made of cane. The bag is of sheepskin (untanned if for use at home, or tanned if the pipes are intended for a tropical climate). The bag has an inner covering of flannel, and an outer one of tartan. The pipes of chiefs' and officers' pipers often have a banner suspended from the large drone, while those of ordinary players have the drones decorated with tartan streamers. The cost of a stand of pipes varies according to their mounting. Those of lairds, chieftains, and chiefs are often embellished with arms, crest, or motto in silver.

An article in the *Highland News*, by Hugh MacLeod, gives a concise technical description of the modern bagpipes :

The Highland bagpipes are of three sizes—first, the Great Highland Bagpipe, the Half-Set or Reel Size, and the Miniature, and there is, of course, the Practising Chanter. It is scarcely necessary to refer in detail to the minor characteristics of these three, which are all alike, but some of you may be interested to know the names of the different parts in Gaelic. The bag, which is usually of sheepskin covered with flannel or other cloth, and an outer garment of tartan or velvet, is called the *màl*. To this is inserted tightly five pieces of well-turned wood, called *stocs*. The chanter is called the *feadan*, and contains eight holes, besides a hole right across and near the base, to give volume and width to the tone. It has a small leather valve, called *siunnach*, to prevent the wind coming out. The reed of the chanter is called the *rifeid*. The bass-drone or *dos-mòr* has two slides used for tuning, while the small drones have only one each, *i.e.* the *duis bheaga*. At the end of each drone is a reed, called, in this case, *na gothan*, being previously widened or closed by moving up or down a string which is tied round each of them. Now, as to the notes of the bagpipe. They are nine in number, beginning with G sharp and end in A natural. The tone of the drones is lowered by lengthening the drones, and when in tune the two small drones should be in unison with one another and with the lower A of the chanter, the bass drone being tuned to an octave lower. . . . One would suppose that, owing to the limited number of notes in the pipe, the capability of producing melody would be very limited, but if you follow any practised player on the pipes you will at once catch what you might call half or mixed notes, called " grace notes." In this way, then, we have an almost unlimited number of tunes or notes, giving rise to an infinite variety of tunes. The chief and noblest, and also the most ancient published class, is *piobaireachd*, or *ceol mor*, in common parlance. *Ceol mor* is of three different kinds. First there is *cruinneachadh*, or gathering ; the *cumha*, or lament ; and the *fàilte*, or salute. The *spaisdearachd*, or march, I consider a minor style of *ceol mor*. A *piobaireachd*

---

[1] See Appendix XXVII.

opens with the *urlar*, or groundwork, played twice, and the rest consists of variations on this theme, such as the *siubhal* ; then the *taorluath, taorluath-breabach*, and a doubling of this ; then comes the *crunluath breabach*, and a doubling of it ; and in large pieces we have *crun luath fosgaille*, and the *crun luath mach*.

We have already seen how the pipes at an early period of Scottish history played their part in municipal economy.[1] They have likewise figured not only in the services of the navy and the army, but of the church as well. There were regular regimental pipers as far back as 1642, and it is believed that the first regiment which had them was the North British (now the 21st Royal Scots) Fusiliers. There were harpers in the navy in the latter part of the seventeenth century. In 1708 we hear of pipers in the navy also. It is not, I think, generally known that there are still pipers on His Majesty's ships. A few years ago, the author was informed by a gallant admiral that when he was commander of one of the guardships in Scottish waters he was allowed one musician on board his vessel. " I chose a piper," said the admiral, " seeing my ship was on a Scottish station. When we were transferred to one of the large naval stations on the south coast of England I took my piper with me ; and he proved to be one of the most successful missionaries I have ever come across. On Sundays the Protestant members of my crew were marched through the dockyard to church, with the piper playing at their head. This distinction was so envied by many of the men who were Catholics that, much to the indignation of the priest, the Catholics forsook their own place of worship in order to march behind the piper to the Protestant church."

The pipes were employed in the church services in Edinburgh in 1536. In 1556 the Queen Regent went in procession, in honour of St. Giles, accompanied by bagpipers and other musicians. During the memory of the present generation the bagpipes have often played a prominent part in the church service not only in St. Giles, but even in an English cathedral. In 1892 at a memorial service in York Minster, after the death of H.R.H. Prince Albert Victor, Duke of Clarence and Avondale (who had resided in York when his regiment was in garrison there), the pipers of the 1st Battalion Royal Scots played a selection of pipe music within the cathedral. In one lonely island in the Hebrides the Roman Catholic worshippers are still called to prayer by the strains of the pipes.

The annual service of the Order of Saint Michael and Saint George,

---

[1] Many local pipe bands ask how to select a tartan, and what crest for their accoutrements. If it is a municipal corporation band these will be the arms of the burgh and the tartan of the superior of the burgh. This is often not the position. In that case, the band should get in touch with some chief or chieftain and invite him to become the band's patron, and in that capacity to accord the band the privilege (it cannot be a " right ") of using, *during the patronage of himself and his successors,* his crest and badge on their accoutrements, and his arms on the drums.

held in St. Paul's Cathedral, London, on the 24th April 1923, possessed a feature of special interest, for, on that occasion, for the first time in the history of the City of London's principal fane, the strains of the *piob-mhòr* resounded beneath its dome. While the banners of the deceased knights were escorted into the chapel, to be laid upon the altar, the solemn procession was headed by the pipers of the King's Own Scottish Borderers, playing laments.

After the Reformation, when the playing of bagpipes was frowned upon by austere Scottish divines, use of the pipes was largely discontinued in the Lowlands. It was the Highlands, therefore, which became the stronghold of bagpipe music. Each chief had his hereditary piper, whose position was an important one. He had lands for his support, and was of superior rank to the other members of the chief's retinue. The piper had a gillie, or servant, to carry his pipes when they were not being used, and the piper's profession was held in such high esteem that he was in all respects accorded the position of a gentleman. Of the hereditary clan pipers the best known were the MacCrimmons or MacCrummens, pipers to the MacLeods of Dunvegan (of whom John MacCrimmon headed the pipers at the Coronation of Charles II. in 1651) ; the MacArthurs, pipers to the MacDonalds of the Isles ; the Mackays, pipers to the MacKenzies of Gairloch ; the Rankins, pipers to the Macleans of Duart and of Coll ; the Campbells, pipers to the Campbells of Mochaster ; and the Macintyres, pipers to the Menzies of Menzies. Of the families of hereditary musicians the Mac-Crimmons were the most celebrated. For years the MacCrimmons had a college for the study of pipe music at Boreraig, in Skye. To this *oilthigh* resorted students from all parts of the Highlands. As many as six to twelve years were devoted to the acquirements of *piobaireachd* alone, for the professors would not permit either reels or quicksteps to be played in their establishment, and some years ago a descendant of this celebrated race was present when a monument was unveiled to those great Celtic musicians. It will generally, however, be found that the opponents of pipe music are those who have formed their opinions from having heard pipe music played in a small hall, where the surroundings are as unfavourable for the exposition of bagpipe-playing as they would be for the performance of the best military brass band. The true home of the Highland bagpipe is on the loch-side and among the hills and glens of the Highlands. Chieftains, however, have always enjoyed alike the morning pipe tune in the courtyard or terrace and the evening one delivered by the pipers marching around the dining-hall complete with heraldic pipe-banner. At least one musical composer, of European celebrity, learnt to appreciate the Great Highland Bagpipe—Mendelssohn, who introduced a theme of its strains into his " Hebrides " overture.

Evil days fell upon bagpipes and pipers after the suppression of the Jacobite Rising of 1745. In this respect they shared in the hatred which was felt by the English Government for everything which savoured of the Highlands. When the Duke of Cumberland was leaving Nairn to meet Prince Charles at Culloden the clan regiments of the Munros, Campbells, and Sutherlands accompanied him. Observing the pipers carrying their pipes, the Duke said to one of his officers, " What are these men going to do with such bundles of sticks ? I can supply them with better implements of war." The officer rejoined, " Your Royal Highness cannot do so. These are the bagpipes—the Highlanders' music in peace or war. Wanting these, all other implements are of no avail, and the Highlanders need not advance another step for they will be of no service." The Butcher Duke evidently learned subsequently what power the pipes possessed when played to Highlanders, for when the Jacobite Rising was being ruthlessly punished, the mere playing of bagpipes was decreed by the Courts of Justice to be a treasonable practice, and the players, therefore, worthy of death. James Reid, a piper, suffered death at York on 15th November 1746 as a rebel. At his trial it was argued in his defence that he had not carried arms. The Court, however, observed, that " a Highland regiment never marched without a piper," and, therefore, in the eye of the law, Reid's bagpipes were an instrument of war.

After the passing of the Heritable Jurisdiction Act of 1747, which attempted to abolish clanship, retinue of chiefs, etc., it became an offence for a chief to have any military followers.[1] One by one, the hereditary pipers were deprived of the lands which were devoted to their maintenance. By a generation later most of the old pipers had disappeared, many of them having emigrated to America.

When bagpipe-playing in Scotland was treated as a treasonable offence, the music of the pipes was kept alive by the Highland emigrants to America, and in the Highland regiments. Bagpipe-playing in Scotland languished from 1747 till 1781, when the Highland Society of London instituted in Scotland a number of competitions for bagpipe-playing.

The revival of pipe-playing towards the close of the eighteenth century was maintained well on into the nineteenth, but at the Disruption many of the Free Church clergy set their faces against instrumental music of any kind, which was regarded as a friend of the devil. The pipes, of course, shared in this general condemnation. It is a matter of congratulation that under those circumstances the pipe bands of the Highland regiments existed to keep alive the flame of the *piobaireachd*. Speaking at a meeting of pipers and lovers of pipe music, 19th December 1903, Lieutenant Edward E. Henderson, of Govan, vigorously attacked these dismal-minded Highland ministers

---

[1] This over-ready assumption was dispelled by Lord Dunedin in the celebrated Dunstaffnage Castle case (1912 S.C. 458), where it was held that only military followings were struck at, not civil and honorary ones (*Tartans of the Clans and Families of Scotland*, p. 21). The question of whether a bagpipe is still an " instrument of war " did not arise ! The decision of the English Court at York is naturally of no authority in Scotland.

for their opposition to the study of music. He said (*Weekly Scotsman* report) that

the pipes had had many enemies, but the greatest enemy which the pipes ever had was, and still is, the Highland minister—especially the Free Church minister. In their eyes to be a piper was to be in league with the evil one. He had visited many villages on the west coast, particularly in Ross-shire, where, if one wished to be respected, they must on the first sound of music put their fingers to their ears. To laugh was to sin, and to look happy on the Sunday was to run the risk of being preached about by the minister.

Since then minds have broadened and the present generation shows a keener zest for the traditions of its natural music, whilst the Church of Scotland is finding its way gradually back to the brighter era of the Celtic Catholic Church.

It is satisfactory to observe the growth of the Highland cadet-corps of many of our public schools in Scotland, to which bands of boy pipers are attached. This is a steady and sure means of developing pipe-playing among the Scottish youth. Canada, as usual, is to the fore where Highland matters are concerned, and has already several Highland cadet-corps of her own.

Scottish regiments seem likely to continue to be the nursery for bagpipe-playing. W. L. Manson, in *The Highland Bagpipe*, remarks :

Nothing has helped more to preserve the bagpipe as our national musical instrument than the fact that it has always been used in connection with the Highland regiments. On several occasions officers, always English it should be noted, have tried to get the bagpipe superseded by instruments more to their own taste, but they have always failed. The sentiment in favour of the pipes was too much for them, and the arguments were too strong to be slighted by the Crown authorities. . . .

In the British (regular) Army there are twenty-two pipe bands, one to each battalion of the following regiments : Scots Guards, Royal Scots, Royal Scots Fusiliers, Borderers (King's Own Scottish Borderers), Cameronians, Royal Highlanders, Highland Light Infantry, Seaforth Highlanders, Gordon Highlanders, Cameron Highlanders, Argyll and Sutherland Highlanders. [The Irish Guards have now *Uilleann* pipes.] The number of men authorised by the War Office to each band as full pipers is six—one sergeant-piper (formerly pipe-major) and five pipers —but each battalion has always ten or twelve men in its pipe band, those above the regulation number being acting pipers. Only the Highland regiments and the Scots Guards are allowed a sergeant in excess of the ordinary strength to perform the duties of sergeant-piper. Members of the band get the same pay as drummers—1d. per day more than ordinary privates—with the opportunity to earn " extras " by playing outside at parties, in public parks, or in any other way. The sergeant-piper and his five comrades are clothed by Government, and a fund is supported by the officers of each battalion, out of which the cost of the pipes, both for full and acting pipers, long hose buckled shoes, etc., and the uniform for the

P*

acting pipers is defrayed.   Captains of companies, however, supply their pipers with banners.   The pipers are all drilled in the same way as other soldiers, their training as pipers only beginning after they have served in the ranks for some time.   Tuition is given free of charge by competent sergeant-pipers, and any lad joining a Highland regiment will be taught the pipes properly if he chooses.   Pipers are generally Highlanders, and it is a remarkable fact that in the time between the middle of the eighteenth and the beginning of the nineteenth century, Skye alone furnished 500 pipers for the British Army—an average of ten a year. . . . When, during the Mutiny, the four Highland regiments marched from Lucknow, their pipers numbered 140, quite a respectable number of fighting musicians.

It is, however, not alone in the British army that bagpipe-playing is being perpetuated.   This has been extended to the Indian army. No European instrumental music so attracts Orientals as that of the pipes.   A pipe band in the East never fails to drawn an admiring crowd of natives who would give merely a passing notice to the finest brass band of the British army.   The first native Indian regiment to adopt pipes was the 1st Punjaub Infantry.   Since then many others have followed the example.   An Order in 1901 by the Commander-in-Chief in India prescribed the setts of tartan to be worn on the ribbons and pipe-bags of the native pipe bands of the different Indian Commands.   Punjaub Command, the Graham tartan ; Bengal Command, Campbell ; Madras Command, Old Stewart sett ; Bombay Command, Old Urquhart tartan.

In MacIan's *Costumes of the Clans* an anecdote is related of a piper from Coire-Garf, in Mar, named Donald Ferguson, who joined Prince Charles's army during " the '45."   When Colonel Roy Stewart surprised and made prisoners a party of Hanoverian troops at Keith, Donald was thrown in the skirmish off the bridge into the Isla. However, he had stuck to his pipes, and these, with great presence of mind, Donald kept blowing with vigour, the inflated bag completely keeping him above water, until he was rescued by some of his comrades. The danger of Donald's situation could not repress the merriment of his companions at the droll appearance the piper presented in the stream.   However, Ferguson afterwards used to say that as long as he was able to blow up his pipes, he would neither die nor drown !

On a later occasion a wounded piper, by means of his pipes and presence of mind, was saved from certain death.   During one of the battles of the Indian Mutiny, this piper, shot through the legs, was lying helpless on the ground, when he observed a native sowar (cavalry-man) bearing down on him with the evident intention of despatching him.   The piper, however, slowly raised himself from the ground, and, sitting up, took deliberate aim at the sowar with the large drone of his bag-pipes.   The mutineer thereupon evidently thinking this some new weapon of war, turned tail, much to the piper's relief.

In *Sketches of the Highlanders*, Stewart of Garth narrates the following incident to show the influence of the bagpipes :

When the late Gordon Fencibles were reviewed in 1794 by His Majesty in Hyde Park, an old friend of mine, a native of the Highlands, which he had left in early life, resided in London. At the commencement of the French Revolution he imbibed many of the new opinions, became an imaginary citizen of the world, and would not allow that he had any country. When the Highland regiment was reviewed he refused to accompany a friend to the review, saying, in his usual style, that he had no country or countrymen. However, he was prevailed upon to go, and when he saw the regiment, the plaids, and the bonnets, and heard the sound of the bagpipes, the memory of former days returned with such force that his heart swelled, his eyes filled with tears, and bursting away from his friend he exclaimed, " I have a country after all : the sight of these poor fellows has given me a truer lesson than all my boasted philosophy." Ever afterwards he used to smile at his sudden conversion, and, as he informed me, never missed an opportunity of visiting his native country.

General Sir Eyre Coote, who, before he had experience of the bagpipes in battle, described them as " a useless relic of the barbarous ages," was completely converted after he had made a campaign in India with the 73rd Highland Regiment. The General particularly noticed the animated manner in which the pipers played, and the effect produced on the minds of the men by the sounds of their native music. The distinctness with which the shrill strains of the *piob-mhòr* made themselves heard through the noise and *melée* of battle, and the influence they seemed to excite, effected a total change in Sir Eyre's opinion. At Port Novo in 1781, Coote, with 8,000 men, of which the 73rd was the only British regiment, defeated Hyder Ali's army of over 150,000 men. The 73rd was on the right of the first line, leading all the attacks, and the notice of the General was particularly attracted by the pipers, who always blew up the most warlike strains when the fire was hottest. This so excited Sir Eyre's admiration that he exclaimed, " Well done, my brave fellows ! you shall have a set of silver pipes for this." The General was as good as his word and the pipes bought had an inscription testifying the high opinion the General had of the pipers.

The story of the storming of the heights of Dargai by the Gordon Highlanders, and the distinguished role played by the pipes may be recalled to the memory of the present generation. The tune played by Piper Findlater, V.C., has been a source of dispute ! Some say it " Haughs of Cromdale " (the Regimental charge-tune), others say was " The Cock o' the North." As a child I always heard it was the latter, to which the following words were sung by the bairns of Deeside :

> Comin' tae Dargai, comin' tae Dargai,
> Comin' tae Dargai heights,
> 'Twas there that Piper Findlater fell,
> An' it's there that he played his pipes.

No doubt he varied his tune in the course of the advance.

The influence of the pipes in the 1899–1902 war in South Africa cannot be over-estimated. There are many, both Highland and Lowland, who can testify how, when toiling footsore and weary across the burning and dusty " veldt," their energies were revived and their drooping spirits cheered by the shrill strains of the bagpipes.

The foregoing remarks were penned in 1904. The events of the Great War, 1914–1918, brought the Highland bagpipe and Scottish pipers into still greater prominence. Instances of the individual bravery of the regimental pipers have been so numerous it would be invidious to narrate how the skirl of the pipes, played at the critical moment, turned many a doubtful action into one of complete victory.[1]

When the original Expeditionary Force landed in France, in 1914, it had seven Scottish battalions with pipe bands. At the time of the Armistice, in 1918, these pipe bands had increased to upwards of one hundred. War had meantime taken heavy toll of the pipers, whose casualties amounted to upwards of 1,100 (500 killed and 600 wounded).

During the Great War the pipers ever took a most distinguished place. On the march, amid the horrors of " going over the top," at the charge, and even in captivity, the Scottish pipers played a worthy and honourable part.

For a time the kilt and bagpipes were banned in Australia (see App. XXIX, 4th Edn.) ; wiser concepts prevailed, and the garb of Caledonia has taken its place (so appropriately with many Scottish names) in the modern Australian forces. A nation is not built of one " uniform " pattern. A forceful realm, like Scotland and other picturesque older kingdoms, embodies variety drawn from many tribal sources, and in all parts of the British Empire, as in Europe of old, the Scot has made a constructive contribution to the kaleidoscope of cultured civilisation. It is pleasing to record (as will be evident, I think, from the list of Canadian regiments given in earlier editions of this book, of which an up-to-date list is in compilation) that Canada has given the other portions of the Empire a lead as regards *her* cult of the kilt, tartan, and pipes.

And who can describe the effect of pipe music when first heard after a lapse of many years by a Scot returned from exile in a foreign land ? He may be pacing the busy streets of the Metropolis, clad in the uninteresting garb and slouch hat of " civilisation," when, in the distance, he hears the skirl of the pipes, which he has not known for long years. It is the band of the Scots Guards or of the lads wearing the " Elcho " tartan which he hears. Does not the back stiffen and the step acquire a new-born spring as the Scot steps out briskly in the direction from which the music proceeds ? And however callous may have grown the heart, or unsentimental the ideas, the exile cannot help feeling just a small lump in the throat and a quickening of the pulse as the kilted laddies come in sight, and the waving tartans and sporrans swing past to the strains of some well-known pipe tune such as " Hielan' Laddie " !

[1] See *The Pipes of War* by Sir Bruce Seton of Abercorn, Bart. (Glasgow, 1920).

We cannot better close this chapter than by quoting the pipe-music preface by the late Rev. Dr. Norman MacLeod of the Barony, reproduced in Queen Victoria's *Leaves from the Journal of a Life in the Highlands* :

The music of the Highlands is the pibroch of the great war-pipe, with its fluttering pennons, fingered by a genuine Celt, in full Highland dress, as he slowly paces a baronial hall, or amidst the wild scenery of his native mountains. The bagpipe is the instrument best adapted for summoning the clans from the far-off glens to rally round the standard of their chiefs, or for leading a Highland regiment to the attack amidst the roar of battle. The pibroch is also constructed to express a welcome to the chief on his return to his clan, and to wail out a lament for him as he is borne by his people to the old burial-place in the glen or in the sainted Isle of Graves. To those who understand its carefully composed music, there is a pathos and depth of feeling suggested by it which a Highlander alone can fully sympathise with ; associated by him as it always is with the most touching memories of his home and country ; recalling the faces and forms of the departed ; spreading forth before his inward eye panoramas of mountain, loch, and glen, and reviving impressions of his early and happiest years. And thus, if it excites the stranger to laughter, it excites the Highlander to tears, as no other music can do, in spite of the most refined culture of his after life. It is thus, too, that what appears to be only a tedious and unmeaning monotony in the music of the genuine pibroch, is not so to one under the magic influence of Highland associations. There is, indeed, in every pibroch a certain monotony of sorrow. It pervades even the " welcome," as if the young chief who arrives recalls the memory of the old chief who has departed. In the " lament " we naturally expect this sadness ; but even in the " summons to battle," with all its fire and energy, it cannot conceal what it seems already to anticipate, sorrow for the slain. In the very reduplication of its hurried notes, and in the repetition of its one idea, there are expressions of vehement passion and of grief—" the joy of grief," as Ossian terms it, which loves to brood upon its own loss, and ever repeats the one desolate thought which fills the heart, and which in the end again breaks forth into the long and loud agonising cry with which it began. All this will no doubt seem both meaningless and extravagant to many, but it is nevertheless a deliberately expressed conviction.

Exponents of Highland and of Scottish music do not, so far, appear to have realised that the same intense local appeal, and high standard of clan and district organisation found in the Scottish clan system and land system, is also noticeable in Scottish music. It would add immensely to the interest of our national music if executants, and the manufacturers of gramophone records were to prepare series of concerts and records based upon the " Music of the Clans," or the " Musics " of the numerous local districts, each of which have peculiarities and local characteristics of their own. Record manufacturers so far seem only to issue heterogeneous " medleys " with (usually) no historical connection. " Clan " and " District " medleys would be equally pleasant and far more interesting, and the chief's arms could be depicted on the label, and a leaflet explanatory of the music and its history supplied.

Our clan societies should each see to this. Such collections, particularly in the case of gramophone records, available for performance, or repetition, at any moment, would add immensely to the knowledge of and enthusiasm for Scottish music, and would also be a means of preserving many clan and district tunes in relation to one another and to their environment, and would prove a source of encouragement to executants and Scottish clan societies throughout the world.

XIII

The Gaelic and other Celtic Languages

ALL that remain in Europe of the Celtic-speaking peoples who over-spread a large portion of that continent two thousand years ago are about 3,200,000 persons, of whom about 1,900,000 are inhabitants of the British Isles, the remaining 1,300,000 being natives of Brittany, or Bretagne (the ancient Armorica), in France. The languages or dialects spoken by these Celtic people have been divided by philologists into two great branches, viz., the *Brythonic*, or Cambro-Celtic, or " P " branch, and the *Goidelic*, or Erse, or " Q " division. To the former division belong the Armoric or Brittany language, the Cymric or Welsh, and the Cornish. Under the latter, or Goidelic branch, are embraced the Erse, or Irish Gaelic, the Manx, or that spoken in the Isle of Man, and the Gaelic of the Highlands of Scotland.

These languages of the present day were originally evolved from one parent stem. Political as well as geographical circumstances, together with the fact that, previous to historic times, the Celts possessed no literature in written form, must alike have combined to evolve the forms of the Celtic language in the various dialects in which it is now found. Whether the original Celts of the British Isles found their way thither in the east from Gaul and the countries bordering on the German Ocean, north-west from these countries, or (as is the tradition with regard to Ireland) north from the Iberian Peninsula the Celts of the British Isles and of France were akin, not only ethno-logically but linguistically.

Aristotle, who wrote 2,300 years ago, mentions Great Britain as Albion and Ireland as Ierna. At the present day the Celtic portion of North Britain is known to its Gaelic-speaking inhabitants as Alba, while the Irish Gael calls his country Eire (obviously Ierna in another form).

Prior to the close of the ninth century, the Gaelic language in Scotland and that in Ireland appear to have been almost identical. Subsequent to that time, and during the period of the Norse kingdoms in the north and west of Scotland (which lasted till the middle of the thirteenth century), the Gaelic of both Scotland and the Isle of Man was considerably influenced by such a close connection of the north of Scotland and the Western Isles with the Scandinavians. To this day, the seaboard of these portions of Scotland and the topography of Man bear evidence, in the nomenclature of lochs, hills, and dales, to Norwegian influence.

In Ireland the Erse, or Irish Gaelic, was the daily language of the nobility and gentry until the reign of King James VI. It was not until 1619 that the use of the Erse in legal documents was discontinued.

The " British language " in Strathclyde, or Scottish Cumbria, appears to have survived till the twelfth century. The people speaking it were known as Walenses. In the ancient chartulary of the bishopric of Glasgow (covering Strathclyde and most South Scotland), charters of King Malcolm IV. and William the Lion are on record in which the inhabitants of the diocese are addressed as : *Francis & Anglicis, Scotis & Galwejensibus, & Walensibus, & omnibus ecclesiae S. Kentegerni de Glasgo, & ejusdem episcopi parochianis.* The *Franci* alluded to are Normans, who had settled in that part of Scotland ; the *Anglici* are non-Norman English folk ; *Galwejenses* are the " Picts " of Galloway ; while the Cymbric population are designated *Walenses.*

The close of the eleventh century witnessed the suppression of Gaelic by Saxon at the Court of the Scottish kings, as well as the introduction of the latter language into the Lowland provinces of Celtic Scotland (*i.e.* those eastern parts north of the Forth). It was not, however, till several centuries later that Gaelic disappeared from these districts. In the fifteenth century it was enacted that the scholars of the Grammar School, Aberdeen, should only speak in French, Hebrew, Latin, Greek, or Gaelic. By King James IV., who was the last Scottish sovereign who spoke Gaelic, King's College, Aberdeen, was founded and its chief object was extension of learning throughout the Highlands. At this College, however, the use of English was prohibited. So late as the reign of Queen Mary, Gaelic was spoken in the Garioch, Aberdeenshire, as well as in other districts of the north-east of Scotland, where that language is now unknown. In 1567 the first book which was printed in Gaelic saw the light. The work was what is generally known as Bishop Carsewell's *Prayer-Book.* It was a translation of John Knox's *Liturgy,* or *Forms of Prayer and Administration of the Sacraments, intended to be Models and Helps for Ministers in the Performance of their Public Duties.* The translator afterwards became Bishop of the Isles.

The Gaelic fell on evil times after the accession of King James VI., for the men who had acquired power during his minority loved neither the Highlanders nor their language. The legislation against both Gaels and Gaelic, especially after he succeeded to the throne of England, became more and more anti-Celtic, as power fell into the hands of those who were so soon to turn against the Royal Authority as well as against the Highlanders, under the force of Genevan fanaticism. Allusion has already been made to the statutes of 1609 which struck at so many old Highland customs, sacred and secular. In 1616 two insulting enactments against the Highlands were promulgated by the Privy Council. The first provided that :

The chiftanes and principal clannit men of the Ylles shall send thair bairnes being past the age of nyne years to the scollis in the Lawlandis to the effect that they may be instructit and trayned to wryte and reid and to speke Inglische ; and that nane of thair bairnis sall be served air unto them nor acknawlegeit nor received as tennentis to his Majestie unless they can wryte, reid, and speik Inglesche.

The second Act contained the following proviso :

Forasmeikle that the Inglesche toung may be universallie planted, and the Irish language, which is one of the chief and principale causes of the continuance of barbaritie and incivillitie among the inhabitantis of the Isles and Highlandis may be abolished and removit, &c.

Notwithstanding all the laws aimed at it, Gaelic died hard in the northern Lowlands, for Burt, in his *Letters from a Gentleman* (written about 1725), says :

The Irish (*i.e.* Gaelic) tongue was, I may say, lately universal in many parts of the Lowlands, and I have heard it from several in Edinburgh that, before the Union, it was the language of the people of Fife. . . . As a proof they told me that, after the Union, it became one condition of an indenture that when a youth of either sex was to be bound on the Edinburgh side of the Forth the apprentice should be taught the English tongue.

Burt, though unacquainted with Gaelic (which he styles Erst or Irish), observed the similarity between Scottish and Irish Gaelic, for he continues :

An Irish gentleman, who never before was in Scotland, and made with me a Highland tour, was perfectly understood even by the common people ; and several of the lairds took me aside to ask me who he was, for that they never heard their language spoken in such purity before. This gentleman told me that he found the dialect to vary as much in different parts of the country as in any two counties of England.

Though by the end of the eighteenth century Gaelic had become a thing of the past in Lowlands, it still held its own in the Highlands, where not only was the old language spoken by high and low, but the old characters were employed in writing. In the *Journal of a Tour in the Highlands and Western Islands of Scotland in* 1800, John Leyden (friend of Sir Stamford Raffles), says :

Some of the MSS. he (MacLaggan, minister of Blair Atholl) showed me were in the handwriting of the Rev. Mr. MacArthur of Kilmore, in Mull, whose father could never read or write the English language or character, though he corresponded constantly with his son in the Irish character while he studied at St. Andrews. This he mentioned as a proof of the current use of the Irish character among the Highlanders, which he asserts was very common.

Gaelic, it must be confessed with regret, has lost much ground in the Highlands since the nineteenth century. This is not due to any extraneous influences or attempts to supersede Gaelic by English, but unfortunately is greatly owing to the action of the Highlanders themselves. Whilst Welshmen have enthusiastically maintained their language, Highlanders, alas, have shown no such pride in theirs. That this is not a recent change is evident from the *Statistical Account of Scotland* (1845). The Rev. Thomas Munro, Kiltearn, Ross, remarks:

> The language generally spoken is an impure dialect of the Gaelic; but it is rapidly losing ground. In the more Highland parts it is better understood than English, but in the low parts, and in Evantown, both languages are spoken indifferently. The Gaelic School Society, by establishing schools throughout the country, have done much to eradicate the language. This may appear paradoxical, but it is actually the case. Those children that had learned to read Gaelic found no difficulty in mastering the English; and they had a strong inducement to do so, because they found in that language more information suited to their capacity and taste than could be found in their own. English being the language universally spoken by the higher classes, the mass of the people attach a notion of superior refinement to the possession of it, which makes them strain every nerve to acquire it; and it is no uncommon thing for those who have lived for a short time in the south to affect, on their return, a total forgetfulness of the language which they had so long been in the habit of using.

This, alas, is equally applicable to the present day, and, says Adam, on one occasion, when interrogating his gillie (a fine (?) old Highlandman) as to why the latter's children were unable to speak Gaelic, the author was met by the rejoinder, " 'Deed, sir, there's no child of mine that I'll be letting learn the Gaelic, for it is the Gaelic that was making the fool of me. I would be twelve years old before I would be knowing the difference from ' yes ' and ' no ' in the English; and that's why I'll not be letting my children know the Gaelic." When such sentiments are prevalent among the rank and file of the passing generation of the Scottish Gael, as compared with the patriotic vigour of the Welsh and Irish, what hope can there be for the survival of Gaelic culture in Scotland? Fortunately this degenerate gillie does *not* seem to be a representative example, for the Registrar-General, in 1931, was able to report that " Gaelic is still largely in use in the homes of the people," and that in the island parishes the percentage has only fallen from 72 per cent. to 62 per cent. since 1891; but whilst this obtains in children up to four years, " after school life is entered upon the Gaelic percentage begins to fall, and declines to insignificant proportions." It is clear that it is the bureaucratic education system which, instead of encouraging local culture, is strangling and extinguishing our Celtic heritage in this, as in every other direction. The Scottish aristocracy now shows a keen interest in Celtic traditions and culture. A great deal has been done by patriotic Celts in all parts of the British Isles to perpetuate the old languages, and a great deal is still being done. A Celtic Chair has been founded in Edinburgh University, and an annual " Gaelic Mod " is now held in Scotland under the auspices of *An Comunn Gaidhealach*, which publishes a Gaelic monthly, *An Gaidheal*. The Welsh gathering of a similar kind is styled the *Eisteddfod*; and the Irish have recently instituted the *Oireachtas*. While all these efforts are most praiseworthy, it is to be feared they will prove nugatory if the Gaelic population of the Highlands do not *themselves* awake to the necessity and the advantage of bringing up their children to speak and read the language of their forefathers. Appendices Nos. XXII. and XXIII. give full information as to the actual position of Gaelic in Scotland, based on the figures of the 1901 to 1951 censuses.

As will be seen by reference to the details in the concluding portion of Appendix No. XXII. (which gives the Gaelic results of the census of 1931), the slump in the number of Gaelic-speaking people points to the likelihood of Gaelic, in Scotland, becoming, within a comparatively short period, one of the dead languages ! The principal reason for this must be attributed, we are now officially shown, not to remissness on the part of the present generations of Gaelic-speaking parents, but to the Anglo-Saxon-minded bureaucracy, and the vulgarian Goths who now usually predominate in local authorities by whom the use of Gaelic is discouraged. It is most inspiriting, from a sentimental point of view, to listen to the stirring strains of *Suas leis a' Ghaidhlig* sung by the audience at a Gaelic Mod or some such Gaelic function. What, however, it may be asked, do such manifestations lead to, from a practical point of view ? Functions such as these may retard, but certainly will not prevent, the decay of Gaelic in Scotland. The dry rot can only be arrested by prompt measures taken at its source —the Gaelic home circle. It is time to tell the Highlanders bluntly that in this they ought to be ashamed of themselves. While the Celts of Ireland, Wales, and Brittany cultivate and are proud of their native tongue, it is in the Highlands of Scotland alone that use of the native langauge is discouraged ! It is to the Dominions one must turn (*not* to the Highlands of Scotland) if one seeks countries where Gaelic is apprised at its true worth. It is deplorable to see the progressive and certain decay of an ancient and distinguished Celtic language through the apathy and indifference of those whose heritage the Gaelic is !

The foregoing is essentially as penned by Mr. Adam, and seems rather to skate around the subject of Gaelic than to say anything definite about Celtic literature in Scotland. Scotland was the centre of a remarkable Gaelic culture, both artistic and linguistic. Unfortunately the latter depended on a tradition of oral transmission, though it is evident that there were at one time many Scottish-Gaelic manuscripts of which now only a few remain. An example of what happened to such is the evidence (in 1808) of Lachlan Mac Mhurrich, whose family had for some fifteen generations been hereditary genealogists of the Macdonalds, and held as such the lands of Staoilgarry. Unfortunately Lachlan's own father had failed to obtemper the condition of instructing him in the ancestral lore, so that Lachlan was illiterate ; the manuscripts, of which it seemed there were a considerable number, were scattered, and some cut up " for tailors measures." This is an example of the decline which took place, so largely in the second half of the eighteenth century.

Most of the manuscripts, and poems, were heroic and genealogical, and on that account of the greater interest ; and many of those collections which survive are of that character. Amongst the earliest, and most important, is that of James Macgregor, Dean of Lismore, which contains many genealogical and " Ossianic " pieces, some cast in a newer " Ballad " form which showed that Gaelic was still a living culture developing in accordance with an advancing civilisation. Perhaps the most interesting feature of the *Book of the Dean of Lismore* is its orthography, which is a sort of phonetic Gaelic. This leads me to say that the orthography, which has unfortunately been adopted in later times, has probably done as much to discourage the preservation and re-extension of Gaelic as anything else. Had the phonetic form of the Dean of Lismore's book (1619) been developed, much greater progress would have resulted. It no doubt presents difficulty to the grammarian, but, since Gaelic was for the most part a spoken rather than a written language, the resort to what is now the " accepted orthography " is only the more to be regretted. Even now I think it would be a good thing to resort to what I might call " the older principle." In Appendix XXVIII. I give : (1) the Dean's text of the first lines of *Bas Dhiarmaid* ; (2) the " modern Gaelic " ; and (3) an English translation. The reader may judge for himself which is most likely to encourage a quick acquisition of an essentially " spoken " language. Since many, who have neither the time nor opportunity to acquire a working knowledge of Gaelic grammar, are yet deeply interested in Gaelic place-names, ready acquaintance with the more usual construction of these and their pronunciation is perhaps the easiest " first step " to a deeper interest in, and knowledge of, the language.

A good vocabulary of words, reasonably correctly pronounced, and subsequently a few verbs and phrases, from a " conversation " manual (such as, be it noticed, are provided for overseas Forces), is the best means of preserving Gaelic as a living language.

PART IV

Highland Forces

PART IV

Highland Forces

XIV

The Highland Regiments, Past and Present [1]

WITH what pride does not only every Highlander, but also every Scot, regard the Highland regiments ; and what exiled Scot, returning to the old country after many years of absence from it, does not feel his heart thrill and the blood course more rapidly in his veins when he meets again, for the first time since many years, a Highland regiment on the march in all its bravery of swinging kilts and waving bonnets.

The character and tradition of a regiment are, however, in general, fixed from the circumstances surrounding its birth, *i.e.* the Colonel who raised it, the circumstances of its embodiment, and the origin of the insignia by which the corps is distinguished.

The subjoined remarks are accordingly not intended to give an account of the services of our Highland regiments. Space does not admit of that being done here ; it has already been performed by many regimental authors. Notes are also included regarding the history of Highland regiments which have ceased to exist, and those which (*a*) exist and have been Highland from the commencement of their existence until the present time and (*b*) commenced their existence as Highland regiments, were afterwards made Lowland corps, and finally became Highland battalions again.

It is scarcely realised what an influence has been exercised by the Highland regiments in perpetuating the use of the Highland dress, when this (after " the '45 ") was denied to any save Highland soldiers in the Government service. The Highland regiments did more ; they kept alive the bagpipes at a time when these were decided by the Government to be a " weapon of war," and anyone carrying them was liable to penalties under the Disarming Act, 1746.

The Black Watch, formed into a regiment in 1739, was the pioneer of the Highland battalions. It was followed by Loudoun's Highlanders, raised in 1745, which, however, were reduced in 1748. Between the latter year and 1757 (when Montgomery's and Fraser's Highland regiments were raised), the officers and soldiers of the Black Watch were the only British subjects who could wear the Highland garb without incurring risk of transportation.

Pitt, Earl of Chatham, gets the credit of being the first to conceive the idea of utilising the military instincts of the disaffected Highland clans by enrolling their members as soldiers of the British army. To the far-seeing Lord President Forbes of Culloden, however, must be given the credit. Knowing the general disaffection towards the

---

[1] See Appendix XXIV. for Scottish Regimental Badges.

439

Hanoverian Government which existed in the North, more especially since the Rising of 1715, he devised a plan he had reason to believe would give scope to the natural military instincts of the Highlanders, while keeping them on the side of the existing Government. Culloden in 1738 communicated his scheme to Lord Milton, the Lord Justice-Clerk, who was managing Scottish affairs under Lord Islay, requesting that if the Lord Justice-Clerk approved of the scheme he would bring it to the notice of Lord Islay :

> I propose that the Government should raise four or five regiments of Highlanders, appointing an English or Scottish officer of undoubted loyalty to be Colonel of each regiment, and naming the lieutenant-colonels, majors, and captains and subalterns from this list in my hand, which comprehends all the chiefs and chieftains of the disaffected clans, who are the very persons whom France and Spain will call upon in case of war to take up arms for the Pretender. If Government pre-engage the Highlanders in the manner I propose, they will not only serve well against the enemy abroad, but will be hostages for the good behaviour of their relatives at home, and I am persuaded it will be absolutely impossible to raise a rebellion in the Highlands.

The Lord President's scheme was by Lord Islay submitted to the Premier (Sir Robert Walpole), who warmly approved of the idea. The scheme as a whole was, however, vetoed by the cabinet, but it did result in the organisation of the Black Watch in 1739, and thus inaugurated the principle of Highland regiments. Eighteen years later (the Rising of 1745 having occurred in the interval) Pitt persuaded the Government to give the scheme a more extensive trial.

Their acquiescence was due to no respect for the Highlanders, but because they saw a good means of draining the best men away from a district in which they had been such a source of apprehension to the Whig Government.

In 1757 Montgomery's (77th) and Fraser's (78th) Highlanders were raised. Between that year and 1766 no less than eleven Highland regiments of the line, besides the Black Watch, had been called into existence, as well as two fencible regiments, whose excellent services fully bore out the forecast which Lord President Forbes had formed many years previously.

In 1766, in his celebrated speech in Parliament on the commencement of the differences with America, Pitt expressed himself regarding the Highland regiments as follows, viz. :

> I sought for merit wherever it was to be found, it is my boast that I was the first minister who looked for it and found it in the mountains of the north. I called it forth and drew into your service a hardy and intrepid race of men, who when left by your jealousy became a prey to the artifice of your enemies, and had gone nigh to have overturned the State in the war before the last. These men in the last war were brought to combat on your side ; they served with fidelity as they fought with valour, and conquered for you in every part of the world.

An anonymous author, a friend of Lord Chatham, noticing how this call to arms was answered, observed :

Battalions on battalions were raised in the remotest parts of the Highlands of those men, who a few years before and while they saw any hope, were devoted to and too long had followed the fate of the race of Stuart. Frasers, Macdonalds, Camerons, Macleans, Macphersons, and others of disaffected names and clans were enrolled, their chiefs or connections obtained commissions, the lower class always ready to follow, they with eagerness endeavoured who should be first enlisted.

When the Highland regiments were first raised, the weapons supplied by Government consisted of a musket, bayonet, and large basket-hilted broadsword, also a pistol and a dirk. In 1769 the officers began to wear light hangers instead of the heavy broadsword, which was only used with full dress. The sergeants were provided with carbines in place of the Lochaber axes with which they had hitherto been armed. In 1776 the broadsword and pistols were laid aside by the men. Many Scottish regiments were, after a time, deprived of their pipes.

When the first Highland regiments were being raised every Highland gentleman of good birth who could raise one hundred men was made a captain, while those who brought with them twenty to thirty men received subaltern's rank.

In the course of the four wars in which Britain had been engaged since the Black Watch was regimented in 1740, the corps embodied in the Highlands amounted to fifty battalions of the line, three reserve, seven militia, besides twenty-six regiments of Fencibles. According to the 1763 *Scots Magazine*, 65,000 Scotsmen were enlisted. Of these a great proportion were Highlanders, whose services were extremely ill-requited. Many of the Highland regiments were disbanded in 1763 :

Were not the Highlanders put upon every hazardous enterprise, where nothing was to be got but broken bones, and are not all these regiments discarded now but the 42nd ? The Scots colonel who entered the Moro Castle (Lieutenant-Colonel James Stuart) is now reduced to half pay, while an English general, whose avarice was the occasion of the death of many thousands of brave men (Lieutenant-General the Earl of Albemarle), is not only on full pay, but in possession of one-fifth of the whole money gained at the Havannah.[1]

This was only too true. The student of Highland regimental history cannot but be struck by the unfair, not to say unjust, treatment meted out to the early Highland regiments by the Government. Not only this, but the repeated attempts, alas, often successful, of the Government to deprive the Highland regiments, who had fought so well for the country, of their national garb, were most cruel and unjust.[2] Indeed, the first half-century of the Highland regiments is one sorry tale of deliberate breaches of enlistment conditions and of attempts

---

[1] *Edinburgh Advertiser*, 6th July 1764.
[2] Numerous instances in this Chapter.

to suppress the Highland dress. It says much for the patriotism of the Highlanders that they continued to come forward.

In the forty years preceding 1837, the island of Skye furnished the army with no fewer than 21 lieutenant-generals and major-generals ; 48 lieutenant-colonels ; 600 majors, captain, and subalterns ; 120 pipers, and 10,000 private soldiers. Also one adjutant-general of the British army. " At the close of the last and the beginning of the present century half the farms in Skye were rented by half-pay officers " (Alexander Smith in *A Summer in Skye*).

The advantage of the Highland garb and its healthiness as a campaigning dress has been abundantly testified, both in the early days of the Highland regiments, as well as at the present day. General Stewart of Garth relates that :

In the march through Holland and Westphalia in 1794 and 1795, when the cold was so intense that brandy froze in bottles, the Highlanders consisting of the 78th, 79th, and the new recruits of the 42nd (very young soldiers) wore their kilts, and yet the loss was out of all comparison less than that sustained by some other corps.

To come down to the present day, the author has seen a letter from an English officer, detached from an English regiment to serve in one of our Highland regiments in South Africa, in which testimony is given to the suitability of the kilt " as a campaigning kit." In October 1900 there appeared in one of the Highland papers a letter from an Orange River colonist to a relative in Ross-shire, saying : " I have a greater opinion than ever of the Highlanders. I think at all hazards their kilts, and therefore their distinctiveness, ought to be preserved." This opinion is one which, no doubt, will be thoroughly endorsed by every person who knows anything about the Highlanders, the Highland dress, and the Highland regiments. In the Boer war, when the Highlanders were offered khaki breeches in place of their kilt, they declined the offer.

In another part of this work it has been pointed out how several successful soldiers, on being given a peerage, have received a Highland soldier as a supporter of their armorial bearings. It will not, therefore, be inappropriate to mention here an instance showing the esteem in which the Highland dress and the Highland regiments were held by one of our most distinguished generals. During the Crimean War the Highland Brigade, under the command of Sir Colin Campbell (afterwards Lord Clyde), behaved with such distinguished gallantry at the battle of the Alma, that Field Marshal Lord Raglan (the Commander-in-Chief of the British Expeditionary Force) requested Sir Colin to ask some boon from him in recognition of the bravery of his Highlanders. The favour asked by Sir Colin, and granted by the Commander-in-Chief, was that he might be permitted during the remainder of the campaign to wear the Highland feather-bonnet in place of a general's cocked hat. If Sir Colin Campbell needed anything to add to the great popularity which he already enjoyed among his Highland soldiers, the above boon asked by and granted to him was the best plan which he could have chosen to endear himself to them.

It is remarkable what a partiality the natives of India have for Highland regiments. The fiery little Ghurkha especially has a profound admiration for the Highlanders, and is always proud to follow the lead of our Highland soldiers. During the relief of Lucknow, in the Indian Mutiny, the 4th Sikhs and the 93rd Highlanders fought side by side, and the constant fraternisation of the Sikhs and Highlanders was a frequent subject of remark. It is said the 4th Sikhs petitioned to be allowed Highland costume for their uniform in the future. Many regiments in the native Indian army have now their own pipe bands, whose members have in many cases received their instruction on the *piob-mhòr* from the pipe-majors of Scottish regiments.

The following pages contain a list of the Highland regiments, past and present, with a short account of the main points in their history.

THE BLACK WATCH

FORMERLY 43RD REGIMENT, AND LATER 42ND REGIMENT, NOW 1ST BATTALION ROYAL HIGHLANDERS, THE BLACK WATCH.

Raised in 1739. *Facings : Blue.*

" Watches " were a system of policy to prevent cattle-lifting. Each Watch was raised by the most powerful chief of the county in which it was to act, and the heads of the clans thus associated were bound for the maintenance of their respective parties, the security of their districts, and to make good to the owner any property stolen within their bounds. In the companies thus raised, the leaders and men supported, clothed, and armed themselves according to the ordinary garb and weapons of the clans before the disarming under Marshal Wade. Cluny Macpherson, Lord Lovat, and the Marquis of Atholl were the principal persons associated with the raising of this armed body.

In 1725 the Government raised six independent companies as part of the armed forces of the kingdom. Three of these companies, of 114 men each, were commanded by Lord Lovat, Sir Duncan Campbell of Lochnell, and Colonel Grant of Ballindalloch, with the rank of captain. The other three, of 70 men each, by Colonel Alexander Campbell of Skipness, John Campbell of Carrick, and George Munro of Culcairn, with the rank of captain-lieutenant. The Watch thus raised was designated *Am Freiceadan Dubh* (the Black Watch) to distinguish them from the regular troops, who, from their uniform of scarlet were called *Saighdearan Dearg* (red soldiers). Its name came from their dark tartan. The privates were, in most cases, of good social position. By the command of George II., two privates were sent to St. James's Palace for the King to approve the tartan and to give an exhibition of Highland sword exercise. On their leaving the Palace the two soldiers were given a guinea a piece, which they threw to the porter at the door. Originally, care was taken to enlist only Highlanders, both officers and privates, who favoured the Hanoverian cause. Later, however, privates were enlisted irrespective of their political proclivities, though the officers were still chosen from Whig families.

The independent companies continued to exist as such until 1739, when the Government resolved to raise four additional companies, and to form the whole into a regiment of the line. For this purpose letters of service, dated 25th October 1739, were addressed to John, 20th Earl of Crawford, who was appointed to command the regiment about to be formed, which was to consist of 1,000 men. The Black Watch was, therefore, embodied as a regiment under the number of the 43rd Regiment in May 1740, and mustered in a field between Tay Bridge and Aberfeldy, in Perthshire.

The first Colonel of the new regiment, known as " the gallant Earl of Crawford," had been bred a Highlander. He was educated under the supervision of John, Duke of Argyll, and passed his boyhood at Inveraray. Lord Crawford entered the army as ensign in 1723, and after brilliant military exploits got command of the Black Watch, but never took command as he was transferred to the Lifeguards.

The uniform of the Black Watch, on its being embodied as a regiment, was a scarlet jacket and waistcoat, with buff facings and white lace, tartan plaid of twelve yards plaited round the middle of the body, the upper part being fixed on the left shoulder, ready to be thrown loose and wrapped over both shoulders and firelock in rainy weather. This plaid was called the " belted plaid," from being kept tight to the body by a belt, and it was worn on guards, reviews, and on all occasions when the men were in full dress. On this belt hung the pistols and dirk when worn. In the barracks, and when not on duty, the little kilt, or philibeg, was worn. The bonnet worn was a blue one, with a border of white, red, and green, arranged in small squares, with a tuft of feathers, or sometimes, from economy or necessity, a small piece of black bearskin. The arms were a musket, a bayonet, and a large basket-hilted broadsword. These were furnished by the Government. Such of the men as chose to supply themselves with pistols and dirks were allowed to carry them, and some of the soldiers carried targets. The sword-belt was of black leather, and the cartouch-box was carried in front, supported by a narrow belt round the middle.

Analysis indicates (Stewart, *Setts of Scottish Tartans*, p. 27) the Black Watch tartan as a " hunting sett " based on the Royal tartan, and that it was adopted and approved for the companies from their formation in 1725. In the eighteenth century it was known as " the Government tartan," and was the natural sett to use for a Royal regiment such as *Am Freiceadan Dubh*. The pipers wore the bright-red Dress Stewart tartan, " so," says General Stewart of Garth, " that they could be more clearly seen at a distance," but the true reason was that this was the " Royal " tartan. When a band of music was added, tartan of the same sett as the pipers was given them.

For fifteen months after the regiment had been raised it remained in the neighbourhood of Tay Bridge. In 1740 the Earl of Crawford was transferred to the Life Guards, and Lord Sempill became Colonel of the Black Watch.

In March 1743 the regiment assembled at Perth and were informed that they were to be marched to England. This order was received with great indignation and suspicion, as the men believed that they had been enlisted for service in the Highlands of Scotland only. Lord President Forbes, who learnt of the intended breach of faith, warned Marshal Wade of the unwisdom of the proposed step, and both Wade and Forbes seem to have received a chilly rebuff from London.[1] The men were pacified by the excuse being given that the King wished to see the regiment. The Black Watch reached London in two divisions on the 29th and 30th April 1743, only to find that the King had sailed for Hanover on the latter day. The regiment, however, was reviewed at Finchley Common by Marshal Wade on the 14th May following. Meanwhile, a rumour had got abroad that not only was the Government about to despatch the 43rd on foreign service but that the destination was to be the American plantations (the Botany Bay of that time). The men were all the readier to believe such reports as they had first been deceived in having been removed from their native country, and then further deceived by the pretence that the King was to review them.

A few days after the regiment had been reviewed by Marshal Wade, the men of the regiment, not knowing what might be their fate if they trusted to the promises of a Government which they had every reason to deem faithless, assembled on a common near Highgate, and thence set out on their return march to the North. The first part of the march was made in the night. The high road was avoided, and the route of march was straight across country. The regiment had reached Oundle, in Northamptonshire, before their route was discovered. The 43rd had entrenched themselves in a wood, and had resolved to be cut to pieces rather than surrender. However, they were ultimately persuaded by General Blakeney, commanding at Northampton, to surrender, the General promising that the most favourable report should be made of them to the lords-justices. The regiment was then disarmed and marched to London. There the mutineers were tried and three of their number selected for execution, viz. Andrew and Samuel Macpherson (brothers) and Fearchar Shaw, all sons of respectable

[1] J. Salmond, *Wade in Scotland*.

gentlemen and members of Clan Chattan. These three were shot on Towerhill on 12th July 1743. In the Highlands they were regarded as heroes and Colonel Lord John Murray placed their portraits in his dining-room.

Two hundred of the Highlanders were then sent to serve in different corps abroad : fifty to Gibraltar, fifty to Minorca, forty to the Leeward Islands, thirty to Jamaica, and thirty to Georgia.

In May 1744 the rest of the regiment was ordered to Flanders, where the Black Watch distinguished itself at Fontenoy in 1745 by covering the retreat of the troops, commanded by that bitter enemy of Highlanders, the Duke of Cumberland.

By withdrawing the Black Watch from Scotland the Government (as the Lord President had anticipated) threw Scotland open to the expedition of 1745, whilst the unfortunate treatment of the Black Watch served much to arouse sympathy with the Jacobites.

During " the '45," the Black Watch was stationed on the coast of Kent. Early in the same year three new companies were raised and added to the regiment. The command of these new companies was given to the gentlemen who recruited the men. These gentlemen were Mackintosh of Mackintosh, Sir Patrick Murray of Ochtertyre, and Campbell of Inverawe.

In 1749, in consequence of the reduction of the old 42nd Regiment (Oglethorp's), the number of the Black Watch, or 43rd Regiment, was changed to 42, the number it has ever since retained.

Three times has a second battalion of the 42nd been raised. The first occasion was in 1758, when, in consideration of the regiment's distinguished services, especially at the battles of Fontenoy and Ticonderoga, letters of service were issued for raising a second battalion, besides an order to make the regiment a " Royal " one, a step which should, logically, have been taken when the independent companies were regimented in 1739. The 2nd Battalion was embodied at Perth in October 1758. This 2nd Battalion was disbanded in Scotland in 1763.

Of all the Highland regiments the Black Watch alone has the privilege of wearing a red heckle, or plume, in their bonnets. The other Highland regiments all wear a white plume in their head-dress. This is the story told of how the 42nd gained the right to wear the red heckle.

In December 1794, when the 42nd were quartered at Thuyl, in the Low Countries, they were ordered on the night of the 31st to march upon Bommell, on the opposite side of the River Waal, which they reached early on 1st January 1795. Here the British attacked the French army, and drove them across the river. The position thus gained was held until the evening of 3rd January, when, the French having been reinforced, a partial retreat of the British took place on the morning of the 4th. The British retired on the village of Guilder-malsen, where the 42nd, along with other regiments, halted, and formed up to cover the retreat through the village. The French cavalry pushed their way through the retreating British picquets with such eagerness that they captured two field-pieces stationed in front of the village to cover the retreat of the picquets, and the French cavalry commenced dragging the guns off. An aide-de-camp came with an order directing the 42nd to advance and retake the guns. The order was fulfilled to the letter and so skilfully that the losses were negligible, and notwithstanding that, since the artillery horses had been disabled, the guns were dragged in by the men of the Black Watch.

On 4th June 1795, when the Black Watch were quartered at Royston, near Cambridge, and after they had fired a *feu de joie* in honour of the birthday of King George III., a box arrived containing red or vulture's feathers, which were served out ; the commanding officer at the same time addressed the regiment, saying that the red plume was conferred upon the regiment as a special Royal recognition of the gallantry it had displayed when retaking the British guns on 4th January 1795. The red heckle has ever since been the distinctive badge of the gallant 42nd.

In the territorial reorganisation of the British army the Black Watch area and headquarters were centred at Perth, the county in which *Am Freiceadan Dubh* had originally been embodied as a regiment.

LOUDOUN'S HIGHLANDERS

Raised in 1745.   Disbanded in 1748.

The great bravery of the 42nd and the admirable service which they rendered at the Battle of Fontenoy, made the Government anxious to avail themselves still further of the military qualities of the Highlanders. Authority, therefore, was given to the Earl of Loudoun to raise another Highland regiment under the patronage of the noblemen, chiefs, and gentlemen of that part of the kingdom, whose sons and connections would be appointed officers.

Lord Loudoun had an easy task as recruits rapidly joined the colours. Soon a body of 750 men assembled at Inverness and the remainder at Perth. The regiment consisted of twelve companies under John, Earl of Loudoun, as Colonel, and John Campbell (afterwards Duke of Argyll), Lieutenant-Colonel. The officers' commissions were dated 6th June 1745.

Before the regiment was disciplined the Rising of "the '45" commenced. So rapid were the movements of Prince Charles's forces that communication between the two parts of the regiment (at Inverness and Perth) was cut off. Eight companies under Lord Loudoun, were occupied in the northern Highlands while the remaining four companies served in the central and southern Highlands.

The force under Lord Loudoun were the victims of the ignominious Rout of Moy, when during the darkness of the night they were put to flight by a handful of the Clan Chattan and the bold tactics of Lady

Mackintosh. At the Battle of Prestonpans every officer and man of three companies was taken prisoner by the Jacobites.

In 1747 Loudoun's Highlanders embarked for Flanders, where they served until the peace of 1748, when they returned to Scotland and were disbanded at Perth.

77TH REGIMENT (MONTGOMERY'S HIGHLANDERS)

Raised in 1757. Disbanded in 1763.

When the Government turned to the Highlands for a third kilted regiment this (the 77th) was recruited from among the Jacobite clans (Frasers, MacDonalds, Camerons, Macleans, and others).

In 1757 letters of service were granted to Major the Hon. Archibald Montgomerie (afterwards 11th Earl of Eglinton) to recruit a regiment from the Highlands. Major Montgomerie was intimately connected with the Highlands and popular among the Highlanders. One of his sisters was married to Sir Alexander MacDonald of Sleate, while another was the wife of the Laird of Abercairney.

The tartan of the regiment was the 42nd. The regiment, which was embodied at Stirling, had thirteen companies of 105 rank and file each, making 1,460 men, including sixty-five sergeants and thirty pipers and drummers. The portrait of its Colonel, Lord Eglinton, is of considerable interest as illustrating the diced bonnet and feathers as worn in the mid-eighteenth century. Its " heraldic " relation to the medieval " cap " is noticeable.

The 77th embarked immediately for Halifax to take part in the operations against the French in America. They later served in the West Indies, and were afterwards quartered in New York. After the termination of hostilities in 1763, both officers and men were given the choice of either settling in America or returning home. Those who elected to remain in America obtained a grant of land in proportion to their rank.

When the American war broke out in 1775, republican sentiments being what they were, many of the old 77th and 78th soldiers again joined the Royal colours and became members of the 84th or Royal Regiment of Highland Emigrants.

78TH REGIMENT (FRASER'S HIGHLANDERS)

Raised in 1757. Disbanded in 1763

The old 78th Regiment must not be confounded with the 2nd Battalion of the present Seaforth Highlanders.

In view of the advice given to King George II. by the great Pitt, to adopt the policy of trying to conciliate the heads of the great Highland Jacobite families, letters of service were in 1757 granted to the Hon. Simon Fraser (son of Lord Lovat, who had been forfeited and executed for his share in " the '45 ") to raise a Highland regiment from the territories of his own family then vested in the Crown. Such was the influence of the Chief of Clan Fraser that, though possessing neither money nor land, he managed to recruit within a few weeks upwards of 600 men. The gentlemen of the country and the officers of the regiment raised some 700 more, so that a battalion was soon formed consisting of thirteen companies of 105 rank and file each, making in all 1,460 men, including sixty-five sergeants and thirty pipers and drummers. The officers' commissions were dated 5th January 1757.

The 78th embarked in 1757 for Halifax, in company with the 77th Regiment, and, like the latter, were employed against the French in America.

When the 78th landed in North America it was proposed to change their uniform, as the Highland garb was said to be unfit for the severe winters and hot summers of that country. The officers and men, however, vehemently protested against any change of garb. On Colonel Fraser representing to the Commander-in-Chief the strong attachment which the men cherished towards their national dress, and the consequences that might be expected to follow if they were deprived of it, the objectionable proposal was dropped. To quote the words of an old veteran of the 78th :

Thanks to our generous chief we were allowed to wear the garb of our fathers, and in the course of six winters showed the doctors that they did not understand our constitutions, for in the coldest winters our men were more healthy than those regiments who wore breeches and warm clothing.

The regiment was quartered alternately in Canada and Nova Scotia till the conclusion of the war, when a number of the officers and men, expressing a desire to settle in the country, all those who elected to do this were discharged and received a grant of land. The rest were sent home and were discharged in Scotland in 1763. Many of the Frasers now in Canada, and who form an important part of the population of that land, claim descent from the members of the old 78th Regiment.

When the war broke out in 1775 between Great Britain and her American colonies, upwards of 300 veterans of the 78th Regiment enlisted in the 84th or Royal Regiment of Highland Emigrants.

87TH & 88TH REGIMENTS (KEITH'S & CAMPBELL'S HIGHLANDERS)

Raised in 1759. Disbanded in 1763.

The first of these regiments was commanded by Major Robert Murray Keith, who had served in the Scots Brigade in Holland, and was a distant relative of the celebrated Field-Marshal Keith. Major Murray Keith returned to Scotland in 1758, where he was appointed

Q

to command three newly raised companies of Highlanders, consisting of 105 men each. With this small corps he joined the Allied army in Germany under Prince Ferdinand in August 1759.

Prince Ferdinand formed such an excellent opinion of Major Keith's little corps that orders were given to augment it to 800 men, with officers in proportion. At the same time orders were also given to raise another regiment in the Highlands, and to place both regiments under the command of Prince Ferdinand.

The command of the second regiment was to be given to Major John Campbell of Dunoon (who was one of the original majors of the Fraser Highlanders). Authority was given to the Earls of Sutherland and of Breadalbane, the Lairds of MacLeod and of Innes, and to other gentlemen in the Highlands, to appoint captains and officers to companies raised on their respective estates. Lord Breadalbane recommended Major Macnab of Macnab, Captain Campbell of Achallader, John Campbell of Avoch, and other officers. MacLeod of MacLeod raised a company in the island of Skye, to which he appointed his nephew, Captain Fothringham of Powrie. Most of the men were raised in the counties of Argyll, Perth, Inverness, Ross, and Sutherland. Within a few weeks the ranks of the regiment were filled.

Keith's regiment was embodied at Perth, and Campbell's regiment at Stirling. The two battalions being embodied at the same time, and ordered on the same service, officers were promoted and removed from the one to the other in the same manner practised at a later period when second battalions were added to the regiments. The two regiments sailed for Germany and joined the Allied army under Prince Ferdinand in 1760, and a graphic account of the campaign was compiled by Captain Sir James Innes of that Ilk.

They served with much distinction during the war. On the conclusion of peace in November 1762 both regiments were ordered home. On their march through Holland to the coast the Highlanders were received in various towns with acclamations, the women presenting laurel leaves to the soldiers. After landing at Tilbury the 87th and 88th Regiments marched through England on their way to Scotland, and were most hospitably received in all the towns through which they passed, their reception at Derby being most remarkable. No payment was taken from them for quarters, and subscriptions were raised to give gratuities to the men. This only shows that the good folk of Derby had not forgotten the exemplary way in which the Highlanders, under Prince Charlie, had behaved when they visited Derby during " the '45."

On arrival in Scotland, Keith's regiment was quartered in Perth and Campbell's in Linlithgow ; both regiments were disbanded in July 1763.

89TH HIGHLAND REGIMENT (DUKE OF GORDON'S HIGHLANDERS)

Raised in 1759. *Disbanded in* 1765.

The 89th Regiment was really the first regiment of Gordon High-landers ever raised. Its genesis was due to the political foresight of the widow of the Duke of Gordon, who had married, as her second husband, Major Staates Long Morris. At that time the Duke of Gordon, son of the Duchess, was in his minority, while the influence of the Duke of Argyll was great in the political world. As a means of strengthening the Gordon influence, and thereby counteracting that of the Argyll family, the Duchess of Gordon prevailed on George II. to allow her husband, Major Morris, to raise a Highland regiment in the Gordon territory. The Duchess knew the country well, as she was a daughter of the Earl of Aberdeen, and, therefore, a native of the district. The efforts of the Duchess were so successful that within a few weeks 960 men assembled at Gordon Castle and marched to Aberdeen, in December 1759. Major Staates Long Morris (afterwards a general) was the lieutenant-colonel-commandant of the new regiment ; George Scott and Hector Munro, who both rose to the rank of general, were the majors ; Alexander, Duke of Gordon, was senior captain ; while his younger brothers, Lords William and George Gordon were, respectively, senior lieutenant and ensign.

The 89th embarked in November 1761 for India. The Duke of Gordon, who was at college, left the university with the intention of accompanying his regiment to the East. This resolution, however, was vetoed by the King, who remarked that as there were only nine Dukes in the kingdom of Scotland, he could not allow one of them to leave his native country ! After serving four years in India the 89th were ordered home and were disbanded in 1765. The regiment acquitted itself in a most exemplary manner during the whole period of its existence.

101ST REGIMENT (JOHNSTONE'S HIGHLANDERS)

Raised in 1760. *Disbanded in* 1763.

In 1760 commissions to raise independent companies in the High-lands, to consist of five sergeants and 105 rank and file each, were given to the following gentlemen, viz. : Captains Colin Graham of Drainie, James Cuthbert of Milncraigs, Peter Gordon of Knockespock, Ludovick Grant of the family of Rothiemurchus, and Robert Campbell of Balliveolin. These officers were to recruit in their own counties of Argyll, Ross, and Inverness.

The recruiting was soon completed and the five companies assembled at Perth, whence they were marched to Newcastle. There they remained until towards the end of 1761, when they were all ordered to reinforce Keith's and Campbell's Highlanders.

After the rank and file had embarked the officers were ordered back to the Highlands in order to raise six additional companies. This was soon performed, and in a few months six more companies assembled at Perth. These were formed into a regiment, numbered the 101st, command of which was given to Major (afterwards Sir) James Johnstone of Westerhall, major-commandant.

The 101st Regiment, however, did not have a chance of seeing service, for, while a detachment was under orders for Portugal in 1763, peace was declared and the regiment was disbanded at Perth in August.

100TH REGIMENT

Raised in 1761. *Disbanded in* 1763.

This regiment was embodied at Stirling, 1761, under command of Major Colin Campbell of Kilberrie. After its inspection the 100th Regiment was ordered to Martinique, where it was stationed until the peace of 1763, when it was ordered to Scotland and disbanded.

105TH REGIMENT (QUEEN'S HIGHLANDERS)

Raised in 1761. *Disbanded in* 1763.

This regiment was raised by Colonel David Graeme of Gorthie in 1761 and embodied at Perth in 1762. Gorthie had been in attendance on Queen Charlotte, hence the compliment given by styling it " The Queen's Highlanders." The 105th was two battalions strong.

Both were ordered to Ireland, and, at the peace in 1763, both were disbanded.

MACLEAN'S HIGHLANDERS

Raised in 1761. *Disbanded in* 1763.

Captain Allan Maclean of Torloisk had the honour of raising the above regiment, of which he was appointed major-commandant. It furnished many recruits to the Highland regiments serving in Germany and in America. It never, however, as a regiment, had the opportunity of seeing service, as the regiment was disbanded at the peace of 1763.

113TH REGIMENT (ROYAL HIGHLAND VOLUNTEERS)

Raised in 1761. *Disbanded in* 1763.

In 1761 a corps was raised and called the Royal Highland Volunteers, and numbered the 113th Regiment. Major James Hamilton was appointed lieutenant-colonel-commandant. The corps never had the opportunity of distinguishing itself, for at the peace of 1763 it was disbanded.

71st REGIMENT (Fraser's Highlanders)

Raised in 1775.   Disbanded in 1783.

Colonel Simon Fraser of Lovat, who raised the 78th, or Fraser's Highlanders (disbanded 1763), became a major-general in 1771. In consideration of the distinguished military services which he had rendered, General Fraser was, in 1774, on the payment of £20,983, granted all the forfeited Lovat estates, which had been lost to the family after the attainder and execution in 1746 of the General's father, the famous Lord Lovat. On the outbreak of the American war in 1775 the Government again had recourse to the influence of the Chief of Clan Fraser to raise forces in the Highlands for the British army. When General (then Mr.) Fraser raised the old 78th Regiment in 1757 he was without lands or territorial influence, yet he succeeded in getting together a fine body of men. In 1775, when again appealed to to use his influence to raise a regiment, his success was still more remarkable and in the meantime the General had obtained possession of his ancestral estates.

Within a few weeks of the issue of letters of service Lovat found himself at the head of 2,340 Highlanders. These were first assembled at Stirling and thence marched to Glasgow, where they were embodied in two battalions in April 1776.

Among the officers of the new regiment there were, in addition to the colonel (Chief of Clan Fraser of Lovat), no less than six chiefs of clans and two sons of chiefs of other clans, besides chieftains and sons of chieftains.

After the Treaty of Paris on 10th February 1763 (when peace was concluded between Great Britain and France), all British regiments bearing numbers above " 70 " had been disbanded. Therefore, when the new regiment of Fraser's Highlanders was raised it was given the number and designation of the 71st Regiment.

Immediately after embodiment the 71st embarked for Boston to join the British forces under Lord Howe. Unfortunately, during their voyage Boston had been evacuated by the British, and as Howe had neglected to station a British war vessel off Boston harbour to warn British transports of the evacuation, one of the transports, with the lieutenant-colonel of the 2nd Battalion on board, sailed into Boston harbour and was captured by the Americans.

The 71st had a distinguished career during the American war, but had the misfortune to form part of Lord Cornwallis's army which capitulated at Yorktown in 1781, when the regiment became prisoners of war.

Despite the inducements offered by the Americans to make the Highlanders desert, not one of the members of the Fraser's Highlanders was gained over by the enemy's proposals. On the conclusion of peace the officers and men of the 71st were shipped to Scotland and the regiment disbanded at Perth in 1783.

Before the 42nd Regiment gained the exclusive right among the Highland regiments (in 1795) to wear the red heckle in their feather-bonnets, the 71st, or Fraser's Highlanders, had adopted the red feather as their special distinction.   In 1776–1777 one of the lieutenant-colonels of the regiment, the Hon. Lieutenant-Colonel Maitland, was so active in his skirmishing tactics as to attract the attention of General Washington.   Some communications having passed between them as old acquaintances, although then opposed as enemies, Colonel Maitland sent intimation to the American General that in future his men would be distinguished by a red feather in their bonnets, so that General Washington could not mistake them, nor avoid doing justice to their ·exploits.   This red feather was worn by the Fraser Highlanders until the conclusion of the war.

THE HIGHLAND LIGHT INFANTRY (1st Battalion)

Lord MacLeod's Highlanders (73rd Regiment), later the 71st Regiment, Highland Light Infantry.

Raised in 1777.   Facings : Buff.

The 73rd (afterwards 71st) Regiment took the name of MacLeod's Highlanders from Lord MacLeod, eldest son of the Earl of Cromartie, who was attainted for the share he took in " the '45." It is the third regiment numbered " 71."

Lord MacLeod received an unconditional pardon on account of his youth.   Deprived of money and ancestral possessions at home, the heir of the MacKenzies, Earls of Cromartie, went abroad to seek his fortune.   He was the guest of the celebrated Marshal Keith at Berlin, and, through the Marshal's interest, obtained a commission in the army of the King of Sweden.   Lord MacLeod served the Swedish sovereigns twenty-seven years and attained the rank of lieutenant-general in the Swedish service.   As with many an exiled Scot, absence from the old country but strengthens the affection for it.   Lord MacLeod returned in 1777 and was presented to King George III., who received him graciously.

Though devoid of lands MacKenzie was still a name to conjure with in the old territories of the Cromartie family.   Lord MacLeod (whose title derived from a claim to represent MacLeod of Lewis) was encouraged to offer to raise a Highland regiment.   His offer was accepted, and 840 Highlanders were recruited and marched to Elgin.

Eventually 1,100 men were embodied under the name of " MacLeod's Highlanders."

On completion of this battalion, letters were granted for a second one, and Lord MacLeod soon found himself at the head of 2,200 men, of whom nearly 1,800 were from the district where once his family had such large possessions.

In 1779 the 1st Battalion embarked for India under command of Lord MacLeod. The 2nd Battalion sailed for Gibraltar under his brother, Hon. Lieutenant-Colonel George MacKenzie. It served in the siege of Gibraltar as part of the garrison, in 1783 returned and at Stirling was disbanded in October 1783.

In 1783 Lord MacLeod (major-general, 1782) returned home, and for his distinguished services the forfeited estates of the Earldom of Cromartie were restored to him in 1784 on payment of £19,000.

MacLeod's Highlanders were uniformed in the kilt and Highland dress, the tartan worn being MacKenzie, quite illogically for a regiment called " MacLeod's Highlanders," an anomaly due to the Earl of Cromarty's attempt to assert chiefship of the MacLeods of Lewis without taking the Name and Arms of that family and whilst remaining in name and tartan a MacKenzie. MacLeod tartan was the only sett proper to a regiment named MacLeod's Highlanders.

In 1785 the Hon. Lieutenant-Colonel George MacKenzie, with several officers from the 2nd Battalion, which had been disbanded two years earlier, joined the 1st Battalion in India. In 1786 the regiment received new colours, and the number was changed to 71st.

In 1804, for the second time, a second battalion was formed and embodied at Dumbarton. Recruiting for this battalion was so successfully carried on in Glasgow that the corps acquired then the name of " The Glasgow Highland Light Infantry." In June 1808 George III. confirmed the title of " Glasgow " to the 71st. On 5th August 1808 :

At a numerous and most respectable meeting of the merchants, manufacturers, and others, inhabitants of this city, held this day in the Town Hall at the request of the Lord Provost and Magistrates, intimated by public advertisement—the following resolutions were proposed by the Lord Provost, seconded by Baillie Dennistoun, and unanimously adopted : Resolved that, as from its ranks being chiefly filled with men raised in this city, his Majesty has lately been graciously pleased to permit the 71st Regiment to assume the appellation of the Glasgow Regiment ; and as the 2nd Battalion of that brave regiment, now quartered here, is nearly in a situation to be able to share in the Glasgow service, in which the 1st Battalion is already engaged, the fund to be raised shall, under the directions of the Lord Provost, Baillie Dennistoun, and Cunningham Corbet, John Hamilton, and John More, Esq., as a Committee, be employed in giving encouragement to those men who shall speedily join the 2nd Battalion of the Glasgow Regiment. An address in terms of these resolutions was then unanimously agreed to, and the Lord Provost requested to subscribe the same in the name of the meeting, and to transmit it to the Right Hon. Lord Hawkesbury, to be presented to his Majesty.

(Signed)
JAMES MacKENZIE, Provost.

In March 1809 the 71st were transformed into a light infantry regiment, when it was directed that the clothing, arming, and discipline should be the same as those of other such regiments. The regiment then ceased to wear the kilt, though permitted to wear the cocked bonnet and retained its pipe band, the members of which were allowed to wear the kilt, but in 1810 the word "Glasgow" apparently was dropped.

The 2nd Battalion was disbanded at Glasgow in 1815. In 1820 the 71st was denominated the 71st Highland Regiment of Foot.

According to a return furnished to the Horse Guards in 1872, the 71st proved then to be a representative national regiment, 710 Scotsmen, 25 Englishmen, and 18 Irish.

In 1875, and again in 1877, the officer commanding the 71st had the chance of having the kilt restored to his regiment. The regiment, however, preferred to retain the trews, as it had thereby the distinction of being then the only Highland regiment wearing the trews.

During 1899 the 1st Battalion Highland Light Infantry (the old 71st) was removed from the Highland Brigade, because the regiment was not a kilted one. Protests were sent to Lord Roberts, and to Major-General Hector MacDonald, commanding the Highland Brigade. The replies were that it was considered the Highland Brigade should consist of kilted regiments only. Later on in the campaign the 71st were allowed to rejoin the Highland Brigade.

In 1901 the regiment, backed by the Corporation, made strong representations to have the kilt and be named The Highland Light Infantry (City of Glasgow) Regiment, and as " The City of Glasgow Regiment," it proudly ranked as one of the oldest of our Highland regiments. The regiment's uniform as worn by the officers was a peaked chaco as headpiece, a Highland doublet, with which trousers of tartan (officially denominated trews) were worn, along with plaid, dirk, and claymore. Eventually the H.L.I. became once more a kilted regiment, but in 1958 lost the kilt on amalgamation with the Royal Scottish Fusiliers becoming part of the *Royal Highland Fusiliers*, a regiment which, had its colonels not resigned over withdrawal of the kilt, was to have been named *The Mar and MacLeod Regiment*.

THE ARGYLL HIGHLANDERS (OLD 74TH HIGHLAND REGIMENT)

Raised in 1778. *Disbanded in* 1783.

In December 1777 letters of service were granted to Colonel John Campbell of Barbreck to raise a regiment in Argyllshire. Barbreck had served first as captain and then as major in the 71st or Fraser's Highlanders. Though all the officers except four were Highlanders, only 590 of the rank and file were from Argyll, the remainder having been recruited from Glasgow and western Scotland. Campbells mustered strong, the three field officers, six captains, and no less than fourteen subalterns being of that clan. Among the officers was The MacQuarrie, who, when he joined, was sixty-two years of age. Financial embarrassments were the reason of this chief embracing the army as a profession at such an advanced age. He died in 1817 in his 102nd year, the last chief of his clan in the direct line.

The regiment mustered 960 rank and file, and were inspected in May 1778. They embarked for America during the following August, and served there until 1783, when they returned home. The regiment was disbanded at Stirling in the autumn of the same year.

MACDONALD'S HIGHLANDERS (OLD 76TH HIGHLAND REGIMENT)

Raised in 1777. *Disbanded in* 1784.

Three regiments in the British army have borne the number " 76," viz. an Irish regiment, MacDonald's Highlanders, and the present 2nd Battalion of the Duke of Wellington's Regiment.

In December 1777 letters of service were granted to Alexander, 1st Lord MacDonald of Sleate, empowering him to raise a regiment in the Highlands. Lord MacDonald was offered the command of this regiment, which, however, he declined. On Lord MacDonald's recommendation command of the regiment was conferred on Major John MacDonell of Lochgarry.

The regimental strength 1,086 was inspected at Inverness in March 1778 by General Skene ; 750 were Highlanders, the remainder being composed of two companies raised in the Lowlands, and a third recruited chiefly in Ireland. As the Colonel of the 76th, Lochgarry, who had been serving in America with Fraser's Highlanders, had been taken prisoner on his passage from there, the command of MacDonald's Highlanders devolved upon Major Donaldson, formerly captain in the 42nd Regiment.

In 1779 the regiment moved to Perth, and thence to Burntisland,
Q*

where they embarked for America. Their commanding officer was then Major Lord Berriedale (eldest son of the 10th Earl of Caithness), Major Donaldson's health not permitting him to embark. The 76th served in different parts of Canada and what is now the United States. They were unfortunately part of the force, under Lord Cornwallis, which surrendered to the Americans at Yorktown in 1781. After the surrender the 76th were marched in detachments as prisoners to different parts of Virginia, where they remained until the peace of 1783. During the regiment's captivity tempting offers were made to the men by their captors to join the American forces. The Mac-Donald Highlanders were, however, proof against all allurements, and not a single soldier was seduced from his allegiance.

When peace was restored the 76th embarked at New York for Scotland, and were disbanded in 1784 at Stirling Castle.

THE ATHOLL HIGHLANDERS (OLD 77TH HIGHLAND REGIMENT)

Raised in 1778. Disbanded in 1783.

On the application of the young Duke of Atholl, the Government granted him letters of service to raise a regiment of 1,000 men for the service of the State, with power to appoint officers. The command of the regiment was given to Colonel James Murray, son of Lord George Murray (uncle to the Duke of Atholl).

The Atholl Highlanders were embodied at Perth, and having marched to Portpatrick, and thence embarked for Ireland, arrived in Dublin 31st May 1778. The terms on which the men had enlisted were service for three years or the duration of the war.

The 77th were quartered in Ireland during the whole war, so had no chance of seeing service. Their record in Ireland, however, was an excellent one.

On the conclusion of hostilities in 1783 the men expected to be disbanded in terms of the agreement, under conditions of which they had enlisted. However, instead of being disbanded the regiment went to Portsmouth for embarkation to the East Indies. On arrival at Portsmouth the men realized that they were the subjects of one of the breaches of faith so characteristic of Government departments, and the order being contrary to their conditions of enlistment the soldiers refused to embark. After some days of disorder, during which the officers lost all control of their men, the Government, seeing the mistake they had made in not implementing their agreement, gave the order to march the regiment to Berwick, where it was disbanded in April 1783, in terms of the original agreement.

Regarding the above unfortunate incident, General Stewart of Garth, in his *History of the Highland Regiments*, remarks :

It is difficult for those who are not in the habit of mixing with the Highlanders to believe the extent of the mischief which this unhappy misunderstanding has occasioned, and the deep and lasting impression it has left behind it. In the course of my recruiting, many years afterwards, I was often reminded of this attempt on the Atholl Highlanders, which was always alleged as a confirmation of what happened at an earlier period to the Black Watch. This transaction, and others of a similar description, have created a distrust in Government and in the integrity of its agents.

If Government had offered a small bounty when the Atholl Highlanders were required to embark, there can be little doubt they would have obeyed their orders, and embarked as cheerfully as they marched into Portsmouth.
. . . An inference in consequence has been drawn, and never forgotten, in the Highlands, that, however unjustifiable in the mode of redress, the men had just cause of complaint.

The Atholl Highlanders were the first regiment to set the military fashion of regimental pipers wearing green doublets.

The title " the Atholl Highlanders " has since the disbandment been the name of the Duke of Atholl's regiment of Highlanders in Blair Atholl. It has been called his " private army." They wear the Atholl district tartan.

THE SEAFORTH HIGHLANDERS

FORMERLY THE 78TH REGIMENT, LATER THE 72ND REGIMENT (THE DUKE OF ALBANY'S OWN HIGHLANDERS), 1ST BATTALION SEAFORTH HIGHLANDERS, (ROSS-SHIRE BUFFS, THE DUKE OF ALBANY'S) AND NOW MERGED WITH THE CAMERONS IN THE " QUEEN'S OWN HIGHLANDERS."

Raised in 1778. Facings : Buff.

The Earl of Seaforth, Chief of the Clan MacKenzie, who had taken part in the Rising of 1715, was attainted and his estates were forfeited. His grandson Kenneth MacKenzie repurchased the family property from the Government. He was raised to the peerage of Ireland in 1764 as Baron Ardelve, in 1766 was created Viscount Fortrose, and eventually, in 1771, Earl of Seaforth.

In order to evince his gratitude for these favours, Lord Seaforth offered King George III. in 1778 to raise a Highland regiment in the territory of the MacKenzies. This offer was gratefully accepted, and in a short time 1,130 men were enlisted. Of this number about 500 men were from the Seaforth estates and about 400 were from the estates of the MacKenzies of Scatwell, Kilcoy, Applecross, and Redcastle, all of whom had sons or brothers in the regiment. The Macraes of Kintail (who have always been such loyal supporters of the Seaforth family) mustered in such force in the new regiment that it was nearly as much a Macrae as a MacKenzie one.

The Seaforth Highlanders were embodied at Elgin in May 1778, and in August marched to Leith for embarkation to (they found) the East Indies. This led to " The Affair of the Wild Macraes." The origin of this mutiny was similar to that which occasioned the mutiny of the Atholl Highlanders, viz., ill faith on the part of

Government. However, through the influence of the Lieutenant-Colonel, Lord Seaforth, and other Highland gentlemen, the matter was amicably arranged without loss of life. The idea of sending the corps to India was for the time abandoned, half the regiment was sent to Guernsey, the other half to Jersey. In April 1781, both divisions assembled at Portsmouth and embarked for India, strength 973. Their chief and commander, Lord Seaforth, accompanied the regiment but unfortunately died at sea in August 1781, to the grief and dismay of his followers. The voyage was a disastrous one for the 78th. Scurvy broke out on board and before arrival at Madras in April 1782, 247 of its strength had died, while of the remainder only 369 were fit for service.

On 12th September 1786 the number of the 78th Regiment was altered to " 72nd " in consequence of the reduction of senior regiments.

On 25th December 1804 a second battalion composed of Aberdeenshire men was raised. Its services were confined to the United Kingdom, and it was disbanded at Londonderry in 1816.

In 1809 the 72nd Highlanders were among the regiments directed by a Royal order to discontinue wearing their national costume as it was "objectionable to the people of South Britain."

In 1823 George IV. authorised the resumption of the Highland dress by the 72nd, trews, however, being substituted for the kilt. The regiment was next re-named The Duke of Albany's Own Highlanders, with plaid and trews of (quite logically) Dress Stewart tartan, and in June 1824 the Duke of Albany's cypher and coronet was assigned for a regimental badge, to be borne on its colours.

Logan (*Scottish Gael*) comments on the substitution of the trews :

It is extraordinary that these two regiments, the oldest embodied clan corps, should wear trowsers, a dress formerly confined to lame, sick, or aged Highlanders. It has been a source of great vexation to their clan and country. Assuredly Lord MacLeod, the eldest son of MacKenzie, Earl of Cromarty, who raised the 73rd now the 71st, and MacKenzie, Earl of Seaforth, who embodied the old 78th now 72nd, would never have thought of an alteration so unnecessary and uncongenial to Celtic feeling.

The trews, however, though of more shapely cut than the government " trousers," were nevertheless a perfectly well recognised " Highland dress " in 1672 and in the eighteenth century.

Since Logan penned his remarks, however, the Highland dress in its entirety has been restored to the 72nd Regiment. In 1881 the 72nd (Duke of Albany's Own) and 78th (Ross-shire Buffs) were formed into a territorial regiment, " The Seaforth Highlanders (Ross-shire Buffs, The Duke of Albany's)," of which the 72nd Highlanders form the 1st Battalion. Both battalions resumed the kilt and the MacKenzie tartan, as again a Clan Regiment.

ABERDEENSHIRE HIGHLAND (81st) REGIMENT

Raised in 1778. *Disbanded in* 1783.

In December 1777 Colonel the Hon. William Gordon, brother of the Earl of Aberdeen, received orders to raise a regiment of Highlanders. Early in 1778, 980 men were embodied, of whom 650 were from the Highlands of Aberdeen. A large contingent of Clan Ross was enlisted through the influence of one of the majors of the regiment, Major Ross. The terms of enlistment were the same as those under which the Atholl Highlanders had been enrolled.

The regiment was marched to Stirling and thence embarked for Ireland where it was stationed three years. Its character during that period was most exemplary. At the end of 1782 the 81st were transferred to England and were quartered at Portsmouth. From there they received orders to embark for India. At first the men made no objection to this order, notwithstanding that it was in violation of the terms on which they had enlisted (viz. service for three years or till the conclusion of the war). However, when they learned what had occurred in the case of the " Atholl Highlanders," the 81st insisted on the terms of their engagement being adhered to. This request was conceded by the authorities and the regiment was marched to Scotland, where it was disbanded in Edinburgh in April 1783.

ROYAL HIGHLAND EMIGRANT (84th) REGIMENT

Embodied in 1775. *Regimented in* 1778. *Disbanded in* 1784.

This regiment was raised in America at the beginning of the American War of Independence. On 12th June 1775 General Gage issued an order to Lieutenant-Colonel Allan Maclean (son of Maclean of Torloisk) residing in Canada, late of the 104th Regiment, empowering him to raise a regiment of Highland emigrants consisting of two battalions of ten companies each, the whole corps to be clothed, armed, and accoutred in like manner with His Majesty's Royal Highland Regiment (Black Watch), and to be called " The Royal Highland Emigrants," and to rendezvous at Lake Champlain.

The uniforms, however, acquired a delightful touch of Canadian colour from the sporrans having to be made of racoons' instead of badgers' skins. The officers wore the broadsword and dirk, and the men a half-basket hilted sword.

The first battalion was to be raised from the Highland emigrants in North America, as well as from the discharged men of the 42nd, of Fraser's and of Montgomery's Highlanders, who had settled in that country after the peace of 1763. Lieutenant-Colonel Maclean commanded the 1st Battalion ; Major-Commandant John Small, 2nd Battalion, recruited in Nova Scotia. MacDonalds of Glenaladale who had settled in Prince Edward's Island with a large number of clansmen from South Uist, helped greatly in raising this regiment.

The 1st Battalion was stationed in Quebec, when Canada was threatened with invasion by the American General Arnold at the head of 3,000 men. So well did Colonel Maclean fulfil his charge, that General Arnold who had been besieging Quebec during the winter, was foiled at every point by his Highland opponent. On the approach of spring Arnold was driven out of Canada.

Notwithstanding the fine service of the Royal Highland Emigrant Regiment, which greatly contributed towards foiling American designs on Canada, the usual Government policy of broken or neglected promises towards Highland regiments followed. Colonel Maclean, at the outset, had been promised that his regiment should be borne on the establishment, and receive precedence according to the date of its embodiment. However, as these promises were not fulfilled at the end of 1776, Colonel Maclean proceeded to England to plead the cause of his regiment. It was not, however, until the close of 1778 that Government implemented its promises. The regiment was then numbered the 84th, the strength of each battalion increased to 1,000 men, and Sir Henry Clinton was appointed Colonel, the former Commandants of the two battalions being the same.

Though many inducements were held out to the 84th Highlanders by the Americans to desert, not one soldier broke his oath of allegiance.

At the conclusion of the American war both battalions were reduced, and grants of land were given to the officers and men, in the proportion of 5,000 acres to a field-officer, 3,000 to a captain, 500 to a subaltern, 200 to a sergeant, and 100 acres to each soldier. All those who had been settled in America previously to the war remained, and took possession of their lands, but many of the others returned home.

The men of Colonel Maclean's (1st) battalion settled in Canada, those of Colonel Small's (2nd) battalion at Douglas in Nova Scotia.

THE 2ND BATTALION ROYAL HIGHLANDERS, THE BLACK WATCH

FORMERLY THE 73RD OR PERTHSHIRE REGIMENT

Raised in 1780. Facings : Blue.

This regiment may be said to have been originally a MacLeod one. In 1780 the Government resolved to add a second battalion to the 42nd (Black Watch). The raising of this battalion was entrusted to Norman MacLeod, 23rd Chief of Macleod, who had already raised a company, of which he was Captain, for the 71st Regiment.

This second battalion was embodied at Perth on 21st March 1780. Lieutenant-Colonel MacLeod of MacLeod afterwards rose to the rank of lieutenant-general in the army.

In December of the same year, the 2nd Battalion Black Watch embarked for India, where they served until 1786. It was then proposed by the authorities to send home the officers and non-commissioned officers of the battalion, and to draft the privates into other regiments. From this fate the 2nd Battalion was saved by the forcible representations made by its lieutenant-colonel, MacLeod of MacLeod.

Colonel MacLeod wrote to Sir Eyre Coote, Commander-in-Chief of the Forces in India :

> I have to observe to Your Excellency that it is the first time ever that this regiment was drafted, and that we were raised upon the idea of being exempted from that misfortune. My own Company are all of my own name and Clan, and if I return to Europe without them I shall be effectually banished from my own home, after having seduced them into a situation from which they thought themselves spared when they enlisted into the service. They are now much reduced, and being on a brisk and actual service, will be still more so before they can be drafted ; their numbers will not then exceed 30 or 40 men. I must entreat Your Excellency to allow me to carry them home with me, that I may not forfeit my honour, credit, and influence in the Highlands, which have been exerted for His Majesty's service.

MacLeod's exertions had their reward. The battalion was not drafted, but, while at Dinapoor, in Bengal, it was on the 18th of April 1786, formed into a separate corps, with green facings, under the designation of the 73rd Regiment.

The 73rd Regiment remained in India until 1805, when it was ordered home. All men, however, who were fit for duty and who preferred to remain in India were allowed a bounty. So many accepted the offer that few came home. In 1809 the ranks were filled up to 800 men, and a second battalion was raised which, however, was disbanded in 1817.

The Highland garb was taken from the regiment in 1809 and it ceased to be a Highland battalion.

It was not until 1881 that the 73rd got back the Highland dress. They were then formed into a territorial regiment, as the 2nd Battalion Black Watch, and now bear the designation of " The Royal Highlanders, The Black Watch."

Two officers and fifty-four privates of the 73rd Regiment were among the band of heroes who went down in the wreck of the *Birkenhead*, off Danger Point on 26th February 1852.

THE HIGHLAND LIGHT INFANTRY (2ND BATTALION)

FORMERLY THE 74TH HIGHLANDERS

Raised in 1787. Facings : Buff.

In 1787 four new regiments were raised—the 74th, 75th, 76th, and 77th. It was directed that the first two should be raised in the north of Scotland, and should be Highland regiments. The regimental establishment of each was to consist of ten companies of seventy-five men each, with the customary number of commissioned and non-commissioned officers. Major-General Sir Archibald Campbell, from half-pay of Fraser's Highlanders, was appointed Colonel of the 74th Regiment, whose Lieutenant-Colonel was Gordon Forbes. The regiment received the designation of the 74th Highland Regiment of Foot.

The uniform was the full Highland one of kilt, plaid, and feather bonnet, the tartan being the same as that of the Black Watch. Before the regiment had been raised to full strength the demand for reinforcements from India was so urgent that 400 men, about one half of whom were Highlanders, were marched to Grangemouth, and embarked for Chatham and sailed for India. It was not till 1789, when the various detachments were united at the cantonments of Poonamalee, that it composed a corps of 750 men. When in India the use of the kilt was forbidden by the military authorities as unsuited to the climate.

The 74th remained in India until 1805, when they embarked for home, and landed in Portsmouth in 1806. They then resumed the kilt, which had been laid aside in India, and proceeded to Scotland to recruit. The regiment left Scotland for Ireland in 1809, and, in May, the War Office ordered that the Highland dress should be discontinued, and that the uniform of the regiment should be the same as that of English regiments of the line. The designation of Highland, however, was retained until 1816. In 1845 was gazetted :

War Office, 8th November 1845.

Memorandum.—Her Majesty has been graciously pleased to approve of the 74th Foot resuming the appellation of the 74th (Highland) Regiment of Foot, and of its being clothed accordingly, that is, to wear the tartan trews instead of the Oxford mixture ; plaid cap instead of the black chaco ; and the plaid scarf as worn by the 71st Regiment. The alteration of the dress is to take place on the next issue of clothing, on 1st April 1846.

Since then recruiting has been carried on in Scotland, and Lamont tartan was adopted as the regimental sett.

In 1881 the 71st and 74th were linked as a territorial regiment (of which the latter became the 2nd Battalion), designated The Highland Light Infantry. The regimental tartan is now unfortunately no longer Lamont (which might have been retained for the 2nd Battalion) but the MacKenzie—inappropriate—from the 1st Battalion. The, uniform of the Highland Light Infantry has been described in the account of the 1st Battalion (71st Regiment).

The 74th are known as the Assaye Regiment from their distinguished bravery at that battle, where every one of their officers was either killed or wounded. It was one of the three regiments to whom the East India Company gave another, or third colour, to be carried " at reviews, inspections, and on gala days." The other two regiments, so honoured, were the 78th Highlanders and 19th Dragoons.

Lieutenant-Colonel Seton of Mounie, 74th Highlanders, was in command of the troops on board the *Birkenhead* when that ill-fated transport went down in Simon's Bay, 26th February 1852, on which occasion, through the Colonel's influence and example, the troops under his command showed the world such a noble example of military discipline and bravery. Besides their Lieutenant-Colonel the 74th lost one officer, two non-commissioned officers, and forty-six privates.

THE GORDON HIGHLANDERS (1st Battalion)

Formerly the 75th Stirlingshire Regiment

Raised in 1787. Facings : Yellow.

Orders for raising of the 74th and the 75th were issued at the same time. The Colonel of the latter was Robert Abercromby of Tullibody, who received his appointment in the autumn of 1787, and the regiment which he was to command was embodied at Stirling in June 1788.

The 75th was despatched to India soon after. There it remained until 1806, when it was ordered home.

In 1809 its designation was changed from the 75th Highlanders to the 75th Foot and the regiment was deprived of its Highland garb. In 1862 it received the name of the 75th Stirlingshire, in remembrance of its origin. At one time it was linked with the 39th Regiment at Dorchester.

In 1881 the 75th Stirlingshire was linked with the Gordon Highlanders as its first battalion, and then had its uniform altered to the full Highland garb, as worn by the 92nd, or 2nd Battalion.

THE SEAFORTH HIGHLANDERS (2nd Battalion)

Ross-shire Buffs, The Duke of Albany's, formerly the 78th Highlanders

Raised in 1793. Facings : Buff.

In 1787, when orders were given to raise the 74th, 75th, 76th, and 77th Regiments, Francis Humberstone MacKenzie of Seaforth, lineal descendant and representative of the old earls of Seaforth, offered to raise a Highland regiment on his estates in Ross-shire and the Hebrides, the regiment to be commanded by himself. Government declined Seaforth's offer, except in as far as procuring recruits for the 74th and 75th Regiments. In 1790 he made a similar offer, which on the ground that the strength of the British army had been fixed at seventy-seven regiments, was again declined.

When, however, war broke out in 1793 Seaforth's patriotic offer was for the third time proferred, and this time accepted. Letters of service were issued empowering Seaforth, as lieutenant-colonel-commandant, to raise a Highland battalion, to be numbered the 78th.

The first Seaforth MacKenzie Regiment had had its number, previously to this, reduced to the 72nd. The 78th Regiment was to consist of one company of grenadiers, one of light infantry, and eight battalion companies. Seaforth appointed as his major his own brother-in-law, Alexander MacKenzie of Belmaduthy, and afterwards of Inverallochy and Castle Fraser, then a captain in the 73rd Regiment (and who took the additional name of " Fraser " on succeeding to Castle Fraser in right of his mother). Many of the recruits were raised by Belmaduthy, and on the estates of MacKenzie of Suddie. The notice, posted throughout the MacKenzie territory, inviting recruits to enlist, expressly stated : " The Lads of this Regiment will live and die together, as they cannot be draughted into other Regiments, and must be reduced in a body in their own country."

Recruits poured in rapidly, and on 10th July 1793 the 78th was inspected at Fort George and passed by Lieutenant-General Sir Hector Munro. Orders were then issued to augment the regiment to 1,000.

In October of the same year Seaforth offered to raise a second battalion for the 78th, and on 30th October received permission to raise 500 additional men on the original letter of service. This was not, however, what Seaforth wanted, and in December 1793 he submitted three alternative proposals to the Government for raising a second battalion. In February 1794 one of these was agreed to. When the scheme had proceeded so far Seaforth was informed that this battalion was to be considered a separate corps. Thereupon he addressed the following protest to the Secretary of State :

St. Alban Street, 8th February 1794.

SIR,—I had sincerely hoped I should not be obliged to trouble you again, but on my going to-day to the War Office about my letter of service (having yesterday, as I thought, finally agreed with Lord Amherst), I was, to my amazement, told that Lord Amherst had ordered that the 1,000 men I am to raise were not to be a second battalion of the 78th, but a separate corps. It will, I am sure, occur to you that should I undertake such a thing, it would destroy my influence among the people of my country entirely ; and instead of appearing as a loyal honest Chieftain calling out his friends to support their King and country, I should be gibbeted as a jobber of the attachment my neighbours bear to me. Recollecting what passed between you and me, I barely state the circumstance ; and I am, with great respect and attachment, sir, your most obliged and obedient servant,

(Signed) F. H. MACKENZIE.

The order for a separate corps was rescinded and a letter of service issued in favour of Seaforth on 10th February 1794, authorising him as lieutenant-colonel-commandant to add the new battalion to his own regiment. The battalion was raised, inspected, and passed at Fort George in June of the same year by Sir Hector Munro ; and in July following the King gave permission to have it named, as a distinctive title, the " Ross-shire Buffs." In August 1794 the 2nd Battalion embarked at Fort George for England, where they remained until 1795 when six companies took part in the expedition which conquered the Cape of Good Hope.

In June 1796 both battalions were amalgamated. Shortly afterwards the lieutenant-colonel (who had been created Lord Seaforth, Baron MacKenzie of Kintail) resigned.

In December 1804, for the second-time, a second battalion of the 78th was raised, and 850 men, under Lieutenant-Colonel Patrick MacLeod of Geanies, assembled at Fort George, and were inspected in January 1805 by Major-General the Marquis of Huntly. Stewart of Garth says :

This being the fourth battalion embodied in that garrison under the influence of the family of Seaforth in the course of thirty years. . . . This corps and the 2nd Battalion of the 79th, raised the same year, were the last corps recruited in the north under the influence of any particular family, or by officers for commissions.

In 1817 the 1st and 2nd Battalions of the 78th were amalgamated. The regiment remained a single battalion one until 1881, when it and the 72nd Regiment were formed into a territorial regiment, of which the 78th is the 2nd Battalion. Both battalions wear full Highland dress and feather bonnet, their tartan being MacKenzie.

The 78th is one of the three regiments who were presented by the East India Company with a third, or honorary, colour, in acknowledgement of their bravery at Assaye. They also enjoy the unique distinction of being the only Highland regiment which bears a Gaelic motto on the colours and appointments, the MacKenzie one, *Cuidich'n Righ.*

The 78th have been justly termed " The Saviours of India," for they contributed largely to stem and eventually turn the tide of battle during the darkest days of the Indian Mutiny. After the Battle of Cawnpore General Havelock addressed their officers thus :

Gentlemen, I am glad of this opportunity of saying a few words to you, which you may repeat to your men. I am now upwards of sixty years old ; I have been forty years in the service ; I have been engaged in action almost seven-and-twenty times ; but in the whole of my career I have never seen any regiment behave better—nay, more, I have never seen any regiment behave so well—as the 78th Highlanders this day. I am proud of you, and if ever I have the good luck to be made a major-general, the first thing I shall do will be to go to the Duke of Cambridge and request that when my turn arrives for a colonelcy of a regiment I may have the 78th Highlanders. And this, gentlemen, you hear from a man who is not in the habit of saying more than he means. I am not a Highlander, but I wish I was one.

The regiment is now (1960) being amalgamated with the Cameron Highlanders as " The Queen's Own Highlanders " whereby two more " clan " regiments virtually vanish.

THE QUEEN'S OWN CAMERON HIGHLANDERS
(1ST AND 2ND BATTALIONS)
79TH CAMERON HIGHLANDERS
Raised in 1793. Facings : Blue.

This distinguished regiment was raised by Lieutenant-General Alan Cameron of Erracht, K.C.B. When a youth, Alan had a dispute with a fellow-clansman, which led to a duel in which the young chieftain slew his opponent. Dreading the vengeance of his late enemy's family, Alan fled to Mull. Thence he removed to Greenock, where he became clerk in the Customs. Finding such employment uncongenial, Alan sailed for America, where he joined the 84th Royal Highland Emigrant Regiment. Erracht was taken prisoner during the war and confined for two years in Philadelphia. After his release he was placed on half-pay, with the rank of lieutenant in Tarleton's Dragoons, and shortly after returned to Lochaber.

Erracht was of an active disposition, and in 1793 conceived the idea of raising a regiment of Highlanders in Lochaber. Letters of service were granted, 17th August 1793, to raise a Highland regiment, and Alan Cameron of Erracht was appointed lieutenant-colonel-commandant. To regiments embodied in this manner the Government generally allowed a bounty, higher or lower, according to time and circumstances. But in this instance no bounty was given, and the men were recruited at the sole expense of Erracht and his officers. Erracht was greatly aided in his recruiting by Ranald MacDonell of Keppoch, who, although he did not join the regiment himself, induced two or three hundred of his clansmen to join. The 79th and the 78th Regiments, both raised in the same year, were the last raised by family influence in the Highlands, or recruited by officers, as a condition of their being given their commissions.

The 79th was from 1793 to 1804 designated the Cameronian Volunteers, and from 1805–1806 the Cameronian Highlanders. This designation was changed in 1807 for " The Cameron Highlanders." The following is an extract from the original recruiting poster. The italics are our own.

All aspiring young men who wish to be serviceable to their King and Country by enlisting into the 79th Regiment, or Cameron Volunteers, will be commanded by the Major (Alan Cameron of Erracht) in person, *who has obtained from his Majesty that they shall not be draughted into any other Regiment ; and when the Reduction is to take place, they shall be marched in to their own Country in a Corps, to be therein disembodied.*

The original facings of the 79th were green.

The regiment was inspected at Stirling in January 1794, and its strength was raised to 1,000 men. Erracht was so determined to have his regiment not merely nominally but really a Highland corps, that he enlisted none but Gaelic speakers, so that the 79th was long familiarly known as the *Cia mar thàs!* The uniform, needless to say, was full Highland dress with feather bonnet. An account of the regimental tartan will be found in Chap. XVI. Sir Henry Campbell-Bannerman, a Scots politician bearing a Highland name, went out of his way in the House of Commons some years ago to describe the sett as a " spurious tartan of the MacDonald Clan " !

After a short time in Ireland and England the 79th embarked for Flanders in August 1794. During the campaign the 79th lost heavily from fever and privation. It returned to England in 1795, when the strength was ordered to be completed to 1,000 men, preparatory to its despatch to India. While its commander, with characteristic energy, was making every effort to fulfil the order he received intimation from the Horse Guards that directions had been given to draft the Cameron Highlanders into four other regiments. This flagrant violation of the conditions on which the regiment had been recruited roused Erracht's wrath. The colonel sought and obtained an interview with the Commander-in-Chief, the Duke of York, when Erracht plainly told the Duke : " To draft the 79th is more than you or your Royal father dare do." The Duke replied : " The King, my father, will certainly send the regiment to the West Indies." Erracht, thereupon losing his temper, warmly rejoined : " You may tell the King, your father, from me, that he may send us to h——l if he likes, and I'll go at the head of them, but he daurna draft us ! " The argument used by the gallant colonel had the desired effect, and the identity of the Cameron Highlanders was preserved.

The 79th were ordered to the West Indies, where they remained until 1797, but suffered so much from the climate that an offer was made to such of the men as were fit for duty to volunteer into other corps. Some 200 entered the Black Watch, while about a dozen joined other regiments. The officers, with the remainder of the regiment, returned to Chatham. Orders were given to fill up the ranks, and by Erracht's exertions a fresh body of 780 men was raised, who assembled at Stirling in June 1798.

In 1804 a second battalion was raised, which was inspected and passed at Stirling on 3rd April 1805. This battalion was never employed on active service, and merely served annually to supply the vacancies caused by casualties in the 1st Battalion. This second battalion was reduced at Dundee on 25th December 1815.

In 1804 the Horse Guards had under consideration the question of abolishing the kilt in all the Highland regiments and substituting for it tartan pantaloons (erroneously denominated trews). In a letter, dated " Horse Guards, 13th October 1804," Colonel Cameron was requested to state his " private opinion as to the expediency of abolishing the kilt in Highland regiments, and substituting in lieu thereof the tartan trews." The colonel's characteristic reply is too long to reproduce *in extenso* here. A few extracts from the letter demonstrate the decided opinion on the subject from so authoritative a source :

The proposed alteration must have proceeded from a whimsical idea more than the mere comfort of the Highland soldier, and a wish to lay aside that national martial garb. . . . From my own experience I feel well founded in saying that if anything was wanted to aid the rack-renting Highland landlords in destroying that source, which hitherto proved so ruitful for keeping up Highland corps, it will be that of abolishing their native garb, which his Royal Highness, the Commander-in-Chief, and the Adjutant-General may rest assured will prove a complete death-warrant to the recruiting service in that respect. But I sincerely hope that his Royal Highness will never acquiesce in so painful and degrading an idea (come from whatever quarter it may) as to strip us of our native garb (admitted hitherto our regimental uniform) and stuff us into a harlequin ·artan pantaloon !

Here, again, Erracht's insistence gained the day, and a few kilted regiments were left to the Scottish nation.

On 10th July 1873 an order was issued that " the 79th Regiment be in future styled The Queen's Own Cameron Highlanders, that the facings be accordingly changed from green to blue, etc." Whilst the change, on Her Majesty's part, was most graciously meant, its instigation may well have been quite otherwise, and the conversion of a " Clan Regiment " into a " Royal Regiment " is historically incongruous, though no doubt precisely what would appeal to Whitehall co-ordinators seeking to eliminate Scots' regimental traditions. In completion of this conversion, the 150th anniversary of the raising of the regiment was commemorated by the Camerons obtaining permission to have their pipers' kilts of the Royal tartan. If a *red* tartan was desired for the kilts of the pipers, it would have been appropriate to request the use of Cameron of Lochiel tartan.

The " Royal regiments " (with blue facings) are those representing the " standing army " of the Crown. The " non-Royal regiments " represent the tribal regiments of the provincial chiefs—and embody the *clan-spirit*, and that of local pride which central authorities are always seeking to break. The history of the " Royal regiments " is such as to inspire every pride ; but so is that of the clan and district regiments. To convert the latter into the former is incompatible with the whole tradition of Highland regiments, other than the 42nd.

At the territorial reorganisation of the army in 1881 the Camerons were the only Highland regiment with one battalion. In 1897 a second battalion was added to the regiment.

In 1960 the Seaforths and Camerons were amalgamated under the name, " The Queen's Own Highlanders, (Seaforth and Cameron) " and have been granted two-coloured facings (blue and buff). Both Mackenzie and Cameron tartans are adjusted for use in the regiment. Owing to Erracht's arms having been deleted from Lyon Register, the only " Cameron " element which survived in the regimental emblem was a spray of Cameron oakleaves around the circlet.

97TH OR STRATHSPEY REGIMENT

Raised in 1794. Disbanded in 1795.

Sir James Grant of Grant, who had already raised the Grant Fencibles, was, in 1794, authorised to raise a Highland regiment of the line, to be of a strength of 1,000 men. It was embodied at Elgin, where it was inspected by Major-General Sir Hector Munro, and afterwards ordered to the south of England.

It served for a few months as marines on board Lord Howe's fleet in the Channel. In the autumn of 1795, in pursuance of the policy of inveigling Highlanders into the army by appeals to clan patriotism and then making service dispositions to break these ancient sentiments (so hated by the exponents of centralised rule) the men and officers were drafted into different regiments, and the two flank companies were transferred to the 42nd (Black Watch) Regiment when that regiment was preparing to embark for the West Indies.

PRINCESS LOUISE'S ARGYLL AND SUTHERLAND HIGHLANDERS (1ST BATTALION)

98TH ARGYLLSHIRE HIGHLANDERS, afterwards 91ST ARGYLLSHIRE HIGHLANDERS, later PRINCESS LOUISE'S ARGYLLSHIRE HIGHLANDERS

Raised in 1794. Facings : Yellow.

In 1794 King George III. expressed a desire to John, 5th Duke of Argyll (a General in the army and Colonel of the Scots Guards) to raise an Argyllshire regiment, and, accordingly, a letter of service, 10th February 1794, was granted, authorising the Duke to raise such a regiment. The regiment was to be complete within three months, and to consist of one grenadier, one light infantry, and eight battalion companies ; the establishment 1,102 officers, non-commissioned officers and men, exclusive of field-officers. Recruits were to be engaged for unlimited service, and " levy money " was granted for 1,064 men, at the rate of five guineas per man.

Duncan Campbell of Lochnell, from the 1st Foot Guards, was appointed Lieutenant-Colonel-Commandant of the new regiment, which was inspected at Stirling on 26th May 1794 by General Lord Adam Gordon, the strength of the battalion being then 738 of all ranks. The following June the regiment was despatched to Netley, and on 9th July the King approved the list of officers, and the regiment was numbered the 98th. Six regiments of the British army have borne the number " 98," the Argyllshire being the third (some say the fourth) to bear it.   At the first inspection, seventeen of its thirty-two officers were Campbells.

Its uniform was the full Highland dress, the tartan being the Argyll-Campbell sett.

On 5th May 1795 the Argyllshire Highlanders embarked at Spithead, as part of the expedition for South Africa to take possession of the Cape.   In October 1798, while the regiment was at Cape Town, its number was changed to the 91st.   When first raised, and in the Cape war, 1795–1796, the regiment had no pipe band, but only drummers and fifers.   In 1802 the regiment returned home.

In August 1804 a second battalion was formed of men from Perth, Argyll, and Bute, and reduced at Perth, 25th December 1815.

In 1809 the War Office ordered that the 91st, along with the 72nd, 73rd, 74th, 75th, and 94th Regiments, should cease to be Highland ones.   This, of course, was breaking faith with the men who had enlisted in these as *Highland Regiments*.   The Highland dress as well as the territorial designation of Argyllshire was taken away from the 91st at that time.   On the eve of the 91st embarking for the disastrous Walcheren expedition in 1809, the tartan for the kilts and plaids reached the regiment, but an order came to make it up into trews. Along with the trews a low flat bonnet with a feather on one side was ordered to be worn.   About a year after, in 1810, even the tartan trews were taken from the 91st, a kind of grey trousers being ordered to be worn instead.   The feather bonnet was taken away at the same time, and the black cap then worn by the ordinary line regiments was substituted.   The pipe bands were then supported by the officers and these stood loyally by their men in maintaining at least that survival of the " Argyllshires " traditions, and we hear of the 91st pipers at the Battle of Toulouse (1814) in Highland garb.   The pipers, however, appear, like the rest, to have had to " thole " the grey trousers.

In 1821 the 91st had its territorial title restored to it, but not the Highland garb, but in 1850, notwithstanding the distinguished services rendered by the 91st ever since its embodiment, the War Office, with customary policy, deprived the unfortunate corps of their pipers.

The retention of the territorial title, however, eventually led to the resuscitation of the 91st as a Highland Regiment.   The first stage was secured when a War Office memo., 3rd May 1864, stated :

Her Majesty has been graciously pleased to approve of the 91st Foot resuming the appellation of the 91st Argyllshire Highlanders, and being clothed and equipped as a non-kilted Highland corps, as follows : Tunic, as worn in all Highland regiments ; trews, of the Campbell tartan ; chaco, blue cloth, with diced band and black braid ; forage cap, Kilmarnock, with diced band.   The officers to wear plaids and claymores.   The alteration of the dress is to take place from 1st April 1865.   The white waistcoat with sleeves, issued to other Highland regiments, will not be worn by the 91st Foot.

The " Campbell tartan," endorsed by the Duke as correct, was the " government sett " with a *red* line.

In 1870 the 91st went to Aldershot, and on 21st March 1871 the regiment furnished a guard of honour on the occasion of the marriage of Her Royal Highness the Princess Louise to the Marquis of Lorne. Shortly after the wedding Her Majesty the Queen commanded that the 91st should always march past in quick time to their pipers. As a further mark of her favour, the Queen commended that the regiment should be designated Princess Louise's Argyllshire Highlanders, and should bear on its colours the crest and motto of the Argyll family —the boar's head, with *Ne obliviscaris*—and with the Princess Louise's coronet and cypher on the three corners of the regimental colour. Prior to conferring the above distinction, Her Majesty desired Lieutenant-Colonel Sprot, commanding the regiment, to report what the regiment would like. Colonel Sprot, after consulting with his oldest officer, suggested the kilt being restored to the 91st. To this Her Majesty readily agreed ; *but the idea was objected to by the military authorities !* The placing of *MacCailein's* crest on the colours had the true clan touch and showed how much Queen Victoria herself grasped the beauty of Scottish clan and military traditions.

In 1881 the 91st and the 93rd Regiments were linked, as a territorial one (the 91st forming the 1st Battalion), under the designation of the Princess Louise's Argyll and Sutherland Highlanders.

The regiment now wears the kilt and the full Highland dress, the tartan being of the sett known as the Sutherland regimental one (a tartan resembling that of the Black Watch, but of a lighter hue).

THE GORDON HIGHLANDERS (2ND BATTALION)

FORMERLY THE 100TH REGIMENT, LATER 92ND REGIMENT

Raised in 1794. Facings : Yellow.

In 1794 the Government accepted an offer made by the Marquis of Huntly, eldest son of the 4th Duke of Gordon (the Marquis being then a captain in the 3rd Foot Guards), to raise a Highland regiment on the Gordon estates. A letter of service was, therefore, granted to the Duke of Gordon, 10th February 1794, authorising him to raise such a regiment, and the commission of Lieutenant-Colonel-Commandant was conferred on his son the Marquis of Huntly. The Duke, Jane (Duchess of Gordon), and the Marquis of Huntly all recruited for the new regiment personally. It is widely told how irresistible the arguments of the lovely Duchess, accompanied by six pipers, proved—namely, a guinea bounty, accompanied by a kiss from her, and she is represented in the well-known picture, riding around on a grey horse in the tunic and head-dress of the regiment. Recruiting proceeded so expeditiously under these circumstances that, within four months, the required number of men was raised ; and on 24th June 1794 the regiment was inspected by Major-General Sir Hector Munro, and embodied under the name of the Gordon Highlanders.

Of the recruits, about three-fourths were from the Highland estates of the Duke of Gordon, while the remaining fourth were drawn from Aberdeenshire, Banff, and Moray.

The Gordon Highlanders embarked for England at Fort George on 9th July 1794, and joined the camp on Netley Common, where the corps was, the following month, put on the establishment as the " 100th Regiment."

The Gordon Highlanders were serving in Ireland in 1799, and thence left for England to join an expedition then being fitted out for Holland. About this time the regimental number was changed to " 92nd," the former regiment of that number having been reduced. The uniform at that time, as now, was the full Highland garb with feather bonnet, and kilt and plaid of Gordon tartan. The yellow facings represent the Gordon livery facings, whilst the crest and motto, *Bydand*, are those of the Gordon Chief.

A second battalion of the 92nd was formed in November 1803, and consisting of 1,000 men, was raised in the counties of Nairn, Inverness, Moray, Banff, and Aberdeen. This battalion served as a feeder to the first battalion during the war. It was disbanded at Edinburgh on 24th October 1814.

The 92nd served with most distinguished gallantry during the Waterloo campaign when it lost its distinguished Colonel, John Cameron, younger, of Fassifern. As a tribute of respect to the memory of this brave soldier, as well as in recognition of his eminent services, the king granted a baronetcy, which has expired, to Ewen Cameron of Fassifern, the Colonel's father. The armorial bearings granted to Fassifern, at the same time, included as supporters, two soldiers of the Gordon Highlanders, which descend to his representatives to-day.

This was the second occasion that the Gordons were singled out to become a permanent heraldic memorial of the services of a brave soldier. The first occasion was during the Peninsular War, when, upon Sir John Moore becoming a knight, and, as such, entitled to supporters to his coat of arms, he chose, as one of the supporters, a soldier of the Gordon Highlanders. On yet a third occasion the Gordons have been favoured in the same way. When Field-Marshal Lord Roberts was granted his peerage he chose, as the right supporter of his coat of arms, a Highland soldier, as a recognition of the help given to him in winning that peerage, during the Afghan war of 1879, by the Highland Brigade, of which the Gordons formed one of the regiments. As the gallant Field-Marshal was, by nationality, not Scots, but Irish, the honour done by him to the Highland regiments is all the greater.

Among the many exploits of the 92nd during the Waterloo campaign was the historical one when the Gordons and the Scots Greys, charging together (the Gordons clinging on to the stirrups of the Greys), scattered a force of French ten times their number, shouting, as they did this, the well-known cry of " Scotland for Ever ! "

In 1881, when the British army was reorganised on a territorial basis, the 92nd Regiment was linked with the 75th Stirlingshire Regiment as a territorial regiment of two battalions as " The Gordon Highlanders," of which the 92nd form the second battalion.

116TH (PERTHSHIRE) REGIMENT

Raised in 1794. Disbanded in 1794.

In 1794 a regiment, under the designation of the Perthshire Highlanders, was raised by Major-General Alexander Campbell of Monzie.

After being a short time stationed in Ireland, the men were drafted to other regiments. Some of the officers accompanied the soldiers, while others remained on full pay, and unattached, till provided for in other regiments.

132ND HIGHLAND REGIMENT

Raised in 1794. Disbanded in 1794.

This regiment was raised in 1794 by Colonel Duncan Cameron of Callart. It was soon, however, reduced, and the men and officers transferred to other regiments.

133RD HIGHLAND REGIMENT

Raised in 1794. Disbanded in 1794.

The 133rd Regiment was raised by Colonel Simon Fraser (afterwards Lieutenant-General). This regiment, however, was soon broken up in the same manner as the 132nd had been, and its men and officers transferred to other regiments.

PRINCESS LOUISE'S ARGYLL AND SUTHERLAND HIGHLANDERS (2ND BATTALION)

FORMERLY 93RD SUTHERLAND HIGHLANDERS

Raised in 1800. Facings : Yellow.

Keltie, in his *History of the Highland Regiments*, remarks of the 93rd as " Perhaps the most Highland of the Highland Regiments."

It was raised on a letter of service, granted in May 1800, to General Wemyss of Wemyss (who had been Commander of the 2nd and 3rd Regiments of Sutherland Fencibles), and was at first known as General

Wemyss's Regiment of Infantry, because no number had been assigned to it.

On the regiment's formation, in 1800, its strength was 596 men and 34 sergeants. Of the soldiers, 460 were Sutherland men ; the remainder were principally from Ross-shire and the neighbouring counties. The strength was later augmented to 1,000, with officers in proportion. In 1811 it numbered 1,049 rank and file, of whom 1,014 were Scots, 18 English, and 17 Irish.

A striking peculiarity in the raising of this regiment was that the original levy was made by a species of conscription, and not by the ordinary mode of recruiting. A census having been taken of the population on the estates of the Countess of Sutherland, her agents requested that a certain proportion of the able-bodied sons of the tenants should join the ranks, as a test of their duty to the Countess and of their loyalty to their Sovereign. The appeal was well responded to, and in a few months the ranks of the regiment were filled up. Naturally, some of the parents grumbled at being deprived of their children. However, the young men themselves never seem to have questioned this claim over their military services. The levy was made up, to a considerable extent, of men who had served in the 3rd Sutherland Fencibles, which had been disbanded about two years previously. Many of the men, as well as the non-commissioned officers, were sons of highly respectable farmers. The officers were mostly well-known gentlemen connected with Sutherlandshire and the adjacent counties.

The recruits, after having enrolled their names on enlistment, were permitted to pursue their callings at home, until it was announced in the various parish churches that their presence was required, when a body of 600 men was assembled, and marched to Inverness in August 1800 for inspection by Major-General Leith Hay, without there being a single absentee. The high character of the class of recruits enlisted is evidenced from that being possible when they were never previously collected together until the final inspection of the corps.

In September 1800 the regiment was numbered the 93rd, and embarked at Fort George for Guernsey, where it remained until September 1802. The 93rd was then ordered home to Scotland to be reduced. However, in consequence of the renewal of the war with France, this order was countermanded, and the regiment was despatched to Aberdeen. In February 1803 it was stationed in Ireland, and in August 1805 embarked at Cork for the Cape of Good Hope. The first lieutenant-colonel of the 93rd was Alexander Halkett, who retained command of the regiment until May 1810.

The uniform of the 93rd was the full Highland garb, with feather bonnet ; the kilt and plaid being of Sutherland tartan. Logan describes this as " the Sutherland tartan, which appears only different from the plain sett of the 42nd in having the green and blue lighter, the former being shown in the kilt and plaid."

The 93rd is one of our few Highland regiments which has since the time of its embodiment worn the kilt up to the present date. About 1845 the regimental pipers were clad in kilt, plaid, and hose of Rob Roy tartan.

In 1813 a second battalion was formed at Inverness, and was originally destined to join the British army in France under the Duke of Wellington. In consequence, however, of the peace of 1814, the destination was changed for Newfoundland, where it remained for sixteen months when it returned to England and was disbanded at Sunderland, 24th December 1815.

During the Crimean War the 93rd made history. Able pens have told the story of " the thin red line," and how, at Balaclava, the 93rd, in line, defeated a Russian cavalry charge. The incident is commemorated in the well-known but technically not altogether accurate painting by Gibb, entitled " The Thin Red Line." The 93rd is the only British infantry regiment entitled to bear the word " Balaclava " on its colours.

In 1881, when the territorial system was introduced into the British army, the 91st and the 93rd Regiments were formed into a territorial regiment, under the designation of Princess Louise's Argyll and Sutherland Highlanders, of which the 93rd became the 2nd Battalion.

The Highland regiments of which an account has been given total thirty-two since the Black Watch was embodied.

SCOTTISH BRIGADES (1958)

In a 1958 reorganisation of the Regular Army the historic Scottish Regiments, Highland and Lowland, have been almost eliminated by being grouped in a Highland and a Lowland Brigade with new cap badges at variance with Scottish regimental tradition, which have superseded the old Scottish clan regimental crests though these still fortunately survive in the territorial battalions. These are insignia rights guaranteed by the Treaty of Union from the Scottish units of the British Army. It seems possible, however, that the old regimental badges may yet survive on the collar-badges of the officers' uniforms.

THE LOVAT SCOUTS AND THE SCOTTISH HORSE

The Boer War led to the raising of two mounted regiments which have since become famous in the Highlands : " The Lovat Scouts," raised in 1900 by Simon Fraser, 14th Lord Lovat ; and " The Scottish Horse," raised in February 1901, on the suggestion of the Caledonian Society of South Africa, by the Marquess of Tullibardine. After the war this unit, popularly known in Scotland as " Tullibardine's Horse," was constituted a yeomanry regiment for the north-east Highlands, and it is a pity the latter title—so characteristically Scottish—was not chosen, since " Scottish Horse "—in Scotland—lacked the individual association so beloved, and there were equally " Scottish " Lowland yeomanry regiments. Both regiments have pipe bands.

The Scottish Horse are now an armoured unit ; the Scouts are partly light anti-aircraft, partly mountain artillery, and wear Lord Lovat's crest Highland-wise in strap and buckle as badge.

FENCIBLE REGIMENTS

That is, regiments for internal defence of the Kingdom (1759–1799).

(1) Argyll Fencibles. Raised in 1759 ; reduced in 1763.

(2) Sutherland Fencibles. Raised in 1759 ; reduced in 1763.

(3) Argyll, or Western Fencibles. Raised in 1778 ; reduced in 1783.

(4) Gordon Fencibles. Raised in 1778 ; reduced in 1783.

(5) Sutherland Fencibles. Raised in 1778 ; reduced in 1783.

(6) Grant, or Strathspey Fencibles. Raised in 1793 ; reduced in 1799.

(7) Breadalbane Fencibles (three battalions). Raised in 1793 to 1794. First and 2nd Battalions were discharged in 1799, while the 3rd Battalion was not reduced until 1802.

(8) Sutherland Fencibles. Raised in 1793 ; reduced in 1797.

(9) Gordon Fencibles. Raised in 1793 ; reduced in 1799.

(10) Argyll Fencibles. Raised in 1793 ; reduced in 1799.

(11) Rothesay and Caithness Fencibles (two battalions). Raised in 1794 to 1795. First Battalion reduced in 1799 and 2nd Battalion in 1802.

(12) Dumbarton Fencibles. Raised in 1794 ; reduced in 1802.

(13) Reay Fencibles. Raised in 1794 ; reduced in 1802.

(14) Inverness-shire Fencibles. Raised in 1794 ; reduced in 1802.

(15) Fraser Fencibles. Raised in 1794 ; reduced in 1802.

(16) Glengarry Fencibles. Raised in 1794 ; reduced in 1802.

(17) Caithness Legion. Raised in 1794 ; reduced in 1802.

(18) Perthshire Fencibles. Raised in 1794 ; reduced shortly after.

(19) Argyll Fencibles. Raised in 1794 ; reduced in 1802.

(20) Lochaber Fencibles. Raised in 1799 ; reduced in 1802.

(21) Clan Alpine Fencibles. Raised in 1799 ; reduced in 1802.

(22) Ross-shire Fencibles. Raised in 1796 ; reduced shortly after.

(23) Regiment of the Isles, or MacDonald Fencibles. Raised in 1799 ; reduced in 1802.

(24) The Argyll Fencibles. Raised in 1799. The service of this regiment extended to any part of Europe. It was, therefore, in 1800, sent to Gibraltar, where it remained until the Peace of Amiens, when it was ordered home, and reduced shortly afterwards.

(25) Ross and Cromarty Rangers. Raised 1799 ; reduced 1802.

(26) MacLeod Fencibles. Raised in 1799 ; reduced in 1802. This was the last Fencible regiment raised in the Highlands.

Though space forbids more than passing notice of the Fencibles, the history of one of these is interwoven with what has proved to be the fortunes of the British Empire.

GLENGARRY FENCIBLES

To the descendants of the members of this corps Canada owes the flourishing settlement of Glengarry in Canada, an *imperium in imperio*, whose inhabitants are even more Gaelic than their fellow Gaels in the Highlands of Scotland.

In 1792 an emigrant ship from the Highlands to America was wrecked, and her passengers landed almost destitute at Greenock. The greater portion were Catholics, and, in Glasgow, they found a friend in Alexander MacDonell, a priest, afterwards Bishop of Kingston, in Canada, by whom situations were found for the poor emigrants in the factories of Glasgow.

In 1794, however, war broke out with France, and export of manufactures to the Continent ceased.

Father MacDonell, along with young MacDonell, Chief of Glengarry, conceived the plan of getting these Highlanders embodied as a Catholic Regiment. The young chief, along with John Fletcher of Dunans, proceeded to London and were graciously received by His Majesty.

Letters of service were issued in August 1794 to Alexander MacDonell of Glengarry to raise the Glengarry Fencible Regiment as a Catholic corps, of which he was appointed Lieutenant-Colonel and Father MacDonell, Chaplain. It was soon after stationed at Guernsey, returned to Scotland in 1802, and was, like other Fencible regiments, reduced.

The Glengarry Highlanders (more than one half from the estate of Glengarry) found themselves as destitute as ever. The brave chaplain proceeded to London in hope of obtaining assistance for his flock to emigrate to Canada. Despite the opposition of not a few Highland chiefs (who feared that this emigration of the Glengarry people might induce their own clansfolk also to leave their native soil), Father MacDonell obtained an order granting 200 acres to each of the Highlanders who should arrive in the province.

The greater part of the Glengarry Fencibles, therefore, under the banner of their chief in person and with their wives and families, emigrated to Upper Canada, and settled in a district to which they gave the name of their native glen. Each head of a family also named his clearing after the farm which he had occupied in Glengarry.

For how Glengarry, in Canada, is populated, and how the Clan Donald name predominates there, see Appendix XV.

When the war of 1812–1814 with the United States broke out, the Glengarry colonists flew to arms and formed a militia regiment, which won laurels in the campaign.

The last occasion on which the fiery cross was sent round among

Highlanders was in the winter of 1812–1813, when the Chief of Glengarry summoned his soldiers to repel an American raid. So proficient in wood-fighting did the Glengarry men become that when, at the end of the Peninsular War, a number of Wellington's soldiers were despatched to Quebec to fight the Americans, the Glengarry men were ordered to teach those veterans how to skirmish in the backwoods of Canada.

Be it remembered that it was Glengarry who carried clanship to Canada.

THE HIGHLAND CADET BATTALION OF MONTREAL

This corps is the only British cadet corps which is a separate organisation, and not attached to any other regiment.

It is entirely self-supporting, as it gets no assistance from the Government except loan of rifles. The corps has four companies of 50 men each when up to strength. It has 6 pipers and a chromatic bugle band of 12 buglers and 4 drummers. The staff consists of a major commanding, 4 captains, 8 lieutenants, adjutant, quartermaster, sergeant-major, orderly-room-sergeant, pipe-major, and drum-major.

The uniform is a silver-grey doublet, blue facings, Glengarry bonnet with a black and white diced border, and a black cock tail feather as plume. The kilt is of MacKenzie tartan, that of the pipers is Fraser. White spats are worn over tartan hose, garter knots red. Black belts are worn. The sporrans of the privates are grey wolf, these of the officers and sergeants of white goat's hair. The piper's doublet is green ; bonnet, Kilmarnock, with a feather.

The kilted lads of Montreal in 1899 carried the Union Jack where it had never been carried until then by a British force since the days of the American Revolution. The occasion for this was on the visit to Boston of the Montreal Highland Cadets, on the invitation of the " Order of Scottish Clans of Massachusetts." The cadets marched through the streets of Boston carrying the Union Jack, and were greeted with immense enthusiasm.

Some years ago H.R.H. the Duke of Connaught presented Montreal with a flag to be competed for annually by the Cadet corps of that city. For many years the Highland corps held the flag against all comers.

Note.—A new list of Overseas Scottish Regiments and Corps, with details of uniforms and tartans, is in process of compilation. It is hoped to include this list in the next edition of this book.

PART V

Clan Insignia and Heraldry

XV

Armorial Bearings in the Clan System

THE noble and ancient science of Heraldry has always had a most intimate connection with clanship and the Highlands, for it is more or less agreed amongst experts that armory originated in the banner, and was reproduced upon the shield,[1] and not only do Celtic records and poetry teem with allusions to the gaily emblazoned banners of olden chieftains, but *An Brataich*, the hereditary standard-bearer, was one of the most important officers of the chief's household. In Scotland, moreover, with its division into great tribal communities, all essentially "noble," armorial bearings have proved indispensable "in authenticating genealogies and distinguishing the various branches of a widely extended clan," and unaided by heraldry,[2] "in the absence of an estate to serve as a designation, who, for example could ever comprehend the endless ramifications" of our widespread families ?

Great Seal of King David II., showing armorial shield, tabard (surcoat), and horse-trappings (ordinary lairds carried their own banners, but the King's banner—also showing the tressured lion rampant—is carried by the Chief of the Scrymgeours). This illustration shows just how arms were used. (No crest is depicted— they were often omitted in battle.)

Highland dress is also the only garb in which armorial bearings continue to be habitually worn in everyday life ; the tartan being still almost invariably worn with the crested-badge-brooch, which marks a man or woman out either as chief or chieftainess, or as clansman or clanswoman, of some historic race or branch ; so that amongst the Scots there must be a far greater relative use of armorial bearings than in any other people.

In full dress, the Highlander is covered with heraldry, from cap-badge and eagle-plumes, to kilt-pin ; the doublet, brooches, buttons, shoulder-belt, claymore, dirk, pistols, and sporran, all display the heraldic charges appropriate to the wearer's rank and position in the

---

[1] Innes of Learney, *Scots Heraldry*, p. 14.
[2] Seton, *Law and Practice of Heraldry in Scotland*, p. 9.

clan ; whilst the bagpipes and pipe-banner also reflect the glory of
the branch to whose chieftain they pertain ; and just as heraldry continues to be more a part of everyday dress in Scotland than it does
elsewhere, so our ancient laws of arms continue to preserve the practical and scientific aspects of the palmiest days of medieval armory ;
and the Court of the Lord Lyon, with its *Public Register of All Arms
and Bearings*, under control of the only Great Officer of State who can
be traced back to the days of our Celtic kings and the tribal form of
society,[1] continues to administer the genealogical jurisdiction of the
High Sennachie, and therewith, " as belonging to his sphere of duty," [2]
the administration of what has been proudly termed " the purest
heraldry in Europe."

The science of Armory, or Heraldry, as a system of identification,
was evolved in the twelfth century. Leaders adopted simple and
outstanding devices which they painted on their shields and banners,
so that their followers might recognise them in war, and the same
device was repeated on the shirt worn over the armour, hence the
term " coat of arms." In Scotland the *leine croich*, or saffron shirt of
war, was in some cases evidently the basis upon which heraldic objects
were depicted, but in other cases a small shield was embroidered on the
back and breast of the yellow *leine croich*. Armorial bearings, when
invented, were a personal mark of identification, but necessarily
became hereditary in the second generation (end of twelfth century),
when the son who succeeded to estate or chiefship naturally continued
the banner, shield, and surcoat which his father's followers had learnt
to recognise ; since a coat of arms could distinguish only one individual,
younger brothers were obliged to bear marks of cadency to distinguish
them from the head of the house (p. 412). In peace the banner above
a house, or arms carved upon it, indicated the owner, and a wax
seal displaying a representation of the owner's shield was attached to
charters, and served as a signature, which could be recognised by
those who could not read.

The shield, helmet, and crest were in use to be hung over the great
fireplace of the chief chymmes—the hearth of the race—beside which
sat the chief's chair, with the arms carven on its back. The " arms "
and other furniture of the " Hall " passed as " heirship moveables "
to each successive *Ceann-tighe*. Later on, a carved heraldic " achievement " representing the olden accoutrements, became the permanent
ornament above the chief's fireplace.

Arms, from their nature and the position of those who first used
them, became marks of nobility, and as grants of nobility included a
grant of arms, a grant of arms became legally a patent of nobility and
proof of inheritance of arms a proof of nobility. A grant, or confirmation of arms to the Representer of a clan or family makes it an
" honourable community," a *communitas* of the realm of Scotland,

---

[1] J. Cameron, *Celtic Law*, p. 197.
[2] Lord Lyon Sir A. Erskine, 1698, *Juridical Review*, September 1940 p. 194.

and the " destination " expressed or implied, of these original arms becomes (subject to variation by re-settlement, *i.e.* tanistry) the line of descent of the chiefship or chieftaincy. All bearing the name and within the limitations, *i.e.* connected with the " stem," form the *daoine-uasail*, viz., the hereditary gentlemen of the clan.

A coat of arms consists of (1) The shield, displaying the arms. This is the most important item, and sometimes the only part existing. (2) The helmet, which varies in shape with the wearer's rank. (3) The mantling, a cap which kept the sun off the helmet. (4) The wreath or torse, covering the joint between helmet and crest, and often depicted as a " wreath bar." (5) The crest, which, until the seventeenth century, was granted only to important personages, but since the seventeenth century to all above the rank of esquire, including ladies who have succeeded to the representation of their house. A crest cannot exist except as subsidiary to a coat of arms. (6) Supporters (sometimes a compartment), an honour only granted to peers, chiefs of clans, and ancient families, feudal barons older than 1592, and Knights Grand Cross. (7) The motto. (8) In the case of chiefs a slogan—to be shouted by their followers. (9) A badge and standard— or rallying flag as distinct from the " personal " flag—*i.e.* the armorial banner.[1] (10) A *chapeau*, or cap-of-dignity, is sometimes substituted for the wreath below the crest. This is the index of a feudal baron, the old *capitani tribuum*. It represents the patriarchal " cap " of family jurisdiction. It is furred with ermine for *Barones Regni Scotiæ*, and furred *contre-ermine* in the case of Barons " of Argyll and the Isles." In order to secure easy recognition, the devices on the shield are simple and conventional, and there are five colours and two metals, which, if they have to be depicted in black-and-white drawing, are distinguished as follows :

Silver	Gold	Red	Blue	Green	Purple	Black	Ermine
Argent	Or	Gules	Azure	Vert	Purpure	Sable	Ermine

A shield may contain one coat of arms, or if impaled (*i.e.* divided down the centre) the arms of a husband and wife : the husband's being on the dexter, *i.e.* his right hand, when the shield is held in front

---

[1] The banner is borne immediately before, or sometimes behind, the chief or chieftain. The standard is flown at his headquarters. Pipe-banners are referred to at p. 420. There are a number of other technical flags, pensils, pennons, ensygnies, pennoncels. A pavilion-pennon (unsplit, 2 feet long), consisting of the chief's " metal and colour " on which the plant-badge is repeated several times, is the admissible flag for Association and such-like tents, not forming part of the chief's administrative headquarters.

of him ; the wife's on the sinister. Quartered shields arise from marrying heiresses, or inheriting offices or fiefs.

To prevent mistakes in battle, and fraud in sealing deeds, etc., the King had to arrange for control of heraldry, and settlement of disputes. Since this involved genealogy the matter was delegated to the Royal Sennachie of Celtic Scotland, as chief genealogist, who became the Lord Lyon King of Arms, and who—since he represents the King—was given a tabard of the Royal Arms. It was soon held that only arms granted or confirmed by Lyon were admissible. In 1592 and 1672, the Scottish Parliament forbade the use of arms not so confirmed, and established the *Public Register of All Arms and Bearings in Scotland*, which is kept in the Court of the Lord Lyon, H.M. Register House, Edinburgh. Under the Act of Parliament it is unlawful to use any arms which have not been matriculated in that Register, or to use the registered arms of any person of whom you are not the lawful heir (*i.e.* senior living descendant in terms of the patent or last confirmation).[1] A coat of arms when registered, descends, like a peerage, to each successive senior heir.[2] If there is no tailzie or destination, arms, unless by consent (*Pringle*, 1938) pass to the heir-of-line, *not* the heir male (*Maclean of Ardgour*, 1938), who, as " Representer," (*i.e.* Chief, per Sir G. Mackenzie) confers the " courtesy " of the arms on her husband (*Cunnyngham of Caprington*, 1829 ; *Carnegie-Arbuthnott of Balnamoon*, 1898 ; *Maclachlan of Maclachlan*, 1950) and transmits the arms undifferenced and un-quartered (*ibid.* and *Graham of Duntrune*, 1896 ; *Lamont of that Ilk*, 1909) as does an only daughter (*Erskine of Linlathen*, 1870 ; *Chisholm*, 1887 and 1938 ; *Rose of Kilravock*, 1946). Keeping the name inherited with the arms is an indispensable condition (G. Seton's *Heraldry*, 356). The heiress-of-line gets the crest (*Farquharson of Invercauld*, 1936 ; *Douglas of Brigton*, 1941 ; *Maclean of Ardgour*, 1941). Rematriculation on succession to " make up title " is a statutory requisite. Daughters (non-heiresses) use the arms for life on a " lozenge," or for impalement in the shield of an armigerous husband. Younger sons must apply to Lyon for a matriculation, costing £20, when the Lord Lyon registers a differenced version of the arms, usually with a bordure indicating the applicant's relationship to the chief or chieftain. " Virtuous and well-deserving persons," who cannot by proof connect their pedigree to a coat of arms already registered, may get a grant of arms (cost £48), and since the fees are payable to H.M. Treasury, the Lyon Court is a source of national revenue. Since armorial bearings are for distinguishing individuals, Scottish clans as such have neither arms nor crests, though the chief's arms form the *basis* of the arms to be accorded to all members of the clan,[3] and a chieftain's arms the *basis*

---

[1] Penalty £100 money and costs for each offence, confiscation of moveables bearing the " unwarrantable " arms and deletion from heritage (*Scots Heraldry*, p. 65.   [2] Unless varied by special provisions ; see pp. 172–5.

[3] See diagram Scheme of Cadency on p. 412.

of arms accorded to all members of his branch. The arms depicted in this book are in every case those of the chief or some prominent chieftain of the clan. Some clan societies have registered arms which are used on stationery, etc. A clan society has no right, as such, to the chief's crest (in any form), or cap-badge, or to any flag. The armorial insignia are the chiefs' and chieftains' machinery for ruling and organising the clan, and right or property in such insignia cannot be conferred by them on others or on Associations.[1]

It was the custom for lords and chiefs to give their followers a silver plate of their crest, to wear as badge, and which was affixed by a strap. When not in use this was coiled round the crest, and this in its conventional form constitutes the crested cap-badge worn in Highland bonnets. A chief, chieftain, or armigerous *duine-uasail* wears his crest and motto alone, or in a plain circlet. A chief surmounts the circlet by three small silver feathers, a chieftain two such feathers. If the wearer is a peer, the circlet is also "ensigned" with the coronet. The strap and buckle implies a clansman, or clanswoman, wearing his chief's or chieftain's crest to indicate that he, or she (ladies wear them to hold sashes and *arisaids*), is the clansman or clanswoman of the chief, chieftain, or chieftainess, whose crest is displayed. It may accordingly be used

Cap Badge of a Chieftain.

by any member of the clan, armigerous or non-armigerous (being one of the privileges in the Law of Arms enjoyed by, and out of, being a "member of the clan"), subject to the chief's pleasure, and presumptively,[2] where he does not expressly apply restrictions. It is, however, often used even by armigerous *daoine-uasail* as indicating their dependance on the chief. In the above sense " non-armigerous " includes all those (save the heir), who have not a substantive right to arms, in virtue of a matriculation, *e.g.* a Duke's younger son, though "Lord George X" is "non-armigerous" until he matriculates, as also all ladies save heretrices (chieftainesses), who bear their own crests. The lion sejant crest seen on Scottish Government stationery is Crown property, like the tressured lion rampant coat of arms, and being an "Ensign of Public Authority," may not be used by unauthorised persons, but any Scotsman may display the silver cross of St. Andrew—as badge or National flag.[3]

---

[1] One clan society got the chief's sanction to show his crest; then put it in a strap and buckle inscribed with the society's name ; but, whilst Lyon has under consideration what form of concession might be made, no decision has yet been issued, but Lyon considered *placing of the Society's name on the belt disloyal, certainly illegal* and *ultra vires* of any chief to sanction. Societies should note this.

[2] Since his clan and following are presumed to be members of his *familia*, and his familial organisation to be in operation.

[3] See fig. on p. 140.

The strap-and-buckle badge is for use on person and accoutrements. The " wearer " has no right to use this or the crest on his plate, stationery, etc.,[1] nor to put them on flags or pipe banners. One must remember they are the Chief's badge for identifying his clansmen.

SLOGANS OR WAR CRIES

The Slughorn, Slogan, or War Cry is reckoned one of the " exterior additaments " of armory.[2] It served as a watchword in cases of sudden alarm, in the thick of battle, or in darkness of the night. In peace it was " shouted out cheerfully " at gatherings and tournaments by the adherents of chiefs on their arrival, or during rival contests. It sometimes consisted of a prominent mountain in the clan district such as " Cruachan," the slogan of the Campbells ; or an island such as " Clar-Innis " in Loch Lomond, associated with the Buchanans. It might also be the remembrance of some gallant deed performed by a prominent clansman, or some act which shed lustre on the clan. Of this latter nature is the warcry of the MacLeans, *Fear eil' airson Eachainn !* (Another for Hector), which records the loyalty of the clansmen to their chief, Sir Hector Roy, at Inverkeithing. Often the name of the chief, twice or thrice repeated—" A Home, a Home, a Home "—was employed. The right to cry a slogan was naturally subject to official control, or grave confusion would have arisen, and they " were not allowed to any but to the chiefs of clans and great men who had many followers, vassals, and dependers." [3] Falling within the jurisdiction of the Law of Arms, they are " allowed " by the King of Arms, and whilst many have latterly been registered as secondary mottoes, the older practice was to record them on a scroll issuing from a be-helmeted head painted beside the achievement.[4] Sometimes they are expressly recorded on the " compartment." [5] Slughorns can still be " cried " at clan and Highland gatherings. To use them on a public occasion without Lyon's official allowance would be a Breach of the Peace as well as of the Law of Arms.

Only admissible form of using cap badge on paper, letter-heads, etc.

[1] At present Lyon Court has, however, under consideration, whether it might be made competent (subject to the chief's pleasure) to use the strap-and-buckle badge on stationery with the words " Member of the Clan MacX . . ." immediately under the badge and words " *Cirean Ceann Cinnidh.*" To print " Member of the Clan MacX . . . Association " would *not* be permissible, that not being the implication of this form of badge. Many members of the clan are not members of a Clan Association ; and some members of some Clan Associations are not members of the clan !

[2] Nisbet, *System of Heraldry*, II., iv., p. 21.

[3] Sir George Mackenzie, *Works*, II., p. 633.

[4] Forman's Lyon Office MSS., and Nisbet's *System of Heraldry*, II., Pl. 3rd.

[5] *Macfarlane*, Lyon Register, I., p. 377 (destined to heirs female).

Technical Descriptions of Armorial Bearings of the Chiefs of Highland Clans, each having their own Tartan

WARNING.—The Armorial Bearings of a Chief or Chieftain fulfil, in a clan or branch, the same functions that the Royal Arms of a Sovereign or Prince do in a Kingdom or Principality, *i.e.* they indicate the presence or authority of the *Princeps/Ceann Cinnidh*. These arms are protected by statutory penalties.

Arms of Chief (or important Chieftain).	Heraldic Description of Armorial Bearings.
 BRODIE OF BRODIE	*Arms :* Argent, a chevron gules between three mullets azure. *Crest :* A right hand holding a bunch of three arrows all proper. *Supporters :* Two savages wreathed about head and middle with laurel, each holding a club resting against his shoulder. *Motto :* " Unite." *Lyon Register*, I, 123.
 BUCHANAN OF THAT ILK	*Arms :* Or, a lion rampant sable, armed and langued gules, within a double tressure flory-counter-flory of the second. *Crest :* A hand coupled holding up a ducal cap proper, tassled with a rose gules, within two laurel branches wreathed, disposed orleways proper. *Supporters :* Two falcons proper garnished or. *Ancient Motto :* above the crest, " Audaces Juvo " (I help the brave) ; below the shield, " Clarior hinc honos " (Brighter hence the honour). *Lyon Register*, I, 122
 CAMERON OF LOCHIEL	*Arms :* Gules, three bars or. *Crest :* A sheaf of five arrows proper, banded gules. *Supporters :* Two savages wreathed about the loins, each shouldering a pole-axe, all proper. *Motto :* above the crest, " Unite." *Lyon Register*, I, 567.

R*

Arms of Chief *(or important Chieftain).*	*Heraldic Description of Armorial Bearings.*

CAMPBELL OF LOCHOW,
DUKE OF ARGYLL

Arms : Quarterly. 1 and 4, Gyrony of eight, or and sable, for the name of Campbell. 2 and 3, are for the Lordship of Lorn—viz., Argent, a galley, sails furled sable, flag and pennons gules. Behind the shield are placed : in bend dexter, A baton gules, semé of thistles or, ensigned with an imperial crown proper, and thereon the crest of Scotland, borne as hereditary Master of the Royal Household ; in bend sinister, A sword proper, hilt and pommel or, indicative of the office of Lord Justice General. *Supporters :* Two lions guardant gules. *Crest :* A boar's head couped or. *Mottoes :* above the shield, " Ne obliviscaris " (Forget not), and, below the shield, " Vix ea nostro voco " (I scarcely call all this my own).

Lyon Register, I, 37.

CAMPBELL OF GLENORCHY,
EARL OF BREADALBANE

Arms : Quarterly. 1 and 4, Gyrony of eight, or and sable, for Campbell. 2, Argent, a lymphad, sails furled sable, for the Lordship of Lorn. 3, Or, a fess chequy azure and argent, for Stewart. *Crest :* A boar's head erased proper. *Supporters :* Two stags proper, attired and unguled or. *Motto :* " Follow me."

Lyon Register, VIII, 13.

CAMPBELL OF CAWDOR

Arms : Quarterly. 1, Or, a hart's head cabossed sable, attired gules, for the name of Calder. 2, Gyrony of eight, or and sable, for Campbell. 3, Argent, a galley with her oars in action sable, for Lorn. 4, Per fess azure and gules a cross or, for Lort of Stack pole. *Crest :* A swan proper crowned or. *Supporters :* Dexter, A lion rampant guardant gules, armed or ; Sinister, A hart proper. *Motto :* " Be mindful."

Lyon Register, I, 133.

Arms of Chief *(or important Chieftain).*	*Heraldic Description of Armorial* *Bearings.*

CAMPBELL OF LOUDOUN

Arms : Gyrony of eight, ermine and gules (being Campbell differenced by change of tinctures), to show relation to the Crawfurds of Loudoun. *Crest :* An eagle displayed with two heads within a flame of fire. *Supporters :* On the dexter side, or, chevalier in armour holding a pike proper ; on the sinister, a lady nobly dressed and holding in her left hand a missive. *Motto :* " I byde my tyme."

Lyon Register, I, 60.

THE CHIEF OF CLAN CHATTAN

Arms : Quarterly. 1, Or, a lion rampant gules. 2, Arg, a hand couped fessways, holding a heart in pale gules, a label of three points azure charged with as many bulls' heads cabossed of the first. 3, Az, a boar's head erased or, armed proper and langued gules. 4, Or, a lymphad sails furled and oars in saltire azure. Over all an inescutcheon or charged with a lymphad sails furled and oars in saltire azure, flagged gules, as chief of Clan Chattan. *Crest :* A wild cat salient proper. *Supporters :* Two wild cats proper. *Motto over :* " Touch not the catt but a glove."

Lyon Register, XXXVI, 36.

THE CHISHOLM

Arms : Gules, a boar's head couped or. *Crest :* A dexter hand with dagger and boar's head transfixed. *Supporters :* Two savages wreathed about the loins, bearing oak staves leaved proper resting on the ground. *Mottoes :* underneath escutcheon, " Vi aut Virtute " (By virtue or valour) and, above escutcheon, " Feros ferio " (To the rough I am rough).

Lyon Register, III, 85 ; XXXIII, 12.

COLQUHOUN OF LUSS

Arms : Argent, a saltire engrailed sable. *Crest :* A hart's head couped gules attired argent. *Supporters :* Two ratch hounds argent, collared sable. *Motto :* " Si je puis " (If I can).

Lyon Register, I, 130 ; XL, 1

Arms of Chief (or important Chieftain).	*Heraldic Description of Armorial Bearings.*
 CUMMING OF ALTYRE	*Arms :* Azure, three garbs or. *Crest :* A lion rampant or, holding in dexter paw a dagger proper. *Supporters :* Two wild horses argent, their manes, tails, and hoofs or. *Motto :* " Courage." *Lyon Register*, I, 281, 569.
 DAVIDSON OF TULLOCH	*Arms :* Quarterly, 1 and 4, Argent, on a fess azure, between a dexter hand couped accompanied by two pheons in chief and a pheon in base, gules, a buck lodged or. 2 and 3, Azure, a wolf's head erased or, armed and langued gules. *Crest :* A stag's head, erased proper. *Motto :* " Sapienter si Sincere " (Wisely if sincerely). *Lyon Register*, XVIII, 62.
 DRUMMOND, EARL OF PERTH	*Arms :* Or, three bars wavy gules. *Crest :* A falcon rising out of a ducal coronet. *Supporters :* Two savages wreathed about the head and loins with oak leaves, bearing each a shouldered club and standing on ground strewn with caltrops. *Motto :* " Virtus coronat honos " (above) ; " Gang warily " (below). The falcon crest is that of his Viscounty of Strathallan. *Lyon Register*, I, 56 ; XL, 77.

| *Arms of Chief* (or important Chieftain). | *Heraldic Description of Armorial Bearings.* |

DUNBAR OF MOCHRUM

Arms : Gules a lion rampant argent within a bordure of the second charged with eight roses of the first. *Crest :* A horse's head couped argent, bridled and reined with garnishing of roses, gules. *Motto* (over): In Promptu. *Supporters :* Two white doves imperially crowned proper. *Motto* (below) : Candoris praemium honos.

Lyon Register. XL, 52.

ERSKINE, EARL OF MAR AND KELLIE

Arms : Argent, a pale sable. Behind the shield are placed in saltire a key, wards, outwards or, and a baton gules, garnished or, and ensigned with a castle. *Crests :* 1st, on a cap of maintenance gules, turned up ermine a dexter hand, holding a skene in pale argent, hilted and pommelled or ; 2nd, on a cap of maintenance gules, turned up ermine a demi-lion rampant guardant gules, armed argent. *Supporters :* Two griffins gules, armed, beaked, and winged or. *Mottos :* above 1st crest " Je Pense Plus " (I think more) ; above 2nd crest ' Decori decus addit avito " (He adds honour to the honour of his ancestors).

Lyon Register, XXVII, 1.

FARQUHARSON OF INVERCAULD

Arms : Quarterly. 1 and 4, Or, a lion rampant gules, armed and langued azure. 2 and 3, Argent, a fir tree growing out of mount in base fructed proper, on a chief gules the Royal standard of Scotland is displayed bendwise on a canton of the field, in allusion to the fight of Pinkie, a hand issuing from the sinister side holding a dagger also proper, point downwards. *Crest :* A demi-lion rampant gules, holding a sword or. *Supporters :* Two wild cats proper. *Motto :* " Fide et Fortitudine " (With faith and fortitude) over Crest, and " I force nae freen, I fear nae foe " below shield.

Lyon Register, I, 300 ; II, 130 ; XXXVII, 95.

Arms of Chief (or important Chieftain).	Heraldic Description of Armorial Bearings.

CLANNFHEARGHUIS OF
STRA-CHUR

Arms : Azure, a round buckle argent traversed by a baton of the second tipped sable, between three boars' heads erased or, langued gules. *Crest :* A lion rampant proper, crowned with an antique crown or, issuant from an antique crown of the last, brandishing in his dexter paw a broadsword proper. *Supporters :* Two griffins proper winged azure, armed gules and langued or. *Motto :* " Clannfhearghuis gu bràth."

Lyon Register, XXXIV, 12.

FORBES,
LORD FORBES

Arms : Azure, three bears' heads couped argent, muzzled gules. *Crest :* A stag's head attired proper. *Supporters :* Two bloodhounds argent, collared gules. *Motto :* " Grace me guide."

Lyon Register, I, 94.

LORD FRASER OF LOVAT

Arms : (Lord Fraser of Lovat), Quarterly. 1 and 4, Azure, three fraises argent. 2 and 3. Argent, three antique crowns gules, for Lovat. *Crest :* A stag's head erased or, attired argent. *Supporters :* Two stags proper. *Motto :* " Je suis prest " (I am ready).

Lyon Register, IV, 15.

| *Arms of Chief* (or important Chieftain). | *Heraldic Description of Armorial Bearings.* |

GORDON,
MARQUESS OF HUNTLY

Arms : Quarterly. 1, Azure, three boars' heads couped or, for Gordon. 2, Or, three lions' heads erased gules, for Badenoch. 3, Or, three crescents within a double tressure flory-counter-flory gules, for Seton. 4, Azure, three fraises argent, for Fraser. *Crest :* A buck's head affronté proper, attired and issuing from a crest coronet, or. *Supporters :* Two deerhounds proper, collars gules each charged with three crescents or. *Mottoes :* above crest, " Bydand " (Abiding or lasting), and, below escutcheon, " Animo non astutia " (By courage not craft).
Lyon Register, I, 42 ; XXXVII, 147.

GRAHAM, EARL OF AIRTH,
MENTEITH AND STRATHEARN

Arms : Quarterly. 1 and 4, Or, on a chief sable three escallops of the first. 2 and 3, Or, fess chequy azure and argent, in a chief a chevron gules. *Crest :* A falcon's head erased proper. *Supporters :* Two lions rampant, guardant gules, each gorged with a collar sable, charged with three escallops or. *Motto :* " Right and Reason."
Seal A.D. 1636 (Pre-Register).

GRAHAM,
DUKE OF MONTROSE

Arms : Quarterly. 1 and 4, Or, on a chief sable three escallops of the first. 2 and 3, Argent, three roses gules, for the title of Montrose. *Crest :* A falcon proper, beaked and armed or, killing a stork proper, armed gules. *Supporters :* Two storks argent, beaked and membered gules. *Motto :* " Ne oublie " (Forget not).
Lyon Register, I, 44.

Arms of Chief *(or important Chieftain).*	*Heraldic Description of Armorial Bearings.*

GRANT OF GRANT
(LORD STRATHSPEY)

Arms : Gules, three Eastern or antique crowns or. *Crest :* A mountain inflamed proper. *Supporters :* Two savages wreathed around the head and loins proper. *Motto :* " Stand fast."

Lyon Register, I, 155 ; XXXVII, 143.

GUNN

Not matriculated as chief.

HAY, EARL OF ERROLL

Arms : Argent, three escutcheons, gules ; on either side of the shield issuant from clouds, two arms armed, each holding a broadsword paleways, and behind the shield, two batons argent, tipped or. *Crest :* Issuing from a crest coronet or, a falcon, rising proper, belled and jessed, or. *Supporters :* Two savages, wreathed about the temples and loins with laurel, each holding on his exterior shoulder, an ox yoke, gules. *Motto :* over, " Serva jugum."

Lyon Register, XXXIV, 44.

INNES OF THAT ILK
(DUKE OF ROXBURGHE)

Arms : Argent, three stars azure. *Crest :* A boar's head erased proper langued gules. *Supporters :* Two greyhounds argent having collars azure charged with three stars of the first. *Motto :* " Be traist."

Lyon Register, I, 168 ; XVIII, 14.

Arms of Chief (or important Chieftain).	*Heraldic Description of Armorial Bearings.*

LAMONT OF LAMONT

Arms : Azure, a lion rampant argent. *Crest :* A dexter hand couped at the wrist proper. *Supporters :* Two savages wreathed about head and middle with laurel and holding in their exterior hands clubs resting on their shoulders all proper. *Motto :* " Ne parcas nec spernas " (Neither destroy nor despise).

Lyon Register, XX, 24 ; XXXIX, 116.

LESLIE, EARL OF ROTHES

Arms : Quarterly. 1 and 4, Argent, on a bend azure three buckles or, for Leslie. 2 and 3, Or, a lion rampant gules debruised with a ribbon sable, for Abernethy. *Crest :* a demi-griffin proper. *Supporters :* Two griffins, wings elevated proper, beaked, armed, and winged or. *Motto :* " Grip fast."

Lyon Register, I, 36.

LINDSAY,
EARL OF CRAWFORD

Arms : Quarterly. 1 and 4, Gules, a fess chequy argent and azure, for Lindsay. 2 and 3, Or, a lion rampant gules debruised with a ribbon sable, for Abernethy. *Crest :* a swan's neck and wings proper issuant from a crest coronet or. *Supporters :* Two lions guardant gules, armed or. *Motto :* " Endure fort " (Suffer bravely).

Lyon Register, I, 50; XI, 48.

Logan

See Maclennan

Arms of Chief (or important Chieftain).	Heraldic Description of Armorial Bearings.

MACALISTAIR OF THE LOUP

Arms : Or, an eagle displayed gules, armed sable ; on its breast a galley, sails furled, oars in action of the last, all within a bordure of the third, charged with three cross-crosslets fiitchée argent. *Crest :* A dexter hand holding a dirk in pale, both proper. *Supporters :* Dexter, a bear pierced by an arrow ; Sinister, an eagle, all proper. *Mottoes :* above escutcheon, " Fortiter " (Bravely) ; and, below escutcheon, " Per mare per terras " (By sea and land).

Lyon Register, IV, 105.

MACARTHUR OF MILTON

Arms : (Milton and Ascog), Azure, a cross moline argent between three antique or Eastern crowns or. *Crest :* Two laurel branches in orle proper. *Motto :* " Fide et opera " (By faith and work).

Lyon Register, I, 506.

GEORGE MACAULAY

Arms : (George MacAulay). Gules, two arrows in saltire argent surmounted by a fess chequy of the first and second, between three buckles or, within a bordure indented or. *Crest :* An antique boot couped at the ankle, with a spur thereon proper. *Motto :* " Dulce periculum " (Sweet is danger).

Lyon Register, I, 359.

MACBAIN OF MACBAIN

Arms : Quarterly, 1st. Or, a lion rampant gules. 2, Argent, a dexter hand couped in pale gules. 3, Argent, a sword in pale proper. 4, A lymphad azure sails furled proper, oars in saltire gu. and flagged of the last. *Crest :* A grey demi-catamountain salient, on his dexter foreleg a highland targe gules. *Motto :* (over) " Touch not a catt bot a targe." *Compartment :* Embellished with two boxwood plants and this slogan, " Kinchyle."

Lyon Register, XLIV.

Arms of Chief *(or important Chieftain).*	*Heraldic Description of Armorial Bearings.*

MACDONALD OF MACDONALD, LORD MACDONALD

Badge: (as Macdonald of Macdonald): An eagle displayed gules, armed and beaked sable, wearing a Lord-Baron's coronet, holding in its talons an escutcheon Or, charged with an eagle displayed gules surmounted of a galley sails furled and oars in action sable. *Crest:* On a crest-coronet Or, a hand in armour fessways couped at the elbow proper, holding a cross-crosslet fitchee, gules. *Motto:* (over) " Per Mare per terras."

Lyon Register, XXXVI, 44.

For blason of full arms see p. 613–614.

MACDONALD OF SLEATE

Arms: Quarterly. 1, Argent, a lion rampant gules. 2, Or, a hand in armour holding a cross-crosslet fitchy gules. 3, Argent, a row galley (or lymphad), the sails furled sable. 4, Vert, a salmon naiant in fess proper. *Crest:* A hand in armour holding a cross-crosslet fitchy gules. *Supporters:* Two leopards tenné, collared or, armed and langued gules. *Motto:* " Per mare per terras " (By sea and land).

Lyon Register, XX, 69.

MACDONALD OF CLAN RANALD

Arms: Quarterly. 1, Argent, a lion rampant gules, armed or. 2, Or, a dexter hand couped fesswise, holding a cross-crosslet fitchy gules. 3, Or, a lymphad or galley, oars in saltire sable, and in base a salmon naiant proper, in sea vert. 4, Argent, an oak tree surmounted by an eagle displayed or. *Crest:* On a castle triple-towered an arm holding a sword proper. *Supporters:* Two bears, each pierced by an arrow through the body proper. *Mottoes:* above escutcheon, " My hope is constant in thee," and, below escutcheon, " Dh'aindeòin có theireadh e " (Gainsay who dare).

Lyon Register, II, 49.

| *Arms of Chief (or important Chieftain).* | *Heraldic Description of Armorial Bearings.* |

MACDONALD (OR MACIAN)
OF ARDNAMURCHAN

Arms : (Rev. William J. McKain). Or, a galley, sails furled, oars in action sable, between, in fess dexter, an eagle displayed gules, and sinister, a buckle of the last. *Crest :* A demi-eagle displayed sable. *Motto :* " In hope I byde."

Lyon Register, XVIII, 20.

MACDONELL OF GLENGARRY

Arms : Or, an eagle displayed gules surmounted by a galley (biorlin) sable, sails furled, in dexter chief a hand couped of the second ; sinister, a cross-crosslet fitchy of the third. *Crest :* A raven proper perched on a rock azure. *Supporters :* Two bears, each pierced with an arrow, in bend proper. *Mottoes :* Over the escutcheon " Creagan-an-Fhitich " (The raven's rock), and, under the escutcheon, " Per mare et terras " (By sea and land).

Lyon Register, I, 576.

MACDONELL OF KEPPOCH

Arms : Or, a lion rampant gules, a canton, argent, charged with a dexter hand couped fessways proper holding a cross-crosslet fitchy of the second.

Lyon Register, 1, 228 ; *s.v.* Michie.

Arms of Chief (or important Chieftain).	Heraldic Description of Armorial Bearings.

MACDOUGALL OF MAC-
DOUGALL AND DUNOLLIE

Arms : Quarterly. 1 and 4, Azure, a lion rampant argent, for MacDougall. 2 and 3, Or, a lymphad (or galley) sable, with a beacon on the topmast proper, for the Lordship of Lorn. *Crest :* An arm in armour embowed fessways couped proper, holding a cross-crosslet fitchy gules. *Supporters :* Two crowned lions proper. *Motto :* " Buaidh no bas."
Lyon Register, XXIX, 68 ; XXXIX, 111.

DUFF OF BRACO, LORD BRACO

Arms : Quarterly. 1 and 4, Or, a lion rampant gules. 2 and 3, Vert, a fess dancetté ermine, between a buck's head cabossed in chief and two escallops in base, or. *Crest :* A demi-lion rampant gules. *Motto :* (over) " Deus Juvat." *Supporters :* Two savages wreathed about the temples and loins with laurel and holding in their exterior hands boughs of oak resting on their shoulders all proper. *Motto :* (under) " Virtute et opera " (With virtue and energy).
Lyon Register, I, 76.

MACFARLANE OF THAT ILK

Arms : Argent, a saltire waved and cantoned with four roses gules. *Crest :* A demi-savage holding a sheaf of arrows in his right hand and pointing with his left to an imperial crown. *Supporters :* Two Highlanders in their native garb, armed with broadswords and bows proper (in the last matriculation they are blazoned " brandishing their broadswords aloft " and stand on a compartment wavy). *Mottoes :* over escutcheon, " This I'll defend," and, under escutcheon, on a compartment wavy, " Loch Sloy."
Lyon Register, I, 184

Arms of Chief *(or important Chieftain).*	*Heraldic Description of Armorial Bearings.*

MACFIE OF DREGHORN

Arms : (House of Macfie of Dreghorn). Per fess nebuly azure and or, in chief a two-handed sword argent hilted and pommelled of the second, and in base a lymphad sable under sail of the third. *Crest :* A demi-lion rampant proper. *Motto :* " Pro Rege " (For the King).

Lyon Register, VII, 89.

MACGILLIVRAY CADET *ex* DUNMAGLASS

Arms : (William Macgillivray, Montreal). Azure, a galley, sails furled, oars in action or, flagged gules, within a bordure argent, on a chief, of the second, a buck's head cabossed sable attired of the third between two cross-crosslets fitchée of the last. *Crest :* A buck's head and neck issuant proper, attired or. *Motto :* " Be mindful."

Lyon Register, I, 584.

MACGREGOR OF MACGREGOR

Arms : Argent, an oak tree eradicated in bend sinister proper, surmounted by a sword azure hilted and pommelled or, in bend supporting on its point, in the dexter canton, an antique crown gules. *Crest :* A lion's head erased proper crowned with an antique crown. *Supporters :* Dexter, a unicorn argent, crowned and horned or (denoting the Royal descent) ; Sinister, a deer proper, tyned azure. *Mottoes :* above escutcheon, " 'S rioghal mo dhream " (Royal is my race) and, below escutcheon, " Ard Choille " (The woody height).

Lyon Register, I, 565, 584 (G. II, 2).

MACINNES
CADET OF MALAGAWATCH

Arms : Quarterly, 1st, azure a castle of two towers or windows and port gules ; 2 and 3, or on a sea in base undy azure and argent a lymphad vert flag and 5 visible oars gules ; 4th, gyronny of eight sable and or ; over all a cross vert charged with a mill-rhind between four pheons argent accompanied by two crosscrosslets in the flanks and as many crosscrosslets fitché, all of the last, in chief and base of the said cross. *Crest :* a sinister arm from the shoulder bendways habited in a close sleeve of the proper tartan of the clan MacInnes (*detailed*) cuff flashed yellow, and three buttons or, the hand grasping a bow vert stringed gules.

Lyon Register, XLIV, 70 ; XLIII, 48.

Arms of Chief (or important Chieftain).	Heraldic Description of Armorial Bearings.

MACINTYRE

Not matriculated for chief ; Cadet-arms for Macintyre of Camus-na-herie.
Motto : " Per ardua."

Lyon Register, XL, 122.

MACKAY

Arms : Azure, on a chevron between three bears' heads couped argent and muzzled gules, a roebuck's head erased, between two hands holding daggers, all proper. *Crest :* A right hand grasping a sword palewise. *Supporters :* Dexter, a pikeman in armour, tunic vert, breeches gules, in his exterior hand a pike proper ; sinister, a similar pikeman, tunic gules, breeches vert, on his exterior shoulder a musket proper.

Lyon Register, I, 229 ; XXXVIII, 99.

MACKENZIE OF SEAFORTH

Arms : Azure, a stag's head cabossed or. *Crest :* A mountain inflamed proper. *Supporters :* Two savages wreathed about the loins and head with laurel, each holding in his exterior hand a baton or club erect and inflamed, all proper. *Motto :* " Luceo non uro " (I shine, not burn).

Lyon Register, I, 59 ; II, 138 ; XII, 27 ; XXXV, 10.

MACKINNON OF MACKINNON

Arms : 1, Vert, a boar's head erased argent, holding in its mouth the shankbone of a deer proper. 2, Azure, a castle triple-towered and embattled argent, masoned sable, windows and portcullis gules. 3, Or, a lymphad, sails furled, the oars saltirewise sable, flags flying gules. 4, Argent, a dexter hand couped fesswise, holding a crosscrosslet fitchy sable. *Crest :* A boar's head erased, holding in its mouth the shank-bone of a deer proper. *Supporters :* Dexter, a lion ; sinister, a leopard, both proper. *Mottoes :* above, " Audentes fortuna juvat " and below, " Cuimhnich bàs Alpin."

Lyon Register, II, 64 ; XXXVI, 153.

Arms of Chief (or important Chieftain).	Heraldic Description of Armorial Bearings.

THE MACKINTOSH

Arms : Quarterly. 1, Or, a lion rampant gules, as descended from MacDuff. 2, Argent, a dexter hand couped fesswise, grasping a man's heart proper. 3, Azure, a boar's head couped or, for Gordon of Lochinvar. 4, Or, a lymphad azure, oars erect in saltire gules, for Clan Chattan. *Crest :* A cat guardant proper. *Supporters :* Two cats proper. *Motto :* " Touch not the cat bot (without) a glove."

Lyon Register, I, 189 ; XXXVI, 40.

MACLACHLAN OF THAT ILK

Arms : Quarterly. 1, Or, a lion rampant gules. 2, Argent, a dexter hand couped in fess, holding a crosslet patté in pale gules. 3, Or, a galley, oars in saltire sable in a sea proper. 4, Argent, in base in the sea undy, vert a salmon naiant proper. *Crest :* (upon a crest-coronet proper) A castle triple-towered on a rock all proper. *Supporters :* Two roebucks proper. *Motto :* " Fortis et fidus " (Brave and faithful).

Lyon Register, I, 189; XXXV, 72.

MACLEAN OF DUART

Arms : Quarterly. 1, Argent, a rock gules. 2, Argent, a dexter hand couped fesswise gules, holding a crosslet fitchy in pale azure. 3, Or, a lymphad, oars in saltire, sails furled sable, flagged gules. 4, Argent, a salmon naiant proper, and in chief two eagles' heads erased respectant gules. *Crest :* A tower embattled argent. *Supporters :* Dexter, a seal proper ; Sinister, an ostrich with a horseshoe in its beak proper. *Motto :* " Virtue mine honour." *Badge :* A Lochaber axe between a laurel branch on the dexter, and cypress on the sinister, proper.

Lyon Register, XX, 1.

MACLAINE OF LOCH BUIE

Arms : Quarterly. 1, Argent, a lion rampant gules. 2, Azure, a tower argent. 3, Or, a dexter hand couped in fess gules, holding a cross-crosslet fitchy azure. 4, Or, a lymphad proper, in base vert a salmon naiant proper. *Crest :* A battle-axe in pale in front of a laurel and cypress branch in saltire, all proper. *Supporters :* Two seals proper. *Motto :* " Vincere vel mori " (Victory or death).

Lyon Register, XVIII, 34.

Arms of Chief (or important Chieftain).	Heraldic Description of Armorial Bearings.

MACLAREN OF MACLAREN

Arms : Or two chevronnells gules, a lymphad sails furled sable in base. *Crest :* A lion's head erased sable langued gules, between two branches of spurge laurel in orle proper. *Supporters :* Two mermaids proper, holding in their exterior hands a branch of spurge laurel proper. *Motto :* (over) " Creag an tuirc " ; (below) " Ab origine fidus."

Lyon Register, XLII, 19

LOGAN OF THAT ILK

Arms : Or three passion nails the two outer most bendways the centre paleways, all meeting at the points and piercing a man's heart gules. *Crest :* A passion nail piercing a human heart proper. *Motto :* " Hoc Majorum virtus " (This is the valour of my ancestors).

Lyon Register, I, 352.

MACLEOD OF MACLEOD

Arms : Quarterly. 1 and 4, Azure, a castle triple-towered and embattled argent, masoned sable, windows and porch gules. 2 and 3, gules three legs armed, conjoined, and flexed at the knees argent (Kingship of Man). *Crest :* A bull's head cabossed sable, between two flags gules staves of the first. *Supporters :* Two lions regardant gules, each holding a dagger proper *Mottoes :* on scroll, below shield, " Murus aheneus esto " (Be a brazen wall), and, above crest, " Hold fast."

Lyon Register, I, 375 ; XXVIII, 12.

Arms of Chief (or important Chieftain).	Heraldic Description of Armorial Bearings.

MACLEOD OF RAASAY

Arms : Or, a burning mountain proper, in the dexter and sinister chief points two crosses patté fitchy gules. *Crest :* The sun in his splendour proper. *Supporters :* Two savages with flames of fire on their heads and hands, each on a burning hillock, all proper. *Motto :* " Luceo non uro " (I shine, not burn).

Lyon Register, I, 352.

MACMILLAN OF MACMILLAN AND KNAP

Arms : Or, a lion rampant sable, in chief three mullets azure. *Crest :* A dexter and a sinister hand brandishing a two-handed sword proper. *Supporters :* Two lions sable collared with collars or, each charged with three mullets azure. *Motto :* " Miseris succurrere disco " (I learn to succour the distressed).

Lyon Register, I, 376 ; XXXVIII, 96.

MACNAB OF THAT ILK

Arms : Sable, on a chevron argent three crescents vert, in base an open boat with oars argent, sailing in a sea proper. *Crest :* The head of a savage affronté proper. *Supporters :* Two dragons sable, armed and langued Or, having wings elevated Argent semee of crescents vert. *Motto :* " Timor omnis abesto " (Be all fear absent).

Lyon Register, I, 229 ; XL.

Arms of Chief (or important Chieftain).	*Heraldic Description of Armorial Bearings.*

MACNAUGHTEN OF
DUNDARAVE

Arms : Quarterly. 1 and 4, Argent, a hand fesswise proper, holding a cross-crosslet fitchy azure. 2 and 3, Argent, a castle embattled gules. *Crest :* A castle embattled gules. *Supporters :* Two roe-bucks proper. *Motto :* (over) " I hope in God."

Lyon Register, X, 39.

MACNEIL OF BARRA

Arms : Quarterly. 1, Vert, a lion rampant or. 2, Argent, in base the sea, with a castle issuant therefrom proper. 3, Or, a lymphad, sails furled sable. 4, Or, a dexter hand palewise couped gules, within an orle of nine fetterlocks. *Crest :* A rock proper. *Supporters :* Two lions proper. *Motto :* " Vincere vel mori " (Victory or death).
Lyon Register, II, 5 ; III, 24 ; XXII, 60; XLVI, 61.

McNEILL OF GIGHA

Arms : Quarterly. 1 and 4, Azure, a lion rampant, armed and langued gules. 2, Argent, a sinister hand couped fessways in chief gules ; in base wavy, azure, a salmon naiant argent. 3, Or, a galley, oars in saltire gules, on a chief gules three mullets or. *Crest :* A mailed arm, the hand holding a dagger proper. *Motto :* " Vincere aut mori " (Conquer or die).

Lyon Register, VII, 74.

Arms of Chief (or important Chieftain).	Heraldic Description of Armorial Bearings.

CLUNY-MACPHERSON

Arms : Party per fess or and azure, a lymphad of the first flagged gules, sails furled, oars in action proper, in the dexter chief point a dexter hand couped fesswise grasping a dagger erect palewise gules, and in the sinister a cross-crosslet fitchée gules. *Crest :* A cat sejant proper. *Supporters :* Two Highlanders (in tartan doublets of the Cluny tartan), their shirts (or " leine chroich ") fastened between their bare thighs, helmets on their heads, dirks by their sides, and targets on their arms. *Motto :* " Touch not the cat bot (without) a glove."
Lyon Register, I, 185 ; IX, 45 ; XXXVII, 10.

MACQUARRIE

Not matriculated.

MACQUEEN

Not matriculated.

MACRAE OF INVERINATE

Arms : Argent a fess azure between three mullets in chief and a lion rampant in base gules. *Crest :* A cubit arm grasping a sword proper. *Motto :* " Fortitudine " (By fortitude).
Lyon Register, XXVII, 16.

MALCOLM OF POLTALLOCH

Arms : Argent, on a saltire azure between four stags' heads erased gules, five mullets or. *Crest :* A tower argent. *Supporters :* Two stags at gaze proper, collared and with chains reflexed over the back or. *Mottoes :* over crest, " In ardua tendit " (Aims at lofty things), and, under crest, " Deus refugium nostrum " (God is our refuge).
Lyon Register, II, 179.

Arms of Chief (or important Chieftain).	Heraldic Description of Armorial Bearings.

HOUSE OF MAR,
EARL OF MAR

Arms : 1 and 4, Azure a bend between six cross-crosslets fitchee. *Crest :* (ancient) on a cap of dignity, gules doubled ermine, two wings erected and addorsed, azure, each charged with a bend between six cross-crosslets or. *Supporters:* Two griffins argent.

Lyon Register, XXX, 67.

MATHESON OF MATHESON

Arms : Gyronny of eight sable and gules, a lion rampant or, armed and langued azure. *Crest :* Issuant from an antique crown or a hand brandishing a scimitar fessways all proper. *Motto :* " Fac et Spera," and on a compartment embellished of roses four-petalled or. This motto " O'Chian."

Lyon Register, XLVI, 137.

MENZIES OF MENZIES

Arms : Argent, a chief gules. *Crest :* A savage's head erased proper. *Supporters :* Two savages wreathed around the head and loins proper. *Motto :* (over) " Vil God I zal."

Lyon Register, I, 186 ; XLII, 141.

MUNRO OF FOULIS

Arms : Or, an eagle's head erased gules. *Crest :* An eagle on the perch proper. *Supporters :* Two eagles proper. *Motto :* " Dread God."

Lyon Register, I, 189 ; XXXIX, 1.

Arms of Chief (or important Chieftain).	Heraldic Description of Armorial Bearings.

MORRISON
(ARMS OF THE HOUSE OF RUCHDI)

Arms : (House of Ruchdi) Per bend sinister, gules and on a bend embattled sinister between a demi-lion rampant issuant, or, armed and langued azure, holding in his paws a battle axe azure, in dexter chief, and in sinister base, issuant from the sea in base undevert and or, a tower sable windows and port gules, an open crown or between two fleurs de lys argent. *Crest :* Issuant from the waves of the sea azure crested argent a mound vert and thereon issuant from an embattled wall azure masoned argent a hand holding a dirk proper. *Motto :* (over) " Teaghlach Phabbay."
Lyon Register, XLIV, 48.

MURRAY OF ATHOLL

Arms : Quarterly. 1, paly of six or and sable, Atholl ; 2, or a fess chequy azure argent, Stewart ; 3, Argent, on a bend azure three stags' heads cabossed or, Stanley ; 4, gules, three legs in armour proper, garnished and spurred or, flexed and conjoined in triangle at the upper part of the thigh. Ensign of Isle of Man ; over all an inescutcheon en surtout azure three mullets argent, within a double tressure flory, ensigned of a Marquess's coronet. *Crests :* 1st a mermaid holding in her dexter hand a mirror and in her sinister a comb, all proper ; 2nd a demi-savage proper, wreathed about the temples and waist with laurel, his arms extended, and holding in his right hand a dagger, in the left a key, all proper. *Supporters :* Dexter, a savage proper wreathed about head and waist vert, his feet in irons, the chain held up by his right hand proper ; Sinister, a lion gules, gorged with a collar azure, thereon three mullets argent. *Motto :* " Furth fortune and fill the fetters."
Lyon Register, I, 73 ; II, 41 ; VII, 24 ; XLIII, 76.

NICOLSON OF SCORRYBRECK

Arms : Or, a chevron between three hawks' heads erased gules. *Crest :* A hawk's head erased gules. *Motto :* (over) " Sgorr-a-bhreac " ; (below) " Generositate non ferocitate."
Lyon Register, XXXI, 21.

Arms of Chief *(or important Chieftain).*	*Heraldic Description of Armorial* *Bearings.*

OGILVY, EARL OF AIRLIE

Arms : Argent, a lion passant guardant gules, crowned with an imperial crown and collared with an open crown or. *Crest :* A woman, from her waist upwards, proper, holding a portcullis gules *Supporters :* Two bulls sable, unguled and horned vert, with a garland of flowers about their necks. *Motto :* " A fin " (To the end).

Lyon Register, I, 63.

ROBERTSON OF STRUAN

Arms : Gules, three wolves' heads erased argent, armed and langued azure. *Crest :* A dexter arm couped in pale holding a regal crown proper. *Compartment :* under the escutcheon a wild man chained proper. *Supporters :* Dexter a serpent vert having a riband of gules around its neck and sinister a dove argent, beaked and membered azure, having on its head a chapeau azure furred ermine. *Motto :* (over) " Virtutis gloria merces " (Glory is the reward of virtue) ; (below the shield) "Garg'n uair dhuisgear."

Lyon Register, I, 206 ; XXXII, 15 ; XL, 14.

ROSE OF KILRAVOCK

Arms : Or, a boar's head couped gules between three water bougets sable. *Crest :* On a cap of estate a harp azure. *Supporters :* Two falcons proper, jessed sable and belled or. *Motto :* " Constant and true."

Lyon Register I, 207 ; XXXVI, 8.

Arms of Chief (or important Chieftain).	*Heraldic Description of Armorial Bearings.*

ROSS OF THAT ILK AND
PITCALNIE

Arms : Gules, three lions rampant, two and one argent. *Crest :* A hand holding a garland of laurel proper. *Supporters :* Two savages wreathed about head and loins with oak, holding clubs resting on their shoulders proper. *Motto :* " Spem successus alit " (Success nourishes hope).

Lyon Register, I, 208; XVIII, 7.

SINCLAIR,
EARL OF CAITHNESS

Arms : Quarterly. 1, Azure, a ship at anchor within a double tressure flory-counter-flory, her oars erect in saltire or, for Orkney. 2 and 3, Or, a lion rampant gules, for Spar. 4, Azure, a ship under sail or, for the title of Caithness, and over all a cross engrailed, quartered, dividing the four quarters argent and sable, for Sinclair. *Crest :* A cock gules winged proper. *Supporters :* Two griffins proper, beaked and membered or. *Motto :* " Commit thy work to God."

Lyon Register, I, 53.

SKENE OF SKENE

Arms : Gules, three sgians (or daggers) palewise in fess argent, hilted and pommelled or, surmounted of as many wolves' heads or. *Crest :* A dexter arm from the shoulder issuing out of a cloud, and holding forth a triumphal crown or garland of laurel leaves proper. *Supporters :* On the dexter side, a Highlander in his proper garb, holding in his right hand a sgian ; and on the sinister, a Highlander in servile habit, his target on the left arm and his dorlach by his side, all proper. *Motto :* " Virtutis regia merces " (Glory is the reward of virtue).

Lyon Register, I, 211.

Arms of Chief *(or important Chieftain).*	*Heraldic Description of Armorial* *Bearings.*

ROYAL ARMS OF SCOTLAND

Arms : Or, a lion rampant gules, armed and langued azure, within a double tressure flory-counter-flory gules, encircled with the Order of Scotland, composed of rue and thistles, with the image of St. Andrew pendent therefrom, having on his breast a cross. *Crest :* above the shield, a sovereign's helmet adorned with an imperial crown and surmounted by a lion sejant affronté, holding in his dexter paw a sword and in the sinister a sceptre. *Supporters :* Two unicorns argent, crowned and gorged with a Royal coronet and chained or. *Mottoes :* In a scroll, above all, " In Defens," and, under escutcheon, " Nemo me impune lacessit " (No one harms me with impunity).

Lyon Register, I, 14.

STEWART OF APPIN

Arms : Quarterly. 1 and 4, Or, a fess chequy azure and argent. 2 and 3, Argent, a galley, sails trussed up, flags, gules, and oars in action. *Crest :* A unicorn's head argent, maned, horned, and bearded or. *Supporters :* Two roebucks proper. *Motto :* " Quhidder will zie " (Whither will ye).

Lyon Register, I, 581.

STEWART OF ATHOLL

Arms : Quarterly. 1 and 4 paley of six or and sable. 2 and 3 or a fess chequey azure and argent. *Crest :* A dexter hand couped at the wrist all proper. *Supporters :* Two wild men in chains wreathed about the head and loins with juniper.

pre. Lyon Register, I.

S

Arms of Chief (or important Chieftain).	*Heraldic Description of Armorial Bearings.*

STEWART,
EARL OF GALLOWAY

Arms : (House of Gorlies) Or, a fess chequy azure and argent, surmounted by a bend engrailed gules, within a tressure flory-counter-flory gules. *Crest :* A pelican argent, winged or, in her nest, feeding her young proper. *Supporters :* Dexter, a savage wreathed about the head and loins with laurel, holding a club on his dexter shoulder, all proper; Sinister, a lion gules. *Motto :* " Virescit vulnere virtus " (Courage grows strong at a wound).

Lyon Register, I, 58; XXXVIII, 11.

EARLDOM OF SUTHERLAND

Countess of Sutherland bears videlicet: Gules, three mullets Or (as the ancient Arms of Sutherland of that Ilk), a bordure of the Second charged of a double tressure flory-counterflory of the First (as an Honourable Augmentation). Coronet, Crest a cat-a mountain sejant rampant proper. Motto : Sans Peur. Supporters, dexter, a savage man wreathed about the head and loins with laurel proper, holding in his exterior hand a club Gules resting upon his shoulder, sinister another like savage sustaining in his sinister hand and against his shoulder, upon a staff ensigned by the coronet of an Earl, a bannerette Gules, chaged of three mullets Or.

URQUHART OF THAT ILK

Arms : Or, three boars' heads erased gules, armed proper and langued azure. Issuant from a crest-coronet Or for *Crest* a naked woman from the waist upwards proper, brandishing in her dexter hand a sword azure, hilted and pommelled gules, and holding in her sinister hand a palm sapling vert, and in an escrol over the same this. *Supporters:* Two greyhounds proper, collared gules and leashed or. *Motto:* "Meane weil, speak weil, and doe weil."

Lyon Register, I, 225; XL111, 44.

Note.—The foregoing arms of chiefs are illustrated for information and identification, like those of peers and baronets, in the annual reference books. They indicate the authority or identity of the respective chiefs, and may not be misappropriated or used for other purposes, or displayed by traders or others, except with the appropriate wording " By Authority of," " Under patronage of," or " By appointment to " the chief concerned—for which permission should be sought through the Standing Council of Scottish Chiefs, 18 Duke St., Edinburgh.

The following paragraph which appeared in the 2nd and 3rd editions deserves comment :

" The adoption of Coats of Arms by Highland Chiefs was a matter of comparatively late date. The introduction of heraldry to the Highlands did not, as a rule, take place till long after it had become universal amongst the feudal lords of the Lowlands."—(Sir J. Balfour Paul, Lord Lyon-King-at-Arms.)

An examination of Scottish armorial seals, however, shows that this rash statement of Sir James Balfour Paul's is quite unfounded. Indeed heraldry spread across the Highlands just as quickly as it spread over the whole of Europe, and was well established amongst West Coast chiefs by the thirteenth to fourteenth century, as appears from their shields on the old carved stones at Iona and elsewhere and the depicting of heraldic bearings on the surface of old Celtic targes.

T. I. of L. Lyon.

A Chief's Insignia for leading the clan. A Chief's shield, helmet, crest and banner (*bratach*)— *Earl of Crawford* (*Le Lindsay*). Regarding mottoes, see p. 400, and slogans, p. 545.

Notes to Armorial Bearings of Clan Chiefs

IN Scotland the motto is normally *over* the crest, but existing blocks have been used where the only defect is that the motto was drawn *below*. Complete arms—*Suaicheantas* ; Crest—*Cirean*.

BRODIE

The *Crest* of the chief shows : A hand holding *three* arrows.

FARQUHARSON

The 1st and 4th quarters are the patrimonial bearing of MacDuff, borne by Mackintosh and Shaw. The 2nd and 3rd quarters which constitute a difference and are in part the feudal arms of the House of Invercauld, contain the pine tree originally borne *en surtout* of the Mackintosh arms as a mark of cadency, and here " composed " along with the Shaws' hand and dagger and the Royal banner, the bearing of which at Pinkie was obtained for Findlay Mór by the Earl of Huntly, *i.e.* Findlay was Deputy Royal Bannerman.

FERGUSON OR FERGUSSON

The heraldic description of the Armorial Bearings of :
FERGUSSON OF KILKERRAN in Ayrshire is :—*Arms :* Azure, a buckle argent between three boars' heads couped or, with the badge of knight-baronet in the dexter chief canton. *Crest :* A bee upon a thistle proper. *Motto :* " Ut prosim aliis " (That I may profit others). *Supporters :* two griffins proper, armed and beaked gules.

Of the Argyll Fergussons the arms recorded by the Chief of Clannfhearghuis of Stra-chur are :

Azure, a buckle or, traversed by a baton fessways argent, all between three boars' heads couped or. *Crest :* issuant from an antique crown or a demi-lion rampant proper, crowned with an antique crown or and grasping in his dexter paw a baton argent. *Motto :* " Clannfhearghuis gu bráth." *Supporters :* Two griffins proper, armed, beaked and winged azure.

INNES

The stars were of five points (see Lindsay of the Mount's Register) until 1672, when they were registered with six. The old form—the five-pointed star—was restored by Lyon decree in 1698, but the 8th Duke of Roxburghe (inadvertently founding on the 1672 registration) reverted to six. The ancient five-point stars, as confirmed by Lord Lyons Sir David Lindsay and Sir Alexander Erskine, are herein illustrated.

MACAULAY

The arms of the chief have not been matriculated.

MACDONALD OF THE ISLES

The earliest knowledge of the arms used by the Lords of the Isles is obtained from the seal of Angus of the Isles, son of Donald, who died about 1292. It shows a galley or lymphad on waves, with four men seated therein. That of Alexander of the Isles, his son, who died about 1300, was a lymphad with two men in it. Donald of the Isles, who succeeded in 1388 and died 1420, has a lymphad surmounted of an eagle, all within the Royal Tressure, the latter to commemorate the marriage of his father, John, with Margaret, daughter of King Robert II.

Alexander of the Isles, who became 10th Earl of Ross in 1429, and died 1449, carried :—Quarterly, 1, A lymphad surmounted of an eagle displayed. 2, Three lions rampant, for Ross. 3, Three garbs, for Cumine of Buchan. 4, On a bend between six crosses couped, three buckles, for Leslie, the whole being within the tressure. Alexander had also another seal which bore : Quarterly, 1 and 4, A lymphad under sail, with one man in it, for the Isles. 2 and 3, Three lions rampant, for Ross. In 1449, John his son had a similar seal, supported by an eagle, whilst in 1471 his arms had been changed to : Quarterly, 1, Three lions. 2, A lymphad under sail. 3, An eagle. 4, A dexter hand issuing from the base, holding a sword in bend sinister, the whole within the tressure. After resigning the Earldom of Ross in 1476, he got a new seal, showing a lymphad surmounted of an eagle displayed, all within the tressure. In the Register of Lord Lyon Sir David Lindsay of the Mount, 1542, the arms of the Lords of the Isles are given as : Or, an eagle displayed gules, surmounted of a lymphad sable—but in Lord Lyon Sir Robert Forman's Register, 1566, there also appears in the dexter canton a sinister hand appaumé gules.

Lord Lyon Sir F. J. Grant, K.C.V.O.

MACDONELL OF KEPPOCH

The Keppoch MacDonalds are stated to have improperly used the arms of Lord MacDonald. The shield here reproduced is from the quartering for Keppoch matriculated in the arms of John Michie in 1761.

MACDUFF

The Armorial Bearings here given are those of the Duke of Fife. The line of the MacDuffs, ancient Earls of Fife, has been for long extinct. In Nisbet's *System of Heraldry* the following passage occurs, viz. : " Sir George MacKenzie, in his *Science of Heraldry*, gives the equestrian side of the seal of MacDuff, Earl of Fife, where he is in armour on horseback, holding in his right hand a sword, and on his left arm his shield of arms, and upon his head his helmet *affronté* and *grillé a capeleine*, with a long tail hanging over his back." Wemyss of Wemyss was held by Lyon Court to represent the Earls of Fife.

MACFARLANE

The arms depicted are those confirmed to the chief in the days of Charles I by Lord Lyon Sir James Balfour of Denmiln. Subsequently, about 1750, Walter Macfarlane of that Ilk, the celebrated antiquary, obtained a resettlement of the armorial achievement in favour of himself and his " heirs " (*i.e.* legally " heirs-female ") and at this time the bows were replaced by broadswords brandished aloft. The entry in the Register is somewhat faded at the point where the edge of the saltire is defined, so that it is not possible to state definitely whether this is waved or engrailed. The former is the more distinctive, as many other families bear saltires engrailed.

MACGILLIVRAY

The arms shown are those recorded by a near kinsman of the chief, and are evidently the galley-coat of Clan Chattan, with the addition of a bordure and of a chief charged, in the centre, with the Calder stag's head. This indicates a sort of very qualified acknowledgement of the traditional descent from the younger son of Parson Muriach. Quite a different form of quarterly arms appear on the stones in the Dunmaglass family burial-ground. Yet a third variety of arms has (on no ascertained use or authority) been attributed to MacGillivray : per pale argent and azure, a hand fessways grasping a dagger proper and a cross-crosslet fitcheé arg. in chief. Dr. Angus MacGillivray, a claimant to chiefship, and whose descent is deduced from the Tacksman of Lagg of Dunmaglass, has recorded (not in the character of chief) another coat (*Lyon Register*, XXII, 32.)

MACGREGOR

The Arms of MacGregor originally displayed the open crown in centre chief—as in Forman's Lyon Office Register (Workman MSS.), where the title is recorded " The Laird of MacGregor of auld."

MACINNES

Two members of this clan have matriculated arms. The shield depicted in former editions appears to have been used by the Speyside McInneses (a branch of the Morayshire *Innes* clan). The Rev. John MacInnes, of *Clan Aonghais* had a seal bearing, quarterly, 1, A castle of two towers. 2 and 3, On the sea in base undy a lymphad, sails furled and flag at prow. 4, Gyronny of eight. *Crest :* A boar's head erased. *Motto :* " Irid Ghipt Dhe agus an Righ " (Ask gifts of God and the King). Details of this are preserved in the Lyon Court records of unauthorised arms. They are consistent with the clan history. They were latterly used without registration (so unlawfully) by Macinnes of Rickerby.

MACKAY

The chief has now matriculated arms as Lord Reay in terms of the statute. Indeed, lawful use of the arms is a condition attached to succession to the peerage. The supporters in the early seventeenth century were dexter, a pikeman fully armed with a *shouldered* musket, but in a manuscript in the Court of the Lord Lyon the musket has its butt on the ground. The older arms, as indicated by carvings on the House of Tongue, seem to have been different and contained stars azure, on argent, along with a hand apparent—the *Bratach Ban*, which still appear on The Chief's pinsel.

MACKINTOSH

The fourth quarter, displaying the lymphad upon the golden field, is the arms borne for, and represented as, those of the " Heretrix of Clan Chattan." Accordingly the arms of Macpherson and MacGillivray show this parted with azure, a major difference of the first variety (see Stevenson, *Heraldry in Scotland*, p. 286).

MACLEAN

The Ardgour MS., which was written about 1765, gives the following description of the Duart Arms, viz. : " First Quarter, Or, a lion rampant gules. Second, Azure, a castle triple-towered argent. Third, Argent, a lymphad with her sails furled up and her oars in action sable. Fourth, A salmon naiant proper and two eagles' heads gules. The whole is *Supported* by Two ostriches with a horseshoe in each of their bills. Underneath are written the words, ' Virtus durissima terit.' The *Crest* is A battle-axe standing upright upon an open helmet, with a laurel and a cypress branch proper tied saltirewise by a ribbon gules about the axe. The *Motto* is ' Altera merces.' "

The DUART *Supporters*, before the chiefship became merged in BROLAS, were Two seals. The *Ancient Motto* of the Macleans was " I am redie." The *Supporters* of the most ancient Armorial Bearings were Two salmon.

The arms shown are, however, those last matriculated in Lyon Register and consequently are the only authorised version.

LOGAN (MACLENNAN)

It is not known whether " George Logan of that Ilk " in whose name these arms were registered was chief of the Highland or Lowland (Restalrig) family. It is unlikely that the *Lobbans* were of either race.

MATHESON

The arms of the Highland Mathesons as confirmed to Achany and others are basically Gyronny of eight, Gules and Sable, a lion rampant Or ; the arms of MacMaken, recorded as Argent, three dexter hands couped erect Gules, in Sir David Lindsay of the Mount's Armorial Register, 1542, have been erroneously supposed to be Matheson arms, but they clearly pertain to south-west Scotland and are analogous to those of Adair and MacMicking.

MURRAY OF TULLIBARDINE

The Tullibardine Arms are now merged in those of the Duke of Atholl, whose second quartering is Azure, three mullets argent within a double tressure flory-counter-flory or, *for Murray of Tullibardine*. According to

Nisbet, and earlier writers whom he cites (*System of Heraldry*, I, p. 253), the blue and silver shield, with its stars, was derived " from the Picts," who painted their bodies in blue, with star-like and other signs, " by which they were distinguished in Kindreds and Clans." Certainly the Banner of Caledonia was azure, the St. Andrew's cross argent, and blue is noticeable in the original arms of the north-eastern mormaerships— Mar, Buchan, and Moray ; so there may be a substratum of truth in the antiquity of the livery colours of the Murray coat ; and the stars must have been a very ancient local cognisance, as they are borne by most other old Morayshire families, which, since they are also borne by the Murrays of the south, would take the device back to almost pre-heraldic times. Indeed, mullets do appear in pre-historic Morayshire cave carvings.

STEWART, ROYAL

Just as the Royal (Stewart) tartan is that of the Scottish Royal line, so the appropriate arms are here not those of the House of Stuart but the Scottish Royal Arms—the tressured lion rampant, with its unicorn supporters. These are borne by the King of Scots, as sovereign, and whilst they have, since the Union of the Crowns (1603), been borne quartered with the Royal Arms of England and Ireland, His Majesty still uses the old Scottish Royal achievement, as for his Lord High Commissioner, and flies the old Lion Banner above the Palace of Holyroodhouse.

STEWART OF GALLOWAY (Earl of Galloway)

Before ascending the throne the Stewarts carried as their armorial sign : Or, a fess chequy of three tracts azure and argent ; and their oldest *Motto* seems to have been " Virescit " (He flourishes). The whole is still the basis of the arms of the Stewarts of Galloway, who appear to be the oldest cadets of the Royal Stewarts, and by failure of the direct line of the House of Stewart the Earl of Galloway is, perhaps, now chief of the clan, but the heirship has not been judicially established.

SUTHERLAND

The undifferenced arms of the Sutherlands, Earls of Sutherland, descended through Elizabeth, the Countess in her own right, to the heirs of line, of whom William, 16th Earl, was duly recorded in the Clan Memorial of 1745 as chief of the clan. Sutherland of Forse, the heir male, was given by Lyon the arms differenced by the bordure or, usually assigned to the premier cadet. In 1716 the 16th Earl of Sutherland received by Royal Warrant the addition of the Royal Tressure. But the Ducal line took to bearing only the surname " Sutherland-Levison-Gower," and in 1928 the Misses Sutherland of Forse obtained a " joint matriculation " of the chief arms. This form of matriculation is inapt, (1941, s.c.) and the present Countess-Heretrix of Sutherland has (1964) been rematriculated the arms and supporters as Countess Chief of the Name.

Flags and Banners

THE ensign has always been an important instrument of command, and figures much in Celtic, as in other medieval literature. Flags are " ensigns armorial," and fall within the Laws of Arms.

BANNER.—This is a square or rectangular flag. Its whole surface is covered by the shield-device of its owner, whose personal flag it is. The best known " banners " are the quartered " Royal Ensign " of H.M. the King and his tressured lion rampant banner of the King of Scots. Most chiefs and chieftains use banners, both as their house-flag and on a pole at Gatherings, where the banner is set near the chief's pavilion or *lonquard*.

STANDARD.—This is a long, narrow flag with St. Andrew's cross next the pole. The remainder of the flag is parted of the livery colours of the chief or chieftain, and upon it is depicted his crest or badge, and his motto or slogan on bands. Sometimes the chief's arms are placed next the pole instead of the national cross. The standard is the rallying flag of the " following." The ancient forms of banner and standard should be carefully adhered to, as they alone combine utility with the simple beauty of ancient heraldry.

Another form of what we might, perhaps, call a " square-standard," the *Ensynzie* developed during the seventeenth century after the carrying of the real heraldic banner became less usual. These later " standards " are rectangular flags with the full heraldic achievement of the chief or chieftain depicted on them. They have been largely used by chiefs in connection with their " private armies," *e.g.* The Invercauld Highlanders, Lonach Highlanders, and so forth. They were the form used by the Highland regiments in " the '45," partly, perhaps, since in many cases the chief was (discreetly) not present in person, so his banner was not displayed, though a " standard " was sent forth with the " Commander of the Clan." The other ground for the popularity of these flags was that they provided an opportunity to depict the coveted distinction of supporters when these existed. A celebrated example of this *sort* of flag is the dubious " Green Banner of Cluny-Macpherson "—actually one of these square-standards.

PINSEL.—A triangular flag, 4 ft. by 2 ft. 6 ins., bearing a golden circlet, emblazoned with the Chief's " Style and Title " as recorded in Lyon Register. It is displayed by the Chief's Officer-in-Command on occasions when the Chief is not present. Within the circlet appears the Chief's " strap and buckle " badge, which is worn by all " his clan," not as " theirs," but as showing that *they* are *his* clan and following. The crest is legally an armorial bearing and the property of the Chief or Chieftain.

PIPE-BANNERS.—These, like other banners, should display the shield-device over their *whole* surface. They should *not* include the crest and supporters. The older examples are of the form above mentioned. Crests, coronets, and supporters are only found in the eighteenth century. The pipe-banners of the Royal Company of Archers, and those recently presented by H.R.H. the Princess Royal to the Scottish Signals are of the ancient form here recommended ; but it is the later form which appears on such pipe-banners as those of the Chief of Clan Grant, in the celebrated picture of his piper. This form (really an " ensygnie ") including

S*

crest and supporters, has become popular, since, as already mentioned, that it enables supporters—where they exist—to be shown. Each of the Highland regiments has its own custom as to which part of the achievement is depicted. In the Gordon Highlanders and K.O.S.B. the full achievement, with supporters if any, is shown. Much discussion has arisen over " what to do " if an officer has no arms, and the matriculation fee is a consideration. If he *can* matriculate, of course, he should ; but the fees on a patent are a considerable expense for many young subalterns —though, of course, not excessive when one recollects they are a patent of hereditary nobility. In the light of examination (pp. 420, 488) it may seem that the " non-armigerous officer " (who, of course, may be an " Honourable " for all that, as a peer's arms only descend to his heir), who is entitled to them with the label (and such achievements are depicted on pipe-banners, *e.g.* that of Burnett of Leys, younger, in K.O.S.B.), might place his chief's or *ceann-tighe's* crest, *within the belt and buckle*, on it, with *cirean ceann cinnidh*. In no circumstances should this be allowed where he *has*, either substantively or as heir apparent or presumptive, a right to arms of his own, otherwise the whole historical and practical point of these banners would be lost. Many lairds and chieftains use their regimental pipe-banners at home after retirement. For this purpose the " regimental " side, with the regimental crest, may, and technically should, be covered over with silk of tartan or the family ' colours," and the badge (if any), whilst the armorial achievement of the owner remains on the other side. I purposely advise " covering up," because the old banner may serve again in case of a future generation serving in the old regiment—a matter of pride and interest. Pipe-banners are used only for chiefs, chieftains and lairds, and in the army for company officers.

A modern idea that regimental pipe-banners were only used indoors is not historically correct. Old accounts and pictures show them being used, like other flags, outside. No doubt an expensive or treasured one *would* only be used indoors ; but at a clan gathering, on a fine day, the chiefs' and chieftains' pipe-banners should certainly be borne outside as well as in. At the castle of the chief of a clan there were, in the morning on the terrace, and in the hall during and after dinner, *three* pipers, whilst in the castles of chieftain—barons there were two, and for ordinary lairds, one. At clan gatherings the three might appear when the chief himself, or herself, is actually present.

USE OF FLAGS.—At gatherings, as above indicated, the chief or chieftain's banner is displayed near his tent, and likewise, where he has one, his standard. When both are available, the banner should technically be hoisted *when* he comes on the field, and *should* be greeted by a horn-fanfare, followed by the chief's salute or march on the pipes. This banner will be struck in the afternoon, when the chief leaves the field.

On the great flagstaff will be flown St. Andrew's Cross—the Scottish national flag ; but if it be a gathering at which the Lord-Lieutenant, Vice-Lieutenant, or a Deputy-Lieutenant directed to represent the Lord-Lieutenant, or (in, so to say, his official capacity, one of the six Great Officers who are *virtute officii* the King's Lieutenants) is to be present ; *then,* on the arrival of H.M. Lieutenant, St. Andrew's Cross is lowered ; and the tressured lion rampant hoisted instead. This should be greeted with a fanfare of trumpets followed by a pibroch, as was the daily practice in the army of the Marquis of Montrose (it was this ceremony which first told the Clan Campbell that Montrose, King Charles's Lieutenant, had crossed the mountains and descended upon Inverlochy), and the other Lieutenants of His Majesty, in the sixteenth and seventeenth centuries (Innes of Learney, *Scots Heraldry*, p. 157 ; J. Buchan, *Montrose*, p. 225).

Whilst the Royal Banners—be it the tressured lion rampant, or the quartered Royal Ensign—must be flown only by those with authority, and in befitting manner, and with befitting ceremony, it is historically impossible to substantiate the theory so stressed in the first quarter of the present century, that the Royal Banner may never be seen except " in the personal presence of the Sovereign "—a principle which, had it been applied in the Middle Ages, would have meant that nobody would have recognised the Royal Banner when it was flown ; and which in the present age has indeed tended to involve the public generally seeing these flags only as cheap decoration. In olden days, when the theory of Lieutenancy was fully understood by everyone, the Royal Lieutenants or Deputy-Lieutenants on occasion, *had* to " display the King's Banner," but only did so in their official capacity, and with the utmost solemnity and Royal Salute—thereby keeping the lieges in mind of their *Ard-righ*, and the authority of his Lieutenancy.

> And haughtily the trumpets peal and gaily dance the bells
> As slow upon the labouring wind the royal blazon swells.

What requires to be emphasised is that the Royal Banners are displayed only with due ceremony on behalf of the sovereign, and when he is personally present or represented. Use of the quartered Royal Ensign is now governed by special provisions. The tressured Lion Rampant, the Royal Banner of Scotland, is still governed by the ancient and relevant provisions of the Scottish Law of Arms.

Use of the Chief's Banner is governed by similar principles. It is displayed when the Chief is present, or when he has commissioned someone to " hold his place " and display his banner—a high responsibility, to be given only by the Chief's written order to a *specific person* for a *specific occasion*.

These Ensigns-Armorial are the legal machinery whereby the Clan is kept together, and whereby the Chief exercised his functions in Warfare or Peaceful Ceremonial. Where their registration or manufacture according to the official blazon involves expense, it is the privilege of the Clan to defray the costs either directly or as at present, just as of old the Chief's state was maintained by *calps, cuiddiche* and *conveth*. There is no reflection in accepting such aid, acceptance of which is officially held proper (*Lyon Reg.* XXXVII, 147). Indeed, it is the Chief's duty to accept it and perform his functions conscientiously. In days of present taxation no chief could maintain the state of a clan without such, any more than a sovereign could, from his personal means, maintain the state of a great kingdom. A clan, like a kingdom, wants its dignity maintained, and its chief provided with everything requisite to the function of hereditarily representing the clan with dignity.

XVI

Notes on the Plates of Clan Tartans

THE plates in Scottish books of tartans have hitherto been intended to give the ordinary reader an " impression " of the tartan as woven material. If the results are " often obscure or inaccurate or misleading," [1] that is partly due to some seventeen or twenty Scottish tartan-weaving firms mostly producing different settings of what is claimed to be the same tartan, which, from one end of the gamut to the other, often varies considerably.

In *Setts of the Scottish Tartans* (Oliver & Boyd, 1950) Donald C. Stewart produced a noteworthy book showing setts of 260 tartans on the " ribband " or " pattern-stick " system, which (as a pictorial medium), along with the $\frac{1}{8}$-inch colour-schemes used by Logan, is the only scientific means of defining and recording setts. Valuable though this book is, its present edition can only be tentative. A number of authentic tartans are not included, and also the bases of a number of the setts shown will not stand scrutiny.

It bears to be based primarily upon (*a*) the published tartan books of Logan, Smibert, Smith, Grant, and D. W. Stewart, and admitting a naturally qualified concession to some *Vestiarium* products, (*b*) the products of tartan-weavers.

Mr. Stewart inferentially [2] seems to place more emphasis on *what the weaver sold*, than what the chiefs preserved in their portraits and private collections, for which he seems to apologise, as these were " less accessible."

We are concerned with " clan/family " tartans, not " trade checks " ; and the distinction could hardly be clearer than in the recent so-called " clan " tartans recently marketed as " Prince Charles " and " Princess Margaret," which, on inquiry from the Lord Chamberlain, Lyon Office learnt had no authority or connection with these personages. [3] I am unable to endorse Mr. Stewart's proposition that *what the weaver sells* can be held " to occupy the position that would in earlier times have been held by unwritten and undated tradition." [4]

---

[1] D. C. Stewart, *Setts of the Scottish Tartans*, p. 122.
[2] *Ibid.*, pp. 6, 22, 120.
[3] If they had, the public would have had no business to use them !
[4] D. C. Stewart, *Setts of the Scottish Tartans*, p. 38

To be a " clan tartan " the sett must have the sanction of the chief, who is the " representative " of the clan and of its founder. No doubt the " dealers in tartan have allowed the public to assume that the patterns they offer represent the traditions of an unbroken succession of craftsmen dating back to a misty period," [1] but, as Stewart himself aptly says (at p. 21), " an error does not become less erroneous as it becomes more widely held," and his most valuable book, in its (I am sure) first edition, just discloses the extent of the confusion and the need for (a) checking by private portraits and collections, (b) obtaining, through reference to the chiefs, some definition and certainty, if not about what this or that clan tartan *was*, at any rate about what it *is to be*.

That has already commenced in various cases before Lyon Court, where, after evidence, remits to the Tartan Committee of the Scottish Woollen Manufacturers' Association, and to the chiefs concerned, " findings in fact " are pronounced, and the " proper " sett (blazoned on the Logan/Stewart system) is recorded in the relative armorial blazon in the *Public Register of All Arms and Bearings*.

A tartan so ascertained, determined, and recorded *is* a " clan/family " tartan of a defined sett. The *legal* effect is that if a merchant thereafter " palms off " on a customer, who asks for " *the* proper Clan X tartan," some *other* sett, then the merchant is responsible to the customer, and liable for deliberately selling him the wrong thing.

Maybe the opinions of the chiefs are " not a safe foundation on which to build claims to ancient usage," [2] but a tartan is not necessarily " right " just because it is supposedly " old " (which is scientifically just snobbery) ; the opinion of a chief, except when he is held to have been trying to build a theory out of a tendencious tartan-claim (as Lyon held, Lyon Reg. XXXVI, p. 7 process, in the case of certain of the Clanranalds), is in general the appropriate foundation for a genuine *clan* tartan.

The following notes explain the sources from which a number of the tartans have been derived and the evidences of antiquity of others. Family records of the chiefs, and plaids in the possession of chiefly families, are of course the best authorities when these exist. It is noticeable that many of the " hunting setts " are modern. They appear to have been adopted after aniline dyes had rendered the old clan setts in fiercer colours than the old vegetable dyes of the Highlands.

BRODIE

The dress sett appears in Allan Ramsay's portrait of James Brodie of Brodie (1744–1824) as a young man about 1770, and indicates this tartan as one of those worn shortly before the repeal of the Proscription Act.

[1] D. C. Stewart, *Setts of the Scottish Tartans*, p. 37.
[2] *Ibid.*, p. 120.

BUCHANAN

The sett shown is that worn by the Clan Buchanan. The *Vestiarium Scoticum* reproduces a sett showing maroon checks on a buff ground, with a black stripe running through the sett. This differs essentially from the bright tartan accepted by the principal authorities as the Buchanan one.

CAMERON, CLAN

The sett shown is that as recorded in Lyon Register, after evidence from Lochiel, in connection with the Dunedin, New Zealand, coat of arms.

CAMERON OF ERRACHT

When the 79th Highlanders (now 1st Battalion Cameron Highlanders) were raised in 1793 by Sir Alan Cameron of Erracht, it was by him designed to be a *Clan Cameron* unit. The tartan selected appears to have been an old Lochaber sett based perhaps on the MacDonald lordship of Lochaber, but elaborated by the colonel perhaps with assistance from Lady Erracht his mother as what they believed to be an old Cameron sett and which probably was an ancient district tartan.

Captain Taylor in *The 79th Magazine* ("News"), September 1954.

Examination shows the modern story about a combination of Cameron's and MacDonald's of Keppoch is untenable, and Sir Alan's mother, Lady Erracht, was, it transpires, not a MacDonald.

This sett has been the tartan of the 79th since its embodiment.

The Erracht tartan is also worn as a hunting sett by the Camerons of Lochiel. It is not illustrated in this book.

CAMERON OF LOCHIEL

There is some confusion with regard to the correct sett of this tartan. The late Lochiel, however, supplied the pattern of the sett which is here reproduced.

CAMPBELL OF ARGYLL

It has been said that the Campbells of Argyll have attempted to appropriate as theirs the " Black Watch " sett of tartan. Frank Adam, who evidently did not like the Campbells, therefore " deemed it right to bring these facts to the notice of his readers " :

(1) Appendix No. XXI shows the authority of Logan that the sett reproduced in Plate No. 7 of this book (with a yellow and a white stripe), is the correct sett of the Argyll Campbell tartan. Logan adds : " This is worn by the Duke of Argyll and the Campbells of Lochow (*i.e.*, the 6th or 7th Duke) "

(2) The author (Adam) acquired a book on clan tartans, published in 1850 by William & Andrew Smith, Mauchline, saying :

The oldest specimen of the Campbell (Argyll) Tartan we could fall in with is nearly the 42nd, with the addition of a stripe of white and yellow alternately ; but we have the authority of his Grace the Duke of Argyll for the specimen here given as the " Argyll Campbell Tartan." It will be observed that the Duke excludes the yellow stripe.

(3) Adam says that he ascertained from an unimpeachable source that a former Duke of Argyll requested the late Lockhart Bogle to visit Inveraray Castle to paint out from some of the ancestral portraits there the yellow and the white stripes on some of the Campbell kilts. Bogle declined to oblige the Duke in this, pointing out that he did not feel justified in tampering with what he considered historical records.

Mr. Adam was faced, therefore, with the following facts : (a) A well-known old firm of manufacturers stating, in 1850, that the oldest sett of Argyll Campbell tartan which they could procure was one which had a white and a yellow stripe alternately. (b) The then Duke of Argyll desired to eliminate the yellow stripe, leaving, however, the white one. (c) A later Duke sought to eliminate both the yellow and the white stripe ; (d) Finally the Clan Campbell of Argyll sought to go a step further, and appropriate the " Black Watch " sett as their own ! (F.A.)

The modern obsession of Campbells to claim that the more or less universal " Government tartan " (now shown to be a dark-based derivative of the " Royal tartan ") is that of Clan Campbell, is a ridiculous phase on which common sense will presumably, in due course, supervene. No one can seriously subscribe to this " nationalisation of the Campbells," which would defeat the very purpose of distinction which tartans have come to serve, and would mean that there is no *Campbell* tartan at all.

There is evidence, however, that there was also a *red* Campbell tartan (*Scots Magazine*, XVI., p. 140), and the existence of this at the commencement of the nineteenth century is referred to by Miss Grant of Rothiemurchus (*Memoirs of a Highland Lady*, p. 259). Examples of this might be these which appear in the Campbell portraits at Loudon Castle, and those formerly at Langton. (*Old and Rare Scottish Tartans*, Plate IV., text.) (T.I. of L.)

CAMPBELL OF BREADALBANE

The tartan here shown is one which, it appears, was, prior to 1820, known simply as " Breadalbane," and differs somewhat from what was then the actual " Campbell of Breadalbane " sett.

CHISHOLM

Mrs. Chisholm, Erchless Castle, supplied the sett here reproduced.

It is usual to have a darker tone of red and green for day wear, the brighter sett being used for full dress.

CLAN CHATTAN

This tartan, recently called " Mackintosh Chief," but also labelled alternatively " Clan Chattan " in the Moy Hall collection, has been held by Lyon Court to be the Clan Chattan tartan, and recorded as such. It was worn, as Chief of Clan Chattan, by The Mackintosh, and is applicable to all tribes of that clan which have no tartan of their own, and for wear along with their own by those who have. The " Macpherson Chief " sett (Stewart, *Setts*, 174), noticeably similar, confirms the common origin and purpose, and that, in a general sense, this tartan was applicable to " the hail kin " of Clan Chattan as such.

CLERGY

Till the eighteenth century the Highland clergy not only wore the kilt and tartan but also carried arms (as members of the church militant). The sett is that which distinguished the Highland minister.

DRUMMOND

This is the ancient and approved sett, recorded by Logan. A portrait alleged to be " Lord John Drummond," and to show its subject in the Grant tartan, is a suggested reason for the " Willoughy " Drummonds and modern weavers attributing to Drummonds the Clan Grant tartan. If the portrait *is* " Lord John," the error probably arose from a plaid connected with his mother, Lady Perth, being widow of a nephew of Lady Lilias Murray, wife of John Grant of Grant. Even if such an error was perpetrated (at Rome) in 1739, for any Drummond to continue wearing Grant tartan instead of his own ancient sett is merely absurd, since the purpose of tartans is distinction.

FERGUSSON

The sett here reproduced is generally acknowledged to be the real clan one. It is worn by Atholl and Aberdeenshire families. There is, however, a sett *without the white stripe*, which was worn by Fergusons of Balquhidder district—sett supplied by Jas. Ferguson of Kinmundy and Rev. R. Menzies Ferguson, Bridge-of-Allan.

42ND OR BLACK WATCH

This has been shown (I think quite credibly) by D. C. Stewart (*Setts &c.*, p. 27), to be a dark sett based of the " Royal " (so-called Royal Stewart) tartan, which explains its wide use and description as the " Government tartan." It was accordingly, as a dark version of the Royal tartan, not only suitable, but the obviously appropriate tartan for Government companies, raised and tartaned in 1725, as is now shown to have occurred. (p. 444)

During the period of the Proscription, it seems to have been tolerated where clan tartans were repressed, and both from connection with the regiment and as supporters of the Hanoverian regime, came to be then worn by a number of anti-Jacobite clans instead of their own former tartans. So Sutherlands, Munros, Grants, and Campbells, amongst others, were found wearing it, and latterly started either the theory that it is "their hunting tartan," or (see above) the claim by Campbells that it is "*the* Campbell tartan," all of which is incompatible with the evidence.

FORBES

The tartan shown (which differs from Lamont only in the black stripes on either side of the white) is stated to have been designed by Miss Forbes of Pitsligo in 1822, apparently to emulate the new 42nd-based Gordon sett. Logan (*see* p. 591) records a similar white-bordered-by-black check on a simpler blue and black base, which was evidently the old Forbes sett, and seems to appear in the portrait of John Forbes of Ballabeg, *ante* 1770, and does, in that of his daughter-in-law (1808), at Newe. It may be styled *Forbes-Ancient* (Stewart, *Setts*, 59).

GORDON

This is the famous sett worn by the Gordon Highlanders, which was apparently prepared for the Duke of Gordon by Forsyth of Huntly at the time the 92nd was raised in 1794. It has, however, an earlier history. The old Gordon tartan, seen in the portrait, *c.* 1700, of Rachel Gordon of Abergeldie, is a brilliant sett. That of William Gordon of Fyvie, 1771, at Fyvie Castle, is somewhat similar, but with broad green stripes *edged with yellow lines*. It is evidently from this that the green with yellow line (in some early patterns, three lines) was incorporated in the Black Watch base for regimental use, and in due course became the ordinary "Gordon tartan." The brilliant Huntly sett was not a clan tartan, but a district one worn by many adherents of the powerful Marquess of Huntly.

GRANT

The Grant tartan is officially registed in Lyon Court and seems the ultimate version of the sett specified in the Laird of Grant's Baron Courts (see p. 124) about 1700. By about 1715 his own clan officers were habited in what may be regarded as the specified tartan, though the chieftains in the Castle Grant portraits were then still wearing various other setts, and some the simpler "barred plaids."

INNES

The sett shown is attributed by Smibert (the first author to repro-duce it) to the Morayshire Clan Innes, by branches of which it has been worn from the early nineteenth century. They wore Highland dress (doubtless plaid and trews) in the seventeenth and eighteenth centuries. It is invariably, by all authors, related to the starred Innes coat of arms and crests. This tartan is dominantly black and red ; another sett dominantly red and green (Stewart, *Setts*, 79, not generally worn) related to a small family around Auchorachan on lower Speyside, who bore badge as a branch of Innes of Blairton (see p. 309), and were held by Lord Lyon Balfour Paul to be an off-shoot from the Morayshire Inneses.

For a hunting sett the red is changed to brown, but Lord Charles' kilt (portrait *c.* 1850 at Floors) is app. 1 az. 6 blk. 1 az. 7 gr. 1 blk. 7 gr., and corresponds with a miniature of Georgina Innes at Edingight.

LENNOX

This tartan is seen on the cloak of the Countess of Lennox, mother of Henry, Lord Darnley, probably *the* earliest painting of a lady in Highland dress. This sett has sometimes been called a " Lennox-district tartan," the Earls of Lennox being then Stewarts. But looking to the association of " clan " with " locality," we may surmise that this was the ancient tartan of the Celtic earls and tribe of The Lennox. A comparison with that of Macfarlane bears this out, for in the centre of the Macfarlane sett are the green and white lines (on a much narrower scale) which form the pattern of the Lennox tartan ; whereof Macfarlane and Kincaid appear " differenced " versions.

LINDSAY

The sett here reproduced is a modern one.

LOGAN OR MACLENNAN

The Logans or Maclennans of Ross-shire are not to be confounded with the Lowland Logans. Macintyre North, in *Book of the Club of the True Highlanders*, says : " The Logan and Maclennan clans are of one descent, and there is no distinction in the tartans, save that the latter prefer it of a broad pattern."

MACAULAY

The sett given is that of the MacAulays of Ardencaple, Dunbarton-shire. Other MacAulays, dependents of the MacLeods of Lewis, wear the MacLeod tartan. The hunting sett is modern.

MACDONELL OF KEPPOCH

The sett illustrated is stated to have been copied from a plaid given by Keppoch to Prince Charlie. There is, however, another sett for which the same claim is made.

MACDOUGALL

Authorities do not agree regarding the correct sett of this clan's tartan. For the sett which is here reproduced Mr. Adam was indebted to MacDougall of that Ilk, and the chief's authority falls to be accepted.

DUFF (MACDUFF)

The hunting sett is a modern one, and the " dress " sett cannot be regarded as very ancient, since by the mid-eighteenth century Wemyss was held representer of Macduff. These tartans were probably produced under the ægis of the Duff family, and are properly *Duff* tartans.

MACGREGOR

MacIan, in *Costumes of the Clans*, says : " The Glengyle branch of the Macgregors wears a peculiar old sett."

There is a well-known sett (black and red checks) called the Rob Roy tartan. It is supposed that this was worn by that well-known MacGregor chieftain as well as by the members of his clan, during the period when the tartan, and, in fact, everything connected with the Clan Gregor, were proscribed. Rob Roy died in 1734.

MACINNES

The sett here shown is the only proper *Clan Aonghais* (Macinnes) tartan, and was produced by John Macinnes of Onich. According to the Macinnes of Rickerby history, they previously wore Campbell tartan, which is consistent with the gyronnated arms used, and with their traditional antecedents.

MACINTYRE

The sett reproduced here is generally recognised as the correct one. There is another sett (alternate green and blue checks on a scarlet ground) which is sometimes reproduced as the Clan Macintyre one. That sett, however, would appear to be, not a clan but a district one, and to have belonged to the Glenorchy district, which was the habitat of the Macintyres.

MACKENZIE

This is the sett worn by the Seaforth Highlanders (72nd and 78th Regiments) and by the Highland Light Infantry (71st and 74th Regiments). The portrait of the Earl of Seaforth at Brahan Castle could, from the bit of plaid shown, give the detail of *one* " old " Mackenzie sett.

MACKINNON

The hunting sett is a modern one.

MACKINTOSH

The sett reproduced is now officially registered. There have, however, been many variations of the Mackintosh setts, perhaps due to the large number of septs which are embraced in the Clan Chattan. Among other Clan Chattan setts is that of Shaw.

MACLACHLAN

The chief's sett is in the *Vestiarium*, but is also used by the chiefs. The clan sett shown is regarded as modern ; the older and brighter one is illustrated in D. W. Stewart, *Old and Rare Scottish Tartans*.

MACLAINE OF LOCHBUIE

The hunting sett (for which Mr Adam was indebted to the courtesy of the late Lochbuie) is a modern one, not illustrated here.

MACLEAN

The hunting sett is the celebrated, and ancient one, described in the young Laird of Maclean's charter of Nerrabolsadh, 19th March 1578–1579, and described in the old Gaelic song :

> Bhu mhian leam am breacan tlath
> Breacan uain' 'us dubh 'us geal ;
> Datha sar Mhich—Ghillian am flath—
> Sud an laoch a fhuair mo ghaol.

> Dear to me is the tartan plaid,
> The plaid of *green and black and white* ;
> The colours of the lordly Maclean,
> The hero of my love.

The sufficiency of the evidence is, however, still questioned.

MACLEOD

There have been many attempts to put forward the MacKenzie sett as a MacLeod one. The origin of this misunderstanding is not far to seek. The 73rd (afterwards 71st) Regiment, viz. 1st Battalion Highland Light Infantry, was in 1777 raised by Lord MacLeod, who, as eldest son of the Earl of Cromarty (a MacKenzie) bore his father's second title of Lord MacLeod. It was but natural that the regiment, raised by Lord MacLeod, and first known as MacLeod's Highlanders, should have been clad in the clan tartan of its first colonel. But, as the Cromarties claimed to be chiefs of the Macleods of Lewis, they *may* have perpetuated some element of the Macleods' hunting sett.

MACMILLAN

The hunting sett is of modern origin.

MACNEIL

The red-lined sett worn by the chiefs of Barra illustrated in D. W. Stewart, *Old and Rare Scottish Tartans*, is regarded as the earliest.

MACPHERSON

This clan has been given a multiplicity of tartans, but those of outstanding interest are the white and grey-based setts. Their nature (like the clan tradition handed down by Cluny himself) indicates them of the type which Stewart (*Setts*, p. 95) considers early. The white-based sett is that regarded as the " Macpherson of Cluny " tartan, peculiar to the chief and the House of Cluny (I presume as distinct from the progeny of the two junior " brothers " of Clan Vurich). It is of this tartan that Cluny wrote to the Smiths, " the light one . . . was known as the *Breacan glas* long before John Sobieski was heard of in that country." He adds that the insertion therein of a yellow line (now only in the " dress " sett) *was* " taken from his MS." but, Cluny insists, " the tartan is an old Macpherson." The so-called " hunting sett " now used as the normal Macpherson clan sett is of the type which J. T. Dunbar (McClintock, *Old Highland Dress*, p. 66) considers early. Is *this* not the " Grey plaid of Badenoch " with probably a district " clan-countrie " origin ? The white-based, so-called " dress " Cluny, is evidently in origin an *arisaid*-sett.

The reddish tartan worn by the Laird of Cluny-Macpherson of *circa* 1700 may be Clan Chattan tartan.

MACRAE

The hunting sett is stated to have been worn at Sheriffmuir by one of the clan. The dress sett closely resembles the " Huntly " tartan, but—as at present used—lacks the yellow lines. Other versions of the dress Macrae do show yellow lines placed differently from those in the Huntly sett. The sett *may* bear on the tradition that the Macraes originally came from Moray—as their starry arms denote. One example of their dress sett was labelled " MacRae tartan plaid worn by Prince Charles Edward in 1745."

MAR

The tartan here shown, which Adam states he got as " Skene " from the Duke of Fife (whose ancestors had owned Mar Lodge from the eighteenth century), differs entirely from the other Skene sett (Stewart, *Setts*, 230), which bears a resemblance—as do the arms— to those of Robertson. This is consistent with the genealogical tradition of the *Clan Donnachaidh-Mhairr*. This name suggests the possibility of confusion in relation to the tartan here shown, which is very different, may well be a " Mar " tartan completely unrelated to the Skene/Donnachie tribe, and as a local sett could have come under the Duff notice at their " Mar estate " (as it was called). The matter deserves further investigation.

MENZIES

The Red and White tartan seems related to the chief's arms, and is the sett commented on as so outstanding at Queen Victoria's visit to Strath Tay in 1842.

MORRISON

The sett which is reproduced is a modern one. The groundwork of the sett appears to be the Mackay sett, with a red stripe running through it.

MUNRO

In addition to the clan dress sett here reproduced, there is another handsome and ancient sett now rarely seen.

MURRAY

It is often maintained that " Murray of Atholl " was originally an Atholl-district sett ; but the Earl of Sutherland's letter, in 1618, to Murray of Pulrossie, requiring him to " remove the red and white lines from the plaids of his men so as to bring their dress into harmony with that of the other septs " (of Clan Sutherland)—see Innes of Learney, *Tartans of the Clans and Families*, p. 9—indicates the possibility that this dark tartan with red (and in the North also white) lines was already, if not a " Murray tartan," anyway a tartan used consciously and with determination by Murrays, as distinct from Sutherlands.

OGILVY

The sett shown has been used, in varying forms, by the Ogilvies from the time of David, 6th Earl of Airlie's marriage to a Drummond in 1812. It appears a compound of earlier Drummond and Ogilvy tartans. The correct, distinctive, and ancient dress Ogilvy sett appears to be (Stewart, *Setts*, 207) seen in the portrait of the Jacobite Lord Ogilvy.

The hunting tartan, often called Ogilvy of Inverquharity, is considered of greater antiquity.

ROBERTSON

In addition to the dress sett here reproduced there is another scarlet one, through which runs a white line. MacIan, in *Costumes of the Clans*, says : " A white stripe has lately been introduced in the tartan, which is hence called the ' New Robertson.' We, of course, reject it." MacIan seems, however, to have been over-hasty. Stewart (*and Old Rare Scottish Tartans*) indicates it was an old variety.

The sett here reproduced as the hunting Robertson is said to have been the special sett of the Kindeace and other Robertsons of the North.

ROSE

The scarlet dress sett appears in but few collections of tartan plates. Mr. Adam was indebted for the pattern of this sett to Colonel Rose of Kilravock, so that it has the chief's authority, and is recorded in Lyon Register.

ROSS

The hunting sett is a modern one, not illustrated here.

SINCLAIR

The hunting sett is, as Stewart indicates, derived from the dress sett. Traditionally it is very old, and related to the green garb worn by the Sinclairs when going south to the Flodden campaign. Both have been recorded in Lyon Court.

SKENE

The sett here shown is the traditional one which is consistent with the arms and traditional descent from Clan Robertson.

STEWART

The Stewart of Appin (later), Stewart of Galloway, Stewart of Atholl, and Stewart of Bute setts are all variants of the " Royal " tartan. An earlier Stewart of Appin sett differs considerably (see D. C. Stewart, Plates 34 and 35). A dark sett, called in old collections " Clan Stewart," and nowadays " Stewart, Ancient " (D. C. Stewart, No. 233 and p. 110), differs completely from the Royal tartan *motif*, and is " unlike any other tartan." This appears to be the *real* Clan Stewart tartan. The " Black Watch," it is now perceived, was the dark setting of the Royal tartan (D. C. Stewart, p. 27), and was the " Government " undress tartan. The other sett, now known as " Hunting Stewart," is not regarded as a " Stewart " tartan at all

(D. C. Stewart, p. 110), and seems to be a differenced and brighter variant of the " Black Watch " motif. It has been used by those who have no tartan of their own, *i.e.* as subjects of the *Ard-Righ Albainn.* It seems really the " National hunting tartan."

The " Royal Stewart " dress tartan is that worn by the pipers of the Scots Guards and members of the Royal Family, and described by H.M. King George V. as " My personal tartan." Historically, it is not a clan tartan at all, but the " Royal tartan," ribbons of which were worn by Charles II. at his coronation. Hence its use even in Hanoverian times. The white-based sett is evidently a lady's " arisaid sett " of the Royal tartan. Is it conceivable that it was really the sett worn by Queen Margaret at the hunting in Atholl in 1529 (Lindsay of Pitscottie's *Chronicles*) ? It was also quite appropriately called " Victoria tartan " during the reign of that great queen, who evidently realised that it was the sett of the *Ban Righ.*

Those who have no clan tartan of their own, or with which they are connected, should wear " Jacobite " tartan, or any of the district setts with which they are associated, *e.g.* Atholl, Strathearn, Dunblane, Lennox, Huntly, etc., and not misappropriate, the Royal or other Stewart setts other than the " Hunting " sett. Englishmen should wear " Childers' Universal " tartan, a nineteenth-century W.O. invention—a converse of the Mackintosh sett.

SUTHERLAND

There are two setts, the ancient one, here reproduced, and that now known as Sutherland. The latter should be styled Argyll and Sutherland Highlanders' regimental sett.

The Sutherland tartan, as such, not being known at the War Office, Mr. Adam concluded that the sett worn by the Argyll and Sutherland Highlanders (91st and 93rd Regiments) is considered by the War Office as a variety of the Black Watch or " Government tartan." Since the Earl of Sutherland took the part of the Government in 1745, and Fencible Regiments were subsequently raised in Sutherland, the use of a version of the Government tartan would easily occur.

The ancient sett (reproduced by both Smibert and Browne as that of the Clan Sutherland) is evidently the correct clan one. This is corroborated by a letter (*Weekly Scotsman*, 16th January 1909), from the widow of John W. Sutherland of Forse : " ' One of the Clan ' was quite correct in his statement that my husband, the late John W. Sutherland of Forse, wore the tartan referred to ' because it was the tartan worn by his ancestors, the ancient Earls of Sutherland.' "

OFFICIALLY AUTHORISED TARTANS

Appendix XXXII gives a list of those tartans which have been ecorded in Lyon Court after consideration of evidence as the distinc-ive and " proper tartans " of the clans concerned.

PART VI

Clan Lists and Statistics

Designations of Highland Clan Chiefs and Chieftains

Am/An styles (though maybe grammatically irregular) are what was actually used along the E.-N.E. " Highland Line "

Highland Designation	English Equivalent
Am Mèinnearach . . .	Menzies of that Ilk.
Am Moireach Mór . . .	The Duke of Atholl (Murray).
An Drumanach Mór . . .	The Earl of Perth (Drummond).
An Gòrdanach *also* . . Coileach an Taobh-tuaith	Chief of Clan Gordon (Marquis of Huntly), *also* " The Cock of the North."
An Granntach	Grant of Grant (Lord Strathspey).
An Greumach Mór . . .	The Duke of Montrose (Graham).
An Siosalach	The Chisholm of Chisholm.
An t-Ailpeanach . . .	MacGregor of MacGregor.
Clann Theàrlach Buidhe . .	Maclean of Dochgarroch.
Clann Fhearghuis Strath-churra .	Fergusson of Strachur.
Mac Pharlain or Mac Pharthaloin	MacFarlane of that Ilk.
Mac' a Phie Cholosaidh . .	Macphee of Colonsay.
Mac-an-Aba	The Macnab.
Mac-ic-Adhamh . . .	Ferguson of Balmacruchie.
Mac Ailein 'ic Ailein . . .	MacDonald of Knoydart.
Mac-an-Lamhaich . . .	Lennie of that Ilk.
Mac-an-Leistear . . .	Fletcher of Achallader.
Mac-Iain Riabhiach . . .	Campbell of Ardkinglass.
Mac-an-Tòisich	The Mackintosh of Mackintosh.
Morair Maghrath . . .	Chief of Clan Mackay.
Mac-Aoidh na Ranna . .	Mackay of Rhinns of Islay.
MacAonghuis an Dùin . .	Campbell of Dunstaffnage (hereditary Captain of Dunstaffnage).
Mac-Cailein-Mór . . .	Campbell (Duke of Argyll).
Mac-Chailein-'ic Dhonnachaidh .	Campbell of Glenorchy (Earl of Breadalbane).
MacAomalan	Bannatyne of that Ilk.
Mac-Coinnich . . . *also* " Caberfeidh " .	Mackenzie of Seaforth and Kintail, (" Deer's antlers ").
MacDhonnachaidh . . .	Campbell of Inverawe.
Mac-Cuaire (or Mac-Ghuaire) .	Macquarrie of Ulva.
Mac-Dhòmnuill Duibh . .	Cameron of Lochiel.
Mac-Dhòmnuill. . . .	The Chief of Clan Donald.
Mac-Dhòmnuill nan Eilean .	MacDonald of the Isles.
Mac-Dhùghaill	MacDougall of MacDougall.
MacDhùghaill Chraignis . .	Campbell of Craignish.
MacFhearghuis Dunfalandaidh .	Fergusson of Dunfallandy.
Mac-Fhionghuin . . .	Mackinnon of Mackinnon.
Mac-Fhionnlaidh . . .	Farquharson of Invercauld.
MacGaradh Mór . . .	Chief of the Hays.
MacGillichattan Mór . . .	Chief of Clan Chattan.

Highland Designation	English Equivalent
Mac-Gill-onaidh . . .	Cameron of Strone.
Mac-Iain	MacDonald of Glencoe.
Mac-Iain-Abrach . . .	Maclean of Coll.
Mac-Iain Aird-nam-murchan .	MacDonald of Ardnamurchan.
Mac-Iain-Duibh . . .	MacAllister of Loup.
Mac-Iain Oig	MacDonald of Glenalladale.
Mac-Iain Stiubhairt na h-Apunn.	Stewart of Appin.
Mac-'ic-Ailein [1] (MacAllan). .	MacDonald of Clanranald.
Mac-'ic-Alasdair . . .	MacDonell of Glengarry.
Mac-'ic-Artair	MacArthur of Tiracladich.
Mac-'ic Dhùgaill (Mhorair) . .	MacDonald of Morar.
Mac-'ic 'Eachuinn-Chinnghearrloch	Maclean of Kingerloch.
Mac-Eoghainn-'ic-Eoghainn .	Cameron of Erracht.
Mac-'ic-Eoghain . . .	Maclean of Lazonby.
Mac-'ic-Iain	MacKenzie of Gairloch.
Mac-'ic-Mhurchaidh . . .	MacKenzie of Achilty.
Mac-'ic-Raonuill . . .	MacDonell of Keppoch.
Mac-'ic-Bhaltair . . .	Stewart of Ardvorlich.
Mac'ill-Eathain . . .	Maclean of Duart.
Mac'ill-Eathain Lochabuidhe, or Sliochd Mhurchaidh Ruaidh	Maclaine of Lochbuie.
Mac-'ille-Chaluim . . .	MacLeod of Raasay.
Mac-'ille Mhoire . . .	Morrison of Lewis.
Mac-Iomhair	Campbell of Asknish.
Mac-Laomuinn	Lamont of Lamont.
MacLeòid	MacLeod of MacLeod and Harris.
Mac-mhaoilean-mór-a'-Cnaip .	Macmillan of Knap.
Mac-'ic-Mhàrtainn . . .	Cameron of Letterfinlay (MacMartin)
MacMhuirich	Macpherson of Cluny-Macpherson.
MacNèill	MacNeil of Barra.
Mac-Phàdruig	Grant of Glenmoriston.
Mac-Sheumais-Chataich . .	Gunn of Braemore.
MacShimidh	Fraser of Lovat (Lord Lovat).
MacUisdein	Fraser of Culbokie.
Morair Chat	The Duke of Sutherland.
Morair Ghallaobh . . .	The Earl of Caithness (Sinclair).
Sliochd a' Chlaidheimh Iarruin .	The Macleans of the Ross of Mull.
Slioch Ferquhard Vic Lauchlan .	Mackintoshes of Kyllachy, heirs male (" senior scion ") of Mackintosh.
Sliochd Phàra Bhig . . .	The Campbells of Barcaldine and Baileveolan.
Tighearna Fólais . . .	Munro of Foulis.

[1] The style *Mac-'ic* used by certain persons of these families is not a " chiefly " title, but (as explained by Sir John Maclean of Duart, Bt.) actually denotes a cadet of the line of the affixed name (*Loyall Dissuasive*, p. 102), usually applied when the person was not actual chief or chieftain, but where there was a dispute in progress, *e.g.* Clan Ranald, where prior to the time of *Ian Moydertach* the title was *MacAllan*.

Badges of Clans and Families

Clan	According to some Authorities	According to Others [1]
Brodie . . .	Periwinkle . .	——
Bruce	Rosemary . .	——
Buchan . . .	Sunflower * . .	——
Buchanan . . .	Bilberry (Blaeberry)	Oak, Birch.
Cameron . . .	Crowberry . .	Oak.
Campbell . . .	Fir Club Moss .	Wild (or Bog) Myrtle.
Chisholm . . .	Fern * . . .	——
Clan Chattan . .	Red Whortleberry *	——
Colquhoun . . .	Hazel * . .	——
Cumin	Cumin Plant .	——
Davidson . . .	Boxwood . .	Red Whortleberry.
Drummond . . .	Holly * . .	——
Farquharson. . .	Scots Fir * . .	Red Whortleberry.
Ferguson (Stra-chur) .	Pine * . . .	——
Do. (Dunfallandy)	Poplar * . .	——
Forbes . . .	Broom . .	——
Fraser	Yew . . .	——
Gordon . . .	Ivy * . . .	——
Graham . . .	Spurge Laurel .	——
Grant	Pine (Scots Fir) * .	——
Gunn	Juniper . .	Rose Root.
Hay	Mistletoe * . .	——
Henderson . . .	Cotton Grass .	——
Home	Broom . .	——
Innes	Great Bulrush * .	——
Johnston . . .	Red Hawthorn .	——
Kennedy . . .	Oak . . .	——
Lamont . . .	Crab-apple Tree .	——
Leslie	Rue . . .	——
Lindsay . . .	Lime Tree . .	——
Logan	Furze . . .	——
MacAlister . . .	Common Heath .	
MacAlpin . . .	Pine (Scots Fir) .	Wild Myrtle.
MacArthur . . .	Wild Thyme .	
MacAulay . . .	Pine (Scots Fir) .	Cranberry.
MacBean . . .	Boxwood . .	Red Whortleberry.
MacDonald . . .	Common Heath (Scots Heather) *	——

[1] As a considerable difference of opinion occurs, even among the best authorities, regarding clan badges, the alternative badges, quoted by these authorities, have been given where no badge is officially recorded. Badges marked with an asterisk have been officially recorded in Lyon Court.

Clan	According to some Authorities	According to Others
Clanranald, Glengarry .	Common Heath* .	——
MacDonell of Keppoch .	Common Heath .	White Heather.
MacDougall . . .	Bell Heather .	——
MacDuff . . .	Boxwood . .	Red Whortleberry, Holly.
MacFarlane . . .	Cranberry . .	Cloudberry.
Macfie . . .	Pine (Scots Fir) .	Oak, Crowberry.
MacGillivray . .	Boxwood . .	Red Whortleberry.
MacGregor . . .	Pine (Scots Fir) * .	——
Macinnes . . .	Holly . . .	——
Macintyre . . .	Common Heath .	——
Mackay . . .	Great Bulrush * .	——
MacKenzie . . .	Variegated Holly .	Deer's Grass.
Mackinnon . . .	Pine (Scots Fir) .	St. John's Wort (St. Columba's Flower).
Mackintosh [1]. . .	Red Whortleberry *	Bearberry.*
MacLachlan . .	Rowan * . .	——
Maclaine of Lochbuie .	Bilberry (Blaeberry)	Bramble.
MacLaren . . .	Laurel * . .	——
Maclean of Duart . .	Crowberry . .	
Ardgour, Coll, Dochgarroch . . .	Holly * . .	——
Maclennan . . .	Furze . . .	——
MacLeod of Macleod .	Juniper . .	——
MacLeod of Lewis . .	Red Whortleberry .	——
Macmillan . . .	Holly * . .	——
Macnab . . .	Stone Bramble * .	——
MacNaughton . .	Trailing Azalea .	——
MacNeil of Barra . .	Dryas . . .	——
McNeill of Gigha . .	Dryas . . .	——
Macpherson . . .	White Heather * .	——
Macquarrie . . .	Pine (Scots Fir) .	——
Macqueen . . .	Boxwood . .	Red Whortleberry.
Macrae . . .	Club Moss . .	——
Malcolm . . .	Rowan Berries .	
Matheson . . .	Broom. . .	Holly.
Menzies . . .	Menzies' Heath * .	——
Morrison . . .	Driftwood . .	——
Munro	Common Club Moss	——
Murray . . .	Butcher's Broom *.	Juniper.
Nicolson . . .	Juniper . .	——
Ogilvie. . . .	Whitethorn . .	——
Robertson . . .	Bracken * . .	——
Rose	Wild Rosemary * .	——
Ross	Juniper . .	Bearberry.

[1] 1947 Mackintosh Judgement, Finding 39.

Clan	According to some Authorities	According to Others
Seton	Yew . . .	—
Sinclair . . .	Furze (Whin) * .	White Clover.
Stewart, Royal [1] . .	Thistle * . .	—
Stewart, Clan . .	Oak . . .	—
Sutherland . . .	Cotton Sedge * .	—
Urquhart . . .	Wallflower *. .	—

Whilst plant badges were occasionally—in special circumstances and large-scale operations—used as a means of distinction (*e.g.* the sprigs of ripe oats used by Montrose's troops during the sack of Aberdeen), it is evident that their use as such would, amongst the smaller clans, have been impracticable and merely a source of confusion. Many of the " badges " given would have been hard to identify, even at a gathering, let alone in battle ; whilst many are such as are only available at a limited season. In Highland forces, as elsewhere, we find from the oldest poems that the gathering symbols were heraldic flags—the banner, standard, and pinsel ; and that the old chiefs had hereditary standard-bearers, just like the *Ard-righ*.

The plant badges have therefore evidently some more subtle origin, and are rather to be regarded as the " race-plant " of the tribe. The confusion which appears from one clan having several such badges is, moreover, almost certainly due, in many cases, to the existence of a district badge, which has been " taken over " when a branch of one race has either " acquired " a whole " country," or inherited it, and taken to using their paternal badge as well as the local *duthus*-badge.

Again, where a large clan-group has come to include a number of great branches, with local associations, it is sometimes found that these have individual badges. The following observations, which have not hitherto appeared (and emerge from a classification made by Messrs. W. & A. K. Johnston), are interesting as throwing some fresh light on what has seemed rather a confusing subject.

(1) The whole Clan Donald group—Macdonald, Macdonell, Macalister, Macintyre (at least those descending from Clan Donald), Macqueen (of Skye)—have Common Heath.

(2) The whole Clan Chattan group—Mackintosh, Macpherson, Mac-Gillivray, MacQueen, Macbean, Farquharson, Davidson—have long borne Red Whortleberry (in Scotland sometimes called " Cranberry ") or Bearberry or Boxwood. Now the leaves of these three plants are, for " practical " purposes, indistinguishable,[2] and it is evident that whichever was available was used. Farquharson, however, uses alternatively Pine (and this appears on the uniforms of " The Invercauld Highlanders "). The origin of this is, that in the first stage of the Invercauld arms a Pine tree was used as mark of cadency from the basic Shaw-Mackintosh arms.[3] It is therefore essentially

---

[1] The badge of the Pictish Kingdom was Rue (*rùgh*), which is seen joined with the thistle in the collar of the " Most Ancient and Most Noble Order of the Thistle."   [2] Cf. *Deeside Field*, VII., p. 15.   [3] *Loyall Dissuasive*, p. 238.

a " district " badge ; but shows how such things arise ; and how the whole Clan Chattan uses the Box-Whortle-Cranberry plant leaves, but that, within the major clan, branch-clans may have additional sub-badges, *drawn, in this case, from the armorial mark of cadency*. The objection to it, *per se*, is that it would suggest a Clan Alpin connection, and, where a local badge of such character exists, it should obviously be borne *along with* the badge of the major clan-group.

(3) Sutherland and Murray both share the Butcher's Broom, whilst as " alternative " the former has Cotton Sedge and the latter Juniper. These seem district badges, and (looking to the very ancient connection of the two lines) the Butcher's Broom *ought* to date back to the early *de Moravia* period ; which, if that house was (as its name suggests), a surviving name-stock of the *Ri-Moreb*, would suggest that Butcher's Broom was an original Moray badge, probably use of which was severely struck at after the suppression of the MacHeth-MacWilliam lines.

(4) The whole Clan Alpin group—Grant, Macgregor, Macaulay, Macfie, Macnab, Mackinnon, MacQuarrie, MacAlpine, and Clann Fhearghuis of Stra-chur—all bear the Pine tree. Macfie, however, is sometimes given Oak and Crowberry as alternative ; Macnab, Common Heath and Stone Bramble ; Grant, Cranberry ; Mackinnon, St. Columba's flower. These are evidently subsidiary clan badges, or ones which have arisen from district or special usage.

(5) The Mackenzie's badge, " Deer's Grass," otherwise called " Heath Club Rush," suggests a possible confusion with " *Club Moss*," alias " *Staghorn* Moss " (used by their " shirt of mail," the Macraes) ; and both would then seem an allusion to the *Caberfeidh* in the Mackenzie coat of arms, as the " Deer's Grass " obviously is. The alternative, " Variegated Holly " may, on investigation, prove related to the Tutor of Kintail's administration in Morvern in the seventeenth century.

(6) It is noticed that the alleged Forbes-Mackay-Urquhart connection does not appear to have a common badge (though Adam *did* give Mackay an " alternative " of Broom). My own examination of the traditions underlying the supposed connection leads me to conclude that no such connection ever existed, and that the events refer to different times and different persons. If the Mackay " broom " was *Butcher's* Broom, it would, however, suggest a Murray-Morayshire connection, which seems a great deal more probable ; as the *oldest* Mackay arms seem to have contained somewhat suggestive *stars*, and the Clan Mackay assuredly claim descent from the Mac-Heth race.

USE OF PLANT BADGES.—These are normally worn as a sprig affixed behind the strap-and-buckle crest badge, affixed to the cap, or which, in the case of ladies, fixes the tartan sash at the shoulder. Where a main and a subsidiary badge both exist, it would seem that these should be worn conjoined behind the brooch, placing the " main " clan badge on the dexter.

The *three* pinion feathers of the native eagle are the distinguishing badge of a *Highland Chief* ; *two* are the badge of a *Chieftain* ; and *one* the badge of a *Gentleman* (*Duine-uasail*), see pp. 136, 487.

The Gaelic equivalent of banner is *bratach* ; of shield, *targaid* ; of badge also) of whole armorial achievement), *suaicheantas* ; and of crest *cirean*.

Slogans or War Cries of Highland Clans

(Slogans marked with asterisks have been officially " allowed " and recorded in Lyon Court, as incident to the chief's arms.)

Clan	Slogan	English Description
Buchanan	Clar Innis	An island in Loch Lomond.
Cameron	Chlanna nan con thigibh a so 's gheibh sibh feòil	Sons of the hounds come here and get flesh.
Campbell	Cruachan	A mountain near Loch Awe.
Clan Chattan	Clan Chattan*	
Colquhoun	Cnoc Ealachain *	
Farquharson	Càrn na cuimhne *	Cairn of Remembrance.
Forbes	Lònach	A mountain in Strathdon.
Fraser	A 'Mhór-fhaiche (and later) Caisteal Dhùni	The Great Field (and later) Castle Downie.
Gordon	An Gordonach *	A Gordon.
Grant [1]	Craig Elachaidh *	
MacAlpin	Cuimhnich bàs Ailpein	Remember the death of Alpin.
MacArthur	Eisd ! O Eisd !	Listen ! O Listen !
MacDonald	Fraoch Eilean *	The Heathery Isle.
MacDonald of Clanranald	Dh' aindeòin có theireadh e *	Gainsay who dare.
MacDonell of Glengarry	Creagan-an-Fhithich *	The Raven's Rock.
MacDonell of Keppoch	Dia 's Naomh Aindrea	God and St. Andrew.
MacDougall	Buaidh no Bàs *	Victory or Death.
MacFarlane	Loch Slòigh *	The Loch of the Host.
MacGillivray	Dunmaghlas.	The name of the chief's castle.
MacGregor	Ard-coille *	Height of the Wood, or High Wood.
Mackay	Bratach bhàn mhic Aoidh *	The White Banner of The Mackay.
MacKenzie	Tulach Ard	The High Hillock.
Mackinnon	Cuimhnich bàs Ailpein	Remember the death of Alpin.

[1] See Appendix. XXVI.

Clan	Slogan	English Description
Mackintosh .	Loch Mòigh * [1] . .	Loch Moy (a loch near the seat of the chief).
MacLaren . .	Creag an Tuirc . .	The Boar's Rock.
Maclean . .	Bàs no Beatha ; *also* Fear eile airson Eachuinn	Death or Life ; *also* Another for Hector. (*These two slogans were used alternately.*)
Maclennan .	Druim nan deur . .	The Ridge of Tears.
MacNab . .	Bovain * . . .	The old MacNab *duthus*.
MacNaughten .	Frechelan . . .	Castle on Loch Awe.
MacNeil . .	Buaidh no Bàs . .	Victory or Death.
Macpherson .	Creag an Dhubh* [1] . .	The Black Rock (near Cluny).
Macquarrie .	An t-Arm breac dearg .	The Red Speckled (or spotted) Army.
Macrae . .	Sgùr Urain . . .	A mountain in Kintail.
Matheson . .	Acha 'n dà thearnaidh .	The Field of the Two Declivities.
Menzies . .	Geal is Dearg a suas .	Up with the Red and White.
Morrison . .	Dun Uisdean . .	Hugh's Castle.
Munro . .	Casteal Fólais na theine *	Foulis Castle on fire.
Robertson or Clan Donnachie	Garg 'n uair dhùisgear *	Fierce when Roused.
Stewart of Appin	Creag-an-Sgairbh . .	The Cormorant's Rock (a rock in Appin).
Sutherland .	Ceann na Drochaide Bige	A bridge at Dunrobin.

[1] Shouted alternately with the slogan of the whole—" Clan Chattan."

HIGHLAND GATHERINGS CEREMONIAL

By immemorial tradition, Scottish conventions/gatherings commence with a ceremonial march in order of precedence (see p. 573) to and around the gathering-place ; *e.g.* the " Riding of Parliament " ; " March of the Chieftains " at Oban ; and " March of the Clansmen " at Braemar and Lonach. In such processions the principle is that the clans or *Estaits* march junior first, but at the head of the procession is that of a Great Officer, or (normally) the " tribe of the land " on which the gathering is held. At Braemar, where the park is part of the old curtilage of the royal castle of Kindrochit, the *Ard-righ's* Balmoral Highlanders lead the march, Farquharsons and Duffs following in normal order. For flag-ceremonials at gatherings, see p. 523.

Distinctive Clan Pipe Music

The following are, respectively, the English and the Gaelic equivalents of descriptions of *Piobaireachd*, (pipe music not dance music), viz. :

English ..	Salute	Gathering	March	Lament
Gaelic ..	Fàilte	Cruinneachadh	Spaidsearachd	Cumha

Clan	*Tune*	*Description*	*English Equivalent*
Cameron .	Fàilte Shir Eòghan [1] .	Salute .	Sir Ewen Cameron of Lochiel's Salute.
	Ceann na Drochaide Móire	Gathering	The Head of the High Bridge.
	Cruinneachadh nan Camronach	Gathering	The Camerons' Gathering.
	Piobaireachd Dhòmnuill Duibh [2]	March .	Pibroch of Donald Dubh.
	Cumha Ailein Oig .	Lament .	Lament of Young Allan.
Campbell of Argyll	Fàilte 'Mharcuis .	Salute .	The Marquis of Argyll's Salute.
	Baile Inbhearaora .	March .	" The Campbells are coming."
	Cumha 'Mharcuis .	Lament .	The Marquis's Lament.
Campbell of Breadalbane	Bodaich nam brigisean	March .	Lord Breadalbane's March, or " The Carles with the breeks."
	Cumha Mhorair Bhread-albainn	Lament .	Lament for Lord Breadalbane.
Campbell of Calder	Fàilte Sheòrais Oig, Tighearna Chaladair	Salute .	Campbell of Calder's Salute.
Chisholm .	Fàilte an t-Siosalaich .	Salute .	The Chisholm's Salute.
	Spaidsearachd Siosal-ach Stratghlais	March .	Chisholm's March.
	Cumha do dh'Uillean Siosal	Lament .	Lament for William Chisholm.
Colquhoun .	Caismeachd Chloinn a' Chompaich	March .	The Colquhouns' March.

[1] This tune is also known as *Gu do bhuidheann Eòghain* (" Away to your tribe, Ewen ! ").

[2] This is also claimed by the MacDonalds, by whom it is styled " Black Donald of the Isles' March."

Clan	Tune	Description	English Equivalent
Colquhoun . —contd.	Ceann na Drochaide Bige	Gathering	The Head of the Little Bridge.
	Ruaig Ghlinne-freoine	Lament .	Rout of Glen Fruin.
Davidson .	Fàilte Thighearna Thulaich	Salute .	Tulloch's Salute.
	Spaidsearachd-Chaisteal Thulaich	March	Tulloch Castle March.
Drummond .	Spaidsearachd Dhiùc Pheairt	March .	The Duke of Perth's March.
	Cumha Dhiùc Pheairt .	Lament .	Lament for the Duke of Perth.
Forbes .	Cath Ghlinn Eurainn .	March .	The Battle of Glen Eurann.
	Cruinneachadh nam Forbasach	Gathering	The Forbes' Gathering (" Gather Glen-Nochty ").
	Cumha Chòirneil Forbes	Lament .	Lament for Colonel Forbes.
Fraser. .	Fàilte Chloinn Shimidh	Salute .	The Frasers' Salute.
	Spaidsearachd Mhic Shimidh	March .	Lovat's March.
	Cumha Mhic Shimidh .	Lament .	Lovat's Lament.
Gordon .	Fàilte nan Gòrdanach .	Salute .	The Gordons' Salute.
	Spaidsearachd nan Gòrdanach	March .	The Gordons' March.
		March .	The Cock o' the North
Graham .	Raon-Ruairidh . .	March .	Killiecrankie.
	Latha Allt-Eire . .	Gathering	Battle of Auldearn.
	Cumha Chlébhers .	Lament	Claverhouse's Lament.
Grant . .	Cruinneachadh nan Granndach	Gathering	The Grants' Gathering.
	Stad 'Chreag Ealach-aidh	March .	Stand Fast, Craig-ellachie.
	Fàilte Elchie . .	Salute .	Elchie's Salute.
	Riobain Gorm nan Granndach	Salute	The Grants' Blue Ribbon.
Gunn . .	Fàilte nan Guinneach	Salute .	The Gunns' Salute.
Innes . .	Spaidsearachd an Iarla Innes	March .	Duke of Roxburghe's March.
	Spaidsearachd Choir-neil Innes na Lairney	March .	Colonel Innes of Learney's March.
Lamont .	Cumha an Fhògraich .	Lament .	The Exile's Lament.
	Mhic Laomainn, ceud fàilte dhuit	Salute .	A Thousand Welcomes Lamont.
	Spaidsearachd Chaip-tein Mhic Laomainn	March .	Captain Lamont's March.

Clan	Tune	Description	English Equivalent
MacBean .	Mo Run Geal Og .	Lament .	My Fair Young Beloved.
MacColl .	Ceann na Drochaide Móire	Gathering	The Head of the High Bridge.
MacCrimmon	Cogadh no Sith . .	March .	War or Peace.
	Cha till, cha till, cha till, Mac Crumein	Lament .	MacCrimmon shall never return.
	Fhuair mi pòg o laimh an Rìgh	Salute .	I got a kiss from the King's hand.
	Cumha na Cloinne .	Lament .	The Lament for the Children.
MacDonald of MacDonald	Fàilte Chlann Dònuill.	Salute .	MacDonald's Salute.
	Làmh dhearg Chlann Dhòmnuill	Gathering	The Red Hand of the MacDonalds.
	Spaidsearachd Mhic Dhòmnuill	March .	March of the MacDonalds.
	Cumha Mhorair Chlann Dhòmnuill	Lament .	Lament for Lord MacDonald.
MacDonald of Sleate	Fàilte Ridir Seumas nan Eilean	Salute .	Sir James MacDonald of the Isles' Salute.
	Fàilte na Bain-tighearna nic Dhòmnuill	Salute .	Lady Margaret MacDonald's Salute.
	Cumha an Ridire Seumas MacDhòmnuill nan Eilean	Lament .	Lament for Sir James MacDonald of the Isles.
	Cumha Bain-tighearna Mhic Dhòmnuill	Lament .	Lament for Lady MacDonald.
MacDonald of Clan Ranald	Fàilte Mhic Mhic Ailein	Salute .	Clan Ranald's Salute.
	Cruinneachadh Mhic Mhic Ailein	Gathering	Clan Ranald's Gathering.
	Spaidsearachd Mhic Mhic Ailein	March .	Clan Ranald's March.
	Cumha Mhic Mhic Ailein	Lament .	Lament for Clan Ranald.
MacDonald of Glencoe	Mort Ghlinne Comhann	Lament .	Massacre of Glencoe.
MacDonell of Glengarry	Fàilte Mhic Alastair .	Salute .	Glengarry's Salute.
	Gille Chriosd . .	Gathering	Gillechrist.
	Spaidsearachd Mhic Mhic - Alastair (or A Sheana Bhean Bhochd)	March .	Glengarry's March.
	Cumha Mhic Mhic-Alastair	Lament .	Glengarry's Lament.
	Cumha Alastair Dheirg	Lament .	Lament for Alexander MacDonell of Glengarry.

Clan	Tune	Description	English Equivalent
MacDonell of Keppoch	Blàr na Maòile Ruaidhe (A mhuinntir a' chàil chaoil, thugaibh am bruthach oirbh)	Salute .	The Battle of Mulroy (1688).
	Spaidsearachd Alasdair Charaich	March .	The March of Alexander I. of Keppoch.
	Latha na Maoile Ruaidhe	March .	The Battle of Mulroy.
	An tarbh breac dearg .	March .	The Red Spreckled Bull.
	Cumha na peathar .	Lament .	The Sister's Lament.
	A' Cheapach na fàsaich	Lament .	Keppoch in desolation.
MacDougall .	Fàilte Iain Chéir .	Salute .	John Ciar's Salute.
	Fàilte Chlann Dùghaill	Salute .	MacDougall's Salute.
	Moladh Móraig . .	March .	The Praise of Marion.
	Caisteal Dhunolla .	March .	Dunolly Castle.
	Brosnachahd - Catha Chlann Dùghaill	March .	Clan Dougall's Incitement to Battle.
	Cumha Iain Chéir .	Lament .	Lament for John Ciar.
	Cumha Chaiptein 'ic Dhùgaill	Lament .	Lament for Captain MacDougall.
	Latha Dhunàbharti .	Lament .	Dunaverty Castle.
	Cumha dubh Shomhairle	Lament .	Sad Lament for Samuel.
MacDuff .	Cruinneachadh Chlann Duibh	Gathering	The MacDuffs' Gathering.
MacFarlane .	'Thogail nam bò .	Gathering	Lifting the Cattle.
	Spaidsearachd Chlann Pharlain	March .	MacFarlane March.
MacGillivray	Spaidsearachd Chlann Mhic Gillebhràth	March .	MacGillivray's March.
MacGregor .	Ruag Ghlinn Fraoin .	Gathering	The Chase of Glen Fruin.
	Fàilte Chlann Ghriogair	Salute .	MacGregor's Salute.
	Cumha Chlann Ghriogair	Lament .	MacGregor's Lament.
	Cumha Mhic Griogair Ruadh-shruth .	Lament .	Lament for MacGregor of Ruaro.
Macintyre .	Fàilte Mhic-an-t-saoir .	Salute .	Macintyre's Salute.
	Cruinneachadh Chlann an t-saoir	Gathering	The Macintyres' Gathering.
	Gabhaidh sinn an rathad mór [1]	March .	We will take the Highway.

[1] The Stewarts of Appin also claim this tune as one belonging to their clan.

Clan	Tune	Description	English Equivalent
Mackay .	Iseabal nic Aoidh .	Salute .	Isabella Mackay.
	Bhratach Bhàn Mhic Aoidh . . .	Gathering	Mackay's White Banner.
	Piobaireachd Chlann Aoidh	March .	Mackay's March.
	Cumha Dhòmnuill Mhic Aoidh	Lament .	Lament for Donald Mackay, first Lord Reay.
	Cumha Shrath Alladail	Lament .	Lament for Mackay of Strath-Halladale.
	Cumha Bain-tighearna Mhic Aoidh	Lament .	Lament for Lady Mackay.
	Cumha Iseabal nic Aoidh	Lament .	Lament for Isabella Mackay.
MacKenzie .	Fàilte Uilleim Dhuibh Mhic Coinnich	Salute .	The Earl of Seaforth's (Black William's) Salute.
	Fàilte Thighearna Gheàrloch	Salute .	MacKenzie of Gairloch's Salute.
	Fàilte Thighearna na Comeraich	Salute .	MacKenzie of Applecross's Salute.
	Co-thional Chlann Choinnich	Gathering	MacKenzie's Gathering.
	Caber Féidh . .	March .	Deer's Antlers.
	Cumha Chailein Ruaidh Mhic Coinnich, no Cumha Mhic Coinnich	Lament .	Lament for Colin Roy.
	Cumha Thighearna Gheàrloch	Lament .	Gairloch's Lament.
Mackintosh .	Bratach Mhic-an-Tòisich	Gathering	The Mackintosh's Banner.
	Creag Dhubh Chlann Chatain	Gathering	The Black Rock of Clan Chattan.
	Cumha Mhic-an-Tòisich	Lament .	Mackintosh's Lament.
MacLachlan .	Moladh Màiri . .	Salute .	The Praise of Mary.
Maclaine of Lochbuie	Cumha Mhic Ghilleathain Lochabuidhe	Lament .	Maclaine of Lochbuie's Lament.
Maclean .	Birlinn Thighearna Cholla	Salute .	Maclean of Coll's Galley.
	Cruinneachadh Chlann Ghilleathain	Gathering	The Macleans' Gathering.
	Spaidsearachd Chlann Ghilleathain	March .	The Macleans' March.
	Caismeachd Eachuinn Mhic Ailein nan Sop	March .	Hector Maclean's Warning.

Clan	Tune	Description	English Equivalent
Maclean —contd.	Cumha Eachuinn Ruaidh nan Cath	Lament .	Hector Roy Maclean's Lament.
	Cumha Iain Ghairbh Mhic Ghilleathain Cholla	Lament .	Lament for John Garve Maclean of Coll.
	Cumha Lachuinn Mhòir (Latha Sròn a' Chlachain)	Lament .	Lament for Lachlan Mor Maclean.
MacLeod •	Fàilte nan Leodach .	Salute .	MacLeod's Salute.
	Port Iomram Mhic Leoid, no Fàilte nan Leòdach	Salute .	MacLeod of MacLeod's Rowing Salute.
	Fàilte Mhic Gille Chaluim Rathasaidh	Salute .	MacLeod of Raasay's Salute.
	Fàilte Ruaraidh Mhòir	Salute .	Rory Mor's (of Harris) Salute.
	Iomradh Mhic Leoid .	March .	MacLeod's Praise.
	Cumha Cheann-Cinnidh na Leodach	Lament .	Lament for MacLeod of MacLeod.
	Cumha Ruaraidh Mhòir	Lament .	Lament for Rory Mor (of Harris).
	Cumha Mhic Gille Chaluim Rathasaidh	Lament .	Lament for MacLeod of Raasay.
Macnab •	Fàilte Mhic an Aba .	Salute .	Macnab's Salute.
	Co-thional Chlann an Aba	Gathering	Macnab's Gathering.
MacNeill •	Spaidsearachd Mhic Nèill Bharra	March .	MacNeill of Barra's March.
	Cumha Mhic Nèill Bharra	Lament .	Lament for MacNeill of Barra.
Macpherson .	Fàilte Fir Chluanaigh .	Salute .	Cluny Macpherson's Salute.
	'S fheudar dhomh fhìn a bhi falbh dhachaidh direach	March .	Macpherson's March.
	Cumha Chluanaigh .	Lament .	Macpherson's Lament.
Macquarrie .	An t-Arm breac dearg	Gathering	The Red-tartaned Army.
Macqueen .	Cumha Mhic Shuain á Roaig	Lament .	Lament for MacSwain of Roag.
Macrae •	Fàilte Loch Duthaich .	Salute .	Loch Duich's Salute.
	Blàr na Pàirc . .	Gathering	Battle of Park.
	Spaidsearachd Chlann Mhicrath	March .	The Macraes' March.
	Cumha Dhònnachaidh Mhic Iain	Lament .	Lament for Duncan Macrae of Kintail.

Clan	Tune	Description	English Equivalent
Menzies .	Fàilte nam Mèinnear-ach	Salute .	The Menzies' Salute.
	Caisteal a' Mhèinnear-aich (Piobaireachd Nuadh)	Gathering	Castle Menzies.
	Piobaireachd a' Mhein-nearaich	March .	Menzie's March.
Munro. .	Fàilte nan Rothach .	Salute .	Munro's Salute.
	Bealach nam Bròg .	March .	Munro's March.
	Cumha Fear Fòláis .	Lament .	Lament for Munro of Foulis.
Murray .	Fàilte Dhiuc Athull .	Salute .	The Duke of Atholl's Salute.
	Fàilte Abarchàrnaig .	Salute .	Abercairney's Salute.
	Cumha Abarchàrnaig .	Lament .	Abercairney's Lament.
Robertson or Clan Donnachie	Fàilte Thigearna an tr Sruthain	Salute .	Struan Robertson's Salute.
	Thainig Clann Donnachaidh	Gathering	The Robertsons have come.
	Till an crodh Dhonn-achaidh	March .	Turn the cattle, Donnachie.
	An Ribean Gorm .	March .	The Blue Ribbon.
	Teachd Chlann Donnachaidh	March .	The coming of the Robertsons.
	Cumha Sruthain .	Lament .	Lament for Robert-son of Struan.
Ross . .	Spaidsearachd Iarla Rois	March .	The Earl of Ross's March.
Sinclair .	Spaidsearachd Mhic nan Ceàrda	March .	The Sinclairs' March.
Stewart .	Earrach an àigh 's a' ghleann	Salute .	Lovely Spring in the Glen.
	Bratach bhàn nan Stiùbhartach	Gathering	The Stewarts' White Banner.
	Birlinn nan tonn .	March .	The Galley of the Waves.
	Creag-an-Sgairbh .	March .	The Cormorant's Rock (Stewart of Appin's March).
	Thàinig mo Rìgh air tìr am Mùideart	March .	My King has landed at Moidart.
Sutherland .	Piobaireachd nan Catach	Gathering	The Sutherlands' Pibroch.
	Spaidsearachd an Iarla Chataich	March .	The Earl of Suther-land's March.

T*

List of Clan Septs and Dependents

(Arranged under the Clans with which they are Connected)

Clan Buchanan	Clan Buchanan —*contd.*	Clan Campbell —*contd.*	Clan Campbell of Loudoun
Colman.	Masterson.	Denoon.	Hastings.
Donleavy.	Murchie.	Denune.	Loudoun.
Donlevy.	Murchison.	Harres.	
Dove.	Risk.	Harris.	**Clan Chattan**
Dow.	Ruskin.	Haws.	See names under
Dowe.	Spittal.	Hawson.	Mackintosh and
Gibb.	Spittel.	MacConnechy.	Macpherson.
Gibson.	Watson.	MacConochie.	
Gilbertson.	Watt.	MacGibbon.	**Clan Colquhoun**
Harper.	Yuill.	Macglasrich.	Cowan.
Harperson.	Yuille.	MacIsaac.	Kilpatrick.
Lennie.	Yule.	MacIver.	Kirkpatrick.
Lenny.		MacIvor.	Macachounich.
Macaldonich.	**Clan Cameron**	MacKellar.	MacCowan.
Macandeoir.	Chalmers.	MacKessock.	
MacAslan.	Clark.	MacKissock.	**Clan Cumming**
MacAuselan.	Kennedy.	MacLaws.	Buchan.[2]
MacAuslan.	MacChlerich.	MacLehose.	Comine.
MacAusland.	MacChlery.	MacNichol.	Comyn.
MacAuslane.	MacGillonie.	MacOran.	MacNiven.
MacCalman.	Macildowie.	MacOwen.	Niven.
MacCalmont.	MacKail.	MacPhedran.	Russell.
MacCammond.	Maclerie.	MacPhun.	
MacChruiter.	MacMartin.	MacTause.	**Clan Davidson**
MacColman.	MacOnie.	MacTavish.[1]	Davie.
MacCormack.	MacOurlic.	MacThomas.	Davis.
Macdonleavy.	MacPhail.	MacUre.	Dawson.
MacGibbon.	MacSorley.	Tawesson.	Dow.
MacGilbert.	MacUlric.	Thomas.	Kay.
Macgreusich.	Macvail.	Thomason.	Macdade.
Macinally.	MacWalrick.	Thompson.[1]	Macdaid.
Macindeor.	Martin.	Thomson.[1]	MacDavid.
Macindoe.	Paul.	Ure.	
Mackinlay.	Sorley.		**Clan Drummond**
Mackinley.	Taylor.	**Clan Campbell of Breadalbane**	Grewar.
MacMaster.		MacDiarmid.	Gruer.
MacMaurice.	**Clan Campbell**	MacDermid.	Maccrouther.
MacMurchie.	Bannatyne.		Macgrewar.
MacMurchy.	Burns.	**Clan Campbell of Cawdor**	Macgrowther.
Macnuyer.	Burnes.	Caddell.	Macgruder.
MacWattie.	Burnett.	Calder.	Macgruther.
MacWhirter.	Connochie.		MacRobbie.

[1] MacTavish is reckoned a clan itself, and Thomson a sept thereof.
[2] Buchan is held a distinct and pre-Cumming Tribe.

554

Clan Farquharson

Brebner.
Coutts.
Farquhar.
Findlay.
Findlayson.
Finlay.
Finlayson.
Greusach.
Hardie.
Hardy.
MacCaig.
MacCardney.
MacCuaig.
MacEarachar.
MacFarquhar.
Machardie.
Machardy.
MacKerchar.
MacKerracher.
Mackindlay.
Mackinlay.
Reoch.
Riach.
Tawse.

Clan Ferguson

Fergus.
Ferries.
MacAdie.
MacFergus.
MacKerras.
MacKersey.

Clan Forbes

Bannerman.
Fordyce.
Michie.
Watson.
Watt.

Clan Fraser

Frissell.
Frizell.
Macimmey.
MacGruer.
MacKim.
MacKimmie.

Clan Fraser
—contd.

MacShimes.
MacSimon.
MacSymon.
Sim.
Sime.
Simson.
Simpson.
Syme.
Symon.
Tweedie.

Clan Gordon

Adam.
Adie.
Crombie.
Edie.
Huntly.
Milne.
Todd.

Clan Graham

Allardice.
Bontein.
Bontine.
Buntain.
Bunten.
Buntine.
MacGibbon.
MacGilvernock.
Macgrime.
Menteith.
Monteith.

Clan Grant

Gilroy.
MacGilroy.
Macilroy.

Clan Gunn

Gallie.
Gaunson.
Georgeson.
Henderson.
Jameson.
Jamieson.
Johnson.
Kean.

Clan Gunn
—contd.

Keene.
MacComas.
MacCorkill.
MacCorkle.
MacIan.
MacKames.
MacKeamish.
MacKean.
MacRob.
MacWilliam.
Manson.
Nelson.
Robison.
Robson.
Sandison.
Swanson.
Williamson.
Wilson.

Clan Innes

Dinnes.
Ennis.
Innie.
McRob.
McTary.
Marnoch.
Mavor.
Middleton.
Mitchell.
Reidfuird.
Thain.
Wilson.

Clan Lamont

Black.
Brown.
Bourdon.
Burdon.
Lamb.
Lambie.
Lammie.
Lamondson.
Landers.
Lemond.
Limond.
Limont.
Lucas.

Clan Lamont
—contd.

Luke.
Lyon.
Macalduie.
MacClymont.
MacGilledow.
MacGillegowie.
Macilzegowie.
Macilwhom.
MacLamond.
MacLucas.
MacLymont.
MacPatrick.
MacPhorich.
MacSorley.
Meikleham.
Patrick.
Sorley.
Toward.
Towart.
Turner.
White.

Clan Leslie

Bartholomew.
Lang.
More.

Clan Lindsay

Crawford.
Deuchar.

Clan MacAllister

Alexander.

Clan MacAulay

MacPhedron.
MacPheidiran.

Clan MacArthur

Arthur.
MacCartair.
MacCarter.

Clan MacBean

Bean.
MacBeath.
MacBeth.
Macilvain.
MacVean.

Clan MacDonald

Beath.
Beaton.
Bethune.
Bowie.
Colson.
Connall.
Connell.
Darroch.
Donald.
Donaldson.
Donillson.
Donnelson.
Drain.
Galbraith.
Gilbride.
Gorrie.
Gowan.
Gowrie.
Hawthorn.
Hewison.
Houstoun.
Howison.
Hughson.
Hutcheonson.
Hutcheson.
Hutchinson.
Hutchison.
Isles.
Kellie.
Kelly.
Kinnell.
Mac a' Challies.
MacBeth.
MacBeath.
MacBheath.
MacBride.
MacCaishe.
MacCall.
MacCash.
MacCeallaich.
MacCodrum.

Clan MacDonald
—contd.

MacColl.
MacConnell.
MacCook.
MacCooish.
MacCrain.
MacCuag.
MacCuish.
MacCuithein.
MacCutcheon.
MacDaniell.
Macdrain.
MacEachern.
MacEachran.
MacElfrish.
MacElheran.
MacGorrie.
MacGorry.
MacGoun.
MacGowan.
MacGown.
MacHugh.
MacHutchen.
MacHutcheon.
MacIan.
Macilreach.
Macilriach.
Macilleriach.
Macilrevie.
Macilvride.
Macilwraith.
MacKean.
MacKellachie.
MacKellaig.
MacKelloch.
MacKiggan.
MacKinnell.
MacLairish.
MacLardie.
MacLardy.
MacLarty.
MacLaverty.
MacLeverty.
MacMurchie.
MacMurdo.
MacMurdoch.
MacO'Shannaig.
MacQuistan.

Clan MacDonald
—contd.

MacQuisten.
MacRaith.
MacRorie.
MacRory.
MacRuer.
MacRurie.
MacRury.
MacShannachan.
MacSorley.
MacSporran.
MacSwan.
MacWhannell.
Martin.
May.
Murchie.
Murchison.
Murdoch.
Murdoson.
O'Drain.
O'May.
O'Shannachan.
O'Shaig.
O'Shannaig.
Purcell.
Revie.
Reoch.
Riach.
Rorison.
Shannon.
Sorley.
Sporran.
Train.
Whannel.

Clan MacDonald of Clanranald

Allan.
Allanson.
Currie.
MacAllan.
MacBurie.
MacEachin.
MacGeachie.
MacGeachin.
MacIsaac.
MacKeachan.

Clan MacDonald of Clanranald
—contd.

Mackechnie.
MacKeochan.
MacKessock.
MacKichan.
MacKissock.
MacMurrich.
MacVarish.
MacVurrich.
MacVurie.

Clan Macdonald of Ardnamurchan

Johnson.
Kean.
Keene.

Clan MacDonald of Glencoe

Henderson.
Johnson.
Kean.
Keene.
MacHenry.
MacIan.
MacKean.

Clan MacDonell of Glengarry

Alexander.
Sanderson.

Clan MacDonell of Keppoch

MacGillivantic.
MacGilp.
Macglasrich.
MacKillop.
MacPhilip.
Philipson.
Ronald.
Ronaldson.

Clan MacDougall	Clan MacFarlane —contd.	Clan MacGregor —contd.	Clan Mackay
Carmichael.	MacGeoch.	Gregorson.	Bain.
Conacher.	Macgreusich.	Gregory.	Bayne.
Cowan.	Macinstalker.	Greig.	MacCay.
Dougall.	MacIock.	Grewar.	MacCrie.
Livingston.	MacJames.	Grier.	Mackee.
Livingstone.	Mackinlay.	Grierson.	Mackie.
MacConacher.	MacNair.	Grigor.	MacPhail.
MacCowan.	MacNeur.	Gruer.	Macquey.
MacCoul.	MacNider.	King.	Macquoid.
MacCulloch.	MacNiter.	Leckie.	Macvail.
MacDulothe.	MacRob.	Lecky.	Neilson.
MacHowell.	MacRobb.	MacAdam.	Paul.
MacKichan.	MacWalter.	Macara.	Polson.
MacLucas.	MacWilliam.	Macaree.	Williamson.
MacLugash.	Miller.	MacChoiter.	
MacLulich.	Monach.	MacConachie.	**Clan MacKenzie**
MacNamell.	Napier.	Maccrouther.	Kenneth.
Macoul.	Parlane.	Macgrewar.	Kennethson.
Macowl.	Robb.	Macgrowther.	MacBeolain.
	Stalker.	Macgruder.	MacConnach.
Clan MacDuff	Thomason.	Macgruther.	MacIver.
Abernethy.	Weaver.	Macilduy.	MacIvor.
Duff.	Weir.	MacLeister.	MacKerlich.
Fife.		MacLiver.	MacMurchie.
Fyfe.	**Clan Macfie**	MacNee.	MacMurchy.
Spence.	Duffie.	MacNeish.	MacVanish.
Spens.	Duffy.	MacNie.	MacVinish.
Wemyss.	MacGuffie.	MacNish.	Murchie.
	Machaffie.	MacPeter.	Murchison.
Clan MacFarlane		MacPetrie.	
Allan.	**Clan MacGillivray**	Malloch.	**Clan Mackinnon**
Allanson.		Neish.	Love.
Bartholomew.	Gilroy.	Nish.	Mackinney.
Caw.	MacGillivour.	Peter.	Mackinring.
Galbraith.	MacGilroy.	White.	Mackinven.
Griesck.	MacGilvra.	Whyte.	MacMorran.
Gruamach.	MacGilvray.		
Kinnieson.	Macilroy.	**Clan Macinnes**	**Clan Mackintosh**
Lennox.	Macilvrae.	Angus.	Adamson.
MacAindra.		MacAngus.	Ayson.
MacAllan.	**Clan MacGregor**	MacCainsh.	Clark.[1]
MacCaa.	Black.	MacCansh.	Clarke.[1]
MacCause.	Caird.	MacMaster.	Clarkson.[1]
MacCaw.	Comrie.		Clerk.[1]
MacCondy.	Dochart.	**Clan Macintyre**	Combie.
MacEoin.	Fletcher.	Tyre.	Crerar.
MacGaw.	Gregor.	MacTear.	Dallas.
		Wright.	

[1] These are directly of Clan Chattan, and not of Mackintosh or Macpherson.

Clan Mackintosh
—contd.

Doles.
Elder.
Esson.
Glen.
Glennie.
Hardie.
Hardy.
MacAndrew.
MacAy.
MacCardney.
MacChlerich.[1]
MacChlery.[1]
MacCombie.
MacCombe.
MacComie.
M'Conchy.
MacFall.[1]
Macglashan.
Machardie.
Machardy.
MacHay.
Mackeggie.
M'Killican.
Maclerie.[1]
MacNiven.[1]
MacOmie.
MacPhail.[1]
Macritchie.
MacThomas.
Macvail.[1]
Niven.
Noble.
Paul.
Ritchie.
Shaw.
Tarrill.
Tosh.
Toshach.

Clan MacLachlan

Ewan.
Ewen.
Ewing.
Gilchrist.

Clan MacLachlan
—contd.

Lachlan.
Lauchlan.
MacEwan.
MacEwen.
MacGilchrist.

Clan Maclaine of Lochbuie

MacCormick.
MacFadyen.
MacFadzean.
MacGilvra.
Macilvora.
MacPhadden.

Clan MacLaurin

MacFater.
MacFeat.
MacPatrick.
MacPhater.
MacGrory.
MacRory.
Paterson.

Clan Maclean

Beath.
Beaton.
Black.
Clanachan.
Garvie.
Lean.
MacBeath.
MacBheath.
MacBeth.
Macilduy.
MacLergain.
MacRankin.
MacVeagh.
MacVey.
Rankin.

Clan Maclennan

Lobban.
Logan.

Clan MacLeod of Harris

Beaton.
Beton.
MacCaig.
MacClure.
MacCrimmon.
MacCuaig.
MacHarold.
Macraild.
Norman.

Clan MacLeod of Lewis

Callum.
Lewis.
MacAskill.
MacAulay.
MacCaskill.
MacLewis.
MacNicol.
Tolmie.

Clan Macmillan

Baxter.
Bell.
Brown.
MacBaxter.

Clan Macnab

Abbot.
Abbotson.
Dewar.
Gilfillan.
Macandeoir.

Clan MacNaughton

Hendrie.
Hendry.
Kendrick.
MacBrayne.
Maceol.
MacHendrie.
MacHendry.

Clan MacNaughton
—contd.

MacKendrick.
MacKenrick.
Macknight.
MacNair.
MacNayer.
MacNiven.
MacNuir.
MacNuyer.
MacVicar.
Niven.
Weir.

Clan MacNeil

MacNeilage.
MacNeiledge.
MacNelly.
Neal.
Neil.
Neill.

Clan Macpherson

Cattanach.[1]
Clark.[1]
Clarke.[1]
Clarkson.[1]
Clerk.[1]
Currie.
Fersen.
Gillespie.
Gillies.
Gow.
Lees.
MacChlerich.[1]
MacChlery.[1]
MacCurrach.[1]
MacGowan.
Maclerie.[1]
MacLeish.
MacLise.
MacMurdo.
MacMurdoch.
MacMurrich.
MacVurrich.

[1] These are directly of Clan Chattan, and not of Mackintosh or Macpherson.

Clan Macpherson
—contd.

Murdoch.
Murdoson.

Clan Macquarrie

MacCorrie.
MacCorry.
MacGorrie.
MacGorry.
MacGuaran.
MacGuire.
Macquaire.
Macquhirr.
Macquire.
MacWhirr.
Wharrie.

Clan Macqueen

MacCunn.
MacSwan.
MacSwen.
MacSween.
MacSwyde.
Swan.

Clan Macrae

Macara.
MacCraw.
Macra.
Macrach.
MacRaith.
MacRath.
Rae.

Clan Malcolm

MacCallum.
Malcolmson.

Mar Tribe

Marr.
Morren.
Strachan.
Tough.

Clan Mathieson

MacMath.
MacPhun.
Mathie.

Clan Menzies

Dewar.
Macindeor.
MacMenzies.
MacMinn.
MacMonies.
Means.
Mein.
Meine.
Mennie.
Meyners.
Minn.
Minnus.
Monzie.

Clan Munro

Dingwall.
Foulis.
MacCulloch.
MacLulich.
Vass.
Wass.

Clan Morison

Brieve.
Gilmore.
MacBrieve.

Clan Murray

MacMurray.
Moray.
Small.
Spalding.

Clan Ogilvy

Airlie.
Gilchrist.
MacGilchrist.
Milne.

Clan Robertson

Collier.
Colyear.
Donachie.
Duncan.
Duncanson.
Dunnachie.
Inches.

Clan Robertson
—contd.

MacConachie.
MacConnechy.
MacDonachie.
Macinroy.
MacIver.
MacIvor.
Maclagan.
MacRobbie.
MacRobie.
MacRobert.
Reid.
Roy.
Stark.
Tonnochy.

Clan Ross

Anderson.
Andrew.
Dingwall.
Gillanders.
MacAndrew.
MacCulloch.
MacLulich.
MacTaggart.
MacTear.
MacTier.
MacTire.
Taggart.
Vass.
Wass.

Clan Sinclair

Caird.
Clouston.
Clyne.
Linklater.
Mason.

Clan Skene

Cariston.
Dis.
Dyce.
Hallyard.
Norie.

Clan Stewart

Boyd.
Garrow.
Menteith.

Clan Stewart
—contd.

Monteith.
Carmichael.
MacMichael.

Stewart, Appin

Carmichael.
Combich.
Livingston.
Livingstone.
MacCombich.
Mackinlay.
Maclae.
Maclay.
Maclea.
Macleay.
MacMichael.

Stewart, Atholl

Crookshanks.
Cruickshank.
Duilach.
Gray.
Macglashan.

Stuart, Bute

Bannatyne.
Fullarton.
Fullerton.
Jameson.
Jamieson.
MacCamie.
MacCloy.
MacCaw.
MacKirdy.
MacLewis.
MacMunn.
Munn.
MacMutrie.

Clan Sutherland

Cheyne.
Federith.
Gray.
Keith.
Mowat.
Oliphant.

Alphabetical List of Clan Septs and Dependents

(Showing the Clans with which they are Connected) [1]

Septs and Dependents	Clans with which they are Connected	Septs and Dependents	Clans with which they are Connected
Abbotson .	Macnab.	Bontein,	Graham of Menteith.
Abbot . .	,,	Bontine,	,,
Abernethy .	MacDuff.	Buntain,	,,
Adam . .	Gordon.	Bunten,	,,
Adie . .	,,	Buntine	,,
Adamson .	Mackintosh.	Bowie . .	MacDonald.
Airlie . .	Ogilvy.	Boyd . .	Stewart (Royal).
Alexander .	MacAlister, Mac-Donell of Glengarry.	Brebner	Farquharson.
		Brieve . .	Morrison.
		Brown . .	Lamont, Macmillan.
Allan . .	MacDonald of Clanranald, MacFarlane.	Buchan	Cumming.
		Burdon or Bourdon	Lamont.
Allanson .	,, ,,	Burns . .	Campbell.
Allardice .	Graham of Menteith.	Burnes . .	,,
Anderson .	Ross.	Burnett . .	,,
Andrew . .	,,		
Angus . .	Macinnes.		
Arthur . .	MacArthur (Campbell of Strachur).	Caird . .	Sinclair, MacGregor.
		Caddell .	Campbell of Cawdor.
Ayson . .	Mackintosh (Shaw).	Calder . .	,,
		Callum . .	MacLeod of Raasay.
Bain . .	Mackay.	Cariston .	Skene.
Bannatyne .	Campbell Stuart of Bute.	Carmichael .	Stewart of Appin, Stewart of Galloway, MacDougall.
Bannerman .	Forbes.		
Bartholomew	MacFarlane, Leslie.	Cattanach .	Clan Chattan.
Baxter . .	Macmillan.	Caw . .	MacFarlane.
Bayne . .	Mackay.	Chalmers .	Cameron.
Bean . .	MacBean.	Cheyne . .	Sutherland.
Beath . .	MacDonald, Maclean.	Clanachan .	Maclean.
		Clark . .	Cameron, Clan Chattan.
Beaton . .	MacDonald, MacLeod.		
		Clarke . .	,, ,,
Bell . .	Macmillan.	Clarkson .	,, ,,
Bethune . .	MacDonald.	Clerk . .	,, ,,
Beton . .	MacLeod.	Clouston .	Sinclair.
Black . .	Lamont, MacGregor, Maclean.	Clyne . .	,,
		Collier . .	Robertson.

Septs and Dependents	Clans with which they are Connected	Septs and Dependents	Clans with which they are Connected
Colman	Buchanan.	Donlevy	Buchanan.
Colson .	MacDonald.	Donnellson .	MacDonald of Antrim.
Colyear	Robertson.		
Combich	Stewart of Appin.	Dougall	,,
Combie	Mackintosh.	Dowall .	,,
Comine	Cumming.	Dowell .	MacDougall.
Comrie .	MacGregor.	Dow	Buchanan, Davidson.
Comyn .	Cumming.		
Conacher	MacDougall.	Dove	Buchanan.
Connall	MacDonald.	Dowe	,,
Connell	,,	Duff	MacDuff.
Conochie	Campbell of Inverawe.	Duffie .	Macfie.
		Duffy .	,,
Coulson	MacDonald.	Duilach	Stewart of Garth.
Coutts .	Farquharson.	Duncan	Robertson.
Cowan .	Colquhoun, MacDougall.	Duncanson	,,
		Dunnachie	,,
Crawford	Lindsay.	Dyce	Skene.
Crerar .	Mackintosh.	Edie	Gordon.
Crookshanks .	Stewart of Garth.	Elder	Mackintosh.
Cruickshank .	,,	Ennis	Innes.
Currie .	MacDonald of Clanranald, Macpherson.	Esson	Mackintosh (Shaw).
		Ewan	MacLachlan.
Dallas .	Mackintosh.	Ewen	,,
Darroch	MacDonald.	Ewing .	,,
Davie .	Davidson.	Farquhar	Farquharson.
Davis .	,,	Federith	Sutherland.
Davison	,,	Fergus .	Ferguson.
Dawson	,,	Ferries .	,,
Denoon	Campbell.	Fersen .	Macpherson.
Denune	,,	Fife	MacDuff.
Deuchar	Lindsay.	Findlay	Farquharson.
Dewar .	Menzies, Macnab.	Findlayson	,,
Dingwall	Munro, Ross.	Finlay .	,,
Dinnes .	Innes.	Finlayson	,,
Dis	Skene.	Fleming	Murray.
Dochart	MacGregor.	Fletcher	MacGregor.
Doles .	Mackintosh.	Fordyce	Forbes.
Donachie	Robertson.	Foulis .	Munro.
Donald .	MacDonald.	Frissell .	Fraser.
Donaldson	,,	Frizell .	,,
Donillson	MacDonald of Antrim.	Fullarton	Stuart of Bute.
		Fullerton	,,
Donleavy	Buchanan.	Fyfe	MacDuff.

Septs and Dependents	Clans with which they are connected	Septs and Dependents	Clans with which they are Connected
Galbraith .	MacDonald, Mac-Farlane.	Hardy . .	Farquharson, Mac-intosh.
Gallie . .	Gunn.	Harper. .	Buchanan.
Garrow .	Stewart.	Harperson .	,,
Garvie .	Maclean.	Harris . .	Campbell.
Gaunson .	Gunn.	Hastings .	Campbell of Loudon.
Georgeson .	,,	Hawes . .	Campbell.
Gibb . .	Buchanan	Haws . .	,,
Gibson . .	,,	Hawson .	,,
Gilbert . .	,,	Hawthorn .	MacDonald.
Gilbertson .	,,	Henderson .	Gunn, MacDonald of Glencoe.
Gilbride .	MacDonald.		
Gilchrist .	MacLachlan, Ogilvy.	Hendrie .	MacNauchten.
Gilfillan .	Macnab.	Hendry .	,,
Gillanders .	Ross.	Hewison .	MacDonald.
Gillespie .	Macpherson.	Houston .	,,
Gillies . .	,,	Howison .	,,
Gilmore .	Morrison.	Hughson .	,,
Gilroy . .	Grant of Glenmoris-ton, MacGillivray.	Huntly . .	Gordon.
		Hutcheonson	MacDonald.
Glen . .	Mackintosh.	Hutcheson .	,,
Glennie .	,,	Hutchinson .	,,
Gorrie . .	MacDonald.	Hutchison .	,,
Gow . .	Macpherson.	Inches . .	Robertson.
Gowan . .	Clan Donald.	Isles . .	MacDonald.
Gowrie . .	,,	Jameson .	Gunn, Stuart of Bute.
Gray . .	Stewart of Atholl, Sutherland.	Jamieson .	,, ,,
		Johnson .	Gunn, MacDonald of Ardnamurchan, and of Glencoe.
Gregor . .	MacGregor.		
Gregorson .	,,		
Gregory .	,,	Kay . .	Davidson.
Greig . .	,,	Kean . .	Gunn, MacDonald of Ardnamurchan, and of Glencoe.
Grier . .	,,		
Grierson .	,,		
Grigor . .	,,	Keene . .	,, ,,
Griesck .	MacFarlane.	Keith . .	Macpherson, Suther-land.
Greusach .	Farquharson.		
Grewar . .	MacGregor, Drum-mond.	Kellie . .	MacDonald.
		Kelly . .	,,
Gruamach .	MacFarlane.	Kendrick .	MacNauchton.
Gruer . .	MacGregor, Drum-mond.	Kennedy .	Cameron.
		Kenneth .	MacKenzie.
Hallyard .	Skene.	Kennethson .	,,
Hardie . .	Farquharson, Mac-kintosh.	Kilpatrick .	Colquhoun.
		King . .	Colquhoun.

Septs and Dependents	Clans with which they are Connected	Septs and Dependents	Clans with which they are Connected
Kirkpatrick .	Colquhoun, Mac-Gregor.	Macandeoir .	Buchanan, Macnab.
		MacAndrew .	Mackintosh.
Kinnell .	MacDonald.	MacAngus .	Macinnes.
Kinnieson .	MacFarlane.	Macara . .	MacGregor, Macrae.
Lamb . .	Lamont.	Macaree .	MacGregor.
Lambie .	,,	MacAskill .	MacLeod of Lewis.
Lammie .	,,	MacAslan .	Buchanan.
Lamondson .	,,	MacAuselan .	,,
Landers .	,,	MacAuslan .	,,
Lachlan .	MacLachlan.	MacAusland .	,,
Lang . .	Leslie.	MacAuslane .	,,
Lauchlan .	MacLachlan.	MacAulay .	MacLeod of Lewis.
Lean . .	Maclean.	MacAy . .	Mackintosh (Shaw).
Lees . .	Macpherson.	MacBaxter .	Macmillan.
Leckie . .	MacGregor.	MacBeolain .	MacKenzie.
Lecky . .	,,	MacBeath .	MacBean, MacDonald, Maclean.
Lemond .	Lamont.		
Lennie . .	Buchanan.	MacBeth .	,, ,,
Lenny . .	,,	MacBheath .	,, ,,
Lennox .	MacFarlane, Stewart.	MacBrayne .	MacNauchton.
		MacBride .	MacDonald.
Lewis . .	MacLeod of Lewis.	MacBrieve .	Morrison.
Limond .	Lamont.	MacBurie .	MacDonald of Clanranald.
Limont .	,,		
Linklater .	Sinclair.	MacCaa .	MacFarlane.
Livingston .	Stewart of Appin, MacDougall.	MacCaig .	Farquharson, MacLeod.
Livingstone .	,, ,,	MacCainsh .	Macinnes.
Lobban .	Maclennan.	MacCaishe .	MacDonald.
Logan . .	,,	MacCall .	,,
Loudoun .	Campbell of Loudoun.	MacCallum .	Malcolm.
Love . .		MacCalman .	Buchanan.
Lucas . .	Mackinnon.	MacCalmont .	,,
Luke . .	Lamont.	MacCammon .	,,
Lyon . .		MacCammond	,,
	Farquharson, Lamont	MacCamie .	Stuart of Bute.
Macachounich	Colquhoun.	MacCansh .	Macinnes.
MacAdam .	MacGregor.	MacCardney .	Farquharson, Mackintosh.
MacAdie .	Ferguson.		
MacAindra .	MacFarlane.	MacCartair .	Campbell of Strachur (MacArthur).
Macaldonich .	Buchanan.		
Macalduie .	Lamont.	MacCarter .	,, ,,
MacAllan .	MacDonald of Clanranald, MacFarlane.	MacCash .	MacDonald.
		MacCaskill .	MacLeod of Lewis.
		MacCaul .	MacDonald.

Septs and Dependents	Clans with which they are Connected	Septs and Dependents	Clans with which they are Connected
MacCause	MacFarlane.	MacCowan	Colquhoun, Mac-
MacCaw	MacFarlane, Stuart		Dougall.
	of Bute.	MacCraw	Macrae.
MacCay	Mackay.	MacCrain	MacDonald.
MacCeallaich.	MacDonald.	MacCrie	Mackay.
Mac a'Challies	,,	MacCrimmon	MacLeod of Harris.
MacChlerich .	Cameron, Clan	Maccrouther .	MacGregor, Drum-
	Chattan.		mond.
MacChlery	,, ,,	MacCuag	MacDonald of Kin-
MacChoiter .	MacGregor.		tyre.
MacChruiter .	Buchanan.	MacCuaig	Farquharson, Mac-
MacCloy	Stuart of Bute.		Leod.
MacClure	MacLeod.	MacCuish	MacDonald.
MacClymont .	Lamont.	MacCuithein .	,,
MacCodrum .	MacDonald.	MacCulloch .	MacDougall, Munro,
MacColl	,,		Ross.
MacColman .	Buchanan.	MacCunn	Macqueen.
MacComas	Gunn.	MacCurrach .	Macpherson.
MacCombe	Mackintosh.	MacCutchen .	MacDonald.
MacCombie	Mackintosh.	MacCutcheon	,,
MacCombich .	Stewart of Appin.	Macdade	Davidson.
MacComie	Mackintosh.	Macdaid	,,
MacConacher	MacDougall.	MacDaniell	MacDonald.
MacConachie.	MacGregor, Robert-	MacDavid	Davidson.
	son.	MacDermid	Campbell of Bread-
MacConchy	Mackintosh.		albane.
MacCondy	MacFarlane.	MacDiarmid .	,, ,,
MacConnach .	MacKenzie.	MacDonachie	Robertson.
MacConnechy	Campbell of Inver-	Macdonleavy.	Buchanan.
	awe, Robertson.	MacDowall	MacDougall.
MacConochie.	,, ,,	MacDowell	,,
MacConnell .	MacDonald.	Macdrain	MacDonald.
MacCooish	,,	MacDuffie	Macfie.
MacCook	MacDonald of Kin-	MacDulothe .	MacDougall.
	tyre.	MacEachan .	MacDonald of Clan-
MacCorkindale	MacLeod of Lewis.		ranald.
MacCorkill	Gunn.	MacEachin .	,, ,,
MacCorkle	,,	MacEachran .	MacDonald.
MacCormack.	Buchanan.	MacEachern .	,,
MacCormick .	Maclaine of Loch-	MacEarachar	Farquharson.
	buie.	MacElfrish	MacDonald.
MacCorquodale	MacLeod of Lewis.	MacElheran .	,,
MacCorrie	Macquarrie.	MacEoin	MacFarlane.
MacCorry	,,	Maceol .	MacNauchtan.
MacCoull	MacDougall.	MacErracher.	MacFarlane.

Septs and Dependents	Clans with which they are Connected	Septs and Dependents	Clans with which they are Connected
MacEwan .	MacLachlan.	MacGowan .	MacDonald, Macpherson.
MacEwen .	,,		
MacFadyen .	Maclaine of Lochbuie.	MacGoun .	MacDonald, MacPherson
MacFadzean .	,, ,,	MacGown .	,, ,,
MacFall .	Clan Chattan.	Macgreusich .	Buchanan, MacFarlane.
MacFarquhar	Farquharson.		
MacFater .	MacLaren.	Macgrewar .	MacGregor, Drummond.
MacFeat .	,,		
MacFergus .	Ferguson.	Macgrime .	Graham of Monteith.
MacGaw .	MacFarlane.		
MacGeachie .	MacDonald of Clanranald.	MacGrory .	MacLaren.
		Macgrowther .	MacGregor, Drummond.
MacGeachin .	,, ,,		
MacGeoch .	MacFarlane.	Macgruder .	,, ,,
Macghee .	Mackay.	Macgruer .	Fraser.
Macghie .	,,	Macgruther .	MacGregor, Drummond.
MacGibbon .	Buchanan of Sallochy, Campbell of Argyll, Graham of Monteith.	MacGuaran .	Macquarrie.
		MacGuffie .	Macfie.
		MacGuire .	Macquarrie.
MacGilbert .	Buchanan of Sallochy.	Machaffie .	Macfie.
		Machardie .	Farquharson, Mackintosh.
MacGilchrist .	MacLachlan, Ogilvy.		
MacGilledow .	Lamont.	Machardy .	,, ,,
MacGillivantic	MacDonell of Keppoch.	MacHarold .	MacLeod.
		MacHay .	Mackintosh (Shaw).
MacGillegowie	Lamont.	MacHendrie .	MacNauchton.
MacGillonie .	Cameron.	MacHendry .	,,
MacGilp .	MacDonell of Keppoch.	MacHenry .	MacDonald (MacIan) of Glencoe.
MacGilroy .	Grant of Glenmoriston, MacGillivray.	MacHowell .	MacDougall.
		MacHugh .	MacDonald.
MacGillivour .	MacGillivray.	MacHutchen .	,,
MacGilvra .	MacGillivray, Maclaine of Lochbuie.	MacHutcheon	,,
		MacIan .	Gunn, MacDonald of Ardnamurchan, MacDonald of Glencoe.
MacGilvray .	MacGillivray.		
MacGilvernock	Graham of Monteith.		
Macglashan .	Mackintosh, Stewart of Atholl.		
		Macildowie .	Cameron.
Macglasrich .	MacIvor, Campbell, MacDonell of Keppoch.	Macilduy .	MacGregor, Maclean
		Macilreach .	MacDonald.
		Macilleriach .	,,
MacGorrie .	MacDonald.	Macilriach .	
MacGorry .	,,	Macilrevie .	

Septs and Dependents	Clans with which they are Connected	Septs and Dependents	Clans with which they are Connected
Macilroy .	MacGillivray, Grant of Glenmoriston.	MacKeochan .	MacDonald of Clanranald.
Macilvain .	MacBean.	MacKerchar .	Farquharson.
Macilvora .	Maclaine of Lochbuie.	MacKerracher	,,
		MacKerlich .	MacKenzie.
Macilvrae .	MacGillivray.	MacKerras .	Ferguson.
Macilvride .	MacDonald.	MacKersey .	,,
Macilwhom .	Lamont.	MacKessock .	Campbell of Craignish, MacDonald
Macilwraith .	MacDonald.		of Clanranald.
Macilzegowie.	Lamont.		
Macimmey .	Fraser.	MacKichan .	MacDonald of Clanranald, Mac-
Macinally .	Buchanan.		Dougall.
Macindeor .	Menzies.		
Macindoe .	Buchanan.	Mackie . .	Mackay.
Macinroy .	Robertson.	MacKiggan .	Clan Donald.
Macinstalker .	MacFarlane.	MacKillican .	Mackintosh.
MacIock .	,,	MacKillop .	MacDonell of Keppoch.
MacIsaac .	Campbell of Craignish, MacDonald	MacKim .	Fraser.
	of Clanranald.	MacKimmie .	,,
		Mackindlay .	Farquharson.
MacIver .	Campbell, Robertson, MacKenzie.	Mackinlay .	Buchanan, Farquharson, Mac-
MacIvor .	,, ,,		Farlane, Stewart
MacJames .	MacFarlane.		of Appin.
MacKail .	Cameron.		
MacKames .	Gunn.	Mackinley .	Buchanan.
MacKeachan .	MacDonald of Clanranald.	MacKinnell .	MacDonald.
		Mackinney .	Mackinnon.
MacKeamish .	Gunn.	Mackinning .	,,
MacKean .	Gunn, MacDonald of Ardnamurchan,	Mackinven .	,,
	MacDonald of	MacKirdy .	Stuart of Bute.
	Glencoe.	MacKissock .	Campbell of Craignish, MacDonald
Mackechnie .	MacDonald of Clanranald.		of Clanranald.
		Macknight .	MacNauchton.
Mackee .	Mackay.	Maclae . .	Stewart of Appin.
Mackeggie .	Mackintosh.	Maclagan .	Robertson.
MacKeith .	Macpherson.	MacLairish .	MacDonald.
MacKellachie	MacDonald.	MacLamond .	Lamont.
MacKellaigh .	,,	MacLardie .	MacDonald.
MacKellaig .	,,	MacLardy .	,,
MacKellar .	Campbell.	MacLarty .	,,
MacKelloch .	MacDonald.	MacLaverty .	,,
MacKendrick	MacNauchton.	MacLaws .	Campbell of Argyll.
MacKenrick .	,,	Maclay . .	Stewart of Appin.

Septs and Dependents	Clans with which they are Connected	Septs and Dependents	Clans with which they are Connected
Maclea .	Stewart of Appin.	MacNair .	MacFarlane, Mac-Nauchton.
Macleay .	,,		
MacLehose .	Campbell of Argyll.	MacNamell .	MacDougall.
MacLergain .	Maclean.	MacNayer .	MacNauchtan.
MacLeish .	Macpherson.	MacNee .	MacGregor.
MacLeister .	MacGregor.	MacNeilage .	MacNeil.
Maclerie .	Cameron, Mackin-tosh, Macpher-son.	MacNeiledge .	,,
		MacNeish .	MacGregor.
		MacNelly .	MacNeil.
MacLeverty .	MacDonald.	MacNeur .	MacFarlane.
MacLewis .	MacLeod of Lewis, Stuart of Bute.	MacNicol .	MacLeod of Lewis.
		MacNichol .	Campbell.
MacLise .	Macpherson.	MacNider .	MacFarlane.
MacLiver .	MacGregor.	MacNie .	MacGregor.
MacLucas .	Lamont, Mac-Dougall.	MacNish .	,,
		MacNiter .	MacFarlane.
MacLugash .	MacDougall.	MacNiven .	Cumming, Mackin-tosh, MacNauch-tan.
MacLulich .	MacDougall, Munro, Ross.		
MacLymont .	Lamont.	MacNuir .	MacNauchtan.
MacMartin .	Cameron.	MacNuyer .	Buchanan Mac-Nauchton, Mac-Farlane.
MacMaster .	Buchanan, Mac-innes.		
MacMath .	Matheson.	MacOmie .	Mackintosh.
MacMaurice .	Buchanan.	MacOnie .	Cameron.
MacMenzies .	Menzies.	MacOran .	Campbell of Melfort.
MacMichael .	Stewart of Appin, Stewart of Gallo-way.	MacO'Shannaig	MacDonald of Kin-tyre.
		Macoul .	MacDougall.
MacMinn .	Menzies.	MacOurlic .	Cameron.
MacMonies .	,,	Macowl .	MacDougall.
MacMunn .	Stuart of Bute.	MacOwen .	Campbell of Argyll.
MacMorran .	Mackinnon.	MacPatrick .	Lamont, MacLaren.
MacMurchie .	Buchanan, Clan Donald, Mac-Kenzie.	MacPeter .	MacGregor.
		MacPetrie .	MacGregor.
		MacPhadden	Maclaine of Loch-buie.
MacMurchy .	,, ,,		
MacMurdo .	Clan Donald, Mac-pherson.	MacPhail .	Cameron, Clan Chattan, Mackay.
MacMurdoch .	,, ,,	MacPhater .	MacLaren.
MacMurray .	Murray.	MacPheidiran	MacAulay.
MacMurrich .	MacDonald of Clan-ranald, Macpher-son.	MacPhedron .	,,
		MacPhedran .	Campbell of Argyll.
		MacPhilip .	MacDonell of Kep-poch.
MacMutrie .	Stuart of Bute.		

Septs and Dependents	Clans with which they are Connected	Septs and Dependents	Clans with which they are Connected
MacPhorich .	Lamont.	MacTary .	Innes.
MacPhun .	Matheson, Campbell.	MacTause .	Campbell.
Macquaire .	Macquarrie.	MacTavish .	,,
Macquey .	Mackay.	MacTear .	Ross, Macintyre.
Macquhirr .	Macquarrie.	MacThomas .	Campbell, Mackintosh.
Macquoid .	Mackay.		
Macquire .	Macquarrie.	MacTier .	Ross.
MacQuistan .	MacDonald.	MacTire .	,,
MacQuisten .	,,	MacUlric .	Cameron.
Macra . .	Macrae.	MacUre .	Campbell of Argyll.
Macrach .	,,	Macvail .	Cameron, Mackay, Clan Chattan
Macraild .	MacLeod of Harris.		
MacRaith .	Macrae, Macilwraith, MacDonald.	MacVanish .	MacKenzie.
		MacVarish .	MacDonald of Clanranald.
MacRankin .	Maclean of Coll.	MacVeagh .	Maclean of Duart.
MacRath .	Macrae.	MacVean .	MacBean.
Macritchie .	Mackintosh.	MacVey .	Maclean of Duart.
MacRob .	Gunn, MacFarlane, Innes.	MacVicar .	MacNauchtan.
		MacVinish .	MacKenzie.
MacRobb .	MacFarlane.	MacVurirch .	MacDonald of Clanranald, Macpherson.
MacRobbie .	Robertson, Drummond.		
MacRobie .	,, ,,	MacVurie .	MacDonald of Clanranald.
MacRobert .	,, ,,		
MacRorie .	MacDonald.	MacWalrick .	Cameron.
MacRory .	MacDonald, MacLaren.	MacWalter .	MacFarlane.
		MacWattie .	Buchanan of Lenny.
MacRuer .	MacDonald.	MacWhannell	MacDonald.
MacRurie .	,,	MacWhirr .	Macquarrie.
MacRury .	,,	MacWhirter .	Buchanan.
MacShannachan	,,	MacWilliam .	Gunn, MacFarlane.
		Malcolmson .	Malcolm.
MacShimes .	Fraser.	Malloch .	MacGregor.
MacSimon .	,,	Manson .	Gunn.
MacSorley .	Cameron, MacDonald, Lamont.	Marnoch .	Innes.
		Marr . .	Mar.
MacSporran .	MacDonald.	Martin .	Cameron, MacDonald.
MacSwan .	Macqueen, MacDonald.		
		Mason .	Sinclair.
MacSwen .	Macqueen.	Masterson .	Buchanan.
MacSween .	,,	Mathie .	Matheson.
MacSwyde .	,,	May . .	MacDonald.
MacSymon .	Fraser.	Means .	Menzies.
MacTaggart .	Ross.	Meikleham .	Lamont.

Septs and Dependents	Clans with which they are Connected	Septs and Dependents	Clans with which they are Connected
Mein . .	Menzies.	Norman .	Sutherland.
Meine . .	,,		
Mennie. .	,,	O'Drain .	MacDonald.
Menteith .	Graham, Stewart (Royal).	Oliphant .	Skene.
		O'May . .	Sutherland.
Meyners .	Menzies.	O'Shannachan	MacDonald.
Michie . .	Forbes.	O'Shannaig .	,,
Middleton .	Innes.	O'Shaig .	,,
Miller . .	MacFarlane.		,,
Milne . .	Gordon, Ogilvy.	Paul . .	
Minn . .	Menzies.		Cameron, Mackintosh, Mackay.
Minnus. .	,,	Parlane .	
Mitchell .	Innes.	Paterson .	MacFarlane.
Monach .	MacFarlane.	Patrick .	MacLaren.
Monteith .	Graham, Stewart.	Peter . .	Lamont.
Monzie. .	Menzies.	Philipson .	MacGregor.
Moray . .	Murray.		MacDonell of Keppoch.
More . .	Leslie.	Pitullich .	
Morren. .	Mar.	Polson . .	MacDonald.
Mowat . .	Sutherland.	Purcell . .	Mackay.
Munn . .	Stuart of Bute.		MacDonald.
Murchie .	Buchanan, Clan Donald, MacKenzie.	Rae . .	
		Rankin .	Macrae.
			Maclean of Coll.
Murchison .	,, ,,	Reid . .	Robertson of Strathloch.
Murdoch .	Clan Donald, Macpherson.		
		Reidfurd .	Innes.
Murdoson .	,, ,,	Revie . .	MacDonald, Clan Donald.
Napier . .	MacFarlane.	Reoch . .	Farquharson, MacDonald.
Neal . .	MacNeil.		
Neil . .	,,	Riach . .	,, ,,
Neill . .	,,	Risk . .	Buchanan.
Neilson. .	Mackay.	Ritchie. .	Mackintosh.
Nelson. .	Gunn.	Robb . .	MacFarlane.
Neish . .	MacGregor.	Robison .	Gunn.
Nicol . .	Nicolson.	Robson .	,,
Nicholl .	,,	Ronald. .	MacDonell of Keppoch.
Nicholson .	,,		
Nish . .	MacGregor.	Ronaldson .	,, ,,
Niven . .	Cumming, Mackintosh, MacNauchton.	Rorison .	MacDonald.
		Roy . .	Robertson.
		Ruskin .	MacCalman (Buchanan).
Noble . .	Mackintosh.		
Norie . .	MacDonald.	Russell. .	Cumming.

Septs and Dependents	Clans with which they are Connected	Septs and Dependents	Clans with which they are Connected
Sanderson .	MacDonell of Glengarry.	Thomson .	Mactavish
		Todd . .	MacTavish, Gordon.
Sandison .	Gunn.	Tolmie . .	MacLeod of Raasay.
Shannon .	MacDonald.	Tonnochy .	Robertson.
Shaw . .	Mackintosh.	Tosh . .	Mackintosh.
Sim . .	Fraser.	Toshach .	,,
Sime . .	,,	Tough .	Mar.
Simpson .	,,	Toward .	Lamont.
Simson .	,,	Towart . .	,,
Small . .	Murray.	Train . .	MacDonald.
Smith . .	Clan Chattan.	Turner . .	Lamont.
Sorley . .	Cameron, MacDonald, Lamont.	Tweedie .	Fraser.
		Tyre . .	Macintyre.
Spalding .	Murray.		
Spence .	MacDuff.	Ure . .	Campbell.
Spens . .	,,		
Spittal .	Buchanan.		
Spittel . .	,,	Vass . .	Munro, Ross.
Sporran .	MacDonald.		
Stalker .	MacFarlane.	Wass . .	,, ,,
Stark . .	Robertson.	Watson .	Buchanan.
Strachan .	Mar.	Watt . .	,,
Swan . .	McQueen.	Weaver .	MacFarlane.
Swanson .	Gunn.	Weir . .	MacNauchtan, MacFarlane.
Syme . .	Fraser.		
Symon . .	,,	Wemyss .	MacDuff.
		Whannell .	MacDonald.
Taggart .	Ross.	Wharrie .	Macquarrie.
Tarrill . .	Mackintosh.	White . .	MacGregor, Lamont.
Tawse . .	Farquharson.		
Tawesson .	Campbell.	Whyte . .	,, ,,
Taylor . .	Cameron.	Williamson .	Gunn, Mackay.
Thain . .	Innes.	Wilson . .	Gunn, Innes.
Thomas .	Campbell, MacTavish.	Wright .	Macintyre.
Thomason .	Campbell, MacFarlane.		
		Yuill . .	Buchanan.
Thompson .	Campbell, MacTavish.	Yuille . .	,,
		Yule . .	,,

APPENDICES

APPENDIX I (PAGE 7)

THE TRIBES OF CALEDONIA (ACCORDING TO PTOLEMY) IN THE SECOND CENTURY A.D.

Tribes	Districts Inhabited by Them
1. Epidii	. Kintyre, Knapdale, Argyll proper, and Lorn.
2. Creones	. Lochaber, Morvern, Moidart, Morar, Knoydart, and Glenelg.
3. Carnonacae	. Wester Ross.
4. Caereni	. Assynt, Edderachylis, and Parish of Durness.
5. Cornavii	. Strathnaver and Caithness.
6. Caledonii	. Badenoch, Stratherrick, Glengarry, Glenmoriston, Glenurquhart, and the Aird, etc., Strathnairn, Strathdearn, and Atholl.
7. Decantae	. Easter Ross.
8. Lugi	. Parishes of Kildonan, South Clyne, Golspie, Dornoch, and Rogart in Sutherland.
9. Smertae	. Parishes of Creich and Lairg in Sutherland.
10. Vacomagi	. The County of Elgin, Strathspey, Strathavon, Braemar, and Strathardle.
11. Venicones	. Mearns, Angus, and Fife.
12. Taixali	. Buchan and Banffshire.
13. Damnonii	. Perthshire, except Atholl.

APPENDIX II (PAGE 12)

THE LEGEND OF THE CORONATION STONE, OR STONE OF DESTINY.

Tradition has quite erroneously identified the Scottish Coronation Stone with the *Lia Fail*—or Stone of Destiny of the *Oir-Righ Eireann* at Tara in Ireland, on which the High-Kings of Eire were inaugurated. The story is that Fergus conveyed the stone to Scotland. It was built into the wall of Dunstaffnage Castle, whence it was removed by King Kenneth, in A.D. 850, to the Church of Scone. The Irish *Lia Fail* was, however, at Tara centuries subsequent to the settlement of King Fergus in Dalriadia, and the Dalriad kings were inaugurated on the stone with the footmark at Dunadd ; so the foregoing story is quite untenable. W. F. Skene, Historiographer-Royal, pointed out [1] that the stone appears to be a natural stone from the neighbourhood of either Scone rock itself, or possibly from Dunstaffnage. Modern scientific geological investigation

---

[1] *The Coronation Stone.*

571

confirms *that not only is the stone Scottish, but that it was " quarried somewhere . . . not far from the ancient seat of the Pictish monarchy at Scone."* [1] It is a block of " Lower Old Red Sandstone age from Scotland," but " the very coarse Old Red Sandstone, on which Dunstaffnage Castle stands, is quite dissimilar from the Stone of Scone."

We are thus now able to affirm that the Stone of Destiny is *a native Scottish stone*, from the neighbourhood of Scone itself, and necessarily *the sacred inaugural seat of the Pictish monarchy of ancient Alba*—the seat of the indigenous line of Caledonian chiefs who ruled in Caledonia long ere the Dalriad kings set foot in Scotland—and that our British sovereigns enthroned on this sacred piece of rock are thus the representatives of an indigenous line of Caledonian high-chiefs, emerging from the very dawn of our national history.

On this Stone of Destiny all the Scottish kings were crowned until 1296, when the English king, Edward I., brought it, along with other Scottish spoils, to London. In Westminster Abbey King Edward I. dedicated the stone to Edward the Confessor, and offered it at the altar of that saint. Since that time the Stone has remained in Westminster Abbey in the Coronation Chair, upon which all the British monarchs are crowned.

A suggestion in the Press (February 1951) that the stone might not be the original seems untenable. Those concerned lived into the Bruce's reign, and it is inconceivable that steps would have been taken in 1328 to recover a bogus stone, or not to denounce it as such if it had been. At Scone the stone evidently lay in a different type of seat from that at Westminster.

An old prophecy says with regard to the Stone of Destiny that, wherever it be found, there a king of Scottish blood shall reign. This prophecy has been fulfilled, for our present king occupies the throne of Great Britain and Ireland in virtue of his descent from King James VI. of Scotland and I. of England. Thus it " dreed its weird " in a manner the English had not dreamed of !

The following is the oracular verse regarding the Stone of Destiny,

" Cinnidh Scuit saor am fine,   Far am faighear an Lia-Fail,
   Mur breug am faistine ;   Dlighe flaitheas do ghabhail."

(" The race of the free Scots shall flourish, if this prediction is not false ; wherever the Stone of Destiny is found, they shall prevail by the right of Heaven.")

and the Latin inscription formerly on the stone is said to have been :

Ni fallat fatam, Scoti, quocunque locatum,
Invenient lapidem, regnare tenentur ibidem.

Unless the Fates are faithless found and Sooth be said in vain,
Where'er this stone shall come to rest, a Scottish king shall reign.

APPENDIX III

CLAN CEREMONIAL

At the opening of a clan gathering, outdoor or indoor, or in connection with a clan-march (in which latter there may sometimes be an advance-guard, led by a special " commander " appointed for the occasion, or particular cadet), the chief, chieftain, or chieftainess, enters preceded by pipers (one for an ordinary laird, two for a chieftain, three for a chief), his *Gillie-brataich*, *Ceann-cath* (with the claymore of state)[2] and *Gillie-sporain*, in front of him, and behind him the

---

[1] C. F. Davidson, *Crown and Empire* (*The Times*, published 1937), p. 127.
[2] Claymore, formerly the great two-handed sword ; since the seventeenth century meant the basket-hilted broadsword, the former having virtually ceased to be used, and the distinction being then from the small-sword, *i.e.* rapier.

Tanist and other officers of his household, and if the *Ban-tighearna* be with him, her attendants behind her, including wives of the clan-officers.

When arranged in state, the *Gillie-brataich* stands with the banner behind the chief or chieftain, the *Ceann-cath* takes place at his or her right [1] and so, with his organised clan around him, the chief or chieftain is ready to preside at council, dance, or *ceilidh*.

At baptisms, marriages, and funerals, Mackenzie emphasises the recital of the pedigree and " exploits " and displaying of portraits of the successive chiefs and *ban-tighearna*.

Where a commissioner, or " commander," has been appointed to represent the chief, his commission is first read. Sometimes it will give him the chief's authority to display his banner, more often to raise his pinsel; in each case, simply for representing the chief and his authority for the occasion. At functions where the chief might be present but is not, his plaid and bonnet are laid on the chiefly chair.

The clan and clan-households all over the world should celebrate certain dates : the " clan day," *i.e.* the day the *duthus* was established (anniversary of its charter, or suchlike) ; the clan-saint's day ; the reigning chief's birthday. On these days the chief's standard will be flown at the *Chymmes* or *duthus*, unless personally present, when his banner will be raised. In branches, the chieftain's standard (if any), and where present his banner, will similarly be flown on the branch-" day " as well.

As to Highland weddings, see p. 418, and at her first appearance in kirk thereafter the bride was received by the eldest member of the *fine* walking backwards ceremoniously.

Funerals were solemn and stately, but not dismal and gloomy ceremonies,[2] and were made the means of re-uniting the clan ; " occasions that whilst they sever our ties with those who are gone, renew the links of kindness with the living." They were accompanied by the pipes, heraldic colour and symbolism, and refreshments, of a ceremony directed to fostering anew the grandeur, strength, and continuity of the clan.

The clan should, under the chief, or a commander appointed by him, hold an annual council, and so should each branch under its chieftain, not merely for social diversion, but also to consider family business interests.

At a formal meeting of two clans—which were most ceremonious—the lesser chief (and they knew their precedence perfectly ; see App. XXV) advances and " vails his bonnet " (doffs it with a flourish and bow) giving a *Benach a' Dhe* to the senior chief.[3] Each chief will be accompanied by *Bladier*, *Gille-choise* and *Leinc-chneas* ; his *Luchd-tighe* and *Ceann-luchd-tighe* remaining adjacent.

APPENDIX IV (PAGE 118)

HOUSEHOLD AND PERSONAL FOLLOWERS OF A HIGHLAND CHIEF

Ard Ghillean an Tighe (Gentlemen of the Household).—The number of these varied according to the importance of the chief.

An Seanachaidh (the Sennachie, or Genealogist of the Chief's House).—At table he sat among the chiefs of families, with precedence of the doctors of medicine. It was his duty to keep the clan register, its records, genealogies, and family history ; to pronounce the addresses of ceremony at clan assemblies, and to deliver the chief's inauguration, birthday, and funeral genealogical orations ; also, as Inaugurator, to invest him on succession.

Am Bard (the Bard).—Often synonymous with the Household Sennachie and generally a hereditary position, but otherwise used of an officer inferior to him.

---

[1] *Loyall Dissuasive*, p. 52 ; *Notes and Queries*, August 1942, Vol. 183, p. 92.
[2] *Proceedings of Soc. of Ant. (Scot.)*, p. 104, 1 (2).
[3] *Loyall Dissuasive*, p. 38. See p. 546 as to Clan Gatherings.

An Clàrsair (the Harper).—This was generally a hereditary office.

Am Marischal Tighe (the Seneschal).—In every great household there were two, the principal of whom was well versed in the genealogies and precedences of all the clans.   At table he assigned to each guest his place by touching the appointed seat with his white wand of office.

Am Bladier, the Spokesman, *i.e.* pursuivant, who carried the chief's messages —which it will be recollected were in primitive days all conveyed orally, not in writing.   He made the chief's proclamations.

Am Fear Sporain (the Treasurer).—This was a hereditary position, and its occupant had a town-land for his service.

Am Fear Brataich (the Standard-bearer or Bannerman).—A hereditary office, as was, too, that of

Am Piobaire (the Piper).

An Gille Mór (the Sword or Armour-bearer).—Also called the *Gall-òglach*, whose duty it was to carry the *clogaid*, or helmet, and the *claidheamh-dà-laimh*, or two-handed sword of the chief.   As armour was not continuously worn he had to carry it when on the march.

An Gille-coise (the Henchman).—This retainer was in continual attendance upon the chief ; he stood fully armed behind the chair of his master at meal-time, and if the peace of the occasion were doubtful the henchman had his pistols loaded.

An Luchd-Tighe (the Body-guard).—These were all young gentlemen, chosen from the finest youths of the clan, and each had one or more attendants of his own.   The members of the bodyguard were all well trained in the use of the sword, the target, and the bow, and were adepts in wrestling, swimming, leaping, and dancing ; and those of the sea-coast and the isles were versed in the sounding and navigation duties of seamanship, and the management of the biorlinns or galleys.   The *Luchd-tighe* always attended the chief when he went abroad, and when his residence was on an island, in a lake, they had barracks and a guard-house on the mainland for keeping open the access to the chief's castle.

Am Fear Fardaiche (the Quartermaster).—His duties were to provide lodgings for all attendants, both at home and abroad.   He held no lands in consideration of his services, but had a duty off the hides of all the cattle killed at the principal festivals, or in a " creach " (or foray).

An Cupair, or *Gille-copain* (the Cup-bearer).—There were several cup-bearers, according to the importance of the chief.   The duty of the principal one was to taste the contents of the cup before it was carried round the board.   The office of principal cup-bearer was hereditary, and its occupant held land granted in charter from the chief.

An Gocaman, the Cockman or Warder, who kept watch on the top of the castle.

Am Forsair (the Forester).—He held by his service a croft and grazing in the forest, and was entitled to claim the hunting-dress and weapons of the chief when he returned home from hunting.   This right, like many ancient perquisites of a similar kind, was only a scale of value, and was compounded by a fee in meal or money.

An Gille-Cas-Fhliuch.—A servant whose duty it was to carry the chief over the fords when the chief was travelling on foot.

An Gille-Couston.—The leader of the chief's horse.

An Gille-Comhsreang.—This was a guide who at dangerous precipices led the chief's horse by a long rein.

An Gille-Trusairneis.—The Baggage-man who had charge of the sumpter-horses.

An Leinc-chneas.—A Confidant or Privy Counsellor.

An Gille-sguain (the Train-bearer).—When the Lords of the Isles were in power we are told that among their train was a person designated *Fear sguabadh dealt*, whose duty it was to brush the dew away before his Royal master.

An Gille Chlarsair.—The Harper's Attendant, who carried his harp.

Gille Phiobaire.—The Piper's Servant, who carried the pipes, presented them to the piper when he was about to play, and received them again when the piper had concluded his performance. This attendant was only, however, attached to pipers of the first rank.

An Gille-Ruith (the Running Footman).

An Cleasaiche (the Fool or Jester).

APPENDIX V (PAGE 203)

Buchanan.—There is a sept bearing this name located in Cowal, which appears to have no connection with and to be of an entirely different origin from the Clan Buchanan of Lochlomondside. The sept alluded to is *Clann a' Chàinich* or *Chananaich of Acha-da-cherran-beg.*

In a paper on Cowal names Lieut.-Col. John MacInnes, V.D., Glendaruel, states : " There is historical evidence that this family has been in possession of their inheritance in Glendaruel for at least five hundred years."

The following information is from the Marquis of Lorne's *The Legends of the Western Highlands* : " When Colin had burnt his house (*i.e.*, at Garvie) he went back to Ardconnel, in Lochawe, to live in the castle there, leaving a *cananach* or *càineach* (from *càin*, a tax), or rent-collector, in Cowal. This man had his farm free of rent, and so he was called ' Baron,' being a small freeholder. There were many small freeholders in Cowal, but there were none of them that did not run into debt and sell their lands before the year 1868, except the descendant of this Colin's *cananach.*"

In the Kirk Session, 18th September 1753, appears *Duncan MacHannanich* of Auchtekerrenbeg ; while on 5th February 1843 appears *Donald MacChananich,* elder. The name seems now to have been modernised as Buchanan.

Alongside the Buchanans of Glendaruel appear the MacGibbons or Gibsons. Both they and the Buchanans of Glendaruel may be classed as septs, or rather dependents, of their more powerful neighbours, the Campbells.

In 1439 the Lennox was ravished by a large body of Islesmen under Lachlan Maclean and Murdoch Gibson. Who this *Murdoch Gibson* was does not appear, but he may have been one of the Gibsons of Glendaruel.

APPENDIX VI (PAGE 204)

Cameron.—There would appear to be a sept bearing this name and deriving it from the village of Cameron, in Fifeshire. This village bore of old the name *Cambrun.* So far back as the days of King Robert the Bruce these Cambruns, de Cambruns, or Camerons appear in the records of the counties of Aberdeen and Perth. It is difficult, therefore, to connect these East Coast Camerons with the Camerons of Lochaber.

" The *Clan Cameron* was *communitas* divided into several distinct clans. The amily which obtained the leadership and whose chief bears the title of Lochiel, has long been known as ' *Clan Dòmhnuill* ' or ' *Conuil,* ' its heads bearing the title ' *MacConuil duibh* ' from ' *Domhnull Dubh,* ' head of the clan in 1429. One of the most frequent forms of this title of the heads of the clan in old writings and histories is ' *MacCoil duibh.* ' This form is of frequent occurrence in the MS. ' History of the Camerons.' In the ' Rentaill of the Lordschippe of Huntlye,' made in 1600 (given in *Spald. Club. Misc.,* IV., 292), we read of ' *Allane Camrone MacOuildowy,* ' and in Moysies' *Memoirs* (98) of ' *Allane MacKildowie.* ' "—(*The MacIntoshes and Clan Chattan,* by A. MacIntosh Shaw.)

APPENDIX VII (PAGE 232)

EXTRACT FROM FRAGMENT OF A MANUSCRIPT HISTORY OF THE MACDONALDS, WRITTEN IN THE REIGN OF CHARLES II.

(From the Gregory Collection)

INSTALLATION OF THE LORDS OF THE ISLES

" The Ceremony of proclaiming the Lord of the Isles. At this the Bishop of the Isles and seven priests were sometimes present ; but a bishop was always present, with the chieftains of all the principal families, and a *Ruler of the Isles*. There was a square stone, seven or eight feet long, and the tract of a man's foot cut thereon, upon which he stood, denoting that he should walk in the footsteps of his predecessors, and that he was installed by right in his possessions. He was clothed in a white habit, to shew his innocence and integrity of heart, that he would be a light to his people, and maintain the true religion. The white apparel did afterwards belong to the poet by right. Then he was to receive a white rod in his hand, intimating that he had power to rule, not with tyranny and partiality, but with discretion and sincerity. Then he received his forefathers' sword, or some other sword, signifying that his duty was to protect and defend them from the incursions of their enemies in peace or war, as the obligations and customs of his predecessors were. The ceremony being over, Mass was said after the blessing of the Bishop and the seven priests, the people pouring their prayer for the success and prosperity of their new created Lord. When they were dismissed, the Lord of the Isles feasted them for a week thereafter ; gave liberally to the monks, poets, bards, and musicians. You may judge that they spent liberally without any exception of persons.

" The constitution or government of the Isles was thus : Macdonald had his council at Island Finlaggan, in Isla, to the number of sixteen, viz. four Thanes, four Armins—that is to say, Lords or sub-Thanes—four Bastards (*i.e.*, Squires), or men of competent estates, who could not come up with Armins or Thanes— that is, freeholders—or men that had their lands in factory, as MacGee of the Rinds of Isla, MacNicoll in Portree in Skye, and MacEachern, Mackay, and MacGillevray in Mull, MacIllemhaoel or Macmillan, etc. There was a table of stone where this council sat in the Isle of Finlaggan ; the which table, with the stone on which MacDonald sat, were carried away by Argyll with the bells that were at Icolumkill. Moreover, there was a judge in every Isle for the discussion of all controversies, who had lands from MacDonald for their trouble, and likewise the eleventh part of every action decided. But there might still be an appeal to the Council of the Isles.

" MacFinnon was obliged to see weights and measures adjusted ; and Mac-Duffie, or Macphie of Colonsay, kept the records of the Isles."

APPENDIX VIII (PAGE 232)

" Mack-Donald, King of the Isles, deliver'd the Rights of their lands to his Vassals in the Isles and Continent, with up-lifted Hands and bended Knees on the black Stones ; and in this Posture, before many Witnesses, he solemnly swore that he would never recall those Rights which he then granted : and this was instead of his Great Seal. Hence it is that when one was certain of what he affirm'd, he said positively, I have freedom to swear this Matter upon the black Stones. . . . The black Stones (of Iona) are so call'd not from their Colour, for that is grey, but from the Effects that Tradition say ensued upon Perjury, if any one became guilty of it after swearing on these Stones in the usual manner ; for an Oath made on them was decisive in all Controversies."—(*A Description of the Western Islands of Scotland*, by M. Martin, Gent., A.D. 1716, s.v. " Island of Iona.")

Note.—I am unable to think this somewhat undignified story has been correctly " taken down " by Martin. The Lord of the Isles made his grants, not kneeling on his knees and calling down imprecations on himself (!) but in the stately formula " I, Macdonald, sitting on Dundonald " (*i.e.*, a moot hill, as a matter of fact, the judgement-seat at the roadside between the hotel and churchyard at Kilmachumaig, near Crinan). That a ceremony of confirmation took place at the Black Stones of Iona, I can well imagine—but I fancy it was the *grantees* who on bended knee did homage and may well have received a confirmation of the promise from Macdonald before the assembled Council of the Isles, when new vassals successively knelt before *him* as patriarch, swearing to " manteine, defende, and support thee, as I wish the Lord in my need to help me."

APPENDIX IX (PAGE 240)

CLAN DONALD CHIEFSHIP : ACT OF THE PRIVY COUNCIL

I

" Apud Edinburgh decimo octavo Julii 1672.

" The Lords of His Majesty's Privy Council considering that by the Laws and Acts of Parliament of the realm, Chieftaines of Clannes are obliged to find caution for their whole name and Clan, that they shall keep the peace, and exhibit and present them to justice, wherever they shall be called. In prosecution of which lawes, the said Lordes, ordaines and commandes Aeneas, Lord Mac-Donald, as Chief of the Name and Clan of MacDonald, to exhibit before the Council, upon the first Tuesday of October next, the persons underwritten, viz., Archibald MacDonald of Keppoch ; MacDonald of Theisit ; MacDonald of Bohauden, and his eldest son ; MacDonald of Killichouat ; MacDonald in Tullich ; MacDonald in Innereymere ; Angus Kennedy in Lenachar ; Mac-Donald of May ; MacDonald of Teinadish ; MacDonald in Armat ; MacDonald of Insh, and MacDonald of Auchnacoshen, to find caution for their men tenants, servants, and indellers upon their lands, roumes, and possessiounes, and the hail persons descended of their Families, etc., etc."

The above Act demonstrates that, so far back as 1672, the Chief of Glengarry was recognised by the Government as *the Chief of the whole Clan of MacDonald*. It will also be seen that among the persons for whom Glengarry is held responsible is MacDonell of Keppoch, who, as has already been shown, was descended from a younger brother of Donald, second Lord of the Isles.

Now the " Chiefship of the Name and Clan of Macdonald," as the Privy Council described it so carefully, has been decided by Lyon Court, 11th April 1947, see Appendix XXXI and *Scots Law Times*, 1950, p. 8.

APPENDIX X (PAGE 116)

THE INAUGURATION OF A CHIEF

Many clans have become chiefless in the past through no proper steps being taken upon the death of the reigning chief with no direct successor ; the more so since they have been ignorant of the principles involved (which, as we have

U

seen, pp. 154, 184, are essentially analogous to those surrounding succession to the Crown, to which Mackenzie, Seton, and Stevenson all equate succession in armorial bearings) ; or have deduced wrongous ideas from the arguments) ɛ tendencious claimants, or of politicians seeking to extinguish the Highland " stocks " on which the survival of clanship depends. We shall indicate accordingly the modern steps which should be taken, as deduced from the regal and feudo-clannish precedents officially recognised.

1. On the death of the chief, or within a short time after, if the heir has not emerged at the funeral, some three prominent chieftains, and/or the Secretary of the Council of chiefs [1] should write to the *Heir at Law*, asking whether he or she *is* the lawful heir to the representation, either at the Common Law of Succession, or under tailzie if any be known (this may be the armorial destination on record in Lyon Court, but there *may* be a testamentary settlement by the late chief, as yet unexecuted and capable of being confirmed by Lyon). The second question, if the heir indicated be of another Name, is, whether he or she *is* to " enter heir " by " taking the name and bearing of the family within due time." [2] If the answer be in the affirmative, steps will proceed ; if in the negative, the next heir will have to be sought and approached.

2. If, after diligent search, no heir, or claimant willing to proceed with his claim, can be found ; then a meeting of the clan should be summoned by advertisement, on, say, forty days' warning, at the instance of the armigerous members of the Honourable Clan : to consider if the chiefship seems *de facto* and *de jure* vacant.[3] If such a resolution is passed at the clan meeting, and no claimant announces challenge in the contrary, with intention to proceed forthwith to make up his title, the armigerous members of the clan (preferably the five or nine oldest or with the most ancient arms) will then aver the vacancy [4] and proceed by themselves, or an *ad hoc derbhfine* consisting of the nine " principal landed men " (chieftains) or *daoine-uasail* as follows.

The *Daoine-uasail* (*i.e.* armigerous members of the clan) will then consider a suitable candidate from amongst the *daoine-uasail* ; and at a further meeting called by the *ad hoc derbhfine* (of nine oldest armigerous *daoine-uasail*), after forty days' warning (sixty if there be armigerous members of the clan known to be overseas), select a candidate for presentation to the Lyon with their recommendation, and direct a roll to be subscribed of those willing to support the candidate. Whilst any " acclamation " or *contra*, would not affect the *derbhfine* resolutions, yet, as Lyon's confirmation is ministerial, not judicial, a " good " acclamation might carry weight. The position is quite different from where there is a nomination or tailzie. Lyon has discretion to confirm or reject.

3. He now petitions the Court of the Lord Lyon for a grant, or confirmation, of the ensigns armorial of the ancient chiefs, lodging in support of his claim the signed roll, along with " Testificats from Persons of Honour," etc. Lyon may be satisfied of the circumstances, or may order intimation and advertisement, or refuse. Any claimant at law may thus still intervene. Lyon, in exercising the Royal Prerogative in Arms (*Macdonell* v. *Macdonald*, 1826), will take any objections into consideration, but (as the Lord Lyon in MacGregor, cf. Balhadie's fourteen votes) will not allow a *liberum veto* of one or two members

---

[1] The Standing Council of Scottish Chiefs, 18 Duke Street, Edinburgh.

[2] *Loyall Dissuasive*, p. 39.

[3] These proceedings presume that only " indeterminate " cadet-*armigeri* are left. For were any surviving affiliated cadet extant, *he* (or she) would be " nearest appearand heir " and no vacancy could be averred. So production of a cadet-matriculation or Official Genealogy, would bar, or void, and make nugatory, any such proceedings.

[4] This cannot be so if anyone petitions Lyon Court claiming rematriculation of (*i.e.* revestiture in) the chiefly arms.

to leave the clan chiefless. What amounts to a sufficient objection for refusal on Lyon's part (he has a complete discretion) remains to be seen by practice. The petitioner in that case is invoking the ministerial power delegated from the *Ard-righ* as " Chief of Chiefs " (see p. 150). If the petitioner is accepted by Lyon, that completes his right, unless the heir under former destination raises a reduction of the Confirmation within twenty years. Thereafter the confirmee and his line are secure, cf. *Mackinnon of Corry*, forced into cadency by Lyon Court, as being too late to reduce Mackinnon of Mackinnon's matriculation of 1811.[1] Lyon would refuse precipitate or unsuitable selectees.

The foregoing refers *solely* to cases where the line of heirs is *lost* ; where you cannot find an heir, or where a supposed heir will not come forward, *i.e.* where the chiefship is *de facto* and *de jure* vacant.

I will now consider the case where there is an heir, or claimant, maybe more than one. In this case there is no room for intervention by the *daoine-uasail*, etc. The question of who is the rightful heir, and chief, as inheritor of the *undifferenced arms* is entirely a matter of legal succession and revestiture by rematriculation, in these arms as the chiefly heritage.

4. Where there is an obvious heir, he or she should be urged to make up his or her title to the ensigns armorial, or at any rate to make good his or her status as representer of the family (the stem of the clan or branch), if not by rematriculation (costing £20 to £36—150 dollars—of Exchequer fees), at any rate by a *Diploma Stemmatis* of maybe simple form, or by adding to the pedigree in the Public Register of Genealogies his or her succession with the style and title of Chief/Representer of the " stem " genealogy. If the initial pedigree is on record, this should cost only a few guineas—maybe not more than £1 (3 or 4 dollars).

5. Where there are several claimants, the situation is that there is a competing claim to incorporeal heritable property of an indivisible nature. The test will be the right and title to " the old family arms," including any supporters, which from their importance have come to be regarded almost as an *index* of chiefship, but are really an *incident* of chiefship—for many people other than chiefs may have supporters.[2] In this contingency, neither the clan, nor the Clan Society, can decide a matter which is *a question of the law of property* ; and recollect, the *clan itself* is an incorporeal " noble fief " (and what " fief " could be nobler ?), of which it is officially laid down there have been " heirs " and " heretrices." In such a controversy, moreover, neither the clan, nor the society, have a *locus* to appear ; for in terms of *Macdonell* v. *Macdonald*, affirmed by the House of Lords in *Seaforth* v. *Allangrange*, no one is entitled to attack a right to arms he does not *himself* claim, unless it is awarded (as indicated in *Macdonell* v. *Macdonald*) in a character which the opponent claims—"He does not say he is the chieftain " (as was observed of Glengarry).[3]

Of course anyone—chieftains or the Clan Society—may take all the steps they can to effect accommodation ; and both in such efforts, and in the litigation which may follow, the records of a well-conducted Clan Society may preserve

---

[1] Lyon Court, 1947, Lyon Register, XXXVI, 27, 153.

[2] See *Tartans of the Clans and Families of Scotland*, p. 52, n. 2.

[3] It is clear, however, that a *duine-uasail* has not a *locus* to intervene to prevent another person being put over him as chief ; Macrae-Gilstrap, second son of Conchra, who intervened against Inverinate on that ground, was only allowed to be heard as to the *existence of the clan* (*i.e.* legally, whether a noble Macrae community existed or not) ; and *he* should not even have been heard on *that* (looking to *MacDonell* and *Seaforth*), it being quite subversive for a cadet of a sub-branch to go over the head of his own branch-*representer* (mark the word). A sub-cadet would need to aver that his own chieftain was incapable, " misguidit," or *incapax*.

any useful points of evidence on the *jus familiare* of that clan ; though in most cases the matter must depend on the terms of prior matriculations and settlements of former representers. For, as Dr. Cameron has explained, *tanistry* (see App. XXX) is really the patriarchal equivalent of *testate succession* ; and the question is, *what*, in exercise of his venerable and parental powers, the dying patriarch has done ; or, if he didn't do anything, what the law, or his predecessors have done about such matters. Lyon has, very properly, rejected resolutions of Clan Societies as bearing on such intestate succession ; and Lord Jamieson made it clear that such are *of no weight*—and fortunately so, for otherwise they would have embarked on a traffic in arms and titles. Their records, as I say, may, if properly kept, come to be very useful evidence ; but they would have to be very different from the records of many such societies at present. I mean they should be repositories of deeds, documents, and other muniments of the clan, which might otherwise perish or be overlooked.

Nor can I give any indication of what may or may not be the principles applicable in any given case. In *Scots Heraldry* (1934), *Tartans of the Clans and Families of Scotland* (1938), *Observations on Armorial Conveyancing* (1941), *Law of Succession in Ensigns Armorial* (1944), and in this volume, I have endeavoured to set forth the principles and considerations which have been applied, and have reported various decisions, with elucidation of what was decided and why. But Lord Lyon Kinnoull laid down in 1824 that every case and competition must be adjudicated according to the principles of law, and Lord Lyon Balfour Paul that " every case must be judged on its merits." All I can do is to state what these general principles have been, and the sort of points regarded as relevant on the merits, *i.e.* the matters which have, or are likely, on relevant *dicta* from the Bench, to receive consideration. In each case the claimant, or competitor, must therefore weigh the whole facts on which he founds ; and as Lord Lyon Grant has said, " Whether opposed or not, every Petitioner must prove his case." Whether the succession in any particular clan or family is to heirs-general, heirs-male, or heirs of tailzie, is entirely the affair of its own chief and his council. As a jurist, what I have to consider is : Which has in any given case been preferred, or what effected ? That is what Lyon Court has to decide after weighing all the relevant considerations placed before it by claimants and counsel. Some of what I have written may enable clans *now* to determine (*a*) how their affairs do stand ; (*b*) how they can be judicially settled ; (*c*) how to go about clearing up dubiety in good time, and effectively arranging the stem-succession in the manner which they and their council do really want, *e.g.* getting their present chief to make a wise settlement.

Let us assume these things have been cleared up, and that either *in foro*, or upon a Petition in ordinary course by an unopposed " appearand heir," the Decree of the Court of Honour has been obtained revesting the heir in " the old family arms "—the constructive shield, armorial *leine-croich*, crest, and banner of the founder of the clan or family (Sir George Mackenzie and Dr. Maclean Watt have, be it remembered, concurred that *clan and family mean the same thing*, and the former that armorial chiefship and Celtic *Ceann-cinnidh* are the same thing) ; and that the Decree has been registered in Lyon's *Public Register* ; and that the heir (thus retoured and invested, in the arms) is formally to take over his parental office and relevant armorial heritage.

6. We now enter on the modern equivalent of the second stage of the ancient Celtic inauguration : what took place " at the stone " and in the presence of the assembled tribe or clan. The " evidence " in those early days was various— maybe the report of the Druid ; sometimes a charter of the chief chymmes ; on other occasions, a charter of chieftainry under the Great Seal—this last representing the patriarchal mandate of the *Ard-righ* ; later, the Lord Lyon's *Diploma* or matriculation (see p. 195).

The clan (or the branch) will be assembled at the *Chymmes*, or wherever else is now the " sacred place " of inauguration. If there *is* a " Bear Stone " like that of the Forbeses, or the " Falcon Stone " of the Hays ; then it should be used.[1] If not, there may be an ancestral chair, such as that of the Leslies, once in Balquhain Castle. If nothing of the kind has survived, you may as well begin now and have one made from timber from the oldest part of the house, or a limb of some aged tree around the *Chymmes* ; and even if the estate has been sold, you may manage to get a branch off such tree. See that the arms are carved on the back of the chair.

Well in front set a table, which may be covered with tartan ; and on the right, some distance away, set the council of the clan, the " Family Council," or the chiefly *derbhfine* of nine persons ; and on the left you may suitably put the officers of the Clan Society.

On either side of the table will be set the harper and the secretary of the Clan Association (as clerk, or in the case of a chieftaincy, the factory-clerk of the *duthus*). Between them is *An Fhear Sporain* with the " old family seal of arms " [2] in an embroidered bag.

An Marischal Tighe (the seneschal) will marshal the proceedings according to the Law of Arms and order of the sennachie, on whose indicating all is ready, the trumpeter will wind his horn, and the new chief's procession will emerge, led by three pipers (two in the case of a chieftain). The standard-bearer, carrying the pinsel, pennon, or standard ; *An Bladier*, the " speaker-household herald," wearing the badge of the chief ; *An Brataich*, the chief's banner-man with the chief's great armorial banner ; *An Sennachie*, the clan bard, in his long robe, carrying the extract matriculation from Lyon Register of the chief's arms. Behind him, *An Boineid-mhor*, or the coronet if the chief be a peer, carried by the most distinguished cadet or senior male relative of the chief,[3] on his right *An Gillemor* carrying the ancestral sword,[4] and on his left, the Baron-Bailie (usually the factor, or solicitor of the chief) carrying the white wand, or rod, denoting parental rule and chiefly authority [5]—the wand of clan justice, the *jus familiare*. Then comes the *Chief*, who may be wearing " the cap of dignity," or his braid bonnet with

---

[1] We have to recollect that the proceedings should represent the fusion of the allodial inauguration with the revestiture as from the *Ard-righ* (the Fountain of Honour), and that, as in the Pictish indigenously Scottish rite, the ceremony consisted essentially of delivery of the symbols, with hortatory addresses ; and that the ceremony rightly treats the new chief as already chief by inheritance, *i.e.* in virtue either of his predecessor's nomination, or the operation of law. The ceremony is so that all may see, hear, and know, who he or she is, and that their representer is *de facto* installed in the coat of the late representer.

[2] *Maclean of Ardgour* v. *Maclean*, 1941 S.C. 713, Finding 27, and see p. 114.

[3] Who has special functions, whether the chief be a male or female, cf. *Memoirs of a Highland Lady*, p. 189.

[4] This may, or should be, some ancestral weapon, if there be one, and not necessarily the sword which will be worn by the chief. A chieftainess would not herself wear a broadsword (claymore, as it is called nowadays), but she would be invested with, and bear formally, " the sword " of office (cf. J. Millington, *Heraldry in History, Poetry, and Romance*, p. 296), and even, like the Empress Maria Theresa, as Queen of that great clan country, the Kingdom of Hungary, wave it to the four winds.

[5] *Scottish Coronations*, p. 33 ; *Tartans of the Clans and Families of Scotland*, p. 30, n. 2 ; I. F. Grant, *Lordship of the Isles*, pp. 74, 155, 353, regarding rods of office, on West Highland tombstones ; and *Scots Peerage*, VIII., p. 270, and *Book of Braemar Gathering*, 1939, p. 105, regarding the long ragged staff found in the tomb of Sir John Lyon of Glamis ; whilst reference may be made to the long white staff held by John, 7th Lord Borthwick, Chief of the Name, in his portrait, *c.* 1580, at Crookston. Although the friend of Mary Queen of Scots, he does not appear to have held any office suggesting a white staff, and it and " the White Lyon's " may well have been the staff of chiefship. Under modern conditions the staff might appropriately be a *cromak* mounted with a chromium-plated band engraved with the shield, motto, and title of the chief or chieftain.

three eagle's feathers, and, if a baron, may be wearing over his Highland dress the old feudo-baronial robe, its train borne by *An Gille Sguain*.[1] In this procession behind the chief, comes, on his right, *An Ceann-Cath* (the principal cadet, or the heir male, where the heir of line is the Chief/*Ceann-cinnidh*) ; to the left, *An Leinc-Chneas* (the chief's eldest councillor) ; and immediately behind, and slightly in the rear of the two foregoing, *An Gille coise*. Behind these follow the *Luchd-tighe* (bodyguard), who take their place behind the chief's chair.

The pipers pass behind the chair, and as the rest get into place, they cease playing. *An Bladier* stands forward to the left of the chair, *An Sennachie* to the right, thence advancing after the chief has taken his first position.

An Marischal-tighe takes his place at the table, on which the seal, sword, and wand have been placed—their bearers passing into the group behind the chair, where the standard-bearer has also placed himself, the banner-man being immediately behind, or slightly to the right of the chair.

An Ceann-Cath takes his place to the right thereof, *An Fear Sporain* also ; and on the left, *An Leinc-Chneas* and *An Gillemor* ; whilst the henchman stands at the back corner of the chair.

The chief takes his place between the chair and table, standing somewhat to the right, and *An Sennachie* advances centrewards near him, facing the table.[2]

All being in position, and the bagpipes having then ceased playing, the proceedings may suitably commence with prayer by the clan chaplain, or the minister occupying the benefice in which the *co-arb* of the clan saint officiated ; and a suitable address on the parental and family character of chiefship and the clan system may be delivered, so that any persons not already informed, may be apprised of the solemn and social significance, and the patriarchal and family nature of the office of chief, and its inaugural ceremonies.

After this, and some suitable vocal, harp, or pipe music, *An Bladier* may himself deliver, or introduce the bard to deliver, a panegyric on the history and glorious deeds of the clan and its chiefs. Thereafter the inauguration itself proceeds.

An Marischal-tighe now " desyres " the sennachie to " Show the Chief's pleasure," and the *Ard-righ's* confirmation.

The Sennachie of the Chiefly House as Inaugurator now addresses the clan :

" Clan MacX . . . I here present unto you A . . . McX . . . of McX . . . the undoubted Chief of this Clan, inheritor thereof by the Laws of God and man, who is willing to accept the Chiefship." [3]

The clan reply, shouting, " God bless our Chief, and us for his cause."

---

[1] This very office of a Celtic train-bearer shows that baronial robes were, on occasion, worn by Highland chiefs—as the portrait of Glenorchy in the *Black Book of Taymouth* illustrates. It may, however, be that the chief will not want to appear *in* cap and robe (although I emphasise the symbolic significance of his entry *with bonnet on*). Many chiefs will think their crested bonnet with the three eagle feathers (real ones, of course, on state occasions) cap enough, as it is certainly symbolic enough. The likewise-crested *Boineid-mhor* borne before him will, as will be seen, be used for another and ceremonial purpose.

[2] At the later stage final grouping, *An Sennachie* stands at the right of the chair and somewhat in front of its line.

[3] In the Scottish " presentation " or " recognition " the people were not even asked whether they be " willing to do service," etc. . . . The pronouncement was simply of the heir's acceptance of the parental office which had devolved upon him. Analogously, the older English presentation specified that the King was " inheritor." What is emphasised is the parental character. Before acceptance of the devolution of the function of being the re-embodiment of the deceased chief, no doubt, steps could be taken to move the first heir to abstain, or devolve the succession otherwise ; or open it to the next heir. The whole concept, however, is tribal and familial—unbroken transmission from patriarch to patriarch.

The Sennachie, Genealogist of the Chiefly House, will then announce :

" There is here produced the Judgement/Diploma of the Lord Lyon King of Arms, His Majesty's Supreme Officer of Honour, confirming unto A . . . McX . . . of McX . . . the ensigns armorial of the House of McX . . . of McX . . . (or avouching the addition to the Genealogy in the Public Register of All Genealogies and Birthbrieves in Scotland, of A . . . McX . . . of McX . . . as now the stem, Representer and Chief, of the House of McX . . . of McX . . .) and the same will now be read by *An Bladier*."

At the conclusion of this reading the sennachie will cry, " God bless the Chief and the Clan." He then calls on the custodian of the inaugural place, or *An Marischal-tighe*, and himself on the right and the *marischal-tighe* on the left, conduct the chief to the chair.

The sennachie now returns to the table, and hands the claymore to the " eldest cadet " (*i.e.* the representer of that house) who delivers the sword to the chief, who demands it,[1] as of right.

The sennachie now delivers the white wand to the latest cadet sprung from the chiefly stem, who delivers it to the chief, who now sits in the ancestral seat invested with the full insignia of chiefly authority. At this point would have occurred imposition of the *boineid-mhor* or diadem, *except* that we have seen the chief-succedant comes in *wearing* his " Hat," and Bute observes there was no " crowning " in the chiefly inauguration, *i.e.* he takes possession, and (per Macleod) *demands* delivery of the insignia of the ancestor whom he now " represents," a solemn and majestic taking upon him/her, of the parenthood.

The Sennachie now advances, and falling on one knee, hails the chief:

" Benach De A mac X McX, nighean y . . . Mac x . . . de (Mac X, or whatever the title may be) *Ceann Cinnidh* Clan MacX . . . (or *Ceann Tighe*, here the territorial title)." (*The genealogy being deduced back, in the case of a chief of a clan to its founder, and of a branch, to the eponymus of the branch.*)

The clan chaplain, or *co-arb*, then submits the chiefly oath :

" Do you promise to be a loving Father/Mother to the Clan McX . . . ? "

The clan sennachie then puts the general oath to the clan—which repeats it, thus :

" I swear and hold up my hand to maintain, defend, and support thee, as I wish the Lord in my need to help me. Amen."

Marischal-tighe now places the chief's *boineid-mhor* with crest-badge on a cushion at the chief's feet, and each cadet-chieftain, sprung directly from the stem, or chieftains of branches not affiliated to the stem, and *sub*-branch chieftains who hold lands or honours *de rege*,[2] or superiors other than the chief or branch chieftains of the clan itself, then advance in their order, and kneeling on one knee, touches the chiefly *boineid*, saying :

" So mote God help me, as I shall support thee."

The last of these having returned to his, or her, place, the clan trumpeter (maybe the baron-officer of the principal fief, or his trumpeter) sounds a fanfare, or anyway " winds his horn," and all cry " Hail to the Chief " three times.

The clan song is sung, and as it concludes (the chiefly insignia having been meantime taken up and delivered again to the bearers) the chief's procession moves out in the same order as it entered, the bagpipes striking up the clan march when the singing has ceased, and forming the indication for the procession to move.

---

[1] R. Macleod of Macleod, *The Macleods of Dunvegan*, p. xiv.

[2] The contingency here is to secure the specific adherence of the clan magnates, and so prevent incidents, such as that in which Coll, on the ground of having got a barony charter, declined to follow Duart, on an important occasion (*Glasgow Archaeological Society*, X., p. 29).

A feast, or "banquet of cake and liquid refreshment" should then follow, at which, after the health of the *Ard-righ*, that of "the chief," and no doubt many others will be given and responded to, and suitable musical accompaniment, from pipes, violin, and *clarsach* rendered.

As already indicated, the portraits (failing originals, photographs of these) of former chiefs, chieftainesses, and *Ban-tighearna* should be on view, and their various achievements (or delinquencies) capably recounted, and likewise copies of illustrations or pictures featuring incidents in which the clan or chiefs took part. During the general gathering, *An Brataich* will throughout keep immediately behind the chief, carrying the hand-*ensynzie*, of prescribed size,[1] this small flag's presence indicating throughout the afternoon the precise whereabouts, amidst the throng, of the chief himself.

This is the primitive ceremony from which our Scots coronation grew. Parts have continued to be used in the old Highland families ; and though few occasions could arise on which the *whole* would be contemplated, use of appropriate portions by some of our great chiefs (to such extent as circumstances may admit), on suitable occasions, not only emphasises the nature of chiefship itself (one of the very purposes of these ceremonies, to which the children of the clan should assuredly be brought, that they may grasp its purport and hand on the details) but reminds us that our sovereign is indeed "Chief of Chiefs" as George IV. was hailed in the Parliament Hall of Edinburgh in 1822, and that our ancient monarchy is the apotheosis of "the clan system" and the supreme glorification of "the family" as a national institution.

APPENDIX XI (PAGE 255)

KENNETH MACKENZIE, "THE BRAHAN SEER" (COINNEACH ODHAR)

This remarkable personage was born at Baile-na-Cille, in the parish of Uig, Island of Lewis, about the beginning of the seventeenth century. He was gifted with wonderful powers of divination and second-sight, said to have been due to the possession of a wonderful stone given to him by fairy agency. Coinneach Odhar's prophecies are well known in Ross-shire and the neighbourhood, and whatever, in these enlightened days, may be thought and said about second-sight, there is no room for doubt that many of the predictions of the Brahan Seer regarding future events and the fate of well-known families have been fulfilled centuries after he had given utterance to them. Several of his prophecies have still to be fulfilled.

During the reign of the 3rd Earl of Seaforth the unfortunate Coinneach Odhar was put to death by his Countess while her Lord was absent in Paris. Before the execution of the Seer he uttered the following remarkable prediction regarding the ultimate extinction of the MacKenzies of Seaforth :

"I see into the far future, and I read the doom of the race of my oppressor. The long-descended line of Seaforth will, ere many generations have passed, end in extinction and in sorrow. I see a chief, the last of his house, both deaf and dumb. He will be the father of four fair sons, all of whom he will follow to the tomb. He will live careworn and die mourning, knowing that the honours of his line are to be extinguished for ever, and that no future chief of the Mac-Kenzies shall bear rule at Brahan or in Kintail. After lamenting over the last and most promising of his sons, he himself shall sink into the grave, and the remnant of his possessions shall be inherited by a white-coifed lassie from the East, and she is to kill her sister. And as a sign by which it may be known that these things are coming to pass, there shall be four great lairds in the days of

---

[1] *Scots Heraldy*, pp. 29–31.

the last deaf and dumb Seaforth (Gairloch, Chisholm, Grant, and Raasay), of whom one shall be buck-toothed, another hare-lipped, another half-witted, and the fourth a stammerer. Chiefs distinguished by these personal marks shall be the allies and neighbours of the last Seaforth ; and when he looks around him and sees them, he may know that his sons are doomed to death, that his broad lands shall pass away to the stranger, and that his race shall come to an end."

Surely enough the Seer's prediction was fulfilled in the time of Francis Humberston MacKenzie, the last Earl of Seaforth, who died in 1815. The Earl was born in full possession of all his faculties, but became stone-deaf, as a consequence of a severe attack of scarlet fever, when he was a boy at school. In the Earl's time lived four Highland lairds who corresponded to the description given by the Brahan Seer—viz. MacKenzie of Gairloch, Chisholm of Chisholm, Grant of Grant, and MacLeod of Raasay, who were distinguished by the peculiarities described by Coinneach Odhar. Owing to losses resulting from his West India estates, Lord Seaforth was compelled to part with much ancestral property, including that of Kintail, the cradle of the Seaforth race. To which it appears the prophecy was *actually* directed : the old idea being that the " house " became " extinct " if or when it lost its chief—and as " Mackenzie of Kintail," both land and *title* have vanished from the race. *Seaforth* has, however, remained along with the armorial honours at Brahan. Seaforth's four sons all predeceased him, and, following on the calamity of the death of his last son, the chief became dumb. And now comes the extraordinary fulfilment of the last part of the Seer's prophecy, viz. " That a white-coifed lassie from the East is to kill her sister."

On the death of the last Earl of Seaforth without male issue, his properties were inherited by his elder daughter, the widow of Admiral Sir Samuel Hood, Bart, K.C.B. Sir Samuel died in the East Indies about the time of Lord Seaforth's decease, and his widow (" the white-coifed lassie "—*i.e.* the lassie in widow's weeds) returned to Scotland to take possession of the property which she had just inherited. Sir Walter Scott commented on her father's death, " Our friend Lady Hood will now be *Caberfeidh* herself." Within a few months of her succession she arrived, and was recognised as *Dame Mary Frederick Hood-Mackenzie of Seaforth*, and, as such, had a confirmation and resettlement of the armorial coat of the Seaforth chiefs. After remaining a widow for some years she married secondly a grandson of the 6th Earl of Galloway, who assumed the name of Stewart-Mackenzie.

Some years after, Lady Stewart-Mackenzie of Seaforth was one day driving her younger sister, the Hon. Caroline MacKenzie, in a pony carriage in the vicinity of Brahan Castle. The ponies suddenly took fright and bolted. Both the ladies were thrown out of the carriage. The Lady Seaforth escaped with a few bruises, but her sister sustained severe injuries, which proved fatal. In this surprising and tragic manner was the last portion of the Brahan Seer's prediction of the doom of Seaforth fulfilled. The late Lord Seaforth, *as chief of the clan*, indeed in 1893, exercising jurisdiction over the name *Mackenzie of Kintail* " exercised " it, by effectively preventing it being given as designation to Mackenzie of Glenmuick in his baronetcy patent. Thus *Seaforth* alone remains as the chief's title.

APPENDIX XII (Page 35)

The old chronicler, " Blind Harry," mentions that Sir William Wallace, when a youth at school in Dundee, wore the Highland dress. " Blind Harry " calls the dress the " *Ersche Mantill*," and, further, states that " it war the kynd to wer."

Logan (in *Scottish Gael*) says : " There is a portrait of Sir William Wallace at Taymouth, a seat of Lord Braidalbane, where the patriot is represented with a plaid of tartan fastened on his breast by a large brooch."

APPENDIX XIII (PAGE 400)

CELTIC NAMES IN KINTYRE

Notes on old Celtic names in Kintyre, extracted from the MSS. of the Rev. Donald Kelly, M.A., minister of the parish of Southend, appeared in the *Campbeltown Courier*, and are so interesting that they were recorded on p. 481 of the 1924 edition of *Clans, Septs and Regiments of the Scottish Highlands*.

APPENDIX XIV (PAGE 396)

SURNAMES IN SCOTLAND

The following list shows the commonest surnames in Scotland and the number of each, according to the census of 1861. It illustrates the great importance of clans and families in Scotland, since the chiefs of these *Names* " represent " such numbers of people, who, if effectively organised (and indeed are as at present loosely so), exert a strong influence on Scottish affairs.

Smith	44,378	Fraser	18,013	Hamilton	12,282
MacDonald	37,572	Murray	17,606	Grant	12,186
Brown	33,820	Maclean	17,375	Hunter	11,829
Robertson	32,600	Cameron	16,802	White, Whyte	11,819
Thomson	32,560	Clark	16,797	Graham	11,709
Stewart	31,836	Young	16,705	Allan	11,578
Campbell	31,555	Henderson	16,394	Kerr	11,146
Wilson	29,741	MacLeod	15,571	MacGregor	11,070
Anderson	28,300	Taylor	15,535	Bell	10,624
Mackay	23,840	Mitchell	15,164	Simpson	10,548
MacKenzie	23,272	Watson	14,933	Martin	10,367
Scott	22,342	Ferguson	14,828	Black	10,151
Johnston	21,569	Walker	14,547	Munro	10,098
Miller	21,318	Morrison	14,482	Sinclair	9,980
Reid	20,047	Davidson	12,683	Sutherland	9,818
Ross	18,254	Gray	12,557	Gibson	9,307
Paterson	18,048	Duncan	12,467		

Total (50 surnames)   907,920

The great clans thus in 1861 comprehended about one-quarter of the population of Scotland.

APPENDIX XV (PAGE 479)

EXTRACT FROM CENSUS RETURN OF 1852, SHOWING NUMBER OF CLAN NAMES THEN IN GLENGARRY, CANADA

MacDonald and MacDonell	3228	Mackintosh	262	Ferguson	110
Macmillan	545	MacGillivray	243	MacLaurin	102
MacDougall	541	Mackinnon	242	MacKenzie	99
Macrae	456	Macpherson	195	Morrison	99
MacLeod	437	Fraser	176	MacCormick	83
Grant	399	Macphee	157	MacMartin	72
MacGillis	359	Macintyre	140	Mackay	72
Kennedy	333	Ross	139	MacArthur	70
Maclennan	322	Chisholm	133	MacLachlan	68
Campbell	304	MacGregor	114	Cattanach	50

APPENDIX XVI (PAGE 412)

ENGLISH AND GAELIC NAMES OF MEN AND WOMEN

Men's Names

Adam	. Adhamh
Albert	. Ailbeart
Alexander	Alasdair
Allan	. Ailean
Alpin	. Ailpean
Andrew	. Aindreas
Angus	. Aonghas
Archibald.	Gilleasbuig
Arthur	. Artair
Bernard	. Bearnard
Charles	. Teàrlach
Christopher	Gillecriosd
Colin	. Cailean
Coll	. Colla
David	. Daibhidh, Dà'idh
Daniel	. Dàniel
Donald	. Dòmhnull
Dugald	. Dùghall
Duncan	. Donnachadh
Edward	. Iomhair
Ewen	. Eoghan
Farquhar .	Fearchar
Finlay	. Fionnladh
Francis	. Fraing
George	. Seòras
Gilbert	. Gillebride
Hugh	. Uisdean

Hector	. Eachann
John	. Iain, Eoin
Joseph	. Iosaiph
James	. Seumas
Kenneth .	Coinneach
Lewis	. Luthais
Malcolm .	Calum
Martin	. Martuin
Michael	. Micheil
Moses	. Maois
Murdoch .	Murcha, Muireach
Nicol	. Neacal
Niel	. Niall
Norman	. Tormaid
Paul	. Pol
Patrick	. Pàruig, Pàdruig
Peter	. Peadair
Richard .	Ruaiseart
Robert	. Raibeart
Roderick.	Ruairidh
Ronald	. Raonull
Samuel	. Somhairle
Simon	. Sim
Thomas	. Tòmas
Torquil	. Torcall
Walter	. Bhaltair
William	. Uilleam

Women's Names

Amelia	. Aimil
Anabella	. Anabala
Ann .	. Anna
Barbara	. Barbara
Beatrice	. Beitris
Bridget	. Bryde
Catherine .	Catrìona
Christian	. Cairistine
Clara	. Sorcha
Dorothy	. Diorbhail
Elizabeth .	Ealasaid
Euphemia .	Oighrig
Flora	. Fionnaghal
Grace	. Giorsal
Helen	. Eilidh
Isabella	. Iseabal
Janet	. Seònaid
Jane.	. Sìne.
Louisa	. Liusaidh
Margaret .	Mairearad
Marjory	. Marsali
Mary	. Màiri,Moire
Muriel	. Mureall
Rachel	. Rachail
Sarah	. Mórag
Sophia	. Beathag
Susan	. Siùsaidh
Winifred .	Una

APPENDIX XVII (PAGE 351)

ENGLISH AND GAELIC EQUIVALENTS FOR PARTS OF HIGHLAND DRESS AND ARMS

English	Gaelic
Tartan .	. Breacan
Bonnet .	Boineid
Shoulder Plaid	. Breacan-guaille
Belted Plaid	. Breacan-féile
Badge .	. Suaicheantas
Brooch .	. Bràisd
Doublet .	. Cotta-geàrr
Kilt .	. Féileadh-beag
Sporran .	. Sporan
Hose .	. Osain
Garters .	. Gartain
Brogues .	. Brogan tionndaidh

English	Gaelic
Trews .	. Triubhas
Belts .	. Criosan
Broadsword or	
Claymore	. Claidheamh-mòr
Dirk .	. Biodag
Dagger .	. Sgian-dubh
Pistols .	. Dagan or Dagaichean
Powder-Horn .	Adharc-fhùdair
Target or Shield	Sgiath
Complete Dress	
and Badge .	Aodach-suaicheantas

APPENDIX XVIII (PAGE 353)

ENGLISH ACTS OF PARLIAMENT PROSCRIBING OLD IRISH GARB

Statute V. of Edward IV., cap. 2, enacts that " Every Irishman dwelling among Englishmen shall go like an Englishman in apparel, and shaving his beard above the mouth."

Statute XXVIII. of Henry VIII., cap. 15, enacts that " None shall wear any short smock, kercher, bendee, neckerchoat, mooket, or lined cap coloured with saffron, nor wear above seven yards of cloth up in their shirts or smocks, and no woman to wear any kestel, or coat tucked up or embroidered with silk, or laid with uske, after the Irish fashion."

APPENDIX XIX (PAGE 381)

HEAD-GEAR OF THE HIGHLAND REGIMENTS

The head-gear of all the Highland regiments of the line for full dress, with the exception of the Highland Light Infantry (71st and 74th Regiments), is the feather bonnet. The Highland Light Infantry wear the shako for full dress. The Black Watch is, of all the Highland regiments, the only one which is entitled to wear the red heckle in the bonnet. The other Highland regiments who wear the feather bonnet carry the white heckle.

The Gordon, Seaforth, and Cameron Highlanders have five " foxtails " (as the drooping plumes of the bonnet are called). The Black Watch, however, has only four " foxtails," while the Argyll and Sutherland Highlanders have no less than six.

APPENDIX XX (PAGE 390)

NATIVE DYES USED IN THE HIGHLANDS OF SCOTLAND

Colour	English Name	Gaelic Name	Latin Name
Black	Water-flag Root	Freumh an t-Seilisdeir	Iris pseud acorus.
Do.	Meadow Sweet	Lus chneas Chuchuilinn	Spiræa ulmaria.
Do.	Alder-tree Bark	Cairt an Fheàrna	Alnus glutinosa.
Do.	Root of Common Dock.	Bun-na-copaig	Rumex obtusifolius.
Do.	Oak Bark and Acorns	Darach	Quercus robur.
Blue	Bilberry (with alum)	Dearc bhraoileag, or Dearc monaidh, or Dearc roide (le alm)	Vaccinium uligonosum.
Do.	Blaeberry (with alum)	Dearcan gorma (le alm)	Vaccinium myrtillus.
Do.	Blaeberry (with copperas)	Lus nan dearcan gorma	Do.
Do.	Elder (with alum)	Druman (le alm)	Sambucus nigra.
Do. (pale)	Elder and Broom (with alum)	Feàrna is Bealaidh (le alm)	Sambucus nigra (elder), Sarothamnus scorparius (broom).
Bluish Black	Common Sloe	Preas nan àirneag	Prunus spinosa.
Do.	Red Bearberry	Grainnseag	Arbutus-uva-ursi.
Brown	Stone Lichen	Crotal	Parmelia saxatilis.
Do.	Common Yellow Wall Lichen	Crotal-buidhe	Parmelia parietina.
Do.	Dulse.	Duileasg	Halymenia edulis or Rhodymenia palmata.
Do. (dark)	Blaeberry (with nut galls)	Lus nan dearcan gorma (le ubhal an daraich)	Vaccinium myrtillus.
Do. (do.)	Currant, Red (with alum)	An dearg dhearcag (le alm)	Ribes rubrum.
Do. (do.)	Walnut Root	Craobh ghall-chnò	Juglans regia.
Do. (do.)	Root of Water Lily	Cairt-an-loch	Nymphia alba.
Do. (light)	Lungwort Lichen	Crotal coille	Sticta pulmonacea.
Crimson (bright)	Corcar Lichen, White (mixed with urine)	Crotal corcuir	Lecanora tartarea.
Do. do.)	White Lichen	Crotal geal	Lecanora palescens.

Colour	English Name	Gaelic Name	Latin Name
Do. (dark) .	Dark Lichen . .	Crotal dubh . . • .	Parmelia ceratophylia.
Drab or Fawn .	Birch Bark . . .	Beithe	Betula alba.
Flesh Colour . .	Willow Bark . .	Cairt-an t-Seilich . .	Salix viminalis.
Green . . .	Teasel or Fuller's Teasel	Liodan an Fhùcadair .	Dipsacus fullonum.
Do. . . .	Privet, Ripe Berries (with salt)	Priobhaid, or Ras chrann sior uaine (le salann)	Ligustrum vulgare.
Do. . . .	Iris Leaf . . .	Selisdeir	Iris pseud acorus.
Do. (bright) .	Broom (Common) .	Bealaidh	Sarothamnus scorparius.
Do. (do.) .	Wild Mignonette (with indigo)	Lus-buidhe mòr . .	Reseda luteola.
Do. (do.) .	Whin or Furze Bark .	Rùsg Conaisg . . .	Ulex Europæus.
Do. (dark) . .	Heather (pulled just before flowering time)	Fraoch-bhadain . .	Erica cinerea.
Grey . . .	Water-flag Root . .	Freumh an t-Seilisdeir .	Iris pseud acorus.
Magenta . .	Dandelion . . .	Bearnan-bride . . .	Leontodon taraxacum.
Orange . . .	Ragweed or Ragwort .	Buadhghallan . . .	Senecio Jacobea.
Do. . . .	Barberry Root . .	Barbrag . . .	Berberis vulgaris.
Do. . . .	Peat Soot (also used for a dirty yellow)	Sùith-fòid-mhòine . .	—
Do. (dark) .	Bramble . . .	Dreas-smeur . . .	Rubus fructicosus.
Purple [1] .	Blaeberry (with alum) .	Lus nan dearc gorma .	Vaccinium myrtillus.
Do. . . .	Spindle Tree (with sal ammonia)	Oir	Eunoymus Europæus.
Do. . . .	Sundew . . .	Lus-na-feàrnaich .	Drosera.
Red [2] . . .	Fir Club Moss . .	Garbhag-an-t-Sléibhe .	Lycopodium selago.
Do. (dark) .	Rock Lichen . .	Crotal-nan-creag .	Ramalina scopulorum.
Do. (do.) .	Blaeberry (with verdigris and sal ammonia)	Lus nan dearc gorma .	Vaccinium myrtillus.
Do. (bright) .	Rue-root or Yellow Bedstraw	Bun-an-Ruadh . .	Galium verum.
Do. (do.) .	Tormentil (also used for tanning)	Leanartach . . .	Tormentilla officinalis.
Saffron . . .	Saffron Flowers . .	Blàth a' Chròich . .	Crocus sativus or Colchicum autumnale.
Scarlet . . .	Limestone Lichen .	Crotal clach-aoil . .	Urceolaria calcarea.
Violet . . .	Cloudberry Shrub .	Lus na h-Oighreig . .	Rubus chamæmorus.
Do. . . .	Watercress . . .	Biolaire	Nasturtium officinalis.
Do. . . .	Bitter Vetch . .	Carra-meille . . .	Orobus tuberosus.
Yellow . . .	Crab-apple Tree . .	Craob-ubhal . . .	Pyrus malus.
	Ash . . .	Uinseann . . .	Fraxinus excelsior.
	Buckthorn . .	Ramh-droighionn . .	Rhamnus catharticus.
	Poplar . . .	Critheann . . .	Populus tremulus.
	Elm	Ailm	Ulmus.
Do. . . .	Bog Myrtle . . .	Roid	Myrica gale.
Do. . . .	Ash-tree Root . .	Freum-na-craobh-uinnseann	Fraxinus excelsior.
Do. . . .	Bracken Root . .	Bun-na-raineach . .	Pteris aquilina.
Do. (bright) .	St. John's Wort . .	Seud-eala-bhuidhe . .	Hypericum perforatum.
Do. (do.) .	Teasel . . .	Liodan-an-Fhùcadair .	Dipsacus sylvestris.
Do. (do.) .	Sundew (with ammonia)	Lus-na-feàrnaich . .	Drosera.
Do. (do.) .	Rhubarb (Monk's) .	Lus-na-purgaid . .	Rumex alpinus.

[1] This colour was obtained from the bilberry or blaeberry, and also from the crowberry boiled with alum or club moss. The lichen called cudbear, or *crotal geal*, was extensively used for dyeing purple. The process of extracting the dye is thus described by Mr. Cameron in his valuable work on *The Gaelic Names of Plants* : " It (the lichen) is first dried in the sun, then pulverised and steeped, commonly in urine, and the vessel made air-tight. In this state it is suffered to remain for three weeks, when it is fit to be boiled in the yarn which it is to colour." The writer then proceeds : " In many Highland districts many of the peasants get their living by scraping off the lichen with an iron hoop and sending it to the Glasgow market." In reviewing the above work the *Northern Chronicle* says : " Mr. Cameron is mistaken in supposing that Highland peasants yet get their living by gathering the *crotal corcur* and sending it to the Glasgow market. The peace of 1815 put an end to that industry. The *crotal* grows undisturbed on mountain stones, and the very scrapers, which were a generation ago to be found in most houses in the Highlands, have, to some, become puzzling curiosities."

" This *crotal geal* or *corcur* is, however, gathered and extensively used to this day for dyeing the far-famed Gairloch hose, and any old Highland woman will tell you that the wearers of hose dyed with a decoction of this lichen are singularly exempted from having their feet inflamed or blistered with walking long distances."—(" H," in the *Celtic Magazine*, March 1883.)

The Highlanders made use of this plant (fir club moss) instead of alum to fix the colours in dyeing.

GAELIC ALPHABET

(*Gaelic Names of Plants*, John Cameron.)

	Gaelic	*English*		*Gaelic*	*English*		*Gaelic*	*English*
A .	Ailm	Elm	G .	Gath	Ivy	O .	Oir	Spindle Tree
B .	Beite	Birch	H .	Huath	Whitethorn	P .	Peith	Pine
C .	Coll	Hazel	I .	Iogh	Yew	R .	Ruis	Elder
D .	Dur	Oak	L .	Luis	Quicken	S .	Suil	Willow
E .	Eagh	Aspen	M .	Muin	Vine	T .	Teine	Furze
F .	Feàrn	Alder	N .	Nuin	Ash	U .	Ur	Heath

APPENDIX XXI (Pages 392 and 524)

Table of clan tartans from Logan's *Descriptions of Clan Tartans*:

" The list here given contains as many specimens as I could procure and authenticate. I have noticed some variations in the patterns worn by different families of the same name, but I have not inserted any fancy tartan. The plan which is adopted in the following table is sufficiently simple. Should anyone desire to supply himself with this pattern, by copying the scale and applying it to the web the object will be accomplished. In like manner these descriptions are a guide to manufacturers, who will now, it is hoped, produce the true patterns.

" A web of tartan is 2 feet 2 inches wide, at least within half an inch, more or less, so that the size of the patterns make no difference in the scale. Commencing at the edge of the cloth, the depth of the colours is stated throughout a square, on which the scale must be reversed or gone through again to the commencement.

" There is, it may be observed, a particular colour in some patterns which can scarcely admit of description, but which is known to the Highlanders, as, for example, the green of the Mackay tartan is light. The plaid which the clergy wore is popularly believed to have been used by the Druids and Culdees. The Highland ministers, it has been shown, went armed and generally dressed in the national costume."

Note that this list is " based " on Logan, varied 1881 by M'Intyre North. Experts should compare Stewart, *Setts of the Scottish Tartans*, p. 119. (*Ed.*)

⅛ of an inch Colours	*⅛ of an inch Colours*	*⅛ of an inch Colours*	*⅛ of an inch Colours*
BUCHANAN.	CAMERON.	CAMERON—*contd.*	CAMPBELL—*contd.*
½ azure.	½ yellow.	1½ red.	1 blue.
8 green.	4 blue.	8 green.	1 black.
½ black.	1½ red.	8 black.	1 blue.
1 azure.	8 blue.	½ red.	8 black.
½ black.	½ red.	8 blue.	8 green.
2 yellow.	8 black.	1½ red.	1 black.
½ black.	8 green.	4 blue.	2 white.
2 yellow.	1½ red.	1 yellow.	1 black.
½ black.	½ green		8 green.
1 azure.	½ red.	CAMPBELL.	8 black.
½ black.	4 green.		8 blue.
8 red.	½ red.	4 blue.	1 black.
1 white.	½ green.	1 black.	1 blue.

⅛ of an inch Colours

CAMPBELL—*contd.*

1 black.
8 blue.
8 black.
8 green.
1 black.
2 yellow.
1 black.
8 green.
8 black.
1 blue.
1 black.
1 blue.
1 black.
4 blue.

This is worn by the Duke of Argyll and the Campbells of Lochow. The Earl of Breadalbane and his clan wear the following pattern :

2 blue.
1 black.
1 blue.
1 black.
1 blue.
7 black.
½ yellow.
11 green.
½ yellow.
7 black.
6 blue.
1 black.
1 blue.

CHISHOLM.

2½ red.
8 green.
2½ red.
2 blue.
1 white.
2 blue.
11 red.
2 blue.
1 white.
2 blue.
2½ red.
8 green.
2½ red.
1 blue.

COLQUHOUN.

½ blue.
1 black.
6 blue.
9 black.
1½ white.
7 green.
1 red.
7 green.

⅛ of an inch Colours

COLQUHOUN—*contd.*

½ white.
9 black.
6 blue.
1 black.
1 blue.

CUMMING.

1 azure.
1 black.
2 azure.
5 black.
½ orange.
5 green.
2 red.
½ white.
2 red.
½ white.
2 red.
5 green.
½ orange.
5 black.
2 azure.
1 black.
2 azure.

DRUMMOND.

¼ white.
1 azure.
1½ blue.
4 red.
8 green.
½ yellow.
1½ blue.
½ white.
17 red.
½ white.
1½ blue.
½ yellow.
8 green.
4 red.
1½ blue.
1 azure.
½ white.

FARQUHARSON.

½ red.
2 blue.
½ black.
½ blue.
½ black.
½ blue.
4 black.
4 green.
1 yellow.
4 green.
4 black.
4 blue.
½ black.
1 red.

⅛ of an inch Colours

FERGUSON.

½ green.
6 blue.
½ red.
6 black.
6 green.
1 black.
6 green.
6 black.
½ red.
6 blue.
1 green.

FORBES.

1 blue.
1 black.
6 blue.
6 black.
6 green.
1 black.
1 white
1 black.
6 green.
6 black.
6 blue.
1 black.
1 blue.

FRASER.

2½ blue.
½ red.
½ blue.
½ red.
5 green.
6½ red.
1 green.
6½ red.
5 green.
5 blue.
½ red.
½ blue.
½ red.
5 blue.
5 green.
6½ red.
1 green.
6½ red.
5 green.
½ red.
½ blue.
½ red.
5 blue.

GORDON.

½ blue.
1 black.
5½ blue.
6 black.
6 green.
1 yellow.
6 green.

⅛ of an inch Colours

GORDON—*contd.*

6 black.
1 blue.
1 black.
1 blue.
1 black.
6 blue.
1 black.
1 blue.
1 black.
1 blue.
6 black.
6 green.
1 yellow.
6 green.
6 black.
5½ blue.
1 black.
1 blue.

GRAHAM.

½ black.
6 smalt.
6 black.
½ green.
1 azure.
8 green.
1 azure.
½ green.
6 black.
6 smalt.
1 black.

GRANT.

1 red.
¼ blue.
½ red.
½ blue.
18 red.
¼ azure.
½ red.
5 blue.
1 red.
½ green.
1 red.
21 green.
½ red.
½ blue.
2½ red.
½ blue.
½ red.
21 green.
1 red.
½ green.
1 red.
5 blue.
½ red.
¼ azure.
18 red.
½ blue.
½ red.
¼ blue.
2½ red.

⅛ of an inch Colours

GUNN.

- ½ green.
- 7 blue.
- ½ green.
- 7 black.
- 7 green.
- 1 red.
- 7 green.
- 7 black.
- ½ green.
- 7 blue.
- 1 green.

LAMONT.

- 2¼ blue.
- 1½ black.
- 1½ blue.
- 1½ black.
- 1½ blue.
- 6 black.
- 6 green.
- 1½ white.
- 6 green.
- 6 black.
- 6 blue.
- 1½ black.
- 1½ blue.
- 1½ black.
- 6 blue.
- 6 black.
- 6 green.
- 1½ white.
- 6 green.
- 6 black.
- 1½ blue.
- 1½ black.
- 1½ blue.
- 1½ black.
- 4½ blue.

LOGAN OR MACLENNAN.

- 1¼ red.
- 1¼ blue.
- ¾ red.
- ¾ blue.
- ¾ red.
- 7 blue.
- 5¼ black.
- 7 green.
- ½ red.
- ½ black.
- 1 yellow.
- ½ black.
- ½ red.
- 7 green.
- 5¼ black.
- 7 blue.

⅛ of an inch Colours

LOGAN OR MACLENNAN—*contd.*

- ¾ red.
- ¾ blue.
- ¾ red.
- 1¼ blue.
- 2¼ red.

MACALASTAIR.

- 4 red.
- ½ light green.
- 3 dark green.
- 1 red.
- 1 azure.
- 1 red.
- ½ white.
- 1 red.
- 1 azure.
- 1 red.
- 3 dark green.
- ½ red.
- ½ white.
- 6 red.
- ½ azure.
- ½ red.
- 11 dark green.
- ½ red.
- ½ azure.
- 16 red.
- ½ azure.
- ½ red.
- 11 dark green.
- ½ red.
- ½ azure.
- 5½ red.
- ½ white.
- ½ red.
- 4 blue.
- ½ red.
- ½ white.
- 2½ red.
- 3 dark green.
- ½ light green.
- 2 red.
- ½ light green.
- 3 dark green.
- ¾ red.
- ½ white.
- ½ red.
- 2½ blue.

MACAULAY.

- ½ black.
- 9 red.
- 3½ green.
- 1½ red.
- 5 green.
- ½ white.

⅛ of an inch Colours

MACAULAY—*contd.*

- 5 green.
- 1½ red.
- 5 green.
- ½ white.
- 5 green.
- 1½ red.
- 3½ green.
- 9 red.
- 1 black.

MACDONALD.[1]

- 2½ green.
- ½ red.
- 1 green.
- 1½ red.
- 8 green.
- 8 black.
- ½ red.
- 8 blue.
- 1½ red.
- ¾ blue.
- ½ red.
- 5 blue.
- ½ red.
- ¾ blue.
- 1½ red.
- 8 blue.
- ½ red.
- 8 black.
- 8 green.
- 1½ red.
- 1 green.
- ½ red.
- 5 green.

MACDOUGALL.

- 3 red.
- 6 green.
- 1 red.
- ½ blue.
- 18 red.
- 2 crimson.
- 18 red.
- ½ blue.
- 1 red.
- 6 green.
- 6 red.
- 6 green.
- 3 crimson.
- 1 red.
- 3 crimson.
- 6 blue.
- 2 red.
- 1 green.
- 2 red.
- 18 green.
- 1 red.
- 1 crimson.

⅛ of an inch Colours

MACDUFF.

- 4 red.
- 3 azure.
- 4 black.
- 6½ green.
- 3½ red.
- 1 black.
- 3½ red.
- 1 black
- 3½ red.
- 6½ green.
- 4 black.
- 3 azure.
- 8 red.

MACFARLANE.

- 10½ red.
- ½ black.
- 6 green.
- 1 white.
- 1½ red.
- ½ black.
- 1½ red.
- 1 white.
- 1 green.
- 6 purple.
- 2 black.
- 1½ red.
- 2 white.
- 1½ green.
- 2 white.
- 1½ red.
- 2 black.
- 6 purple.
- 1 green.
- 1 white.
- 1½ red.
- ½ black.
- 1½ red.
- 1 white.
- 6 green.
- ½ black.
- 21 red.

MACGILLIVRAY.

- ½ blue.
- 2 red.
- ¼ azure.
- 2 red.
- 9 green.
- 1 red.
- 7 blue.
- ½ red.
- ½ azure.
- 18 red.
- ¼ blue.
- ¼ azure.
- 2 red.

[1] There is a white stripe introduced for distinction by the Glengarry Clan, and Lord MacDonald wears a pattern composed of red and green.

⅛ of an inch Colours

MacGillivray—*contd.*

¼ azure.
¼ blue.
18 red.
½ azure.
½ red.
7 blue.
1 red.
9 green.
2 red.
¼ azure.
2 red.
½ blue.

MACGREGOR.

12 red.
6 green.
2½ red.
3 green.
½ black.
1 white.
½ black.
3 green.
2½ red.
6 green.
24 red.

MACINTOSH.[1]

12 red.
6 blue.
2½ red.
10½ green.
4 red.
½ blue.
4 red.
10½ green.
2½ red.
6 blue.
24 red.

MACKAY.

¾ green.
7 corbeau.
1 green.
7 black.
7 green.
1½ black.
7 green.
7 black.
1 green.
7 corbeau.
1½ green.

MACKENZIE.

3½ blue.
1½ black.
1½ blue.

⅛ of an inch Colours

MacKenzie—*contd.*

1½ black.
1½ blue.
7 black.
7 green.
1½ black.
1½ white.
1½ black.
7 green.
7 black.
7 blue.
1½ black.
1½ red.
1½ black
7 blue.
7 black.
7 green.
1½ black.
1½ white.
1½ black.
7 green.
7 black.
1½ blue.
1½ black.
1½ blue.
1½ black.
7 blue.

MACKINNON.

½ white.
1½ red.
1 green.
1 blue.
3 red.
8 green.
1 red.
2 blue.
1 green.
8 red.
4 green.
1 white.
2 red.
1 white.
2 red.
1 white.
4 green.
8 red.
1 green.
2 blue.
1 red.
8 green.
3 red.
1 blue.
1 green.
1½ red.
1 white.

MACLACHLAN.

4 red.
1 black.
1 red.

⅛ of an inch Colours

Maclachlan—*contd.*

1 black.
1 red.
8 black.
8 blue.
1½ green.
8 blue.
8 black.
8 red.
1 black.
1 red.

MACLAREN.

9½ blue.
4 black.
1½ green.
1½ red.
3 green.
½ black.
1 yellow.
½ black.
3 green.
1½ red.
1½ green.
5 black.
18 blue.
5 black.

MACLEAN.

½ black.
1½ red.
1 azure.
11 red.
5 green.
1 black.
1½ white.
1 black.
½ yellow.
2 black.
3½ azure.
2 black.
½ yellow.
1 black.
1½ white.
1 black.
5 green.
11 red.
1 azure.
1½ red.
1 black.

MACLEOD.

1 yellow.
½ black.
6 blue.
6 black.
6 green.
½ black.
2 red.
½ black.

⅛ of an inch Colours

Macleod—*contd.*

6 green.
6 black.
6 blue.
½ black.
2 yellow.

MACNAB.

1 green.
1 crimson.
6 green.
6 crimson.
6 red.
1 crimson.
6 red.
6 crimson.
1 green.
1 crimson.
1 green.
1 crimson.
6 green.
1 crimson.
1 green.
1 crimson.
1 green.
6 crimson.
6 red.
1 crimson.
6 red.
6 crimson.
6 green.
1 crimson.

MACNAUGHTEN.

¼ black.
½ azure.
8 red.
8 green.
6 black.
4½ azure.
8 red.
½ azure.
½ black.
½ azure.
8 red.
4½ azure.
6 black.
8 green.
8 red.
½ azure.
½ black.

MACNEILL.

1 white.
6 smalt.
6 black.
6 green.
2½ black.
½ yellow.
2½ black.

[1] The chief also wears a particular tartan of a very showy pattern (Clan Chattan sett.—*Ed.*).

⅛ of an inch Colours

MACNEILL—*contd.*

6 green.
6 black.
6 smalt.
½ white.

MACPHERSON.[1]

¼ red.
½ black.
½ white.
5½ red.
2 azure.
½ black.
½ azure.
½ black.
2 azure.
3 black.
½ yellow.
4 green.
5½ red.
1 azure.
5½ red.
1 azure.
5½ red.
4 green.
½ yellow.
3 black.
2 azure.
½ black.
½ azure.
½ black.
2 azure.
5½ red.
½ white.
½ black.
½ red.

MACQUARRIE.

2½ red.
12 blue.
15 red.
¼ azure.
2 red.
¼ azure.
15 red.
12 blue.
5 red.
16 green.
7 red.

MACRAE.

5½ green.
2½ black.
11 green.
2 red.
3 green.
1 black.
3 blue.
1 white.

⅛ of an inch Colours

MACRAE—*contd.*

3 blbue.
1 black.
3 green.
2 red.
11 green.
2½ black.
11 green.
2½ black.
11 green.

MATHESON.

½ red.
1 green.
6 red.
5 dark blue.
1½ azure.
5 green.
1 red.
1 green.
1 red.
5 green.
6 red.
1 green.
1 red.

MENZIES.

12 red.
9 green.
1 white.
3 azure.
24 red.
3 azure.
1 white.
9 green.

MENZIES (DRESS).

14¼ red.
3½ white.
1½ red.
3½ white.
3 red.
1½ white.
¾ red.
7 white.
¾ red.
1½ white.
3½ red.
3½ white.
1½ red.
3½ white.
28½ red.

MUNRO.

6½ red.
½ yellow.
½ blue.
1½ red.

⅛ of an inch Colours

MUNRO—*contd.*

13 green.
1½ red.
½ blue.
½ yellow
1½ red.
3 blue.
1½ red.
½ yellow
½ blue.
13 red.
1½ green.
1½ red.
1½ green.
1½ red.
1½ green.
13 red.

MURRAY.

1 blue.
1 black.
6 blue.
6 black.
6 green.
2 red.
6 green.
6 black.
1 blue.
1 black.
1 blue.
1 black.
6 blue.
1 black.
1 blue.
1 black.
1 blue.
6 black.
6 green.
2 red.
6 green.
6 black.
6 blue.
1 black.
2 blue.

OGILVY

1 red.
¼ white.
½ black.
½ yellow.
1 purple.
½ yellow.
1½ green.
½ yellow.
½ black
½ red.
½ black.
½ red.

⅛ of an inch Colours

OGILVIE—*contd.*

½ black.
½ red.
½ black.
1 yellow.
2 green.
1 yellow.
½ black.
2 red.
½ white.
2 red.
½ black.
½ yellow.
2 green.
½ white.
2 green.
½ yellow.
½ purple.
1 red.
½ black.
3½ red.
¼ white.
½ blue.
¼ white.
3½ red.
¼ white.
½ blue.
3½ red.
½ black.
1 red.
½ green.
1 yellow.
1½ green.
½ yellow.
1½ green.
1 yellow.
3 black.
¼ white.
1 blue.
¼ white.
3 black.
2 red.
½ white.
2 red.
½ white.
2 red.
½ black.
½ yellow.
3½ green.
1 black.
3½ green.
1 black.
3½ green.
½ yellow.
½ black.
2 red.
½ white.
2 red.
½ white.
2 red.
½ black.
½ yellow.

[1] The chief has recently dressed in a different pattern, which is said to have been formerly worn by his family (Macpherson of Cluny sett, which *is* ancient.—*Ed.*).

⅛ of an inch Colours	⅛ of an inch Colours	⅛ of an inch Colours	⅛ of an inch Colours
OGILVIE—contd.	ROSE.	SKENE—contd.	SUTHERLAND—contd.
2 green.	½ red.	12 green.	8 black.
⅛ white.	5 blue.	2 black.	8 green.
2 green.	5 black.	1½ red.	1 black.
⅛ yellow.	5 green.	2 black.	8 green.
⅛ black.	⅛ white.	12 blue.	8 black.
2 red.	2 black.	2 black.	1 blue.
⅛ white.	⅛ white.		1 black.
2 red.	5 green.	STEWART.	1 blue.
⅛ white.	5 black.	⅛ white.	1 black.
2 red.	5 blue.	1½ red.	11 blue.
⅛ black.	1 red.	1 black.	
1 yellow.		4 red.	URQUHART.
3½ green.	ROSS.	8 green.	4 green.
1 black.	4½ green.	1 black.	1 black.
1¾ green.	1 red.	1 white.	1 green.
	9 green.	1 black.	1 black.
ROBERTSON.	9 red.	⅛ yellow.	1 green.
⅛ red.	1 green.	5 black.	8 black.
1 green.	2 red.	3 azure.	8 blue.
8½ red.	1 green.	16 red.	1 red.
1 blue.	9 red.	3 azure.	8 blue.
1 red.	9 blue.	5 black.	8 black.
8½ green.	1 red.	⅛ yellow.	8 green.
8½ green.	9 blue.	1 black.	1 black.
1 red.	9 red.	1 white.	1 green.
1 green.	½ blue.	1 black.	
8½ red.	½ red.	8 green.	BREACAN NAN
1 green.	1 blue.	4 red.	CLEIREACH, OR
1 red.	½ red.	1 black.	TARTAN OF THE
1 green.	½ blue.	1½ red.	CLERGY.
8½ red.	9 red.	1 white.	¼ white.
1 green.			2½ black.
1 red.	SINCLAIR.	SUTHERLAND.	¼ white.
8½ blue.	9 red.	5½ blue.	2 grey.
1 red.	10 green.	1 black.	¼ white.
8½ green.	2½ black.	1 blue.	5 black.
1 red.	⅛ white.	1 black.	2½ grey.
1 blue.	4 azure.	1 blue.	1 black.
8½ red.	18 red.	8 black.	2½ grey.
1 green.		8 green.	5 black.
1 red.	SKENE.	1 black.	¼ white.
1 green.	1 black.	8 green.	13 black.
8½ red.	1½ red.	8 black.	¼ white.
1 blue.	12 green.	8 blue.	2 grey.
1 red.	2 black.	1 black.	¼ white.
8½ green.	1½ orange.	1 blue.	2½ black.
½ red.	2 black.	1 black.	¼ white.
		8 blue.	

M'Intyre North, in *Book of the Club of True Highlanders*, says :

" We have already referred to the list of tartans compiled by James Logan, and the following tables, based on [1] his authority, will show the proportionate quantity of material in each colour comprising the several tartans. Logan (1847) says : ' The web of the tartan is from twenty-four inches to twenty-six inches in width. All clan tartans ought to have the colours so proportioned that they can be made up in the form of a kilt or the belted plaid—that is, the stripes should be so arranged that, in box plaiting, the distinguishing bars should appear without any overlaying, which prevents the free play of the feile-beg, and destroys the pleasing effect of loose drapery.'

" In the list twelve threads have been reckoned to the one-eighth of an inch, and the figures denote one-eighths of an inch, or parts of one-eighth of an inch (*i.e.* one-half on the list would be equal to one-sixteenth). The length only of the pattern is given (commencing from the selvage), as the pattern is the same, whether for warp or woof. Logan's plan of describing the tartans, admirable as it is for the use of the weaver, is rather confusing to others ; we have, therefore, added opposite each tartan a table showing the proportionate amount of each colour in one-eighths lineal displayed in each, and the width in inches occupied by each pattern. The reader will thus be able to form a better general idea of the effect and appearance of each tartan."

[1] Note, and cf. p. 590. (*Ed.*)

TABLE OF CLAN TARTANS TO SCALE

Clan	*Proportions of each Colour in Eighths of an Inch.*						*Width of Sett Inches*
MacDonald[1]	G. 25½	Bl. 22½	Bk. 16	R. 9	—	—	= 9 1/8
MacAlaster	R. 44¾	Dk. G. 34	Bl. 6½	A. 4	Lt. G. 1½	W. 2½	= 11 21/32
MacDougall	R. 53	G. 37	C. 9	Bl. 7	—	—	= 13¼
MacNeill	Bk. 17	G. 12	S. 12	W. 1½	Y. ½	—	= 5 3/8
MacLachlan	Bk. 19	Bl. 16	R. 15	G. 1½	—	—	= 6 7/16
Lamont	Bk. 33	Bl. 26¼	G. 24	W. 3	—	—	= 10 13/16
Skene	G. 24	Bl. 12	Bk. 11	R. 3	Or. 1½	—	= 6 7/16
Macpherson	R. 28¼	A. 11	Bk. 9	G. 8	Y. 1	W. 1	= 7 9/32
Macintosh	R. 49	G. 21	Bl. 12½	—	—	—	= 10 5/16
MacNaughten	R. 32	G. 16	Bk. 13¼	A. 11	—	—	= 9 1/32
Robertson	R. 52½	G. 41	Bl. 11½	—	—	—	= 13 1/8
MacFarlane	R. 36	G. 11¾	Dk. Bl. 10	W. 7	Bl. 4	—	= 8 13/32
MacGillivray	R. 49	G. 18	Bl. 16	A. 2	—	—	= 10 5/8
Farquharson	Bk. 9½	G. 8	Bl. 7	R. 1½	Y. 1	—	= 3 3/8
Cameron	Bl. 24	G. 21	Bk. 16	R. 8	Y. 1½	—	= 8 13/16
Munro	R. 41½	G. 17½	Bl. 4½	Y. 2½	—	—	= 8¼
Mackay[2]	G. 18¼	Bk. 15½	Cu. 14	—	—	—	= 5 31/32
Sutherland	Bk. 40	Bl. 37½	G. 32	—	—	—	= 13 11/16
Gunn	G. 16½	Bk. 14	Bl. 14	R. 7	—	—	= 5 11/16
Macrae	G. 55½	Bk. 9½	Bl. 6	R. 4	W. 1	—	= 9½
Sinclair	R. 27	G. 10	A. 4	Bk. 2½	W. ½	—	= 5½
Ross	R. 41	Bl. 20	G. 15½	—	—	—	= 9 9/16
MacKenzie	Bk. 43	Bl. 30½	G. 28½	W. 3	R. 1½	—	= 13¼
Rose	Bk. 12	Bl. 10	G. 10	R. 1½	W. 1	—	= 4 5/16
Matheson	R. 15½	G. 13	Dk. Bl. 5	A. 1½	—	—	= 4 3/8
Logan and Maclennan[3]	Bl. 18	G. 14	Bk. 11½	R. 7½	Y. 1	—	= 6½
MacGregor	R. 41	G. 18	W. 1	Bk. ½	—	—	= 7 9/16
Grant	R. 4¼	G. 43	Bl. 12½	A. ½	—	—	= 13 5/32
Mackinnon	R. 31	G. 28	Bl. 6	W. 4½	—	—	= 8 7/16
Macquarrie	R. 46½	Bl. 24	G. 16	A. ½	—	—	= 10 7/8
Macnab	C. 32	R. 24	G. 23	—	—	—	= 9 7/8
MacDuff	R. 22½	G. 13	Bk. 10	A. 6	—	—	= 6 7/16
MacAulay	R. 21	G. 17	Bk. 1½	W. ½	—	—	= 5
Macinnes[4]	R. 16½	G. 14	A. 6	Bk. 2	Y. 1	W 1	= 5 1/16
Stewart	R. 27	Bk. 16	G. 16	A. 6	W. 3¼	Y. 1	= 8 21/32
Menzies	R. 53¾	W. 24	—	—	—	—	= 9 23/32
Drummond	R. 25	G. 16	Bl. 6	A. 2	W. 1¾	Y. 1	= 6 15/32
Gordon	Bk. 30	G. 24	Bl. 22½	Y. 2	—	—	= 9 13/16
Graham	Bk. 13½	S. 12	G. 9	A. 2	—	—	= 4 9/16
Ogilvy	R. 33	G. 27¼	Bk. 14	Y. 10	W. 5½	Bl.2, P.1½	= 11 21/32
Ferguson	G. 13½	Bk. 13	Bl. 12	R. 1	—	—	= 4 15/16
Forbes	Bk. 16	Bl. 14	G. 12	W. 1	—	—	= 5 3/8
Urquhart	Bk. 19	Bl. 16	G. 15	R. 1	—	—	= 6 3/8
Fraser	R. 29	G. 22	Bl. 19	—	—	—	= 8¾
Chisholm	R. 21	G. 16	Bl. 9	W. 2	—	—	= 6

[1] There are four great divisions of Clan Donald besides the chief branch, distinguished as of "*The Isles*," viz.: *Clan Ranald*, *Glengarry*, *Keppoch*, and *Glencoe*. The *Glengarry* tartan has a white stripe in the centre of the green division; and in that of *Clan Ranald* two have been introduced, one on each side of the same division. (There are *five* divisions—Sleate, Glengarry, Clan Ranald, Keppoch, Glencoe.—*Ed.*)

[2] This is the original colour from a native dye, but it is now usually dark blue.

[3] These two clans are of one descent, and there is no distinction in the tartans save that the latter prefer it of a broad pattern.

[4] Omitted by Logan/Adam in the "Table," and a variant of the *Innes* recorded by Smibert.

Clan	*Proportions of each Colour in Eighths of an Inch*						*Width of Sett Inches*
Murray . . .	Bk. 30	Bl. 25	G. 24	R. 4	—	—	$=10\frac{3}{8}$
MacLeod. . .	Bk. 14	Bl. 12	G. 12	Y. 3	R. 2	—	$=5\frac{3}{8}$
Campbell of Argyll .	Bk. 42	G. 32	Bl. 29	Y. 2	W. 2	—	$=13\frac{3}{8}$
Campbell of Breadal-bane . . .	Bk. 17	Bl. 11	G. 11	Y. 1	—	—	$=5$
Cumming . .	Bk. 12	G. 10	A. 7	R. 4	O. 1	W. $\frac{1}{2}$	$=4\frac{5}{16}$
Maclean . . .	R. 25	G. 10	Bl. $9\frac{1}{2}$	A. $5\frac{1}{2}$	W. 3	Y. 1	$=6\frac{3}{4}$
MacLaren . .	Bl. $27\frac{1}{4}$	Bk. 15	G. 9	R. 3	Y. 1	—	$=6\frac{29}{32}$
Buchanan . .	G. 8	R. 8	A. $2\frac{1}{2}$	Bk. 2	Y. 2	W. 1	$=2\frac{15}{16}$
Colquhoun . .	Bk. 20	G. 14	Bl. $13\frac{1}{2}$	W. 3	R. 1	—	$=6\frac{7}{16}$

"We have analysed the foregoing in order to see whether the simplicity or otherwise of the tartan (like as in heraldry) is any guide to its antiquity. We find that in twenty-six, red is predominant; in seventeen, black (the effect of this is, however, counterbalanced by the combined colours of blue and green); in six, green predominates; in three, blue; in one, crimson; and in one the red and green are equal. The Buchanan is the narrowest pattern, with three inches, bare; the Sutherland the widest, with thirteen and three-quarter inches; Menzies, the simplest, with two colours and fifteen divisions; Ogilvy, the most complicated, with seven colours and eighty-one divisions.

RED PREDOMINANT

Clan	*Approximate Proportion of Dominant Colour*	*No. of Colours*	*No. of Divisions*	*Clan*	*Approximate Proportion of Dominant Colour*	*No. of Colours*	*No. of Divisions*
Menzies . . .	$\frac{3}{4}$	2	15	Matheson . .	$\frac{3}{7}$	4	13
Macintosh . .	$\frac{2}{3}$	3	11	MacDuff . . .	$\frac{3}{7}$	4	13
Robertson . .	$\frac{1}{2}$	3	31	Chisholm. . .	$\frac{3}{7}$	4	14
Fraser . . .	$\frac{3}{7}$	3	23	Mackinnon . .	$\frac{1}{3}$	4	27
Ross . . .	$\frac{1}{4}$	3	18	Sinclair . . .	$\frac{3}{5}$	5	6
Munro . . .	$\frac{7}{11}$	4	20	MacFarlane . .	$\frac{6}{11}$	5	27
MacGregor . .	$\frac{2}{3}$	4	11	Drummond . .	$\frac{1}{2}$	6	17
MacGillivray . .	$\frac{4}{7}$	4	25	Maclean . . .	$\frac{1}{2}$	6	21
MacAulay . .	$\frac{1}{2}$	4	11	Macpherson . .	$\frac{1}{2}$	6	29
Macquarrie . .	$\frac{1}{2}$	4	11	MacAlaster . .	$\frac{1}{2}$	6	41
MacDougall . .	$\frac{1}{2}$	4	22	Macinnes. . .	$\frac{2}{3}$	6	23
Grant . . .	$\frac{1}{2}$	4	29	Stewart . . .	$\frac{3}{8}$	6	23
MacNaughten . .	$\frac{4}{9}$	4	17	Ogilvy . . .	$\frac{1}{3}$	7	81

BLACK PREDOMINANT

Sutherland . .	$\frac{4}{11}$	3	25	Graham . . .	$\frac{1}{3}$	4	11
Gordon . . .	$\frac{5}{6}$	4	25	Campbell of Argyll .	$\frac{3}{5}$	5	29
Murray . . .	$\frac{5}{9}$	4	13	MacNeill. . .	$\frac{3}{7}$	5	11
Urquhart . .	$\frac{2}{5}$	4	13	Colquhoun . .	$\frac{2}{5}$	5	13
Campbell of Breadal-				MacKenzie . .	$\frac{2}{5}$	5	29
bane . . .	$\frac{2}{5}$	4	13	Rose . . .	$\frac{1}{3}$	5	11
Forbes . . .	$\frac{4}{11}$	4	13	MacLeod. . .	$\frac{1}{3}$	5	13
MacLachlan . .	$\frac{1}{3}$	4	13	Farquharson . .	$\frac{1}{3}$	5	14
Lamont . . .	$\frac{3}{8}$	4	25	Cumming . .	$\frac{1}{3}$	6	15

GREEN PREDOMINANT

Clan	Approximate Proportion of Dominant Colour	No. of Colours	No. of Divisions	Clan	Approximate Proportion of Dominant Colour	No. of Divisions	No. of Colours
Mackay . . .	$\frac{3}{8}$	3	11	MacDonald . .	$\frac{1}{2}$	4	21
Gunn . . .	$\frac{4}{9}$	4	11	Macrae . . .	$\frac{4}{9}$	5	17
Ferguson . . .	$\frac{1}{3}$	4	11	Skene . . .	$\frac{4}{9}$	5	12

BLUE PREDOMINANT

MacLaren . .	$\frac{1}{2}$	5	14	Logan and Maclennan . . .	$\frac{1}{3}$	5	23
Cameron . .	$\frac{1}{3}$	5	21				

CRIMSON PREDOMINANT   RED AND GREEN EQUAL

Macnab . . .	$\frac{2}{5}$	3	24	Buchanan . .	$\frac{1}{3}$ each	6	11

" We submit these tables in the hope that, in abler hands, they may be the means of elucidating many obscure points in clan history."

APPENDIX XXII (PAGE 435)

THE GAELIC CENSUS AS ON 31st MARCH 1901

A census report was presented to Parliament in January 1902 showing the number of persons in the different Parliamentary burghs and counties in Scotland who speak Gaelic only, and the number who speak both Gaelic and English. The appended table relates to the Parliamentary burghs :

Parliamentary Burghs	Total Population	Gaelic only	Gaelic and English	Parliamentary Burghs	Total Population	Gaelic only	Gaelic and English
Aberdeen—				Elgin District—			
1. North Div. .	65,793	2	262	Banff . .	7,149	—	25
2. South Div. .	77,935	4	410	Cullen . .	1,936	—	8
Ayr District—				Elgin . .	8,407	1	168
Ayr . . .	27,529	3	114	Inverurie . .	3,454	—	14
Campbeltown .	8,234	—	793	Kintore . .	789	—	—
Inverary . .	662	—	206	Peterhead . .	11,763	—	28
Irvine . .	9,604	—	79				
Oban . .	4,848	68	2,418	Falkirk District—			
				Airdrie . .	16,288	1	107
Dumfries District—				Falkirk . .	20,505	1	175
Annan . .	4,302	—	8	Hamilton . .	32,775	1	282
Dumfries . .	18,685	—	48	Lanark . .	5,084	—	22
Kirkcudbright .	2,386	—	7	Linlithgow .	4,279	—	38
Lochmaben .	1,051	—	7				
Sanquhar .	1,375	—	—	Glasgow—			
				1. Bridgeton Div.	91,242	1	781
Dundee Burgh .	159,040	6	720	2. Camlachie Div.	78,011	4	618
				3. St. Rollox Div.	118,626	12	2,271
Edinburgh—				4. Central Div. .	74,601	9	3,238
1. East Div. .	73,181	18	794	5. College Div. .	112,492	19	3,825
2. West Div. .	55,464	15	1,007	6. Tradeston Div.	71,278	—	2,718
3. Central Div. .	62,262	18	823	7. Blackfriars .	76,122	10	985
4. South Div. .	107,206	17	1,710	Greenock Burgh .	67,672	24	2,494

Parliamentary Burghs	Total Population	Gaelic only	Gaelic and English	Parliamentary Burghs	Total Population	Gaelic only	Gaelic and English
Hawick District—				Montrose District—*contd.*			
Galashiels . .	12,822	—	30	Inverbervie .	1,207	—	1
Hawick . .	17,303	—	26	Montrose . .	12,401	—	25
Selkirk . .	5,701	—	6				
				Paisley Burgh .	79,354	8	964
Inverness District—							
Forres . .	4,313	—	229	Perth City . .	32,866	2	787
Fortrose . .	1,065	—	120				
Inverness . .	21,177	60	5,000	St. Andrews Dist.—			
Nairn . .	4,327	—	375	Anstruther-E. .	1,190	—	4
				Anstruther-W. .	501	—	—
Kilmarnock Dist.—				Crail . . .	1,087	—	1
Dumbarton .	18,836	—	462	Cupar . .	4,511	—	25
Kilmarnock .	34,165	9	115	Kilrenny . .	2,542	—	2
Port-Glasgow .	16,840	2	127	Pittenweem .	1,859	—	3
Renfrew . .	9,296	—	159	St. Andrews .	7,621	—	74
Rutherglen .	17,206	—	94				
				Stirling District—			
Kirkcaldy District—				Culross . .	335	—	1
Burntisland .	4,725	—	40	Dunfermline .	22,039	—	75
Dysart . .	15,256	—	25	Inverkeithing .	1,909	—	5
Kinghorn . .	1,550	—	4	Queensferry .	1,850	—	11
Kirkcaldy . .	22,346	2	65	Stirling . .	18,403	4	428
Leith District—				Wick District—			
Leith . .	76,668	1	589	Cromarty . .	1,233	—	87
Musselburgh .	11,706	—	26	Dingwall . .	2,490	21	765
Portobello . .	9,180	—	84	Dornoch . .	583	—	241
				Kirkwall . .	3,660	—	19
Montrose District—				Tain . . .	1,645	3	492
Arbroath . .	22,375	—	57	Wick . . .	7,882	1	207
Brechin . .	8,941	—	30				
Forfar . .	11,397	1	30	Total of Parl. Burghs	2,036,483	348	39,113

The following table deals with the Parliamentary districts of counties :

Parliamentary Counties	Total Population	Gaelic only	Gaelic and English	Parliamentary Counties	Total Population	Gaelic only	Gaelic and English
Aberdeenshire—				Dumfries . .	52,586	1	121
East . . .	77,433	—	187	Edinburgh . .	91,887	6	709
West. . .	65,893	2	432	Elgin and Nairn—			
Argyll . . .	60,270	3,287	31,381	Moray . .	32,176	1	1,472
Ayrshire				Nairnshire .	5,799	21	1.500
North . .	87,946	3	926	Fife—			
South . .	94,833	1	418	1. Eastern. .	51,475	1	267
Banff . . .	52,846	—	455	2. Western .	77,037	—	241
Berwick . .	30,888	1	74	Forfar . . .	69,658	6	458
Bute . . .	18,641	20	2,713	Haddington . .	38,798	7	462
Caithness . .	25,741	19	2,658	Inverness . .	67,700	11,623	37,537
Clackmannan, etc.—				Kincardine . .	39,846	—	102
Clackmannan Por.	32,669	1	181	Kirkcudbright .	31,503	—	83
Kinross Por. .	7,212	—	67	Lanark—			
Perth (Muckart)	475	—	8	1. Govan . .	103,978	20	3,971
Fife (Culross) .	2,647	—	15	2. Partick . .	115,528	12	3,696
Stirling (Logie) .	312	—	6	3. North-W. .	100,209	1	881
Dumbarton . .	90,722	12	2,512	4. North-E . .	119,349	4	855

Parliamentary Counties	Total Population	Gaelic only	Gaelic and English	Parliamentary Counties	Total Population	Gaelic only	Gaelic and English
5. Mid Div.	90,966	—	507	Renfrew—			
6. Southern Div.	56,504	1	358	1. Eastern Div.	84,773	8	1,815
Linlithgow	58,667	5	526	2. Western Div.	68,160	4	1,514
Orkney & Shetland—				Ross and Cromarty	68,908	12,132	37,289
Orkney	24,067	—	51	Roxburgh	31,702	—	108
Shetland	27,736	—	52	Stirling	105,637	7	1,455
Peebles & Selkirk—		1		Sutherland	20,656	469	13,835
Peebles Portion	15,065		72	Wigtown	32,593	—	84
Selkirk Portion	4,544	—	19				
Perth—				Total of County Districts	2,425,764	27,752	162,700
1. Eastern Div.	42,330	1	1,121				
2. Western Div.	47,399	75	9,506				

The following table gives the gross totals, inclusive of shipping :

Population of Scotland and of the Parliamentary Counties and Burghs, with the Number of Persons on board Ships in Scottish Waters	Total Population	Persons speaking Gaelic only	Persons speaking Gaelic and English
Parliamentary Counties	2,425,764	27,752	162,700
Parliamentary Burghs	2,036,483	348	39,113
Persons on board Ships in Scottish Waters	9,856	6	887
Total in Scotland	4,472,103	28,106	202,700

INTERESTING POINTS IN THE SCOTTISH CENSUS OF 1901

THE COUNTY GROUPS

Many interesting points are detailed in a Blue Book on the census of Scotland, taken on the 31st March 1901.

The area of land in Scotland is 19,069,500 acres, or about 29,796 square miles. A table gives the distribution of the population over this area, and from it is seen that at the census there were 150 persons to each square mile in the country ; that the number of acres to each person was 4·3 (inland waters, tidal rivers, and foreshores not included) ; and that the proximity or distance from person to person was 154 lineal yards.

The county most sparsely populated is Sutherland, where there are but 11 persons to each square mile ; the most densely so being Lanark, where in a corresponding area there would be 1,523 individuals.

WOMEN PREDOMINATE

The number of the inhabitants of Scotland at the date of the census is 4,472,103, of whom 2,173,755 are of the male sex and 2,298,348 of the female, the latter exceeding the former by 124,593, and giving the proportion of 105·7 females to every 100 males—a lower proportion than has occurred at any previous census. The highest rate was 118·5 to 100 at the census of 1811, since when it has steadily fallen.

GAELIC-SPEAKING POPULATION

A table in the Appendix gives the number and proportion of those in Scotland in its divisions and counties who speak Gaelic only or both Gaelic and English, and on this occasion children under three years of age are not included. Throughout the country 28,106, or 0·63 per cent., of the inhabitants, spoke Gaelic only, while in addition 202,700, or 4·53 per cent., spoke both Gaelic and English. The largest number of persons speaking Gaelic are found in the north-western and west midland divisions of the country, in the former of which 23,893, or 14·34 per cent., spoke Gaelic only, and 82,573, or 49·58 per cent., both Gaelic and English ; and in the latter 3,357, or 0·96 per cent., spoke Gaelic only, and 42,315, or 12·14 per cent., spoke both languages. In the southern divisions 720,495, or 0·26 per cent., of the population, were able to speak Gaelic. As to the counties of Ross and Cromarty, 12,171, or 15·92 per cent., of the population, speak Gaelic only, and 39,929, or 41·39 per cent., both Gaelic and English. In Inverness 11,722, or 13·01 per cent., speak Gaelic only, while 43,287, or 48·03 per cent., both Gaelic and English. In these two counties are included the Western Isles, Lewis, Harris, etc., in which the greater portion of the inhabitants speak either Gaelic alone or Gaelic with their English. In Sutherland 479, or 2·19 per cent. of the population, speak Gaelic only, and 14,083, or 65·68 per cent., both Gaelic and English. Argyll follows with 3,313, or 4·49 per cent. of its inhabitants speaking Gaelic alone, and 34,428, or 46·75 per cent., both languages. The counties in which the lowest proportion of their inhabitants speak Gælic are Shetland, Orkney, Kincardine, Berwick, Selkirk, and Dumfries.

EXTRACT FROM REPORT ON 13TH CENSUS (1921) OF SCOTLAND

POPULATION OF SCOTLAND

The population of Scotland on 19th June 1921 amounted to 4,882,288, of whom 2,348,403 were male and 2,533,885 were female. The total population is 121,384 more than at the time of the previous census, 2nd April 1911, and the intercensal increase is equivalent to 2·5 per cent. of the 1911 figure.

The first official census of Scotland was taken in 1801, and at that time the population was found to be 1,608,420. Since then a census has been taken every ten years, and each successive census has shown an increase of population. The population of Scotland exceeded 2,000,000 for the first time in 1821, exceeded 3,000,000 for the first time in 1861, and 4,000,000 for the first time in 1891. It is now fully three times what it was in 1801, and fully twice what it was in 1831, but unfortunately the increase is entirely urban.

GAELIC-SPEAKING POPULATION

Table IX is designed to show the number of persons returned in the schedules as able to speak Gaelic, these being divided into two classes, the one, those able to speak Gaelic only, and the other, those able to speak Gaelic and English. The total number in Scotland of the former, that is those able to speak Gaelic but not English, amounts to 10,314, and the total number of the latter, those able to speak both Gaelic and English, 151,159. Compared with the numbers at the time of the previous census, those speaking Gaelic only are 8,086 fewer, and those speaking Gaelic as well as English, 32,839 fewer. Both these numbers have shown a steady decline during the last thirty years. In 1891 those speaking Gaelic but not English numbered 43,738 ; in 1901 this number had fallen to 28,106 ; in 1911 to 18,400, and it is now, as above stated, 10,314, or less than one-quarter of what it was thirty years ago. The number of persons speaking Gaelic and English in 1891 was 210,677 ; in 1901 it had fallen to 202,700 ; in 1911 to 183,998, and it is now 151,159. In 1891 6·3 per cent. of the total population of Scotland were able to talk Gaelic, the corresponding figure is now 3·3 per cent. There are three counties in Scotland containing a considerable number of persons able to speak Gaelic only, these being Ross and Cromarty, Inverness, and Argyll, in the first of which those able to speak Gaelic only numbered 4,860, in the second 4,660, and in the third 599. Outside these three counties only 195 persons have been returned as speaking Gaelic but not English. In the county of Ross and Cromarty 57·5 per cent. of the population was returned as being able to speak Gaelic ; in Sutherland, 50·0 per cent. ; in Inverness, 48·8 per cent., and in Argyll, 33·1 per cent.

X*

TABLE IX.—NUMBER OF PERSONS SPEAKING GAELIC (1921 AND 1931)

Counties	1921 Population (both Sexes)	1921 Persons Speaking		1931 Persons Speaking		1921 Percentage of Total Population Speaking	
		Gaelic Only	Gaelic and English	Gaelic Only	Gaelic and English	Gaelic Only	Gaelic and English
Aberdeen	300,980	1	874	19	752	—	0·29
Argyll	76,856	599	24,813	335	20,913	0·78	32·29
Ayr	299,254	4	1,451	4	1,160	—	0·48
Banff	57,293	—	258	4	156	—	0·45
Berwick	28,395	—	82	—	74	—	0·29
Bute	33,711	—	1 453	—	927	—	4·31
Caithness	28,284	—	1,005	—	633	—	3·55
Clackmannan	32,543	—	151	1	186	—	0·46
Dumfries	75,365	1	153	10	228	—	0·20
Dunbarton	150,868	9	2,252	—	1,866	0·01	1·49
Fife	292,902	3	972	4	810	—	0·33
Forfar, Angus	270,950	14	748	5	762	0·01	0·23
Haddington	47,487	—	319	1	213	—	0·67
Inverness	82,446	4,660	35,577	3,123	31,474	5·65	43·15
Kincardine	41,779	1	111	—	102	—	0·27
Kinross	7,963	—	61	—	54	—	0·77
Kirkcudbright	37,156	4	103	—	83	0·01	0·28
Lanark	1,539,307	42	19,196	58	18,121	—	1·25
Linlithgow	83,966	—	224	5	170	—	0·26
Midlothian	506,378	9	3,473	19	3,269	—	0·69
Moray (Elgin)	41,561	—	816	—	532	—	1·96
Nairn	8,790	—	542	—	411	—	6·17
Orkney	24,109	1	63	—	58	—	0·26
Peebles	15,330	—	69	—	64	—	0·45
Perth	125,515	16	6,303	11	4,828	0·01	5·02
Renfrew	298,887	14	3,828	5	3,042	—	1·28
Ross and Cromarty	70,790	4,860	35,810	3,435	31,098	6·87	50·59
Roxburgh	44,989	—	95	—	99	—	0·21
Selkirk	22,606	—	47	1	61	—	0·21
Shetland	25,520	3	104	—	33	0·01	0·41
Stirling	161,726	5	1,272	4	1,073	—	0·79
Sutherland	17,800	68	8,831	24	6,763	0·38	49·61
Wigtown	30,782	—	103	1	98	—	0·33

In the Report on the 1931 Census the Registrar-General observes :

In the island parishes the proportion of the children aged three to four years returned as speaking Gaelic without English, viz. 62·71 per cent., shows comparatively little diminution since 1891, when it was 72·6 per cent. From this it may be inferred that Gaelic is still largely in use in the homes of the people. After school life has been entered on, the Gaelic percentage begins to fall and declines to insignificant proportions.

It is observed that in certain of the age periods the decline has been very considerable. In the 25 to 29 age period, this decrease has been from 33·6 per cent. in 1891 to 0·6 per cent. in 1931.

Census	Population	Gaelic Only	Percentage	Gaelic and English	Percentage
1901	4,472,103	28,106	0·62	202,700	4·51
1921	4,882,288	10,314	0·21	151,159	3·10
1931	4,888,909	6,716	0·14	129,419	2·76
1951	5,095,969	2,652	0·05	91,630	1·80

APPENDIX XXIII (Page 435)

Celtic population of Wales, Ireland, Scotland, and Isle of Man (1901 census)

WALES.—*Welsh speakers*, out of a total population of 2,012,876
(of whom 280,905 spoke Welsh only) 949,824
IRELAND.—*Irish speakers*, representing 14·4 of the population
(of whom 38,000 spoke Erse only) 641,142
SCOTLAND.—*Gaelic speakers*, out of a total population of 4,472,103
(of whom 28,106 spoke Gaelic only) 230,806
ISLE OF MAN.—*Manx speakers*, out of a total population of 54,572
(of whom 59 spoke Manx only) 4,657

Total 1,826,429

BRITTANY (France).—*Breton speakers* (679,000 spoke Breton
only) 1,322,000

APPENDIX XXIV (Page 439)

SCOTTISH REGIMENTAL BADGES

The Royal Arms—which are by warrant the special device of the regiments of Household Cavalry, the Royal Artillery, and Royal Engineers—are allowed to be worn on appointments by two Scottish regiments, the Scots Greys and the Scots Fusiliers, for it will be found hidden in the grenade that forms the plume-socket of the head-dress of these two regiments. The Greys are the only cavalry regiment that wears the grenade and the bearskin head-dress, a distinction they earned at Ramillies by charging and sweeping away three battalions of French grenadiers. A century later, and only a few miles from the scene of their previous heroism, they won at Waterloo the " Eagle " badge. At this great battle the Greys, together with the Royals and Inniskillings, formed the " Union Brigade," and in one of the charges the " Eagle " of the 45th French Infantry was captured by Sergeant Charles Ewart of the Greys, the incident being the subject of a well-known picture and engraving.

Two Scottish corps also wear the light infantry, " bugle," viz. the Cameronians (Scottish Rifles) and the Highland Light Infantry. The former derive the honour from their 2nd Battalion, the old 90th Perthshire Light Infantry, which was raised in 1794, and trained as light infantry. It is the oldest light infantry corps in the Service, for it was not till three years later that a light infantry battalion was added to the 60th, then an ordinary regiment of foot. In the case of the Highland Light Infantry " a French horn " is substituted for the ordinary light infantry " bugle and strings." This the Highland Light Infantry derive from their 1st Battalion, the 71st Highland Light Infantry, and the distinction is almost unique, as they share it only with the 51st, now 1st Yorkshire Light Infantry. Both regiments received the distinction for their services in the Corunna campaign, on their return from which they were made light infantry, and undoubtedly copied their form of the light infantry emblem from that in vogue with our friends the enemy. Of special campaign badges, Scottish regiments can show the Sphinx, the Tiger, the Elephant, and the China Dragon. The first was conferred for Abercromby's campaign in Egypt. The old 42nd, now 1st Black Watch, used to display the emblem on their colours on red ground, to commemorate successfully wiping out, at Alexandria, a French demi-brigade known as " the Invincibles "—they lost 26 out of 31 officers and more than half the rank and file. The distinction is also held by the Scots Guards, Royal Scots, Gordons, and Camerons.

For assiduous service in India the Highland Light Infantry and Seaforths display the badge of the "Elephant," and the Gordons the "Tiger." The Highland Light Infantry derive their badge from their 2nd Battalion, the old 74th, and couple with it the legend Assaye. They have, moreover, the proud distinction of being the only corps in the Service that can couple the legends Seringapatam and Assaye amongst their battle honours. For their distinguished conduct at the great battle where Wellington "against the myriads of Assaye clashed with his fiery few and won," the 74th received from the East India Company a third colour—a white silken flag bearing in the centre the "Elephant,'

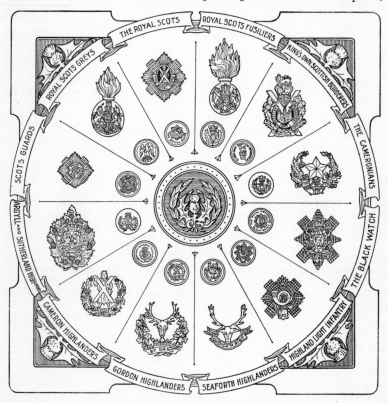

surrounded by a laurel wreath, and from this the badge is derived. The Sea-forths also wear the legend Assaye in right of their 2nd Battalion, the 78th or Ross-shire Buffs, which also received a third colour from the East India Company. The Gordons derive their "Tiger" badge from their 1st Battalion, the old 75th Regiment. This corps was one of the four extra regiments of foot provided at the cost of the East India Company in 1787, and they gained the badge by nineteen years' hard service in India. Only one Scottish regiment shows the China Dragon, the distinguishing badge of the 1st Batt. Scottish Rifles or Cameronians, which served in the China War of 1840–1842.

Clan or family insignia figure largely amongst the regimental badges of the Scottish corps. The Scottish Rifles display the "mullet" or star, the cognisance of the Douglas family, and derive it from their 1st Battalion, the old 26th, raised by a Douglas.

The *caberfeidh* of the MacKenzies, a stag's head and antlers with the Gaelic motto " Cuidich an Righ " (Help the King), is worn by the Seaforth Highlanders, both of the regiments which now form its two battalions having been raised by Earls of Seaforth, heads of Clan MacKenzie. They also wear on some of their appointments the mottoes " Cabar Féidh " (Antlers of the deer), the slogan or war-cry of Seaforth, and " Tulach Ard " (the high hill), the slogan of Kintail, the home of the MacKenzies and the mustering-place of the clansmen.

The Gordon cognisance, a stag's head with the motto " Bydand " (Watchful), commemorates that the 2nd Battalion of the Gordon Highlanders, the old 92nd, was raised by Alexander, 4th Duke of Gordon, and first commanded by his son, the Marquess of Huntly, afterwards 5th and last Duke of Gordon. The Duchess, one of the most charming and fascinating women of the period, greatly stimulated the recruiting of the regiment. Going from clachan to clachan with the recruiting party, she offered the luxury of a kiss on her ripe lips as well as the bounty to all who took the shilling, and the bait was one that took royally. The insignia of two ducal houses are worn by the Argyll and Sutherland Highlanders. Its 1st Battalion, the 91st, late Princess Louise's Argyllshire Highlanders, was raised in 1794 by the Duke of Argyll, and hence the regiment wears *MacCailein Mór's* " Boar's Head " and motto " Ne obliviscaris," surrounded by a wreath of myrtle, the badge of the Campbells. The 2nd Battalion, late 93rd Sutherland Highlanders, was raised in 1800 mainly on the estates of the Countess of Sutherland, and hence the regiment wears the Sutherland crest with the motto " Sans peur," surrounded by a wreath of Butcher's broom, the badge of the clan. Both badges are worn conjointly, and imposed on the whole is a label of three points, the " mark of cadency " or heraldic distinction borne on the Arms of H.R.H. the Princess Louise.

Beyond the above family mottoes and the " In veritate religionis confido " which accompanies the King's (English !) crest amongst the badges of the Scottish Borderers, the most common motto amongst Scottish regiments is " Nemo me impune lacessit," the motto of the Order of the Thistle. The Greys have adopted a very distinctive motto, " Second to None," which they assumed when they took their present position on the British establishment as the 2nd Dragoons, having previously ranked by seniority as the 4th Dragoons. This grand old regiment descends directly from certain troops of Horse and Dragoons placed on the Scottish establishment in 1678. In 1681 the troops of Horse were regimented under Graham of Claverhouse—" Bonnie Dundee "—those of Dragoons under Sir Thomas Dalziel. Claverhouse's men wore the Royal livery of red faced with yellow ; Dalziel clad his men in a stone-grey uniform, which probably accounts for the name of the corps and the custom that always prevailed (derived from his heraldic liveries) of mounting the regiment on grey horses.

APPENDIX XXV (PAGE 574)

CLAN PRECEDENCE

The Scottish people, and Highlanders in particular, were most ceremonious,[1] each chief or chieftain knowing exactly to whom " pertained " the ceremonious " vailing of the bonnet," etc., as well as place on public or warlike occasions. Excepting certain special grants of " place " in warfare, the *Precedence of Clans depends on the precedence of the Chief* (who is " Representer " of the race). The order (ascertain from p. 618 and books of reference) runs, (1) Peers, (2) Baronets, (3) Feudal Barons in their order of erection, (4) Confirmations or grants of arms, for those of non-baronial rank. The above *hereditary* order is now and then (temporarily) varied where a chief holds higher personal rank (by reason of knighthood or companioncy of orders) than he holds hereditary rank.

---

[1] *Loyall Dissuasive*, p. 38 ; J. Riddell, *Peerage Law*, pp. 482, 487.

APPENDIX XXVI (Pages 224, 545)

THE GRANT'S SLOGAN, " STAND FAST, CRAIGELLACHIE ! "

(John Ruskin, in *Two Paths*)

" In one of the loveliest districts of Scotland, where the peat cottages are darkest, just at the western foot of the great mass of the Grampians, which encircles the sources of the Spey and the Dee, the main road, which traverses the chain, winds round the foot of a broken rock, called the Crag or Craig-ellachie. There is nothing remarkable in either its height or form ; it is darkened with a few scattered pines and birch trees, and touched along the summit with a flush of heather ; but it constitutes a sort of headland or leading promontory in the group of hills to which it belongs—a sort of initial letter of the mountains ; and thus stands in the mind of the inhabitants of the district—the Clan Grant—for a type of the country upon themselves. Their sense of this is beautifully indicated by the war-cry of the clan, ' Stand Fast, Craigellachie ! ' You may think long over these words without exhausting the deep wells of feeling and thought contained in them—the love of the native land and the assurance of faithfulness to it."

APPENDIX XXVII (Page 421)

Much information, historical and otherwise, regarding the bagpipe will be found in the following interesting works :

The Highland Bagpipe : Its History, Literature, and Music, by W. L. Manson. Paisley : Alexander Gardner. 1901.

Some Reminiscences and the Bagpipe, by Alexander Duncan Fraser, M.D. Edinburgh : W. J. Hay. 1907.

The Pipes of War, by Brevet-Colonel Sir Bruce-Seton of Abercorn, Bart., and Pipe-Major John Grant. Glasgow : MacLehose, Jackson & Co. 1920.

The Pipes in Peace and War, by C. A. Malcolm.

A Bibliography of the Bagpipe, by Gilbert Askew (Northumberland Pipers Society, Pub. 1933), gives a useful and compendious list of most works on the pipes.

The Story of the Bagpipe, by W. H. G. Flood. London : Walter Scott Publishing Co. 1911.

APPENDIX XXVIII (Page 436)

(1) Phonetic Gaelic text of the opening stanza of " *Bas Dhiarmaid,*" from the *Book of the Dean of Lismore* (James McGregor, 1619) :

> Glenuschee in glenn so rame heive
> A binn feig agus lon
> Menik redeis in nane
> Ar on trath so in dey agon.

(2) The same four lines in modern Gaelic orthography :

> Gleannsith an gleann so ri'm thaobh
> 'S am binn feidh agus loin
> Is minich a rachas an Fheinn
> Air an t-srath so an deigh an con.

(3) English translation :

> Glenshee the vale that close beside me lies
> Where sweetest sounds are heard of deer and elk
> And where the Feinn did oft pursue the chase
> Following their hounds along the lengthening vale.

The Dean's phonetic system may be far from perfect, but as between this and the modern orthography, the non-Gaelic-speaking reader will gain a much quicker, and an intelligible, impression of what Gaelic—and a Gaelic poem— sounds like from the text of 1619, than from the modern version, wherewith (unless he has put in a deal of preliminary study) he will be completely " stumped."

APPENDIX XXIX (PAGE 47)

The account on page 47 (but with some additional exposition of the *curiae militaris* aspects, not apparent to the layman) is that handed down in the Clan Chattan, *as see* Lach. Shaw, *History of the Province of Moray* (J. F. S. G. Ed.), III, pp. 115–117. Here he says " our historians have not sufficiently explained who they were or what was the cause of the dispute," and that the result was regarded as " a royal sentence in favour of the Macphersons "—as indeed it was —*versus* Davidson. Upon that construction Shaw, the Historian of the Roses, Skene, and Neilson all concur that it was on a matter of " precedence "—which is exactly why it was determinable *in curia militaris*, and by combat. The account is therefore not mine, though, as we see, the *matter of honour* arose indirectly out of the land-dispute with the Camerons.

APPENDIX XXX (PAGE 102)

EXPERT EVIDENCE ON CLANSHIP, ETC., IN *MACLEAN OF ARDGOUR* v. *MACLEAN*, 1938

EVIDENCE OF JOHN CAMERON, Solicitor, D.Ph., author of *Celtic Law*

Excerpts from Minutes of Evidence, 4 *July* 1938

(P. 7) (Q.) In the early Celtic system, at least in Ireland and Wales, the social group called the *clann* or children is essentially similar in conception to the Family or Name of later times ? (A.) I agree that that is so. (*Referred to Skene, " Celtic Scotland," III,* p. 306, *s.v. Law Clan Macduff.*) (Q.) Do you agree with the suggestion that the Law Clan Macduff is suggestive of a *derbhfine* system having existed in early Scotland ? (A.) Yes. . . . (*Referred to Sir J. Skene, " De Verborum Significatione," s.v. Law Clan Macduff, re Arbuthnott and Spens.*) (Q.) Essentially it suggests the idea of *derbhfine* was not restricted to males ? (A.) That is so : might be that. (Q.) Isn't that also a necessary deduction from the Pictish order of succession described by Bede ? (A.) Yes. . . . (P. 12) (Q.) It was stated that " after their mothers they take sovereignty and every other inheritance besides." You think that would include the lesser chiefships amongst the Picts, too, therefore ? (A.) I think so.

(Q.) Do you consider that such a primitive order of succession (*as that attributed to the Picts*) including females and descendants would be a natural preliminary to the evolution of a non-Salic as distinct from a Salic order of common law succession ? (A.) Quite likely. Yes. (*Referred to Sir H. Maine, " Ancient Law,"* 1930 *ed., p.* 205, " The family was in fact a corporation and he was the representative, or we might almost say, its public officer.") (Q.) (p. 15) Would you say that tanistry, nomination or designation, was a means for the reigning chief or patriarch to nominating the person who is to be his successor as representative of the family ? (A.) Yes. . . . (Q.) Tanistry in that sense is really more analogous to the settlement or testate succession than to succession by operation of a common law succession, is it not ? (A.) Yes, I think you could call it perhaps testate succession without writing. (Q.) Have you noticed that on occasion in the Scottish peerage the title of " Master " is applied . . . to someone such as a brother ? . . . (A.) Yes. I consider that it is a form of tanistry. (Q.) A survival in the Scottish peerage of the tanistry of earlier times ? (A.) Yes. (Q.) And you are aware that a number of Scottish peers had power of nominating the succession to their dignities ? (A.) Yes. (Q.) In other words, these things suggest to you that considerable relics of the system of tanistry or nomination survived from Celtic times into our medieval Scottish peerage ? (A.) I think that is the case.

(P. 21) (Q.) Would you regard the thaneage as being the demesne of the *toshach* ? (A.) Yes. (*Referred to C. Innes, " Thanes of Cawdor," p. 4.*) (Q.) Does it strike you as important that this charter refers to a period when thaneage-tenure was still a working system ? (A.) Yes, I notice the destination is one to " heirs." (Q.) And not to heirs male ? (A.) Yes. . . . (Q.) The men who owned Cawdor under the Calder charter would continue to be known as thane ? (A.) Yes, he was a thane of Calder. (Q.) And the thane in your opinion is *derbhfine*-successor of the *toshach* or tribe-chief ? (A.) Yes. (Q.) Then isn't it an important part of the charter that we find the devolution of thane or *derbhfine-toshach* is non-Salic and to " heirs " including heirs female ? (A.) Yes, undoubtedly the destination is to " heirs," which I presume is one to heirs female. (Q.) According to what was shown by Lord Hailes in the " Additional Case for the Countess of Sutherland " ? (A.) Yes.

(P. 24) (Q.) Is it a well-founded view that the King was the greatest sort of chiefs ? (A.) Yes. (Q.) But only a bigger thing ? (A.) Yes.[1] (*Referred to Nisbet's " Heraldry," Vol. II, p. 172 ; Bute, " Scottish Coronations," p. 155.*)

(*Referred to Kenkynol charters, " Great Seal," Vol. I, No. 509.*) (Q.) Do you assume from this that the office *caput toties progenii* was regarded as a possession held from the Crown and which could be resigned to the Crown for re-destination ? (A.) Yes, there was apparently a resignation. (Q.) So that the office of *cean-cinnidh*, which was held under the first charter to " heirs " including heirs female, is resigned to the Crown and a re-destination taken to Kennedy and his heirs male ? (A.) Yes, these are the terms. . . . (Q.) . . . unless one apply for a tailzied order of succession, a *cean-cinnidh* was a thing descendable like other impartible inheritance in Scotland in a non-Salic line ? (A.) Yes, all our evidence, I think, is to that effect. (Q.) Unless you got an express tailzied it went to heirs of line ? (A.) Yes. (Q.) That is a Celtic chiefship is considered at that period as a subject tenable from the Crown with whatever destination the Crown agrees to put in ? (A.) Yes. (Q.) Is that not rather consistent with the development of the theory of the Crown as the fountain of honour ? (A.) Yes. Of course, the chiefship was an office of honour.

(P. 28) (Q.) You find that under Celtic conditions women could own land ? (A.) Yes. (Q.) You find reference in Celtic law to women being of chieftain grade ? (A.) That is referred to in the ancient laws of Ireland . . . my own opinion is that these laws were applied to a very great extent in Scotland. (Q.) And a woman could also own service to a higher chief, I see you say on p. 68 ? (A.) Yes, that is so.

(P. 33) (Q.) In your view, banners have a practical connection with the exercise of the chief's position ? (A.) I would say so. (Q.) And that heraldry, therefore, was closely related to a social system ? (A.) I consider so. (Q.) Even to what is called the clan system ? (A.) Yes.

---

[1] Cf. p. 296, evidence of A. Boyd, whose ancestor came in on the galley with the 1st Ardgour : " What is the Crown more than an estate ? " (Q.) With regard to the expression *Cean-tighe* . . . if you wanted to make that apply to a lady, wouldn't you say *ban-tighe* ? (A.) No. Among the crofters some of the women are known as *cean-tighe*. (Q.) Did you ever hear Miss Catriona referred to as *cean-tighe* ? (A.) We call her nothing else but *cean-tighe*. (Q.) You call her that ? (A.) Yes. (Q.) Did you ever hear any other lady on an estate called *cean-tighe* ? (A.) Yes, they are called *cean-tighe* where there is no man.

(P. 37) (Q.) I refer you to Sir A. Macpherson, *Loyall Dissuasive*, p. 118 : Is that not a definite and positive statement by Macpherson that he considers the chieftainship of a West Highland clan such as the Macdonalds was transmissable through a female ? (A.) Yes, just as it was transmissable to all the others through a female. (Q.) His views are therefore left in no doubt ? (A.) No.

(P. 34) *(Referred to " Irish Law of Kingship," " Proceedings of Roy. Irish Academy," Vol. 40, p.* 190, " *Aedh Ua Domhnaill* intervened in virtue of the suzerainty claimed by the *Cinel Conaill* over Connaught and proclaimed Theobald Burke chieftain.") (Q.) Do you regard that as an exercise of the authority of *Aedh Ua Domhnaill* to determine a dispute about chiefship ? (A.) Yes, it appears to be so. (Q.) Do you think that it was analogous to the King of Scots' confirmation and warrandice of the *Kenkynol* ? (A.) It seemed to be analogous to that.

(P. 46) *(Referred to " Letters of Sir Walter Scott,"* 1903 *ed., p.* 14, " Lady Hood will now be *caberfae* herself . . .") (A.) Yes, he regarded her as a chief. (Q.) He regarded her as chief of the Mackenzies ? (A.) Yes. (Q.) And the achievement *(of Arms)* she got would suggest to you, looking at it, that it was the achievement of the chief of the Mackenzies ? (A.) It looks that.

5 *July* 1942

(P. 69) (Q.) We were dealing yesterday with the patronymic *Mac mhic* . . . Do you agree whoever is entitled to that is the head of the family so far as the Highlands is concerned ? (A.) No. . . . I don't think that patronymics were generally applied. *(Referred to Skene's " Highlanders," McBain Ed., p.* 106, " In the Highlands it was quite different, for there the property of the clan was, by the law of gavel, divided . . . while females were altogether excluded from succession either to chiefship or to property.") (Q.) Do you agree with Dr. Skene ? (A.) No, the theory that the land belonged altogether to the clan is one which is not true.

(P. 81. That a woman could not succeed.) (A.) Could not succeed to what ? (Q.) In any way, either to lands or chiefship, or anything else, just what Skene said. (A.) I hold that that view is not correct.

(P. 87) (Q.) Do you seriously suggest that the theory of succession to the Crown prior to 1400 is of any assistance in this case ? (A.) Yes, I am of opinion that the system of succession to chiefship would be analogous. . . . (Q.) Is your view that chiefships were descendable in a non-Salic order based upon an analogy from thaneages and the Crown prior to 1400 ? (A.) Yes, I think those thaneages and the Crown, in my opinion, show Celtic custom and Celtic succession to a great extent came down through thaneages. It was incorporated into it.

(P. 101) (Q.) You frequently found the same person being a feudal lord and a Celtic chief ? (A.) I wouldn't go that length. . . . These offices existed, and I think they gradually came down and were evolved, as it were, into a feudal system, these leaders going perhaps under different names ; but I think the Celtic system was one which very readily adapted itself to the feudal system because it was a system which in many of its aspects was of a feudal nature. . . . (Q.) Is it your view that by the year 1300 the Celtic and the feudal system had coalesced in the Highlands of Scotland ? (A.) Yes, I think they had pretty well become merged.

(P. 122) *(Referred to Brown's " History of the Highlands," p.* 397.) (Q.) Does the charter to Brian Vicar Mackay suggest that the tenure of land in the Highlands was solely on a basis on which women could not succeed to property ? (A.) The destination in the Gaelic charter is to " heirs." (Q.) Have you found that a number of *(old charters in the West Highlands)* contain destinations to " heirs " ? (A.) Yes. (Q.) Therefore Mr. Brown's statement in that respect is not consistent with what you find in actual records ? (A.) No, it is not consistent with these records.

(P. 124) (Q.) You are aware Skene held the theory *thane* was a development of *toshach* ?   (A.) Yes, with all its qualifications.   (Q.) Does it not follow from that, that Skene's later opinion was that in its late form the *toshach*-head was capable of descending in the form of the thane and thaneage in heirs female ? (A.) That would appear to be his view.   (Q.) Then it would appear, writing in his second book, Skene departs from his youthful Salic supposition ?   (A.) He would appear to have departed from the earlier view.

(P. 30) (Q.)   (*The Crown*) had in fact feudalised these Celtic dignities ?   (A.) Yes, I would say the Celtic dignities merged into the feudal system.   (Q.) And became governed by the new laws of descent the Crown was applying ?   (A.) That is my view.   (Q.) They came to be held as incorporeal feudal dignities *de Rege* ?   (A.) Yes.   (Q.) In these circumstances, is it not inconsistent to suggest that the clan could determine a chiefship ?   (A.) Well, I don't think it was consistent that they could do so.

EVIDENCE OF W. MACKAY MACKENZIE, LL.D., F.S.A., Secretary to the Royal
Commission on Ancient Monuments.

5 *July* 1938

(P. 220) (Q.) In your view, what does the word " clan " mean ?   (A.) It has a general meaning of family, ordinary meaning of family, but there is a peculiar sense in which it is used for this quasi-feudal organisation in the Highlands, or you might say feudal organisation.   (Q.) But its primary meaning, I think, is family ?   (A.) Yes.

(Q.) In your view, did the clans in fact consist either of persons linked by blood or persons linked by reason of place of dwelling in a territory ?   (A.) That is the definition of the Act of Parliament.
(*Reference Acts* 1587, & *Act of* 11 *Sect*, 1593, *A.P.S.*, *IV*, *p.* 40.) (Q.) Do you see a reference there to the pretence of blood or place of dwelling ?   (A.) Yes.   (Q.) Are those familiar terms ?   (A.) Quite familiar.   Pretence means claim. . . . (Q.) So that in your view do you get this dual element entering into the composition of the clan, blood-relation and place of dwelling ?   (A.) Oh, yes, you have both.

(Q.) Have you considered at all the question of rule of succession operating the descent of the chiefship of the clan or the family unit ?   (A.) Well, it would be the ordinary feudal rule of succession.

(Q.) Do you know of examples of the case of a daughter who has no brothers marrying, and her husband coming in and being regarded as the chief of the clan or unit ?   (A.) Yes. . . . (Q.) In addition do you get cases of children becoming chiefs through succession through a female ?   (A.) The female would marry normally and her husband taking the name could be accepted as chief.   Then, of course, the son would succeed in normal course :   Colquhoun for example.

(Q.) The chiefship succession could transmit through a female ?   (A.) Yes, she is described as heiress of the Clan Chattan.

(Q.) In your view, about what date did the clan system first become apparent in Scotland ?   (A.) I should say it began to take shape in the Highlands, and in the Borders—which must not be forgotten about—about the same time, about the end of the fourteenth century.   (Q.) From that time down to at least 1715 have you come across or do you know of any examples of a person being regarded as head or chief of the clan or family who did not own the territory ? . . . (A.) No.   I think the two things are incompatible.   What is the good of a chief who did not own land and did not have a following ?   (Q.) At least down to the time of 1715 do you know of any example of landless chiefs ?   (A.) Except the Mac-Gregors.   (Q.) And I think they were outlaws ?   (A.) Yes.   (Q.) Can they be regarded as very special ?   (A.) Oh, dear !   Yes.   (Q.) It has been suggested that there was a rule of succession governing the headships to clans and families by which females were excluded from that succession.   Do you know of such a rule ?

(A.) I do not know it.   (Q.) Have you come across any examples of such a rule ?
(A.) No.

(Q.) It has been suggested that the office of the chiefship of a clan or headship of a family was elective.   (A.) No.   (Q.) Have you come across any examples
of elected heads or chiefs ?   (A.) No.   How could they draw up clan genealogies
if they were going to be interrupted by general election ?

(Q.) Do you say that the chiefship was territorial rather than personal ?
(A.) No.   I do not say that.   (Q.) You think the personal element was an important
one ?   (A.) The personal element entered into the whole of Scottish procedure.
All land-holding in Scotland was marked by the personal element.   (*Then,
reference to " Burt's Letters," II, p.* 108 ; *and re McBain's ed. of Skene's " Highlanders of Scotland," p.* 102, *line* 16, " the officer of engineers was Captain Burt.")
Dr. M. Mackenzie :   " Burt was not a captain and he was not an engineer.   (A.)
I think the personal loyalty was a very strong element in the clan.   It was an
element in all land-holding in Scotland.   It was through all Scottish feudalism,
but circumstances made it more significant in the north and on the Borders.

(Q.) Do you say that the element of recognition by the clan had nothing to
do with the question of chiefship ?   (A.) I don't think it had.

(Q.) Did the person who held the principal fief or the principal portion of
the land hold the chiefship ?   (A.) I think so, being of the line bearing the name.
(Q.) And as a general principle, did the person who inherited the land inherit
the chiefship ?   (A.) Yes.

(Q.) Coming down to modern times : Let us assume the land had vanished,
. . . do you see any reason why the chiefship . . . should not continue to descend
according to the same rule by which it apparently descended while there was
and ? . . . (A.) I see no reason, no.

EVIDENCE OF THE VERY REV. LACHLAN MACLEAN WATT, LL.D., " Bard of the
   Clan Maclean Association."

*This witness had been largely examined on poetry, etc., but the following points
in cross relate to the clan/family organisation.*

(P. 517) (Q.) (*Referred to Mackenzie's " Works," II,* 574, 618 : " The French
have constantly and the Scots frequently taken such differences or brisures as
might . . . distinguish their families from that of *their chief, for so we call the
Representative of the Family* from the French word *chef* or head, *and* in the Irish
with us *the chief of the family is called the " Head of the Clan."*)   (Q.) Do you deduce
that Sir G. Mackenzie considered that from a heraldic point of view the " head
of the clan," the " chief of the clan," or the " representative of the family "
all meant the same thing ?   (A.) I respectfully suggest that it is a matter of
" Head of a Family " and " Head of a Clan."   He was a Highlander and he
knew that clan means a family.   Clan and family mean exactly the same thing.

(P. 522) (Q.) Did you come to the conclusion from reading in the *Book of
Deer* that the *toiseach* had an interest in land ?   (A.) Of course, he naturally had.
(Q.) Does that not suggest the *toiseach* had a territorial character ?   (A.) Yes,
of course it had then.   (Q.) You consider the *toiseach* was in the nature of a lesser
chief ?   (A.) He was a chief and he had a territorial character and he had mensal
property.   (Q.) That you understand to mean a piece of land that supported
a chief and descended to the successor holding the office of chief ?   (A.) Yes.
It was not divided up.   (P. 524) (Q.) What do you take to be the meaning of
the word *cean-tighe* of " house " ?   (A.) First of all, as a rule, a house where
people lived.   That is to found a house of which one becomes the head.   It means
that when the people had lived there it became a community.   (Q.) Your impression is that the house originated in a literal structural house ?   (A.) Yes, it began
as the household and grew until then figuratively used to represent the community descending from the first householder . . . (A.) (On p. 525) The *ceunn-
tighe* mean the living representative of the man who founded the house.

(Q). You said that all members were members of the house ?   (A.) You misunderstood me.   You asked me, did the head of a house who became the representer remain chief of that house.   Yes, the head of the stock is the word. Stem or stock is a good word perfectly understandable in dealing with Highland matters.[1]

(Q.) (*Referred to Garth's " Sketches of the Highlanders," p.* 24.)   The members of each clan considered themselves, and actually were, branches and descendants of the same family.   The central stem of this family was the chief ?   (A.) Certainly.

(P. 544) (Q.) You stated that the office of *Ceann-cinnidh* means that of chief ?   (A.) Yes, head of a clan.   (*Referred to the Kenkynol of Carrick, " Great Seal Charter," Vol. I, No.* 509.)   (Q.) In this case a lady might have succeeded as leader in peace and war ?   (A.) Yes.

APPENDIX XXXI (PAGE 238)

THE COURTS AND THE CLAN

In the *Scots Law Times*, 1950, will be found (abbreviated) legal reports of Decisions of the Court of the Lord Lyon, covering in a number of cases *Chiefship of Clans*, where the Lyon Court has given effect to the law, as laid down in earlier decisions, and by the House of Lords (where clan chiefship and its relation to arms was before the Court—in relation to whether either of the coats of arms was of that character—in *Seaforth* v. *Allangrange*, 1922, S.C., H.L., p. 39) by decisions of which both Lyon Court and the Court of Session are bound, and (so far as relevant) *Maclean of Ardgour* v. *Maclean*, Court of Session, 1941, as regards succession to arms, but where clan chiefship was not *sub judice*, and no chiefly rights nor jurisdiction regarding clan chiefship were or could be affected.

Illustrative findings of Lyon Court, from *e.g.* chiefships of Clan Farquharson and Macdonald, are subjoined, and represent the ruling legal decisions upon the subject : [2]

(*a*) That " Clan " is a *nomen juris* in Scotland, and membership or Headship of a Clan involves, or may involve, rights such as rights of Name, or rights to Ensigns Armorial, cognisable in the Law of Arms and justiciable in the Court of the Lord Lyon.

(*b*) That Headship of a Clan is cognisable in the Law of Arms in relation to (*a*) undifferenced arms, (*b*) supporters, (*c*) badge, slogan, and standard, (*d*) name, and is a description relevant and relative to such arms, supporters, or external additaments and name.

(*c*) That Sir George Mackenzie of Rosehaugh, His Majesty's Advocate, states in the 21st Chapter of his treatise, *The Science of Herauldrie*, that " the marks whereby the cadets or younger sons do distinguish their arms from those of the principal house or the chiefhouse, as we say in Scotland, are called brisurs," and further that such brisurs " distinguish their families from that of their Chief, for so we call the Representative of the family from the French word *chef*, an head, and in the Irish with us, the Chief of the family is called the Head of the Clan," and thus identifies the terms and character " Head of the Clan " in Gaelic with " Representative of the Family " in Scots, and both these with proprietorship of the ancestral arms without brisur or mark of cadency, and that the Lords Dunedin, Shaw, and Sumner likewise held on 12th December 1921 that the Chief of a Clan is the member of the family entitled to the undifferenced ancestral arms.

---

[1] The term " stock " is used in the Lyon Court Act, 1592 c. 125, and " stem " in birthbrief preambles.

[2] See 1950 *Scots Law Times*, Lyon Court Reports.

(*d*) That the Representation of an armigerous family, and *id est* Headship of an Honourable Clan, is capable of conveyance or resettlement by *inter alia* (*a*) Resignation in the Lord Lyon's hands and Regrant, or (*b*) confirmation of a " designation " or settlement in tailzie of, or indicative of, the undifferenced or absolute Ensigns Armorial by the representative of such family or clan.

(*e*) That a resettlement of the undifferenced arms within the blood, or *in familia heraldica*, including a resettlement conferring armorial courtesy upon the husband of an heiress in blood or a daughter of the family, does not require the consent of the family, *id est* clan.

(*f*) That as Inheritor of the arms of Farquharson of Invercauld without brisur or mark of cadency, the Petitioner, being now " Representer " and " Chief, for so we call the Head of the family," of the Family of Farquharson of Invercauld, is accordingly " in the Gaelic, Head of the Clan " Farquharson, as set forth by, and in the words of, Sir George Mackenzie of Rosehaugh in his *Science of Herauldrie* (*Works*, Vol. II, p. 618, line 16).

(*g*) That as Inheritor of the baronial estate of Invercauld with which the family history of the Chiefs of Clan Farquharson is bound up, and being nominee in tailzie of the Ensigns Armorial of Farquharson of Invercauld without brisur or mark of cadency, the Petitioner, having assumed the surname of Farquharson of Invercauld without addition or diminution, is, subject to confirmation and reinvestiture of the arms by the Lord Lyon, now Representer, *id est* Representative of the House and Family of Farquharson of Invercauld and of the Name or Clan Farquharson.

As an example of the Executive documents following, and in this instance embodying superimposed ministerial procedure (embodying regrant and publication of antecedent Lyon Court decision and matriculation-warrant), the operative part of LORD MACDONALD's Letters Patent, 1st May 1947, is subjoined, and runs :

KNOW YE THEREFORE that WE, having in His Majesty's Name and Authority Officially-Recognised the Petitioner's assumption of the surname of " MACDONALD OF MACDONALD," Do by these Presents Restore, Ratify and Confirm unto the Petitioner and his heirs in the lands and Barony of Macdonald, or ancestral castle of Dunscaith, within the said Barony, and to the heir-general of the last heir in the heritage aforesaid, if it so fall out—bearing the name " Macdonald of Macdonald " without alteration, addition, or diminution, except such as may be congruous to their rank or dignity for the time, the following Ensigns Armorial, *videlicet* : *Or, an eagle displayed Gules, surmounted of a lymphad, sails furled, oars in action Sable* (for Macdonald of Macdonald) along with *two leopards proper* for supporters, set upon a compartment of *rocks and heather proper, issuant from waves undy*, along with this Motto *FRAOCH EILEAN*, and for Badge *an eagle displayed Gules armed and beaked Sable, having a chapeau Gules furred Ermine, holding in its talons an escutcheon as afore-blasoned*, which Ensigns are to borne as marshalled in the matriculation on the 44 folio of the 36th Volume of Our Public Register of All Arms and Bearings in Scotland of even date with these Presents, wherein We CERTIFY AND MAKE KNOWN that the Ensigns Armorial appertaining and belonging unto the said Right Honourable ALEXANDER GODFREY MACDONALD OF MACDONALD, LORD MACDONALD, Baron of the Barony of Macdonald in the Isle of Skye, Representative of the Family of Macdonald of Macdonald, Chief of the Name and Arms of Macdonald, are matriculated conform to these Presents Our Letters Patent, and are thus blasoned, *videlicet* : quarterly, 1st, *Argent, a lion rampant Gules, armed and langued Azure ;* 2nd, *Or, a hand in armour fessways holding a cross-crosslet fitchée Gules ;* 3rd, *Or, a lymphad sails furled and oars in action Sable, flagged Gules ;* 4th, *Vert, a salmon naiant in fess proper ;* over all, on an inescutcheon *en surtout, Or, an eagle displayed Gules, surmounted of a lymphad, sails furled, oars in action Sable* (as Chief of the Name and Arms of Macdonald) ; above the shield is placed his Lordship's coronet, thereon an Helmet befitting his degree with a Mantling Gules doubled Ermine, and *on a crest-coronet Or* is set for Crest *a hand in armour fessways couped at the elbow proper, holding a cross-crosslet fitchée Gules,* and in an Escrol over the same this Motto PER MARE PER TERRAS, and on a Compartment of rocks and heather proper issuant from waves undy along with this Motto FRAOCH EILEAN are set for Supporters *two leopards proper* ; for his Lordship's badge *an eagle displayed Gules, armed and beaked Sable, having a Chapeau Gules furred Ermine* (for which his Lordship and his successors, Lords Macdonald, may at their pleasure substitute their peerage coronet) *holding in its talons an escutcheon Or charged wtih an eagle displayed Gules surmounted of a lymphad sails furled and oars in action Sable,* which is depicted in the first compartment, with the crest in the second compartment and a sprig of heather in the third compartment of a standard five yards in length, with his Lordship's arms in the hoist, of these Liveries, *Or and Gules, and upon two transverse bands Sable this Slughorn FRAOCH EILEAN in letters also Or ;* by demonstration of which Ensigns Armorial he and his successors therein are to be Accounted, Taken and Received as *Chief of the Name and Arms of Macdonald,* Representative of the noble and princely family of Macdonald, and, in the sense and words of Sir George Mackenzie of Rosehaugh, His Majesty's Advocate, " *Head of the Clan* " *Macdonald,* amongst all Nobles and in All Places of Honour.

APPENDIX XXXII

Setts of Tartans officially Authorised and Recorded in the Court of the Lord Lyon

The setts are " blazoned " according to the system devised by James Logan (see Appendix XXI) and also employed by Donald C. Stewart in *Setts of the Scottish Tartans,* already referred to on p. 524. The system provides *relative proportions of colour,* and is applicable to any increase or reduction of the width of the whole pattern.

Actually, as in the case of Logan's scale, the proportions are given, as in *eighths of an inch,* relative to the measurements across the sett, in the normal size appropriate to *an adult kilt sett.*

When reduced for use in small-scale silk, and *e.g.* neck-tie, weaves, some distortion is frequently inevitable (unless relatively thinner threads of suitable size happen to be available) owing to thread-thickness and to the consideration that for practical purposes *two threads* is the narrowest " line " that can be woven.

As D. C. Stewart observes,[1] any such distortions, arising out of what should be purely practical weaving requirements, should be confined to the minimum deviation from the standard sett.[2] Many of the divergencies found in trade

---

[1] *Setts of the Scottish Tartans,* p. 41.

[2] It has been suggested that deviation in band-widths might be justified in " over-size " settings on the ground that some colours become more dominant when seen in quantity. The Lord Lyon is by no means satisfied that there is *any* ground for deviation on *that* account. Skilful variation in *colour-shade* more correctly meets such considerations where they arise. The point is, however, to be investigated by *Episcope* in connection with certain tartans at present *sub judice.*

evidently arise from one weaver " enlarging " for normal weave from a " reduced " pattern of some other weaver who, having distorted the sett in reduction, *his* deviation has become enlarged in the next man's normal-sized weave, one error thus leading to another on a larger scale. Publication of the officially authorised setts will prevent new firms falling into such errors, and also enable clans-folk to check up whether they are being sold needlessly, or erroneously, distorted patterns.[1]

Reference : Az., Azure ; B., Black ; Bl., Blue ; G., Green ; R., Red ; Y., Yellow.

BOYD 7th March 1956. *Lyon Court Book.*

BURNETT[2] OF LEYS[3] 20th October 1838. *Lyon Register,* IV, 33.

$2\frac{1}{2}$ B., $2\frac{1}{2}$ R., 1 W., $2\frac{1}{2}$ R., 1 G., $2\frac{1}{2}$ R., 1 Y., $2\frac{1}{2}$ R., 1 G., $2\frac{1}{2}$ R., 1 W., $2\frac{1}{2}$ R., $2\frac{1}{2}$ Bl., 30 R.

CAMERON 25th November 1947. *Lyon Register,* XXXVI, 86.

1 Y., 15 R., $5\frac{1}{2}$ G., 1 R., $5\frac{1}{2}$ G., 1 R., $5\frac{1}{2}$ G., 1 R., $5\frac{1}{2}$ G., 15 R.

CLAN CHATTAN (CHIEF) 9th April 1947. *Lyon Register,* XXXVI, 38.

$\frac{1}{2}$ W., 15 R., 1 B., $\frac{1}{2}$ W., 8 G., 1 W., $1\frac{3}{4}$ Y., $1\frac{3}{4}$ R., $\frac{1}{2}$ B., $1\frac{3}{4}$ R., $1\frac{3}{4}$ Y., 1 W., 8 Az., 2 B., 2 R., 3 Y., 1 W.

CLAN CHATTAN

$30\frac{1}{2}$ R., 1 B., $\frac{1}{2}$ W., 8 G., 1 W., $1\frac{3}{4}$ Y., $1\frac{3}{4}$ R., $\frac{1}{2}$ B., $1\frac{3}{4}$ R., $1\frac{3}{4}$ Y., 1 W., 8 Az., 2 B., 2 R., 3 Y., 1 W.

FARQUHARSON 6th February 1946. *Lyon Register,* XXXV, 71.

$\frac{1}{2}$ R., 2 Bl., $\frac{1}{2}$ B., $\frac{1}{2}$ Bl., $\frac{1}{2}$ B., $\frac{1}{2}$ Bl., 4 B., 4 G., 1 Y., 4 G., 4 B., 4 Bl., $\frac{1}{2}$ B., 1 R.

GRANT 20th November 1946. *Lyon Register,* XXXV, 74v.

3 R., 1 Bl., 1 R., 1 Bl., 12 R., 1 Az., 1 R., 3 Bl., 1 R., 1 G., 1 R., 10 G., 1 R., 1 Bl., 3 R.

INNES[4] 30th August 1951. *Lyon Register,* XXXVIII, 89.

6 R., 1 B., 1 R., 1 B., 1 R., 6 B., $1\frac{1}{4}$ Az., 6 B., 1 R., 1 B., 1 R., 1 B., 6 R., 1 Y., $1\frac{1}{2}$ R., 3 Bl., $1\frac{1}{2}$ R., 1 B., 5 G., 1 B., $1\frac{1}{2}$ R., 1 W., $1\frac{1}{2}$ R., 1 B., 5 G., 1 B., $1\frac{1}{2}$ R., 3 Bl., $1\frac{1}{2}$ R., 1 Y.

MACDONALD OF CLANRANALD

11th October 1946. *Lyon Register,* XXXVI, 7v.

$5\frac{1}{2}$ B., 1 R., 6 Bl., $1\frac{1}{2}$ R., 1 Bl., 1 R., 3 Bl., 1 R., 1 Bl., $1\frac{1}{2}$ R., 6 Bl., 1 R., $5\frac{1}{2}$ B., 1 W., $5\frac{1}{2}$ G., $1\frac{1}{2}$ R., 1 G., 1 R., 3 G.

MACFARLANE 17th May 1957. *Lyon Register,* XLII, 55.

MACINTYRE 29th December 1955. *Lyon Register,* XL, 122.

---

[1] As indicated by Logan (see p. 592 *supra*) there were often minor family-variations of a generic clan-tartan, cf. the " *Prince Charles Edward* " sett of the *Royal* (*Stewart*) tartan. Some may be real " Branch-variations," others mere accident, whilst some others are a special weave to suit some individual member's idiosyncrasy. Lyon has already found instances in which such were likely to have slipped into becoming " the " clan-pattern—as made by " this " or " that " firm ! Such instances, which can rightly be (and anciently would have been) denominated " *So and So's* Fancy," should be carefully noted by makers and tailors. Henceforth, reference to the *Authoritative sett,* gives all concerned the opportunity to check up, and note the extent (and look for the source) of such " Fancy " or " tradesmen's error " devagations from the correct clan sett.

[2] Recorded by de-painting, and above is weaving count approved by Lord Lyon. [3] Distinct from Barns, etc.

[4] Decided with Lord High Constable as Assessor in judgment on petition of Charles S. Innes, Washington, U.S.A.

MACKINTOSH   29th March 1951. *Lyon Court Book.*
  22 R., 5 Bl., 2 R., 11 G., 3 R., 1 Bl., 3 R., 11 G., 2 R., 5 Bl.

MACKINTOSH (HUNTING)   29th March 1951. *Lyon Court Book.*
  $10\frac{1}{2}$ G., 1 Y., $10\frac{1}{2}$ G., 5 Bl., 2 R., 11 G., 3 R., 1 Bl., 3 R., 11 G., 2 R., 5 Bl.

MACPHERSON OF CLUNY [1]
                    6th September 1948.   *Lyon Register*, XXXVII, 13.
  $1\frac{12}{16}$ B., $\frac{4}{16}$ W., $\frac{11}{16}$ B., $\frac{2}{16}$ W., $\frac{11}{16}$ B., $\frac{4}{16}$ W., $1\frac{12}{16}$ B., $2\frac{3}{16}$ W., $\frac{3}{16}$ R., $\frac{5}{16}$ W.,
  $\frac{3}{16}$ R., $2\frac{3}{16}$ W., $1\frac{12}{16}$ B., $\frac{4}{16}$ W., $\frac{11}{16}$ B., $\frac{2}{16}$ W., $\frac{11}{16}$ B., $\frac{4}{16}$ W.

ROSE (DRESS)   10th November 1946.   *Lyon Register*, XXXVI, 10.
  1 G., 14 R., 3 Bl., $2\frac{1}{2}$ R., 1 Bl., 1 R., 1 Bl., $5\frac{1}{2}$ R., 1 W.

SINCLAIR (HUNTING)   25th March 1947.   *Lyon Register*, XXXVI, 33.
  12 G., 1 R., 4 G., 1 R., 12 G., 6 B., 1 W., 7 Bl., $2\frac{1}{2}$ R.

SINCLAIR (DRESS)   29th June 1951.   *Lyon Court Book.*
  15 R., 6 G., $2\frac{1}{2}$ B., 1 W., 3 Bl., 15 R., 3 Bl., 1 W., $2\frac{1}{2}$ B., 6 G.

WALLACE [2]   *In causa*, S. Wallace, K.C., 1951.
  $1\frac{1}{2}$ B., 12 R., 12 B., $1\frac{1}{2}$ Y., 12 B., 12 R.

Several other tartans have been recorded in the Public Register by small-scale de-painting, but have not yet been fractionally defined as have the foregoing.   From 1952 onwards, tartans have been in process of determination and registration.

---

[1] Recorded by de-painting (with yellow central line in 1873 and without yellow line, 1948) but, as regards rematriculation, subject to fractional recording, still subject to confirmation.   The foregoing is the count of Cluny-Macpherson's plaid, as laid before Lyon Court.   The " Hunting Macpherson " has been recorded by de-painting (but not yet fractionally blazoned) in the supporter of the arms of Lord Strathcarron.

[2] The count approved by Wallace of that Ilk, and laid before Lyon Court, and provisionally approved by the Lord Lyon, pending decerniture in the Petition for arms whereto inclusion of the tartan is relative.

Chieftain's Calling Card

LIST OF COLOURED PLATES OF TARTANS

(AT END OF VOLUME)

LIST OF COLOURED PLATES OF TARTANS—*continued*

94. Nicolson or Macnicol
95. Ogilvy, Dress
96. Ogilvy, Hunting
97. Rattray
98. Robertson, Dress
99. Robertson, Hunting
100. Rose, Dress
101. Rose, Hunting
102. Ross
103. Sinclair, Dress

104. Sinclair, Hunting
105. Skene
106. Stewart of Atholl
107. Stewart of Bute
108. Royal Stewart, " The Royal Tartan "
109. Stewart, Hunting
110. Stewart, Royal (Arisaid)
111. Sutherland (Ancient)
112. Urquhart

LIST OF HEREDITARY PRECEDENCE OF SCOTTISH CLANS AND NAMES

Table of ranking of clans (in reference to pp. 573 and 605) for use at general clan-functions, and deriving from the hereditary precedence of the Chiefs. Some dormant names, and certain others not yet " ascertained " and of (as yet) " un-erected " clans, are omitted.

PART I. DERIVING FROM PEERAGES AND BARONETCIES

Precedence from

1. *Dukedoms*
   Hamilton
   Lennox
   Scott
   Campbell
   Graham
2. *Marquesses*
   Gordon
   Kerr
   Stuart of Bute
   Kennedy

3. *Earldoms*
   Sutherland
   Lindsay
   Hay
   Leslie
   Montgomerie
   Sinclair
   Erskine
   Home
   Drummond
   Bruce
   Carnegie

   Ramsay
   Ogilvy
   Keith
   Innes
4. *Viscounty*
   Arbuthnott
5. *Lordships*
   Forbes
   Fraser of Lovat
   Mackay
   Macdonald
   (Clan Donald)

   Grant
6. *Baronetcies*
   Macdonald
   of Sleat
   Burnett
   Maclean
   Elliott
   Colquhoun
   Macgregor
   Cumming
   Macnaghten

PART II. DERIVING FROM BARONAGE AND ARMORIAL BEARINGS

Precedence from

1. *Barony*
   Ross, 1160
   Wemyss, 1202
   Rose, 1292
   Rattray, 1315
   Macdougall, 1344
   Stewart of Appin, 1363
   Dundas, 1451

   Robertson, 1451
   Chisholm, 1457
   Lamont, 1472
   Mackenzie, 1508
   Cameron, 1528
   Brodie, 1529
   Clanranald, 1531
   Buchan, 1596
   Macleod, 1611
   Wallace, 1620

   Glengarry, 1629
   Maclachlan, 1680
   Macneil, 1688
   Munro, 1699
   Fergusson, 1701
   Farquharson, 1708 [1]
2. *Sasine of Arms*
   Clan Chattan,
   spec. prec.
   Macfarlane, 1646
   Macpherson, 1672

   Mackintosh, 1679
   Macmillan, 1742
   Macnab, 1765
   Macbrayne, 1770
   Mactavish, 1793
   Darroch, 1797
   Mackinnon, 1811
   Malcolm, 1818
   Gillon, 1824
   Macalastair, 1847
   Nicolson

[1] *Per se* as regards other clans, and *not* in relation to Mackintosh and Clan Chattan.

INDEX

For individual Clans, see Chap. VII ; for names of Septs, see pp. 560–570 *and Chap. VIII.*

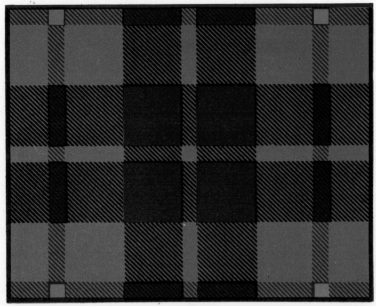

1. BARCLAY

2. BRODIE, DRESS

3. BRODIE, HUNTING

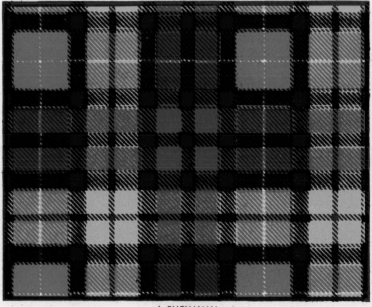

4. BUCHANAN

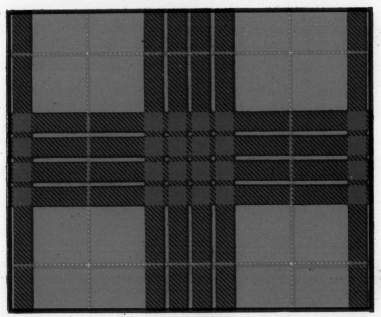

5. CLAN CAMERON

6. CAMERON OF LOCHIEL

7. CAMPBELL OF ARGYLL (CLAN CAMPBELL)

8. CAMPBELL OF BREADALBANE

9. CAMPBELL OF CAWDOR

10. CLAN CHATTAN

11. CHISHOLM

12. CLERGY

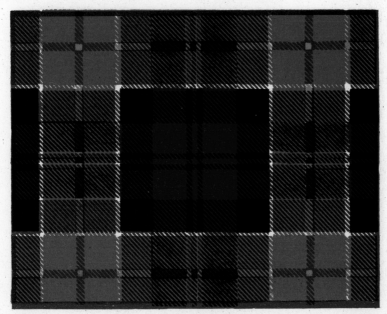

13. COLQUHOUN

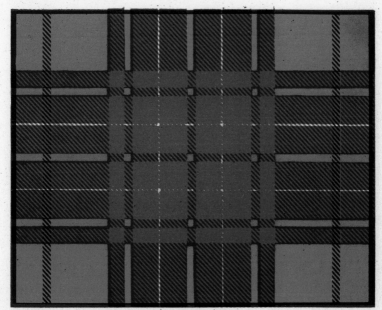

14. CUMMING, DRESS

15. CUMMING, HUNTING

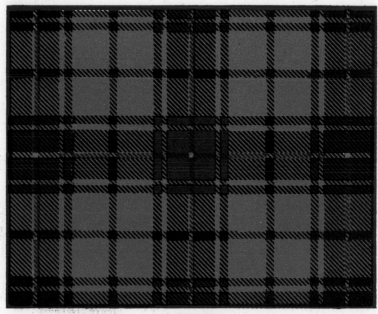

16. DAVIDSON

17. DRUMMOND

18. DUNBAR

19. ERSKINE

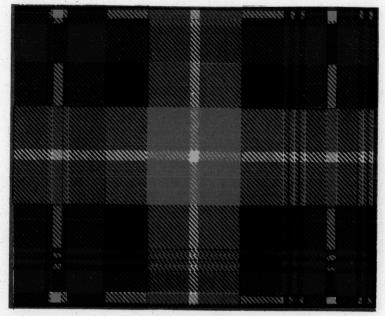

20. FARQUHARSON

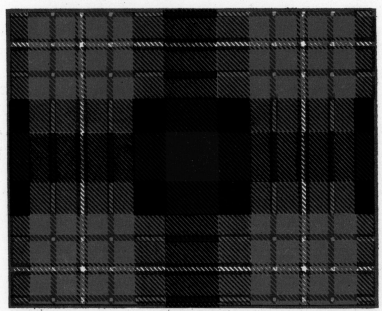

21. FERGUSSON

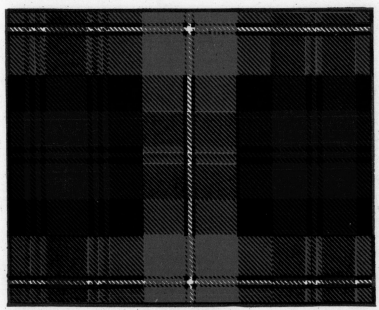

22. FORBES

23. FORTY-SECOND REGIMENT (BLACK WATCH)

24. FRASER, DRESS

25. FRASER, HUNTING

26. GORDON

27. GRAHAM OF MONTROSE

28. GRAHAM OF MENTEITH

29. GRANT

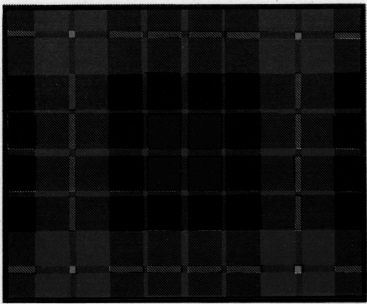

30. GUNN

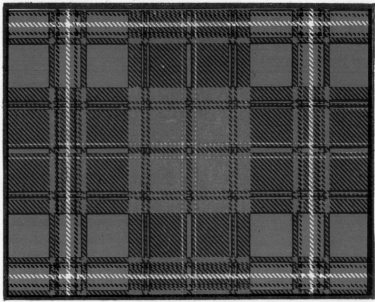

31. HAY

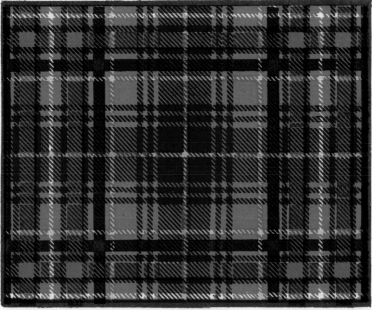

32. INNES

33. LAMONT

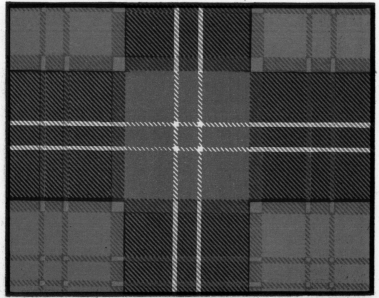

34. LENNOX, DISTRICT

B

35. LESLIE, DRESS

36. LESLIE, HUNTING

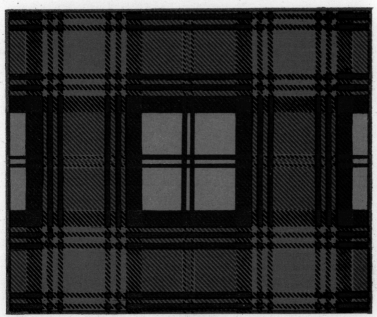

37. LINDSAY

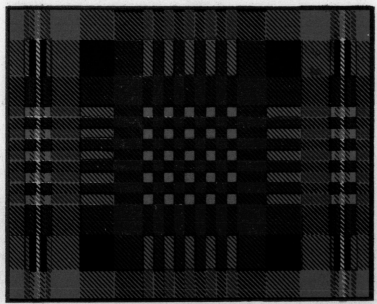

38. LOGAN OR MACLENNAN

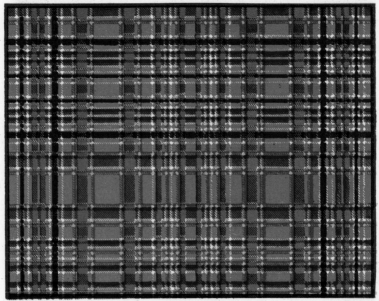

39. MACALISTER

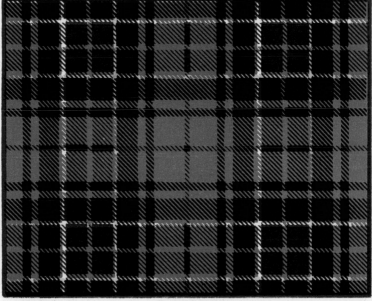

40. MACALPINE

41. MACARTHUR

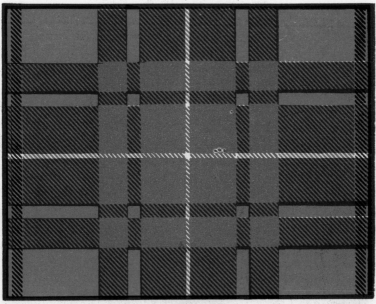

42. MACAULAY

43. MACBEAN

44. MACDONALD (CLAN DONALD)

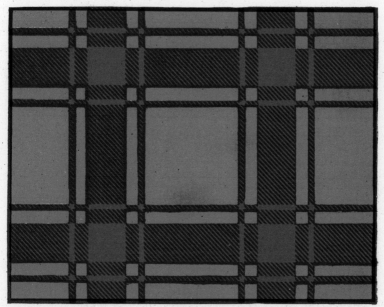

45. MACDONALD OF SLEAT, DRESS

46. MACDONALD OF SLEAT, HUNTING

47. MACDONALD OF CLANRANALD

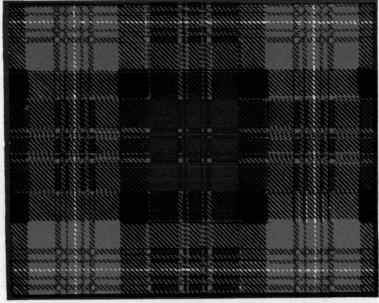

48. MACDONELL OF GLENGARRY

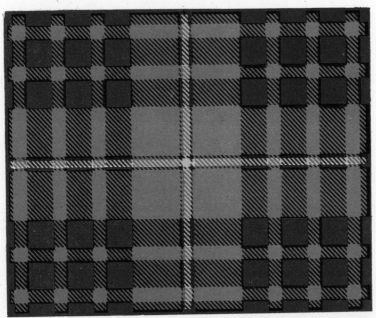

49. MACDONALD (OR MACIAN) OF ARDNAMURCHAN

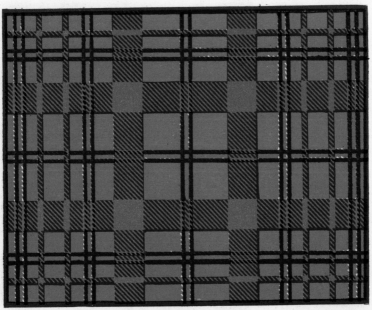

50. MACDONELL OF KEPPOCH

51. MACDOUGALL

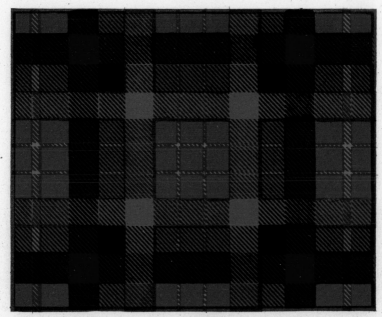

52. MACDUFF

53. MACFARLANE

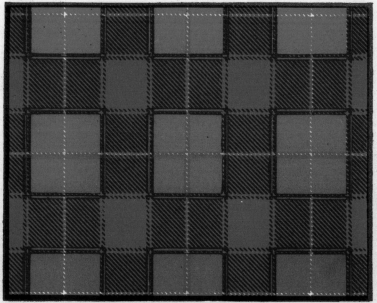

54. MACFIE

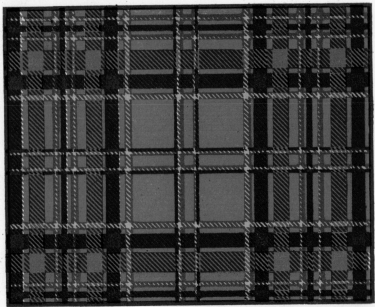

55. MACGILLIVRAY

56. MACGREGOR

57. MACINNES (CLAN AONGHAIS)

58. MACINTYRE

59. MACKAY

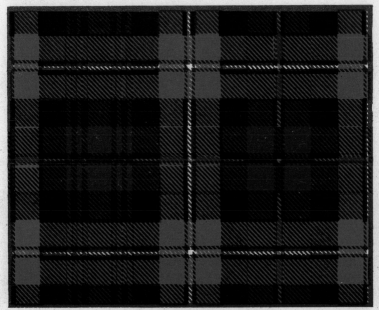

60. MACKENZIE

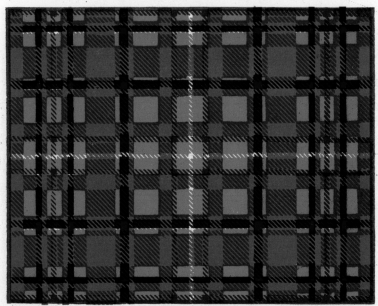

61. MACKINNON, DRESS

62. MACKINNON, HUNTING

63. MACKINTOSH

64. MACLACHLAN, DRESS

65. MÀCLACHLAN

66. MACLAINE OF LOCHBUIE

67. MACLAREN

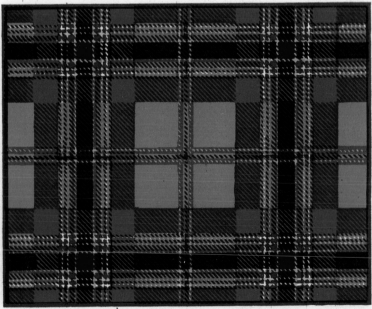

68. MACLEAN OF DUART, DRESS

69. MACLEAN, HUNTING

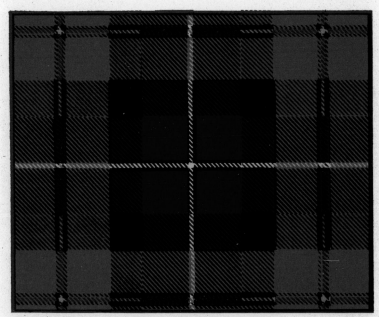

70. MACLEOD OF MACLEOD AND HARRIS

71. MACLEOD OF LEWIS AND RAASAY

72. MACMILLAN, DRESS

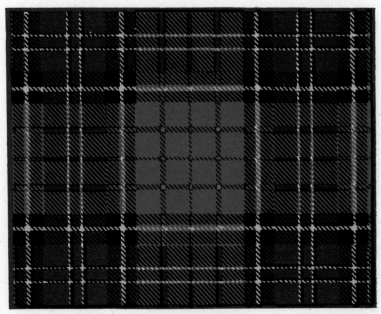

73. MACMILLAN, HUNTING

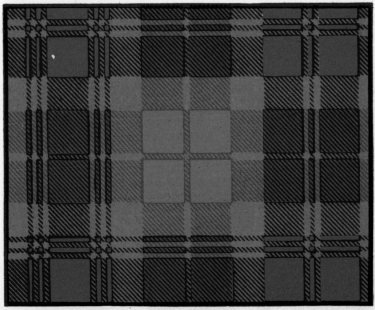

74. MACNAB

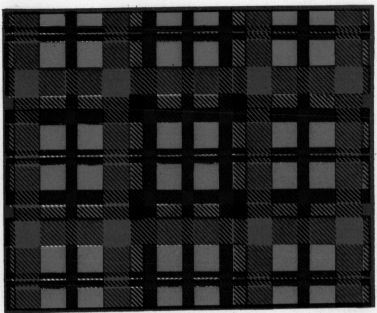

75. MACNAUGHTEN

76. MACNEIL OF BARRA

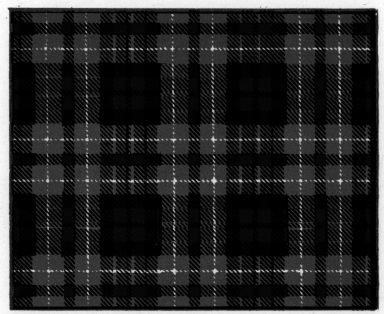

77. McNEILL OF COLONSAY

78. MACPHERSON, "CHIEF" (ARISAID?)

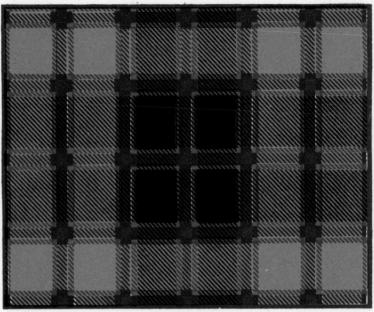

79. MACPHERSON

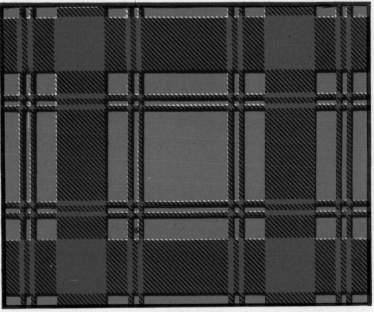

80. MACQUARRIE

81. MACQUEEN

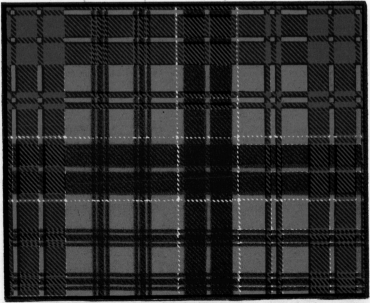

82. MACRAE, DRESS

C*

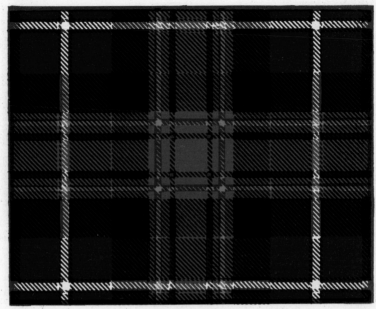

83. MACRAE, HUNTING

84. MACTAVISH

85. MALCOLM (McCALLUM)

86. MAR, DISTRICT

87. MATHESON

88. MENZIES, DRESS

89. MENZIES, HUNTING

90. MORRISON

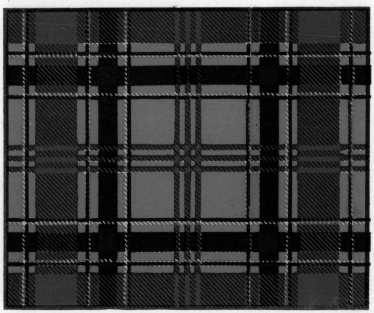

91. MUNRO

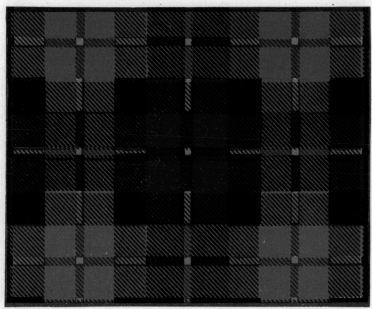

92. MURRAY OF ATHOLL

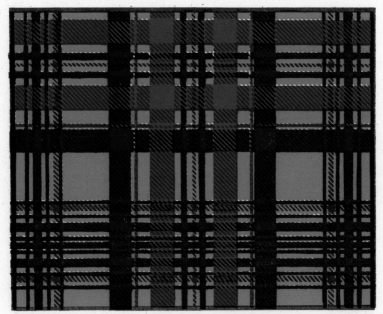

93. MURRAY OF TULLIBARDINE

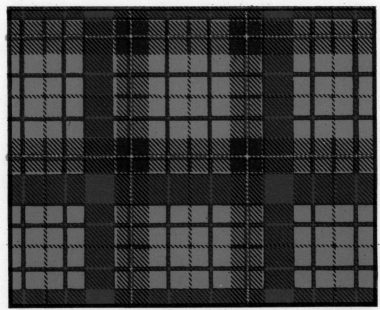

94. NICOLSON OR MACNICOL

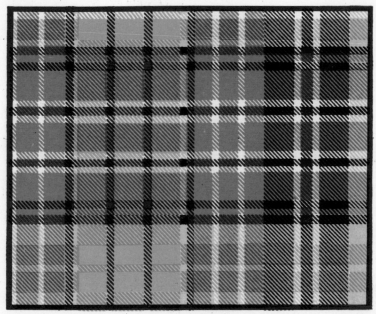

95. OGILVY, DRESS

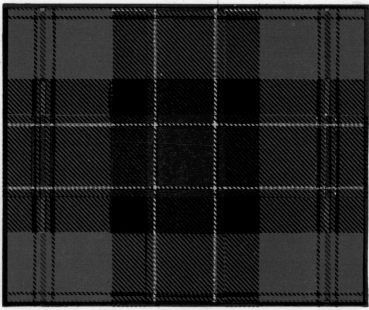

96. OGILVY, HUNTING

97. RATTRAY

98. ROBERTSON, DRESS

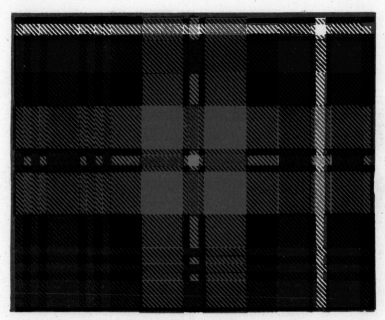

99. ROBERTSON, HUNTING

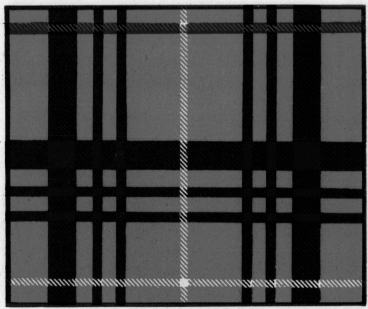

100. ROSE, DRESS

101. ROSE, HUNTING

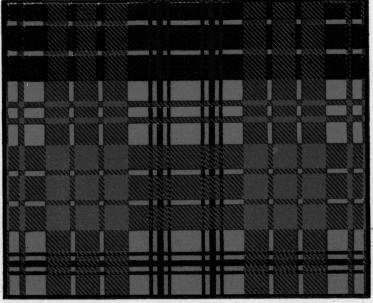

102. ROSS

103. SINCLAIR, DRESS

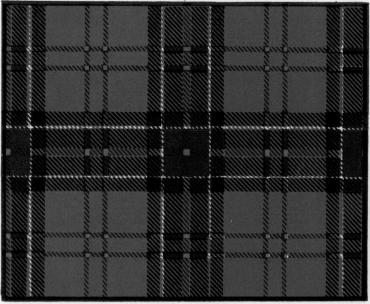

104. SINCLAIR, HUNTING

105. SKENE

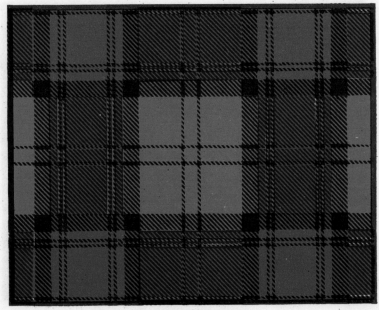

106. STEWART OF ATHOLL

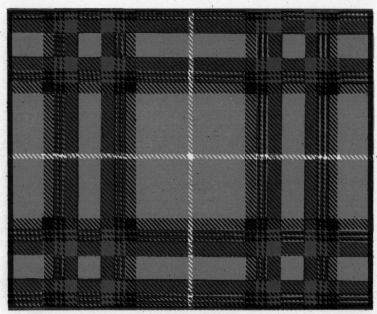

107. STEWART OF BUTE

108. ROYAL STEWART, " THE ROYAL TARTAN "

109. STEWART, HUNTING

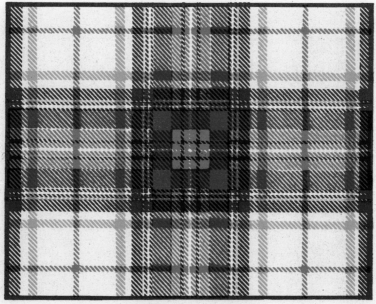

110. STEWART, ROYAL (ARISAID)

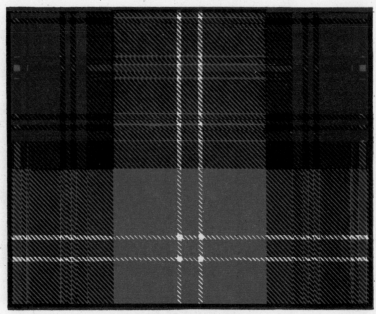

111. SUTHERLAND (ANCIENT)

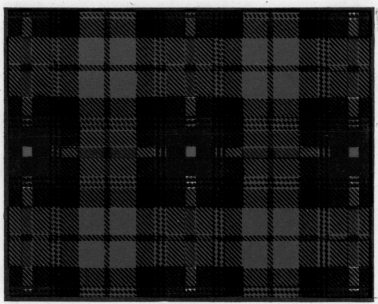

112. URQUHART